THE DOVER READER

G. K. Chesterton

DOVER PUBLICATIONS, INC.
Mineola, New York

DOVER THRIFT EDITIONS

General Editor: Mary Carolyn Waldrep

Editor of This Volume: Jim Miller

Copyright

Bibliographical Note

G. K. Chesterton: The Dover Reader, first published by Dover Publications, Inc., in 2014, is a new compilation of works by G. K. Chesterton, reprinted from authoritative sources. The Note has been specially prepared for this Dover edition.

International Standard Book Number
ISBN-13: 978-0-486-79114-2
ISBN-10: 0-486-79114-9

Manufactured in the United States by Courier Corporation
79114901 2014
www.doverpublications.com

Note

GILBERT KEITH CHESTERTON was born in London on May 29th, 1874, and before the turn of the century established himself as a free-lance journalist and reviewer. From the publication of his first book of poetry, *The Wild Knight*, until his death in 1936, Chesterton was one of the most prolific and best-known figures on the English literary scene. During those three and a half decades he turned out dozens of volumes of political and social commentary, literary criticism and biography, theological essays, poems, short stories, and novels. This collection contains a broad spectrum of Chesterton's work, including *The Man Who Was Thursday*, perhaps his best-known novel. It also includes six short stories featuring the priest-sleuth Father Brown, *Orthodoxy*, *The Club of Queer Trades*, and a selection of essays on a wide range of subjects. G. K. Chesterton's literary output was so enormous and his subjects so varied that one can only hope to impart a little of the wit, humor, and intelligence that made him the "Prince of Paradox."

Contents

Father Brown

Contents

THE BLUE CROSS

BETWEEN THE silver ribbon of morning and the green glittering ribbon of sea, the boat touched Harwich and let loose a swarm of folk like flies, among whom the man we must follow was by no means conspicuous—nor wished to be. There was nothing notable about him, except a slight contrast between the holiday gaiety of his clothes and the official gravity of his face. His clothes included a slight, pale grey jacket, a white waistcoat, and a silver straw hat with a grey-blue ribbon. His lean face was dark by contrast, and ended in a curt black beard that looked Spanish and suggested an Elizabethan ruff. He was smoking a cigarette with the seriousness of an idler. There was nothing about him to indicate the fact that the grey jacket covered a loaded revolver, that the white waistcoat covered a police card, or that the straw hat covered one of the most powerful intellects in Europe. For this was Valentin himself, the head of the Paris police and the most famous investigator of the world; and he was coming from Brussels to London to make the greatest arrest of the century.

Flambeau was in England. The police of three countries had tracked the great criminal at last from Ghent to Brussels, from Brussels to the Hook of Holland; and it was conjectured that he would take some advantage of the unfamiliarity and confusion of the Eucharistic Congress, then taking place in London. Probably he would travel as some minor clerk or secretary connected with it; but, of course, Valentin could not be certain; nobody could be certain about Flambeau.

It is many years now since this colossus of crime suddenly ceased keeping the world in a turmoil; and when he ceased, as they said after the death of Roland, there was a great quiet upon the earth. But in his best days (I mean, of course, his worst) Flambeau was a figure as statuesque and international as the Kaiser. Almost every morning the daily paper announced that he had escaped the consequences of one extraordinary crime by committing another. He was a Gascon of gigantic stature and bodily daring; and the wildest tales were told of his outbursts of athletic humour; how he turned the *juge d'instruction* upside down and stood him on his head, "to clear his mind"; how he ran down the Rue de Rivoli with a policeman under each arm. It is due to him to say that his fantastic physical strength was generally employed in such bloodless though undignified scenes; his real crimes were chiefly those of ingenious and wholesale robbery. But each of his thefts was almost a new sin, and would make a story by itself. It was he who ran the great Tyrolean Dairy Company in London, with no dairies, no cows, no carts, no milk, but with some thousand subscribers. These he served by the simple operation of moving the little milk-cans outside people's doors to the doors of his own customers. It was he who had kept up an unaccountable and close correspondence with a young lady whose whole letter-bag was intercepted, by the extraordinary trick of photographing his messages infinitesimally small upon the slides of a microscope. A sweeping simplicity, however, marked many of his experiments. It is said he once repainted all the numbers in a street in the dead of night merely to divert one traveller into a trap. It is quite certain that he invented a portable pillar-box, which he put up at corners in quiet suburbs on the chance of strangers dropping postal orders into it. Lastly he was known to be a startling acrobat; despite his huge figure, he could leap like a grasshopper and melt into the treetops like a monkey. Hence the great Valentin, when he set out to find Flambeau, was perfectly well aware that his adventures would not end when he had found him.

But how was he to find him? On this the great Valentin's ideas were still in process of settlement.

There was one thing which Flambeau, with all his dexterity of disguise, could not cover, and that was his singular height. If Valentin's quick eye had caught a tall apple-woman, a tall grenadier, or even a tolerably tall duchess, he might have arrested them on the spot. But all along his train there was nobody that could be a disguised Flambeau, any more than a cat could be a disguised giraffe. About the people on the boat he had already satisfied himself; and the people picked up at Harwich or on the journey limited themselves with certainty to six. There was a short railway official travelling up to the terminus, three fairly short market-gardeners picked up two stations afterwards, one very short widow lady going up from a small Essex town, and a very short Roman Catholic priest going up from a small Essex village. When it came to the last case, Valentin gave it up and almost laughed. The little priest was so much the essence of those Eastern flats: he had a face as round and dull as a Norfolk dumpling; he had eyes as empty as the North Sea; he had several brown-paper parcels which he was quite incapable of collecting. The Eucharistic Congress had doubtless sucked out of their local stagnation many such creatures, blind and helpless, like moles disinterred. Valentin was a sceptic in the severe style of France, and could have no love for priests. But he could have pity for them, and this one might have provoked pity in anybody. He had a large, shabby umbrella, which constantly fell on the floor. He did not seem to know which was the right end of his return ticket. He explained with a moon-calf simplicity to everybody in the carriage that he had to be careful, because he had something made of real silver "with blue stones" in one of his brown-paper parcels. His quaint blending of Essex flatness with saintly simplicity continuously amused the Frenchman till the priest arrived (somehow) at Stratford with all his parcels, and came back for his umbrella. When he did the last, Valentin even had the good nature to warn him not to take care of the silver by telling everybody about it. But to whomever he talked, Valentin kept his eye open for someone else; he looked out steadily for anyone, rich or poor, male or female, who was well up to six feet; for Flambeau was four inches above it.

He alighted at Liverpool Street, however, quite conscientiously secure that he had not missed the criminal so far. He then went to Scotland Yard to regularize his position and arrange for help in case of need; he then lit another cigarette and went for a long stroll in the streets of London. As he was walking in the streets and squares beyond Victoria, he paused suddenly and stood. It was a quaint, quiet square, very typical of London, full of an accidental stillness. The tall, flat houses round looked at once prosperous and uninhabited; the square of shrubbery in the centre looked as deserted as a green Pacific islet. One of the four sides was much higher than the rest, like a dais; and the line of this side was broken by one of London's admirable accidents—a restaurant that looked as if it had strayed from Soho. It was an unreasonably attractive object, with dwarf plants in pots and long, striped blinds of lemon yellow and white. It stood specially high above the street, and in the usual patchwork way of London, a flight of steps from the street ran up to meet the front door almost as a fire-escape might run up to a first-floor window. Valentin stood and smoked in front of the yellow-white blinds and considered them long.

The most incredible thing about miracles is that they happen. A few clouds in heaven do come together into the staring shape of one human eye. A tree does stand up in the landscape of a doubtful journey in the exact and elaborate shape of a note of interrogation. I have seen both these things myself within the last few days. Nelson does die in the instant of victory; and a man named Williams does quite accidentally murder a man named Williamson; it sounds like a sort of infanticide. In short, there is in life an element of elfin coincidence which people reckoning on the prosaic may perpetually miss. As it has been well expressed in the paradox of Poe, wisdom should reckon on the unforeseen.

Aristide Valentin was unfathomably French; and the French intelligence is intelligence specially and solely. He was not "a thinking machine"; for that is a brainless phrase of modern fatalism and materialism. A machine only *is* a machine because it cannot think. But he was a thinking man, and a plain man at the same time. All his wonderful successes, that looked like conjuring, had been gained by plodding logic, by clear and commonplace French thought. The French electrify the world not by starting any paradox, they electrify it by carrying out a truism. They carry a truism so far—as in the French Revolution. But exactly because Valentin understood reason, he understood the limits of reason. Only a man who knows nothing of motors talks of motoring without petrol; only a man who knows nothing of reason talks of reasoning without strong, undisputed first principles. Here he had no strong first principles. Flambeau had been missed at Harwich; and if he was in London at all, he might be anything from a tall tramp on Wimbledon Common to a tall toastmaster at the Hôtel Métropole. In such a naked state of nescience, Valentin had a view and a method of his own.

In such cases he reckoned on the unforeseen. In such cases, when he could not follow the train of the reasonable, he coldly and carefully followed the train of the unreasonable. Instead of going to the right places—banks, police-stations, rendezvous—he systematically went to the wrong places; knocked at every empty house, turned down every *cul de sac,* went up every lane blocked with rubbish, went round every crescent that led him uselessly out of the way. He defended this crazy course quite logically. He said that if one had a clue this was the worst way; but if one had no clue at all it was the best, because there was just the chance that any oddity that caught the eye of the pursuer might be the same that had caught the eye of the pursued. Somewhere a man must begin, and it had better be just where another man might stop. Something about that flight of steps up to the shop, something about the quietude and quaintness of the restaurant, roused all the detective's rare romantic fancy and made him resolve to strike at random. He went up the steps, and sitting down by the window, asked for a cup of black coffee.

It was half-way through the morning, and he had not breakfasted; the slight litter of other breakfasts stood about on the table to remind him of his hunger; and adding a poached egg to his order, he proceeded musingly to shake some white sugar into his coffee, thinking all the time about Flambeau. He remembered how Flambeau had escaped, once by a pair of nail scissors, and once by a house on fire; once by having to pay for an unstamped letter, and once by getting people to look through a telescope at a comet that might destroy the world. He thought his detective brain as good as the criminal's, which was true. But he fully realized the disadvantage. "The criminal is the creative artist; the detective only the critic," he said with a sour smile, and lifted his coffee cup to his lips slowly, and put it down very quickly. He had put salt in it.

He looked at the vessel from which the silvery powder had come; it was certainly a sugar-basin; as unmistakably meant for sugar as a champagne-bottle for champagne. He wondered why they should keep salt in it. He looked to see if there were any more orthodox vessels. Yes, there were two salt-cellars quite full. Perhaps there was some speciality in the condiment in the salt-cellars. He tasted it; it was sugar. Then he looked round at the restaurant with a refreshed air of interest, to see if there were any other traces of that singular artistic taste which puts the sugar in the salt-cellars and the salt in the sugar-basin. Except for an odd splash of some dark fluid on one of the white-papered walls, the whole place appeared neat, cheerful and ordinary. He rang the bell for the waiter.

When that official hurried up, fuzzy-haired and somewhat blear-eyed at that early hour, the detective (who was not without an appreciation of the simpler forms of humour) asked him to taste the sugar and see if it was up to the high reputation of the hotel. The result was that the waiter yawned suddenly and woke up.

"Do you play this delicate joke on your customers every morning?" inquired Valentin. "Does changing the salt and sugar never pall on you as a jest?"

The waiter, when this irony grew clearer, stammeringly assured him that the establishment had certainly no such intention; it must be a most curious mistake. He picked up the sugar-basin and looked at it; he picked up the salt-cellar and looked at that, his face growing more and more bewildered. At last he abruptly excused himself, and hurrying away, returned in a few seconds with the proprietor. The proprietor also examined the sugar-basin and then the salt-cellar; the proprietor also looked bewildered.

Suddenly the waiter seemed to grow inarticulate with a rush of words.

"I zink," he stuttered eagerly, "I zink it is those two clergymen."

"What two clergymen?"

"The two clergymen," said the waiter, "that threw soup at the wall."

"Threw soup at the wall?" repeated Valentin, feeling sure this must be some Italian metaphor.

"Yes, yes," said the attendant excitedly, and pointing at the dark splash on the white paper; "threw it over there on the wall."

Valentin looked his query at the proprietor, who came to his rescue with fuller reports.

"Yes, sir," he said, "it's quite true, though I don't suppose it has anything to do with the sugar and salt. Two clergymen came in and drank soup here very early, as soon as the shutters were taken down. They were both very quiet, respectable people; one of them paid the bill and went out; the other, who seemed a slower coach altogether, was some minutes longer getting his things together. But he went at last. Only, the instant before he stepped into the street he deliberately picked up his cup, which he had only half emptied, and threw the soup slap on the wall. I was in the back room myself, and so was the waiter; so I could only rush out in time to find the wall splashed and the shop empty. It didn't do any particular damage, but it was confounded cheek; and I tried to catch the men in the street. They were too far off though; I only noticed they went round the corner into Carstairs Street."

The detective was on his feet, hat settled and stick in hand. He had already decided that in the universal darkness of his mind he could only follow the first odd finger that pointed; and this finger was odd enough. Paying his bill and clashing the glass doors behind him, he was soon swinging round into the other street.

It was fortunate that even in such fevered moments his eye was cool and quick. Something in a shop-front went by him like a mere flash; yet he went back to look at it. The shop was a popular greengrocer and fruiterer's, an array of goods set out in the open air and plainly ticketed with their names and prices. In the two most prominent compartments were two heaps, of oranges and of nuts respectively. On the heap of nuts lay a scrap of cardboard, on which was written in bold, blue chalk, "Best tangerine oranges, two a penny." On the oranges was the equally clear and exact description, "Finest Brazil nuts, 4d. a lb." M. Valentin looked at these two placards and fancied he had met this highly subtle form of humour before, and that somewhat recently. He drew the attention of the red-faced fruiterer, who was looking rather sullenly up and down the street, to this inaccuracy in his advertisements. The fruiterer said nothing, but sharply put each card into its proper place. The detective, leaning elegantly on his walking-cane, continued to scrutinize the shop. At last he said: "Pray excuse my apparent irrelevance, my good sir, but I should like to ask you a question in experimental psychology and the association of ideas."

The red-faced shopman regarded him with an eye of menace; but he continued gaily, swinging his cane. "Why," he pursued, "why are two tickets wrongly placed in a greengrocer's shop like a shovel hat that has come to London for a holiday? Or, in case I do not make myself clear, what is the mystical association which connects the idea of nuts marked as oranges with the idea of two clergymen, one tall and the other short?"

The eyes of the tradesman stood out of his head like a snail's; he really seemed for an instant likely to fling himself upon the stranger. At last he stammered angrily: "I don't know what you 'ave to do with it, but if you're one of their friends, you can tell 'em from me that I'll knock their silly 'eads off, parsons or no parsons, if they upset my apples again."

"Indeed?" asked the detective, with great sympathy. "Did they upset your apples?"

"One of 'em did," said the heated shopman; "rolled 'em all over the street. I'd 'ave caught the fool but for havin' to pick 'em up."

"Which way did these parsons go?" asked Valentin.

"Up that second road on the left-hand side, and then across the square," said the other promptly.

"Thanks," said Valentin, and vanished like a fairy. On the other side of the second square he found a policeman, and said: "This is urgent, constable; have you seen two clergymen in shovel hats?"

The policeman began to chuckle heavily. "I 'ave, sir; and if you arst me, one of 'em was drunk. He stood in the middle of the road that bewildered that——"

"Which way did they go?" snapped Valentin.

"They took one of them yellow buses over there," answered the man; "them that go to Hampstead."

Valentin produced his official card and said very rapidly: "Call up two of your men to come with me in pursuit," and crossed the road with such contagious energy that the ponderous policeman was moved to almost agile obedience. In a minute and a half the French detective was joined on the opposite pavement by an inspector and a man in plain clothes.

"Well, sir," began the former, with smiling importance, "and what may——?"

Valentin pointed suddenly with his cane. "I'll tell you on the top of that omnibus," he said, and was darting and dodging across the tangle of the traffic. When all three sank panting on the top seats of the yellow vehicle, the inspector said: "We could go four times as quick in a taxi."

"Quite true," replied their leader placidly, "if we only had an idea of where we were going."

"Well, where *are* you going?" asked the other, staring.

Valentin smoked frowningly for a few seconds; then, removing his cigarette, he said: "If you *know* what a man's doing, get in front of him; but if you want to guess what he's doing, keep behind him. Stray when he strays; stop when he stops; travel as slowly as he. Then you may see what he saw and may act as he acted. All we can do is to keep our eyes skinned for a queer thing."

"What sort of a queer thing do you mean?" asked the inspector.

"Any sort of queer thing," answered Valentin, and relapsed into obstinate silence.

The yellow omnibus crawled up the northern roads for what seemed like hours on end; the great detective would not explain further, and perhaps his assistants felt a silent and growing doubt of his errand. Perhaps, also, they felt a silent and growing desire for lunch, for the hours crept long past the normal luncheon hour, and the long roads of the North London suburbs seemed to shoot out into length after length like an infernal telescope. It was one of those journeys on which a man perpetually feels that now at last he must have come to the end of the universe, and then finds he has only come to the beginning of Tufnell Park. London died away in draggled taverns and dreary scrubs, and then was unaccountably born again in blazing high streets and blatant hotels. It was like passing through thirteen separate vulgar cities all just touching each other. But though the winter twilight was already threatening the road ahead of them, the Parisian detective still sat silent and watchful, eyeing the frontage of the streets that slid by on either side. By the time they had left Camden Town behind, the policemen were nearly asleep; at least, they gave something like a jump as Valentin leapt erect, struck a hand on each man's shoulder, and shouted to the driver to stop.

They tumbled down the steps into the road without realizing why they had been dislodged; when they looked round for enlightenment they found Valentin triumphantly pointing his finger towards a window on the left side of the road. It was a large window, forming part of the long facade of a gilt and palatial public-house; it was the part reserved for respectable dining, and labelled "Restaurant." This window, like all the rest along the frontage of the hotel, was of frosted and figured glass, but in the middle of it was a big, black smash, like a star in the ice.

"Our cue at last," cried Valentin, waving his stick; "the place with the broken window."

"What window? What cue?" asked his principal assistant. "Why, what proof is there that this has anything to do with them?"

Valentin almost broke his bamboo stick with rage.

"Proof!" he cried. "Good God! the man is looking for proof! Why, of course, the chances are twenty to one that it has *nothing* to do with them. But what else can we do? Don't you see we must either follow one wild possibility or else go home to bed?" He banged his way into the restaurant, followed by his companions, and they were soon seated at a late luncheon at a little table, and looking at the star of smashed glass from the inside. Not that it was very informative to them even then.

"Got your window broken, I see," said Valentin to the waiter, as he paid his bill.

"Yes, sir," answered the attendant, bending busily over the change, to which Valentin silently added an enormous tip. The waiter straightened himself with mild but unmistakable animation.

"Ah, yes, sir," he said. "Very odd thing, that, sir."

"Indeed? Tell us about it," said the detective with careless curiosity.

"Well, two gents in black came in," said the waiter; "two of those foreign parsons that are running about. They had a cheap and quiet little lunch, and one of them paid for it and went out. The other was just going out to join him when I looked at my change again and found he'd paid me more than three times too much. 'Here,' I says to the chap who was nearly out of the door, 'you've paid too much.' 'Oh,' he says, very cool, 'have we?' 'Yes,' I says, and picks up the bill to show him. Well, that was a knock-out."

"What do you mean?" asked his interlocutor.

"Well, I'd have sworn on seven Bibles that I'd put 4s. on that bill. But now I saw I'd put 14s., as plain as paint."

"Well?" cried Valentin, moving slowly, but with burning eyes, "and then?"

"The parson at the door he says, all serene, 'Sorry to confuse your accounts, but it'll pay for the window.' 'What window?' I says. 'The one I'm going to break,' he says, and smashed that blessed pane with his umbrella."

All the inquirers made an exclamation; and the inspector said under his breath: "Are we after escaped lunatics?" The waiter went on with some relish for the ridiculous story:

"I was so knocked silly for a second, I couldn't do anything. The man marched out of the place and joined his friend just round the corner. Then they went so quick up Bullock Street that I couldn't catch them, though I ran round the bars to do it."

"Bullock Street," said the detective, and shot up that thoroughfare as quickly as the strange couple he pursued.

Their journey now took them through bare brick ways like tunnels; streets with few lights and even with few windows; streets that seemed built out of the blank backs of everything and everywhere. Dusk was deepening, and it was not easy even for the London policemen to guess in what exact direction they were treading. The inspector, however, was pretty certain that they would eventually strike some part of Hampstead Heath. Abruptly one bulging and gas-lit window broke the blue twilight like a bull's-eye lantern; and Valentin stopped an instant before a little garish sweetstuff shop. After an instant's hesitation he went in; he stood amid the gaudy colours of the confectionery with entire gravity and bought thirteen chocolate cigars with a certain care. He was clearly preparing an opening; but he did not need one.

An angular, elderly young woman in the shop had regarded his elegant appearance with a merely automatic inquiry; but when she saw the door behind him blocked with the blue uniform of the inspector, her eyes seemed to wake up.

"Oh," she said, "if you've come about that parcel, I've sent it off already."

"Parcel!" repeated Valentin; and it was his turn to look inquiring.

"I mean the parcel the gentleman left—the clergyman gentleman."

"For goodness' sake," said Valentin, leaning forward with his first real confession of eagerness, "for Heaven's sake tell us what happened exactly."

"Well," said the woman, a little doubtfully, "the clergymen came in about half an hour ago and bought some peppermints and talked a bit, and then went off towards the Heath. But a second after, one of them runs back into the shop and says, 'Have I left a parcel?' Well, I looked everywhere and couldn't see one; so he says, 'Never mind; but if it should turn up, please post it to this address,' and he left me the address and a shilling for my trouble. And sure enough, though I thought I'd looked everywhere, I found he'd left a brown-paper parcel, so I posted it to the place he said. I can't remember the address now; it was somewhere in Westminster. But as the thing seemed so important, I thought perhaps the police had come about it."

"So they have," said Valentin shortly. "Is Hampstead Heath near here?"

"Straight on for fifteen minutes," said the woman, "and you'll come right out on the open." Valentin sprang out of the shop and began to run. The other detectives followed him at a reluctant trot.

The street they threaded was so narrow and shut in by shadows that when they came out unexpectedly into the void common and vast sky they were startled to find the evening still so light and clear. A perfect dome of peacock-green sank into gold amid the blackening trees and the dark violet distances. The glowing green tint was just deep enough to pick out in points of crystal one or two stars. All that was left of the daylight lay in a golden glitter across the edge of Hampstead and that popular hollow which is called the Vale of Health. The holiday makers who roam this region had not wholly dispersed: a few couples sat shapelessly on benches; and here and there a distant girl still shrieked in one of the swings. The glory of heaven deepened and darkened around the sublime vulgarity of man; and standing on the slope and looking across the valley, Valentin beheld the thing which he sought.

Among the black and breaking groups in that distance was one especially black which did not break—a group of two figures clerically clad. Though they seemed as small as insects, Valentin could see that one of them was much smaller than the other. Though the other had a student's stoop and an inconspicuous manner, he could see that the man was well over six feet high. He shut his teeth and went forward, whirling his stick impatiently. By the time he had substantially diminished the distance and magnified the two black figures as in a vast microscope, he had perceived something else; something which startled him, and yet which he had somehow expected. Whoever was the tall priest, there could be no doubt about the identity of the short one. It was his friend of the Harwich train, the stumpy little *curé* of Essex whom he had warned about his brown-paper parcels.

Now, so far as this went, everything fitted in finally and rationally enough. Valentin had learned by his inquiries that morning that a Father Brown from Essex was bringing up a silver cross with sapphires, a relic of considerable value, to show some of the foreign priests at the congress. This undoubtedly was the "silver with blue stones"; and Father Brown undoubtedly was the little greenhorn in the train. Now there was nothing wonderful about the fact that what Valentin had found out Flambeau had also found out; Flambeau found out everything. Also there was nothing wonderful in the fact that when Flambeau heard of a sapphire cross he should try to steal it; that was the most natural thing in all natural history. And most certainly there was nothing wonderful about the fact that Flambeau should have it all his own way with such a silly sheep as the man with the umbrella and the parcels. He was the sort of man whom anybody could lead on a string to the North Pole; it was not surprising that an actor like Flambeau, dressed as another priest, could lead him to Hampstead Heath. So far the crime seemed clear enough; and while the detective pitied the priest for his helplessness, he almost despised Flambeau for condescending to so gullible a victim. But when Valentin thought of all that had happened in between, of all that had led him to his triumph, he racked his brains for the smallest rhyme or reason in it. What had the stealing of a blue-and-silver cross from a priest from Essex to do with chucking soup at wallpaper? What had it to do with calling nuts oranges, or with paying for windows first and breaking them afterwards? He had come to the end of his chase; yet somehow he had missed the middle of it. When he failed (which was seldom), he had usually grasped the clue, but nevertheless missed the criminal. Here he had grasped the criminal, but still he could not grasp the clue.

The two figures that they followed were crawling like black flies across the huge green contour of a hill. They were evidently sunk in conversation, and perhaps did not notice where they were going; but they were certainly going to the wilder and more silent heights of the Heath. As their pursuers gained on them, the latter had to use the undignified attitudes of the deer-stalker, to crouch behind clumps of trees and even to crawl prostrate in deep grass. By these ungainly ingenuities the hunters even came close enough to the quarry to hear the murmur of the discussion, but no word could be distinguished except the word "reason" recurring frequently in a high and almost childish voice. Once, over an abrupt dip of land and a dense tangle of thickets, the detectives actually lost the two figures they were following. They did not find the trail again for an agonizing ten minutes, and then it led round the brow of a great dome of hill overlooking an amphitheatre of rich and desolate sunset scenery. Under a tree in this commanding yet neglected spot was an old ramshackle wooden seat. On this seat sat the two priests still in serious speech together. The gorgeous green and gold still clung to the darkening horizon; but the dome above was turning slowly from peacock-green to peacock-blue, and the stars detached themselves more and more like solid jewels. Mutely motioning to his followers, Valentin contrived to creep up behind the big branching tree, and, standing there in deathly silence, heard the words of the strange priests for the first time.

After he had listened for a minute and a half, he was gripped by a devilish doubt. Perhaps he had dragged the two English policemen to the wastes of a nocturnal heath on an errand no saner than seeking figs on thistles. For the two priests were talking exactly like priests, piously, with learning and leisure, about the most aerial enigmas of theology. The little Essex priest spoke the more simply, with his round face turned to the strengthening stars; the other talked with his head bowed, as if he were not even worthy to look at them. But no more innocently clerical conversation could have been heard in any white Italian cloister or black Spanish cathedral.

The first he heard was the tail of one of Father Brown's sentences, which ended: "…what they really meant in the Middle Ages by the heavens being incorruptible."

The taller priest nodded his bowed head and said:

"Ah, yes, these modern infidels appeal to their reason; but who can look at those millions of worlds and not feel that there may well be wonderful universes above us where reason is utterly unreasonable?"

"No," said the other priest; "reason is always reasonable, even in the last limbo, in the lost borderland of things. I know that people charge the Church with lowering reason, but it is just the other way. Alone on earth, the Church makes reason really supreme. Alone on earth, the Church affirms that God Himself is bound by reason."

The other priest raised his austere face to the spangled sky and said:

"Yet who knows if in that infinite universe——?"

"Only infinite physically," said the little priest, turning sharply in his seat, "not infinite in the sense of escaping from the laws of truth."

Valentin behind his tree was tearing his finger-nails with silent fury. He seemed almost to hear the sniggers of the English detectives whom he had brought so far on a fantastic guess only to listen to the metaphysical gossip of two mild old parsons. In his impatience he lost the equally elaborate answer of the tall cleric, and when he listened again it was again Father Brown who was speaking:

"Reason and justice grip the remotest and the loneliest star. Look at those stars. Don't they look as if they were single diamonds and sapphires? Well, you can imagine any mad botany or geology you please. Think of forests of adamant with leaves of brilliants. Think the moon is a blue moon, a single elephantine sapphire. But don't fancy that all that frantic astronomy would make the smallest difference to the reason and justice of conduct. On plains of opal, under cliffs cut out of pearl, you would still find a notice-board, 'Thou shalt not steal.' "

Valentin was just in the act of rising from his rigid and crouching attitude and creeping away as softly as might be, felled by the one great folly of his life. But something in the very silence of the tall priest made him stop until the latter spoke. When at last he did speak, he said simply, his head bowed and his hands on his knees:

"Well, I still think that other worlds may perhaps rise higher than our reason. The mystery of heaven is unfathomable, and I for one can only bow my head."

Then, with brow yet bent and without changing by the faintest shade his attitude or voice, he added:

"Just hand over that sapphire cross of yours, will you? We're all alone here, and I could pull you to pieces like a straw doll."

The utterly unaltered voice and attitude added a strange violence to that shocking change of speech. But the guarder of the relic only seemed to turn his head by the smallest section of the compass. He seemed still to have a somewhat foolish face turned to the stars. Perhaps he had not understood. Or, perhaps, he had understood and sat rigid with terror.

"Yes," said the tall priest, in the same low voice and in the same still posture, "yes, I am Flambeau."

Then, after a pause, he said:

"Come, will you give me that cross?"

"No," said the other, and the monosyllable had an odd sound.

Flambeau suddenly flung off all his pontifical pretensions. The great robber leaned back in his seat and laughed low but long.

"No," he cried; "you won't give it me, you proud prelate. You won't give it me, you little celibate simpleton. Shall I tell you why you won't give it me? Because I've got it already in my own breast-pocket."

The small man from Essex turned what seemed to be a dazed face in the dusk, and said, with the timid eagerness of "The Private Secretary":

"Are—are you sure?"

Flambeau yelled with delight.

"Really, you're as good as a three-act farce," he cried. "Yes, you turnip, I am quite sure. I had the sense to make a duplicate of the right parcel, and now, my friend, you've got the duplicate, and I've got the jewels. An old dodge, Father Brown—a very old dodge."

"Yes," said Father Brown, and passed his hand through his hair with the same strange vagueness of manner. "Yes, I've heard of it before."

The colossus of crime leaned over to the little rustic priest with a sort of sudden interest.

"*You* have heard of it?" he asked. "Where have *you* heard of it?"

"Well, I mustn't tell you his name, of course," said the little man simply. "He was a penitent, you know. He had lived prosperously for about twenty years entirely on duplicate brown-paper parcels. And so, you see, when I began to suspect you, I thought of this poor chap's way of doing it at once."

"Began to suspect me?" repeated the outlaw with increased intensity. "Did you really have the gumption to suspect me just because I brought you up to this bare part of the heath?"

"No, no," said Brown with an air of apology. "You see, I suspected you when we first met. It's that little bulge up the sleeve where you people have the spiked bracelet."

"How in Tartarus," cried Flambeau, "did you ever hear of the spiked bracelet?"

"Oh, one's little flock, you know!" said Father Brown, arching his eyebrows rather blankly. "When I was a curate in Hartlepool, there were three of them with spiked bracelets. So, as I suspected you from the first, don't you see, I made sure that the cross should go safe, anyhow. I'm afraid I watched you, you know. So at last I saw you change the parcels. Then, don't you see, I changed them back again. And then I left the right one behind."

"Left it behind?" repeated Flambeau, and for the first time there was another note in his voice beside his triumph.

"Well, it was like this," said the little priest, speaking in the same unaffected way. "I went back to that sweet-shop and asked if I'd left a parcel, and gave them a particular address if it turned up. Well, I knew I hadn't; but when I went away again I did. So, instead of running after me with that valuable parcel, they have sent it flying to a friend of mine in Westminster." Then he added rather sadly: "I learnt that, too, from a poor fellow in Hartlepool. He used to do it with handbags he stole at railway stations, but he's in a monastery now. Oh, one gets to know, you know," he added, rubbing his head again with the same sort of desperate apology. "We can't help being priests. People come and tell us these things."

Flambeau tore a brown-paper parcel out of his inner pocket and rent it in pieces. There was nothing but paper and sticks of lead inside it. He sprang to his feet with a gigantic gesture, and cried:

"I don't believe you. I don't believe a bumpkin like you could manage all that. I believe you've still got the stuff on you, and if you don't give it up—why, we're all alone, and I'll take it by force!"

"No," said Father Brown simply, and stood up also; "you won't take it by force. First, because I really haven't still got it. And, second, because we are not alone."

Flambeau stopped in his stride forward.

"Behind that tree," said Father Brown, pointing, "are two strong policemen and the greatest detective alive. How did they come here, do you ask? Why, I brought them, of course! How did I do it? Why, I'll tell you if you like! Lord bless you, we have to know twenty such things when we work among the criminal classes! Well, I wasn't sure you were a thief, and it would never do to make a scandal against one of our own clergy. So I just tested you to see if anything would make you show yourself. A man generally makes a small scene if he finds salt in his coffee; if he doesn't, he has some reason for keeping quiet. I changed the salt and sugar, and *you* kept quiet. A man generally objects if his bill is three times too big. If he pays it, he has some motive for passing unnoticed. I altered your bill, and *you* paid it."

The world seemed waiting for Flambeau to leap like a tiger. But he was held back as by a spell; he was stunned with the utmost curiosity.

"Well," went on Father Brown, with lumbering lucidity, "as you wouldn't leave any tracks for the police, of course somebody had to. At every place we went to, I took care to do something that would get us talked about for the rest of the day. I didn't do much harm—a splashed wall, spilt apples, a broken window; but I saved the cross, as the cross will always be saved. It is at Westminster by now. I rather wonder you didn't stop it with the Donkey's Whistle."

"With the what?" asked Flambeau.

"I'm glad you've never heard of it," said the priest, making a face. "It's a foul thing. I'm sure you're too good a man for a Whistler. I couldn't have countered it even with the Spots myself; I'm not strong enough in the legs."

"What on earth are you talking about?" asked the other.

"Well, I did think you'd know the Spots," said Father Brown, agreeably surprised. "Oh, you can't have gone so very wrong yet!"

"How in blazes do you know all these horrors?" cried Flambeau.

The shadow of a smile crossed the round, simple face of his clerical opponent.

"Oh, by being a celibate simpleton, I suppose," he said. "Has it never struck you that a man who does next to nothing but hear men's real sins is not likely to be wholly unaware of human evil? But, as a matter of fact, another part of my trade, too, made me sure you weren't a priest."

"What?" asked the thief, almost gaping.

"You attacked reason," said Father Brown. "It's bad theology."

And even as he turned away to collect his property, the three policemen came out from under the twilight trees. Flambeau was an artist and a sportsman. He stepped back and swept Valentin a great bow.

"Do not bow to me, *mon ami*," said Valentin, with silver clearness. "Let us both bow to our master."

And they both stood an instant uncovered, while the little Essex priest blinked about for his umbrella.

THE SINS OF PRINCE SARADINE

WHEN FLAMBEAU took his month's holiday from his office in Westminster he took it in a small sailing-boat, so small that it passed much of its time as a rowing-boat. He took it, moreover, on little rivers in the Eastern counties, rivers so small that the boat looked like a magic boat sailing on land through meadows and cornfields. The vessel was just comfortable for two people; there was room only for necessities, and Flambeau had stocked it with such things as his special philosophy considered necessary. They reduced themselves, apparently, to four essentials: tins of salmon, if he should want to eat; loaded revolvers, if he should want to fight; a bottle of brandy, presumably in case he should faint; and a priest, presumably in case he should die. With this light luggage he crawled down the little Norfolk rivers, intending to reach the Broads at last, but meanwhile delighting in the over-hanging gardens and meadows, the mirrored mansions or villages, lingering to fish in the pools and corners, and in some sense hugging the shore.

Like a true philosopher, Flambeau had no aim in his holiday; but, like a true philosopher, he had an excuse. He had a sort of half purpose, which he took just so seriously that its success would crown the holiday, but just so lightly that its failure would not spoil it. Years ago, when he had been a king of thieves and the most famous figure in Paris, he had often received wild communications of approval, denunciation or even love; but one had, somehow, stuck in his memory. It consisted simply of a visiting-card, in an envelope with an English postmark. On the back of the card was written in French and in green ink: "If you ever retire and become respectable, come and see me. I want to meet you, for I have met all the other great men of my time. That trick of yours of getting one detective to arrest the other was the most splendid scene in French history." On the front of the card was engraved in the formal fashion, "Prince Saradine, Reed House, Reed Island, Norfolk."

He had not troubled much about the prince then, beyond ascertaining that he had been a brilliant and fashionable figure in southern Italy. In his youth, it was said, he had eloped with a married woman of high rank; the escapade was scarcely startling in his social world, but it had clung to men's minds because of an additional tragedy: the alleged suicide of the insulted husband, who appeared to have flung himself over a precipice in Sicily. The prince then lived in Vienna for a time, but his more recent years seemed to have been passed in perpetual and restless travel. But when Flambeau, like the prince himself, had left European celebrity and settled in England, it occurred to him that he might pay a surprise visit to this eminent exile in the Norfolk Broads. Whether he should find the place he had no idea; and, indeed, it was sufficiently small and forgotten. But, as things fell out, he found it much sooner than he expected.

They had moored their boat one night under a bank veiled in high grasses and short pollarded trees. Sleep, after heavy sculling, had come to them early, and by a corresponding accident they awoke before it was light. To speak more strictly, they awoke before it was daylight; for a large lemon moon was only just setting in the forest of high grass above their heads, and the sky was of a vivid violet-blue, nocturnal but bright. Both men had simultaneously a reminiscence of childhood, of the elfin and adventurous time when tall weeds close over us like woods. Standing up thus against the large low moon the daisies really seemed to be giant daisies, the dandelions to be giant dandelions. Somehow it reminded them of the dado of a nursery wall-paper. The drop of the river-bed sufficed to sink them under the roots of all shrubs and flowers and make them gaze upwards at the grass.

"By Jove!" said Flambeau; "it's like being in fairyland."

Father Brown sat bolt upright in the boat and crossed himself. His movement was so abrupt that his friend asked him, with a mild stare, what was the matter.

"The people who wrote the mediæval ballads," answered the priest, "knew more about fairies than you do. It isn't only nice things that happen in fairyland."

"Oh, bosh!" said Flambeau. "Only nice things could happen under such an innocent moon. I am for pushing on now and seeing what does really come. We may die and rot before we ever see again such a moon or such a mood."

"All right," said Father Brown. "I never said it was always wrong to enter fairyland. I only said it was always dangerous."

They pushed slowly up the brightening river; the glowing violet of the sky and the pale gold of the moon grew fainter and fainter, and faded into that vast colourless cosmos that precedes the colours of the dawn. When the first faint stripes of red and gold and grey split the horizon from end to end they were broken by the black bulk of a town or village which sat on the river just ahead of them. It was already an easy twilight, in which all things were visible, when they came under the hanging roofs and bridges of this riverside hamlet. The houses, with their long, low, stooping roofs, seemed to come down to drink at the river, like huge grey and red cattle. The broadening and whitening dawn had already turned to working daylight before they saw any living creature on the wharves and bridges of that silent town. Eventually they saw a very placid and prosperous man in his shirt sleeves, with a face as round as the recently sunken moon, and rays of red whisker around the low arc of it, who was leaning on a post above the sluggish tide. By an impulse not to be analysed, Flambeau rose to his full height in the swaying boat and shouted at the man to ask if he knew Reed Island or Reed House. The prosperous man's smile grew slightly more expansive, and he simply pointed up the river towards the next bend of it. Flambeau went ahead without further speech.

The boat took many such grassy corners and followed many such reedy and silent reaches of river; but before the search had become monotonous they had swung round a specially sharp angle and come into the silence of a sort of pool or lake, the sight of which instinctively arrested them. For in the middle of this wider piece of water, fringed on every side with rushes, lay a long, low islet along which ran a long, low house or bungalow built of bamboo or some kind of tough tropic cane. The upstanding rods of bamboo which made the walls were pale yellow, the sloping rods that made the roof were of darker red or brown, otherwise the long house was a thing of repetition and monotony. The early morning breeze rustled the reeds round the island and sang in the strange ribbed house as in a giant pan-pipe.

"By George!" cried Flambeau; "here is the place, after all! Here is Reed Island, if ever there was one. Here is Reed House, if it is anywhere. I believe that fat man with whiskers was a fairy."

"Perhaps," remarked Father Brown impartially. "If he was, he was a bad fairy."

But even as he spoke the impetuous Flambeau had run his boat ashore in the rattling reeds, and they stood on the long, quaint islet beside the old and silent house.

The house stood with its back, as it were, to the river and the only landing-stage; the main entrance was on the other side, and looked down the long island garden. The visitors approached it, therefore, by a small path running round nearly three sides of the house, close under the low eaves. Through three different windows on three different sides they looked in on the same long, well-lit room, panelled in light wood, with a large number of looking-glasses, and laid out as for an elegant lunch. The front door, when they came round to it at last, was flanked by two turquoise-blue flower-pots. It was opened by a butler of the drearier type—long, lean, grey and listless—who murmured that Prince Saradine was from home at present, but was expected hourly; the house being kept ready for him and his guests. The exhibition of the card with the scrawl of green ink awoke a flicker of life in the parchment face of this depressed retainer, and it was with a certain shaky courtesy that he suggested that the strangers should remain. "His Highness may be here any minute," he said, "and would be distressed to have just missed any gentleman he had invited. We have orders always to keep a little cold lunch for him and his friends, and I am sure he would wish it to be offered."

Moved with curiosity to this minor adventure, Flambeau assented gracefully, and followed the old man, who ushered him ceremoniously into the long, lightly panelled room. There was nothing very notable about it, except the rather unusual alternation of many long, low windows with many long, low oblongs of looking-glass, which gave a singular air of lightness and unsubstantialness to the place. It was somehow like lunching out of doors. One or two pictures of a quiet kind hung in the corners: one a large grey photograph of a very young man in uniform, another a red chalk sketch of two long-haired boys. Asked by Flambeau whether the soldierly person was the prince, the butler answered shortly in the negative; it was the prince's younger brother, Captain Stephen Saradine, he said. And with that the old man seemed to dry up suddenly and lose all taste for conversation.

After lunch had tailed off with exquisite coffee and liqueurs, the guests were introduced to the garden, the library, and the housekeeper—a dark handsome lady, of no little majesty, and rather like a plutonic Madonna. It appeared that she and the butler were the only survivors of the prince's original foreign *ménage,* all the other servants now in the house being new and collected in Norfolk by the housekeeper. This latter lady went by the name of Mrs. Anthony, but she spoke with a slight Italian accent, and Flambeau did not doubt that Anthony was a Norfolk version of some more Latin name. Mr. Paul, the butler, also had a faintly foreign air, but he was in tongue and training English, as are many of the most polished men-servants of the cosmopolitan nobility.

Pretty and unique as it was, the place had about it a curious luminous sadness. Hours passed in it like days. The long, well-windowed rooms were full of daylight, but it seemed a dead daylight. And through all other incidental noises, the sound of talk, the clink of glasses, or the passing feet of servants, they could hear on all sides of the house the melancholy noise of the river.

"We have taken a wrong turning and come to a wrong place," said Father Brown, looking out of the window at the grey-green sedges and the silver flood. "Never mind; one can sometimes do good by being the right person in the wrong place."

Father Brown, though commonly a silent, was an oddly sympathetic little man, and in those few but endless hours he unconsciously sank deeper into the secrets of Reed House than his professional friend. He had that knack of friendly silence which is so essential to gossip; and saying scarcely a word, he probably obtained from his new acquaintances all that in any case they would have told. The butler indeed was naturally uncommunicative. He betrayed a sullen and almost animal affection for his master, who, he said, had been very badly treated. The chief offender seemed to be his highness's brother, whose name alone would lengthen the old man's lantern jaws and pucker his parrot nose into a sneer. Captain Stephen was a ne'er-do-well, apparently, and had drained his benevolent brother of hundreds and thousands; forced him to fly from fashionable life and live quietly in this retreat. That was all Paul, the butler, would say, and Paul was obviously a partisan.

The Italian housekeeper was somewhat more communicative, being, as Brown fancied, somewhat less content. Her tone about her master was faintly acid, though not without a certain awe. Flambeau and his friend were standing in the room of the looking-glasses examining the red sketch of the two boys when the housekeeper swept in swiftly on some domestic errand. It was a peculiarity of this glittering, glass-panelled place that anyone entering was reflected in four or five mirrors at once; and Father Brown, without turning round, stopped in the middle of a sentence of family criticism. But Flambeau, who had his face close up to the picture, was already saying in a loud voice: "The brothers Saradine, I suppose. They both look innocent enough. It would be hard to say which is the good brother and which the bad." Then realizing the lady's presence, he turned the conversation with some triviality, and strolled out into the garden. But Father Brown still gazed steadily at the red crayon sketch; and Mrs. Anthony still gazed steadily at Father Brown.

She had large and tragic brown eyes, and her olive face glowed darkly with a curious and painful wonder—as of one doubtful of a stranger's identity or purpose. Whether the little priest's coat and creed touched some southern memories of confession, or whether she fancied he knew more than he did, she said to him in a low voice, as to a fellow plotter: "He is right enough in one way, your friend. He says it would be hard to pick out the good and bad brothers. Oh, it would be hard, it would be mighty hard, to pick out the good one."

"I don't understand you," said Father Brown, and began to move away.

The woman took a step nearer to him, with thunderous brows and a sort of savage stoop, like a bull lowering his horns.

"There isn't a good one," she hissed. "There was badness enough in the captain taking all that money, but I don't think there was much goodness in the prince giving it. The captain's not the only man with something against him."

A light dawned on the cleric's averted face, and his mouth formed silently the word "blackmail." Even as he did so the woman turned an abrupt white face over her shoulder and almost fell. The door had opened soundlessly and the pale Paul stood like a ghost in the doorway. By the weird trick of the reflecting walls, it seemed as if five Pauls had entered by five doors simultaneously.

"His Highness," he said, "has just arrived."

In the same flash the figure of a man had passed outside the first window, crossing the sunlit pane like a lighted stage. An instant later he passed at the second window, and the many mirrors repainted in successive frames the same eagle profile and marching figure. He was erect and alert, but his hair was white and his complexion of an odd ivory yellow. He had that short, curved Roman nose which generally goes with long, lean cheeks and chin, but these were partly masked by moustache and imperial. The moustache was much darker than the beard, giving an effect slightly theatrical, and he was dressed up to the same dashing part, having a white top hat, an orchid in his coat, a yellow waistcoat and yellow gloves which he flapped and swung as he walked. When he came round to the front door they heard the stiff Paul open it, and heard the new arrival say cheerfully: "Well, you see I have come." The stiff Mr. Paul bowed and answered in his inaudible manner; for a few minutes their conversation could not be heard. Then the butler said: "Everything is at your disposal"; and the glove-flapping Prince Saradine came gaily into the room to greet them. They beheld once more that spectral scene—five princes entering a room with five doors.

The prince put the white hat and yellow gloves on the table and offered his hand quite cordially.

"Delighted to see you here, Mr. Flambeau," he said. "Know you very well by reputation, if that's not an indiscreet remark."

"Not at all," answered Flambeau, laughing. "I am not sensitive. Very few reputations are gained by unsullied virtue."

The prince flashed a sharp look at him to see if the retort had any personal point; then he laughed also and offered chairs to everyone, including himself.

"Pleasant little place this, I think," he said with a detached air. "Not much to do, I fear; but the fishing is really good."

The priest, who was staring at him with the grave stare of a baby, was haunted by some fancy that escaped definition. He looked at the grey, carefully curled hair, yellow-white visage, and slim, somewhat foppish figure. These were not unnatural, though perhaps a shade *prononcé*, like the outfit of a figure behind the footlights. The nameless interest lay in something else, in the very framework of the face; Brown was tormented with a half memory of having seen it somewhere before. The man looked like some old friend of his dressed up. Then he remembered the mirrors, and put his fancy down to some psychological effect of that multiplication of human masks.

Prince Saradine distributed his social attentions between his guests with great gaiety and tact. Finding the detective of a sporting turn and eager to employ his holiday, he guided Flambeau and Flambeau's boat down to the best fishing spot in the stream, and was back in his own canoe in twenty minutes to join Father Brown in the library and plunge equally politely into the priest's more philosophic pleasures. He seemed to know a great deal both about the fishing and the books, though of these not the most edifying; he spoke five or six languages, though chiefly the slang of each. He had evidently lived in varied cities and very motley societies, for some of his cheerfullest stories were about gambling hells and opium dens, Australian bushrangers or Italian brigands. Father Brown knew that the once celebrated Saradine had spent his last few years in almost ceaseless travel, but he had not guessed that the travels were so disreputable or so amusing.

Indeed, with all his dignity of a man of the world, Prince Saradine radiated, to such sensitive observers as the priest, a certain atmosphere of the restless and even the unreliable. His face was fastidious, but his eye was wild; he had little nervous tricks, like a man shaken by drink or drugs; and he neither had, nor professed to have, his hand on the helm of household affairs. All these were left to the two old servants, especially to the butler, who was plainly the central pillar of the house. Mr. Paul, indeed, was not so much a butler as a sort of steward, or even, chamberlain; he dined privately, but with almost as much pomp as his master; he was feared by all the servants; and he consulted with the prince decorously, but somewhat unbendingly—rather as if he were the prince's solicitor. The sombre housekeeper was a mere shadow in comparison; indeed, she seemed to efface herself and wait only on the butler, and Brown heard no more of those volcanic whispers which had half told him of the younger brother who blackmailed the elder. Whether the prince was really being thus bled by the absent captain he could not be certain, but there was something insecure and secretive about Saradine that made the tale by no means incredible.

When they went once more into the long hall with the windows and the mirrors yellow evening was dropping over the waters and the willowy banks, and a bittern sounded in the distance like an elf upon his dwarfish drum. The same singular sentiment of some sad and evil fairyland crossed the priest's mind again like a grey cloud. "I wish Flambeau were back," he muttered.

"Do you believe in doom?" asked the restless Prince Saradine suddenly.

"No," answered his guest. "I believe in Doomsday."

The prince turned from the window and stared at him in a singular manner, his face in shadow against the sunset. "What do you mean?" he asked.

"I mean that we here are on the wrong side of the tapestry," answered Father Brown. "The things that happen here do not seem to mean anything; they mean something somewhere else. Somewhere else retribution will come on the real offender. Here it often seems to fall on the wrong person."

The prince made an inexplicable noise like an animal; in his shadowed face the eyes were shining queerly. A new and shrewd thought exploded silently in the other's mind. Was there another meaning in Saradine's blend of brilliancy and abruptness? Was the prince—— Was he perfectly sane? He was repeating, "The wrong person—the wrong person," many more times than was natural in a social exclamation.

Then Father Brown awoke tardily to a second truth. In the mirrors before him he could see the silent door standing open, and the silent Mr. Paul standing in it, with his usual pallid impassiveness.

"I thought it better to announce at once," he said, with the same stiff respectfulness as of an old family lawyer, "a boat rowed by six men has come to the landing-stage, and there's a gentleman sitting in the stern."

"A boat!" repeated the prince; "a gentleman?" and he rose to his feet.

There was a startled silence punctuated only by the odd noise of the bird in the sedge; and then, before anyone could speak again, a new face and figure passed in profile round the three sunlit windows, as the prince had passed an hour or two before. But except for the accident that both outlines were aquiline, they had little in common. Instead of the new white topper of Saradine, was a black one of antiquated or foreign shape; under it was a young and very solemn face, clean shaven, blue about its resolute chin, and carrying a faint suggestion of the young Napoleon. The association was assisted by something old and odd about the whole get-up, as of a man who had never troubled to change the fashions of his fathers. He had a shabby blue frock coat, a red, soldierly looking waistcoat, and a kind of coarse white trousers common among the early Victorians, but strangely incongruous to-day. From all this old clothes-shop his olive face stood out strangely young and monstrously sincere.

"The deuce!" said Prince Saradine, and clapping on his white hat he went to the front door himself, flinging it open on the sunset garden.

By that time the new-comer and his followers were drawn up on the lawn like a small stage army. The six boatmen had pulled the boat well up on shore, and were guarding it almost menacingly, holding their oars erect like spears. They were swarthy men, and some of them wore earrings. But one of them stood forward beside the olive-faced young man in the red waistcoat, and carried a large black case of unfamiliar form.

"Your name," said the young man, "is Saradine?"

Saradine assented rather negligently.

The new-comer had dull, dog-like brown eyes, as different as possible from the restless and glittering grey eyes of the prince. But once again Father Brown was tortured with a sense of having seen somewhere a replica of the face; and once again he remembered the repetitions of the glass-panelled room, and put down the coincidence to that. "Confound this crystal palace!" he muttered. "One sees everything too many times. It's like a dream."

"If you are Prince Saradine," said the young man, "I may tell you that my name is Antonelli."

"Antonelli," repeated the prince languidly. "Somehow I remember the name."

"Permit me to present myself," said the young Italian.

With his left hand he politely took off his old-fashioned top hat; with his right he caught Prince Saradine so ringing a crack across the face that the white top hat rolled down the steps and one of the blue flower-pots rocked upon its pedestal.

The prince, whatever he was, was evidently not a coward; he sprang at his enemy's throat and almost bore him backwards to the grass. But his enemy extricated himself with a singularly inappropriate air of hurried politeness.

"That is all right," he said, panting and in halting English. "I have insulted. I will give satisfaction. Marco, open the case."

The man beside him with the earrings and the big black case proceeded to unlock it. He took out of it two long Italian rapiers, with splendid steel hilts and blades, which he planted point downwards in the lawn. The strange young man standing facing the entrance with his yellow and vindictive face, the two swords standing up in the turf like two crosses in a cemetery, and the line of the ranked rowers behind, gave it all an odd appearance of being some barbaric court of justice. But everything else was unchanged, so sudden had been the interruption. The sunset gold still glowed on the lawn, and the bittern still boomed as announcing some small but dreadful destiny.

"Prince Saradine," said the man called Antonelli; "when I was an infant in the cradle you killed my father and stole my mother;

my father was the more fortunate. You did not kill him fairly, as I am going to kill you. You and my wicked mother took him driving to a lonely pass in Sicily, flung him down a cliff, and went on your way. I could imitate you if I chose, but imitating you is too vile. I have followed you all over the world, and you have always fled from me. But this is the end of the world—and of you. I have you now, and I give you the chance you never gave my father. Choose one of those swords."

Prince Saradine, with contracted brows, seemed to hesitate a moment, but his ears were still singing with the blow, and he sprang forward and snatched at one of the hilts. Father Brown had also sprung forward, striving to compose the dispute; but he soon found his personal presence made matters worse. Saradine was a French Freemason and a fierce atheist, and a priest moved him by the law of contraries. And for the other man neither priest nor layman moved him at all. This young man with the Bonaparte face and the brown eyes was something far sterner than a puritan—a pagan. He was a simple slayer from the morning of the earth; a man of the stone age—a man of stone.

One hope remained, the summoning of the household; and Father Brown ran back into the house. He found, however, that all the under-servants had been given a holiday ashore by the autocrat Paul, and that only the sombre Mrs. Anthony moved uneasily about the long rooms. But the moment she turned a ghastly face upon him, he resolved one of the riddles of the house of mirrors. The heavy brown eyes of Antonelli were the heavy brown eyes of Mrs. Anthony, and in a flash he saw half the story.

"Your son is outside," he said, without wasting words; "either he or the prince will be killed. Where is Mr. Paul?"

"He is at the landing-stage," said the woman faintly. "He is—he is—signalling for help."

"Mrs. Anthony," said Father Brown seriously, "there is no time for nonsense. My friend has his boat down the river, fishing. Your son's boat is guarded by your son's men. There is only this one canoe; what is Mr. Paul doing with it?"

"Santa Maria! I do not know," she said; and swooned all her length on the matted floor.

Father Brown lifted her to a sofa, flung a pot of water over her, shouted for help, and then rushed down to the landing-stage of the little island. But the canoe was already in mid-stream, and old Paul was pulling and pushing it up the river with an energy incredible at his years.

"I will save my master," he cried, his eyes blazing maniacally. "I will save him yet!"

Father Brown could do nothing but gaze after the boat as it struggled up-stream, and pray that the old man might waken the little town in time.

"A duel is bad enough," he muttered, rubbing up his rough dust-coloured hair, "but there's something wrong about this duel, even as a duel. I feel it in my bones. But what can it be?"

As he stood staring at the water, a wavering mirror of sunset, he heard from the other end of the island garden a small but unmistakable sound—the cold concussion of steel. He turned his head.

Away on the farthest cape or headland of the long islet, on a strip of turf beyond the last rank of roses, the duellists had already crossed swords. Evening above them was a dome of virgin gold, and, distant as they were, every detail was picked out. They had cast off their coats, but the yellow waistcoat and white hair of Saradine, the red waistcoat and white trousers of Antonelli, glittered in the level light like the colours of the dancing clockwork dolls. The two swords sparkled from point to pommel like two diamond pins. There was something frightful in the two figures appearing so little and so gay. They looked like two butterflies trying to pin each other to a cork.

Father Brown ran as hard as he could, his little legs going like a wheel. But when he came to the field of combat he found he was both too late and too early—too late to stop the strife, under the shadow of the grim Sicilians leaning on their oars, and too early to anticipate any disastrous issue of it. For the two men were singularly well matched, the prince using his skill with a sort of cynical confidence, the Sicilian using his with a murderous care. Few finer fencing matches can ever have been seen in crowded amphitheatres than that which tinkled and sparkled on that forgotten island in the reedy river. The dizzy fight was balanced so long that hope began to revive in the protesting priest; by all common probability Paul must soon come back with the police. It would be some comfort even if Flambeau came back from his fishing, for Flambeau, physically speaking, was worth four other men. But there was no sign of Flambeau, and, what was much queerer, no sign of Paul or the police. No other raft or stick was left to float on; in that lost island in that vast nameless pool, they were cut off as on a rock in the Pacific.

Almost as he had the thought the ringing of the rapiers quickened to a rattle, the prince's arms flew up, and the point shot out behind between his shoulder-blades. He went over with a great whirling movement, almost like one throwing the half of a boy's cart-wheel. The sword flew from his hand like a shooting star, and dived into the distant river; and he himself sank with so earth-shaking a subsidence that he broke a big rose-tree with his body and shook up into the sky a cloud of red earth—like the smoke of some heathen sacrifice. The Sicilian had made blood-offering to the ghost of his father.

The priest was instantly on his knees by the corpse, but only to make too sure that it was a corpse. As he was still trying some last hopeless tests he heard for the first time voices from farther up the river, and saw a police-boat shoot up to the landing-stage with constables and other important people, including the excited Paul. The little priest rose with a distinctly dubious grimace.

"Now, why on earth," he muttered, "why on earth couldn't he have come before?"

Some seven minutes later the island was occupied by an invasion of townsfolk and police, and the latter had put their hands on the victorious duellist, ritually reminding him that anything he said might be used against him.

"I shall not say anything," said the monomaniac, with a wonderful and peaceful face. "I shall never say anything any more. I am very happy, and I only want to be hanged."

Then he shut his mouth as they led him away, and it is the strange but certain truth that he never opened it again in this world, except to say "Guilty" at his trial.

Father Brown had stared at the suddenly crowded garden, the arrest of the man of blood, the carrying away of the corpse after its examination by the doctor, rather as one watches the break-up of some ugly dream; he was motionless, like a man in a nightmare. He gave his name and address as a witness, but declined their offer of a boat to the shore, and remained alone in the island garden, gazing at the broken rose bush and the whole green theatre of that swift and inexplicable tragedy. The light died along the river; mist rose in the marshy banks; a few belated birds flitted fitfully across.

Stuck stubbornly in his sub-consciousness (which was an unusually lively one) was an unspeakable certainty that there was something still unexplained. This sense that had clung to him all day could not be fully explained by his fancy about "looking-glass land."

Somehow he had not seen the real story, but some game or masque. And yet people do not get hanged or run through the body for the sake of a charade.

As he sat on the steps of the landing-stage ruminating he grew conscious of the tall, dark streak of a sail coming silently down the shining river, and sprang to his feet with such a back-rush of feeling that he almost wept.

"Flambeau!" he cried, and shook his friend by both hands again and again, much to the astonishment of that sportsman, as he came on shore with his fishing tackle. "Flambeau," he said, "so you're not killed?"

"Killed!" repeated the angler in great astonishment. "And why should I be killed?"

"Oh, because nearly everybody else is," said his companion rather wildly. "Saradine got murdered, and Antonelli wants to be hanged, and his mother's fainted, and I, for one, don't know whether I'm in this world or the next. But, thank God, you're in the same one." And he took the bewildered Flambeau's arm.

As they turned from the landing-stage they came under the eaves of the low bamboo house and looked in through one of the windows, as they had done on their first arrival. They beheld a lamp-lit interior well calculated to arrest their eyes. The table in the long dining-room had been laid for dinner when Saradine's destroyer had fallen like a storm-bolt on the island. And the dinner was now in placid progress, for Mrs. Anthony sat somewhat sullenly at the foot of the table, while at the head of it was Mr. Paul, the *major domo*: eating and drinking of the best, his bleared, bluish eyes standing queerly out of his face, his gaunt countenance inscrutable, but by no means devoid of satisfaction.

With a gesture of powerful impatience, Flambeau rattled at the window, wrenched it open, and put an indignant head into the lamp-lit room.

"Well!" he cried; "I can understand you may need some refreshment, but really to steal your master's dinner while he lies murdered in the garden——"

"I have stolen a great many things in a long and pleasant life," replied the strange old gentleman placidly; "this dinner is one of the few things I have not stolen. This dinner and this house and garden happen to belong to me."

A thought flashed across Flambeau's face. "You mean to say," he began, "that the will of Prince Saradine——"

"I am Prince Saradine," said the old man, munching a salted almond.

Father Brown, who was looking at the birds outside, jumped as if he were shot, and put in at the window a pale face like a turnip.

"You are *what*?" he repeated in a shrill voice.

"Paul Prince Saradine, *à vos ordres*," said the venerable person politely, lifting a glass of sherry. "I live here very quietly, being a domestic kind of fellow; and for the sake of modesty I am called Mr. Paul, to distinguish me from my unfortunate brother Mr. Stephen. He died, I hear, recently—in the garden. Of course, it is not my fault if enemies pursue him to this place. It is owing to the regrettable irregularity of his life. He was not a domestic character."

He relapsed into silence, and continued to gaze at the opposite wall just above the bowed and sombre head of the woman. They saw plainly the family likeness that had haunted them in the dead man. Then his old shoulders began to heave and shake a little, as if he were choking, but his face did not alter.

"My God!" cried Flambeau after a pause; "he's laughing!"

"Come away," said Father Brown, who was quite white. "Come away from this house of hell. Let us get into an honest boat again."

Night had sunk on rushes and river by the time they had pushed off from the island, and they went down-stream in the dark, warming themselves with two big cigars that glowed like crimson ships' lanterns. Father Brown took his cigar out of his mouth and said:

"I suppose you can guess the whole story now? After all, it's a primitive story. A man had two enemies. He was a wise man. And so he discovered that two enemies are better than one."

"I do not follow that," answered Flambeau.

"Oh, it's really simple," rejoined his friend. "Simple, though anything but innocent. Both the Saradines were scamps: but the prince, the elder, was the sort of scamp that gets to the top; and the younger, the captain, was the sort that sinks to the bottom. This squalid officer fell from beggar to blackmailer, and one ugly day he got his hold upon his brother the prince. Obviously it was for no light matter, for Prince Paul Saradine was frankly 'fast,' and had no reputation to lose as to the mere sins of society. In plain fact, it was a hanging matter, and Stephen literally had a rope round his brother's neck. He had somehow discovered the truth about the Sicilian affair, and could prove that Paul murdered old Antonelli in the mountains. The captain raked in the hush money heavily for ten years, until even the prince's splendid fortune began to look a little foolish.

"But Prince Saradine bore another burden besides his blood-sucking brother. He knew that the son of Antonelli, a mere child at the time of the murder, had been trained in savage Sicilian loyalty, and lived only to avenge his father, not with the gibbet (for he lacked Stephen's legal proof), but with the old weapons of vendetta. The boy had practised arms with a deadly perfection, and about the time that he was old enough to use them Prince Saradine began, as the society papers said, to travel. The fact is that he began to flee for his life, passing from place to place like a hunted criminal; but with one relentless man upon his trail. That was Prince Paul's position, and by no means a pretty one. The more money he spent on eluding Antonelli the less he had to silence Stephen. The more he gave to silence Stephen the less chance there was of finally escaping Antonelli. Then it was that he showed himself a great man—a genius like Napoleon.

"Instead of resisting his two antagonists, he surrendered suddenly to both of them. He gave way, like a Japanese wrestler, and his foes fell prostrate before him. He gave up the race round the world, and he gave up his address to young Antonelli; then he gave up everything to his brother. He sent Stephen money enough for smart clothes and easy travel, with a letter saying roughly: 'This is all I have left. You have cleaned me out. I still have a little house in Norfolk, with servants and a cellar, and if you want more from me you must take that. Come and take possession if you like, and I will live there quietly as your friend or agent or anything.' He knew that the Sicilian had never seen the Saradine brothers save, perhaps, in pictures; he knew they were somewhat alike, both having grey, pointed beards. Then he shaved his own face and waited. The trap worked. The unhappy captain, in his new clothes, entered the house in triumph as a prince, and walked upon the Sicilian's sword.

"There was one hitch, and it is to the honour of human nature. Evil spirits like Saradine often blunder by never expecting the virtues of mankind. He took it for granted that the Italian's blow, when it came, would be dark, violent and nameless, like the blow it avenged; that the victim would be knifed at night, or shot from behind a hedge, and so die without speech. It was a bad minute for Prince Paul when Antonelli's chivalry proposed a formal duel, with all its possible explanations. It was then that I found him putting off in his boat with wild eyes. He was fleeing, bareheaded, in an open boat before Antonelli should learn who he was.

"But, however agitated, he was not hopeless. He knew the adventurer and he knew the fanatic. It was quite probable that Stephen, the adventurer, would hold his tongue, through his mere histrionic pleasure in playing a part, his lust for clinging to his new cosy quarters, his rascal's trust in luck, and his fine fencing. It was certain that Antonelli, the fanatic, would hold his tongue, and be hanged without telling tales of his family. Paul hung about on the river till he knew the fight was over. Then he roused the town, brought police, saw his two vanquished enemies taken away for ever, and sat down smiling to his dinner."

"Laughing, God help us!" said Flambeau with a strong shudder. "Do they get such ideas from Satan?"

"He's got that idea from you," answered the priest.

"God forbid!" ejaculated Flambeau. "From me? What do you mean?"

The priest pulled a visiting-card from his pocket and held it up in the faint glow of his cigar; it was scrawled with green ink.

"Don't you remember his original invitation to you?" he asked; "and the compliment to your criminal exploit? 'That trick of yours,' he says, 'of getting one detective to arrest the other?' He has just copied your trick. With an enemy on each side of him he slipped swiftly out of the way and let them collide and kill each other."

Flambeau tore Prince Saradine's card from the priest's hands and rent it savagely in small pieces.

"There's the last of that old skull and crossbones," he said as he scattered the pieces upon the dark and disappearing waves of the stream; "but I should think it would poison the fishes."

The last gleam of white card and green ink was drowned and darkened; a faint and vibrant colour as of morning changed the sky, and the moon behind the grasses grew paler. They drifted in silence.

"Father," said Flambeau suddenly, "do you think it was all a dream?"

The priest shook his head, whether in dissent or agnosticism, but remained mute. A smell of hawthorn and of orchards came to them through the darkness, telling them that a wind was awake; the next moment it swayed their little boat and swelled their sail, and carried them onward down the winding river to happier places and the homes of harmless men.

THE SIGN OF THE BROKEN SWORD

THE THOUSAND ARMS of the forest were grey, and its million fingers silver. In a sky of dark green-blue-like slate the stars were bleak and brilliant like splintered ice. All that thickly wooded and sparsely tenanted countryside was stiff with a bitter and brittle frost. The black hollows between the trunks of the trees looked like bottomless, black caverns of that heartless Scandinavian hell, a hell of incalculable cold. Even the square stone tower of the church looked northern to the point of heathenry, as if it were some barbaric tower among the sea rocks of Iceland. It was a queer night for anyone to explore a churchyard. But, on the other hand, perhaps it was worth exploring.

It rose abruptly out of the ashen wastes of forest in a sort of hump or shoulder of green turf that looked grey in the starlight. Most of the graves were on a slant, and the path leading up to the church was as steep as a staircase. On the top of the hill, in the one flat and prominent place, was the monument for which the place was famous. It contrasted strangely with the featureless graves all round, for it was the work of one of the greatest sculptors of modern Europe; and yet his fame was at once forgotten in the fame of the man whose image he had made. It showed, by touches of the small silver pencil of starlight, the massive metal figure of a soldier recumbent, the strong hands sealed in an everlasting worship, the great head pillowed upon a gun. The venerable face was bearded, or rather whiskered, in the old, heavy Colonel Newcome fashion. The uniform, though suggested with the few strokes of simplicity, was that of modern war. By his right side lay a sword, of which the tip was broken off; on the left side lay a Bible. On glowing summer afternoons wagonettes came full of Americans and cultured suburbans to see the sepulchre; but even then they felt the vast forest land with its one dumpy dome of churchyard and church as a place oddly dumb and neglected. In this freezing darkness of mid-winter one would think he might be left alone with the stars. Nevertheless, in the stillness of those stiff woods a wooden gate creaked, and two dim figures dressed in black climbed up the little path to the tomb.

So faint was that frigid starlight that nothing could have been traced about them except that while they both wore black, one man was enormously big, and the other (perhaps by contrast) almost startlingly small. They went up to the great graven tomb of the historic warrior, and stood for a few minutes staring at it. There was no human, perhaps no living, thing for a wide circle; and a morbid fancy might well have wondered if they were human themselves. In any case, the beginning of their conversation might have seemed strange. After the first silence the small man said to the other:

"Where does a wise man hide a pebble?"

And the tall man answered in a low voice: "On the beach."

The small man nodded, and after a short silence said: "Where does a wise man hide a leaf?"

And the other answered: "In the forest."

There was another stillness, and then the tall man resumed: "Do you mean that when a wise man has to hide a real diamond he has been known to hide it among sham ones?"

"No, no," said the little man with a laugh, "we will let bygones be bygones."

He stamped his cold feet for a second or two and then said: "I'm not thinking of that at all, but of something else; something rather peculiar. Just strike a match, will you?"

The big man fumbled in his pocket, and soon a scratch and a flare painted gold the whole flat side of the monument. On it was cut in black letters the well-known words which so many Americans had reverently read: "Sacred to the Memory of General Sir Arthur St. Clare, Hero and Martyr, who Always Vanquished his Enemies and Always Spared Them, and Was Treacherously Slain by Them at Last. May God in Whom he Trusted both Reward and Revenge him."

The match burnt the big man's fingers, blackened, and dropped. He was about to strike another, but his small companion stopped him. "That's all right, Flambeau, old man; I saw what I wanted. Or, rather, I didn't see what I didn't want. And now we must walk a mile and a half along the road to the next inn, and I will try to tell you all about it. For Heaven knows a man should have fire and ale when he dares tell such a story."

They descended the precipitous path, they re-latched the rusty gate, and set off at a stamping, ringing walk down the frozen forest road. They had gone a full quarter of a mile before the smaller man spoke again. He said: "Yes; the wise man hides a pebble on the beach. But what does he do if there is no beach? Do you know anything of the great St. Clare trouble?"

"I know nothing about English generals, Father Brown," answered the large man, laughing, "though a little about English policemen. I only know that you have dragged me a precious long dance to all the shrines of this fellow, whoever he is. One would think he got buried in six different places. I've seen a memorial to General St. Clare in Westminster Abbey; I've seen a ramping equestrian statue of General St. Clare on the Embankment; I've seen a medallion of General St. Clare in the street he was born in; and another in the street he lived in; and now you drag me after dark to his coffin in the village churchyard. I am beginning to be a bit tired of his magnificent personality, especially as I don't in the least know who he was. What are you hunting for in all these crypts and effigies?"

"I am only looking for one word," said Father Brown. "A word that isn't there."

"Well," asked Flambeau, "are you going to tell me anything about it?"

"I must divide it into two parts," remarked the priest. "First there is what everybody knows; and then there is what I know. Now, what everybody knows is short and plain enough. It is also entirely wrong."

"Right you are," said the big man called Flambeau cheerfully. "Let's begin at the wrong end. Let's begin with what everybody knows, which isn't true."

"If not wholly untrue, it is at least very inadequate," continued Brown; "for in point of fact, all that the public knows amounts precisely to this: The public knows that Arthur St. Clare was a great and successful English general. It knows that after splendid yet careful campaigns both in India and Africa he was in command against Brazil when the great Brazilian patriot Olivier issued his ultimatum. It knows that on that occasion St. Clare with a very small force attacked Olivier with a very large one, and was captured after heroic resistance. And it knows that after his capture, and to the abhorrence of the civilized world, St. Clare was hanged on the nearest tree. He was found swinging there after the Brazilians had retired, with his broken sword hung round his neck."

"And that popular story is untrue?" suggested Flambeau.

"No," said his friend quietly; "that story is quite true, so far as it goes."

"Well, I think it goes far enough!" said Flambeau, "but if the popular story is true, what is the mystery?"

They had passed many hundreds of grey and ghostly trees before the little priest answered. Then he bit his finger reflectively and said: "Why, the mystery is a mystery of psychology. Or, rather, it is a mystery of two psychologies. In that Brazilian business two of the most famous men of modern history acted flat against their characters. Mind you, Olivier and St. Clare were both heroes—the old thing, and no mistake; it was like the fight between Hector and Achilles. Now, what would you say to an affair in which Achilles was timid and Hector was treacherous?"

"Go on," said the large man impatiently as the other bit his finger again.

"Sir Arthur St. Clare was a soldier of the old religious type—the type that saved us during the Mutiny," continued Brown. "He was always more for duty than for dash; and with all his personal courage was decidedly a prudent commander, particularly indignant at any needless waste of soldiers. Yet, in this last battle, he attempted something that a baby could see was absurd. One need not be a strategist to see it was as wild as wind; just as one need not be a strategist to keep out of the way of a motor-bus. Well, that is the first mystery; what had become of the English general's head? The second riddle is, what had become of the Brazilian general's heart? President Olivier might be called a visionary or a nuisance; but even his enemies admitted that he was magnanimous to the point of knight errantry. Almost every other prisoner he had ever captured had been set free, or even loaded with benefits. Men who had really wronged him came away touched by his simplicity and sweetness. Why the deuce should he diabolically revenge himself only once in his life; and then for the one particular blow that could not have hurt him? Well, there you have it. One of the wisest men in the world acted like an idiot for no reason. One of the best men in the world acted like a fiend for no reason. That's the long and short of it; and I leave it to you, my boy."

"No, you don't," said the other with a snort. "I leave it to you; and you jolly well tell me all about it."

"Well," resumed Father Brown, "it's not fair to say that the public impression is just what I've said, without adding that two things have happened since. I can't say they threw a new light, for nobody can make sense of them. But they threw a new kind of darkness, they threw the darkness in new directions. The first was this. The family physician of the St. Clares quarrelled with that family and began publishing a violent series of articles, in which he said that the late general was a religious maniac; but as far as the tale went, this seemed to mean little more than a religious man. Anyhow, the story fizzled out. Everyone knew, of course, that St. Clare had some of the eccentricities of puritan piety. The second incident was much more arresting. In the luckless and unsupported regiment which made that rash attempt at the Black River there was a certain Captain Keith, who was at that time engaged to St. Clare's daughter, and who afterwards married her. He was one of those who were captured by Olivier, and, like all the rest except the general, appears to have been bounteously treated and promptly set free. Some twenty years afterwards this man, then Lieutenant-Colonel Keith, published a sort of autobiography called 'A British Officer in Burmah and Brazil.' In the place where the reader looks eagerly for some account of the mystery of St. Clare's disaster may be found the following words: 'Everywhere else in this book I have narrated things exactly as they occurred, holding as I do the old-fashioned opinion that the glory of England is old enough to take care of itself. The exception I shall make is in this matter of the defeat by the Black River; and my reasons, though private, are honourable and compelling. I will, however, add this in justice to the memories of two distinguished men. General St. Clare has been accused of incapacity on this occasion; I can at least testify that this action, properly understood, was one of the most brilliant and sagacious of his life. President Olivier by similar report is charged with savage injustice. I think it due to the honour of an enemy to say that he acted on this occasion with even more than his characteristic good feeling. To put the matter popularly, I can assure my countrymen that St. Clare was by no means such a fool, nor Olivier such a brute as he looked. This is all I have to say; nor shall any earthly consideration induce me to add a word.' "

A large frozen moon like a lustrous snowball began to show through the tangle of twigs in front of them, and by its light the narrator had been able to refresh his memory of Captain Keith's text from a scrap of printed paper. As he folded it up and put it back in his pocket Flambeau threw up his hand with a French gesture.

"Wait a bit, wait a bit," he cried excitedly. "I believe I can guess it at the first go."

He strode on, breathing hard, his black head and bull neck forward, like a man winning a walking race. The little priest, amused and interested, had some trouble in trotting beside him. Just before them the trees fell back a little to left and right, and the road swept downwards across a clear, moonlit valley, till it dived again like a rabbit into the wall of another wood. The entrance to the farther forest looked small and round, like the black hole of a remote railway tunnel. But it was within some hundred yards, and gaped like a cavern before Flambeau spoke again.

"I've got it," he cried at last, slapping his thigh with his great hand. "Four minutes' thinking, and I can tell you the whole story myself."

"All right," assented his friend. "You tell it."

Flambeau lifted his head, but lowered his voice. "General Sir Arthur St. Clare," he said, "came of a family in which madness was hereditary; and his whole aim was to keep this from his daughter, and even, if possible, from his future son-in-law. Rightly or wrongly, he thought the final collapse was close, and resolved on suicide. Yet ordinary suicide would blazon the very idea he dreaded. As the campaign approached the clouds came thicker on his brain, and at last in a mad moment he sacrificed his public duty to his private. He rushed rashly into battle, hoping to fall by the first shot. When he found that he had only attained capture and discredit, the sealed bomb in his brain burst, and he broke his own sword and hanged himself."

He stared firmly at the grey facade of forest in front of him, with the one black gap in it, like the mouth of the grave, into which their path plunged. Perhaps something menacing in the road thus suddenly swallowed reinforced his vivid vision of the tragedy, for he shuddered.

"A horrid story," repeated the priest with bent head; "but not the real story."

Then he threw back his head with a sort of despair and cried: "Oh, I wish it had been."

The tall Flambeau faced round and stared at him.

"Yours is a clean story," cried Father Brown, deeply moved. "A sweet, pure, honest story, as open and white as that moon. Madness and despair are innocent enough. There are worse things, Flambeau."

Flambeau looked up wildly at the moon thus invoked; and from where he stood one black tree-bough curved across it exactly like a devil's horn.

"Father—Father," cried Flambeau with the French gesture and stepping yet more rapidly forward, "do you mean it was worse than that?"

"Worse than that," said the other like a grave echo. And they plunged into the black cloister of the woodland, which ran by them in a dim tapestry of trunks, like one of the dark corridors in a dream.

They were soon in the most secret entrails of the wood, and felt close about them the foliage that they could not see, when the priest said again:

"Where does a wise man hide a leaf? In the forest. But what does he do if there is no forest?"

"Well—well," cried Flambeau irritably, "what does he do?"

"He grows a forest to hide it in," said the priest in an obscure voice. "A fearful sin."

"Look here," cried his friend impatiently, for the dark wood and the dark sayings got a little on his nerves; "will you tell me this story or not? What other evidence is there to go on?"

"There are three more bits of evidence," said the other, "that I have dug up in holes and corners, and I will give them in logical rather than chronological order. First of all, of course, our authority for the issue and event of the battle is in Olivier's own dispatches, which are lucid enough. He was entrenched with two or three regiments on the heights that swept down to the Black River, on the other side of which was lower and more marshy ground. Beyond this again was gently rising country, on which was the first English outpost, supported by others which lay, however, considerably in its rear. The British forces as a whole were greatly superior in numbers; but this particular regiment was just far enough from its base to make Olivier consider the project of crossing the river to cut it off. By sunset, however, he had decided to retain his own position, which was a specially strong one. At daybreak next morning he was thunderstruck to see that this stray handful of English, entirely unsupported from their rear, had flung themselves across the river, half by the bridge to the right, and the other half by a ford higher up, and were massed upon the marshy bank below him.

"That they should attempt an attack with such numbers against such a position was incredible enough; but Olivier noticed something yet more extraordinary. For instead of attempting to seize more solid ground, this mad regiment, having put the river in its rear by one wild charge, did nothing more, but stuck there in the mire like flies in treacle. Needless to say, the Brazilians blew great gaps in them with artillery, which they could only return with spirited but lessening rifle fire. Yet they never broke; and Olivier's curt account ends with a strong tribute of admiration for the mystic valour of these imbeciles. 'Our line then advanced finally,' writes Olivier, 'and drove them into the river; we captured General St. Clare himself and several other officers. The colonel and the major had both fallen in the battle. I cannot resist saying that few finer sights can have been seen in history than the last stand of this extraordinary regiment; wounded officers picking up the rifles of dead soldiers, and the general himself facing us on horseback bareheaded and with a broken sword.' On what happened to the general afterwards Olivier is as silent as Captain Keith."

"Well," grunted Flambeau, "get on to the next bit of evidence."

"The next evidence," said Father Brown, "took some time to find, but it will not take long to tell. I found at last, in an almshouse down in the Lincolnshire Fens, an old soldier who not only was wounded at the Black River, but had actually knelt beside the colonel of the regiment when he died. This latter was a certain Colonel Clancy, a big bull of an Irishman; and it would seem that he died almost as much of rage as of bullets. He, at any rate, was not responsible for that ridiculous raid; it must have been imposed on him by the general. His last edifying words, according to my informant, were these: 'And there goes the damned old donkey with the end of his sword knocked off. I wish it was his head.' You will remark that everyone seems to have noticed this detail about the broken sword blade, though most people regard it somewhat more reverently than did the late Colonel Clancy. And now for the third fragment."

Their path through the woodland began to go upward, and the speaker paused a little for breath before he went on. Then he continued in the same business-like tone:

"Only a month or two ago a certain Brazilian official died in England, having quarrelled with Olivier and left his country. He was a well-known figure both here and on the Continent, a Spaniard named Espado; I knew him myself, a yellow-faced old dandy, with a hooked nose. For various private reasons I had permission to see the documents he had left; he was a Catholic, of course, and I had been with him towards the end. There was nothing of his that lit up any corner of the black St. Clare business, except five or six common exercise books filled with the diary of some English soldier. I can only suppose that it was found by the Brazilians on one of those that fell. Anyhow, it stopped abruptly the night before the battle.

"But the account of that last day in the poor fellow's life was certainly worth reading. I have it on me; but it's too dark to read it here, and I will give you a résumé. The first part of that entry is full of jokes, evidently flung about among the men, about somebody called the Vulture. It does not seem as if this person, whoever he was, was one of themselves, nor even an Englishman; neither is he exactly spoken of as one of the enemy. It sounds rather as if he were some local go-between and non-combatant; perhaps a guide or a journalist. He has been closeted with old Colonel Clancy; but is more often seen talking to the major. Indeed, the major is somewhat prominent in this soldier's narrative; a lean, dark-haired man, apparently, of the name of Murray—a north of Ireland man and a Puritan. There are continual jests about the contrast between this Ulsterman's austerity and the conviviality of Colonel Clancy. There is also some joke about the Vulture wearing bright-coloured clothes.

"But all these levities are scattered by what may well be called the note of a bugle. Behind the English camp, and almost parallel to the river, ran one of the few great roads of that district. Westward the road curved round towards the river, which it crossed by the bridge before mentioned. To the east the road swept backwards into the wilds, and some two miles along it was the next English outpost. From this direction there came along the road that evening a glitter and clatter of light cavalry, in which even the simple diarist could recognize with astonishment the general with his staff. He rode the great white horse which you have seen so often in illustrated papers and Academy pictures; and you may be sure that the salute they gave him was not merely ceremonial. He, at least, wasted no time on ceremony, but, springing from the saddle immediately, mixed with the group of officers, and fell into emphatic though confidential speech. What struck our friend the diarist most was his special disposition to discuss matters with Major Murray; but, indeed, such a selection, so long as it was not marked, was in no way unnatural. The two men were made for sympathy; they were men who 'read their Bibles'; they were both the old Evangelical type of officer. However this may be, it is certain that when the general mounted again he was still talking earnestly to Murray; and that as he walked his horse slowly down the road towards the river, the tall Ulsterman still walked by his bridle-rein in earnest debate. The soldiers watched the two until they vanished behind a clump of trees where the road turned towards the river. The colonel had gone back to his tent, and the men to their pickets; the man with the diary lingered for another four minutes, and saw a marvellous sight.

"The great white horse which had marched slowly down the road, as it had marched in so many processions, flew back, galloping up the road towards them as if it were mad to win a race. At first they thought it had run away with the man on its back; but they soon saw that the general, a fine rider, was himself urging it to full speed. Horse and man swept up to them like a whirlwind; and then, reining up the reeling charger, the general turned on them a face like flame, and called for the colonel like the trumpet that wakes the dead.

"I conceive that all the earthquake events of that catastrophe tumbled on top of each other rather like lumber in the minds of men such as our friend with the diary. With the dazed excitement of a dream, they found themselves falling—literally falling—into their ranks, and learned that an attack was to be led at once across the river. The general and the major, it was said, had found out something at the bridge, and there was only just time to strike for life. The major had gone back at once to call up the reserve along the road behind; it was doubtful if even with that prompt appeal help could reach them in time. But they must pass the stream that night, and seize the heights by morning. It is with the very stir and throb of that romantic nocturnal march that the diary suddenly ends."

Father Brown had mounted ahead; for the woodland path grew smaller, steeper, and more twisted, till they felt as if they were ascending a winding staircase. The priest's voice came from above out of the darkness.

"There was one other little and enormous thing. When the general urged them to their chivalric charge he drew half his sword from the scabbard; and then, as if ashamed of such melodrama, thrust it back again. The sword again, you see."

A half-light broke through the network of boughs above them, flinging the ghost of a net about their feet; for they were mounting again to the faint luminosity of the naked night. Flambeau felt truth all round him as an atmosphere, but not as an idea. He answered with bewildered brain: "Well, what's the matter with the sword? Officers generally have swords, don't they?"

"They are not often mentioned in modern war," said the other dispassionately; "but in this affair one falls over the blessed sword everywhere."

"Well, what is there in that?" growled Flambeau; "it was a two-pence coloured sort of incident; the old man's blade breaking in his last battle. Anyone might bet the papers would get hold of it, as they have. On all these tombs and things it's shown broken at the point. I hope you haven't dragged me through this Polar expedition merely because two men with an eye for a picture saw St. Clare's broken sword."

"No," cried Father Brown, with a sharp voice like a pistol shot; "but who saw his unbroken sword?"

"What do you mean?" cried the other, and stood still under the stars. They had come abruptly out of the grey gates of the wood.

"I say, who saw his unbroken sword?" repeated Father Brown obstinately. "Not the writer of the diary, anyhow; the general sheathed it in time."

Flambeau looked about him in the moonlight, as a man struck blind might look in the sun; and his friend went on for the first time with eagerness:

"Flambeau," he cried, "I cannot prove it, even after hunting through the tombs. But I am sure of it. Let me add just one more tiny fact that tips the whole thing over. The colonel, by a strange chance, was one of the first struck by a bullet. He was struck long before the troops came to close quarters. But he saw St. Clare's sword broken. Why was it broken? How was it broken? My friend, it was broken before the battle."

"Oh!" said his friend, with a sort of forlorn jocularity; "and pray where is the other piece?"

"I can tell you," said the priest promptly. "In the north-east corner of the cemetery of the Protestant Cathedral at Belfast."

"Indeed?" inquired the other. "Have you looked for it?"

"I couldn't," replied Brown, with frank regret. "There's a great marble monument on top of it; a monument to the heroic Major Murray, who fell fighting gloriously at the famous Battle of the Black River."

Flambeau seemed suddenly galvanized into existence. "You mean," he cried hoarsely, "that General St. Clare hated Murray, and murdered him on the field of battle because——"

"You are still full of good and pure thoughts," said the other. "It was worse than that."

"Well," said the large man, "my stock of evil imagination is used up."

The priest seemed really doubtful where to begin, and at last he said again:

"Where would a wise man hide a leaf? In the forest."

The other did not answer.

"If there were no forest, he would make a forest. And if he wished to hide a dead leaf, he would make a dead forest."

There was still no reply, and the priest added still more mildly and quietly:

"And if a man had to hide a dead body, he would make a field of dead bodies to hide it in."

Flambeau began to stamp forward with an intolerance of delay in time or space; but Father Brown went on as if he were continuing the last sentence:

"Sir Arthur St. Clare, as I have already said, was a man who read his Bible. That was what was the matter with *him*. When will people understand that it is useless for a man to read his Bible unless he also reads everybody else's Bible? A printer reads a Bible for misprints. A Mormon reads his Bible and finds polygamy; a Christian Scientist reads his and finds we have no arms and legs. St. Clare was an old Anglo-Indian Protestant soldier. Now, just think what that might mean; and, for Heaven's sake, don't cant about it. It might mean a man physically formidable living under a tropic sun in an Oriental society, and soaking himself without sense or guidance in an Oriental book. Of course, he read the Old Testament rather than the New. Of course, he found in the Old Testament anything that he wanted—lust, tyranny, treason. Oh, I dare say he was honest, as you call it. But what is the good of a man being honest in his worship of dishonesty?

"In each of the hot and secret countries to which that man went he kept a harem, he tortured witnesses, he amassed shameful gold; but certainly he would have said with steady eyes that he did it to the glory of the Lord. My own theology is sufficiently expressed by asking which Lord? Anyhow, there is this about such evil, that it opens door after door in hell, and always into smaller and smaller chambers. This is the real case against crime, that a man does not become wilder and wilder, but only meaner and meaner. St. Clare was soon suffocated by difficulties of bribery and blackmail; and needed more and more cash. And by the time of the battle of the Black River he had fallen from world to world to that place which Dante makes the lowest floor of the universe."

"What do you mean?" asked his friend again.

"I mean *that*," retorted the cleric, and suddenly pointed at a puddle sealed with ice that shone in the moon. "Do you remember whom Dante put in the last circle of ice?"

"The traitors," said Flambeau, and shuddered. As he looked round at the inhuman landscape of trees, with taunting and almost obscene outlines, he could almost fancy he was Dante, and the priest with the rivulet of a voice was, indeed, a Virgil leading him through a land of eternal sins.

The voice went on: "Olivier, as you know, was quixotic, and would not permit a secret service and spies. The thing, however, was done, like many other things, behind his back. It was managed by my old friend Espado; he was the bright-clad fop, whose hook nose got him called the Vulture. Posing as a sort of philanthropist at the front, he felt his way through the English Army, and at last got his fingers on its one corrupt man—please God!—and that man at the top. St. Clare was in foul need of money, and mountains of it. The discredited family doctor was threatening those extraordinary exposures that afterwards began and were broken off; tales of monstrous and prehistoric things in Park Lane; things done by an English Evangelical that smelt like human sacrifice and hordes of slaves. Money was wanted, too, for his daughter's dowry; for to him the fame of wealth was as sweet as wealth itself. He snapped the last thread, whispered the word to Brazil, and wealth poured in from the enemies of England. But another man had talked to Espado the Vulture as well as he. Somehow the dark, grim young major from Ulster had guessed the hideous truth; and when they walked slowly together down that road towards the bridge Murray was telling the general that he must resign instantly, or be court-martialled and shot. The general temporized with him till they came to the fringe of tropic trees by the bridge; and there by the singing river and the sunlit palms (for I can see the picture) the general drew his sabre and plunged it through the body of the major."

The wintry road curved over a ridge in cutting frost, with cruel black shapes of bush and thicket; but Flambeau fancied that he saw beyond it faintly the edge of an aureole that was not starlight and moonlight, but some fire such as is made by men. He watched it as the tale drew to its close.

"St. Clare was a hell-hound, but he was a hound of breed. Never, I'll swear, was he so lucid and so strong as when poor Murray lay a cold lump at his feet. Never in all his triumphs, as Captain Keith said truly, was the great man so great as he was in this last world-despised defeat. He looked coolly at his weapon to wipe off the blood; he saw the point he had planted between his victim's shoulders had broken off in the body. He saw quite calmly as, through a club window-pane, all that must follow. He saw that men must find the unaccountable corpse; must extract the unaccountable sword-point; must notice the unaccountable broken sword—or absence of sword. He had killed, but not silenced. But his imperious intellect rose against the facer—there was one way yet. He could make the corpse less unaccountable. He could create a hill of corpses to cover this one. In twenty minutes eight hundred English soldiers were marching down to their death."

The warmer glow behind the black winter wood grew richer and brighter, and Flambeau strode on to reach it. Father Brown also quickened his stride; but he seemed merely absorbed in his tale.

"Such was the valour of that English thousand, and such the genius of their commander, that if they had at once attacked the hill, even their mad march might have met some luck. But the evil mind that played with them like pawns had other aims and reasons. They must remain in the marshes by the bridge at least till British corpses should be a common sight there. Then for the last grand scene: the silver-haired soldier-saint would give up his shattered sword to save further slaughter. Oh, it was well organized for an impromptu. But I think (I cannot prove), I think that it was while they stuck there in the bloody mire that someone doubted—and someone guessed."

He was mute a moment, and then said: "There is a voice from nowhere that tells me the man who guessed was the lover . . . the man to wed the old man's child."

"But what about Olivier and the hanging?" asked Flambeau.

"Olivier, partly from chivalry, partly from policy, seldom encumbered his march with captives," explained the narrator. "He released everybody in most cases. He released everybody in this case."

"Everybody but the general," said the tall man.

"Everybody," said the priest.

Flambeau knitted his black brows. "I don't grasp it all yet," he said.

"There is another picture, Flambeau," said Brown in his more mystical undertone. "I can't prove it; but I can do more—I can see it. There is a camp breaking up on the bare, torrid hills at morning, and Brazilian uniforms massed in blocks and columns to march. There is the red shirt and long black beard of Olivier, which blows as he stands, his broad-brimmed hat in his hand. He is saying farewell to the great enemy he is setting free—the simple, snow-headed English veteran, who thanks him in the name of his men. The English remnant stand behind at attention; beside them are stores and vehicles for the retreat. The drums roll; the Brazilians are moving; the English are still like statues. So they abide till the last hum and flash of the enemy have faded from the tropic horizon. Then they alter their postures all at once, like dead men coming to life; they turn their fifty faces upon the general—faces not to be forgotten."

Flambeau gave a great jump. "Ah," he cried. "You don't mean——"

"Yes," said Father Brown in a deep, moving voice. "It was an English hand that put the rope around St. Clare's neck; I believe the hand that put the ring on his daughter's finger. They were English hands that dragged him up to the tree of shame; the hands of men that had adored him and followed him to victory. And they were English souls (God pardon and endure us all!) who stared at him swinging in that foreign sun on the green gallows of palm, and prayed in their hatred that he might drop off it into hell."

As the two topped the ridge there burst on them the strong scarlet light of a red-curtained English inn. It stood sideways in the road, as if standing aside in the amplitude of hospitality. Its three doors stood open with invitation; and even where they stood they could hear the hum and laughter of humanity happy for a night.

"I need not tell you more," said Father Brown. "They tried him in the wilderness and destroyed him; and then, for the honour of England and of his daughter, they took an oath to seal up for ever the story of the traitor's purse and the assassin's sword blade. Perhaps—Heaven help them—they tried to forget it. Let us try to forget it, anyhow; here is our inn."

"With all my heart," said Flambeau, and was just striding into the bright, noisy bar when he stepped back and almost fell on the road.

"Look there, in the devil's name!" he cried, and pointed rigidly at the square wooden sign that overhung the road. It showed dimly the crude shape of a sabre hilt and a shortened blade; and was inscribed in false archaic lettering, "The Sign of the Broken Sword."

"Were you not prepared?" asked Father Brown gently. "He is the god of this country; half the inns and parks and streets are named after him and his story."

"I thought we had done with the leper," cried Flambeau, and spat on the road.

"You will never have done with him in England," said the priest, looking down, "while brass is strong and stone abides. His marble statues will erect the souls of proud, innocent boys for centuries, his village tomb will smell of loyalty as of lilies. Millions who never knew him shall love him like a father—this man whom the last few that knew him dealt with like dung. He shall be a saint; and the truth shall never be told of him, because I have made up my mind at last. There is so much good and evil in breaking secrets, that I put my conduct to a test. All these newspapers will perish; the anti-Brazil boom is already over; Olivier is already honoured everywhere. But I told myself that if anywhere, by name, in metal or marble that will endure like the pyramids, Colonel Clancy, or Captain Keith, or President Olivier, or any innocent man was wrongly blamed, then I would speak. If it were only that St. Clare was wrongly praised, I would be silent. And I will."

They plunged into the red-curtained tavern, which was not only cosy, but even luxurious inside. On a table stood a silver model of the tomb of St. Clare, the silver head bowed, the silver sword broken. On the walls were coloured photographs of the same scene, and of the system of wagonettes that took tourists to see it. They sat down on the comfortable padded benches.

"Come, it's cold," cried Father Brown; "let's have some wine or beer."

"Or brandy," said Flambeau.

THE MAN IN THE PASSAGE

TWO MEN APPEARED simultaneously at the two ends of a sort of passage running along the side of the Apollo Theatre in the Adelphi. The evening daylight in the streets was large and luminous, opalescent and empty. The passage was comparatively long and dark, so each man could see the other as a mere black silhouette at the other end. Nevertheless, each man knew the other, even in that inky outline, for they were both men of striking appearance, and they hated each other.

The covered passage opened at one end on one of the steep streets of the Adelphi, and at the other on a terrace overlooking the sunset-coloured river. One side of the passage was a blank wall, for the building it supported was an old unsuccessful theatre restaurant, now shut up. The other side of the passage contained two doors, one at each end. Neither was what was commonly called the stage door; they were a sort of special and private stage doors, used by very special performers, and in this case by the star actor and actress in the Shakespearean performance of the day. Persons of that eminence often like to have such private exits and entrances, for meeting friends or avoiding them.

The two men in question were certainly two such friends, men who evidently knew the doors and counted on their opening, for each approached the door at the upper end with equal coolness and confidence. Not, however, with equal speed; but the man who walked fast was the man from the other end of the tunnel, so they both arrived before the secret stage door almost at the same instant. They saluted each other with civility, and waited a moment before one of them, the sharper walker, who seemed to have the shorter patience, knocked at the door.

In this and everything else each man was opposite and neither could be called inferior. As private persons, both were handsome, capable, and popular. As public persons, both were in the first public rank. But everything about them, from their glory to their good looks, was of a diverse and incomparable kind. Sir Wilson Seymour was the kind of man whose importance is known to everybody who knows. The more you mixed with the innermost ring in every polity or profession, the more often you met Sir Wilson Seymour. He was the one intelligent man on twenty unintelligent committees—on every sort of subject, from the reform of the Royal Academy to the project of bimetallism for Greater Britain. In the arts especially he was omnipotent. He was so unique that nobody could quite decide whether he was a great aristocrat who had taken up art, or a great artist whom the aristocrats had taken up. But you could not meet him for five minutes without realising that you had really been ruled by him all your life.

His appearance was "distinguished" in exactly the same sense; it was at once conventional and unique. Fashion could have found no fault with his high silk hat; yet it was unlike anyone else's hat—a little higher, perhaps, and adding something to his natural height. His tall, slender figure had a slight stoop, yet it looked the reverse of feeble. His hair was silver-grey, but he did not look old; it was worn longer than the common, yet he did not look effeminate; it was curly, but it did not look curled. His carefully pointed beard made him look more manly and militant rather than otherwise, as it does in those old admirals of Velasquez with whose dark portraits his house was hung. His grey gloves were a shade bluer, his silver-knobbed cane a shade longer than scores of such gloves and canes flapped and flourished about the theatres and the restaurants.

The other man was not so tall, yet would have struck nobody as short, but merely as strong and handsome. His hair also was curly, but fair and cropped close to a strong, massive head—the sort of head you break a door with, as Chaucer said of the Miller's. His military moustache and the carriage of his shoulders showed him a soldier, but he had a pair of those peculiar, frank, and piercing blue eyes which are more common in sailors. His face was somewhat square, his jaw was square, his shoulders were square, even his jacket was square. Indeed, in the wild school of caricature then current, Mr. Max Beerbohm had represented him as a proposition in the fourth book of Euclid.

For he also was a public man, though with quite another sort of success. You did not have to be in the best society to have heard of Captain Cutler, of the siege of Hong-Kong and the great march across China. You could not get away from hearing of him wherever you were; his portrait was on every other postcard; his maps and battles in every other illustrated paper; songs in his honour in every other music-hall turn or on every other barrel-organ. His fame, though probably more temporary, was ten times more wide, popular, and spontaneous than the other man's. In thousands of English homes he appeared enormous above England, like Nelson. Yet he had infinitely less power in England than Sir Wilson Seymour.

The door was opened to them by an aged servant or "dresser," whose broken-down face and figure and black shabby coat and trousers contrasted queerly with the glittering interior of the great actress's dressing-room. It was fitted and filled with looking-glasses at every angle of refraction, so that they looked like the hundred facets of one huge diamond—if one could get inside a diamond. The other features of luxury, a few flowers, a few coloured cushions, a few scraps of stage costume, were multiplied by all the mirrors into the madness of the Arabian Nights, and danced and changed places perpetually as the shuffling attendant shifted a mirror outwards or shot one back against the wall.

They both spoke to the dingy dresser by name, calling him Parkinson, and asking for the lady as Miss Aurora Rome. Parkinson said she was in the other room, but he would go and tell her. A shade crossed the brow of both visitors; for the other room was the private room of the great actor with whom Miss Aurora was performing, and she was of the kind that does not inflame admiration without inflaming jealousy. In about half a minute, however, the inner door opened, and she entered as she always did, even in private life, so that the very silence seemed to be a roar of applause, and one well deserved. She was clad in a somewhat strange garb of peacock green and peacock blue satins, that gleamed like blue and green metals, such as delight children and æsthetes, and her heavy, hot brown hair framed one of those magic faces which are dangerous to all men, but especially to boys and to men growing grey. In company with her male colleague, the great American actor, Isidore Bruno, she was producing a particularly poetical and fantastic interpretation of the *Midsummer Night's Dream,* in which the artistic prominence was given to Oberon and Titania, or in other words to Bruno and herself. Set in dreamy and exquisite scenery, and moving in mystical dances, the green costume, like burnished beetle-wings, expressed all the elusive individuality of an elfin queen. But when personally confronted in what was still broad daylight, a man looked only at the woman's face.

She greeted both men with the beaming and baffling smile which kept so many males at the same just dangerous distance from her. She accepted some flowers from Cutler, which were as tropical and expensive as his victories; and another sort of present from Sir Wilson Seymour, offered later on and more nonchalantly by that gentleman. For it was against his breeding to show eagerness, and against his conventional unconventionality to give anything so obvious as flowers. He had picked up a trifle, he said, which was rather a curiosity; it was an ancient Greek dagger of the Mycenean Epoch, and might have been well worn in the time of Theseus and Hippolyta. It was made of brass like all the Heroic weapons, but, oddly enough, sharp enough to prick anyone still. He had really been attracted to it by the leaflike shape; it was as perfect as a Greek vase. If it was of any interest to Miss Rome or could come in anywhere in the play, he hoped she would——

The inner door burst open and a big figure appeared, who was more of a contrast to the explanatory Seymour than even Captain Cutler. Nearly six-foot-six, and of more than theatrical thews and muscles, Isidore Bruno, in the gorgeous leopard skin and golden-brown garments of Oberon, looked like a barbaric god. He leaned on a sort of hunting-spear, which across a theatre looked a slight, silvery wand, but which in the small and comparatively crowded room looked as plain as a pikestaff—and as menacing. His vivid, black eyes rolled volcanically, his bronzed face, handsome as it was, showed at that moment a combination of high cheekbones with set white teeth, which recalled certain American conjectures about his origin in the Southern plantations.

"Aurora," he began, in that deep voice like a drum of passion that had moved so many audiences, "will you——"

He stopped indecisively because a sixth figure had suddenly presented itself just inside the doorway—a figure so incongruous in the scene as to be almost comic. It was a very short man in the black uniform of the Roman secular clergy, and looking (especially in such a presence as Bruno's and Aurora's) rather like the wooden Noah out of an ark. He did not, however, seem conscious of any contrast, but said with dull civility: "I believe Miss Rome sent for me."

A shrewd observer might have remarked that the emotional temperature rather rose at so unemotional an interruption. The detachment of a professional celibate seemed to reveal to the others that they stood round the woman as a ring of amorous rivals; just as a stranger coming in with frost on his coat will reveal that a room is like a furnace. The presence of the one man who did not care about her increased Miss Rome's sense that everybody else was in love with her, and each in a somewhat dangerous way: the actor with all the appetite of a savage and a spoilt child; the soldier with all the simple selfishness of a man of will rather than mind; Sir Wilson with that daily hardening concentration with which old Hedonists take to a hobby; nay, even the abject Parkinson, who had known her before her triumphs, and who followed her about the room with eyes or feet, with the dumb fascination of a dog.

A shrewd person might also have noted a yet odder thing. The man like a black wooden Noah (who was not wholly without shrewdness) noted it with a considerable but contained amusement. It was evident that the great Aurora, though by no means indifferent to the admiration of the other sex, wanted at this moment to get rid of all the men who admired her and be left alone with the man who did not—did not admire her in that sense, at least; for the little priest did admire and even enjoy the firm feminine diplomacy with which she set about her task. There was, perhaps, only one thing that Aurora Rome was clever about, and that was one half of humanity—the other half. The little priest watched, like a Napoleonic campaign, the swift precision of her policy for expelling all while banishing none. Bruno, the big actor, was so babyish that it was easy to send him off in brute sulks, banging the door. Cutler, the British officer, was pachydermatous to ideas, but punctilious about behaviour. He would ignore all hints, but he would die rather than ignore a definite commission from a lady. As to old Seymour he had to be treated differently; he had to be left to the last. The only way to move him was to appeal to him in confidence as an old friend, to let him into the secret of the clearance. The priest did really admire Miss Rome as she achieved all these three objects in one selected action.

She went across to Captain Cutler and said in her sweetest manner: "I shall value all these flowers because they must be your favourite flowers. But they won't be complete, you know, without *my* favourite flower. Do go over to that shop round the corner and get me some lilies-of-the-valley and then it will be *quite lovely.*"

The first object of her diplomacy, the exit of the enraged Bruno, was at once achieved. He had already handed his spear in a lordly style like a sceptre to the piteous Parkinson, and was about to assume one of the cushioned seats like a throne. But at this open appeal to his rival there glowed in his opal eyeballs all the sensitive insolence of the slave; he knotted his enormous brown fists for an instant, and then, dashing open the door, disappeared into his own apartments beyond. But meanwhile Miss Rome's experiment in mobilising the British Army had not succeeded so simply as seemed probable. Cutler had indeed risen stiffly and suddenly, and walked towards the door, hatless, as if at a word of command. But perhaps there was something ostentatiously elegant about the languid figure of Seymour leaning against one of the looking-glasses, that brought him up short at the entrance, turning his head this way and that like a bewildered bulldog.

"I must show this stupid man where to go," said Aurora in a whisper to Seymour, and ran out to the threshold to speed the parting guest.

Seymour seemed to be listening, elegant and unconscious as was his posture, and he seemed relieved when he heard the lady call out some last instructions to the Captain, and then turn sharply and run laughing down the passage towards the other end, the end on the terrace above the Thames. Yet a second or two after, Seymour's brow darkened again. A man in his position has so many rivals, and he remembered that at the other end of the passage was the corresponding entrance to Bruno's private room. He did not lose his dignity; he said some civil words to Father Brown about the revival of Byzantine architecture in the Westminster Cathedral, and then, quite naturally, strolled out himself into the upper end of the passage. Father Brown and Parkinson were left alone, and they were neither of them men with a taste for superfluous conversation. The dresser went round the room, pulling out looking-glasses and pushing them in again, his dingy dark coat and trousers looking all the more dismal since he was still holding the festive fairy spear of King Oberon. Every time he pulled out the frame of a new glass, a new black figure of Father Brown appeared; the absurd glass chamber was full of Father Browns, upside down in the air like angels, turning somersaults like acrobats, turning their backs to everybody like very rude persons.

Father Brown seemed quite unconscious of this cloud of witnesses, but followed Parkinson with an idly attentive eye till he took himself and his absurd spear into the farther room of Bruno. Then he abandoned himself to such abstract meditations as always amused him—calculating the angles of the mirrors, the angles of each refraction, the angle at which each must fit into the wall . . . when he heard a strong but strangled cry.

He sprang to his feet and stood rigidly listening. At the same instant Sir Wilson Seymour burst back into the room, white as ivory. "Who's that man in the passage?" he cried. "Where's that dagger of mine?"

Before Father Brown could turn in his heavy boots, Seymour was plunging about the room looking for the weapon. And before he could possibly find that weapon or any other, a brisk running of feet broke upon the pavement outside, and the square face of Cutler was thrust into the same doorway. He was still grotesquely grasping a bunch of lilies-of-the-valley. "What's this?" he cried. "What's that creature down the passage? Is this some of your tricks?"

"My tricks!" hissed his pale rival, and made a stride towards him.

In the instant of time in which all this happened Father Brown stepped out into the top of the passage, looked down it, and at once walked briskly towards what he saw.

At this the other two men dropped their quarrel and darted after him, Cutler calling out: "What are you doing? Who are you?"

"My name is Brown," said the priest sadly, as he bent over something and straightened himself again. "Miss Rome sent for me, and I came as quickly as I could. I have come too late."

The three men looked down, and in one of them at least the life died in that late light of afternoon. It ran along the passage like a path of gold, and in the midst of it Aurora Rome lay lustrous in her robes of green and gold, with her dead face turned upwards. Her dress was torn away as in a struggle, leaving the right shoulder bare, but the wound from which the blood was welling was on the other side. The brass dagger lay flat and gleaming a yard or so away.

There was a blank stillness for a measurable time; so that they could hear far off a flower-girl's laugh outside Charing Cross, and someone whistling furiously for a taxicab in one of the streets off the Strand. Then the Captain, with a movement so sudden that it might have been passion or play-acting, took Sir Wilson Seymour by the throat.

Seymour looked at him steadily without either fight or fear. "You need not kill me," he said, in a voice quite cold; "I shall do that on my own account."

The Captain's hand hesitated and dropped; and the other added with the same icy candour: "If I find I haven't the nerve to do it with that dagger, I can do it in a month with drink."

"Drink isn't good enough for me," replied Cutler, "but I'll have blood for this before I die. Not yours—but I think I know whose."

And before the others could appreciate his intention he snatched up the dagger, sprang at the other door at the lower end of the passage, burst it open, bolt and all, and confronted Bruno in his dressing-room. As he did so, old Parkinson tottered in his wavering way out of the door and caught sight of the corpse lying in the passage. He moved shakily towards it; looked at it weakly with a working face; then moved shakily back into the dressing-room again, and sat down suddenly on one of the richly cushioned chairs. Father Brown instantly ran across to him, taking no notice of Cutler and the colossal actor, though the room already rang with their blows and they began to struggle for the dagger. Seymour, who retained some practical sense, was whistling for the police at the end of the passage.

When the police arrived it was to tear the two men from an almost apelike grapple; and, after a few formal inquiries, to arrest Isidore Bruno upon a charge of murder, brought against him by his furious opponent. The idea that the great national hero of the hour had arrested a wrongdoer with his own hand doubtless had its weight with the police, who are not without elements of the journalist. They treated Cutler with a certain solemn attention, and pointed out that he had got a slight slash on the hand. Even as Cutler bore him back across tilted chair and table, Bruno had twisted the dagger out of his grasp and disabled him just below the wrist. The injury was really slight, but till he was removed from the room the half-savage prisoner stared at the running blood with a steady smile.

"Looks a cannibal sort of chap, don't he?" said the constable confidentially to Cutler.

Cutler made no answer, but said sharply a moment after: "We must attend to the . . . the death . . . " and his voice escaped from articulation.

"The two deaths," came in the voice of the priest from the farther side of the room. "This poor fellow was gone when I got across to him." And he stood looking down at old Parkinson, who sat in a black huddle on the gorgeous chair. He also had paid his tribute, not without eloquence, to the woman who had died.

The silence was first broken by Cutler, who seemed not untouched by a rough tenderness. "I wish I was him," he said huskily. "I remember he used to watch her wherever she walked more than—anybody. She was his air, and he's dried up. He's just dead."

"We are all dead," said Seymour, in a strange voice, looking down the road.

They took leave of Father Brown at the corner of the road, with some random apologies for any rudeness they might have shown. Both their faces were tragic, but also cryptic.

The mind of the little priest was always a rabbit-warren of wild thoughts that jumped too quickly for him to catch them. Like the white tail of a rabbit, he had the vanishing thought that he was certain of their grief, but not so certain of their innocence.

"We had better all be going," said Seymour heavily; "we have done all we can to help."

"Will you understand my motives," asked Father Brown quietly, "if I say you have done all you can to hurt?"

They both started as if guiltily, and Cutler said sharply: "To hurt whom?"

"To hurt yourselves," answered the priest. "I would not add to your troubles if it weren't common justice to warn you. You've done nearly everything you could do to hang yourselves, if this actor should be acquitted. They'll be sure to subpœna me; I shall be bound to say that after the cry was heard, each of you rushed into the room in a wild state and began quarrelling about a dagger. As far as my words on oath can go, you might either of you have done it. You hurt yourselves with that; and then Captain Cutler must hurt himself with the dagger."

"Hurt myself!" exclaimed the Captain, with contempt. "A silly little scratch."

"Which drew blood," replied the priest, nodding. "We know there's blood on the brass now. And so we shall never know whether there was blood on it before."

There was a silence; and then Seymour said, with an emphasis quite alien to his daily accent: "But I saw a man in the passage."

"I know you did," answered the cleric Brown, with a face of wood; "so did Captain Cutler. That's what seems so improbable."

Before either could make sufficient sense of it even to answer, Father Brown had politely excused himself and gone stumping up the road with his stumpy old umbrella.

As modern newspapers are conducted, the most honest and most important news is the police news. If it be true that in the twentieth century more space was given to murder than to politics, it was for the excellent reason that murder is a more serious subject. But even this would hardly explain the enormous omnipresence and widely distributed detail of "The Bruno Case," or "The Passage Mystery," in the Press of London and the provinces. So vast was the excitement that for some weeks the Press really told the truth; and the reports of examination and cross-examination, if interminable, even if intolerable, are at least reliable. The true reason, of course, was the coincidence of persons. The victim was a popular actress; the accused was a popular actor; and the accused had been caught red-handed, as it were, by the most popular soldier of the patriotic season. In those extraordinary circumstances the Press was paralysed into probity and accuracy; and the rest of this somewhat singular business can practically be recorded from the reports of Bruno's trial.

The trial was presided over by Mr. Justice Monkhouse, one of those who are jeered at as humorous judges, but who are generally much more serious than the serious judges, for their levity comes from a living impatience of professional solemnity; while the serious judge is really filled with frivolity, because he is filled with vanity. All the chief actors being of a worldly importance, the barristers were well balanced; the prosecutor for the Crown was Sir Walter Cowdray, a heavy but weighty advocate of the sort that knows how to seem English and trustworthy, and how to be rhetorical with reluctance. The prisoner was defended by Mr. Patrick Butler, K.C., who was mistaken for a mere *flâneur* by those who misunderstand the Irish character—and those who had not been examined by him. The medical evidence involved no contradictions, the doctor whom Seymour had summoned on the spot, agreeing with the eminent surgeon who had later examined the body. Aurora Rome had been stabbed with some sharp instrument such as a knife or dagger; some instrument, at least, of which the blade was short. The wound was just over the heart, and she had died instantly. When the first doctor saw her she could hardly have been dead for twenty minutes. Therefore when Father Brown found her she could hardly have been dead for three.

Some official detective evidence followed, chiefly concerned with the presence or absence of any proof of a struggle: the only suggestion of this was the tearing of the dress at the shoulder, and this did not seem to fit in particularly well with the direction and finality of the blow. When these details had been supplied, though not explained, the first of the important witnesses was called.

Sir Wilson Seymour gave evidence as he did everything else that he did at all—not only well, but perfectly. Though himself much more of a public man than the judge, he conveyed exactly the fine shade of self-effacement before the King's Justice; and though everyone looked at him as they would at the Prime Minister or the Archbishop of Canterbury, they could have said nothing of his part in it but that it was that of a private gentleman, with an accent on the noun. He was also refreshingly lucid, as he was on the committees. He had been calling on Miss Rome at the theatre; he had met Captain Cutler there; they had been joined for a short time by the accused, who had then returned to his own dressing-room; they had then been joined by a Roman Catholic priest, who asked for the deceased lady and said his name was Brown. Miss Rome had then gone just outside the theatre to the entrance of the passage, in order to point out to Captain Cutler a flower-shop at which he was to buy her some more flowers; and the witness had remained in the room, exchanging a few words with the priest. He had then distinctly heard the deceased, having sent the Captain on his errand, turn round laughing and run down the passage towards its other end, where was the prisoner's dressing-room. In idle curiosity as to the rapid movements of his friends, he had strolled out to the head of the passage himself and looked down it towards the prisoner's door. Did he see anything in the passage? Yes, he saw something in the passage.

Sir Walter Cowdray allowed an impressive interval, during which the witness looked down, and for all his usual composure seemed to have more than his usual pallor. Then the barrister said in a lower voice, which seemed at once sympathetic and creepy: "Did you see it distinctly?"

Sir Wilson Seymour, however moved, had his excellent brains in full working order. "Very distinctly as regards its outline, but quite indistinctly—indeed not at all—as regards the details inside the outline. The passage is of such length that anyone in the middle of it appears quite black against the light at the other end." The witness lowered his steady eyes once more and added: "I had noticed the fact before, when Captain Cutler first entered it." There was another silence, and the judge leaned forward and made a note.

"Well," said Sir Walter patiently, "what was the outline like? Was it, for instance, like the figure of the murdered woman?"

"Not in the least," answered Seymour quietly.

"What did it look to you like?"

"It looked to me," replied the witness, "like a tall man."

Everyone in court kept his eyes riveted on his pen or his umbrella handle or his book or his boots or whatever he happened to be looking at. They seemed to be holding their eyes away from the prisoner by main force; but they felt his figure in the dock, and they felt it as gigantic. Tall as Bruno was to the eye, he seemed to swell taller and taller when all eyes had been torn away from him.

Cowdray was resuming his seat with his solemn face, smoothing his black silk robes and white silk whiskers. Sir Wilson was leaving the witness-box, after a few final particulars to which there were many other witnesses, when the counsel for the defence sprang up and stopped him.

"I shall only detain you a moment," said Mr. Butler, who was a rustic-looking person with red eyebrows and an expression of partial slumber. "Will you tell his lordship how you knew it was a man?"

A faint, refined smile seemed to pass over Seymour's features. "I'm afraid it is the vulgar test of trousers," he said. "When I saw daylight between the long legs I was sure it was a man, after all."

Butler's sleepy eyes opened as suddenly as some silent explosion. "After all!" he repeated slowly. "So you did think first it was a woman?"

Seymour looked troubled for the first time. "It is hardly a point of fact," he said, "but if his lordship would like me to answer for my impression, of course I shall do so. There was something about the thing that was not exactly a woman and yet was not quite a man; somehow the curves were different. And it had something that looked like long hair."

"Thank you," said Mr. Butler, K.C., and sat down suddenly, as if he had got what he wanted.

Captain Cutler was a far less plausible and composed witness than Sir Wilson, but his account of the opening incidents was solidly the same. He described the return of Bruno to his dressing-room, the dispatching of himself to buy a bunch of lilies-of-the-valley, his return to the upper end of the passage, the thing he saw in the passage, his suspicion of Seymour, and his struggle with Bruno. But he could give little artistic assistance about the black figure that he and

Seymour had seen. Asked about its outline, he said he was no art critic—with a somewhat too obvious sneer at Seymour. Asked if it was a man or a woman, he said it looked more like a beast—with a too obvious snarl at the prisoner. But the man was plainly shaken with sorrow and sincere anger, and Cowdray quickly excused him from confirming facts that were already fairly clear.

The defending counsel also was again brief in his cross-examination; although (as was his custom) even in being brief, he seemed to take a long time about it. "You used a rather remarkable expression," he said, looking at Cutler sleepily. "What do you mean by saying that it looked more like a beast than a man or a woman?"

Cutler seemed seriously agitated. "Perhaps I oughtn't to have said that," he said, "but when the brute has huge humped shoulders like a chimpanzee, and bristles sticking out of its head like a pig——"

Mr. Butler cut short his curious impatience in the middle. "Never mind whether its hair was like a pig's," he said; "was it like a woman's?"

"A woman's!" cried the soldier. "Great Scott, no!"

"The last witness said it was," commented the counsel, with unscrupulous swiftness. "And did the figure have any of those serpentine and semi-feminine curves to which eloquent allusion has been made? No? No feminine curves? The figure, if I understand you, was rather heavy and square than otherwise?"

"He may have been bending forward," said Cutler, in a hoarse and rather faint voice.

"Or again, he may not," said Mr. Butler, and sat down suddenly for the second time.

The third witness called by Sir Walter Cowdray was the little Catholic clergyman, so little compared with the others, that his head seemed hardly to come above the box, so that it was like cross-examining a child. But unfortunately Sir Walter had somehow got it into his head (mostly by some ramifications of his family's religion) that Father Brown was on the side of the prisoner, because the prisoner was wicked and foreign and even partly black. Therefore, he took Father Brown up sharply whenever that proud pontiff tried to explain anything; and told him to answer yes or no, and tell the plain facts without any jesuitry. When Father Brown began, in his simplicity, to say who he thought the man in the passage was, the barrister told him that he did not want his theories.

"A black shape was seen in the passage. And you say you saw the black shape. Well, what shape was it?"

Father Brown blinked as under rebuke; but he had long known the literal nature of obedience. "The shape," he said, "was short and thick, but had two sharp, black projections curved upwards on each side of the head or top, rather like horns, and——"

"Oh! the devil with horns, no doubt," ejaculated Cowdray, sitting down in triumphant jocularity. "It was the devil come to eat Protestants."

"No," said the priest dispassionately; "I know who it was."

Those in court had been wrought up to an irrational but real sense of some monstrosity. They had forgotten the figure in the dock and thought only of the figure in the passage. And the figure in the passage, described by three capable and respectable men who had all seen it, was a shifting nightmare: one called it a woman, and the other a beast, and the other a devil. . . .

The judge was looking at Father Brown with level and piercing eyes. "You are a most extraordinary witness," he said, "but there is something about you that makes me think you are trying to tell the truth. Well, who was the man you saw in the passage?"

"He was myself," said Father Brown.

Butler, K.C., sprang to his feet in an extraordinary stillness, and said quite calmly: "Your lordship will allow me to cross-examine?" And then, without stopping, he shot at Brown the apparently disconnected question: "You have heard about this dagger; you know the experts say the crime was committed with a short blade?"

"A short blade," assented Brown, nodding solemnly like an owl, "but a very long hilt."

Before the audience could quite dismiss the idea that the priest had really seen himself doing murder with a short dagger with a long hilt (which seemed somehow to make it more horrible), he had himself hurried on to explain.

"I mean daggers aren't the only things with short blades. Spears have short blades. And spears catch at the end of the steel just like daggers, if they're that sort of fancy spear they have in theatres; like the spear poor old Parkinson killed his wife with, just when she'd sent for me to settle their family troubles—and I came just too late, God forgive me! But he died penitent—he just died of being penitent. He couldn't bear what he'd done."

The general impression in court was that the little priest, who was gabbling away, had literally gone mad in the box. But the judge still looked at him with bright and steady eyes of interest; and the counsel for the defence went on with his questions, unperturbed.

"If Parkinson did it with that pantomime spear," asked Butler, "he must have thrust from four yards away. How do you account for signs of struggle, like the dress dragged off the shoulder?" He had slipped into treating this mere witness as an expert; but no one noticed it now.

"The poor lady's dress was torn," said the witness, "because it was caught in a panel that slid to just behind her. She struggled to free herself, and as she did so Parkinson came out of the prisoner's room and lunged with the spear."

"A panel?" repeated the barrister in a curious voice.

"It was a looking-glass on the other side," explained Father Brown. "When I was in the dressing-room I noticed that some of them could probably be slid out into the passage."

There was another vast and unnatural silence, and this time it was the judge who spoke. "So you really mean that, when you looked down that passage, the man you saw was yourself—in a mirror?"

"Yes, my lord; that was what I was trying to say," said Brown, "but they asked me for the shape; and our hats have corners just like horns, and so I——"

The judge leaned forward, his old eyes yet more brilliant, and said in specially distinct tones: "Do you really mean to say that when Sir Wilson Seymour saw that wild what-you-call-him with curves and a woman's hair and a man's trousers, what he saw was Sir Wilson Seymour?"

"Yes, my lord," said Father Brown.

"And you mean to say that when Captain Cutler saw that chimpanzee with humped shoulders and hog's bristles, he simply saw himself?"

"Yes, my lord."

The judge leaned back in his chair with a luxuriance in which it was hard to separate the cynicism and the admiration. "And can you tell us why," he asked, "you should know your own figure in a looking-glass, when two such distinguished men don't?"

Father Brown blinked even more painfully than before; then he stammered: "Really, my lord, I don't know . . . unless it's because I don't look at it so often."

THE PERISHING OF THE PENDRAGONS

Father Brown was in no mood for adventures. He had lately fallen ill with over-work, and when he began to recover, his friend Flambeau had taken him on a cruise in a small yacht with Sir Cecil Fanshaw, a young Cornish squire and an enthusiast for Cornish coast scenery. But Brown was still rather weak; he was no very happy sailor; and though he was never of the sort that either grumbles or breaks down, his spirits did not rise above patience and civility. When the other two men praised the ragged violet sunset or the ragged volcanic crags, he agreed with them. When Flambeau pointed out a rock shaped like a dragon, he looked at it and thought it very like a dragon. When Fanshaw more excitedly indicated a rock that was like Merlin he looked at it, and signified assent. When Flambeau asked whether this rocky gate of the twisted river was not the gate of Fairyland, he said "Yes." He heard the most important things and the most trivial with the same tasteless absorption. He heard that the coast was death to all but careful seamen; he also heard that the ship's cat was asleep. He heard that Fanshaw couldn't find his cigar-holder anywhere; he also heard the pilot deliver the oracle "Both eyes bright, she's all right; one eye winks, down she sinks." He heard Flambeau say to Fanshaw that no doubt this meant the pilot must keep both eyes open and be spry. And he heard Fanshaw say to Flambeau that, oddly enough, it didn't mean this: it meant that while they saw two of the coast-lights, one near and the other distant, exactly side by side, they were in the right river-channel; but that if one light was hidden behind the other, they were going on the rocks. He heard Fanshaw add that his county was full of such quaint fables and idioms; it was the very home of romance; he even pitted this part of Cornwall against Devonshire, as a claimant to the laurels of Elizabethan seamanship. According to him there had been captains among these coves and islets compared with whom Drake was practically a landsman. He heard Flambeau laugh, and ask if, perhaps, the adventurous title of "Westward Ho!" only meant that all Devonshire men wished they were living in Cornwall. He heard Fanshaw say there was no need to be silly; that not only had Cornish captains been heroes, but that they were heroes still: that near that very spot there was an old admiral, now retired, who was scarred by thrilling voyages full of adventures; and who had in his youth found the last group of eight Pacific Islands that was added to the chart of the world. This Cecil Fanshaw was, in person, of the kind that commonly urges such crude but pleasing enthusiasms; a very young man, light-haired, high-coloured, with an eager profile; with a boyish bravado of spirits, but an almost girlish delicacy of tint and type. The big shoulders, black brows and black mousquetaire swagger of Flambeau were a great contrast.

All these trivialities Brown heard and saw; but heard them as a tired man hears a tune in the railway wheels or saw them as a sick man sees the pattern of his wall-paper. No one can calculate the turns of mood in convalescence; but Father Brown's depression must have had a great deal to do with his mere unfamiliarity with the sea. For as the river-mouth narrowed like the neck of a bottle, and the water grew calmer and the air warmer and more earthy, he seemed to wake up and take notice like a baby. They had reached that phase just after sunset when air and water both look bright, but earth and all its growing things look almost black by comparison. About this particular evening, however, there was something exceptional. It was one of those rare atmospheres in which a smoked glass slide seems to have been slid away from between us and Nature; so that even dark colours on that day look more gorgeous than bright colours on cloudier days. The trampled earth of the river-banks and the peaty stain in the pools did not look drab but glowing umber, and the dark woods astir in the breeze did not look, as usual, dim blue with mere depth or distance, but more like wind-tumbled masses of some vivid violet blossom. This magic clearness and intensity in the colours was further forced on Brown's slowly reviving senses by something romantic and even secret in the very form of the landscape.

The river was still well wide and deep enough for a pleasure boat so small as theirs; but the curves of the country-side suggested that it was closing in on either hand; the woods seemed to be making broken and flying attempts at bridge-building; as if the boat were passing from the romance of a valley to the romance of a hollow and so to the supreme romance of a tunnel. Beyond this mere look of things there was little for Brown's freshening fancy to feed on; he saw no human beings, except some gypsies trailing along the river-bank, with faggots and osiers cut in the forest; and one sight no longer unconventional, but in such remote parts still uncommon: a dark-haired lady bare-headed, and paddling her own canoe. If Father Brown ever attached any importance to either of these, he certainly forgot them at the next turn of the river, which brought in sight a singular object.

The water seemed to widen and split, being cloven by the dark wedge of a fish-shaped and wooded islet. With the rate at which they went, the islet seemed to swim towards them like a ship; a ship with a very high prow—or, to speak more strictly, a very high funnel. For at the extreme point nearest them stood up an odd-looking building, unlike anything they could remember or connect with any purpose. It was not specially high, but it was too high for its breadth to be called anything but a tower. Yet it appeared to be built entirely of wood, and that in a most unequal and eccentric way. Some of the planks and beams were of good, seasoned oak; some of such wood cut raw and recent; some again of white pine-wood and a great deal more of the same sort of wood painted black with tar. These black beams were set crooked or criss-cross at all kinds of angles; giving the whole a most patchy and puzzling appearance. There were one or two windows, which appeared to be coloured and leaded in an old-fashioned but more elaborate style. The travellers looked at it with that paradoxical feeling we have when something reminds us of something, and yet we are certain it is something very different.

Father Brown, even when he was mystified, was clever in analysing his own mystification. And he found himself reflecting that the oddity seemed to consist in a particular shape cut out in an incongruous material; as if one saw a top-hat made of tin or a frock-coat cut out of tartan. He was sure he had seen timbers of different tints arranged like that somewhere, but never in such architectural proportions. The next moment a glimpse through the dark trees told him all he wanted to know; and he laughed. Through a gap in the foliage there appeared for a moment one of those old wooden houses, faced with black beams, which are still to be found here and there in England, but which most of us see imitated in some show called "Old London" or "Shakespeare's England." It was in view only long enough for the priest to see that, however old-fashioned, it was a comfortable and well-kept country-house, with flower beds in front of it. It had none of the piebald and crazy look of the tower that seemed made out of its refuse.

"What on earth's this?" said Flambeau, who was still staring at the tower.

Fanshaw's eyes were shining and he spoke triumphantly. "Aha, you've not seen a place quite like this before, I fancy; that's why I've brought you here, my friend. Now you shall see whether I exaggerate about the mariners of Cornwall. This place belongs to Old Pendragon, whom we call the Admiral; though he retired before getting the rank. The spirit of Raleigh and Hawkins is a memory with the Devon folk; it's a modern fact with the Pendragons. If Queen Elizabeth were to rise from the grave and come up this river in a gilded barge, she would be received by the Admiral in a house exactly such as she was accustomed to, in every corner and casement, in every panel on the wall or plate on the table. And she would find an English Captain still talking fiercely of fresh lands to be found in little ships, as much as if she had dined with Drake."

"She'd find a rum sort of thing in the garden," said Father Brown, "which would not please her Renaissance eye. That Elizabethan domestic architecture is charming in its way; but it's against the very nature of it to break out into turrets."

"And yet," answered Fanshaw, "that's the most romantic and Elizabethan part of the business. It was built by the Pendragons in the very days of the Spanish wars; and though it's needed patching and even rebuilding for another reason, it's always been rebuilt in the old way. The story goes that the lady of Sir Peter Pendragon built it in this place and to this height, because from the top you can just see the corner where vessels turn into the river-mouth; and she wished to be the first to see her husband's ship, as he sailed home from the Spanish main."

"For what other reason," asked Father Brown, "do you mean that it has been rebuilt?"

"Oh, there's a strange story about that too," said the young squire with relish. "You are really in a land of strange stories; King Arthur was here and Merlin and the fairies before him. The story goes that Sir Peter Pendragon, who (I fear) had some of the faults of the pirates as well as the virtues of the sailor, was bringing home three Spanish gentlemen in honourable captivity, intending to escort them to Elizabeth's court. But he was a man of flaming and tigerish temper; and coming to high words with one of them, he caught him by the throat and flung him, by accident or design, into the sea. A second Spaniard, who was the brother of the first, instantly drew his sword and flew at Pendragon, and after a short but furious combat in which both got three wounds in as many minutes, Pendragon drove his blade through the other's body and the second Spaniard was accounted for. As it happened the ship had already turned into the river-mouth and was close to comparatively shallow water. The third Spaniard sprang over the side of the ship, struck out for the shore, and was soon near enough to it to stand up to his waist in water. And turning again to face the ship, and holding up both arms to Heaven like a prophet calling plagues upon a wicked city, he called out to Pendragon in a piercing and terrible voice, that he at least was yet living, that he would go on living, that he would live for ever; and that generation after generation the house of Pendragon should never see him or his, but should know by very certain signs that he and his vengeance were alive. With that he dived under the wave, and was either drowned or swam so long under water that no hair of his head was seen afterwards."

"There's that girl in the canoe again," said Flambeau irrelevantly, for good-looking young women would call him off any topic. "She seems bothered by the queer tower just as we were."

Indeed, the black-haired young lady was letting her canoe float slowly and silently past the strange islet; and was looking intently up at the strange tower, with a strong glow of curiosity on her oval and olive face.

"Never mind girls," said Fanshaw impatiently, "there are plenty of them in the world, but not many things like the Pendragon Tower. As you may easily suppose, plenty of superstitions and scandals have followed in the track of the Spaniard's curse; and no doubt, as you would put it, any accident happening to this Cornish family would be connected with it by rural credulity. But it is perfectly true that this tower has been burnt down two or three times; and the family can't be called lucky, for more than two, I think, of the Admiral's near kin have perished by shipwreck; and one at least, to my own knowledge, on practically the same spot where Sir Peter threw the Spaniard overboard."

"What a pity!" exclaimed Flambeau. "She's going."

"When did your friend the Admiral tell you this family history?" asked Father Brown, as the girl in the canoe paddled off, without showing the least intention of extending her interest from the tower to the yacht, which Fanshaw had already caused to lie alongside the island.

"Many years ago," replied Fanshaw; "he hasn't been to sea for some time now, though he is as keen on it as ever. I believe there's a family compact or something. Well, here's the landing-stage; let's come ashore and see the old boy."

They followed him on to the island just under the tower; and Father Brown, whether from the mere touch of dry land, or the interest of something on the other bank of the river (which he stared at very hard for some seconds), seemed singularly improved in briskness. They entered a wooded avenue between two fences of thin greyish wood, such as often enclose parks or gardens; and over the top of which the dark trees tossed to and fro like black and purple plumes upon the hearse of a giant. The tower, as they left it behind, looked all the quainter, because such entrances are usually flanked by two towers; and this one looked lopsided. But for this, the avenue had the usual appearance of the entrance to a gentleman's grounds; and, being so curved that the house was now out of sight, somehow looked a much larger park than any plantation on such an island could really be. Father Brown was, perhaps, a little fanciful in his fatigue, but he almost thought the whole place must be growing larger, as things do in a nightmare. Anyhow, a mystical monotony was the only character of their march, until Fanshaw suddenly stopped, and pointed to something sticking out through the grey fence—something that looked at first rather like the imprisoned horn of some beast. Closer observation showed that it was a slightly curved blade of metal that shone faintly in the fading light.

Flambeau, who like all Frenchmen had been a soldier, bent over it and said in a startled voice: "Why, it's a sabre! I believe I know the sort; heavy and curved, but shorter than the cavalry; they used to have them in the artillery and the——"

As he spoke the blade plucked itself out of the crack it had made and came down again with a more ponderous slash, splitting the fissiparous fence to the bottom, with a rending noise. Then it was pulled out again, flashed above the fence some feet farther along, and again split it half-way down with the first stroke; and after waggling a little to extricate itself (accompanied with curses in the darkness) split it down to the ground with a second. Then a kick of devilish energy sent the whole loosened square of thin wood flying into the pathway, and a great gap of dark coppice gaped in the paling.

Fanshaw peered into the dark opening, and uttered an exclamation of astonishment. "My dear Admiral!" he exclaimed, "do you—er—do you generally cut out a new front door whenever you want to go for a walk?"

The voice in the gloom swore again, and then broke into a jolly laugh. "No," it said; "I've really got to cut down this fence somehow; it's spoiling all the plants, and no one else here can do it. But I'll only carve another bit off the front door, and then come out and welcome you."

And sure enough, he heaved up his weapon once more, and, hacking twice, brought down another and similar strip of fence, making the opening about fourteen feet wide in all. Then through this larger forest gateway he came out into the evening light, with a chip of grey wood sticking to his sword-blade.

He momentarily fulfilled all Fanshaw's fable of an old piratical Admiral; though the details seemed afterwards to decompose into accidents. For instance, he wore an ordinary broad-brimmed hat as against the sun; but the front flap of it was turned up straight to the sky and the two corners pulled down lower than the ears; so that it stood across his forehead in a crescent like the old cocked hat worn by Nelson. He wore an ordinary dark-blue jacket, with nothing special about the buttons, but the combination of it with white linen trousers somehow had a sailorish look. He was tall and loose, and walked with a sort of swagger, which was not a sailor's roll, and yet somehow suggested it. And he held in his hand a short sabre which was like a navy cutlass, but about twice as big. Under the bridge of the hat, his eagle face looked eager, all the more because it was not only clean-shaven, but without eyebrows. It seemed almost as if all the hair had come off his face from his thrusting it through a throng of elements. His eyes were prominent and piercing. His colour was curiously attractive, while partly tropical; it reminded one vaguely of a blood-orange. That is, that while it was ruddy and sanguine, there was a yellow in it that was in no way sickly, but seemed rather to glow like gold apples of the Hesperides. Father Brown thought he had never seen a figure so expressive of all the romances about the countries of the Sun.

When Fanshaw had presented his two friends to their host, he fell again into a tone of rallying the latter about his wreckage of the fence and his apparent rage of profanity. The Admiral pooh-poohed it at first as a piece of necessary but annoying garden work; but at length the ring of real energy came back into his laughter, and he cried with a mixture of impatience and good humour:

"Well, perhaps I do go at it a bit rabidly, and feel a kind of pleasure in smashing anything. So would you if your only pleasure was in cruising about to find some new Cannibal Islands, and you had to stick on this muddy little rockery in a sort of rustic pond. When I remember how I've cut down a mile and a half of green poisonous jungle with an old cutlass half as sharp as this; and then remember I must stop here and chop this matchwood, because of some confounded old bargain scribbled in a family Bible, why, I——"

He swung up the heavy steel again; and this time sundered the wall of wood from top to bottom at one stroke.

"I feel like that," he said laughing, but furiously flinging the sword some yards down the path, "and now let's go up to the house; you must have some dinner."

The semicircle of lawn in front of the house was varied by three circular garden beds, one of red tulips, a second of yellow tulips, and the third of some white waxen-looking blossoms that the visitors did not know and presumed to be exotic. A heavy, hairy and rather sullen-looking gardener was hanging up a heavy coil of garden hose. The corners of the expiring sunset which seemed to cling about the corners of the house gave glimpses here and there of the colours of remoter flower beds; and in a treeless space on one side of the house opening upon the river stood a tall brass tripod on which was tilted a big brass telescope. Just outside the steps of the porch stood a little painted green garden table, as if someone had just had tea there. The entrance was flanked with two of those half-featured lumps of stone with holes for eyes that are said to be South Sea idols; and on the brown oak beam across the doorway were some confused carvings that looked almost as barbaric.

As they passed indoors, the little cleric hopped suddenly on to the table, and standing on it peered unaffectedly through the spectacles at the mouldings in the oak. Admiral Pendragon looked very much astonished, though not particularly annoyed; while Fanshaw was so amused with what looked like a performing pigmy on his little stand, that he could not control his laughter. But Father Brown was not likely to notice either the laughter or the astonishment.

He was gazing at three carved symbols, which, though very worn and obscure, seemed still to convey some sense to him. The first seemed to be the outline of some tower or other building, crowned with what looked like curly pointed ribbons. The second was clearer; an old Elizabethan galley with decorative waves beneath it, but interrupted in the middle by a curious jagged rock, which was either a fault in the wood or some conventional representation of the water coming in. The third represented the upper half of a human figure, ending in an escalloped line like the waves; the face was rubbed and featureless; and both arms were held very stiffly up in the air.

"Well," muttered Father Brown, blinking, "here is the legend of the Spaniard plain enough. Here he is holding up his arms and cursing in the sea; and here are the two curses: the wrecked ship and the burning of Pendragon Tower."

Pendragon shook his head with a kind of venerable amusement. "And how many other things might it not be?" he said. "Don't you know that that sort of half man, like a half lion or half stag, is quite common in heraldry? Might not that line through the ship be one of those *parti-per-pale* lines, *indented,* I think they call it? And though the third thing isn't very heraldic, it would be more heraldic to suppose it a tower crowned with laurel than with fire; and it looks just as like it."

"But it seems rather odd," said Flambeau, "that it should exactly confirm the old legend."

"Ah," replied the sceptical traveller, "but you don't know how much of the old legend may have been made up from the old figures. Besides, it isn't the only old legend. Fanshaw, here, who is fond of such things, will tell you there are other versions of the tale, and much more horrible ones. One story credits my unfortunate ancestor with having had the Spaniard cut in two; and that will fit the pretty picture also. Another obligingly credits our family with the possession of a tower full of snakes and explains those little, wriggly things in that way. And a third theory supposes the crooked line on the ship to be a conventionalised thunderbolt; but that alone, if seriously examined, would show what a very little way these unhappy coincidences really go."

"Why, how do you mean?" asked Fanshaw.

"It so happens," replied his host coolly, "that there was no thunder and lightning at all in the two or three shipwrecks I know of in our family."

"Oh!" said Father Brown, and jumped down from the little table.

There was another silence in which they heard the continuous murmur of the river; then Fanshaw said, in a doubtful and perhaps disappointed tone: "Then you don't think there is anything in the tales of the tower in flames?"

"There are the tales, of course," said the Admiral, shrugging his shoulders, "and some of them, I don't deny, on evidence as decent as one ever gets for such things. Someone saw a blaze hereabout, don't you know, as he walked home through a wood; someone keeping sheep on the uplands inland thought he saw a flame hovering over Pendragon tower. Well, a damp dab of mud like this confounded island seems the last place where one would think of fires."

"What is that fire over there?" asked Father Brown, with a gentle suddenness pointing to the woods on the left river-bank. They were all thrown a little off their balance, and the more fanciful Fanshaw had even some difficulty in recovering his, as they saw a long, thin stream of blue smoke ascending silently into the end of the evening light.

Then Pendragon broke into a scornful laugh again. "Gypsies!" he said; "they've been camping about here for a week. Gentlemen, you want your dinner," and he turned as if to enter the house.

But the antiquarian superstition in Fanshaw was still quivering; and he said hastily, "But, Admiral, what's that hissing noise quite near the island? It's very like fire."

"It's more like what it is," said the Admiral, laughing as he led the way; "it's only some canoe going by."

Almost as he spoke the butler, a lean man in black, with very black hair and a very long, yellow face, appeared in the doorway and told him that dinner was served.

The dining-room was as nautical as the cabin of a ship; but its note was rather that of the modern than the Elizabethan captain. There were, indeed, three antiquated cutlasses in a trophy over the fireplace and one brown sixteenth-century map, with Tritons and little ships dotted about a curly sea. But such things were less prominent on the white panelling than some cases of quaint coloured South American birds, very scientifically stuffed, fantastic shells from the Pacific, and several instruments so rude and queer in shape that savages might have used them either to kill their enemies or to cook them. But the alien colour culminated in the fact that, besides the butler, the Admiral's only servants were two negroes, somewhat quaintly clad in tight uniforms of yellow. The priest's instinctive trick of analysing his own impressions told him that the colour and the little neat coat-tails of these bipeds had suggested the word

"Canary," and so by a mere pun connected them with Southward travel. Towards the end of the dinner they took their yellow clothes and black faces out of the room, leaving only the black clothes and yellow face of the butler.

"I'm rather sorry you take this so lightly," said Fanshaw to the host, "for the truth is I've brought these friends of mine with the idea of their helping you, as they know a good deal of these things. Don't you really believe in the family story at all?"

"I don't believe in anything," answered Pendragon very briskly, with a bright eye cocked at a red tropical bird. "I'm a man of science."

Rather to Flambeau's surprise, his clerical friend, who seemed to have entirely woke up, took up the digression and talked natural history with his host with a flow of words and much unexpected information, until the dessert and decanters were set down and the last of the servants vanished. Then he said, without altering his tone:

"Please don't think me impertinent, Admiral Pendragon. I don't ask for curiosity, but really for my guidance and your convenience. Have I made a bad shot if I guess you don't want these old things talked of before your butler?"

The Admiral lifted the hairless arches over his eyes and exclaimed, "Well, I don't know where you got it; but the truth is I can't stand the fellow, though I've no excuse for discharging a family servant. Fanshaw, with his fairy tales, would say my blood moved against men with that black, Spanish-looking hair."

Flambeau struck the table with his heavy fist. "By Jove!" he cried, "and so had that girl!"

"I hope it'll all end to-night," continued the Admiral, "when my nephew comes back safe from his ship. You look surprised. You won't understand, I suppose, unless I tell you the story. You see, my father had two sons; I remained a bachelor, but my elder brother married, and had a son who became a sailor like all the rest of us, and will inherit the proper estate. Well, my father was a strange man; he somehow combined Fanshaw's superstition with a good deal of my scepticism; they were always fighting in him; and after my first voyages, he developed a notion which he thought somehow would settle finally whether the curse was truth or trash. If all the Pendragons sailed about anyhow, he thought there would be too much chance of natural catastrophes to prove anything. But if we went to sea one at a time in strict order of succession to the property, he thought it might show whether any connected fate followed the family as a family. It was a silly notion, I think, and I quarrelled with my father pretty heartily; for I was an ambitious man and was left to the last, coming, by succession, after my own nephew."

"And your father and brother," said the priest, very gently, "died at sea, I fear."

"Yes," groaned the Admiral; "by one of those brutal accidents on which are built all the lying mythologies of mankind, they were both shipwrecked. My father, coming up this coast out of the Atlantic, was washed up on these Cornish rocks. My brother's ship was sunk, no one knows where, on the voyage home from Tasmania. His body was never found. I tell you it was from perfectly natural mishap; lots of other people besides Pendragons were drowned; and both disasters are discussed in a normal way by navigators. But, of course, it set this forest of superstition on fire; and men saw the flaming tower everywhere. That's why I say it will be all right when Walter returns. The girl he's engaged to was coming to-day; but I was so afraid of some chance delay frightening her that I wired her not to come till she heard from me. But he's practically sure to be here some time to-night; and then it'll all end in smoke—tobacco smoke. We'll crack that old lie when we crack a bottle of this wine."

"Very good wine," said Father Brown, gravely lifting his glass, "but, as you see, a very bad wine-bibber. I most sincerely beg your pardon": for he had spilt a small spot of wine on the table-cloth. He drank and put down the glass with a composed face; but his hand had started at the exact moment when he became conscious of a face looking in through the garden window just behind the Admiral—the face of a woman, swarthy, with Southern hair and eyes, and young, but like a mask of tragedy.

After a pause the priest spoke again in his mild manner. "Admiral," he said, "will you do me a favour? Let me, and my friends if they like, stop in that tower of yours just for to-night? Do you know that in my business you're an exorcist almost before anything else?"

Pendragon sprang to his feet and paced swiftly to and fro across the window, from which the face had instantly vanished. "I tell you there is nothing in it," he cried, with ringing violence. "There is one thing I know about this matter. You may call me an atheist. I am an atheist." Here he swung round and fixed Father Brown with a face of frightful concentration. "This business is perfectly natural. There is no curse in it at all."

Father Brown smiled. "In that case," he said, "there can't be any objection to my sleeping in your delightful summer-house."

"The idea is utterly ridiculous," replied the Admiral, beating a tattoo on the back of his chair.

"Please forgive me for everything," said Brown in his most sympathetic tone, "including spilling the wine. But it seems to me you are not quite so easy about the flaming tower as you try to be."

Admiral Pendragon sat down again as abruptly as he had risen; but he sat quite still, and when he spoke again it was in a lower voice. "You do it at your own peril," he said; "but wouldn't *you* be an atheist to keep sane in all this devilry?"

Some three hours afterwards Fanshaw, Flambeau and the priest were still dawdling about the garden in the dark; and it began to dawn on the other two that Father Brown had no intention of going to bed either in the tower or the house.

"I think the lawn wants weeding," said he dreamily. "If I could find a spud or something I'd do it myself."

They followed him, laughing and half remonstrating; but he replied with the utmost solemnity, explaining to them, in a maddening little sermon, that one can always find some small occupation that is helpful to others. He did not find a spud; but he found an old broom made of twigs, with which he began most energetically to brush the fallen leaves off the grass.

"Always some little thing to be done," he said with idiot cheerfulness; "as George Herbert says, 'Who sweeps an Admiral's garden in Cornwall as for Thy laws makes that and the action fine.' And now," he added, suddenly slinging the broom away, "let's go and water the flowers."

With the same mixed emotions, they watched him uncoil some considerable lengths of the large garden hose, saying with an air of wistful discrimination, "The red tulips before the yellow, I think. Look a bit dry, don't you think?"

He turned the little tap on the instrument, and the water shot out straight and solid as a long rod of steel.

"Look out, Samson," cried Flambeau; "why, you've cut off the tulip's head."

Father Brown stood ruefully contemplating the decapitated plant.

"Mine does seem to be a rather kill or cure sort of watering," he admitted, scratching his head. "I suppose it's a pity I didn't find the spud. You should have seen me with the spud! Talking of tools, you've got that swordstick, Flambeau, you always carry? That's right; and Sir Cecil could have that sword the Admiral threw away by the fence here. How grey everything looks!"

"The mist's rising from the river," said the staring Flambeau.

Almost as he spoke the huge figure of the hairy gardener appeared on a higher ridge of the trenched and terraced lawn, hailing them with a brandished rake and a horribly bellowing voice. "Put down that hose," he shouted; "put down that hose and go to your——"

"I am fearfully clumsy," replied the reverend gentleman weakly; "do you know, I upset some wine at dinner." He made a wavering half-turn of apology towards the gardener, with the hose still spouting in his hand. The gardener caught the cold crash of the water full in his face like the crash of a cannon-ball; staggered, slipped and went sprawling with his boots in the air.

"How very dreadful!" said Father Brown, looking round in a sort of wonder. "Why, I've hit a man!"

He stood with his head forward for a moment as if looking or listening; and then set off at a trot towards the tower, still trailing the hose behind him. The tower was quite close, but its outline was curiously dim.

"Your river mist," he said, "has a rum smell."

"By the Lord it has," cried Fanshaw, who was very white. "But you can't mean——"

"I mean," said Father Brown, "that one of the Admiral's scientific predictions is coming true to-night. This story is going to end in smoke."

As he spoke a most beautiful rose-red light seemed to burst into blossom like a gigantic rose; but accompanied with a crackling and rattling noise that was like the laughter of devils.

"My God! what is this?" cried Sir Cecil Fanshaw.

"The sign of the flaming tower," said Father Brown, and sent the driving water from his hose into the heart of the red patch.

"Lucky we hadn't gone to bed!" ejaculated Fanshaw. "I suppose it can't spread to the house."

"You may remember," said the priest quietly, "that the wooden fence that might have carried it was cut away."

Flambeau turned electrified eyes upon his friend, but Fanshaw only said rather absently, "Well, nobody can be killed, anyhow."

"This is rather a curious kind of tower," observed Father Brown; "when it takes to killing people, it always kills people who are somewhere else."

At the same instant the monstrous figure of the gardener with the streaming beard stood again on the green ridge against the sky, waving others to come on; but now waving not a rake but a cutlass. Behind him came the two negroes, also with the old crooked cutlasses out of the trophy. But in the blood-red glare, with their black faces and yellow figures, they looked like devils carrying instruments of torture. In the dim garden behind them a distant voice was heard calling out brief directions. When the priest heard the voice, a terrible change came over his countenance.

But he remained composed; and never took his eye off the patch of flame which had begun by spreading, but now seemed to shrink a little as it hissed under the torch of the long silver spear of water. He kept his finger along the nozzle of the pipe to ensure the aim, and attended to no other business, knowing only by the noise and that semi-conscious corner of the eye, the exciting incidents that began to tumble themselves about the island garden. He gave two brief directions to his friends. One was, "Knock these fellows down somehow and tie them up, whoever they are; there's rope down by those faggots. They want to take away my nice hose." The other was, "As soon as you get a chance, call out to that canoeing girl; she's over on the bank with the gypsies. Ask her if they could get some buckets across and fill them from the river." Then he closed his mouth and continued to water the new red flower as ruthlessly as he had watered the red tulip.

He never turned his head to look at the strange fight that followed between the foes and friends of the mysterious fire. He almost felt the island shake when Flambeau collided with the huge gardener; he merely imagined how it would whirl round them as they wrestled. He heard the crashing fall; and his friend's gasp of triumph as he dashed on to the first negro; and the cries of both the blacks as Flambeau and Fanshaw bound them. Flambeau's enormous strength more than redressed the odds in the fight, especially as the fourth man still hovered near the house, only a shadow and a voice. He heard also the water broken by the paddles of a canoe; the girl's voice giving orders, the voices of gypsies answering and coming nearer, the plumping and sucking noise of empty buckets plunged into a full stream; and finally the sound of many feet around the fire. But all this was less to him than the fact that the red rent, which had lately once more increased, had once more slightly diminished.

Then came a cry that very nearly made him turn his head. Flambeau and Fanshaw, now reinforced by some of the gypsies, had rushed after the mysterious man by the house; and he heard from the other end of the garden the Frenchman's cry of horror and astonishment. It was echoed by a howl not to be called human, as the being broke from their hold and ran along the garden. Three times at least it raced round the whole island, in a way that was as horrible as the chase of a lunatic, both in the cries of the pursued and the ropes carried by the pursuers; but was more horrible still, because it somehow suggested one of the chasing games of children in a garden. Then, finding them closing in on every side, the figure sprang upon one of the higher river banks and disappeared with a splash into the dark and driving river.

"You can do no more, I fear," said Brown in a voice cold with pain. "He has been washed down to the rocks by now, where he has sent so many others. He knew the use of a family legend."

"Oh, don't talk in these parables," cried Flambeau impatiently. "Can't you put it simply in words of one syllable?"

"Yes," answered Brown, with his eye on the hose. "'Both eyes bright, she's all right; one eye blinks, down she sinks.'"

The fire hissed and shrieked more and more, like a strangled thing, as it grew narrower and narrower under the flood from the pipe and buckets, but Father Brown still kept his eye on it as he went on speaking:

"I thought of asking this young lady if it were morning yet, to look through that telescope at the river-mouth and the river. She might have seen something to interest her: the sign of the ship; or Mr. Walter Pendragon coming home; and perhaps even the sign of the half-man, for though he is certainly safe by now, he may very well have waded ashore. He has been within a shave of another shipwreck; and would never have escaped it, if the lady hadn't had the sense to suspect the old Admiral's telegram and come down to watch him. Don't let's talk about the old Admiral. Don't let's talk about anything. It's enough to say that whenever this tower, with its pitch and resin-wood, really caught fire, the spark on the horizon always looked like the twin light to the coast lighthouse."

"And that," said Flambeau, "is how the father and brother died. The wicked uncle of the legends very nearly got his estate, after all."

Father Brown did not answer; indeed, he did not speak again, save for civilities, till they were all safe round a cigar-box in the cabin of the yacht. He saw that the frustrate fire was extinguished; and then refused to linger, though he actually heard young Pendragon, escorted by an enthusiastic crowd, come tramping up the river-bank; and might (had he been moved by romantic curiosities) have received the combined thanks of the man from the ship and the girl from the canoe. But his fatigue had fallen on him once more; and he only started once, when Flambeau abruptly told him he had dropped cigar-ash on his trousers.

"That's no cigar-ash," he said rather wearily. "That's from the fire, but you don't think so because you're all smoking cigars. That's just the way I got my first faint suspicion about the chart."

"Do you mean Pendragon's chart of his Pacific Islands?" asked Fanshaw.

"You thought it was a chart of the Pacific Islands," answered Brown. "Put a feather with a fossil and a bit of coral and everyone will think it's a specimen. Put the same feather with a ribbon and an artificial flower and everyone will think it's for a lady's hat. Put the same feather with an ink-bottle, a book, and a stack of writing-paper, and most men will swear they've seen a quill pen. So you saw that map among tropic birds and shells and thought it was a map of Pacific Islands. It was the map of this river."

"But how do you know?" asked Fanshaw.

"I saw the rock you thought was like a dragon, and the one like Merlin, and——"

"You seem to have noticed a lot as we came in," cried Fanshaw. "We thought you were rather abstracted."

"I was sea-sick," said Father Brown simply. "I felt simply horrible. But feeling horrible has nothing to do with not seeing things." And he closed his eyes.

"Do you think most men would have seen that?" asked Flambeau. He received no answer: Father Brown was asleep.

THE SALAD OF COLONEL CRAY

FATHER BROWN WAS walking home from Mass on a white weird morning when the mists were slowly lifting—one of those mornings when the very element of light appears as something mysterious and new. The scattered trees outlined themselves more and more out of the vapour, as if they were first drawn in grey chalk and then in charcoal. At yet more distant intervals appeared the houses upon the broken fringe of the suburb; their outlines became clearer and clearer until he recognised many in which he had chance acquaintances, and many more the names of whose owners he knew. But all the windows and doors were sealed; none of the people were of the sort that would be up at such a time, or still less on such an errand. But as he passed under the shadow of one handsome villa with verandas and wide ornate gardens, he heard a noise that made him almost involuntarily stop. It was the unmistakable noise of a pistol or carbine or some light firearm discharged; but it was not this that puzzled him most. The first full noise was immediately followed by a series of fainter noises—as he counted them, about six. He supposed it must be the echo; but the odd thing was that the echo was not in the least like the original sound. It was not like anything else that he could think of; the three things nearest to it seemed to be the noise made by siphons of soda-water, one of the many noises made by an animal, and the noise made by a person attempting to conceal laughter. None of which seemed to make much sense.

Father Brown was made of two men. There was a man of action, who was as modest as a primrose and as punctual as a clock; who went his small round of duties and never dreamed of altering it. There was also a man of reflection, who was much simpler but much stronger, who could not easily be stopped; whose thought was always (in the only intelligent sense of the words) free thought. He could not help, even unconsciously, asking himself all the questions that there were to be asked, and answering as many of them as he could; all that went on like his breathing or circulation. But he never consciously carried his actions outside the sphere of his own duty; and in this case the two attitudes were aptly tested. He was just about to resume his trudge in the twilight, telling himself it was no affair of his, but instinctively twisting and untwisting twenty theories about what the odd noises might mean. Then the grey sky-line brightened into silver, and in the broadening light he realised that he had been to the house which belonged to an Anglo-Indian Major named Putnam; and that the Major had a native cook from Malta who was of his communion. He also began to remember that pistol-shots are sometimes serious things; accompanied with consequences with which he was legitimately concerned. He turned back and went in at the garden gate, making for the front door.

Half-way down one side of the house stood out a projection like a very low shed; it was, as he afterwards discovered, a large dustbin. Round the corner of this came a figure, at first a mere shadow in the haze, apparently bending and peering about. Then, coming nearer, it solidified into a figure that was, indeed, rather unusually solid. Major Putnam was a bald-headed, bull-necked man, short and very broad, with one of those rather apoplectic faces that are produced by a prolonged attempt to combine the oriental climate with the occidental luxuries. But the face was a good-humoured one, and even now, though evidently puzzled and inquisitive, wore a kind of innocent grin. He had a large palm-leaf hat on the back of his head (suggesting a halo that was by no means appropriate to the face), but otherwise he was clad only in a very vivid suit of striped scarlet and yellow pyjamas; which, though glowing enough to behold, must have been, on a fresh morning, pretty chilly to wear. He had evidently come out of his house in a hurry; and the priest was not surprised when he called out without further ceremony: "Did you hear that noise?"

"Yes," answered Father Brown. "I thought I had better look in, in case anything was the matter."

The Major looked at him rather queerly with his good-humoured gooseberry eyes. "What do you think the noise was?" he asked.

"It sounded like a gun or something," replied the other, with some hesitation; "but it seemed to have a singular sort of echo."

The Major was still looking at him quietly, but with protruding eyes, when the front door was flung open, releasing a flood of gaslight on the face of the fading mist; and another figure in pyjamas sprang or tumbled out into the garden. The figure was much longer, leaner, and more athletic; the pyjamas, though equally tropical, were comparatively tasteful, being of white with a light lemon-yellow stripe. The man was haggard, but handsome, more sunburned than the other; he had an aquiline profile and rather deep-sunken eyes, and a slight air of oddity arising from the combination of coal-black hair with a much lighter moustache. All this Father Brown absorbed in detail more at leisure. For the moment he only saw one thing about the man: which was the revolver in his hand.

"Cray!" exclaimed the Major, staring at him, "did you fire that shot?"

"Yes, I did," retorted the black-haired gentleman hotly, "and so would you in my place. If you were chased everywhere by devils and nearly——"

The Major seemed to intervene rather hurriedly. "This is my friend Father Brown," he said. And then to Brown: "I don't know whether you've met Colonel Cray of the Royal Artillery."

"I have heard of him, of course," said the priest innocently. "Did you—did you hit anything?"

"I thought so," answered Cray with gravity.

"Did he——" asked Major Putnam, in a lowered voice, "did he fall or cry out, or anything?"

Colonel Cray was regarding his host with a strange and steady stare "I'll tell you exactly what he did," he said. "He sneezed."

Father Brown's hand went half-way to his head, with the gesture of a man remembering somebody's name. He knew now what it was that was neither soda-water nor the snorting of a dog.

"Well," ejaculated the staring Major, "I never heard before that a service revolver was a thing to be sneezed at."

"Nor I," said Father Brown faintly. "It's lucky you didn't turn your artillery on him, or you might have given him quite a bad cold." Then, after a bewildered pause, he said: "Was it a burglar?"

"Let us go inside," said Major Putnam, rather sharply, and led the way into his house.

The interior exhibited a paradox often to be marked in such morning hours: that the rooms seemed brighter than the sky outside; even after the Major had turned out the one gaslight in the front hall. Father Brown was surprised to see the whole dining-table set out as for a festive meal, with napkins in their rings, and wine-glasses of some six unnecessary shapes set beside every plate. It was common enough, at that time of the morning, to find the remains of a banquet overnight; but to find it freshly spread so early was unusual.

While he stood wavering in the hall Major Putnam rushed past him and sent a raging eye over the whole oblong of the tablecloth. At last he spoke, spluttering: "All the silver gone!" he gasped. "Fish-knives and forks gone. Old cruet-stand gone. Even old silver cream-jug gone. And now, Father Brown, I am ready to answer your question of whether it was a burglar."

"They're simply a blind," said Cray stubbornly. "I know better than you why people persecute this house; I know better than you why——"

The Major patted him on the shoulder with a gesture almost peculiar to the soothing of a sick child, and said: "It was a burglar. Obviously it was a burglar."

"A burglar with a bad cold," observed Father Brown, "that might assist you to trace him in the neighbourhood."

The Major shook his head in a sombre manner. "He must be far beyond tracing now, I fear," he said.

Then, as the restless man with the revolver turned again towards the door into the garden, he added in a husky, confidential voice: "I doubt whether I should send for the police, for fear my friend here has been a little too free with his bullets, and got on the wrong side of the law. He's lived in very wild places; and, to be frank with you, I think he sometimes fancies things."

"I think you once told me," said Brown, "that he believes some Indian secret society is pursuing him."

Major Putnam nodded, but at the same time shrugged his shoulders. "I suppose we'd better follow him outside," he said. "I don't want any more—shall we say, sneezing?"

They passed out into the morning light, which was now even tinged with sunshine, and saw Colonel Cray's tall figure bent almost double, minutely examining the condition of gravel and grass. While the Major strolled unobtrusively towards him, the priest took an equally indolent turn, which took him round the next corner of the house to within a yard or two of the projecting dustbin.

He stood regarding this dismal object for some minute and a half; then he stepped towards it, lifted the lid, and put his head inside. Dust and other discolouring matter shook upwards as he did so; but

Father Brown never observed his own appearance, whatever else he observed. He remained thus for a measurable period, as if engaged in some mysterious prayers. Then he came out again, with some ashes on his hair, and walked unconcernedly away.

By the time he came round to the garden door again he found a group there which seemed to roll away morbidities as the sunlight had already rolled away the mists. It was in no way rationally reassuring; it was simply broadly comic, like a cluster of Dickens's characters. Major Putnam had managed to slip inside and plunge into a proper shirt and trousers, with a crimson cummer-bund, and a light square jacket over all; thus normally set off, his red festive face seemed bursting with a commonplace cordiality. He was indeed emphatic, but then he was talking to his cook—the swarthy son of Malta, whose lean, yellow, and rather careworn face contrasted quaintly with his snow-white cap and costume. The cook might well be careworn, for cookery was the Major's hobby. He was one of those amateurs who always know more than the professional. The only other person he even admitted to be a judge of an omelette was his friend Cray—and as Brown remembered this, he turned to look for the other officer. In the new presence of daylight and people clothed and in their right mind, the sight of him was rather a shock. The taller and more elegant man was still in his night-garb, with tousled black hair, and now crawling about the garden on his hands and knees, still looking for traces of the burglar; and now and again, to all appearance, striking the ground with his hand in anger at not finding him. Seeing him thus quadrupedal in the grass, the priest raised his eyebrows rather sadly; and for the first time guessed that "fancies things" might be an euphemism.

The third item in the group of the cook and the epicure was also known to Father Brown: it was Audrey Watson, the Major's ward and housekeeper; and at this moment, to judge by her apron, tucked-up sleeves, and resolute manner, much more the housekeeper than the ward.

"It serves you right," she was saying: "I always told you not to have that old-fashioned cruet-stand."

"I prefer it," said Putnam placably. "I'm old-fashioned myself; and the things keep together."

"And vanish together, as you see," she retorted. "Well, if you are not going to bother about the burglar, I shouldn't bother about the lunch. It's Sunday, and we can't send for vinegar and all that in the town; and you Indian gentlemen can't enjoy what you call a dinner without a lot of hot things. I wish to goodness now you hadn't asked Cousin Oliver to take me to the musical service. It isn't over till half-past twelve, and the Colonel has to leave by then. I don't believe you men can manage alone."

"Oh, yes, we can, my dear," said the Major, looking at her very amiably. "Marco has all the sauces; and we've often done ourselves well in very rough places, as you might know by now. And it's time you had a treat, Audrey; you mustn't be a housekeeper every hour of the day; and I know you want to hear the music."

"I want to go to church," she said, with rather severe eyes.

She was one of those handsome women who will always be handsome, because the beauty is not in an air or a tint, but in the very structure of the head and features. But though she was not yet middle-aged and her auburn hair was of a Titianesque fullness in form and colour, there was a look in her mouth and around her eyes which suggested that some sorrows wasted her, as winds waste at last the edges of a Greek temple. For indeed the little domestic difficulty of which she was now speaking so decisively was rather comic than tragic. Father Brown gathered, from the course of the conversation, that Cray, the other *gourmet*, had to leave before the usual lunch-time; but that Putnam, his host, not to be done out of a final feast with an old crony, had arranged for a special *déjeuner* to be set out and consumed in the course of the morning, while Audrey and other graver persons were at morning service. She was going there under the escort of a relative and old friend of hers, Dr. Oliver Oman, who, though a scientific man of a somewhat bitter type, was enthusiastic for music, and would go even to church to get it. There was nothing in all this that could conceivably concern the tragedy in Miss Watson's face; and by a half-conscious instinct, Father Brown turned again to the seeming lunatic grubbing about in the grass.

When he strolled across to him, the black unbrushed head was lifted abruptly, as if in some surprise at his continued presence. And indeed, Father Brown, for reasons best known to himself, had lingered much longer than politeness required; or even, in the ordinary sense, permitted.

"Well!" cried Cray, with wild eyes. "I suppose you think I'm mad, like the rest?"

"I have considered the thesis," answered the little man composedly. "And I incline to think you are not."

"What do you mean?" snapped Cray quite savagely.

"Real madmen," explained Father Brown, "always encourage their own morbidity. They never strive against it. But you are trying to find traces of the burglar; even when there aren't any. You are struggling against it. You want what no madman ever wants."

"And what is that?"

"You want to be proved wrong," said Brown.

During the last words, Cray had sprung or staggered to his feet and was regarding the cleric with agitated eyes. "By hell, but that is a true word!" he cried. "They are all at me here that the fellow was only after the silver—as if I shouldn't be only too pleased to think so! *She's* been at me," and he tossed his tousled black head towards Audrey, but the other had no need of the direction, "she's been at me to-day about how cruel I was to shoot a poor harmless housebreaker, and how I have the devil in me against poor harmless natives. But I was a good-natured man once—as good-natured as Putnam."

After a pause he said: "Look here, I've never seen you before; but you shall judge of the whole story: Old Putnam and I were friends in the same mess; but, owing to some accidents on the Afghan border, I got my regiment much sooner than most men; only we were both invalided home for a bit. I was engaged to Audrey out there; and we all travelled back together. But on the journey back things happened. Curious things. The result of them was that Putnam wants it broken off, and even Audrey keeps it hanging on—and I know what they mean. I know what they think I am. So do you.

"Well, these are the facts: The last day we were in an Indian city, I asked Putnam if I could get some Trichinopoli cigars; he directed me to a little place opposite his lodgings. I have since found he was quite right; but 'opposite' is a dangerous word when one decent house stands opposite five or six squalid ones: and I must have mistaken the door. It opened with difficulty, and then only on darkness; but as I turned back, the door behind me sank back and settled into its place with a noise as of innumerable bolts. There was nothing to do but to walk forward; which I did through passage after passage, pitch-dark. Then I came to a flight of steps, and then to a blind door, secured by a latch of elaborate Eastern iron-work, which I could only trace by touch, but which I loosened at last. I came out again upon gloom, which was half turned into a greenish twilight by a multitude of small but steady lamps below. They showed merely the feet or fringes of some huge and empty architecture. Just in front of me was something that looked like a mountain. I confess I nearly fell on the great stone platform on which I had emerged, to realise that it was an idol. And, worst of all, an idol with its back to me.

"It was hardly half human, I guessed; to judge by the small squat head, and still more by a thing like a tail or extra limb turned up behind and pointing, like a loathsome large finger, at some symbol graven in the centre of the vast stone back. I had begun, in the dim light, to guess at the hieroglyphic, not without horror, when a more horrible thing happened. A door opened silently in the temple wall behind me and a man came out, with a brown face and a black coat. He had a carved smile on his face, of copper flesh and ivory teeth; but I think the most hateful thing about him was that he was in European dress. I was prepared, I think, for shrouded priests or naked fakirs. But this seemed to say that the devilry was over all the earth. As indeed I found it to be.

" 'If you had only seen the Monkey's Feet,' he said, smiling steadily and without other preface, 'we should have been very gentle—you would only be tortured and die. If you had seen the Monkey's Face, still we should be very moderate, very tolerant—you would only be tortured and live. But as you have seen the Monkey's Tail, we must pronounce the worst sentence. Which is—Go Free.'

"When he said the words I heard the elaborate iron latch with which I had struggled automatically unlock itself: and then far down the dark passages I had passed I heard the heavy street-door shifting its own bolts backwards.

" 'It is vain to ask for mercy; you must go free,' said the smiling man. 'Henceforth a hair shall slay you like a sword, and a breath shall bite you like an adder; weapons shall come against you out of nowhere; and you shall die many times.' And with that he was swallowed once more in the wall behind; and I went out into the street."

Cray paused: and Father Brown unaffectedly sat down on the lawn and began to pick daisies.

Then the soldier continued: "Putnam, of course, with his jolly common sense, pooh-poohed all my fears; and from that time dates his doubt of my mental balance. Well, I'll simply tell you, in the fewest words, the three things that have happened since; and you shall judge which of us is right.

"The first happened in an Indian village on the edge of the jungle, but hundreds of miles from the temple, or town, or type of tribes and customs where the curse had been put on me. I woke in black midnight, and lay thinking of nothing in particular, when

I felt a faint tickling thing, like a thread or a hair, trailed across my throat. I shrank back out of its way, and could not help thinking of the words in the temple. But when I got up and sought lights and a mirror, the line across my neck was a line of blood.

"The second happened in a lodging in Port Said, later, on our journey home together. It was a jumble of tavern and curiosity-shop; and though there was nothing there remotely suggesting the cult of the Monkey, it is, of course, possible that some of its images or talismans were in such a place. Its curse was there, anyhow. I woke again in the dark with a sensation that could not be put in colder or more literal words than that a breath bit like an adder. Existence was an agony of extinction; I dashed my head against walls until I dashed it against a window; and fell rather than jumped into the garden below. Putnam, poor fellow, who had called the other thing a chance scratch, was bound to take seriously the fact of finding me half insensible on the grass at dawn. But I fear it was my mental state he took seriously; and not my story.

"The third happened in Malta. We were in a fortress there; and as it happened our bedrooms overlooked the open sea, which almost came up to our window-sills, save for a flat white outer wall as bare as the sea. I woke up again; but it was not dark. There was a full moon, as I walked to the window; I could have seen a bird on the bare battlement, or a sail on the horizon. What I did see was a sort of stick or branch circling self-supported in the empty sky. It flew straight in at my window and smashed the lamp beside the pillow I had just quitted. It was one of those queer-shaped war-clubs some Eastern tribes use. But it had come from no human hand."

Father Brown threw away a daisy chain he was making, and rose with a wistful look. "Has Major Putnam," he asked, "got any Eastern curios, idols, weapons, and so on, from which one might get a hint?"

"Plenty of those, though not much use, I fear," replied Cray; "but by all means come into his study."

As they entered they passed Miss Watson buttoning her gloves for church, and heard the voice of Putnam downstairs still giving a lecture on cookery to the cook. In the Major's study and den of curios they came suddenly on a third party, silk-hatted and dressed for the street, who was poring over an open book on the smoking-table—a book which he dropped rather guiltily, and turned.

Cray introduced him civilly enough, as Dr. Oman, but he showed such disfavour in his very face that Brown guessed the two men, whether Audrey knew it or not, were rivals. Nor was the priest wholly unsympathetic with the prejudice. Dr. Oman was a very well-dressed gentleman indeed; well-featured, though almost dark enough for an Asiatic. But Father Brown had to tell himself sharply that one should be in charity even with those who wax their pointed beards, who have small gloved hands, and who speak with perfectiy modulated voices.

Cray seemed to find something specially irritating in the small prayer-book in Oman's dark-gloved hand. "I didn't know that was in your line," he said rather rudely.

Oman laughed mildly, but without offence. "This is more so, I know," he said, laying his hand on the big book he had dropped, "a dictionary of drugs and such things. But it's rather too large to take to church." Then he closed the larger book, and there seemed again the faintest touch of hurry and embarrassment.

"I suppose," said the priest, who seemed anxious to change the subject, "all these spears and things are from India?"

"From everywhere," answered the doctor. "Putnam is an old soldier, and has been in Mexico and Australia, and the Cannibal Islands for all I know."

"I hope it was not in the Cannibal Islands," said Brown, "that he learnt the art of cookery." And he ran his eye over the stew-pots or other strange utensils on the wall.

At this moment the jolly subject of their conversation thrust his laughing, lobsterish face into the room. "Come along, Cray," he cried. "Your lunch is just coming in. And the bells are ringing for those who want to go to church."

Cray slipped upstairs to change; Dr. Oman and Miss Watson betook themselves solemnly down the street, with a string of other churchgoers; but Father Brown noticed that the doctor twice looked back and scrutinised the house; and even came back to the corner of the street to look at it again.

The priest looked puzzled. "*He* can't have been at the dustbin," he muttered. "Not in those clothes. Or was he here earlier to-day?"

Father Brown, touching other people, was as sensitive as a barometer; but to-day he seemed about as sensitive as a rhinoceros. By no social law, rigid or implied, could he be supposed to linger round the lunch of the Anglo-Indian friends; but he lingered, covering his position with torrents of amusing but quite needless conversation. He was the more puzzling because he did not seem to want any lunch. As one after another of the most exquisitely balanced kedgerees or curries, accompanied with their appropriate vintages, were laid before the other two, he only repeated that it was one of his fast-days, and munched a piece of bread and sipped and then left untasted a tumbler of cold water. His talk, however, was exuberant.

"I'll tell you what I'll do for you," he cried; "I'll mix you a salad! I can't eat it, but I'll mix it like an angel! You've got a lettuce there."

"Unfortunately it's the only thing we have got," answered the good-humoured Major. "You must remember that mustard, vinegar, oil, and so on vanished with the cruet and the burglar."

"I know," replied Brown, rather vaguely. "That's what I've always been afraid would happen. That's why I always carry a cruet-stand about with me. I'm so fond of salads."

And to the amazement of the two men he took a pepper-pot out of his waistcoat pocket and put it on the table.

"I wonder why the burglar wanted mustard, too," he went on, taking a mustard-pot from another pocket. "A mustard plaster, I suppose. And vinegar," producing that condiment, "haven't I heard something about vinegar and brown paper? As for oil, which I think I put in my left——"

His garrulity was an instant arrested; for lifting his eyes, he saw what no one else saw—the black figure of Dr. Oman standing on the sunlit lawn and looking steadily into the room. Before he could quite recover himself, Cray had cloven in.

"You're an astounding card," he said, staring. "I shall come and hear your sermons if they're as amusing as your manners." His voice changed a little, and he leaned back in his chair.

"Oh, there are sermons in a cruet-stand, too," said Father Brown, quite gravely. "Have you heard of faith like a grain of mustard-seed; or charity that anoints with oil? And as for vinegar, can any soldiers forget that solitary soldier, who, when the sun was darkened——"

Colonel Cray leaned forward a little and clutched the tablecloth.

Father Brown, who was making the salad, tipped two spoonfuls of the mustard into the tumbler of water beside him; stood up, and said in a new, loud and sudden voice—"Drink that!"

At the same moment the motionless doctor in the garden came running and bursting open a window, cried, "Am I wanted? Has he been poisoned?"

"Pretty near," said Brown, with the shadow of a smile; for the emetic had very suddenly taken effect. And Cray lay in a deck-chair, gasping as for life, but alive.

Major Putnam had sprung up, his purple face mottled. "A crime!" he cried hoarsely. "I will go for the police!"

The priest could hear him dragging down his palm-leaf hat from the peg and tumbling out of the front door; he heard the garden gate slam. But he only stood looking at Cray; and after a silence said quietly:

"I shall not talk to you much; but I will tell you what you want to know. There is no curse on you. The Temple of the Monkey was either a coincidence or a part of the trick; the trick was the trick of a white man. There is only one weapon that will bring blood with that mere feathery touch: a razor held by a white man. There is one way of making a common room full of invisible overpowering poison: turning on the gas—the crime of a white man. And there is only one kind of club that can be thrown out of a window, turn in mid air and come back to the window next to it: the Australian boomerang. You'll see some of them in the Major's study."

With that he went outside and spoke for a moment to the doctor. The moment after, Audrey Watson came rushing into the house and fell on her knees beside Cray's chair. He could not hear what they said to each other; but their faces moved with amazement, not unhappiness. The doctor and the priest walked slowly towards the garden gate.

"I suppose the Major was in love with her, too," he said, with a sigh; and when the other nodded observed: "You were very generous, doctor. You did a fine thing. But what made you suspect?"

"A very small thing," said Oman; "but it kept me restless in church till I came back to see that all was well. That book on his table was a work on poisons; and was put down open at the place where it stated that a certain Indian poison, though deadly and difficult to trace, was particularly easily reversible by the use of the commonest emetics. I suppose he read that at the last moment——"

"And remembered that there were emetics in the cruet-stand," said Father Brown. "Exactly. He threw the cruet in the dustbin, where I found it, along with other silver, for the sake of a burglary blind. But if you look at that pepper-pot I put on the table, you'll see a small hole. That's where Cray's bullet struck, shaking up the pepper and making the criminal sneeze."

There was a silence. Then Dr. Oman said grimly: "The Major is a long time looking for the police."

"Or the police in looking for the Major?" said the priest. "Well, goodbye."

The Man Who Was Thursday

A NIGHTMARE

Contents

To Edmund Clerihew Bentley.

A cloud was on the mind of men, and wailing went the weather,
Yea, a sick cloud upon the soul when we were boys together.
Science announced nonentity and art admired decay;
The world was old and ended: but you and I were gay;
Round us in antic order their crippled vices came—
Lust that had lost its laughter, fear that had lost its shame.
Like the white lock of Whistler, that lit our aimless gloom,
Men showed their own white feather as proudly as a plume.
Life was a fly that faded, and death a drone that stung;
The world was very old indeed when you and I were young.
They twisted even decent sin to shapes not to be named:
Men were ashamed of honour; but we were not ashamed.
Weak if we were and foolish, not thus we failed, not thus;
When that black Baal blocked the heavens he had no hymns from us.
Children we were—our forts of sand were even as weak as we,
High as they went we piled them up to break that bitter sea.
Fools as we were in motley, all jangling and absurd,
When all church bells were silent our cap and bells were heard.

Not all unhelped we held the fort, our tiny flags unfurled;
Some giants laboured in that cloud to lift it from the world.
I find again the book we found, I feel the hour that flings
Far out of fish-shaped Paumanok some cry of cleaner things;
And the Green Carnation withered, as in forest fires that pass,
Roared in the wind of all the world ten million leaves of grass;
Or sane and sweet and sudden as a bird sings in the rain—
Truth out of Tusitala spoke and pleasure out of pain.
Yea, cool and clear and sudden as a bird sings in the grey,
Dunedin to Samoa spoke, and darkness unto day.
But we were young; we lived to see God break their bitter charms.
God and the good Republic come riding back in arms:
We have seen the City of Mansoul, even as it rocked, relieved—
Blessed are they who did not see, but being blind, believed.

This is a tale of those old fears, even of those emptied hells,
And none but you shall understand the true thing that it tells—
Of what colossal gods of shame could cow men and yet crash,
Of what huge devils hid the stars, yet fell at a pistol flash.
The doubts that were so plain to chase, so dreadful to withstand—
Oh, who shall understand but you; yea, who shall understand?
The doubts that drove us through the night as we two talked amain,
And day had broken on the streets e'er it broke upon the brain.
Between us, by the peace of God, such truth can now be told;
Yea, there is strength in striking root, and good in growing old.
We have found common things at last, and marriage and a creed,
And I may safely write it now, and you may safely read.

G. K. C.

To Edmund Clerihew Bentley

A cloud was on the mind of men, and wailing went the weather,
Yea, a sick cloud upon the soul when we were boys together.
Science announced nonentity and art admired decay;
The world was old and ended: but you and I were gay.
Round us in antic order their crippled vices came—
Lust that had lost its laughter, fear that had lost its shame.
Like the white lock of Whistler, that lit our aimless gloom,
Men showed their own white feather as proudly as a plume.
Life was a fly that faded, and death a drone that stung;
The world was very old indeed when you and I were young.
They twisted even decent sin to shapes not to be named:
Men were ashamed of honour; but we were not ashamed.
Weak if we were and foolish, not thus we failed, not thus;
When that black Baal blocked the heavens he had no hymns from us.
Children we were—our forts of sand were even as weak as we,
High as they went we piled them up to break that bitter sea.
Fools as we were in motley, all jangling and absurd,
When all church bells were silent our cap and bells were heard.

Not all unhelped we held the fort, our tiny flags unfurled;
Some giants laboured in that cloud to lift it from the world.
I find again the book we found, I feel the hour that flings
Far out of fish-shaped Paumanok some cry of cleaner things;
And the Green Carnation withered, as in forest fires that pass,
Roared in the wind of all the world ten million leaves of grass;
Or sane and sweet and sudden as a bird sings in the rain—
Truth out of Tusitala spoke and pleasure out of pain.
Yea, cool and clear and sudden as a bird sings in the grey,
Dunedin to Samoa spoke, and darkness unto day.
But we were young; we lived to see God break their bitter charms,
God and the good Republic come riding back in arms:
We have seen the City of Mansoul, even as it rocked, relieved—
Blessed are they who did not see, but being blind, believed.

This is a tale of those old fears, even of those emptied hells,
And none but you shall understand the true thing that it tells—
Of what colossal gods of shame could cow men and yet crash,
Of what huge devils hid the stars, yet fell at a pistol flash.
The doubts that were so plain to chase, so dreadful to withstand—
Oh, who shall understand but you; yea, who shall understand?
The doubts that drove us through the night as we two talked amain,
And day had broken on the streets e'er it broke upon the brain.
Between us, by the peace of God, such truth can now be told;
Yea, there is strength in striking root, and good in growing old.
We have found common things at last, and marriage and a creed,
And I may safely write it now, and you may safely read.

I

THE TWO POETS OF SAFFRON PARK

THE SUBURB of Saffron Park lay on the sunset side of London, as red and ragged as a cloud of sunset. It was built of a bright brick throughout; its sky-line was fantastic, and even its ground plan was wild. It had been the outburst of a speculative builder, faintly tinged with art, who called its architecture sometimes Elizabethan and sometimes Queen Anne, apparently under the impression that the two sovereigns were identical. It was described with some justice as an artistic colony, though it never in any definable way produced any art. But although its pretensions to be an intellectual centre were a little vague, its pretensions to be a pleasant place were quite indisputable. The stranger who looked for the first time at the quaint red houses could only think how very oddly shaped the people must be who could fit in to them. Nor when he met the people was he disappointed in this respect. The place was not only pleasant, but perfect, if once he could regard it not as a deception but rather as a dream. Even if the people were not "artists," the whole was nevertheless artistic. That young man with the long, auburn hair and the impudent face—that young man was not really a poet; but surely he was a poem. That old gentleman with the wild, white beard and the wild, white hat—that venerable humbug was not really a philosopher; but at least he was the cause of philosophy in others. That scientific gentleman with the bald, egg-like head and the bare, bird-like neck had no real right to the airs of science that he assumed. He had not discovered anything new in biology; but what biological creature could he have discovered more singular than himself? Thus, and thus only, the whole place had properly to be regarded; it had to be considered not so much as a workshop for artists, but as a frail but finished work of art. A man who stepped into its social atmosphere felt as if he had stepped into a written comedy.

More especially this attractive unreality fell upon it about nightfall, when the extravagant roofs were dark against the afterglow and the whole insane village seemed as separate as a drifting cloud. This again was more strongly true of the many nights of local festivity, when the little gardens were often illuminated, and the big Chinese lanterns glowed in the dwarfish trees like some fierce and monstrous fruit. And this was strongest of all on one particular evening, still vaguely remembered in the locality, of which the auburn-haired poet was the hero. It was not by any means the only evening of which he was the hero. On many nights those passing by his little back garden might hear his high, didactic voice laying down the law to men and particularly to women. The attitude of women in such cases was indeed one of the paradoxes of the place. Most of the women were of the kind vaguely called emancipated, and professed some protest against male supremacy. Yet these new women would always pay to a man the extravagant compliment which no ordinary woman ever pays to him, that of listening while he is talking. And Mr. Lucian Gregory, the red-haired poet, was really (in some sense) a man worth listening to, even if one only laughed at the end of it. He put the old cant of the lawlessness of art and the art of lawlessness with a certain impudent freshness which gave at least a momentary pleasure. He was helped in some degree by the arresting oddity of his appearance, which he worked, as the phrase goes, for all it was worth. His dark red hair parted in the middle was literally like a woman's, and curved into the slow curls of a virgin in a pre-Raphaelite picture. From within this almost saintly oval, however, his face projected suddenly broad and brutal, the chin carried forward with a look of cockney contempt. This combination at once tickled and terrified the nerves of a neurotic population. He seemed like a walking blasphemy, a blend of the angel and the ape.

This particular evening, if it is remembered for nothing else, will be remembered in that place for its strange sunset. It looked like the end of the world. All the heaven seemed covered with a quite vivid and palpable plumage; you could only say that the sky was full of feathers, and of feathers that almost brushed the face. Across the great part of the dome they were grey, with the strangest tints of violet and mauve and an unnatural pink or pale green; but towards the west the whole grew past description, transparent and passionate, and the last red-hot plumes of it covered up the sun like something too good to be seen. The whole was so close about the earth, as to express nothing but a violent secrecy. The very empyrean seemed to be a secret. It expressed that splendid smallness which is the soul of local patriotism. The very sky seemed small.

I say that there are some inhabitants who may remember the evening if only by that oppressive sky. There are others who may remember it because it marked the first appearance in the place of the second poet of Saffron Park. For a long time the red-haired revolutionary had reigned without a rival; it was upon the night of the sunset that his solitude suddenly ended. The new poet, who introduced himself by the name of Gabriel Syme, was a very mild-looking mortal, with a fair, pointed beard and faint, yellow hair. But an impression grew that he was less meek than he looked. He signalised his entrance by differing with the established poet, Gregory, upon the whole nature of poetry. He said that he (Syme) was a poet of law, a poet of order; nay, he said he was a poet of respectability. So all the Saffron Parkers looked at him as if he had that moment fallen out of that impossible sky.

In fact, Mr. Lucian Gregory, the anarchic poet, connected the two events.

"It may well be," he said, in his sudden lyrical manner, "it may well be on such a night of clouds and cruel colours that there is brought forth upon the earth such a portent as a respectable poet. You say you are a poet of law; I say you are a contradiction in terms. I only wonder there were not comets and earthquakes on the night you appeared in this garden."

The man with the meek blue eyes and the pale, pointed beard endured these thunders with a certain submissive solemnity. The third party of the group, Gregory's sister Rosamond, who had her brother's braids of red hair, but a kindlier face underneath them, laughed with such mixture of admiration and disapproval as she gave commonly to the family oracle.

Gregory resumed in high oratorical good-humour.

"An artist is identical with an anarchist," he cried. "You might transpose the words anywhere. An anarchist is an artist. The man who throws a bomb is an artist, because he prefers a great moment to everything. He sees how much more valuable is one burst of blazing light, one peal of perfect thunder, than the mere common bodies of a few shapeless policemen. An artist disregards all governments, abolishes all conventions. The poet delights in disorder only. If it were not so, the most poetical thing in the world would be the Underground Railway."

"So it is," said Mr. Syme.

"Nonsense!" said Gregory, who was very rational when any one else attempted paradox. "Why do all the clerks and navvies in the railway trains look so sad and tired, so very sad and tired? I will tell you. It is because they know that the train is going right. It is because they know that whatever place they have taken a ticket for that place they will reach. It is because after they have passed Sloane Square they know that the next station must be Victoria, and nothing but Victoria. Oh, their wild rapture! oh, their eyes like stars and their souls again in Eden, if the next station were unaccountably Baker Street!"

"It is you who are unpoetical," replied the poet Syme. "If what you say of clerks is true, they can only be as prosaic as your poetry. The rare, strange thing is to hit the mark; the gross, obvious thing is to miss it. We feel it is epical when man with one wild arrow strikes a distant bird. Is it not also epical when man with one wild engine strikes a distant station? Chaos is dull; because in chaos the train might indeed go anywhere, to Baker Street or to Bagdad. But man is a magician, and his whole magic is in this, that he does say Victoria, and lo! it is Victoria. No, take your books of mere poetry and prose; let me read a time table, with tears of pride. Take your Byron, who commemorates the defeats of man; give me Bradshaw, who commemorates his victories. Give me Bradshaw, I say!"

"Must you go?" inquired Gregory sarcastically.

"I tell you," went on Syme with passion, "that every time a train comes in I feel that it has broken past batteries of besiegers, and that man has won a battle against chaos. You say contemptuously that when one has left Sloane Square one must come to Victoria. I say that one might do a thousand things instead, and that whenever I really come there I have the sense of hair-breadth escape. And when I hear the guard shout out the word 'Victoria,' it is not an unmeaning word. It is to me the cry of a herald announcing conquest. It is to me indeed 'Victoria'; it is the victory of Adam."

Gregory wagged his heavy, red head with a slow and sad smile.

"And even then," he said, "we poets always ask the question, 'And what is Victoria now that you have got there?' You think Victoria is like the New Jerusalem. We know that the New Jerusalem will only be like Victoria. Yes, the poet will be discontented even in the streets of heaven. The poet is always in revolt."

"There again," said Syme irritably, "what is there poetical about being in revolt? You might as well say that it is poetical to be seasick. Being sick is a revolt. Both being sick and being rebellious may be the wholesome thing on certain desperate occasions; but I'm hanged if I can see why they are poetical. Revolt in the abstract is—revolting. It's mere vomiting."

The girl winced for a flash at the unpleasant word, but Syme was too hot to heed her.

"It is things going right," he cried, "that is poetical! Our digestions, for instance, going sacredly and silently right, that is the foundation of all poetry. Yes, the most poetical thing, more poetical than the flowers, more poetical than the stars—the most poetical thing in the world is not being sick."

"Really," said Gregory, superciliously, "the examples you choose——"

"I beg your pardon," said Syme grimly, "I forgot we had abolished all conventions."

For the first time a red patch appeared on Gregory's forehead.

"You don't expect me," he said, "to revolutionise society on this lawn?"

Syme looked straight into his eyes and smiled sweetly.

"No, I don't," he said; "but I suppose that if you were serious about your anarchism, that is exactly what you would do."

Gregory's big bull's eyes blinked suddenly like those of an angry lion, and one could almost fancy that his red mane rose.

"Don't you think, then," he said in a dangerous voice, "that I am serious about my anarchism?"

"I beg your pardon?" said Syme.

"Am I not serious about my anarchism?" cried Gregory, with knotted fists.

"My dear fellow!" said Syme, and strolled away.

With surprise, but with a curious pleasure, he found Rosamond Gregory still in his company.

"Mr. Syme," she said, "do the people who talk like you and my brother often mean what they say? Do you mean what you say now?"

Syme smiled.

"Do you?" he asked.

"What do you mean?" asked the girl, with grave eyes.

"My dear Miss Gregory," said Syme gently, "there are many kinds of sincerity and insincerity. When you say 'thank you' for the salt, do you mean what you say? No. When you say 'the world is round,' do you mean what you say? No. It is true, but you don't mean it. Now, sometimes a man like your brother really finds a thing he does mean. It may be only a half-truth, quarter-truth, tenth-truth; but then he says more than he means—from sheer force of meaning it."

She was looking at him from under level brows; her face was grave and open, and there had fallen upon it the shadow of that unreasoning responsibility which is at the bottom of the most frivolous woman, the maternal watch which is as old as the world.

"Is he really an anarchist, then?" she asked.

"Only in that sense I speak of," replied Syme; "or if you prefer it, in that nonsense."

She drew her broad brows together and said abruptly—

"He wouldn't really use—bombs or that sort of thing?"

Syme broke into a great laugh, that seemed too large for his slight and somewhat dandified figure.

"Good Lord, no!" he said, "that has to be done anonymously."

And at that the corners of her own mouth broke into a smile, and she thought with a simultaneous pleasure of Gregory's absurdity and of his safety.

Syme strolled with her to a seat in the corner of the garden, and continued to pour out his opinions. For he was a sincere man, and in spite of his superficial airs and graces, at root a humble one. And it is always the humble man who talks too much; the proud man watches himself too closely. He defended respectability with violence and exaggeration. He grew passionate in his praise of tidiness and propriety. All the time there was a smell of lilac all round him. Once he heard very faintly in some distant street a barrel-organ begin to play, and it seemed to him that his heroic words were moving to a tiny tune from under or beyond the world.

He stared and talked at the girl's red hair and amused face for what seemed to be a few minutes; and then, feeling that the groups in such a place should mix, rose to his feet. To his astonishment, he discovered the whole garden empty. Every one had gone long ago, and he went himself with a rather hurried apology. He left with a sense of champagne in his head, which he could not afterwards explain. In the wild events which were to follow this girl had no part at all; he never saw her again until all his tale was over. And yet, in some indescribable way, she kept recurring like a motive in music through all his mad adventures afterwards, and the glory of her strange hair ran like a red thread through those dark and ill-drawn tapestries of the night. For what followed was so improbable, that it might well have been a dream.

When Syme went out into the starlit street, he found it for the moment empty. Then he realised (in some odd way) that the silence was rather a living silence than a dead one. Directly outside the door stood a street lamp, whose gleam gilded the leaves of the tree that bent out over the fence behind him. About a foot from the lamp-post stood a figure almost as rigid and motionless as the lamp-post itself. The tall hat and long frock-coat were black; the face, in an abrupt shadow, was almost as dark. Only a fringe of fiery hair against the light, and also something aggressive in the attitude, proclaimed that it was the poet Gregory. He had something of the look of a masked bravo waiting sword in hand for his foe.

He made a sort of doubtful salute, which Syme somewhat more formally returned.

"I was waiting for you," said Gregory. "Might I have a moment's conversation?"

"Certainly. About what?" asked Syme in a sort of weak wonder.

Gregory struck out with his stick at the lamp-post, and then at the tree.

"About *this* and *this*," he cried; "about order and anarchy. There is your precious order, that lean, iron lamp, ugly and barren; and there is anarchy, rich, living, reproducing itself—there is anarchy, splendid in green and gold."

"All the same," replied Syme patiently, "just at present you only see the tree by the light of the lamp. I wonder when you would ever see the lamp by the light of the tree." Then after a pause he said, "But may I ask if you have been standing out here in the dark only to resume our little argument?"

"No," cried out Gregory, in a voice that rang down the street, "I did not stand here to resume our argument, but to end it forever."

The silence fell again, and Syme, though he understood nothing, listened instinctively for something serious. Gregory began in a smooth voice and with a rather bewildering smile.

"Mr. Syme," he said, "this evening you succeeded in doing something rather remarkable. You did something to me that no man born of woman has ever succeeded in doing before."

"Indeed!"

"Now I remember," resumed Gregory reflectively, "one other person succeeded in doing it. The captain of a penny steamer (if I remember correctly) at Southend. You have irritated me."

"I am very sorry," replied Syme with gravity.

"I am afraid my fury and your insult are too shocking to be wiped out even with an apology," said Gregory very calmly. "No duel could wipe it out. If I struck you dead I could not wipe it out. There is only one way by which that insult can be erased, and that way I choose. I am going, at the possible sacrifice of my life and honour, to *prove* to you that you were wrong in what you said."

"In what I said?"

"You said I was not serious about being an anarchist."

"There are degrees of seriousness," replied Syme. "I have never doubted that you were perfectly sincere in this sense, that you thought what you said well worth saying, that you thought a paradox might wake men up to a neglected truth."

Gregory stared at him steadily and painfully.

"And in no other sense," he asked, "you think me serious? You think me a *flâneur* who lets fall occasional truths. You do not think that in a deeper, a more deadly sense, I am serious."

Syme struck his stick violently on the stones of the road.

"Serious!" he cried. "Good Lord! is this street serious? Are these damned Chinese lanterns serious? Is the whole caboodle serious? One comes here and talks a pack of bosh, and perhaps some sense as well, but I should think very little of a man who didn't keep something in the background of his life that was more serious, whether it was religion or only drink."

"Very well," said Gregory, his face darkening, "you shall see something more serious than either drink or religion."

Syme stood waiting with his usual air of mildness until Gregory again opened his lips.

"You spoke just now of having a religion. Is it really true that you have one?"

"Oh," said Syme with a beaming smile, "we are all Catholics now."

"Then may I ask you to swear by whatever gods or saints your religion involves that you will *not* reveal what I am now going to tell you to any son of Adam, and especially not to the police? Will you swear that! If you will take upon yourself this awful abnegation, if you will consent to burden your soul with a vow that you should never make and a knowledge you should never dream about, I will promise you in return——"

"You will promise me in return?" inquired Syme, as the other paused.

"I will promise you a very entertaining evening."

Syme suddenly took off his hat.

"Your offer," he said, "is far too idiotic to be declined. You say that a poet is always an anarchist. I disagree; but I hope at least that he is always a sportsman. Permit me, here and now, to swear as a Christian, and promise as a good comrade and a fellow-artist, that I will not report anything of this, whatever it is, to the police. And now, in the name of Colney Hatch, what is it?"

"I think," said Gregory, with placid irrelevancy, "that we will call a cab."

He gave two long whistles, and a hansom came rattling down the road. The two got into it in silence. Gregory gave through the trap the address of an obscure public-house on the Chiswick bank of the river. The cab whisked itself away again, and in it these two fantastics quitted their fantastic town.

II

THE SECRET OF GABRIEL SYME

THE CAB pulled up before a particularly dreary and greasy beershop, into which Gregory rapidly conducted his companion. They seated themselves in a close and dim sort of bar-parlour, at a stained wooden table with one wooden leg. The room was so small and dark, that very little could be seen of the attendant who was summoned, beyond a vague and dark impression of something bulky and bearded.

"Will you take a little supper?" asked Gregory politely. "The *pâté de foie gras* is not good here, but I can recommend the game."

Syme received the remark with stolidity, imagining it to be a joke. Accepting the vein of humour, he said, with a well-bred indifference—

"Oh, bring me some lobster mayonnaise."

To his indescribable astonishment, the man only said, "Certainly, sir!" and went away apparently to get it.

"What will you drink?" resumed Gregory, with the same careless yet apologetic air. "I shall only have a *crême de menthe* myself; I have dined. But the champagne can really be trusted. Do let me start you with a half-bottle of Pommery at least?"

"Thank you!" said the motionless Syme. "You are very good."

His further attempts at conversation, somewhat disorganised in themselves, were cut short finally as by a thunderbolt by the actual appearance of the lobster. Syme tasted it, and found it particularly good. Then he suddenly began to eat with great rapidity and appetite.

"Excuse me if I enjoy myself rather obviously!" he said to Gregory, smiling. "I don't often have the luck to have a dream like this. It is new to me for a nightmare to lead to a lobster. It is commonly the other way."

"You are not asleep, I assure you," said Gregory. "You are, on the contrary, close to the most actual and rousing moment of your existence. Ah, here comes your champagne! I admit that there may be a slight disproportion, let us say, between the inner arrangements of this excellent hotel and its simple and unpretentious exterior. But that is all our modesty. We are the most modest men that ever lived on earth."

"And who are *we?*" asked Syme, emptying his champagne glass.

"It is quite simple," replied Gregory. "*We* are the serious anarchists, in whom you do not believe."

"Oh!" said Syme shortly. "You do yourselves well in drinks."

"Yes, we are serious about everything," answered Gregory.

Then after a pause he added—

"If in a few moments this table begins to turn round a little, don't put it down to your inroads into the champagne. I don't wish you to do yourself an injustice."

"Well, if I am not drunk, I am mad," replied Syme with perfect calm; "but I trust I can behave like a gentleman in either condition. May I smoke?"

"Certainly!" said Gregory, producing a cigar-case. "Try one of mine."

Syme took the cigar, clipped the end off with a cigar-cutter out of his waistcoat pocket, put it in his mouth, lit it slowly, and let out a long cloud of smoke. It is not a little to his credit that he performed these rites with so much composure, for almost before he had begun them the table at which he sat had begun to revolve, first slowly, and then rapidly, as if at an insane séance.

"You must not mind it," said Gregory; "it's a kind of screw."

"Quite so," said Syme placidly, "a kind of screw! How simple that is!"

The next moment the smoke of his cigar, which had been wavering across the room in snaky twists, went straight up as if from a factory chimney, and the two, with their chairs and table, shot down through the floor as if the earth had swallowed them. They went rattling down a kind of roaring chimney as rapidly as a lift cut loose, and they came with an abrupt bump to the bottom. But when Gregory threw open a pair of doors and let in a red subterranean light, Syme was still smoking, with one leg thrown over the other, and had not turned a yellow hair.

Gregory led him down a low, vaulted passage, at the end of which was the red light. It was an enormous crimson lantern, nearly as big as a fireplace, fixed over a small but heavy iron door. In the door there was a sort of hatchway or grating, and on this Gregory struck five times. A heavy voice with a foreign accent asked him who he was. To this he gave the more or less unexpected reply, "Mr. Joseph Chamberlain." The heavy hinges began to move; it was obviously some kind of password.

Inside the doorway the passage gleamed as if it were lined with a network of steel. On a second glance, Syme saw that the glittering pattern was really made up of ranks and ranks of rifles and revolvers, closely packed or interlocked.

"I must ask you to forgive me all these formalities," said Gregory; "we have to be very strict here."

"Oh, don't apologise," said Syme. "I know your passion for law and order," and he stepped into the passage lined with the steel weapons. With his long, fair hair and rather foppish frock-coat, he looked a singularly frail and fanciful figure as he walked down that shining avenue of death.

They passed through several such passages, and came out at last into a queer steel chamber with curved walls, almost spherical in shape, but presenting, with its tiers of benches, something of the appearance of a scientific lecture-theatre. There were no rifles or pistols in this apartment, but round the walls of it were hung more dubious and dreadful shapes, things that looked like the bulbs of iron plants, or the eggs of iron birds. They were bombs, and the very room itself seemed like the inside of a bomb. Syme knocked his cigar ash off against the wall, and went in.

"And now, my dear Mr. Syme," said Gregory, throwing himself in an expansive manner on the bench under the largest bomb, "now we are quite cosy, so let us talk properly. Now, no human words can give you any notion of why I brought you here. It was one of those quite arbitrary emotions, like jumping off a cliff or falling in love. Suffice it to say that you were an inexpressibly irritating fellow, and, to do you justice, you are still. I would break twenty oaths of secrecy for the pleasure of taking you down a peg. That way you have of lighting a cigar would make a priest break the seal of confession. Well, you said that you were quite certain I was not a serious anarchist. Does this place strike you as being serious?"

"It does seem to have a moral under all its gaiety," assented Syme; "but may I ask you two questions? You need not fear to give me information, because, as you remember, you very wisely extorted from me a promise not to tell the police, a promise I shall certainly keep. So it is in mere curiosity that I make my queries. First of all, what is it really all about? What is it you object to? You want to abolish Government?"

"To abolish God!" said Gregory, opening the eyes of a fanatic. "We do not only want to upset a few despotisms and police regulations; that sort of anarchism does exist, but it is a mere branch of the Nonconformists. We dig deeper and we blow you higher. We wish to deny all those arbitrary distinctions of vice and virtue, honour and treachery, upon which mere rebels base themselves. The silly sentimentalists of the French Revolution talked of the Rights of Man! We hate Rights as we hate Wrongs. We have abolished Right and Wrong."

"And Right and Left," said Syme with a simple eagerness, "I hope you will abolish them too. They are much more troublesome to me."

"You spoke of a second question," snapped Gregory.

"With pleasure," resumed Syme. "In all your present acts and surroundings there is a scientific attempt at secrecy. I have an aunt who lived over a shop, but this is the first time I have found people living from preference under a public-house. You have a heavy iron door. You cannot pass it without submitting to the humiliation of calling yourself Mr. Chamberlain. You surround yourself with steel instruments which make the place, if I may say so, more impressive than homelike. May I ask why, after taking all this trouble to barricade yourselves in the bowels of the earth, you then parade your whole secret by talking about anarchism to every silly woman in Saffron Park?"

Gregory smiled.

"The answer is simple," he said. "I told you I was a serious anarchist, and you did not believe me. Nor do *they* believe me. Unless I took them into this infernal room they would not believe me."

Syme smoked thoughtfully, and looked at him with interest. Gregory went on.

"The history of the thing might amuse you," he said. "When first I became one of the New Anarchists I tried all kinds of respectable disguises. I dressed up as a bishop. I read up all about bishops in our anarchist pamphlets, in *Superstition the Vampire* and *Priests of Prey*. I certainly understood from them that bishops are strange and terrible old men keeping a cruel secret from mankind. I was misinformed. When on my first appearing in episcopal gaiters in a drawing-room I cried out in a voice of thunder, 'Down! down! presumptuous human reason!' they found out in some way that I was not a bishop at all. I was nabbed at once. Then I made up as a millionaire; but I defended Capital with so much intelligence that a fool could see that I was quite poor. Then I tried being a major. Now I am a humanitarian myself, but I have, I hope, enough intellectual breadth to understand the position of those who, like Nietzsche, admire violence—the proud, mad war of Nature and all that, you know. I threw myself into the major. I drew my sword and waved it constantly. I called out 'Blood!' abstractedly, like a man calling for wine. I often said, 'Let the weak perish; it is the Law.' Well, well, it seems majors don't do this. I was nabbed again. At last I went in despair to the President of the Central Anarchist Council, who is the greatest man in Europe."

"What is his name?" asked Syme.

"You would not know it," answered Gregory. "That is his greatness. Cæsar and Napoleon put all their genius into being heard of, and they *were* heard of. He puts all his genius into not being heard of, and he is not heard of. But you cannot be for five minutes in the room with him without feeling that Cæsar and Napoleon would have been children in his hands."

He was silent and even pale for a moment, and then resumed—

"But whenever he gives advice it is always something as startling as an epigram, and yet as practical as the Bank of England. I said to him, 'What disguise will hide me from the world? What can I find more respectable than bishops and majors?' He looked at me with his large but indecipherable face. 'You want a safe disguise, do you? You want a dress which will guarantee you harmless; a dress in which no one would ever look for a bomb?' I nodded. He suddenly lifted his lion's voice. 'Why, then, dress up as an *anarchist*, you fool!' he roared so that the room shook. 'Nobody will ever expect you to do anything dangerous then.' And he turned his broad back on me without another word. I took his advice, and have never regretted it. I preached blood and murder to those women day and night, and—by God!—they would let me wheel their perambulators."

Syme sat watching him with some respect in his large, blue eyes. "You took me in," he said. "It is really a smart dodge."

Then after a pause he added—

"What do you call this tremendous President of yours?"

"We generally call him Sunday," replied Gregory with simplicity. "You see, there are seven members of the Central Anarchist Council, and they are named after days of the week. He is called Sunday, by some of his admirers Bloody Sunday. It is curious you should mention the matter, because the very night you have dropped in (if I may so express it) is the night on which our London branch, which assembles in this room, has to elect its own deputy to fill a vacancy in the Council. The gentleman who has for some time past played, with propriety and general applause, the difficult part of Thursday, has died quite suddenly. Consequently, we have called a meeting this very evening to elect a successor."

He got to his feet and strolled across the room with a sort of smiling embarrassment.

"I feel somehow as if you were my mother, Syme," he continued casually. "I feel that I can confide anything to you, as you have promised to tell nobody. In fact, I will confide to you something that I would not say in so many words to the anarchists who will be coming to the room in about ten minutes. We shall, of course, go through a form of election; but I don't mind telling you that it is practically certain what the result will be." He looked down for a moment modestly. "It is almost a settled thing that I am to be Thursday."

"My dear fellow," said Syme heartily, "I congratulate you. A great career!"

Gregory smiled in deprecation, and walked across the room, talking rapidly.

"As a matter of fact, everything is ready for me on this table," he said, "and the ceremony will probably be the shortest possible."

Syme also strolled across to the table, and found lying across it a walking-stick, which turned out on examination to be a sword-stick, a large Colt's revolver, a sandwich case, and a formidable flask of brandy. Over the chair, beside the table, was thrown a heavy-looking cape or cloak.

"I have only to get the form of election finished," continued Gregory with animation, "then I snatch up this cloak and stick, stuff these other things into my pocket, step out of a door in this cavern, which opens on the river, where there is a steam-tug already waiting for me, and then—then—oh, the wild joy of being Thursday!" And he clasped his hands.

Syme, who had sat down once more with his usual insolent languor, got to his feet with an unusual air of hesitation.

"Why is it," he asked vaguely, "that I think you are quite a decent fellow? Why do I positively like you, Gregory?" He paused a moment, and then added with a sort of fresh curiosity, "Is it because you are such an ass?"

There was a thoughtful silence again, and then he cried out—

"Well, damn it all! this is the funniest situation I have ever been in in my life, and I am going to act accordingly. Gregory, I gave you a promise before I came into this place. That promise I would keep under red-hot pincers. Would you give me, for my own safety, a little promise of the same kind?"

"A promise?" asked Gregory, wondering.

"Yes," said Syme very seriously, "a promise. I swore before God that I would not tell your secret to the police. Will you swear by Humanity, or whatever beastly thing you believe in, that you will not tell my secret to the anarchists?"

"Your secret?" asked the staring Gregory. "Have you got a secret?"

"Yes," said Syme, "I have a secret." Then after a pause, "Will you swear?"

Gregory glared at him gravely for a few moments, and then said abruptly—

"You must have bewitched me, but I feel a furious curiosity about you. Yes, I will swear not to tell the anarchists anything you tell me. But look sharp, for they will be here in a couple of minutes."

Syme rose slowly to his feet and thrust his long, white hands into his long, grey trousers' pockets. Almost as he did so there came five knocks on the outer grating, proclaiming the arrival of the first of the conspirators.

"Well," said Syme slowly, "I don't know how to tell you the truth more shortly than by saying that your expedient of dressing up as an aimless poet is not confined to you or your President. We have known the dodge for some time at Scotland Yard."

Gregory tried to spring up straight, but he swayed thrice.

"What do you say?" he asked in an inhuman voice.

"Yes," said Syme simply, "I am a police detective. But I think I hear your friends coming."

From the doorway there came a murmur of "Mr. Joseph Chamberlain." It was repeated twice and thrice, and then thirty times, and the crowd of Joseph Chamberlains (a solemn thought) could be heard trampling down the corridor.

III
THE MAN WHO WAS THURSDAY

BEFORE ONE of the fresh faces could appear at the doorway, Gregory's stunned surprise had fallen from him. He was beside the table with a bound, and a noise in his throat like a wild beast. He caught up the Colt's revolver and took aim at Syme. Syme did not flinch, but he put up a pale and polite hand.

"Don't be such a silly man," he said, with the effeminate dignity of a curate. "Don't you see it's not necessary? Don't you see that we're both in the same boat? Yes, and jolly seasick."

Gregory could not speak, but he could not fire either, and he looked his question.

"Don't you see we've checkmated each other?" cried Syme. "I can't tell the police you are an anarchist. You can't tell the anarchists I'm a policeman. I can only watch you, knowing what you are; you can only watch me, knowing what I am. In short, it's a lonely, intellectual duel, my head against yours. I'm a policeman deprived of the help of the police. You, my poor fellow, are an anarchist deprived of the help of that law and organisation which is so essential to anarchy. The one solitary difference is in your favour. You are not surrounded by inquisitive policemen; I am surrounded by inquisitive anarchists. I cannot betray you, but I might betray myself. Come, come! wait and see me betray myself. I shall do it so nicely."

Gregory put the pistol slowly down, still staring at Syme as if he were a sea-monster.

"I don't believe in immortality," he said at last, "but if, after all this, you were to break your word, God would make a hell only for you, to howl in forever."

"I shall not break my word," said Syme sternly, "nor will you break yours. Here are your friends."

The mass of the anarchists entered the room heavily, with a slouching and somewhat weary gait; but one little man, with a black beard and glasses—a man somewhat of the type of Mr. Tim Healy—detached himself, and bustled forward with some papers in his hand.

"Comrade Gregory," he said, "I suppose this man is a delegate?"

Gregory, taken by surprise, looked down and muttered the name of Syme; but Syme replied almost pertly—

"I am glad to see that your gate is well enough guarded to make it hard for any one to be here who was not a delegate."

The brow of the little man with the black beard was, however, still contracted with something like suspicion.

"What branch do you represent?" he asked sharply.

"I should hardly call it a branch," said Syme, laughing; "I should call it at the very least a root."

"What do you mean?"

"The fact is," said Syme serenely, "the truth is I am a Sabbatarian. I have been specially sent here to see that you show a due observance of Sunday."

The little man dropped one of his papers, and a flicker of fear went over all the faces of the group. Evidently the awful President, whose name was Sunday, did sometimes send down such irregular ambassadors to such branch meetings.

"Well, comrade," said the man with the papers after a pause, "I suppose we'd better give you a seat in the meeting?"

"If you ask my advice as a friend," said Syme with severe benevolence, "I think you'd better."

When Gregory heard the dangerous dialogue end, with a sudden safety for his rival, he rose abruptly and paced the floor in painful thought. He was, indeed, in an agony of diplomacy. It was clear that Syme's inspired impudence was likely to bring him out of all merely accidental dilemmas. Little was to be hoped from them. He could not himself betray Syme, partly from honour, but partly also because, if he betrayed him and for some reason failed to destroy him, the Syme who escaped would be a Syme freed from all obligation of secrecy, a Syme who would simply walk to the nearest police station. After all, it was only one night's discussion, and only one detective who would know of it. He would let out as little as possible of their plans that night, and then let Syme go, and chance it.

He strode across to the group of anarchists, which was already distributing itself along the benches.

"I think it is time we began," he said; "the steam-tug is waiting on the river already. I move that Comrade Buttons takes the chair."

This being approved by a show of hands, the little man with the papers slipped into the presidential seat.

"Comrades," he began, as sharp as a pistol-shot, "our meeting tonight is important, though it need not be long. This branch has always had the honour of electing Thursdays for the Central European Council. We have elected many and splendid Thursdays. We all lament the sad decease of the heroic worker who occupied the post until last week. As you know, his services to the cause were considerable. He organised the great dynamite coup of Brighton which, under happier circumstances, ought to have killed everybody on the pier. As you also know, his death was as self-denying as his life, for he died through his faith in a hygienic mixture of chalk and water as a substitute for milk, which beverage he regarded as barbaric, and as involving cruelty to the cow. Cruelty, or anything approaching to cruelty, revolted him always. But it is not to acclaim his virtues that we are met, but for a harder task. It is difficult properly to praise his qualities, but it is more difficult to replace them. Upon you, comrades, it devolves this evening to choose out of the company present the man who shall be Thursday. If any comrade suggests a name I will put it to the vote. If no comrade suggests a name, I can only tell myself that that dear dynamiter, who is gone from us, has carried into the unknowable abysses the last secret of his virtue and his innocence."

There was a stir of almost inaudible applause, such as is sometimes heard in church. Then a large old man, with a long and venerable white beard, perhaps the only real working-man present, rose lumberingly and said—

"I move that Comrade Gregory be elected Thursday," and sat lumberingly down again.

"Does any one second?" asked the chairman.

A little man with a velvet coat and pointed beard seconded.

"Before I put the matter to the vote," said the chairman, "I will call on Comrade Gregory to make a statement."

Gregory rose amid a great rumble of applause. His face was deadly pale, so that by contrast his queer red hair looked almost scarlet. But he was smiling, and altogether at ease. He had made up his mind, and he saw his best policy quite plain in front of him like a white road. His best chance was to make a softened and ambiguous speech, such as would leave on the detective's mind the impression that the anarchist brotherhood was a very mild affair after all. He believed in his own literary power, his capacity for suggesting fine shades and picking perfect words. He thought that with care he could succeed, in spite of all the people around him, in conveying an impression of the institution, subtly and delicately false. Syme had once thought that anarchists, under all their bravado, were only playing the fool. Could he not now, in the hour of peril, make Syme think so again?

"Comrades," began Gregory, in a low but penetrating voice, "it is not necessary for me to tell you what is my policy, for it is your policy also. Our belief has been slandered, it has been disfigured, it has been utterly confused and concealed, but it has never been altered. Those who talk about anarchism and its dangers go everywhere and anywhere to get their information, except to us, except to the fountain head. They learn about anarchists from sixpenny novels; they learn about anarchists from tradesmen's newspapers; they learn about anarchists from *Ally Sloper's Half-Holiday* and the *Sporting Times*. They never learn about anarchists from anarchists. We have no chance of denying the mountainous slanders which are heaped upon our heads from one end of Europe to another. The man who has always heard that we are walking plagues has never heard our reply. I know that he will not hear it to-night, though my passion were to rend the roof. For it is deep, deep under the earth that the persecuted are permitted to assemble, as the Christians assembled in the Catacombs. But if, by some incredible accident, there were here to-night a man who all his life had thus immensely misunderstood us, I would put this question to him: 'When those Christians met in those Catacombs, what sort of moral reputation had they in the streets above? What tales were told of their atrocities by one educated Roman to another? Suppose' (I would say to him), 'suppose that we are only repeating that still mysterious paradox of history. Suppose we seem as shocking as the Christians because we are really as harmless as the Christians. Suppose we seem as mad as the Christians because we are really as meek.' "

The applause that had greeted the opening sentences had been gradually growing fainter, and at the last word it stopped suddenly. In the abrupt silence, the man with the velvet jacket said, in a high, squeaky voice—

"I'm not meek!"

"Comrade Witherspoon tells us," resumed Gregory, "that he is not meek. Ah, how little he knows himself! His words are, indeed, extravagant; his appearance is ferocious, and even (to an ordinary taste) unattractive. But only the eye of a friendship as deep and delicate as mine can perceive the deep foundation of solid meekness which lies at the base of him, too deep even for himself to see. I repeat, we are the true early Christians, only that we come too late. We are simple, as they were simple—look at Comrade Witherspoon. We are modest, as they were modest—look at me. We are merciful—"

"No, no!" called out Mr. Witherspoon with the velvet jacket.

"I say we are merciful," repeated Gregory furiously, "as the early Christians were merciful. Yet this did not prevent their being accused of eating human flesh. We do not eat human flesh—"

"Shame!" cried Witherspoon. "Why not?"

"Comrade Witherspoon," said Gregory, with a feverish gaiety, "is anxious to know why nobody eats him (laughter). In our society, at any rate, which loves him sincerely, which is founded upon love——"

"No, no!" said Witherspoon, "down with love."

"Which is founded upon love," repeated Gregory, grinding his teeth, "there will be no difficulty about the aims which we shall pursue as a body, or which I should pursue were I chosen as the representative of that body. Superbly careless of the slanders that represent us as assassins and enemies of human society, we shall pursue, with moral courage and quiet, intellectual pressure, the permanent ideals of brotherhood and simplicity."

Gregory resumed his seat and passed his hand across his forehead. The silence was sudden and awkward, but the chairman rose like an automaton, and said in a colourless voice—

"Does any one oppose the election of Comrade Gregory?"

The assembly seemed vague and sub-consciously disappointed, and Comrade Witherspoon moved restlessly on his seat and muttered in his thick beard. By the sheer rush of routine, however, the motion would have been put and carried. But as the chairman was opening his mouth to put it, Syme sprang to his feet and said in a small and quiet voice—

"Yes, Mr. Chairman, I oppose."

The most effective fact in oratory is an unexpected change in the voice. Mr. Gabriel Syme evidently understood oratory. Having said these first formal words in a moderated tone and with a brief simplicity, he made his next word ring and volley in the vault as if one of the guns had gone off.

"Comrades!" he cried, in a voice that made every man jump out of his boots, "have we come here for this? Do we live underground like rats in order to listen to talk like this? This is talk we might listen to while eating buns at a Sunday-school treat. Do we line these walls with weapons and bar that door with death lest any one should come and hear Comrade Gregory saying to us, 'Be good, and you will be happy,' 'Honesty is the best policy,' and 'Virtue is its own reward'? There was not a word in Comrade Gregory's address to which a curate could not have listened with pleasure (hear, hear). But I am not a curate (loud cheers), and I did not listen to it with pleasure (renewed cheers). The man who is fitted to make a good curate is not fitted to make a resolute, forcible, and efficient Thursday (hear, hear).

"Comrade Gregory has told us, in only too apologetic a tone, that we are not the enemies of society. But I say that we are the enemies of society, and so much the worse for society. We are the enemies of society, for society is the enemy of humanity, its oldest and its most pitiless enemy (hear, hear). Comrade Gregory has told you (apologetically again) that we are not murderers. There I agree. We are not murderers, we are executioners (cheers)."

Ever since Syme had risen Gregory had sat staring at him, his face idiotic with astonishment. Now in the pause his lips of clay parted, and he said, with an automatic and lifeless distinctness—

"You damnable hypocrite!"

Syme looked straight into those frightful eyes with his own pale blue ones, and said with dignity—

"Comrade Gregory accuses me of hypocrisy. He knows as well as I do that I am keeping all my engagements and doing nothing but my duty. I do not mince words. I do not pretend to. I say that Comrade Gregory is unfit to be Thursday for all his amiable qualities. He is unfit to be Thursday because of his amiable qualities. We do not want the Supreme Council of Anarchy infected with a maudlin mercy (hear, hear). This is no time for ceremonial politeness, neither is it a time for ceremonial modesty. I set myself against Comrade Gregory as I would set myself against all the Governments of Europe, because the anarchist who has given himself to anarchy has forgotten modesty as much as he has forgotten pride (cheers). I am not a man at all; I am a cause (renewed cheers). I set myself against Comrade Gregory as impersonally and as calmly as I should choose one pistol rather than another out of that rack upon the wall; and I say that rather than have Gregory and his milk-and-water methods on the Supreme Council, I would offer myself for election—"

His sentence was drowned in a deafening cataract of applause. The faces, that had grown fiercer and fiercer with approval as his tirade grew more and more uncompromising, were now distorted with grins of anticipation or cloven with delighted cries. At the moment when he announced himself as ready to stand for the post of Thursday, a roar of excitement and assent broke forth, and became uncontrollable, and at the same moment Gregory sprang to his feet, with foam upon his mouth, and shouted against the shouting.

"Stop, you blasted madmen!" he cried, at the top of a voice that tore his throat. "Stop, you—"

But louder than Gregory's shouting and louder than the roar of the room came the voice of Syme, still speaking in a peal of pitiless thunder—

"I do not go to the Council to rebut that slander that calls us murderers; I go to earn it (loud and prolonged cheering). To the priest who says these men are the enemies of religion, to the judge who says these men are the enemies of law, to the fat parliamentarian who says these men are the enemies of order and public decency, to all these I will reply, 'You are false kings, but you are true prophets. I am come to destroy you, and to fulfill your prophecies.' "

The heavy clamour gradually died away, but before it had ceased Witherspoon had jumped to his feet, his hair and beard all on end, and had said—

"I move, as an amendment, that Comrade Syme be appointed to the post."

"Stop all this, I tell you!" cried Gregory, with frantic face and hands. "Stop it, it is all—"

The voice of the chairman clove his speech with a cold accent.

"Does any one second this amendment?" he said.

A tall, tired man, with melancholy eyes and an American chin beard, was observed on the back bench to be slowly rising to his feet. Gregory had been screaming for some time past; now there was a change in his accent, more shocking than any scream.

"I end all this!" he said, in a voice as heavy as stone. "This man cannot be elected. He is a—"

"Yes," said Syme, quite motionless, "what is he?"

Gregory's mouth worked twice without sound; then slowly the blood began to crawl back into his dead face.

"He is a man quite inexperienced in our work," he said, and sat down abruptly.

Before he had done so, the long, lean man with the American beard was again upon his feet, and was repeating in a high American monotone—

"I beg to second the election of Comrade Syme."

"The amendment will, as usual, be put first," said Mr. Buttons, the chairman, with mechanical rapidity. "The question is that Comrade Syme—"

Gregory had again sprung to his feet, panting and passionate.

"Comrades," he cried out, "I am not a madman."

"Oh, oh!" said Mr. Witherspoon.

"I am not a madman," reiterated Gregory, with a frightful sincerity which for a moment staggered the room, "but I give you a counsel which you can call mad if you like. No, I will not call it a counsel, for I can give you no reason for it. I will call it a command. Call it a mad command, but act upon it. Strike, but hear me! Kill me, but obey me! Do not elect this man."

Truth is so terrible, even in fetters, that for a moment Syme's slender and insane victory swayed like a reed. But you could not have guessed it from Syme's bleak blue eyes. He merely began—

"Comrade Gregory commands—"

Then the spell was snapped, and one anarchist called out to Gregory—

"Who are you? You are not Sunday;" and another anarchist added in a heavier voice, "And you are not Thursday."

"Comrades," cried Gregory, in a voice like that of a martyr who in an ecstasy of pain has passed beyond pain, "it is nothing to me whether you detest me as a tyrant or detest me as a slave. If you will not take my command, accept my degradation. I kneel to you. I throw myself at your feet. I implore you. Do not elect this man."

"Comrade Gregory," said the chairman after a painful pause, "this is really not quite dignified."

For the first time in the proceedings there was for a few seconds a real silence. Then Gregory fell back in his seat, a pale wreck of a man, and the chairman repeated, like a piece of clockwork suddenly started again—

"The question is that Comrade Syme be elected to the post of Thursday on the General Council."

The roar rose like the sea, the hands rose like a forest, and three minutes afterwards Mr. Gabriel Syme, of the Secret Police Service, was elected to the post of Thursday on the General Council of the Anarchists of Europe.

Every one in the room seemed to feel the tug waiting on the river, the sword-stick and the revolver, waiting on the table. The instant the election was ended and irrevocable, and Syme had received the paper proving his election, they all sprang to their feet, and the fiery groups moved and mixed in the room. Syme found himself, somehow or other, face to face with Gregory, who still regarded him with a stare of stunned hatred. They were silent for many minutes.

"You are a devil!" said Gregory at last.

"And you are a gentleman," said Syme with gravity.

"It was you that entrapped me," began Gregory, shaking from head to foot, "entrapped me into—"

"Talk sense," said Syme shortly. "Into what sort of devils' parliament have you entrapped me, if it comes to that? You made me swear before I made you. Perhaps we are both doing what we think right. But what we think right is so damned different that there can be nothing between us in the way of concession. There is nothing possible between us but honour and death," and he pulled the great cloak about his shoulders and picked up the flask from the table.

"The boat is quite ready," said Mr. Buttons, bustling up. "Be good enough to step this way."

With a gesture that revealed the shopwalker, he led Syme down a short, iron-bound passage, the still agonised Gregory following feverishly at their heels. At the end of the passage was a door, which Buttons opened sharply, showing a sudden blue and silver picture of the moonlit river, that looked like a scene in a theatre. Close to the opening lay a dark, dwarfish steam-launch, like a baby dragon with one red eye.

Almost in the act of stepping on board, Gabriel Syme turned to the gaping Gregory.

"You have kept your word," he said gently, with his face in shadow. "You are a man of honour, and I thank you. You have kept it even down to a small particular. There was one special thing you promised me at the beginning of the affair, and which you have certainly given me by the end of it."

"What do you mean?" cried the chaotic Gregory. "What did I promise you?"

"A very entertaining evening," said Syme, and he made a military salute with the sword-stick as the steamboat slid away.

IV

THE TALE OF A DETECTIVE

GABRIEL SYME was not merely a detective who pretended to be a poet; he was really a poet who had become a detective. Nor was his hatred of anarchy hypocritical. He was one of those who are driven early in life into too conservative an attitude by the bewildering folly of most revolutionists. He had not attained it by any tame tradition. His respectability was spontaneous and sudden, a rebellion against rebellion. He came of a family of cranks, in which all the oldest people had all the newest notions. One of his uncles always walked about without a hat, and another had made an unsuccessful attempt to walk about with a hat and nothing else. His father cultivated art and self-realisation; his mother went in for simplicity and hygiene. Hence the child, during his tenderer years, was wholly unacquainted with any drink between the extremes of absinth and cocoa, of both of which he had a healthy dislike. The more his mother preached a more than Puritan abstinence the more did his father expand into a more than pagan latitude; and by the time the former had come to enforcing vegetarianism, the latter had pretty well reached the point of defending cannibalism.

Being surrounded with every conceivable kind of revolt from infancy, Gabriel had to revolt into something, so he revolted into the only thing left—sanity. But there was just enough in him of the blood of these fanatics to make even his protest for common-sense a little too fierce to be sensible. His hatred of modern lawlessness had been crowned also by an accident. It happened that he was walking in a side street at the instant of a dynamite outrage. He had been blind and deaf for a moment, and then seen, the smoke clearing, the broken windows and the bleeding faces. After that he went about as usual—quiet, courteous, rather gentle; but there was a spot on his mind that was not sane. He did not regard anarchists, as most of us do, as a handful of morbid men, combining ignorance with intellectualism. He regarded them as a huge and pitiless peril, like a Chinese invasion.

He poured perpetually into newspapers and their waste-paper baskets a torrent of tales, verses and violent articles, warning men of this deluge of barbaric denial. But he seemed to be getting no nearer his enemy, and, what was worse, no nearer a living. As he paced the Thames embankment, bitterly biting a cheap cigar and brooding on the advance of Anarchy, there was no anarchist with a bomb in his pocket so savage or so solitary as he. Indeed, he always felt that Government stood alone and desperate, with its back to the wall. He was too quixotic to have cared for it otherwise.

He walked on the Embankment once under a dark red sunset. The red river reflected the red sky, and they both reflected his anger. The sky, indeed, was so swarthy, and the light on the river relatively so lurid, that the water almost seemed of fiercer flame than the sunset it mirrored. It looked like a stream of literal fire winding under the vast caverns of a subterranean country.

Syme was shabby in those days. He wore an old-fashioned black chimney-pot hat; he was wrapped in a yet more old-fashioned cloak, black and ragged; and the combination gave him the look of the early villains in Dickens and Bulwer Lytton. Also his yellow beard and hair were more unkempt and leonine than when they appeared long afterwards, cut and pointed, on the lawns of Saffron Park. A long, lean, black cigar, bought in Soho for twopence, stood out from between his tightened teeth, and altogether he looked a very satisfactory specimen of the anarchists upon whom he had vowed a holy war. Perhaps this was why a policeman on the Embankment spoke to him, and said "Good evening."

Syme, at a crisis of his morbid fears for humanity, seemed stung by the mere stolidity of the automatic official, a mere bulk of blue in the twilight.

"A good evening is it?" he said sharply. "You fellows would call the end of the world a good evening. Look at that bloody red sun and that bloody river! I tell you that if that were literally human blood, spilt and shining, you would still be standing here as solid as ever, looking out for some poor harmless tramp whom you could move on. You policemen are cruel to the poor, but I could forgive you even your cruelty if it were not for your calm."

"If we are calm," replied the policeman, "it is the calm of organised resistance."

"Eh?" said Syme, staring.

"The soldier must be calm in the thick of the battle," pursued the policeman. "The composure of an army is the anger of a nation."

"Good God, the Board Schools!" said Syme. "Is this undenominational education?"

"No," said the policeman sadly, "I never had any of those advantages. The Board Schools came after my time. What education I had was very rough and old-fashioned, I am afraid."

"Where did you have it?" asked Syme, wondering.

"Oh, at Harrow," said the policeman.

The class sympathies which, false as they are, are the truest things in so many men, broke out of Syme before he could control them. "But, good Lord, man," he said, "you oughtn't to be a policeman!"

The policeman sighed and shook his head.

"I know," he said solemnly, "I know I am not worthy."

"But why did you join the police?" asked Syme with rude curiosity.

"For much the same reason that you abused the police," replied the other. "I found that there was a special opening in the service for those whose fears for humanity were concerned rather with the aberrations of the scientific intellect than with the normal and excusable, though excessive, outbreaks of the human will. I trust I make myself clear."

"If you mean that you make your opinion clear," said Syme, "I suppose you do. But as for making yourself clear, it is the last thing you do. How comes a man like you to be talking philosophy in a blue helmet on the Thames embankment?"

"You have evidently not heard of the latest development in our police system," replied the other. "I am not surprised at it. We are keeping it rather dark from the educated class, because that class contains most of our enemies. But you seem to be exactly in the right frame of mind. I think you might almost join us."

"Join you in what?" asked Syme.

"I will tell you," said the policeman slowly. "This is the situation: The head of one of our departments, one of the most celebrated detectives in Europe, has long been of opinion that a purely intellectual conspiracy would soon threaten the very existence of civilisation. He is certain that the scientific and artistic worlds are silently bound in a crusade against the Family and the State. He has, therefore, formed a special corps of policemen, policemen who are also philosophers. It is their business to watch the beginnings of this conspiracy, not merely in a criminal but in a controversial sense. I am a democrat myself, and I am fully aware of the value of the ordinary man in matters of ordinary valour or virtue. But it would obviously be undesirable to employ the common policeman in an investigation which is also a heresy hunt."

Syme's eyes were bright with a sympathetic curiosity.

"What do you do, then?" he said.

"The work of the philosophical policeman," replied the man in blue, "is at once bolder and more subtle than that of the ordinary detective. The ordinary detective goes to pot-houses to arrest thieves; we go to artistic tea-parties to detect pessimists. The ordinary detective discovers from a ledger or a diary that a crime has been committed. We discover from a book of sonnets that a crime will be committed. We have to trace the origin of those dreadful thoughts that drive men on at last to intellectual fanaticism and intellectual crime. We were only just in time to prevent the assassination at Hartlepool, and that was entirely due to the fact that our Mr. Wilks (a smart young fellow) thoroughly understood a triolet."

"Do you mean," asked Syme, "that there is really as much connection between crime and the modern intellect as all that?"

"You are not sufficiently democratic," answered the policeman, "but you were right when you said just now that our ordinary treatment of the poor criminal was a pretty brutal business. I tell you I am sometimes sick of my trade when I see how perpetually it means merely a war upon the ignorant and the desperate. But this new movement of ours is a very different affair. We deny the snobbish English assumption that the uneducated are the dangerous criminals. We remember the Roman Emperors. We remember the great poisoning princes of the Renaissance. We say that the dangerous criminal is the educated criminal. We say that the most dangerous criminal now is the entirely lawless modern philosopher. Compared to him, burglars and bigamists are essentially moral men; my heart goes out to them. They accept the essential ideal of man; they merely seek it wrongly. Thieves respect property. They merely wish the property to become their property that they may more perfectly respect it. But philosophers dislike property as property; they wish to destroy the very idea of personal possession. Bigamists respect marriage, or they would not go through the highly ceremonial and even ritualistic formality of bigamy. But philosophers despise marriage as marriage. Murderers respect human life; they merely wish to attain a greater fulness of human life in themselves by the sacrifice of what seems to them to be lesser lives. But philosophers hate life itself, their own as much as other people's."

Syme struck his hands together.

"How true that is," he cried. "I have felt it from my boyhood, but never could state the verbal antithesis. The common criminal is a bad man, but at least he is, as it were, a conditional good man. He says that if only a certain obstacle be removed—say a wealthy uncle—he is then prepared to accept the universe and to praise God. He is a reformer, but not an anarchist. He wishes to cleanse the edifice, but not to destroy it. But the evil philosopher is not trying to alter things, but to annihilate them. Yes, the modern world has retained all those parts of police work which are really oppressive and ignominious, the harrying of the poor, the spying upon the unfortunate. It has given up its more dignified work, the punishment of powerful traitors in the State and powerful heresiarchs in the Church. The moderns say we must not punish heretics. My only doubt is whether we have a right to punish anybody else."

"But this is absurd!" cried the policeman, clasping his hands with an excitement uncommon in persons of his figure and costume, "but it is intolerable! I don't know what you're doing, but you're wasting your life. You must, you shall, join our special army against anarchy. Their armies are on our frontiers. Their bolt is ready to fall. A moment more, and you may lose the glory of working with us, perhaps the glory of dying with the last heroes of the world."

"It is a chance not to be missed, certainly," assented Syme, "but still I do not quite understand. I know as well as anybody that the modern world is full of lawless little men and mad little movements. But, beastly as they are, they generally have the one merit of disagreeing with each other. How can you talk of their leading one army or hurling one bolt. What is this anarchy?"

"Do not confuse it," replied the constable, "with those chance dynamite outbreaks from Russia or from Ireland, which are really the outbreaks of oppressed, if mistaken, men. This is a vast philosophic movement, consisting of an outer and an inner ring. You might even call the outer ring the laity and the inner ring the priesthood. I prefer to call the outer ring the innocent section, the inner ring the supremely guilty section. The outer ring—the main mass of their supporters—are merely anarchists; that is, men who believe that rules and formulas have destroyed human happiness. They believe that all the evil results of human crime are the results of the system that has called it crime. They do not believe that the crime creates the punishment. They believe that the punishment has created the crime. They believe that if a man seduced seven women he would naturally walk away as blameless as the flowers of spring. They believe that if a man picked a pocket he would naturally feel exquisitely good. These I call the innocent section."

"Oh!" said Syme.

"Naturally, therefore, these people talk about 'a happy time coming'; 'the paradise of the future'; 'mankind freed from the bondage of vice and the bondage of virtue,' and so on. And so also the men of the inner circle speak—the sacred priesthood. They also speak to applauding crowds of the happiness of the future, and of mankind freed at last. But in their mouths"—and the policeman lowered his voice—"in their mouths these happy phrases have a horrible meaning. They are under no illusions; they are too intellectual to think that man upon this earth can ever be quite free of original sin and the struggle. And they mean death. When they say that mankind shall be free at last, they mean that mankind shall commit suicide. When they talk of a paradise without right or wrong, they mean the grave. They have but two objects, to destroy first humanity and then themselves. That is why they throw bombs instead of firing pistols. The innocent rank and file are disappointed because the bomb has not killed the king; but the high-priesthood are happy because it has killed somebody."

"How can I join you?" asked Syme, with a sort of passion.

"I know for a fact that there is a vacancy at the moment," said the policeman, "as I have the honour to be somewhat in the confidence of the chief of whom I have spoken. You should really come and see him. Or rather, I should not say see him, nobody ever sees him; but you can talk to him if you like."

"Telephone?" inquired Syme, with interest.

"No," said the policeman placidly, "he has a fancy for always sitting in a pitch-dark room. He says it makes his thoughts brighter. Do come along."

Somewhat dazed and considerably excited, Syme allowed himself to be led to a side-door in the long row of buildings of Scotland Yard. Almost before he knew what he was doing, he had been passed through the hands of about four intermediate officials, and was suddenly shown into a room, the abrupt blackness of which startled him like a blaze of light. It was not the ordinary darkness, in which forms can be faintly traced; it was like going suddenly stone-blind.

"Are you the new recruit?" asked a heavy voice.

And in some strange way, though there was not the shadow of a shape in the gloom, Syme knew two things: first, that it came from a man of massive stature; and second, that the man had his back to him.

"Are you the new recruit?" said the invisible chief, who seemed to have heard all about it. "All right. You are engaged."

Syme, quite swept off his feet, made a feeble fight against this irrevocable phrase.

"I really have no experience," he began.

"No one has any experience," said the other, "of the Battle of Armageddon."

"But I am really unfit——"

"You are willing, that is enough," said the unknown.

"Well, really," said Syme, "I don't know any profession of which mere willingness is the final test."

"I do," said the other—"martyrs. I am condemning you to death. Good-day."

Thus it was that when Gabriel Syme came out again into the crimson light of evening, in his shabby black hat and shabby, lawless cloak, he came out a member of the New Detective Corps for the frustration of the great conspiracy. Acting under the advice of his friend the policeman (who was professionally inclined to neatness), he trimmed his hair and beard, bought a good hat, clad himself in an exquisite summer suit of light blue-grey, with a pale yellow flower in the buttonhole, and, in short, became that elegant and rather insupportable person whom Gregory had first encountered in the little garden of Saffron Park. Before he finally left the police premises his friend provided him with a small blue card, on which was written, "The Last Crusade," and a number, the sign of his official authority. He put this carefully in his upper waistcoat pocket, lit a cigarette, and went forth to track and fight the enemy in all the drawing-rooms of London. Where his adventure ultimately led him we have already seen. At about half-past one on a February night he found himself steaming in a small tug up the silent Thames, armed with sword-stick and revolver, the duly elected Thursday of the Central Council of Anarchists.

When Syme stepped out on to the steam-tug he had a singular sensation of stepping out into something entirely new; not merely into the landscape of a new land, but even into the landscape of a new planet. This was mainly due to the insane yet solid decision of that evening, though partly also to an entire change in the weather and the sky since he entered the little tavern some two hours before. Every trace of the passionate plumage of the cloudy sunset had been swept away, and a naked moon stood in a naked sky. The moon was so strong and full, that (by a paradox often to be noticed) it seemed like a weaker sun. It gave, not the sense of bright moonshine, but rather of a dead daylight.

Over the whole landscape lay a luminous and unnatural discoloration, as of that disastrous twilight which Milton spoke of as shed by the sun in eclipse; so that Syme fell easily into his first thought, that he was actually on some other and emptier planet, which circled round some sadder star. But the more he felt this glittering desolation in the moonlit land, the more his own chivalric folly glowed in the night like a great fire. Even the common things he carried with him—the food and the brandy and the loaded pistol—took on exactly that concrete and material poetry which a child feels when he takes a gun upon a journey or a bun with him to bed. The sword-stick and the brandy-flask, though in themselves only the tools of morbid conspirators, became the expressions of his own more healthy romance. The sword-stick became almost the sword of chivalry, and the brandy the wine of the stirrup-cup. For even the most dehumanised modern fantasies depend on some older and simpler figure; the adventures may be mad, but the adventurer must be sane. The dragon without St. George would not even be grotesque. So this inhuman landscape was only imaginative by the presence of a man really human. To Syme's exaggerative mind the bright, bleak houses and terraces by the Thames looked as empty as the mountains of the moon. But even the moon is only poetical because there is a man in the moon.

The tug was worked by two men, and with much toil went comparatively slowly. The clear moon that had lit up Chiswick had gone down by the time that they passed Battersea, and when they came under the enormous bulk of Westminster day had already begun to break. It broke like the splitting of great bars of lead, showing bars of silver; and these had brightened like white fire when the tug, changing its onward course, turned inward to a large landing stage rather beyond Charing Cross.

The great stones of the Embankment seemed equally dark and gigantic as Syme looked up at them. They were big and black against the huge white dawn. They made him feel that he was landing on the colossal steps of some Egyptian palace; and indeed the thing suited his mood, for he was, in his own mind, mounting to attack the solid thrones of horrible and heathen kings. He leapt out of the boat on to one slimy step, and stood, a dark and slender figure, amid the enormous masonry. The two men in the tug put her off again and turned up stream. They had never spoken a word.

V
THE FEAST OF FEAR

At first the large stone stair seemed to Syme as deserted as a pyramid; but before he reached the top he had realised that there was a man leaning over the parapet of the Embankment and looking out across the river. As a figure he was quite conventional, clad in a silk hat and frock-coat of the more formal type of fashion; he had a red flower in his buttonhole. As Syme drew nearer to him step by step, he did not even move a hair; and Syme could come close enough to notice even in the dim, pale morning light that his face was long, pale and intellectual, and ended in a small triangular tuft of dark beard at the very point of the chin, all else being clean-shaven. This scrap of hair almost seemed a mere oversight; the rest of the face was of the type that is best shaven—clear-cut, ascetic, and in its way noble. Syme drew closer and closer, noting all this, and still the figure did not stir.

At first an instinct had told Syme that this was the man whom he was meant to meet. Then, seeing that the man made no sign, he had concluded that he was not. And now again he had come back to a certainty that the man had something to do with his mad adventure. For the man remained more still than would have been natural if a stranger had come so close. He was as motionless as a wax-work, and got on the nerves somewhat in the same way. Syme looked again and again at the pale, dignified and delicate face, and the face still looked blankly across the river. Then he took out of his pocket the note from Buttons proving his election, and put it before that sad and beautiful face. Then the man smiled; and his smile was a shock, for it was all on one side, going up in the right cheek and down in the left.

There was nothing, rationally speaking, to scare any one about this. Many people have this nervous trick of a crooked smile, and in many it is even attractive. But in all Syme's circumstances, with the dark dawn and the deadly errand and the loneliness on the great dripping stones, there was something unnerving in it. There was the silent river and the silent man, a man of even classic face. And there was the last nightmare touch that his smile suddenly went wrong.

The spasm of smile was instantaneous, and the man's face dropped at once into its harmonious melancholy. He spoke without further explanation or inquiry, like a man speaking to an old colleague.

"If we walk up towards Leicester Square," he said, "we shall just be in time for breakfast. Sunday always insists on an early breakfast. Have you had any sleep?"

"No," said Syme.

"Nor have I," answered the man in an ordinary tone. "I shall try to get to bed after breakfast."

He spoke with casual civility, but in an utterly dead voice that contradicted the fanaticism of his face. It seemed almost as if all friendly words were to him lifeless conveniences, and that his only life was hate. After a pause the man spoke again.

"Of course, the Secretary of the branch told you everything that can be told. But the one thing that can never be told is the last notion of the President, for his notions grow like a tropical forest. So in case you don't know, I'd better tell you that he is carrying out his notion of concealing ourselves by not concealing ourselves to the most extraordinary lengths just now. Originally, of course, we met in a cell underground, just as your branch does. Then Sunday made us take a private room at an ordinary restaurant. He said that if you didn't seem to be hiding nobody hunted you out. Well, he is the only man on earth, I know; but sometimes I really think that his huge brain is going a little mad in its old age. For now we flaunt ourselves before the public. We have our breakfast on a balcony—on a balcony, if you please—overlooking Leicester Square."

"And what do the people say?" asked Syme.

"It's quite simple what they say," answered his guide. "They say we are a lot of jolly gentlemen who pretend they are anarchists."

"It seems to me a very clever idea," said Syme.

"Clever! God blast your impudence! Clever!" cried out the other in a sudden, shrill voice which was as startling and discordant as his crooked smile. "When you've seen Sunday for a split second you'll leave off calling him clever."

With this they emerged out of a narrow street, and saw the early sunlight filling Leicester Square. It will never be known, I suppose, why this square itself should look so alien and in some ways so continental. It will never be known whether it was the foreign look that attracted the foreigners or the foreigners who gave it the foreign look. But on this particular morning the effect seemed singularly bright and clear. Between the open square and the sunlit leaves and the statue and the Saracenic outlines of the Alhambra, it looked the replica of some French or even Spanish public place. And this effect increased in Syme the sensation, which in many shapes he had had through the whole adventure, the eerie sensation of having strayed into a new world. As a fact, he had bought bad cigars round Leicester Square ever since he was a boy. But as he turned that corner, and saw the trees and the Moorish cupolas, he could have sworn that he was turning into an unknown Place de something or other in some foreign town.

At one corner of the square there projected a kind of angle of a prosperous but quiet hotel, the bulk of which belonged to a street behind. In the wall there was one large French window, probably the window of a large coffee-room; and outside this window, almost literally overhanging the square, was a formidably buttressed balcony, big enough to contain a dining-table. In fact, it did contain a dining-table, or more strictly a breakfast-table; and round the breakfast-table, glowing in the sunlight and evident to the street, were a group of noisy and talkative men, all dressed in the insolence of fashion, with white waistcoats and expensive buttonholes. Some of their jokes could almost be heard across the square. Then the grave Secretary gave his unnatural smile, and Syme knew that this boisterous breakfast party was the secret conclave of the European Dynamiters.

Then, as Syme continued to stare at them, he saw something that he had not seen before. He had not seen it literally because it was too large to see. At the nearest end of the balcony, blocking up a great part of the perspective, was the back of a great mountain of a man. When Syme had seen him, his first thought was that the weight of him must break down the balcony of stone. His vastness did not lie only in the fact that he was abnormally tall and quite incredibly fat. This man was planned enormously in his original proportions, like a statue carved deliberately as colossal. His head, crowned with white hair, as seen from behind looked bigger than a head ought to be. The ears that stood out from it looked larger than human ears. He was enlarged terribly to scale; and this sense of size was so staggering, that when Syme saw him all the other figures seemed quite suddenly to dwindle and become dwarfish. They were still sitting there as before with their flowers and frock-coats, but now it looked as if the big man was entertaining five children to tea.

As Syme and the guide approached the side door of the hotel, a waiter came out smiling with every tooth in his head.

"The gentlemen are up there, sare," he said. "They do talk and they do laugh at what they talk. They do say they will throw bombs at ze king."

And the waiter hurried away with a napkin over his arm, much pleased with the singular frivolity of the gentlemen up-stairs.

The two men mounted the stairs in silence.

Syme had never thought of asking whether the monstrous man who almost filled and broke the balcony was the great President of whom the others stood in awe. He knew it was so, with an unaccountable but instantaneous certainty. Syme, indeed, was one of those men who are open to all the more nameless psychological influences in a degree a little dangerous to mental health. Utterly devoid of fear in physical dangers, he was a great deal too sensitive to the smell of spiritual evil. Twice already that night little unmeaning things had peeped out at him almost pruriently, and given him a sense of drawing nearer and nearer to the headquarters of hell. And this sense became overpowering as he drew nearer to the great President.

The form it took was a childish and yet hateful fancy. As he walked across the inner room towards the balcony, the large face of Sunday grew larger and larger; and Syme was gripped with a fear that when he was quite close the face would be too big to be possible, and that he would scream aloud. He remembered that as a child he would not look at the mask of Memnon in the British Museum, because it was a face, and so large.

By an effort braver than that of leaping over a cliff, he went to an empty seat at the breakfast-table and sat down. The men greeted him with good-humoured raillery as if they had always known him. He sobered himself a little by looking at their conventional coats and solid, shining coffee-pot; then he looked again at Sunday. His face was very large, but it was still possible to humanity.

In the presence of the President the whole company looked sufficiently commonplace; nothing about them caught the eye at first, except that by the President's caprice they had been dressed up with a festive respectability, which gave the meal the look of a wedding breakfast. One man indeed stood out at even a superficial glance. He at least was the common or garden Dynamiter. He wore, indeed, the high white collar and satin tie that were the uniform of the occasion; but out of this collar there sprang a head quite unmanageable and quite unmistakable, a bewildering bush of brown hair and beard that almost obscured the eyes like those of a Skye terrier. But the eyes did look out of the tangle, and they were the sad eyes of some Russian serf. The effect of this figure was not terrible like that of the President, but it had every diablerie that can come from the utterly grotesque. If out of that stiff tie and collar there had come abruptly the head of a cat or a dog, it could not have been a more idiotic contrast.

The man's name, it seemed, was Gogol; he was a Pole, and in this circle of days he was called Tuesday. His soul and speech were incurably tragic; he could not force himself to play the prosperous and frivolous part demanded of him by President Sunday. And, indeed, when Syme came in the President, with that daring disregard of public suspicion which was his policy, was actually chaffing Gogol upon his inability to assume conventional graces.

"Our friend Tuesday," said the President in a deep voice at once of quietude and volume, "our friend Tuesday doesn't seem to grasp the idea. He dresses up like a gentleman, but he seems to be too great a soul to behave like one. He insists on the ways of the stage conspirator. Now if a gentleman goes about London in a top hat and a frock-coat, no one need know that he is an anarchist. But if a gentleman puts on a top hat and a frock-coat, and then goes about on his hands and knees—well, he may attract attention. That's what Brother Gogol does. He goes about on his hands and knees with such inexhaustible diplomacy, that by this time he finds it quite difficult to walk upright."

"I am not good at goncealment," said Gogol sulkily, with a thick foreign accent; "I am not ashamed of the cause."

"Yes you are, my boy, and so is the cause of you," said the President good-naturedly. "You hide as much as anybody; but you can't do it, you see, you're such an ass! You try to combine two inconsistent methods. When a householder finds a man under his bed, he will probably pause to note the circumstance. But if he finds a man under his bed in a top hat, you will agree with me, my dear Tuesday, that he is not likely even to forget it. Now when you were found under Admiral Biffin's bed——"

"I am not good at deception," said Tuesday gloomily, flushing.

"Right, my boy, right," said the President with a ponderous heartiness, "you aren't good at anything."

While this stream of conversation continued, Syme was looking more steadily at the men around him. As he did so, he gradually felt all his sense of something spiritually queer return.

He had thought at first that they were all of common stature and costume, with the evident exception of the hairy Gogol. But as he looked at the others, he began to see in each of them exactly what he had seen in the man by the river, a demoniac detail somewhere. That lopsided laugh, which would suddenly disfigure the fine face of his original guide, was typical of all these types. Each man had something about him, perceived perhaps at the tenth or twentieth glance, which was not normal, and which seemed hardly human. The only metaphor he could think of was this, that they all looked as men of fashion and presence would look, with the additional twist given in a false and curved mirror.

Only the individual examples will express this half-concealed eccentricity. Syme's original cicerone bore the title of Monday; he was the Secretary of the Council, and his twisted smile was regarded with more terror than anything, except the President's horrible, happy laughter. But now that Syme had more space and light to observe him, there were other touches. His fine face was so emaciated, that Syme thought it must be wasted with some disease; yet somehow the very distress of his dark eyes denied this. It was no physical ill that troubled him. His eyes were alive with intellectual torture, as if pure thought was pain.

He was typical of each of the tribe; each man was subtly and differently wrong. Next to him sat Tuesday, the towzle-headed Gogol, a man more obviously mad. Next was Wednesday, a certain Marquis de St. Eustache, a sufficiently characteristic figure. The first few glances found nothing unusual about him, except that he was the only man at table who wore the fashionable clothes as if they were really his own. He had a black French beard cut square and a black English frock-coat cut even squarer. But Syme, sensitive to such things, felt somehow that the man carried a rich atmosphere with him, a rich atmosphere that suffocated. It reminded one irrationally of drowsy odours and of dying lamps in the darker poems of Byron and Poe. With this went a sense of his being clad, not in lighter colours, but in softer materials; his black seemed richer and warmer than the black shades about him, as if it were compounded of profound colour. His black coat looked as if it were only black by being too dense a purple. His black beard looked as if it were only black by being too deep a blue. And in the gloom and thickness of the beard his dark red mouth showed sensual and scornful. Whatever he was he was not a Frenchman; he might be a Jew; he might be something deeper yet in the dark heart of the East. In the bright coloured Persian tiles and pictures showing tyrants hunting, you may see just those almond eyes, those blue-black beards, those cruel, crimson lips.

Then came Syme, and next a very old man, Professor de Worms, who still kept the chair of Friday, though every day it was expected that his death would leave it empty. Save for his intellect, he was in the last dissolution of senile decay. His face was as grey as his long grey beard, his forehead was lifted and fixed finally in a furrow of mild despair. In no other case, not even that of Gogol, did the bridegroom brilliancy of the morning dress express a more painful contrast. For the red flower in his buttonhole showed up against a face that was literally discoloured like lead; the whole hideous effect was as if some drunken dandies had put their clothes upon a corpse. When he rose or sat down, which was with long labour and peril, something worse was expressed than mere weakness, something indefinably connected with the horror of the whole scene. It did not express decrepitude merely, but corruption. Another hateful fancy crossed Syme's quivering mind. He could not help thinking that whenever the man moved a leg or arm might fall off.

Right at the end sat the man called Saturday, the simplest and the most baffling of all. He was a short, square man with a dark, square face clean-shaven, a medical practitioner going by the name of Bull. He had that combination of *savoir-faire* with a sort of well-groomed coarseness which is not uncommon in young doctors. He carried his fine clothes with confidence rather than ease, and he mostly wore a set smile. There was nothing whatever odd about him, except that he wore a pair of dark, almost opaque spectacles. It may have been merely a crescendo of nervous fancy that had gone before, but those black discs were dreadful to Syme; they reminded him of half-remembered ugly tales, of some story about pennies being put on the eyes of the dead. Syme's eye always caught the black glasses and the blind grin. Had the dying Professor worn them, or even the pale Secretary, they would have been appropriate. But on the younger and grosser man they seemed only an enigma. They took away the key of the face. You could not tell what his smile or his gravity meant. Partly from this, and partly because he had a vulgar virility wanting in most of the others, it seemed to Syme that he might be the wickedest of all those wicked men. Syme even had the thought that his eyes might be covered up because they were too frightful to see.

VI
THE EXPOSURE

SUCH WERE the six men who had sworn to destroy the world. Again and again Syme strove to pull together his common sense in their presence. Sometimes he saw for an instant that these notions were subjective, that he was only looking at ordinary men, one of whom was old, another nervous, another short-sighted. The sense of an unnatural symbolism always settled back on him again. Each figure seemed to be, somehow, on the borderland of things, just as their theory was on the borderland of thought. He knew that each one of these men stood at the extreme end, so to speak, of some wild road of reasoning. He could only fancy, as in some old-world fable, that if a man went westward to the end of the world he would find something—say a tree—that was more or less than a tree, a tree possessed by a spirit; and that if he went east to the end of the world he would find something else that was not wholly itself—a tower, perhaps, of which the very shape was wicked. So these figures seemed to stand up, violent and unaccountable, against an ultimate horizon, visions from the verge. The ends of the earth were closing in.

Talk had been going on steadily as he took in the scene; and not the least of the contrasts of that bewildering breakfast-table was the contrast between the easy and unobtrusive tone of talk and its terrible purport. They were deep in the discussion of an actual and immediate plot. The waiter down-stairs had spoken quite correctly when he said that they were talking about bombs and kings. Only three days afterwards the Czar was to meet the President of the French Republic in Paris, and over their bacon and eggs upon their sunny balcony these beaming gentlemen had decided how both should die. Even the instrument was chosen; the black-bearded Marquis, it appeared, was to carry the bomb.

Ordinarily speaking, the proximity of this positive and objective crime would have sobered Syme, and cured him of all his merely mystical tremors. He would have thought of nothing but the need of saving at least two human bodies from being ripped in pieces with iron and roaring gas. But the truth was that by this time he had begun to feel a third kind of fear, more piercing and practical than either his moral revulsion or his social responsibility. Very simply, he had no fear to spare for the French President or the Czar; he had begun to fear for himself. Most of the talkers took little heed of him, debating now with their faces closer together, and almost uniformly grave, save when for an instant the smile of the Secretary ran aslant across his face as the jagged lightning runs aslant across the sky. But there was one persistent thing which first troubled Syme and at last terrified him. The President was always looking at him, steadily, and with a great and baffling interest. The enormous man was quite quiet, but his blue eyes stood out of his head. And they were always fixed on Syme.

Syme felt moved to spring up and leap over the balcony. When the President's eyes were on him he felt as if he were made of glass. He had hardly the shred of a doubt that in some silent and extraordinary way Sunday had found out that he was a spy. He looked over the edge of the balcony, and saw a policeman standing abstractedly just beneath, staring at the bright railings and the sunlit trees.

Then there fell upon him the great temptation that was to torment him for many days. In the presence of these powerful and repulsive men, who were the princes of anarchy, he had almost forgotten the frail and fanciful figure of the poet Gregory, the mere æsthete of anarchism. He even thought of him now with an old kindness, as if they had played together when children. But he remembered that he was still tied to Gregory by a great promise. He had promised never to do the very thing that he now felt himself almost in the act of doing. He had promised not to jump over that balcony and speak to that policeman. He took his cold hand off the cold stone balustrade. His soul swayed in a vertigo of moral indecision. He had only to snap the thread of a rash vow made to a villainous society, and all his life could be as open and sunny as the square beneath him. He had, on the other hand, only to keep his antiquated honour, and be delivered inch by inch into the power of this great enemy of mankind, whose very intellect was a torture-chamber. Whenever he looked down into the square he saw the comfortable policeman, a pillar of common-sense and common order. Whenever he looked back at the breakfast-table he saw the President still quietly studying him with big, unbearable eyes.

In all the torrent of his thought there were two thoughts that never crossed his mind. First, it never occurred to him to doubt that the President and his Council could crush him if he continued to stand alone. The place might be public, the project might seem impossible. But Sunday was not the man who would carry himself thus easily without having, somehow or somewhere, set open his iron trap. Either by anonymous poison or sudden street accident, by hypnotism or by fire from hell, Sunday could certainly strike him. If he defied the man he was probably dead, either struck stiff there in his chair or long afterwards as by an innocent ailment. If he called in the police promptly, arrested every one, told all, and set against them the whole energy of England, he would probably escape; certainly not otherwise. They were a balconyful of gentlemen overlooking a bright and busy square; but he felt no more safe with them than if they had been a boatful of armed pirates overlooking an empty sea.

There was a second thought that never came to him. It never occurred to him to be spiritually won over to the enemy. Many moderns, inured to a weak worship of intellect and force, might have wavered in their allegiance under this oppression of a great personality. They might have called Sunday the super-man. If any such creature be conceivable, he looked, indeed, somewhat like it, with his earth-shaking abstraction, as of a stone statue walking. He might have been called something above man, with his large plans, which were too obvious to be detected, with his large face, which was too frank to be understood. But this was a kind of modern meanness to which Syme could not sink even in his extreme morbidity. Like any man, he was coward enough to fear great force; but he was not quite coward enough to admire it.

The men were eating as they talked, and even in this they were typical. Dr. Bull and the Marquis ate casually and conventionally of the best things on the table—cold pheasant or Strasbourg pie. But the Secretary was a vegetarian, and he spoke earnestly of the projected murder over half a raw tomato and three quarters of a glass of tepid water. The old Professor had such slops as suggested a sickening second childhood. And even in this President Sunday preserved his curious predominance of mere mass. For he ate like twenty men; he ate incredibly, with a frightful freshness of appetite, so that it was like watching a sausage factory. Yet continually, when he had swallowed a dozen crumpets or drunk a quart of coffee, he would be found with his great head on one side staring at Syme.

"I have often wondered," said the Marquis, taking a great bite out of a slice of bread and jam, "whether it wouldn't be better for me to do it with a knife. Most of the best things have been brought off with a knife. And it would be a new emotion to get a knife into a French President and wriggle it round."

"You are wrong," said the Secretary, drawing his black brows together. "The knife was merely the expression of the old personal quarrel with a personal tyrant. Dynamite is not only our best tool, but our best symbol. It is as perfect a symbol of us as is incense of the prayers of the Christians. It expands; it only destroys because it broadens; even so, thought only destroys because it broadens. A man's brain is a bomb," he cried out, loosening suddenly his strange passion and striking his own skull with violence. "My brain feels like a bomb, night and day. It must expand! It must expand! A man's brain must expand, if it breaks up the universe."

"I don't want the universe broken up just yet," drawled the Marquis. "I want to do a lot of beastly things before I die. I thought of one yesterday in bed."

"No, if the only end of the thing is nothing," said Dr. Bull with his sphinx-like smile, "it hardly seems worth doing."

The old Professor was staring at the ceiling with dull eyes.

"Every man knows in his heart," he said, "that nothing is worth doing."

There was a singular silence, and then the Secretary said—

"We are wandering, however, from the point. The only question is how Wednesday is to strike the blow. I take it we should all agree with the original notion of a bomb. As to the actual arrangements, I should suggest that to-morrow morning he should go first of all to——"

The speech was broken off short under a vast shadow. President Sunday had risen to his feet, seeming to fill the sky above them.

"Before we discuss that," he said in a small, quiet voice, "let us go into a private room. I have something very particular to say."

Syme stood up before any of the others. The instant of choice had come at last, the pistol was at his head. On the pavement below he could hear the policeman idly stir and stamp, for the morning, though bright, was cold.

A barrel-organ in the street suddenly sprang with a jerk into a jovial tune. Syme stood up taut, as if it had been a bugle before the battle. He found himself filled with a supernatural courage that came from nowhere. That jingling music seemed full of the vivacity, the vulgarity, and the irrational valour of the poor, who in all those unclean streets were all clinging to the decencies and the charities of Christendom. His youthful prank of being a policeman had faded from his mind; he did not think of himself as the representative of the corps of gentlemen turned into fancy constables, or of the old eccentric who lived in the dark room. But he did feel himself as the ambassador of all these common and kindly people in the street, who every day marched into battle to the music of the barrel-organ. And this high pride in being human had lifted him unaccountably to an infinite height above the monstrous men around him. For an instant, at least, he looked down upon all their sprawling eccentricities from the starry pinnacle of the commonplace. He felt towards them all that unconscious and elementary superiority that a brave man feels over powerful beasts or a wise man over powerful errors. He knew that he had neither the intellectual nor the physical strength of President Sunday; but in that moment he minded it no more than the fact that he had not the muscles of a tiger or a horn on his nose like a rhinoceros. All was swallowed up in an ultimate certainty that the President was wrong and that the barrel-organ was right. There clanged in his mind that unanswerable and terrible truism in the song of Roland—

> "Païens ont tort et Chrétiens ont droit,"

which in the old nasal French has the clang and groan of great iron. This liberation of his spirit from the load of his weakness went with a quite clear decision to embrace death. If the people of the barrel-organ could keep their old-world obligations, so could he. This very pride in keeping his word was that he was keeping it to miscreants. It was his last triumph over these lunatics to go down into their dark room and die for something that they could not even understand. The barrel-organ seemed to give the marching tune with the energy and the mingled noises of a whole orchestra; and he could hear deep and rolling, under all the trumpets of the pride of life, the drums of the pride of death.

The conspirators were already filing through the open window and into the rooms behind. Syme went last, outwardly calm, but with all his brain and body throbbing with romantic rhythm. The President led them down an irregular side stair, such as might be used by servants, and into a dim, cold, empty room, with a table and benches, like an abandoned board-room. When they were all in, he closed and locked the door.

The first to speak was Gogol, the irreconcilable, who seemed bursting with inarticulate grievance.

"Zso! Zso!" he cried, with an obscure excitement, his heavy Polish accent becoming almost impenetrable. "You zay you nod 'ide. You zay you show himselves. It is all nuzzinks. Ven you vant talk importance you run yourselves in a dark box!"

The President seemed to take the foreigner's incoherent satire with entire good humour.

"You can't get hold of it, Gogol," he said in a fatherly way. "When once they have heard us talking nonsense on that balcony they will not care where we go afterwards. If we had come here first, we should have had the whole staff at the keyhole. You don't seem to know anything about mankind."

"I die for zem," cried the Pole in thick excitement, "and I slay zare oppressors. I care not for these games of gonzealment. I would zmite ze tyrant in ze open square."

"I see, I see," said the President, nodding kindly as he seated himself at the top of a long table. "You die for mankind first, and then you get up and smite their oppressors. So that's all right. And now may I ask you to control your beautiful sentiments, and sit down with the other gentlemen at this table. For the first time this morning something intelligent is going to be said."

Syme, with the perturbed promptitude he had shown since the original summons, sat down first. Gogol sat down last, grumbling in his brown beard about gombromise. No one except Syme seemed to have any notion of the blow that was about to fall. As for him, he had merely the feeling of a man mounting the scaffold with the intention, at any rate, of making a good speech.

"Comrades," said the President, suddenly rising, "we have spun out this farce long enough. I have called you down here to tell you something so simple and shocking that even the waiters up-stairs (long inured to our levities) might hear some new seriousness in my voice. Comrades, we were discussing plans and naming places. I propose, before saying anything else, that those plans and places should not be voted by this meeting, but should be left wholly in the control of some one reliable member. I suggest Comrade Saturday, Dr. Bull."

They all stared at him; then they all started in their seats, for the next words, though not loud, had a living and sensational emphasis. Sunday struck the table.

"Not one word more about the plans and places must be said at this meeting. Not one tiny detail more about what we mean to do must be mentioned in this company."

Sunday had spent his life in astonishing his followers; but it seemed as if he had never really astonished them until now. They all moved feverishly in their seats, except Syme. He sat stiff in his, with his hand in his pocket, and on the handle of his loaded revolver. When the attack on him came he would sell his life dear. He would find out at least if the President was mortal.

Sunday went on smoothly—

"You will probably understand that there is only one possible motive for forbidding free speech at this festival of freedom. Strangers overhearing us matters nothing. They assume that we are joking. But what would matter, even unto death, is this, that there should be one actually among us who is not of us, who knows our grave purpose, but does not share it, who——"

The Secretary screamed out suddenly like a woman.

"It can't be!" he cried, leaping. "There can't——"

The President flapped his large flat hand on the table like the fin of some huge fish.

"Yes," he said slowly, "there is a spy in this room. There is a traitor at this table. I will waste no more words. His name——"

Syme half rose from his seat, his finger firm on the trigger.

"His name is Gogol," said the President. "He is that hairy humbug over there who pretends to be a Pole."

Gogol sprang to his feet, a pistol in each hand. With the same flash three men sprang at his throat. Even the Professor made an effort to rise. But Syme saw little of the scene, for he was blinded with a beneficent darkness; he had sunk down into his seat shuddering, in a palsy of passionate relief.

VII

THE UNACCOUNTABLE CONDUCT OF PROFESSOR DE WORMS

"SIT DOWN!" said Sunday in a voice that he used once or twice in his life, a voice that made men drop drawn swords.

The three who had risen fell away from Gogol, and that equivocal person himself resumed his seat.

"Well, my man," said the President briskly, addressing him as one addresses a total stranger, "will you oblige me by putting your hand in your upper waistcoat pocket and showing me what you have there?"

The alleged Pole was a little pale under his tangle of dark hair, but he put two fingers into the pocket with apparent coolness and pulled out a blue strip of card. When Syme saw it lying on the table, he woke up again to the world outside him. For although the card lay at the other extreme of the table, and he could read nothing of the inscription on it, it bore a startling resemblance to the blue card in his own pocket, the card which had been given to him when he joined the anti-anarchist constabulary.

"Pathetic Slav," said the President, "tragic child of Poland, are you prepared in the presence of that card to deny that you are in this company—shall we say *de trop?*"

"Right oh!" said the late Gogol. It made every one jump to hear a clear, commercial and somewhat cockney voice coming out of that forest of foreign hair. It was irrational, as if a Chinaman had suddenly spoken with a Scotch accent.

"I gather that you fully understand your position," said Sunday.

"You bet," answered the Pole. "I see it's a fair cop. All I say is, I don't believe any Pole could have imitated my accent like I did his."

"I concede the point," said Sunday. "I believe your own accent to be inimitable, though I shall practice it in my bath. Do you mind leaving your beard with your card?"

"Not a bit," answered Gogol; and with one finger he ripped off the whole of his shaggy head-covering, emerging with thin red hair and a pale, pert face. "It was hot," he added.

"I will do you the justice to say," said Sunday, not without a sort of brutal admiration, "that you seem to have kept pretty cool under it. Now listen to me. I like you. The consequence is that it would annoy me for just about two and a half minutes if I heard that you had died in torments. Well, if you ever tell the police or any human soul about us, I shall have that two and a half minutes of discomfort. On your discomfort I will not dwell. Good-day. Mind the step."

The red-haired detective who had masqueraded as Gogol rose to his feet without a word, and walked out of the room with an air of perfect nonchalance. Yet the astonished Syme was able to realise that this ease was suddenly assumed; for there was a slight stumble outside the door, which showed that the departing detective had not minded the step.

"Time is flying," said the President in his gayest manner, after glancing at his watch, which like everything about him seemed bigger than it ought to be. "I must get off at once; I have to take the chair at a Humanitarian meeting."

The Secretary turned to him with working eyebrows.

"Would it not be better," he said a little sharply, "to discuss further the details of our project, now that the spy has left us?"

"No, I think not," said the President with a yawn like an unobtrusive earthquake. "Leave it as it is. Let Saturday settle it. I must be off. Breakfast here next Sunday."

But the late loud scenes had whipped up the almost naked nerves of the Secretary. He was one of those men who are conscientious even in crime.

"I must protest, President, that the thing is irregular," he said. "It is a fundamental rule of our society that all plans shall be debated in full council. Of course, I fully appreciate your forethought when in the actual presence of a traitor——"

"Secretary," said the President seriously, "if you'd take your head home and boil it for a turnip it might be useful. I can't say. But it might."

The Secretary reared back in a kind of equine anger.

"I really fail to understand——" he began in high offence.

"That's it, that's it," said the President, nodding a great many times. "That's where you fail right enough. You fail to understand. Why, you dancing donkey," he roared, rising, "you didn't want to be overheard by a spy, didn't you? How do you know you aren't overheard now?"

And with these words he shouldered his way out of the room, shaking with incomprehensible scorn.

Four of the men left behind gaped after him without any apparent glimmering of his meaning. Syme alone had even a glimmering, and such as it was it froze him to the bone. If the last words of the President meant anything, they meant that he had not after all passed unsuspected. They meant that while Sunday could not denounce him like Gogol, he still could not trust him like the others.

The other four got to their feet grumbling more or less, and betook themselves elsewhere to find lunch, for it was already well past midday. The Professor went last, very slowly and painfully. Syme sat long after the rest had gone, revolving his strange position. He had escaped a thunderbolt, but he was still under a cloud. At last he rose and made his way out of the hotel into Leicester Square. The bright, cold day had grown increasingly colder, and when he came out into the street he was surprised by a few flakes of snow. While he still carried the sword-stick and the rest of Gregory's portable luggage, he had thrown the cloak down and left it somewhere, perhaps on the steam-tug, perhaps on the balcony. Hoping, therefore, that the snow-shower might be slight, he stepped back out of the street for a moment and stood up under the doorway of a small and greasy hair-dresser's shop, the front window of which was empty, except for a sickly wax lady in evening dress.

Snow, however, began to thicken and fall fast; and Syme, having found one glance at the wax lady quite sufficient to depress his spirits, stared out instead into the white and empty street. He was considerably astonished to see, standing quite still outside the shop and staring into the window, a man. His top hat was loaded with snow like the hat of Father Christmas, the white drift was rising round his boots and ankles; but it seemed as if nothing could tear him away from the contemplation of the colourless wax doll in dirty evening dress. That any human being should stand in such weather looking into such a shop was a matter of sufficient wonder to Syme; but his idle wonder turned suddenly into a personal shock; for he realised that the man standing there was the paralytic old

Professor de Worms. It scarcely seemed the place for a person of his years and infirmities.

Syme was ready to believe anything about the perversions of this dehumanised brotherhood; but even he could not believe that the Professor had fallen in love with that particular wax lady. He could only suppose that the man's malady (whatever it was) involved some momentary fits of rigidity or trance. He was not inclined, however, to feel in this case any very compassionate concern. On the contrary, he rather congratulated himself that the Professor's stroke and his elaborate and limping walk would make it easy to escape from him and leave him miles behind. For Syme thirsted first and last to get clear of the whole poisonous atmosphere, if only for an hour. Then he could collect his thoughts, formulate his policy, and decide finally whether he should or should not keep faith with Gregory.

He strolled away through the dancing snow, turned up two or three streets, down through two or three others, and entered a small Soho restaurant for lunch. He partook reflectively of four small and quaint courses, drank half a bottle of red wine, and ended up over black coffee and a black cigar, still thinking. He had taken his seat in the upper room of the restaurant, which was full of the chink of knives and the chatter of foreigners. He remembered that in old days he had imagined that all these harmless and kindly aliens were anarchists. He shuddered, remembering the real thing. But even the shudder had the delightful shame of escape. The wine, the common food, the familiar place, the faces of natural and talkative men, made him almost feel as if the Council of the Seven Days had been a bad dream; and although he knew it was nevertheless an objective reality, it was at least a distant one. Tall houses and populous streets lay between him and his last sight of the shameful seven; he was free in free London, and drinking wine among the free. With a somewhat easier action, he took his hat and stick and strolled down the stair into the shop below.

When he entered that lower room he stood stricken and rooted to the spot. At a small table, close up to the blank window and the white street of snow, sat the old anarchist Professor over a glass of milk, with his lifted livid face and pendent eyelids. For an instant Syme stood as rigid as the stick he leant upon. Then with a gesture as of blind hurry, he brushed past the Professor, dashing open the door and slamming it behind him, and stood outside in the snow.

"Can that old corpse be following me?" he asked himself, biting his yellow moustache. "I stopped too long up in that room, so that even such leaden feet could catch me up. One comfort is, with a little brisk walking I can put a man like that as far away as Timbuctoo. Or am I too fanciful? Was he really following me? Surely Sunday would not be such a fool as to send a lame man?"

He set off at a smart pace, twisting and whirling his stick, in the direction of Covent Garden. As he crossed the great market the snow increased, growing blinding and bewildering as the afternoon began to darken. The snowflakes tormented him like a swarm of silver bees. Getting into his eyes and beard, they added their unremitting futility to his already irritated nerves; and by the time that he had come at a swinging pace to the beginning of Fleet Street, he lost patience, and finding a Sunday tea-shop, turned into it to take shelter. He ordered another cup of black coffee as an excuse. Scarcely had he done so, when Professor de Worms hobbled heavily into the shop, sat down with difficulty and ordered a glass of milk.

Syme's walking-stick had fallen from his hand with a great clang, which confessed the concealed steel. But the Professor did not look round. Syme, who was commonly a cool character, was literally gaping as a rustic gapes at a conjuring trick. He had seen no cab following; he had heard no wheels outside the shop; to all mortal appearances the man had come on foot. But the old man could only walk like a snail, and Syme had walked like the wind. He started up and snatched his stick, half crazy with the contradiction in mere arithmetic, and swung out of the swinging doors, leaving his coffee untasted. An omnibus going to the Bank went rattling by with an unusual rapidity. He had a violent run of a hundred yards to reach it; but he managed to spring, swaying upon the splash-board, and pausing for an instant to pant, he climbed on to the top. When he had been seated for about half a minute, he heard behind him a sort of heavy and asthmatic breathing.

Turning sharply, he saw rising gradually higher and higher up the omnibus steps a top hat soiled and dripping with snow, and under the shadow of its brim the short-sighted face and shaky shoulders of Professor de Worms. He let himself into a seat with characteristic care, and wrapped himself up to the chin in the mackintosh rug.

Every movement of the old man's tottering figure and vague hands, every uncertain gesture and panic-stricken pause, seemed to put it beyond question that he was helpless, that he was in the last imbecility of the body. He moved by inches, he let himself down with little gasps of caution. And yet, unless the philosophical entities called time and space have no vestige even of a practical existence, it appeared quite unquestionable that he had run after the omnibus.

Syme sprang erect upon the rocking car, and after staring wildly at the wintry sky, that grew gloomier every moment, he ran down the steps. He had repressed an elemental impulse to leap over the side.

Too bewildered to look back or to reason, he rushed into one of the little courts at the side of Fleet Street as a rabbit rushes into a hole. He had a vague idea, if this incomprehensible old Jack-in-the-box was really pursuing him, that in that labyrinth of little streets he could soon throw him off the scent. He dived in and out of those crooked lanes, which were more like cracks than thoroughfares; and by the time that he had completed about twenty alternate angles and described an unthinkable polygon, he paused to listen for any sound of pursuit. There was none; there could not in any case have been much, for the little streets were thick with the soundless snow. Somewhere behind Red Lion Court, however, he noticed a place where some energetic citizen had cleared away the snow for a space of about twenty yards, leaving the wet, glistening cobblestones. He thought little of this as he passed it, only plunging into yet another arm of the maze. But when a few hundred yards farther on he stood still again to listen, his heart stood still also, for he heard from that space of rugged stones the clinking crutch and labouring feet of the infernal cripple.

The sky above was loaded with the clouds of snow, leaving London in a darkness and oppression premature for that hour of the evening. On each side of Syme the walls of the alley were blind and featureless; there was no little window or any kind of eye. He felt a new impulse to break out of this hive of houses, and to get once more into the open and lamp-lit street. Yet he rambled and dodged for a long time before he struck the main thoroughfare. When he did so, he struck it much farther up than he had fancied. He came out into what seemed the vast and void of Ludgate Circus, and saw St. Paul's Cathedral sitting in the sky.

At first he was startled to find these great roads so empty, as if a pestilence had swept through the city. Then he told himself that some degree of emptiness was natural; first because the snow-storm was even dangerously deep, and secondly because it was Sunday. And at the very word Sunday he bit his lip; the word was henceforth for him like some indecent pun. Under the white fog of snow high up in the heaven the whole atmosphere of the city was turned to a very queer kind of green twilight, as of men under the sea. The sealed and sullen sunset behind the dark dome of St. Paul's had in it smoky and sinister colours—colours of sickly green, dead red or decaying bronze, that were just bright enough to emphasise the solid whiteness of the snow. But right up against these dreary colours rose the black bulk of the cathedral; and upon the top of the cathedral was a random splash and great stain of snow, still clinging as to an Alpine peak. It had fallen accidentally, but just so fallen as to half drape the dome from its very topmost point, and to pick out in perfect silver the great orb and the cross. When Syme saw it he suddenly straightened himself, and made with his sword-stick an involuntary salute.

He knew that that evil figure, his shadow, was creeping quickly or slowly behind him, and he did not care. It seemed a symbol of human faith and valour that while the skies were darkening that high place of the earth was bright. The devils might have captured heaven, but they had not yet captured the cross. He had a new impulse to tear out the secret of this dancing, jumping and pursuing paralytic; and at the entrance of the court as it opened upon the Circus he turned, stick in hand, to face his pursuer.

Professor de Worms came slowly round the corner of the irregular alley behind him, his unnatural form outlined against a lonely gas-lamp, irresistibly recalling that very imaginative figure in the nursery rhymes, "the crooked man who went a crooked mile." He really looked as if he had been twisted out of shape by the tortuous streets he had been threading. He came nearer and nearer, the lamp-light shining on his lifted spectacles, his lifted, patient face. Syme waited for him as St. George waited for the dragon, as a man waits for a final explanation or for death. And the old Professor came right up to him and passed him like a total stranger, without even a blink of his mournful eyelids.

There was something in this silent and unexpected innocence that left Syme in a final fury. The man's colourless face and manner seemed to assert that the whole following had been an accident. Syme was galvanised with an energy that was something between bitterness and a burst of boyish derision. He made a wild gesture as if to knock the old man's hat off, called out something like "Catch me if you can," and went racing away across the white, open Circus. Concealment was impossible now; and looking back over his shoulder, he could see the black figure of the old gentleman coming after him with long, swinging strides like a man winning a mile race. But the head upon that bounding body was still pale, grave and professional, like the head of a lecturer upon the body of a harlequin.

This outrageous chase sped across Ludgate Circus, up Ludgate Hill, round St. Paul's Cathedral, along Cheapside, Syme remembering all the nightmares he had ever known. Then Syme broke away towards the river, and ended almost down by the docks. He saw the yellow panes of a low, lighted public-house, flung himself into it and ordered beer. It was a foul tavern, sprinkled with foreign sailors, a place where opium might be smoked or knives drawn.

A moment later Professor de Worms entered the place, sat down carefully, and asked for a glass of milk.

VIII
THE PROFESSOR EXPLAINS

WHEN GABRIEL Syme found himself finally established in a chair, and opposite to him, fixed and final also, the lifted eyebrows and leaden eyelids of the Professor, his fears fully returned. This incomprehensible man from the fierce council, after all, had certainly pursued him. If the man had one character as a paralytic and another character as a pursuer, the antithesis might make him more interesting, but scarcely more soothing. It would be a very small comfort that he could not find the Professor out, if by some serious accident the Professor should find him out. He emptied a whole pewter pot of ale before the Professor had touched his milk.

One possibility, however, kept him hopeful and yet helpless. It was just possible that this escapade signified something other than even a slight suspicion of him. Perhaps it was some regular form or sign. Perhaps the foolish scamper was some sort of friendly signal that he ought to have understood. Perhaps it was a ritual. Perhaps the new Thursday was always chased along Cheapside, as the new Lord Mayor is always escorted along it. He was just selecting a tentative inquiry, when the old Professor opposite suddenly and simply cut him short. Before Syme could ask the first diplomatic question, the old anarchist had asked suddenly, without any sort of preparation—

"Are you a policeman?"

Whatever else Syme had expected, he had never expected anything so brutal and actual as this. Even his great presence of mind could only manage a reply with an air of rather blundering jocularity.

"A policeman?" he said, laughing vaguely. "Whatever made you think of a policeman in connection with me?"

"The process was simple enough," answered the Professor patiently. "I thought you looked like a policeman. I think so now."

"Did I take a policeman's hat by mistake out of the restaurant?" asked Syme, smiling wildly. "Have I by any chance got a number stuck on to me somewhere? Have my boots got that watchful look? Why must I be a policeman? Do, do let me be a postman."

The old Professor shook his head with a gravity that gave no hope, but Syme ran on with a feverish irony.

"But perhaps I misunderstood the delicacies of your German philosophy. Perhaps policeman is a relative term. In an evolutionary sense, sir, the ape fades so gradually into the policeman, that I myself can never detect the shade. The monkey is only the policeman that may be. Perhaps a maiden lady on Clapham Common is only the policeman that might have been. I don't mind being the policeman that might have been. I don't mind being anything in German thought."

"Are you in the police service?" said the old man, ignoring all Syme's improvised and desperate raillery. "Are you a detective?"

Syme's heart turned to stone, but his face never changed.

"Your suggestion is ridiculous," he began. "Why on earth——"

The old man struck his palsied hand passionately on the rickety table, nearly breaking it.

"Did you hear me ask a plain question, you paltering spy?" he shrieked in a high, crazy voice. "Are you, or are you not, a police detective?"

"No!" answered Syme, like a man standing on the hangman's drop.

"You swear it," said the old man, leaning across to him, his dead face becoming as it were loathsomely alive. "You swear it! You swear it! If you swear falsely, will you be damned? Will you be sure that the devil dances at your funeral? Will you see that the nightmare sits on your grave? Will there really be no mistake? You are an anarchist, you are a dynamiter! Above all, you are not in any sense a detective? You are not in the British police?"

He leant his angular elbow far across the table, and put up his large loose hand like a flap to his ear.

"I am not in the British police," said Syme with insane calm.

Professor de Worms fell back in his chair with a curious air of kindly collapse.

"That's a pity," he said, "because I am."

Syme sprang up straight, sending back the bench behind him with a crash.

"Because you are what?" he said thickly. "You are what?"

"I am a policeman," said the Professor with his first broad smile, and beaming through his spectacles. "But as you think policeman only a relative term, of course I have nothing to do with you. I am in the British police force; but as you tell me you are not in the British police force, I can only say that I met you in a dynamiter's club. I suppose I ought to arrest you." And with these words he laid on the table before Syme an exact facsimile of the blue card which Syme had in his own waistcoat pocket, the symbol of his power from the police.

Syme had for a flash the sensation that the cosmos had turned exactly upside down, that all trees were growing downwards and that all stars were under his feet. Then came slowly the opposite conviction. For the last twenty-four hours the cosmos had really been upside down, but now the capsized universe had come right side up again. This devil from whom he had been fleeing all day was only an elder brother of his own house, who on the other side of the table lay back and laughed at him. He did not for the moment ask any questions of detail; he only knew the happy and silly fact that this shadow, which had pursued him with an intolerable oppression of peril, was only the shadow of a friend trying to catch him up. He knew simultaneously that he was a fool and a free man. For with any recovery from morbidity there must go a certain healthy humiliation. There comes a certain point in such conditions when only three things are possible: first a perpetuation of Satanic pride, secondly tears, and third laughter. Syme's egotism held hard to the first course for a few seconds, and then suddenly adopted the third. Taking his own blue police ticket from his own waistcoat pocket, he tossed it on to the table; then he flung his head back until his spike of yellow beard almost pointed at the ceiling, and shouted with a barbaric laughter.

Even in that close den, perpetually filled with the din of knives, plates, cans, clamorous voices, sudden struggles and stampedes, there was something Homeric in Syme's mirth which made many half-drunken men look round.

"What yer laughing at, guv'nor?" asked one wondering labourer from the docks.

"At myself," answered Syme, and went off again into the agony of his ecstatic reaction.

"Pull yourself together," said the Professor, "or you'll get hysterical. Have some more beer. I'll join you."

"You haven't drunk your milk," said Syme.

"My milk!" said the other, in tones of withering and unfathomable contempt, "my milk! Do you think I'd look at the beastly stuff when I'm out of sight of the bloody anarchists? We're all Christians in this room, though perhaps," he added, glancing around at the reeling crowd, "not strict ones. Finish my milk? Great blazes! yes, I'll finish it right enough!" and he knocked the tumbler off the table, making a crash of glass and a splash of silver fluid.

Syme was staring at him with a happy curiosity.

"I understand now," he cried; "of course, you're not an old man at all."

"I can't take my face off here," replied Professor de Worms. "It's rather an elaborate make-up. As to whether I'm an old man, that's not for me to say. I was thirty-eight last birthday."

"Yes, but I mean," said Syme impatiently, "there's nothing the matter with you."

"Yes," answered the other dispassionately, "I am subject to colds."

Syme's laughter at all this had about it a wild weakness of relief. He laughed at the idea of the paralytic Professor being really a young actor dressed up as if for the footlights. But he felt that he would have laughed as loudly if a pepper-pot had fallen over.

The false Professor drank and wiped his false beard.

"Did you know," he asked, "that that man Gogol was one of us?"

"I? No, I didn't know it," answered Syme in some surprise. "But didn't you?"

"I knew no more than the dead," replied the man who called himself de Worms. "I thought the President was talking about me, and I rattled in my boots."

"And I thought he was talking about me," said Syme, with his rather reckless laughter. "I had my hand on my revolver all the time."

"So had I," said the Professor grimly; "so had Gogol evidently."

Syme struck the table with an exclamation.

"Why, there were three of us there!" he cried. "Three out of seven is a fighting number. If we had only known that we were three!"

The face of Professor de Worms darkened, and he did not look up.

"We were three," he said. "If we had been three hundred we could still have done nothing."

"Not if we were three hundred against four?" asked Syme, jeering rather boisterously.

"No," said the Professor with sobriety, "not if we were three hundred against Sunday."

And the mere name struck Syme cold and serious; his laughter had died in his heart before it could die on his lips. The face of the unforgettable President sprang into his mind as startling as a coloured photograph, and he remarked this difference between Sunday and all his satellites, that their faces, however fierce or sinister, became gradually blurred by memory like other human faces, whereas Sunday's seemed almost to grow more actual during absence, as if a man's painted portrait should slowly come alive.

They were both silent for a measure of moments, and then Syme's speech came with a rush, like the sudden foaming of champagne.

"Professor," he cried, "it is intolerable. Are you afraid of this man?"

The Professor lifted his heavy lids, and gazed at Syme with large, wide-open, blue eyes of an almost ethereal honesty.

"Yes, I am," he said mildly. "So are you."

Syme was dumb for an instant. Then he rose to his feet erect, like an insulted man, and thrust the chair away from him.

"Yes," he said in a voice indescribable, "you are right. I am afraid of him. Therefore I swear by God that I will seek out this man whom I fear until I find him, and strike him on the mouth. If heaven were his throne and the earth his footstool, I swear that I would pull him down."

"How?" asked the staring Professor. "Why?"

"Because I am afraid of him," said Syme; "and no man should leave in the universe anything of which he is afraid."

De Worms blinked at him with a sort of blind wonder. He made an effort to speak, but Syme went on in a low voice, but with an undercurrent of inhuman exaltation——

"Who would condescend to strike down the mere things that he does not fear? Who would debase himself to be merely brave, like any common prizefighter? Who would stoop to be fearless—like a tree? Fight the thing that you fear. You remember the old tale of the English clergyman who gave the last rites to the brigand of Sicily, and how on his death-bed the great robber said, 'I can give you no money, but I can give you advice for a lifetime: your thumb on the blade, and strike upwards.' So I say to you, strike upwards, if you strike at the stars."

The other looked at the ceiling, one of the tricks of his pose.

"Sunday is a fixed star," he said.

"You shall see him a falling star," said Syme, and put on his hat.

The decision of his gesture drew the Professor vaguely to his feet.

"Have you any idea," he asked, with a sort of benevolent bewilderment, "exactly where you are going?"

"Yes," replied Syme shortly, "I am going to prevent this bomb being thrown in Paris."

"Have you any conception how?" inquired the other.

"No," said Syme with equal decision.

"You remember, of course," resumed the soi-disant de Worms, pulling his beard and looking out of the window, "that when we broke up rather hurriedly the whole arrangements for the atrocity were left in the private hands of the Marquis and Dr. Bull. The Marquis is by this time probably crossing the Channel. But where he will go and what he will do it is doubtful whether even the President knows; certainly we don't. The only man who does know is Dr. Bull."

"Confound it!" cried Syme. "And we don't know where he is."

"Yes," said the other in his curious, absent-minded way, "I know where he is myself."

"Will you tell me?" asked Syme with eager eyes.

"I will take you there," said the Professor, and took down his own hat from a peg.

Syme stood looking at him with a sort of rigid excitement.

"What do you mean?" he asked sharply. "Will you join me? Will you take the risk?"

"Young man," said the Professor pleasantly, "I am amused to observe that you think I am a coward. As to that I will say only one word, and that shall be entirely in the manner of your own philosophical rhetoric. You think that it is possible to pull down the President. I know that it is impossible, and I am going to try it," and opening the tavern door, which let in a blast of bitter air, they went out together into the dark streets by the docks.

Most of the snow was melted or trampled to mud, but here and there a clot of it still showed grey rather than white in the gloom. The small streets were sloppy and full of pools, which reflected the flaming lamps irregularly, and by accident, like fragments of some other and fallen world. Syme felt almost dazed as he stepped through this growing confusion of lights and shadows; but his companion walked on with a certain briskness towards where, at the end of the street, an inch or two of the lamplit river looked like a bar of flame.

"Where are you going?" Syme inquired.

"Just now," answered the Professor, "I am going just round the corner to see whether Dr. Bull has gone to bed. He is hygienic, and retires early."

"Dr. Bull!" exclaimed Syme. "Does he live round the corner?"

"No," answered his friend. "As a matter of fact he lives some way off, on the other side of the river, but we can tell from here whether he has gone to bed."

Turning the corner as he spoke, and facing the dim river, flecked with flame, he pointed with his stick to the other bank. On the Surrey side at this point there ran out into the Thames, seeming almost to overhang it, a bulk and cluster of those tall tenements, dotted with lighted windows, and rising like factory chimneys to an almost insane height. Their special poise and position made one block of buildings especially look like a Tower of Babel with a hundred eyes. Syme had never seen any of the sky-scraping buildings in America, so he could only think of the buildings in a dream.

Even as he stared, the highest light in this innumerably lighted turret abruptly went out, as if this black Argus had winked at him with one of his innumerable eyes.

Professor de Worms swung round on his heel, and struck his stick against his boot.

"We are too late," he said, "the hygienic Doctor has gone to bed."

"What do you mean?" asked Syme. "does he live over there, then?"

"Yes," said de Worms, "behind that particular window which you can't see. Come along and get some dinner. We must call on him to-morrow morning."

Without further parley, he led the way through several by-ways until they came out into the flare and clamour of the East India Dock Road. The Professor, who seemed to know his way about the neighbourhood, proceeded to a place where the line of lighted shops fell back into a sort of abrupt twilight and quiet, in which an old white inn, all out of repair, stood back some twenty feet from the road.

"You can find good English inns left by accident everywhere, like fossils," explained the Professor. "I once found a decent place in the West End."

"I suppose," said Syme, smiling, "that this is the corresponding decent place in the East End?"

"It is," said the Professor reverently, and went in. In that place they dined and slept, both very thoroughly. The beans and bacon, which these unaccountable people cooked well, the astonishing emergence of Burgundy from their cellars, crowned Syme's sense of a new comradeship and comfort. Through all this ordeal his root horror had been isolation, and there are no words to express the abyss between isolation and having one ally. It may be conceded to the mathematicians that four is twice two. But two is not twice one; two is two thousand times one. That is why, in spite of a hundred disadvantages, the world will always return to monogamy.

Syme was able to pour out for the first time the whole of his outrageous tale, from the time when Gregory had taken him to the little tavern by the river. He did it idly and amply, in a luxuriant monologue, as a man speaks with very old friends. On his side, also, the man who had impersonated Professor de Worms was not less communicative. His own story was almost as silly as Syme's.

"That's a good get-up of yours," said Syme, draining a glass of Macon; "a lot better than old Gogol's. Even at the start I thought he was a bit too hairy."

"A difference of artistic theory," replied the Professor pensively. "Gogol was an idealist. He made up as the abstract or platonic ideal of an anarchist. But I am a realist. I am a portrait painter. But, indeed, to say that I am a portrait painter is an inadequate expression. I am a portrait."

"I don't understand you," said Syme.

"I am a portrait," repeated the Professor. "I am a portrait of the celebrated Professor de Worms, who is, I believe, in Naples."

"You mean you are made up like him," said Syme. "But doesn't he know that you are taking his nose in vain?"

"He knows it right enough," replied his friend cheerfully.

"Then why doesn't he denounce you?"

"I have denounced him," answered the Professor.

"Do explain yourself," said Syme.

"With pleasure, if you don't mind hearing my story," replied the eminent foreign philosopher. "I am by profession an actor, and my name is Wilks. When I was on the stage I mixed with all sorts of Bohemian and blackguard company. Sometimes I touched the edge of the turf, sometimes the riffraff of the arts, and occasionally the political refugee. In some den of exiled dreamers I was introduced to the great German Nihilist philosopher, Professor de Worms. I did not gather much about him beyond his appearance, which was very disgusting, and which I studied carefully. I understood that he had proved that the destructive principle in the universe was God; hence he insisted on the need for a furious and incessant energy, rending all things in pieces. Energy, he said, was the All. He was lame, short-sighted, and partially paralytic. When I met him I was in a frivolous mood, and I disliked him so much that I resolved to imitate him. If I had been a draughtsman I would have drawn a caricature. I was only an actor, I could only act a caricature. I made myself up into what was meant for a wild exaggeration of the old Professor's dirty old self. When I went into the room full of his supporters I expected to be received with a roar of laughter, or (if they were too far gone) with a roar of indignation at the insult. I cannot describe the surprise I felt when my entrance was received with a respectful silence, followed (when I had first opened my lips) with a murmur of admiration. The curse of the perfect artist had fallen upon me. I had been too subtle, I had been too true. They thought I really was the great Nihilist Professor. I was a healthy-minded young man at the time, and I confess that it was a blow. Before I could fully recover, however, two or three of these admirers ran up to me radiating indignation, and told me that a public insult had been put upon me in the next room. I inquired its nature. It seemed that an impertinent fellow had dressed himself up as a preposterous parody of myself. I had drunk more champagne than was good for me, and in a flash of folly I decided to see the situation through. Consequently it was to meet the glare of the company and my own lifted eyebrows and freezing eyes that the real Professor came into the room.

"I need hardly say there was a collision. The pessimists all round me looked anxiously from one Professor to the other Professor to see which was really the more feeble. But I won. An old man in poor health, like my rival, could not be expected to be so impressively feeble as a young actor in the prime of life. You see, he really had paralysis, and working within this definite limitation, he couldn't be so jolly paralytic as I was. Then he tried to blast my claims intellectually. I countered that by a very simple dodge. Whenever he said something that nobody but he could understand, I replied with something which I could not even understand myself. 'I don't fancy,' he said, 'that you could have worked out the principle that evolution is only negation, since there inheres in it the introduction of lacunæ, which are an essential of differentiation.' I replied quite scornfully, 'You read all that up in Pinckwerts; the notion that involution functioned eugenically was exposed long ago by Glumpe.' It is unnecessary for me to say that there never were such people as Pinckwerts and Glumpe. But the people all round (rather to my surprise) seemed to remember them quite well, and the Professor, finding that the learned and mysterious method left him rather at the mercy of an enemy slightly deficient in scruples, fell back upon a more popular form of wit. 'I see,' he sneered, 'you prevail like the false pig in Æsop.' 'And you fail,' I answered, smiling, 'like the hedgehog in Montaigne.' Need I say that there is no hedgehog in Montaigne? 'Your claptrap comes off,' he said; 'so would your beard.' I had no intelligent answer to this, which was quite true and rather witty. But I laughed heartily, answered, 'Like the Pantheist's boots,' at random, and turned on my heel with all the honours of victory. The real Professor was thrown out, but not with violence, though one man tried very patiently to pull off his nose. He is now, I believe, received everywhere in Europe as a delightful impostor. His apparent earnestness and anger, you see, make him all the more entertaining."

"Well," said Syme, "I can understand your putting on his dirty old beard for a night's practical joke, but I don't understand your never taking it off again."

"That is the rest of the story," said the impersonator. "When I myself left the company, followed by reverent applause, I went limping down the dark street, hoping that I should soon be far enough away to be able to walk like a human being. To my astonishment, as I was turning the corner, I felt a touch on the shoulder, and turning, found myself under the shadow of an enormous policeman. He told me I was wanted. I struck a sort of paralytic attitude, and cried in a high German accent, 'Yes, I am wanted—by the oppressed of the world. You are arresting me on the charge of being the great anarchist, Professor de Worms.' The policeman impassively consulted a paper in his hand. 'No, sir,' he said civilly, 'at least, not exactly sir. I am arresting you on the charge of not being the celebrated anarchist, Professor de Worms.' This charge, if it was criminal at all, was certainly the lighter of the two, and I went along with the man, doubtful, but not greatly dismayed. I was shown into a number of rooms, and eventually into the presence of a police officer, who explained that a serious campaign had been opened against the centres of anarchy, and that this, my successful masquerade, might be of considerable value to the public safety. He offered me a good salary and this little blue card. Though our conversation was short, he struck me as a man of very massive common sense and humour; but I cannot tell you much about him personally, because——"

Syme laid down his knife and fork.

"I know," he said, "because you talked to him in a dark room."

Professor de Worms nodded and drained his glass.

IX

THE MAN IN SPECTACLES

"BURGUNDY IS a jolly thing," said the Professor sadly, as he set his glass down.

"You don't look as if it were," said Syme; "you drink it as if it were medicine."

"You must excuse my manner," said the Professor dismally, "my position is rather a curious one. Inside I am really bursting with boyish merriment; but I acted the paralytic Professor so well, that now I can't leave off. So that when I am among friends, and have no need at all to disguise myself, I still can't help speaking slow and wrinkling my forehead—just as if it were my forehead. I can be quite happy, you understand, but only in a paralytic sort of way. The most buoyant exclamations leap up in my heart, but they come out of my mouth quite different. You should hear me say, 'Buck up, old cock!' it would bring tears to your eyes."

"It does," said Syme; "but I cannot help thinking that apart from all that you are really a bit worried."

The Professor started a little and looked at him steadily.

"You are a very clever fellow," he said, "it is a pleasure to work with you. Yes, I have rather a heavy cloud in my head. There is a great problem to face," and he sank his bald brow in his two hands.

Then he said in a low voice—

"Can you play the piano?"

"Yes," said Syme in simple wonder, "I'm supposed to have a good touch."

Then, as the other did not speak, he added—

"I trust the great cloud is lifted."

After a long silence, the Professor said out of the cavernous shadow of his hands—

"It would have done just as well if you could work a typewriter."

"Thank you," said Syme, "you flatter me."

"Listen to me," said the other, "and remember whom we have to see to-morrow. You and I are going to-morrow to attempt something which is very much more dangerous than trying to steal the Crown Jewels out of the Tower. We are trying to steal a secret from a very sharp, very strong, and very wicked man. I believe there is no man, except the President, of course, who is so seriously startling and formidable as that little grinning fellow in goggles. He has not perhaps the white-hot enthusiasm unto death, the mad martyrdom for anarchy, which marks the Secretary. But then that very fanaticism in the Secretary has a human pathos, and is almost a redeeming trait. But the little Doctor has a brutal sanity that is more shocking than the Secretary's disease. Don't you notice his detestable virility and vitality? He bounces like an india-rubber ball. Depend on it, Sunday was not asleep (I wonder if he ever sleeps?) when he locked up all the plans of this outrage in the round, black head of Dr. Bull."

"And you think," said Syme, "that this unique monster will be soothed if I play the piano to him?"

"Don't be an ass," said his mentor. "I mentioned the piano because it gives one quick and independent fingers. Syme, if we are to go through this interview and come out sane or alive, we must have some code of signals between us that this brute will not see. I have made a rough alphabetical cypher corresponding to the five fingers—like this, see," and he rippled with his fingers on the wooden table—"B A D, bad, a word we may frequently require."

Syme poured himself out another glass of wine, and began to study the scheme. He was abnormally quick with his brains at puzzles, and with his hands at conjuring, and it did not take him long to learn how he might convey simple messages by what would seem to be idle taps upon a table or knee. But wine and companionship had always the effect of inspiring him to a farcical ingenuity, and the Professor soon found himself struggling with the too vast energy of the new language, as it passed through the heated brain of Syme.

"We must have several word-signs," said Syme seriously—"words that we are likely to want, fine shades of meaning. My favourite word is 'coeval.' What's yours?"

"Do stop playing the goat," said the Professor plaintively. "You don't know how serious this is."

" 'Lush,' too," said Syme, shaking his head sagaciously, "we must have 'lush,'—word applied to grass, don't you know?"

"Do you imagine," asked the Professor furiously, "that we are going to talk to Dr. Bull about grass?"

"There are several ways in which the subject could be approached," said Syme reflectively, "and the word introduced without appearing forced. We might say, 'Dr. Bull, as a revolutionist, you remember that a tyrant once advised us to eat grass; and indeed many of us, looking on the fresh lush grass of summer——' "

"Do you understand," said the other, "that this is a tragedy?"

"Perfectly," replied Syme; "always be comic in a tragedy. What the deuce else can you do? I wish this language of yours had a wider scope. I suppose we could not extend it from the fingers to the toes? That would involve pulling off our boots and socks during the conversation, which however unobtrusively performed——"

"Syme," said his friend with a stern simplicity, "go to bed!"

Syme, however, sat up in bed for a considerable time mastering the new code. He was awakened next morning while the east was still sealed with darkness, and found his grey-bearded ally standing like a ghost beside his bed.

Syme sat up in bed blinking; then slowly collected his thoughts, threw off the bedclothes, and stood up. It seemed to him in some curious way that all the safety and sociability of the night before fell with the bedclothes off him, and he stood up in an air of cold danger. He still felt an entire trust and loyalty towards his companion; but it was the trust between two men going to the scaffold.

"Well," said Syme with a forced cheerfulness as he pulled on his trousers, "I dreamt of that alphabet of yours. Did it take you long to make it up?"

The Professor made no answer, but gazed in front of him with eyes the colour of a wintry sea; so Syme repeated his question.

"I say, did it take you long to invent all this? I'm considered good at these things, and it was a good hour's grind. Did you learn it all on the spot?"

The Professor was silent; his eyes were wide open, and he wore a fixed but very small smile.

"How long did it take you?"

The Professor did not move.

"Confound you, can't you answer?" called out Syme, in a sudden anger that had something like fear underneath. Whether or no the Professor could answer, he did not.

Syme stood staring back at the stiff face like parchment and the blank, blue eyes. His first thought was that the Professor had gone mad, but his second thought was more frightful. After all, what did he know about this queer creature whom he had heedlessly accepted as a friend? What did he know, except that the man had been at the anarchist breakfast and had told him a ridiculous tale? How improbable it was that there should be another friend there beside Gogol! Was this man's silence a sensational way of declaring war? Was this adamantine stare after all only the awful sneer of some threefold traitor, who had turned for the last time? He stood and strained his ears in this heartless silence. He almost fancied he could hear dynamiters come to capture him shifting softly in the corridor outside.

Then his eye strayed downwards, and he burst out laughing. Though the Professor himself stood there as voiceless as a statue, his five dumb fingers were dancing alive upon the dead table. Syme watched the twinkling movements of the talking hand, and read clearly the message—

"I will only talk like this. We must get used to it."

He rapped out the answer with the impatience of relief—

"All right. Let's get out to breakfast."

They took their hats and sticks in silence; but as Syme took his sword-stick, he held it hard.

They paused for a few minutes only to stuff down coffee and coarse thick sandwiches at a coffee stall, and then made their way across the river, which under the grey and growing light looked as desolate as Acheron. They reached the bottom of the huge block of buildings which they had seen from across the river, and began in silence to mount the naked and numberless stone steps, only pausing now and then to make short remarks on the rail of the banisters. At about every other flight they passed a window; each window showed them a pale and tragic dawn lifting itself laboriously over London. From each the innumerable roofs of slate looked like the leaden surges of a grey, troubled sea after rain. Syme was increasingly conscious that his new adventure had somehow a quality of cold sanity worse than the wild adventures of the past. Last night, for instance, the tall tenements had seemed to him like a tower in a dream. As he now went up the weary and perpetual steps, he was daunted and bewildered by their almost infinite series. But it was not the hot horror of a dream or of anything that might be exaggeration or delusion. Their infinity was more like the empty infinity of arithmetic, something unthinkable, yet necessary to thought. Or it was like the stunning statements of astronomy about the distance of the fixed stars. He was ascending the house of reason, a thing more hideous than unreason itself.

By the time they reached Dr. Bull's landing, a last window showed them a harsh, white dawn edged with banks of a kind of coarse red, more like red clay than red cloud. And when they entered Dr. Bull's bare garret it was full of light.

Syme had been haunted by a half historic memory in connection with these empty rooms and that austere daybreak. The moment he saw the garret and Dr. Bull sitting writing at a table, he remembered what the memory was—the French Revolution. There should have been the black outline of a guillotine against that heavy red and white of the morning. Dr. Bull was in his white shirt and black breeches only; his cropped, dark head might well have just come out of its wig; he might have been Marat or a more slipshod Robespierre.

Yet when he was seen properly, the French fancy fell away. The Jacobins were idealists; there was about this man a murderous materialism. His position gave him a somewhat new appearance. The strong, white light of morning coming from one side creating sharp shadows, made him seem both more pale and more angular than he had looked at the breakfast on the balcony. Thus the two black glasses that encased his eyes might really have been black cavities in his skull, making him look like a death's-head. And indeed, if ever Death himself sat writing at a wooden table, it might have been he.

He looked up and smiled brightly enough as the men came in, and rose with the resilient rapidity of which the Professor had spoken. He set chairs for both of them, and going to a peg behind the door, proceeded to put on a coat and waistcoat of rough, dark tweed; he buttoned it up neatly, and came back to sit down at his table.

The quiet good humour of his manner left his two opponents helpless. It was with some momentary difficulty that the Professor broke silence and began, "I'm sorry to disturb you so early, comrade," said he, with a careful resumption of the slow de Worms manner. "You have no doubt made all the arrangements for the Paris affair?" Then he added with infinite slowness, "We have information which renders intolerable anything in the nature of a moment's delay."

Dr. Bull smiled again, but continued to gaze on them without speaking. The Professor resumed, a pause before each weary word—

"Please do not think me excessively abrupt; but I advise you to alter those plans, or if it is too late for that, to follow your agent with all the support you can get for him. Comrade Syme and I have had an experience which it would take more time to recount than we can afford, it we are to act on it. I will, however, relate the occurrence in detail, even at the risk of losing time, if you really feel that it is essential to the understanding of the problem we have to discuss."

He was spinning out his sentences, making them intolerably long and lingering, in the hope of maddening the practical little Doctor into an explosion of impatience which might show his hand. But the little Doctor continued only to stare and smile, and the monologue was uphill work. Syme began to feel a new sickness and despair. The Doctor's smile and silence were not at all like the cataleptic stare and horrible silence which he had confronted in the Professor half an hour before. About the Professor's make-up and all his antics there was always something merely grotesque, like a gollywog. Syme remembered those wild woes of yesterday as one remembers being afraid of Bogy in childhood. But here was daylight: here was a healthy, square-shouldered man in tweeds, not odd save for the accident of his ugly spectacles, not glaring or grinning at all, but smiling steadily and not saying a word. The whole had a sense of unbearable reality. Under the increasing sunlight the colours of the Doctor's complexion, the pattern of his tweeds, grew and expanded outrageously, as such things grow too important in a realistic novel. But his smile was quite slight, the pose of his head polite; the only uncanny thing was his silence.

"As I say," resumed the Professor, like a man toiling through heavy sand, "the incident that has occurred to us and has led us to ask for information about the Marquis, is one which you may think it better to have narrated; but as it came in the way of Comrade Syme rather than me——"

His words he seemed to be dragging out like words in an anthem; but Syme, who was watching, saw his long fingers rattle quickly on the edge of the crazy table. He read the message, "You must go on. This devil has sucked me dry!"

Syme plunged into the breach with that bravado of improvisation which always came to him when he was alarmed.

"Yes, the thing really happened to me," he said hastily. "I had the good fortune to fall into conversation with a detective who took me, thanks to my hat, for a respectable person. Wishing to clinch my reputation for respectability, I took him and made him very drunk at the Savoy. Under this influence he became friendly, and told me in so many words that within a day or two they hope to arrest the Marquis in France. So unless you or I can get on his track——"

The Doctor was still smiling in the most friendly way, and his protected eyes were still impenetrable. The Professor signalled to Syme that he would resume his explanation, and he began again with the same elaborate calm.

"Syme immediately brought this information to me, and we came here together to see what use you would be inclined to make of it. It seems to me unquestionably urgent that——"

All this time Syme had been staring at the Doctor almost as steadily as the Doctor stared at the Professor, but quite without the smile. The nerves of both comrades-in-arms were near snapping under that strain of motionless amiability, when Syme suddenly leant forward and idly tapped the edge of the table. His message to his ally ran, "I have an intuition."

The Professor, with scarcely a pause in his monologue, signalled back, "Then sit on it."

Syme telegraphed, "It is quite extraordinary."

The other answered, "Extraordinary rot!"

Syme said, "I am a poet."

The other retorted, "You are a dead man."

Syme had gone quite red up to his yellow hair, and his eyes were burning feverishly. As he said, he had an intuition, and it had risen to a sort of light-headed certainty. Resuming his symbolic taps, he signalled to his friend, "You scarcely realise how poetic my intuition is. It has that sudden quality we sometimes feel in the coming of spring."

He then studied the answer on his friend's fingers. The answer was, "Go to hell!"

The Professor then resumed his merely verbal monologue addressed to the Doctor.

"Perhaps I should rather say," said Syme on his fingers, "that it resembles that sudden smell of the sea which may be found in the heart of lush woods."

His companion disdained to reply.

"Or yet again," tapped Syme, "it is positive, as is the passionate red hair of a beautiful woman."

The Professor was continuing his speech, but in the middle of it Syme decided to act. He leant across the table, and said in a voice that could not be neglected—

"Dr. Bull!"

The Doctor's sleek and smiling head did not move, but they could have sworn that under his dark glasses his eyes darted towards Syme.

"Dr. Bull," said Syme, in a voice peculiarly precise and courteous, "would you do me a small favour? Would you be so kind as to take off your spectacles?"

The Professor swung round on his seat, and stared at Syme with a sort of frozen fury of astonishment. Syme, like a man who has thrown his life and fortune on the table, leaned forward with a fiery face. The Doctor did not move.

For a few seconds there was a silence in which one could hear a pin drop, split once by the single hoot of a distant steamer on the Thames. Then Dr. Bull rose slowly, still smiling, and took off his spectacles.

Syme sprang to his feet, stepping backwards a little, like a chemical lecturer from a successful explosion. His eyes were like stars, and for an instant he could only point without speaking.

The Professor had also started to his feet, forgetful of his supposed paralysis. He leant on the back of the chair and stared doubtfully at Dr. Bull, as if the Doctor had been turned into a toad before his eyes. And indeed it was almost as great a transformation scene.

The two detectives saw sitting in the chair before them a very boyish-looking young man, with very frank and happy hazel eyes, an open expression, cockney clothes like those of a city clerk, and an unquestionable breath about him of being very good and rather commonplace. The smile was still there, but it might have been the first smile of a baby.

"I knew I was a poet," cried Syme in a sort of ecstasy. "I knew my intuition was as infallible as the Pope. It was the spectacles that did it! It was all the spectacles! Given those beastly black eyes, and all the rest of him, his health and his jolly looks, made him a live devil among dead ones."

"It certainly does make a queer difference," said the Professor shakily. "But as regards the project of Dr. Bull——"

"Project be damned!" roared Syme, beside himself. "Look at him! Look at his face, look at his collar, look at his blessed boots! You don't suppose, do you, that that thing's an anarchist?"

"Syme!" cried the other in an apprehensive agony.

"Why, by God," said Syme, "I'll take the risk of that myself! Dr. Bull, I am a police officer. There's my card," and he flung down the blue card upon the table.

The Professor still feared that all was lost; but he was loyal. He pulled out his own official card and put it beside his friend's. Then the third man burst out laughing, and for the first time that morning they heard his voice.

"I'm awfully glad you chaps have come so early," he said, with a sort of schoolboy flippancy, "for we can all start for France together. Yes, I'm in the force right enough," and he flicked a blue card towards them lightly as a matter of form.

Clapping a brisk bowler on his head and resuming his goblin glasses, the Doctor moved so quickly towards the door, that the others instinctively followed him. Syme seemed a little distrait, and as he passed under the doorway he suddenly struck his stick on the stone passage so that it rang.

"But Lord God Almighty," he cried out, "if this is all right, there were more damned detectives than there were damned dynamiters at the damned Council!"

"We might have fought easily," said Bull; "we were four against three."

The Professor was descending the stairs, but his voice came up from below.

"No," said the voice, "we were not four against three—we were not so lucky. We were four against One."

The others went down the stairs in silence.

The young man called Bull, with an innocent courtesy characteristic of him, insisted on going last until they reached the street; but there his own robust rapidity asserted itself unconsciously, and he walked quickly on ahead towards a railway inquiry office, talking to the others over his shoulder.

"It is jolly to get some pals," he said. "I've been half dead with the jumps, being quite alone. I nearly flung my arms round Gogol and embraced him, which would have been imprudent. I hope you won't despise me for having been in a blue funk."

"All the blue devils in blue hell," said Syme, "contributed to my blue funk! But the worst devil was you and your infernal goggles."

The young man laughed delightedly.

"Wasn't it a rag?" he said. "Such a simple idea—not my own. I haven't got the brains. You see, I wanted to go into the detective service, especially the anti-dynamite business. But for that purpose they wanted some one to dress up as a dynamiter; and they all swore by blazes that I could never look like a dynamiter. They said my very walk was respectable, and that seen from behind I looked like the British Constitution. They said I looked too healthy and too optimistic, and too reliable and benevolent; they called me all sorts of names at Scotland Yard. They said that if I had been a criminal, I might have made my fortune by looking so like an honest man; but as I had the misfortune to be an honest man, there was not even the remotest chance of my assisting them by ever looking like a criminal. But at last I was brought before some old josser who was high up in the force, and who seemed to have no end of a head on his shoulders. And there the others all talked hopelessly. One asked whether a bushy beard would hide my nice smile; another said that if they blacked my face I might look like a negro anarchist; but this old chap chipped in with a most extraordinary remark. 'A pair of smoked spectacles will do it,' he said positively. 'Look at him now; he looks like an angelic office boy. Put him on a pair of smoked spectacles, and children will scream at the sight of him.' And so it was, by George! When once my eyes were covered all the rest, smile and big shoulders and short hair, made me look a perfect little devil. As I say, it was simple enough when it was done, like miracles; but that wasn't the really miraculous part of it. There was one really staggering thing about the business, and my head still turns at it."

"What was that?" asked Syme.

"I'll tell you," answered the man in spectacles. "This big pot in the police who sized me up so that he knew how the goggles would go with my hair and socks—by God, he never saw me at all!"

Syme's eyes suddenly flashed on him.

"How was that?" he asked. "I thought you talked to him."

"So I did," said Bull brightly; "but we talked in a pitch-dark room like a coal cellar. There, you would never have guessed that."

"I could not have conceived it," said Syme gravely.

"It is indeed a new idea," said the Professor.

Their new ally was in practical matters a whirlwind. At the inquiry office he asked with businesslike brevity about the trains for Dover. Having got his information, he bundled the company into a cab, and put them and himself inside a railway carriage before they had properly realised the breathless process. They were already on the Calais boat before conversation flowed freely.

"I had already arranged," he explained, "to go to France for my lunch; but I am delighted to have some one to lunch with me. You see, I had to send that beast, the Marquis, over with his bomb, because the President had his eye on me, though God knows how.

I'll tell you the story some day. It was perfectly choking. Whenever I tried to slip out of it I saw the President somewhere, smiling out of the bow-window of a club or taking off his hat to me from the top of an omnibus. I tell you, you can say what you like, that fellow sold himself to the devil; he can be in six places at once."

"So you sent the Marquis off, I understand," asked the Professor. "Was it long ago? Shall we be in time to catch him?"

"Yes," answered the new guide, "I've timed it all. He'll still be at Calais when we arrive."

"But when we do catch him at Calais," said the Professor, "what are we going to do?"

At this question the countenance of Dr. Bull fell for the first time. He reflected a little, and then said—

"Theoretically, I suppose, we ought to call the police."

"Not I," said Syme. "Theoretically I ought to drown myself first. I promised a poor fellow, who was a real modern pessimist, on my word of honour not to tell the police. I'm no hand at casuistry, but I can't break my word to a modern pessimist. It's like breaking one's word to a child."

"I'm in the same boat," said the Professor. "I tried to tell the police and I couldn't, because of some silly oath I took. You see, when I was an actor I was a sort of all-round beast. Perjury or treason is the only crime I haven't committed. If I did that I shouldn't know the difference between right and wrong."

"I've been through all that," said Dr. Bull, "and I've made up my mind. I gave my promise to the Secretary—you know him, man who smiles upside down. My friends, that man is the most utterly unhappy man that was ever human. It may be his digestion, or his conscience, or his nerves, or his philosophy of the universe, but he's damned, he's in hell! Well, I can't turn on a man like that, and hunt him down. It's like whipping a leper. I may be mad, but that's how I feel; and there's jolly well the end of it."

"I don't think you're mad," said Syme. "I knew you would decide like that when first you——"

"Eh?" said Dr. Bull.

"When first you took off your spectacles."

Dr. Bull smiled a little, and strolled across the deck to look at the sunlit sea. Then he strolled back again, kicking his heels carelessly, and a companionable silence fell between the three men.

"Well," said Syme, "it seems that we have all the same kind of morality or immorality, so we had better face the fact that comes of it."

"Yes," assented the Professor, "you're quite right; and we must hurry up, for I can see the Grey Nose standing out from France."

"The fact that comes of it," said Syme seriously, "is this, that we three are alone on this planet. Gogol has gone, God knows where; perhaps the President has smashed him like a fly. On the Council we are three men against three, like the Romans who held the bridge. But we are worse off than that, first because they can appeal to their organisation and we cannot appeal to ours, and second because——"

"Because one of those other three men," said the Professor, "is not a man."

Syme nodded and was silent for a second or two, then he said—

"My idea is this. We must do something to keep the Marquis in Calais till to-morrow midday. I have turned over twenty schemes in my head. We cannot denounce him as a dynamiter; that is agreed. We cannot get him detained on some trivial charge, for we should have to appear; he knows us, and he would smell a rat. We cannot pretend to keep him on anarchist business; he might swallow much in that way, but not the notion of stopping in Calais while the Czar went safely through Paris. We might try to kidnap him, and lock him up ourselves; but he is a well-known man here. He has a whole body-guard of friends; he is very strong and brave, and the event is doubtful. The only thing I can see to do is actually to take advantage of the very things that are in the Marquis's favour. I am going to profit by the fact that he is a highly respected nobleman. I am going to profit by the fact that he has many friends and moves in the best society."

"What the devil are you talking about?" asked the Professor.

"The Symes are first mentioned in the fourteenth century," said Syme; "but there is a tradition that one of them rode behind Bruce at Bannockburn. Since 1350 the tree is quite clear."

"He's gone off his head," said the little Doctor, staring.

"Our bearings," continued Syme calmly, "are 'argent a chevron gules charged with three cross crosslets of the field.' The motto varies."

The Professor seized Syme roughly by the waistcoat.

"We are just inshore," he said. "Are you seasick or joking in the wrong place?"

"My remarks are almost painfully practical," answered Syme, in an unhurried manner. "The house of St. Eustache also is very ancient. The Marquis cannot deny that he is a gentleman. He cannot deny that I am a gentleman. And in order to put the matter of my social position quite beyond a doubt, I propose at the earliest opportunity to knock his hat off. But here we are in the harbour."

They went on shore under the strong sun in a sort of daze. Syme, who had now taken the lead as Bull had taken it in London, led them along a kind of marine parade until he came to some cafés, embowered in a bulk of greenery and overlooking the sea. As he went before them his step was slightly swaggering, and he swung his stick like a sword. He was making apparently for the extreme end of the line of cafés, but he stopped abruptly. With a sharp gesture he motioned them to silence, but he pointed with one gloved finger to a café table under a bank of flowering foliage at which sat the Marquis de St. Eustache, his teeth shining in his thick, black beard, and his bold, brown face shadowed by a light yellow straw hat and outlined against the violet sea.

X

THE DUEL

SYME SAT down at a café table with his companions, his blue eyes sparkling like the bright sea below, and ordered a bottle of Saumur with a pleased impatience. He was for some reason in a condition of curious hilarity. His spirits were already unnaturally high; they rose as the Saumur sank, and in half an hour his talk was a torrent of nonsense. He professed to be making out a plan of the conversation which was going to ensue between himself and the deadly Marquis. He jotted it down wildly with a pencil. It was arranged like a printed catechism, with questions and answers, and was delivered with an extraordinary rapidity of utterance.

"I shall approach. Before taking off his hat, I shall take off my own. I shall say, 'The Marquis de Saint Eustache, I believe.' He will say, 'The celebrated Mr. Syme, I presume.' He will say in the most exquisite French, 'How are you?' I shall reply in the most exquisite Cockney, 'Oh, just the Syme——' "

"Oh, shut it!" said the man in spectacles. "Pull yourself together, and chuck away that bit of paper. What are you really going to do?"

"But it was a lovely catechism," said Syme pathetically. "Do let me read it you. It has only forty-three questions and answers, and some of the Marquis's answers are wonderfully witty. I like to be just to my enemy."

"But what's the good of it all?" asked Dr. Bull in exasperation.

"It leads up to my challenge, don't you see," said Syme, beaming. "When the Marquis has given the thirty-ninth reply, which runs——"

"Has it by any chance occurred to you," asked the Professor, with a ponderous simplicity, "that the Marquis may not say all the forty-three things you have put down for him? In that case, I understand, your own epigrams may appear somewhat more forced."

Syme struck the table with a radiant face.

"Why, how true that is," he said, "and I never thought of it. Sir, you have an intellect beyond the common. You will make a name."

"Oh, you're as drunk as an owl!" said the Doctor.

"It only remains," continued Syme quite unperturbed, "to adopt some other method of breaking the ice (if I may so express it) between myself and the man I wish to kill. And since the course of a dialogue cannot be predicted by one of its parties alone (as you have pointed out with such recondite acumen), the only thing to be done, I suppose, is for the one party, as far as possible, to do all the dialogue by himself. And so I will, by George!" And he stood up suddenly, his yellow hair blowing in the slight sea breeze.

A band was playing in a *café chantant* hidden somewhere among the trees, and a woman had just stopped singing. On Syme's heated head the bray of the brass band seemed like the jar and jingle of that barrel-organ in Leicester Square, to the tune of which he had once stood up to die. He looked across to the little table where the Marquis sat. The man had two companions now, solemn Frenchmen in frock-coats and silk hats, one of them with the red rosette of the Legion of Honour, evidently people of a solid social position. Beside these black, cylindrical costumes, the Marquis, in his loose straw hat and light spring clothes, looked Bohemian and even barbaric; but he looked the Marquis. Indeed, one might say that he looked the king, with his animal elegance, his scornful eyes, and his proud head lifted against the purple sea. But he was no Christian king, at any rate; he was, rather, some swarthy despot, half Greek, half Asiatic, who in the days when slavery seemed natural looked down on the Mediterranean, on his galley and his groaning slaves. Just so, Syme thought, would the brown-gold face of such a tyrant have shown against the dark green olives and the burning blue.

"Are you going to address the meeting?" asked the Professor peevishly, seeing that Syme still stood up without moving.

Syme drained his last glass of sparkling wine.

"I am," he said, pointing across to the Marquis and his companions, "that meeting. That meeting displeases me. I am going to pull that meeting's great ugly, mahogany-coloured nose."

He stepped across swiftly, if not quite steadily. The Marquis, seeing him, arched his black Assyrian eyebrows in surprise, but smiled politely.

"You are Mr. Syme, I think," he said.

Syme bowed.

"And you are the Marquis de Saint Eustache," he said gracefully. "Permit me to pull your nose."

He leant over to do so, but the Marquis started backwards, upsetting his chair, and the two men in top hats held Syme back by the shoulders.

"This man has insulted me!" said Syme, with gestures of explanation.

"Insulted you?" cried the gentleman with the red rosette, "when?"

"Oh, just now," said Syme recklessly. "He insulted my mother."

"Insulted your mother!" exclaimed the gentleman incredulously.

"Well, anyhow," said Syme, conceding a point, "my aunt."

"But how can the Marquis have insulted your aunt just now?" said the second gentleman with some legitimate wonder. "He has been sitting here all the time."

"Ah, it was what he said!" said Syme darkly.

"I said nothing at all," said the Marquis, "except something about the band. I only said that I liked Wagner played well."

"It was an allusion to my family," said Syme firmly. "My aunt played Wagner badly. It was a painful subject. We are always being insulted about it."

"This seems most extraordinary," said the gentleman who was *décoré*, looking doubtfully at the Marquis.

"Oh, I assure you," said Syme earnestly, "the whole of your conversation was simply packed with sinister allusions to my aunt's weaknesses."

"This is nonsense!" said the second gentleman. "I for one have said nothing for half an hour except that I liked the singing of that girl with black hair."

"Well, there you are again!" said Syme indignantly. "My aunt's was red."

"It seems to me," said the other, "that you are simply seeking a pretext to insult the Marquis."

"By George!" said Syme, facing round and looking at him, "what a clever chap you are!"

The Marquis started up with eyes flaming like a tiger's.

"Seeking a quarrel with me!" he cried. "Seeking a fight with me! By God! there was never a man who had to seek long. These gentlemen will perhaps act for me. There are still four hours of daylight. Let us fight this evening."

Syme bowed with a quite beautiful graciousness.

"Marquis," he said, "your action is worthy of your fame and blood. Permit me to consult for a moment with the gentlemen in whose hands I shall place myself."

In three long strides he rejoined his companions, and they, who had seen his champagne-inspired attack and listened to his idiotic explanations, were quite startled at the look of him. For now that he came back to them he was quite sober, a little pale, and he spoke in a low voice of passionate practicality.

"I have done it," he said hoarsely. "I have fixed a fight on the beast. But look here, and listen carefully. There is no time for talk. You are my seconds, and everything must come from you. Now you must insist, and insist absolutely, on the duel coming off after seven to-morrow, so as to give me the chance of preventing him from catching the 7:45 for Paris. If he misses that he misses his crime. He can't refuse to meet you on such a small point of time and place. But this is what he will do. He will choose a field somewhere near a wayside station, where he can pick up the train. He is a very good swordsman, and he will trust to killing me in time to catch it. But I can fence well too, and I think I can keep him in play, at any rate, until the train is lost. Then perhaps he may kill me to console his feelings. You understand? Very well then, let me introduce you to some charming friends of mine," and leading them quickly across the parade, he presented them to the Marquis's seconds by two very aristocratic names of which they had not previously heard.

Syme was subject to spasms of singular common sense, not otherwise a part of his character. They were (as he said of his impulse about the spectacles) poetic intuitions, and they sometimes rose to the exaltation of prophecy.

He had correctly calculated in this case the policy of his opponent. When the Marquis was informed by his seconds that Syme could only fight in the morning, he must fully have realised that an obstacle had suddenly arisen between him and his bomb-throwing business in the capital. Naturally he could not explain this objection to his friends, so he chose the course which Syme had predicted. He induced his seconds to settle on a small meadow not far from the railway, and he trusted to the fatality of the first engagement.

When he came down very coolly to the field of honour, no one could have guessed that he had any anxiety about a journey; his hands were in his pockets, his straw hat on the back of his head, his handsome face brazen in the sun. But it might have struck a stranger as odd that there appeared in his train, not only his seconds carrying the sword-case, but two of his servants carrying a portmanteau and a luncheon basket.

Early as was the hour, the sun soaked everything in warmth, and Syme was vaguely surprised to see so many spring flowers burning gold and silver in the tall grass in which the whole company stood almost knee-deep.

With the exception of the Marquis, all the men were in sombre and solemn morning-dress, with hats like black chimney-pots; the little Doctor especially, with the addition of his black spectacles, looked like an undertaker in a farce. Syme could not help feeling a comic contrast between this funereal church parade of apparel and the rich and glistening meadow, growing wild flowers everywhere. But, indeed, this comic contrast between the yellow blossoms and the black hats was but a symbol of the tragic contrast between the yellow blossoms and the black business. On his right was a little wood; far away to his left lay the long curve of the railway line, which he was, so to speak, guarding from the Marquis, whose goal and escape it was. In front of him, behind the black group of his opponents, he could see, like a tinted cloud, a small almond bush in flower against the faint line of the sea.

The member of the Legion of Honour, whose name it seemed was Colonel Ducroix, approached the Professor and Dr. Bull with great politeness, and suggested that the play should terminate with the first considerable hurt.

Dr. Bull, however, having been carefully coached by Syme upon this point of policy, insisted, with great dignity and in very bad French, that it should continue until one of the combatants was disabled. Syme had made up his mind that he could avoid disabling the Marquis and prevent the Marquis from disabling him for at least twenty minutes. In twenty minutes the Paris train would have gone by.

"To a man of the well-known skill and valour of Monsieur de St. Eustache," said the Professor solemnly, "it must be a matter of indifference which method is adopted, and our principal has strong reasons for demanding the longer encounter, reasons the delicacy of which prevent me from being explicit, but for the just and honourable nature of which I can——"

"*Peste!*" broke from the Marquis behind, whose face had suddenly darkened, "let us stop talking and begin," and he slashed off the head of a tall flower with his stick.

Syme understood his rude impatience, and instinctively looked over his shoulder to see whether the train was coming in sight. But there was no smoke on the horizon.

Colonel Ducroix knelt down and unlocked the case, taking out a pair of twin swords, which took the sunlight and turned to two streaks of white fire. He offered one to the Marquis, who snatched it without ceremony, and another to Syme, who took it, bent it, and poised it with as much delay as was consistent with dignity. Then the Colonel took out another pair of blades, and taking one himself and giving another to Dr. Bull, proceeded to place the men.

Both combatants had thrown off their coats and waistcoats, and stood sword in hand. The seconds stood on each side of the line of fight with drawn swords also, but still sombre in their dark frock-coats and hats. The principals saluted. The Colonel said quietly, "Engage!" and the two blades touched and tingled.

When the jar of the joined iron ran up Syme's arm, all the fantastic fears that have been the subject of this story fell from him like dreams from a man waking up in bed. He remembered them clearly and in order as mere delusions of the nerves—how the fear of the Professor had been the fear of the tyrannic accidents of nightmare, and how the fear of the Doctor had been the fear of the airless vacuum of science. The first was the old fear that any miracle might happen, the second the more hopeless modern fear that no miracle can ever happen. But he saw that these fears were fancies, for he found himself in the presence of the great fact of the fear of death, with its coarse and pitiless common sense. He felt like a man who had dreamed all night of falling over precipices, and had woke up on the morning when he was to be hanged. For as soon as he had seen the sunlight run down the channel of his foe's foreshortened blade, and as soon as he had felt the two tongues of steel touch, vibrating like two living things, he knew that his enemy was a terrible fighter, and that probably his last hour had come.

He felt a strange and vivid value in all the earth around him, in the grass under his feet; he felt the love of life in all living things. He could almost fancy that he heard the grass growing; he could almost fancy that even as he stood fresh flowers were springing up and breaking into blossom in the meadow—flowers blood-red and burning gold and blue, fulfilling the whole pageant of the spring. And whenever his eyes strayed for a flash from the calm, staring, hypnotic eyes of the Marquis, they saw the little tuft of almond tree against the skyline. He had the feeling that if by some miracle he escaped he would be ready to sit forever before that almond tree, desiring nothing else in the world.

But while earth and sky and everything had the living beauty of a thing lost, the other half of his head was as clear as glass, and he was parrying his enemy's point with a kind of clockwork skill of which he had hardly supposed himself capable. Once his enemy's point ran along his wrist, leaving a slight streak of blood, but it either was not noticed or was tacitly ignored. Every now and then he *riposted,* and once or twice he could almost fancy that he felt his point go home, but as there was no blood on blade or shirt he supposed he was mistaken. Then came an interruption and a change.

At the risk of losing all, the Marquis, interrupting his quiet stare, flashed one glance over his shoulder at the line of railway on his right. Then he turned on Syme a face transfigured to that of a fiend, and began to fight as if with twenty weapons. The attack came so fast and furious, that the one shining sword seemed a shower of shining arrows. Syme had no chance to look at the railway; but also he had no need. He could guess the reason of the Marquis's sudden madness of battle—the Paris train was in sight.

But the Marquis's morbid energy overreached itself. Twice Syme, parrying, knocked his opponent's point far out of the fighting circle; and the third time his *riposte* was so rapid, that there was no doubt about the hit this time. Syme's sword actually bent under the weight of the Marquis's body, which it had pierced. Syme was as certain that he had stuck his blade into his enemy as a gardener that he has stuck his spade into the ground. Yet the Marquis sprang back from the stroke without a stagger, and Syme stood staring at his own sword-point like an idiot. There was no blood on it at all.

There was an instant of rigid silence, and then Syme in his turn fell furiously on the other, filled with a flaming curiosity. The Marquis was probably, in a general sense, a better fencer than he, as he had surmised at the beginning, but at the moment the Marquis seemed distraught and at a disadvantage. He fought wildly and even weakly, and he constantly looked away at the railway line, almost as if he feared the train more than the pointed steel. Syme, on the other hand, fought fiercely but still carefully, in an intellectual fury, eager to solve the riddle of his own bloodless sword. For this purpose, he aimed less at the Marquis's body, and more at his throat and head. A minute and a half afterwards he felt his point enter the man's neck below the jaw. It came out clean. Half mad, he thrust again, and made what should have been a bloody scar on the Marquis's cheek. But there was no scar.

For one moment the heaven of Syme again grew black with supernatural terrors. Surely the man had a charmed life. But this new spiritual dread was a more awful thing than had been the mere spiritual topsy-turvydom symbolised by the paralytic who pursued him. The Professor was only a goblin; this man was a devil—perhaps he was the Devil! Anyhow, this was certain, that three times had a human sword been driven into him and made no mark. When Syme had that thought he drew himself up, and all that was good in him sang high up in the air as a high wind sings in the trees. He thought of all the human things in his story—of the Chinese lanterns in Saffron Park, of the girl's red hair in the garden, of the honest, beer-swilling sailors down by the dock, of his loyal companions standing by. Perhaps he had been chosen as a champion of all these fresh and kindly things to cross swords with the enemy of all creation. "After all," he said to himself, "I am more than a devil; I am a man. I can do the one thing which Satan himself cannot do—I can die," and as the word went through his head, he heard a faint and far-off hoot, which would soon be the roar of the Paris train.

He fell to fighting again with a supernatural levity, like a Mohammedan panting for Paradise. As the train came nearer and nearer he fancied he could see people putting up the floral arches in Paris; he joined in the growing noise and the glory of the great Republic whose gate he was guarding against Hell. His thoughts rose higher and higher with the rising roar of the train, which ended, as if proudly, in a long and piercing whistle. The train stopped.

Suddenly, to the astonishment of every one, the Marquis sprang back quite out of sword reach and threw down his sword. The leap was wonderful, and not the less wonderful because Syme had plunged his sword a moment before into the man's thigh.

"Stop!" said the Marquis in a voice that compelled a momentary obedience. "I want to say something."

"What is the matter?" asked Colonel Ducroix, staring. "Has there been foul play?"

"There has been foul play somewhere," said Dr. Bull, who was a little pale. "Our principal has wounded the Marquis four times at least, and he is none the worse."

The Marquis put up his hand with a curious air of ghastly patience.

"Please let me speak," he said. "It is rather important. Mr. Syme," he continued, turning to his opponent, "we are fighting to-day, if I remember right, because you expressed a wish (which I thought irrational) to pull my nose. Would you oblige me by pulling my nose now as quickly as possible? I have to catch a train."

"I protest that this is most irregular," said Dr. Bull indignantly.

"It is certainly somewhat opposed to precedent," said Colonel Ducroix, looking wistfully at his principal. "There is, I think, one case on record (Captain Bellegarde and the Baron Zumpt) in which the weapons were changed in the middle of the encounter at the request of one of the combatants. But one can hardly call one's nose a weapon."

"Will you or will you not pull my nose?" said the Marquis in exasperation. "Come, come, Mr. Syme! You wanted to do it, do it! You can have no conception of how important it is to me. Don't be so selfish! Pull my nose at once, when I ask you!" and he bent slightly forward with a fascinating smile. The Paris train, panting and groaning, had grated into a little station behind the neighbouring hill.

Syme had the feeling he had more than once had in these adventures—the sense that a horrible and sublime wave lifted to heaven was just toppling over. Walking in a world he half understood, he took two paces forward and seized the Roman nose of this remarkable nobleman. He pulled it hard, and it came off in his hand.

He stood for some seconds with a foolish solemnity, with the pasteboard proboscis still between his fingers, looking at it, while the sun and the clouds and the wooded hills looked down upon this imbecile scene.

The Marquis broke the silence in a loud and cheerful voice.

"If any one has any use for my left eyebrow," he said, "he can have it. Colonel Ducroix, do accept my left eyebrow! It's the kind of thing that might come in useful any day," and he gravely tore off one of his swarthy Assyrian brows, bringing about half his brown forehead with it, and politely offered it to the Colonel, who stood crimson and speechless with rage.

"If I had known," he spluttered, "that I was acting for a poltroon who pads himself to fight——"

"Oh, I know, I know!" said the Marquis, recklessly throwing various parts of himself right and left about the field. "You are making a mistake; but it can't be explained just now. I tell you the train has come into the station!"

"Yes," said Dr. Bull fiercely, "and the train shall go out of the station. It shall go out without you. We know well enough for what devil's work——"

The mysterious Marquis lifted his hands with a desperate gesture. He was a strange scarecrow, standing there in the sun with half his old face peeled off, and half another face glaring and grinning from underneath.

"Will you drive me mad?" he cried. "The train——"

"You shall not go by the train," said Syme firmly, and grasped his sword.

The wild figure turned towards Syme, and seemed to be gathering itself for a sublime effort before speaking.

"You great fat, blasted, blear-eyed, blundering, thundering, brainless, God-forsaken, doddering, damned fool!" he said without taking breath. "You great silly, pink-faced, towheaded turnip! You——"

"You shall not go by this train," repeated Syme.

"And why the infernal blazes," roared the other, "should I want to go by the train?"

"We know all," said the Professor sternly. "You are going to Paris to throw a bomb!"

"Going to Jericho to throw a Jabberwock!" cried the other, tearing his hair, which came off easily. "Have you all got softening of the brain, that you don't realise what I am? Did you really think I wanted to catch that train? Twenty Paris trains might go by for me. Damn Paris trains!"

"Then what did you care about?" began the Professor.

"What did I care about? I didn't care about catching the train; I cared about whether the train caught me, and now, by God! it has caught me."

"I regret to inform you," said Syme with restraint, "that your remarks convey no impression to my mind. Perhaps if you were to remove the remains of your original forehead and some portion of what was once your chin, your meaning would become clearer. Mental lucidity fulfils itself in many ways. What do you mean by saying that the train has caught you? It may be my literary fancy, but somehow I feel that it ought to mean something."

"It means everything," said the other, "and the end of everything. Sunday has us now in the hollow of his hand."

"Us!" repeated the Professor, as if stupefied. "What do you mean by 'us'?"

"The police, of course!" said the Marquis, and tore off his scalp and half his face.

The head which emerged was the blonde, well-brushed, smooth-haired head which is common in the English constabulary, but the face was terribly pale.

"I am Inspector Ratcliffe," he said, with a sort of haste that verged on harshness. "My name is pretty well known to the police, and I can see well enough that you belong to them. But if there is any doubt about my position, I have a card——" and he began to pull a blue card from his pocket.

The Professor gave a tired gesture.

"Oh, don't show it us," he said wearily; "we've got enough of them to equip a paper-chase."

The little man named Bull had, like many men who seem to be of a mere vivacious vulgarity, sudden movements of good taste. Here he certainly saved the situation. In the midst of this staggering transformation scene he stepped forward with all the gravity and responsibility of a second, and addressed the two seconds of the Marquis.

"Gentlemen," he said, "we all owe you a serious apology; but I assure you that you have not been made the victims of such a low joke as you imagine, or indeed of anything undignified in a man of honour. You have not wasted your time; you have helped to save the world. We are not buffoons, but very desperate men at war with a vast conspiracy. A secret society of anarchists is hunting us like hares; not such unfortunate madmen as may here or there throw a bomb through starvation or German philosophy, but a rich and powerful and fanatical church, a church of eastern pessimism, which holds it holy to destroy mankind like vermin. How hard they hunt us you can gather from the fact that we are driven to such disguises as those for which I apologise, and to such pranks as this one by which you suffer."

The younger second of the Marquis, a short man with a black moustache, bowed politely, and said——

"Of course, I accept the apology; but you will in your turn forgive me if I decline to follow you further into your difficulties, and permit myself to say good-morning! The sight of an acquaintance and distinguished fellow-townsman coming to pieces in the open air is unusual, and, upon the whole, sufficient for one day. Colonel Ducroix, I would in no way influence your actions, but if you feel with me that our present society is a little abnormal, I am now going to walk back to the town."

Colonel Ducroix moved mechanically, but then tugged abruptly at his white moustache and broke out—

"No, by George! I won't. If these gentlemen are really in a mess with a lot of low wreckers like that, I'll see them through it. I have fought for France, and it is hard if I can't fight for civilisation."

Dr. Bull took off his hat and waved it, cheering as at a public meeting.

"Don't make too much noise," said Inspector Ratcliffe, "Sunday may hear you."

"Sunday!" cried Bull, and dropped his hat.

"Yes," retorted Ratcliffe, "he may be with them."

"With whom?" asked Syme.

"With the people out of that train," said the other.

"What you say seems utterly wild," began Syme. "Why, as a matter of fact—— But, my God," he cried out suddenly, like a man who sees an explosion a long way off, "by God! if this is true the whole bally lot of us on the Anarchist Council were against anarchy! Every born man was a detective except the President and his personal secretary. What can it mean?"

"Mean!" said the new policeman with incredible violence. "It means that we are struck dead! Don't you know Sunday? Don't you know that his jokes are always so big and simple that one has never thought of them? Can you think of anything more like Sunday than this, that he should put all his powerful enemies on the Supreme Council, and then take care that it was not supreme? I tell you, he has bought every trust, he has captured every cable, he has control of every railway line—especially of *that* railway line!" and he pointed a shaking finger towards the small wayside station. "The whole movement was controlled by him; half the world was ready to rise for him. But there were just five people, perhaps, who would have resisted him. . . and the old devil put them on the Supreme Council, to waste their time in watching each other. Idiots that we are, he planned the whole of our idiocies! Sunday knew that the Professor would chase Syme through London, and that Syme would fight me in France. And he was combining great masses of capital, and seizing great lines of telegraphy, while we five idiots were running after each other like a lot of confounded babies playing blind man's buff."

"Well?" asked Syme with a sort of steadiness.

"Well," replied the other with sudden serenity, "he has found us playing blind man's buff to-day in a field of great rustic beauty and extreme solitude. He has probably captured the world; it only remains to him to capture this field and all the fools in it. And since you really want to know what was my objection to the arrival of that train, I will tell you. My objection was that Sunday or his Secretary has just this moment got out of it."

Syme uttered an involuntary cry, and they all turned their eyes towards the far-off station. It was quite true that a considerable bulk of people seemed to be moving in their direction. But they were too distant to be distinguished in any way.

"It was a habit of the late Marquis de St. Eustache," said the new policeman, producing a leather case, "always to carry a pair of opera-glasses. Either the President or the Secretary is coming after us with that mob. They have caught us in a nice quiet place where we are under no temptations to break our oaths by calling the police. Dr. Bull, I have a suspicion that you will see better through these than through your own highly decorative spectacles."

He handed the field-glasses to the Doctor, who immediately took off his spectacles and put the apparatus to his eyes.

"It cannot be as bad as you say," said the Professor, somewhat shaken. "There are a good number of them certainly, but they may easily be ordinary tourists."

"Do ordinary tourists," asked Bull, with the field-glasses to his eyes, "wear black masks half-way down the face?"

Syme almost tore the glasses out of his hand, and looked through them. Most men in the advancing mob really looked ordinary enough; but it was quite true that two or three of the leaders in front wore black half-masks almost down to their mouths. This disguise is very complete, especially at such a distance, and Syme found it impossible to conclude anything from the clean-shaven jaws and chins of the men talking in the front. But presently as they talked they all smiled, and one of them smiled on one side.

XI

THE CRIMINALS CHASE THE POLICE

SYME PUT the field-glasses from his eyes with an almost ghastly relief.

"The President is not with them, anyhow," he said, and wiped his forehead.

"But surely they are right away on the horizon," said the bewildered Colonel, blinking and but half recovered from Bull's hasty though polite explanation. "Could you possibly know your President among all those people?"

"Could I know a white elephant among all those people!" answered Syme somewhat irritably. "As you very truly say, they are on the horizon; but if he were walking with them . . . by God! I believe this ground would shake."

After an instant's pause the new man called Ratcliffe said with gloomy decision—

"Of course the President isn't with them. I wish to Gemini he were. Much more likely the President is riding in triumph through Paris, or sitting on the ruins of St. Paul's Cathedral."

"This is absurd!" said Syme. "Something may have happened in our absence; but he cannot have carried the world with a rush like that. It is quite true," he added, frowning dubiously at the distant fields that lay towards the little station, "it is certainly true that there seems to be a crowd coming this way; but they are not all the army that you make out."

"Oh, they," said the new detective contemptuously; "no, they are not a very valuable force. But let me tell you frankly that they are precisely calculated to our value—we are not much, my boy, in Sunday's universe. He has got hold of all the cables and telegraphs himself. But to kill the Supreme Council he regards as a trivial matter, like a post-card; it may be left to his private secretary," and he spat on the grass.

Then he turned to the others and said somewhat austerely—

"There is a great deal to be said for death; but if any one has any preference for the other alternative, I strongly advise him to walk after me."

With these words, he turned his broad back and strode with silent energy towards the wood. The others gave one glance over their shoulders, and saw that the dark cloud of men had detached itself from the station and was moving with a mysterious discipline across the plain. They saw already, even with the naked eye, black blots on the foremost faces, which marked the masks they wore. They turned and followed their leader, who had already struck the wood, and disappeared among the twinkling trees.

The sun on the grass was dry and hot. So in plunging into the wood they had a cool shock of shadow, as of divers who plunge into a dim pool. The inside of the wood was full of shattered sunlight and shaken shadows. They made a sort of shuddering veil, almost recalling the dizziness of a cinematograph. Even the solid figures walking with him Syme could hardly see for the patterns of sun and shade that danced upon them. Now a man's head was lit as with a light of Rembrandt, leaving all else obliterated; now again he had strong and staring white hands with the face of a negro. The ex-Marquis had pulled the old straw hat over his eyes, and the black shade of the brim cut his face so squarely in two that it seemed to be wearing one of the black half-masks of their pursuers. The fancy tinted Syme's overwhelming sense of wonder. Was he wearing a mask? Was any one wearing a mask? Was any one anything? This wood of witchery, in which men's faces turned black and white by turns, in which their figures first swelled into sunlight and then faded into formless night, this mere chaos of chiaroscuro (after the clear daylight outside), seemed to Syme a perfect symbol of the world in which he had been moving for three days, this world where men took off their beards and their spectacles and their noses, and turned into other people. That tragic self-confidence which he had felt when he believed that the Marquis was a devil had strangely disappeared now that he knew that the Marquis was a friend. He felt almost inclined to ask after all these bewilderments what was a friend and what an enemy. Was there anything that was apart from what it seemed? The Marquis had taken off his nose and turned out to be a detective.

Might he not just as well take off his head and turn out to be a hobgoblin? Was not everything, after all, like this bewildering woodland, this dance of dark and light? Everything only a glimpse, the glimpse always unforeseen, and always forgotten. For Gabriel Syme had found in the heart of that sun-splashed wood what many modern painters had found there. He had found the thing which the modern people call Impressionism, which is another name for that final scepticism which can find no floor to the universe.

As a man in an evil dream strains himself to scream and wake, Syme strove with a sudden effort to fling off this last and worst of his fancies. With two impatient strides he overtook the man in the Marquis's straw hat, the man whom he had come to address as Ratcliffe. In a voice exaggeratively loud and cheerful, he broke the bottomless silence and made conversation.

"May I ask," he said, "where on earth we are all going to?"

So genuine had been the doubts of his soul, that he was quite glad to hear his companion speak in an easy, human voice.

"We must get down through the town of Lancy to the sea," he said. "I think that part of the country is least likely to be with them."

"What can you mean by all this?" cried Syme. "They can't be running the real world in that way. Surely not many working men are anarchists, and surely if they were, mere mobs could not beat modern armies and police."

"Mere mobs!" repeated his new friend with a snort of scorn. "So you talk about mobs and the working classes as if they were the question. You've got that eternal idiotic idea that if anarchy came it would come from the poor. Why should it? The poor have been rebels, but they have never been anarchists; they have more interest than any one else in there being some decent government. The poor man really has a stake in the country. The rich man hasn't; he can go away to New Guinea in a yacht. The poor have sometimes objected to being governed badly; the rich have always objected to being governed at all. Aristocrats were always anarchists, as you can see from the barons' wars."

"As a lecture on English history for the little ones," said Syme, "this is all very nice; but I have not yet grasped its application."

"Its application is," said his informant, "that most of old Sunday's right-hand men are South African and American millionaires. That is why he has got hold of all the communications; and that is why the last four champions of the anti-anarchist police force are running through a wood like rabbits."

"Millionaires I can understand," said Syme thoughtfully, "they are nearly all mad. But getting hold of a few wicked old gentlemen with hobbies is one thing; getting hold of great Christian nations is another. I would bet the nose off my face (forgive the allusion) that Sunday would stand perfectly helpless before the task of converting any ordinary healthy person anywhere."

"Well," said the other, "it rather depends what sort of person you mean."

"Well, for instance," said Syme, "we could never convert that person," and he pointed straight in front of him.

They had come to an open space of sunlight, which seemed to express to Syme the final return of his own good sense; and in the middle of this forest clearing was a figure that might well stand for that common sense in an almost awful actuality. Burnt by the sun and stained with perspiration, and grave with the bottomless gravity of small necessary toils, a heavy French peasant was cutting wood with a hatchet. His cart stood a few yards off, already half full of timber; and the horse that cropped the grass was, like his master, valorous but not desperate; like his master, he was even prosperous, but yet was almost sad. The man was a Norman, taller than the average of the French and very angular; and his swarthy figure stood dark against a square of sunlight, almost like some allegoric figure of labour frescoed on a ground of gold.

"Mr. Syme is saying," called out Ratcliffe to the French Colonel, "that this man, at least, will never be an anarchist."

"Mr. Syme is right enough there," answered Colonel Ducroix, laughing, "if only for the reason that he has plenty of property to defend. But I forgot that in your country you are not used to peasants being wealthy."

"He looks poor," said Dr. Bull doubtfully.

"Quite so," said the Colonel; "that is why he is rich."

"I have an idea," called out Dr. Bull suddenly; "how much would he take to give us a lift in his cart? Those dogs are all on foot, and we could soon leave them behind."

"Oh, give him anything!" said Syme eagerly. "I have piles of money on me."

"That will never do," said the Colonel; "he will never have any respect for you unless you drive a bargain."

"Oh, if he haggles!" began Bull impatiently.

"He haggles because he is a free man," said the other. "You do not understand; he would not see the meaning of generosity. He is not being tipped."

And even while they seemed to hear the heavy feet of their strange pursuers behind them, they had to stand and stamp while the French Colonel talked to the French wood-cutter with all the leisurely badinage and bickering of market-day. At the end of the four minutes, however, they saw that the Colonel was right, for the wood-cutter entered into their plans, not with the vague servility of a tout too-well paid, but with the seriousness of a solicitor who had been paid the proper fee. He told them that the best thing they could do was to make their way down to the little inn on the hills above Lancy, where the innkeeper, an old soldier who had become *dévot* in his latter years, would be certain to sympathise with them, and even to take risks in their support. The whole company, therefore, piled themselves on top of the stacks of wood, and went rocking in the rude cart down the other and steeper side of the woodland. Heavy and ramshackle as was the vehicle, it was driven quickly enough, and they soon had the exhilarating impression of distancing altogether those, whoever they were, who were hunting them. For, after all, the riddle as to where the anarchists had got all these followers was still unsolved. One man's presence had sufficed for them; they had fled at the first sight of the deformed smile of the Secretary. Syme every now and then looked back over his shoulder at the army on their track.

As the wood grew first thinner and then smaller with distance, he could see the sunlit slopes beyond it and above it; and across these was still moving the square black mob like one monstrous beetle. In the very strong sunlight and with his own very strong eyes, which were almost telescopic, Syme could see this mass of men quite plainly. He could see them as separate human figures; but he was increasingly surprised by the way in which they moved as one man. They seemed to be dressed in dark clothes and plain hats, like any common crowd out of the streets; but they did not spread and sprawl and trail by various lines to the attack, as would be natural in an ordinary mob. They moved with a sort of dreadful and wicked woodenness, like a staring army of automatons.

Syme pointed this out to Ratcliffe.

"Yes," replied the policeman, "that's discipline. That's Sunday. He is perhaps five hundred miles off, but the fear of him is on all of them, like the finger of God. Yes, they are walking regularly; and you bet your boots that they are talking regularly, yes, and thinking regularly. But the one important thing for us is that they are disappearing regularly."

Syme nodded. It was true that the black patch of the pursuing men was growing smaller and smaller as the peasant belaboured his horse.

The level of the sunlit landscape, though flat as a whole, fell away on the farther side of the wood in billows of heavy slope towards the sea, in a way not unlike the lower slopes of the Sussex downs. The only difference was that in Sussex the road would have been broken and angular like a little brook, but here the white French road fell sheer in front of them like a waterfall. Down this direct descent the cart clattered at a considerable angle, and in a few minutes, the road growing yet steeper, they saw below them the little harbour of Lancy and a great blue arc of the sea. The travelling cloud of their enemies had wholly disappeared from the horizon.

The horse and cart took a sharp turn around a clump of elms, and the horse's nose nearly struck the face of an old gentleman who was sitting on the benches outside the little café of "Le Soleil d'Or." The peasant grunted an apology, and got down from his seat. The others also descended one by one, and spoke to the old gentleman with fragmentary phrases of courtesy, for it was quite evident from his expansive manner that he was the owner of the little tavern.

He was a white-haired, apple-faced old boy, with sleepy eyes and grey moustache; stout, sedentary, and very innocent, of a type that may often be found in France, but is still commoner in Catholic Germany. Everything about him, his pipe, his pot of beer, his flowers, his beehive, suggested an ancestral peace; only when his visitors looked up as they entered the inn-parlour, they saw the sword upon the wall.

The Colonel, who greeted the innkeeper as an old friend, passed rapidly into the inn-parlour, and sat down ordering some ritual refreshment. The military decision of his action interested Syme, who sat next to him, and he took the opportunity when the old innkeeper had gone out of satisfying his curiosity.

"May I ask you, Colonel," he said in a low voice, "why we have come here?"

Colonel Ducroix smiled behind his bristly white moustache.

"For two reasons, sir," he said; "and I will give first, not the most important, but the most utilitarian. We came here because this is the only place within twenty miles in which we can get horses."

"Horses!" repeated Syme, looking up quickly.

"Yes," replied the other; "if you people are really to distance your enemies it is horses or nothing for you, unless of course you have bicycles and motor-cars in your pocket."

"And where do you advise us to make for?" asked Syme doubtfully.

"Beyond question," replied the Colonel, "you had better make all haste to the police station beyond the town. My friend, whom I seconded under somewhat deceptive circumstances, seems to me to exaggerate very much the possibilities of a general rising; but even he would hardly maintain, I suppose, that you were not safe with the gendarmes."

Syme nodded gravely; then he said abruptly—

"And your other reason for coming here?"

"My other reason for coming here," said Ducroix soberly, "is that it is just as well to see a good man or two when one is possibly near to death."

Syme looked up at the wall, and saw a crudely-painted and pathetic religious picture. Then he said—

"You are right," and then almost immediately afterwards, "Has any one seen about the horses?"

"Yes," answered Ducroix, "you may be quite certain that I gave orders the moment I came in. Those enemies of yours gave no impression of hurry, but they were really moving wonderfully fast, like a well-trained army. I had no idea that the anarchists had so much discipline. You have not a moment to waste."

Almost as he spoke, the old innkeeper with the blue eyes and white hair came ambling into the room, and announced that six horses were saddled outside.

By Ducroix's advice the five others equipped themselves with some portable form of food and wine, and keeping their duelling swords as the only weapons available, they clattered away down the steep, white road. The two servants, who had carried the Marquis's luggage when he was a marquis, were left behind to drink at the café by common consent, and not at all against their own inclination.

By this time the afternoon sun was slanting westward, and by its rays Syme could see the sturdy figure of the old innkeeper growing smaller and smaller, but still standing and looking after them quite silently, the sunshine in his silver hair. Syme had a fixed, superstitious fancy, left in his mind by the chance phrase of the Colonel, that this was indeed, perhaps, the last honest stranger whom he should ever see upon the earth.

He was still looking at this dwindling figure, which stood as a mere grey blot touched with a white flame against the great green wall of the steep down behind him. And as he stared, over the top of the down behind the innkeeper, there appeared an army of black-clad and marching men. They seemed to hang above the good man and his house like a black cloud of locusts. The horses had been saddled none too soon.

XII

THE EARTH IN ANARCHY

URGING THE horses to a gallop, without respect to the rather rugged descent of the road, the horsemen soon regained their advantage over the men on the march, and at last the bulk of the first buildings of Lancy cut off the sight of their pursuers. Nevertheless, the ride had been a long one, and by the time they reached the real town the west was warming with the colour and quality of sunset. The Colonel suggested that, before making finally for the police station, they should make the effort, in passing, to attach to themselves one more individual who might be useful.

"Four out of the five rich men in this town," he said, "are common swindlers. I suppose the proportion is pretty equal all over the world. The fifth is a friend of mine, and a very fine fellow; and what is even more important from our point of view, he owns a motor-car."

"I am afraid," said the Professor in his mirthful way, looking back along the white road on which the black, crawling patch might appear at any moment, "I am afraid we have hardly time for afternoon calls."

"Doctor Renard's house is only three minutes off," said the Colonel.

"Our danger," said Dr. Bull, "is not two minutes off."

"Yes," said Syme, "if we ride on fast we must leave them behind, for they are on foot."

"He has a motor-car," said the Colonel.

"But we may not get it," said Bull.

"Yes, he is quite on your side."

"But he might be out."

"Hold your tongue," said Syme suddenly. "What is that noise?"

For a second they all sat as still as equestrian statues, and for a second—for two or three or four seconds—heaven and earth seemed equally still. Then all their ears, in an agony of attention, heard along the road that indescribable thrill and throb that means only one thing—horses!

The Colonel's face had an instantaneous change, as if lightning had struck it, and yet left it scatheless.

"They have done us," he said, with brief military irony. "Prepare to receive cavalry!"

"Where can they have got the horses?" asked Syme, as he mechanically urged his steed to a canter.

The Colonel was silent for a little, then he said in a strained voice—

"I was speaking with strict accuracy when I said that the 'Soleil d'Or' was the only place where one can get horses within twenty miles."

"No!" said Syme violently, "I don't believe he'd do it. Not with all that white hair."

"He may have been forced," said the Colonel gently. "They must be at least a hundred strong, for which reason we are all going to see my friend Renard, who has a motor-car."

With these words he swung his horse suddenly round a street corner, and went down the street with such thundering speed, that the others, though already well at the gallop, had difficulty in following the flying tail of his horse.

Dr. Renard inhabited a high and comfortable house at the top of a steep street, so that when the riders alighted at his door they could once more see the solid green ridge of the hill, with the white road across it, standing up above all the roofs of the town. They breathed again to see that the road as yet was clear, and they rang the bell.

Dr. Renard was a beaming, brown-bearded man, a good example of that silent but very busy professional class which France has preserved even more perfectly than England. When the matter was explained to him he pooh-poohed the panic of the ex-Marquis altogether; he said, with the solid French scepticism, that there was no conceivable probability of a general anarchist rising. "Anarchy," he said, shrugging his shoulders, "it is childishness!"

"*Et ça*," cried out the Colonel suddenly, pointing over the other's shoulder, "and that is childishness, isn't it?"

They all looked round, and saw a curve of black cavalry come sweeping over the top of the hill with all the energy of Attila. Swiftly as they rode, however, the whole rank still kept well together, and they could see the black vizards of the first line as level as a line of uniforms. But although the main black square was the same, though travelling faster, there was now one sensational difference which they could see clearly upon the slope of the hill, as if upon a slanted map. The bulk of the riders were in one block; but one rider flew far ahead of the column, and with frantic movements of hand and heel urged his horse faster and faster, so that one might have fancied that he was not the pursuer but the pursued. But even at that great distance they could see something so fanatical, so unquestionable in his figure, that they knew it was the Secretary himself.

"I am sorry to cut short a cultured discussion," said the Colonel, "but can you lend me your motor-car now, in two minutes?"

"I have a suspicion that you are all mad," said Dr. Renard, smiling sociably; "but God forbid that madness should in any way interrupt friendship. Let us go round to the garage."

Dr. Renard was a mild man with monstrous wealth; his rooms were like the Musée de Cluny, and he had three motor-cars. These, however, he seemed to use very sparingly, having the simple tastes of the French middle class, and when his impatient friends came to examine them, it took them some time to assure themselves that one of them even could be made to work. This with some difficulty they brought round into the street before the Doctor's house. When they came out of the dim garage they were startled to find that twilight had already fallen with the abruptness of night in the tropics. Either they had been longer in the place than they imagined, or some unusual canopy of cloud had gathered over the town. They looked down the steep streets, and seemed to see a slight mist coming up from the sea.

"It is now or never," said Dr. Bull. "I hear horses."

"No," corrected the Professor, "a horse."

And as they listened, it was evident that the noise, rapidly coming nearer on the rattling stones, was not the noise of the whole cavalcade but that of the one horseman, who had left it far behind—the insane Secretary.

Syme's family, like most of those who end in the simple life, had once owned a motor, and he knew all about them. He had leapt at once into the chauffeur's seat, and with flushed face was wrenching and tugging at the disused machinery. He bent his strength upon one handle, and then said quite quietly—

"I am afraid it's no go."

As he spoke, there swept round the corner a man, rigid on his rushing horse, with the rush and rigidity of an arrow. He had a smile that thrust out his chin as if it were dislocated. He swept alongside of the stationary car, into which its company had crowded, and laid his hand on the front. It was the Secretary, and his mouth went quite straight in the solemnity of triumph.

Syme was leaning hard upon the steering wheel, and there was no sound but the rumble of the other pursuers riding into the town. Then there came quite suddenly a scream of scraping iron, and the car leapt forward. It plucked the Secretary clean out of his saddle, as a knife is whipped out of its sheath, trailed him kicking terribly for twenty yards, and left him flung flat upon the road far in front of his frightened horse. As the car took the corner of the street with a splendid curve, they could just see the other anarchists filling the street and raising their fallen leader.

"I can't understand why it has grown so dark," said the Professor at last in a low voice.

"Going to be a storm, I think," said Dr. Bull. "I say, it's a pity we haven't got a light on this car, if only to see by."

"We have," said the Colonel, and from the floor of the car he fished up a heavy, old-fashioned, carved iron lantern with a light inside it. It was obviously an antique, and it would seem as if its original use had been in some way semi-religious, for there was a rude moulding of a cross upon one of its sides.

"Where on earth did you get that?" asked the Professor.

"I got it where I got the car," answered the Colonel, chuckling, "from my best friend. While our friend here was fighting with the steering wheel, I ran up the front steps of the house and spoke to Renard, who was standing in his own porch, you will remember. 'I suppose,' I said, 'there's no time to get a lamp.' He looked up, blinking amiably at the beautiful arched ceiling of his own front hall. From this was suspended, by chains of exquisite ironwork, this lantern, one of the hundred treasures of his treasure house. By sheer force he tore the lamp out of his own ceiling, shattering the painted panels, and bringing down two blue vases with his violence. Then he handed me the iron lantern, and I put it in the car. Was I not right when I said that Dr. Renard was worth knowing?"

"You were," said Syme seriously, and hung the heavy lantern over the front. There was a certain allegory of their whole position in the contrast between the modern automobile and its strange, ecclesiastical lamp.

Hitherto they had passed through the quietest part of the town, meeting at most one or two pedestrians, who could give them no hint of the peace or the hostility of the place. Now, however, the windows in the houses began one by one to be lit up, giving a greater sense of habitation and humanity. Dr. Bull turned to the new detective who had led their flight, and permitted himself one of his natural and friendly smiles.

"These lights make one feel more cheerful."

Inspector Ratcliffe drew his brows together.

"There is only one set of lights that make me more cheerful," he said, "and they are those lights of the police station which I can see beyond the town. Please God we may be there in ten minutes."

Then all Bull's boiling good sense and optimism broke suddenly out of him.

"Oh, this is all raving nonsense!" he cried. "If you really think that ordinary people in ordinary houses are anarchists, you must be madder than an anarchist yourself. If we turned and fought these fellows, the whole town would fight for us."

"No," said the other with an immovable simplicity, "the whole town would fight for them. We shall see."

While they were speaking the Professor had leant forward with sudden excitement.

"What is that noise?" he said.

"Oh, the horses behind us, I suppose," said the Colonel. "I thought we had got clear of them."

"The horses behind us! No," said the Professor, "it is not horses, and it is not behind us."

Almost as he spoke, across the end of the street before them two shining and rattling shapes shot past. They were gone almost in a flash, but every one could see that they were motor-cars, and the Professor stood up with a pale face and swore that they were the other two motor-cars from Dr. Renard's garage.

"I tell you they were his," he repeated, with wild eyes, "and they were full of men in masks!"

"Absurd!" said the Colonel angrily. "Dr. Renard would never give them his cars."

"He may have been forced," said Ratcliffe quietly. "The whole town is on their side."

"You still believe that," asked the Colonel incredulously.

"You will all believe it soon," said the other with a hopeless calm.

There was a puzzled pause for some little time, and then the Colonel began again abruptly—

"No, I can't believe it. The thing is nonsense. The plain people of a peaceable French town——"

He was cut short by a bang and a blaze of light, which seemed close to his eyes. As the car sped on it left a floating patch of white smoke behind it, and Syme had heard a shot shriek past his ear.

"My God!" said the Colonel, "some one has shot at us."

"It need not interrupt conversation," said the gloomy Ratcliffe. "Pray resume your remarks, Colonel. You were talking, I think, about the plain people of a peaceable French town."

The staring Colonel was long past minding satire. He rolled his eyes all round the street.

"It is extraordinary," he said, "most extraordinary."

"A fastidious person," said Syme, "might even call it unpleasant. However, I suppose those lights out in the field beyond this street are the Gendarmerie. We shall soon get there."

"No," said Inspector Ratcliffe, "we shall never get there."

He had been standing up and looking keenly ahead of him. Now he sat down and smoothed his sleek hair with a weary gesture.

"What do you mean?" asked Bull sharply.

"I mean that we shall never get there," said the pessimist placidly. "They have two rows of armed men across the road already; I can see them from here. The town is in arms, as I said it was. I can only wallow in the exquisite comfort of my own exactitude."

And Ratcliffe sat down comfortably in the car and lit a cigarette, but the others rose excitedly and stared down the road. Syme had slowed down the car as their plans became doubtful, and he brought it finally to a standstill just at the corner of a side street that ran down very steeply to the sea.

The town was mostly in shadow, but the sun had not sunk; wherever its level light could break through, it painted everything a burning gold. Up this side street the last sunset light shone as sharp and narrow as the shaft of artificial light at the theatre. It struck the car of the five friends, and lit it like a burning chariot. But the rest of the street, especially the two ends of it, was in the deepest twilight, and for some seconds they could see nothing. Then Syme, whose eyes were the keenest, broke into a little bitter whistle, and said—

"It is quite true. There is a crowd or an army or some such thing across the end of that street."

"Well, if there is," said Bull impatiently, "it must be something else—a sham fight or the mayor's birthday or something. I cannot and will not believe that plain, jolly people in a place like this walk about with dynamite in their pockets. Get on a bit, Syme, and let us look at them."

The car crawled about a hundred yards farther and then they were all startled by Dr. Bull breaking into a high crow of laughter.

"Why, you silly mugs!" he cried, "what did I tell you. That crowd's as law-abiding as a cow, and if it weren't, it's on our side."

"How do you know?" asked the Professor, staring.

"You blind bat," cried Bull, "don't you see who is leading them?"

They peered again, and then the Colonel, with a catch in his voice, cried out—

"Why, it's Renard!"

There was, indeed, a rank of dim figures running across the road, and they could not be clearly seen; but far enough in front to catch the accident of the evening light was stalking up and down the unmistakable Dr. Renard, in a white hat, stroking his long brown beard, and holding a revolver in his left hand.

"What a fool I've been!" exclaimed the Colonel. "Of course, the dear old boy has turned out to help us."

Dr. Bull was bubbling over with laughter, swinging the sword in his hand as carelessly as a cane. He jumped out of the car and ran across the intervening space, calling out—

"Dr. Renard! Dr. Renard!"

An instant after Syme thought his own eyes had gone mad in his head. For the philanthropic Dr. Renard had deliberately raised his revolver and fired twice at Bull, so that the shots rang down the road.

Almost at the same second as the puff of white cloud went up from this atrocious explosion a long puff of white cloud went up also from the cigarette of the cynical Ratcliffe. Like all the rest he turned a little pale, but he smiled. Dr. Bull, at whom the bullets had been fired, just missing his scalp, stood quite still in the middle of the road without a sign of fear, and then turned very slowly and crawled back to the car, and climbed in with two holes through his hat.

"Well," said the cigarette smoker slowly, "what do you think now?"

"I think," said Dr. Bull with precision, "that I am lying in bed at No. 217 Peabody Buildings, and that I shall soon wake up with a jump; or, if that's not it, I think that I am sitting in a small cushioned cell in Hanwell, and that the doctor can't make much of my case. But if you want to know what I don't think, I'll tell you. I don't think what you think. I don't think, and I never shall think, that the mass of ordinary men are a pack of dirty modern thinkers. No, sir, I'm a democrat, and I still don't believe that Sunday could convert one average navvy or counter-jumper. No, I may be mad, but humanity isn't."

Syme turned his bright blue eyes on Bull with an earnestness which he did not commonly make clear.

"You are a very fine fellow," he said. "You can believe in a sanity which is not merely your sanity. And you're right enough about humanity, about peasants and people like that jolly old innkeeper. But you're not right about Renard. I suspected him from the first. He's rationalistic, and, what's worse, he's rich. When duty and religion are really destroyed, it will be by the rich."

"They are really destroyed now," said the man with a cigarette, and rose with his hands in his pockets. "The devils are coming on!"

The men in the motor-car looked anxiously in the direction of his dreamy gaze, and they saw that the whole regiment at the end of the road was advancing upon them, Dr. Renard marching furiously in front, his beard flying in the breeze.

The Colonel sprang out of the car with an intolerant exclamation.

"Gentlemen," he cried, "the thing is incredible. It must be a practical joke. If you knew Renard as I do—it's like calling Queen Victoria a dynamiter. If you had got the man's character into your head——"

"Dr. Bull," said Syme sardonically, "has at least got it into his hat."

"I tell you it can't be!" cried the Colonel, stamping. "Renard shall explain it. He shall explain it to me," and he strode forward.

"Don't be in such a hurry," drawled the smoker. "He will very soon explain it to all of us."

But the impatient Colonel was already out of earshot, advancing towards the advancing enemy. The excited Dr. Renard lifted his pistol again, but perceiving his opponent, hesitated, and the Colonel came face to face with him with frantic gestures of remonstrance.

"It is no good," said Syme. "He will never get anything out of that old heathen. I vote we drive bang through the thick of them, bang as the bullets went through Bull's hat. We may all be killed, but we must kill a tidy number of them."

"I won't 'ave it," said Dr. Bull, growing more vulgar in the sincerity of his virtue. "The poor chaps may be making a mistake. Give the Colonel a chance."

"Shall we go back, then?" asked the Professor.

"No," said Ratcliffe in a cold voice, "the street behind us is held too. In fact, I seem to see there another friend of yours, Syme."

Syme spun round smartly, and stared backwards at the track which they had travelled. He saw an irregular body of horsemen gathering and galloping towards them in the gloom. He saw above the foremost saddle the silver gleam of a sword, and then as it grew nearer the silver gleam of an old man's hair. The next moment, with shattering violence, he had swung the motor round and sent it dashing down the steep side street to the sea, like a man that desired only to die.

"What the devil is up?" cried the Professor, seizing his arm.

"The morning star has fallen!" said Syme, as his own car went down the darkness like a falling star.

The others did not understand his words, but when they looked back at the street above they saw the hostile cavalry coming round the corner and down the slopes after them; and foremost of all rode the good innkeeper, flushed with the fiery innocence of the evening light.

"The world is insane!" said the Professor, and buried his face in his hands.

"No," said Dr. Bull in adamantine humility, "it is I."

"What are we going to do?" asked the Professor.

"At this moment," said Syme, with a scientific detachment, "I think we are going to smash into a lamp-post."

The next instant the automobile had come with a catastrophic jar against an iron object. The instant after that four men had crawled out from under a chaos of metal, and a tall, lean lamp-post that had stood up straight on the edge of the marine parade stood out, bent and twisted, like the branch of a broken tree.

"Well, we smashed something," said the Professor, with a faint smile. "That's some comfort."

"You're becoming an anarchist," said Syme, dusting his clothes with his instinct of daintiness.

"Every one is," said Ratcliffe.

As they spoke, the white-haired horseman and his followers came thundering from above, and almost at the same moment a dark string of men ran shouting along the sea-front. Syme snatched a sword, and took it in his teeth; he stuck two others under his armpits, took a fourth in his left hand and the lantern in his right, and leapt off the high parade on to the beach below.

The others leapt after him, with a common acceptance of such decisive action, leaving the débris and the gathering mob above them.

"We have one more chance," said Syme, taking the steel out of his mouth. "Whatever all this pandemonium means, I suppose the police station will help us. We can't get there, for they hold the way. But there's a pier or breakwater runs out into the sea just here, which we could defend longer than anything else, like Horatius and his bridge. We must defend it till the Gendarmerie turn out. Keep after me."

They followed him as he went crunching down the beach, and in a second or two their boots broke not on the sea gravel, but on broad, flat stones. They marched down a long, low jetty, running out in one arm into the dim, boiling sea, and when they came to the end of it they felt that they had come to the end of their story. They turned and faced the town.

That town was transfigured with uproar. All along the high parade from which they had just descended was a dark and roaring stream of humanity, with tossing arms and fiery faces, groping and glaring towards them. The long dark line was dotted with torches and lanterns; but even where no flame lit up a furious face, they could see in the farthest figure, in the most shadowy gesture, an organised hate. It was clear that they were the accursed of all men, and they knew not why.

Two or three men, looking little and black like monkeys, leapt over the edge as they had done and dropped on to the beach. These came ploughing down the deep sand, shouting horribly, and strove to wade into the sea at random. The example was followed, and the whole black mass of men began to run and drip over the edge like black treacle.

Foremost among the men on the beach Syme saw the peasant who had driven their cart. He splashed into the surf on a huge carthorse, and shook his axe at them.

"The peasant!" cried Syme. "They have not risen since the Middle Ages."

"Even if the police do come now," said the Professor mournfully, "they can do nothing with this mob."

"Nonsense!" said Bull desperately; "there must be some people left in the town who are human."

"No," said the hopeless Inspector, "the human being will soon be extinct. We are the last of mankind."

"It may be," said the Professor absently. Then he added in his dreamy voice, "What is all that at the end of the 'Dunciad'?

" 'Nor public flame, nor private, dares to shine
Nor human life is left, nor glimpse divine!
Lo! thy dread Empire, Chaos, is restored;
Light dies before thine uncreating word:
Thy hand, great Anarch, lets the curtain fall;
And universal darkness buries all.' "

"Stop!" cried Bull suddenly, "the gendarmes are out."

The low lights of the police station were indeed blotted and broken with hurrying figures, and they heard through the darkness the clash and jingle of a disciplined cavalry.

"They are charging the mob!" cried Bull in ecstasy or alarm.

"No," said Syme, "they are formed along the parade."

"They have unslung their carbines," cried Bull, dancing with excitement.

"Yes," said Ratcliffe, "and they are going to fire on us."

As he spoke there came a long crackle of musketry, and bullets seemed to hop like hailstones on the stones in front of them.

"The gendarmes have joined them!" cried the Professor, and struck his forehead.

"I am in the padded cell," said Bull solidly.

There was a long silence, and then Ratcliffe said, looking out over the swollen sea, all a sort of grey purple—

"What does it matter who is mad or who is sane? We shall all be dead soon."

Syme turned to him and said—

"You are quite hopeless, then?"

Mr. Ratcliffe kept a stony silence; then at last he said quietly—

"No; oddly enough I am not quite hopeless. There is one insane little hope that I cannot get out of my mind. The power of this whole planet is against us, yet I cannot help wondering whether this one silly little hope is hopeless yet."

"In what or whom is your hope?" asked Syme with curiosity.

"In a man I never saw," said the other, looking at the leaden sea.

"I know what you mean," said Syme in a low voice, "the man in the dark room. But Sunday must have killed him by now."

"Perhaps," said the other steadily; "but if so, he was the only man whom Sunday found it hard to kill."

"I heard what you said," said the Professor, with his back turned. "I also am holding hard on to the thing I never saw."

All of a sudden Syme, who was standing as if blind with introspective thought, swung round and cried out, like a man waking from sleep—

"Where is the Colonel? I thought he was with us!"

"The Colonel! Yes," cried Bull, "where on earth is the Colonel?"

"He went to speak to Renard," said the Professor.

"We cannot leave him among all those beasts," cried Syme. "Let us die like gentlemen if——"

"Do not pity the Colonel," said Ratcliffe, with a pale sneer. "He is extremely comfortable. He is——"

"No! no! no!" cried Syme in a kind of frenzy, "not the Colonel too! I will never believe it!"

"Will you believe your eyes?" asked the other, and pointed to the beach.

Many of their pursuers had waded into the water shaking their fists, but the sea was rough, and they could not reach the pier. Two or three figures, however, stood on the beginning of the stone footway, and seemed to be cautiously advancing down it. The glare of a chance lantern lit up the faces of the two foremost. One face wore a black half-mask, and under it the mouth was twisting about in such a madness of nerves that the black tuft of beard wriggled round and round like a restless, living thing. The other was the red face and white moustache of Colonel Ducroix. They were in earnest consultation.

"Yes, he is gone too," said the Professor, and sat down on a stone. "Everything's gone. I'm gone! I can't trust my own bodily machinery. I feel as if my own hand might fly up and strike me."

"When my hand flies up," said Syme, "it will strike somebody else," and he strode along the pier towards the Colonel, the sword in one hand and the lantern in the other.

As if to destroy the last hope or doubt, the Colonel, who saw him coming, pointed his revolver at him and fired. The shot missed Syme, but struck his sword, breaking it short at the hilt. Syme rushed on, and swung the iron lantern above his head.

"Judas before Herod!" he said, and struck the Colonel down upon the stones. Then he turned to the Secretary, whose frightful mouth was almost foaming now, and held the lamp high with so rigid and arresting a gesture, that the man was, as it were, frozen for a moment, and forced to hear.

"Do you see this lantern?" cried Syme in a terrible voice. "Do you see the cross carved on it, and the flame inside? You did not make it. You did not light it. Better men than you, men who could believe and obey, twisted the entrails of iron and preserved the legend of fire. There is not a street you walk on, there is not a thread you wear, that was not made as this lantern was, by denying your philosophy of dirt and rats. You can make nothing. You can only destroy. You will destroy mankind; you will destroy the world. Let that suffice you. Yet this one old Christian lantern you shall not destroy. It shall go where your empire of apes will never have the wit to find it."

He struck the Secretary once with the lantern so that he staggered; and then, whirling it twice round his head, sent it flying far out to sea, where it flared like a roaring rocket and fell.

"Swords!" shouted Syme, turning his flaming face to the three behind him. "Let us charge these dogs, for our time has come to die."

His three companions came after him sword in hand. Syme's sword was broken, but he rent a bludgeon from the fist of a fisherman, flinging him down. In a moment they would have flung themselves upon the face of the mob and perished, when an interruption came. The Secretary, ever since Syme's speech, had stood with his hand to his stricken head as if dazed; now he suddenly pulled off his black mask.

The pale face thus peeled in the lamplight revealed not so much rage as astonishment. He put up his hand with an anxious authority.

"There is some mistake," he said. "Mr. Syme, I hardly think you understand your position. I arrest you in the name of the law."

"Of the law?" said Syme, and dropped his stick.

"Certainly!" said the Secretary. "I am a detective from Scotland Yard," and he took a small blue card from his pocket.

"And what do you suppose we are?" asked the Professor, and threw up his arms.

"You," said the Secretary stiffly, "are, as I know for a fact, members of the Supreme Anarchist Council. Disguised as one of you, I——"

Dr. Bull tossed his sword into the sea.

"There never was any Supreme Anarchist Council," he said. "We were all a lot of silly policemen looking at each other. And all these nice people who have been peppering us with shot thought we were the dynamiters. I knew I couldn't be wrong about the mob," he said, beaming over the enormous multitude, which stretched away to the distance on both sides. "Vulgar people are never mad. I'm vulgar myself, and I know. I am now going on shore to stand a drink to everybody here."

XIII
THE PURSUIT OF THE PRESIDENT

NEXT MORNING five bewildered but hilarious people took the boat for Dover. The poor old Colonel might have had some cause to complain, having been first forced to fight for two factions that didn't exist, and then knocked down with an iron lantern. But he was a magnanimous old gentleman, and being much relieved that neither party had anything to do with dynamite, he saw them off on the pier with great geniality.

The five reconciled detectives had a hundred details to explain to each other. The Secretary had to tell Syme how they had come to wear masks originally in order to approach the supposed enemy as fellow-conspirators; Syme had to explain how they had fled with such swiftness through a civilised country. But above all these matters of detail which could be explained, rose the central mountain of the matter that they could not explain. What did it all mean? If they were all harmless officers, what was Sunday? If he had not seized the world, what on earth had he been up to? Inspector Ratcliffe was still gloomy about this.

"I can't make head or tail of old Sunday's little game any more than you can," he said. "But whatever else Sunday is, he isn't a blameless citizen. Damn it! do you remember his face?"

"I grant you," answered Syme, "that I have never been able to forget it."

"Well," said the Secretary, "I suppose we can find out soon, for to-morrow we have our next general meeting. You will excuse me," he said, with a rather ghastly smile, "for being well acquainted with my secretarial duties."

"I suppose you are right," said the Professor reflectively. "I suppose we might find it out from him; but I confess that I should feel a bit afraid of asking Sunday who he really is."

"Why," asked the Secretary, "for fear of bombs?"

"No," said the Professor, "for fear he might tell me."

"Let us have some drinks," said Dr. Bull, after a silence.

Throughout their whole journey by boat and train they were highly convivial, but they instinctively kept together. Dr. Bull, who had always been the optimist of the party, endeavoured to persuade the other four that the whole company could take the same hansom cab from Victoria; but this was overruled, and they went in a four-wheeler, with Dr. Bull on the box, singing. They finished their journey at an hotel in Piccadilly Circus, so as to be close to the early breakfast next morning in Leicester Square. Yet even then the adventures of the day were not entirely over. Dr. Bull, discontented with the general proposal to go to bed, had strolled out of the hotel at about eleven to see and taste some of the beauties of London. Twenty minutes afterwards, however, he came back and made quite a clamour in the hall. Syme, who tried at first to soothe him, was forced at last to listen to his communication with quite new attention.

"I tell you I've seen him!" said Dr. Bull, with thick emphasis.

"Whom?" asked Syme quickly. "Not the President?"

"Not so bad as that," said Dr. Bull, with unnecessary laughter, "not so bad as that. I've got him here."

"Got whom here?" asked Syme impatiently.

"Hairy man," said the other lucidly, "man that used to be hairy man—Gogol. Here he is," and he pulled forward by a reluctant elbow the identical young man who five days before had marched out of the Council with thin red hair and a pale face, the first of all the sham anarchists who had been exposed.

"Why do you worry with me?" he cried. "You have expelled me as a spy."

"We are all spies!" whispered Syme.

"We're all spies!" shouted Dr. Bull. "Come and have a drink."

Next morning the battalion of the reunited six marched stolidly towards the hotel in Leicester Square.

"This is more cheerful," said Dr. Bull; "we are six men going to ask one man what he means."

"I think it is a bit queerer than that," said Syme. "I think it is six men going to ask one man what they mean."

They turned in silence into the Square, and though the hotel was in the opposite corner, they saw at once the little balcony and a figure that looked too big for it. He was sitting alone with bent head, poring over a newspaper. But all his councillors, who had come to vote him down, crossed that square as if they were watched out of heaven by a hundred eyes.

They had disputed much upon their policy, about whether they should leave the unmasked Gogol without and begin diplomatically, or whether they should bring him in and blow up the gunpowder at once. The influence of Syme and Bull prevailed for the latter course, though the Secretary to the last asked them why they attacked Sunday so rashly.

"My reason is quite simple," said Syme. "I attack him rashly because I am afraid of him."

They followed Syme up the dark stair in silence, and they all came out simultaneously into the broad sunlight of the morning and the broad sunlight of Sunday's smile.

"Delightful!" he said. "So pleased to see you all. What an exquisite day it is. Is the Czar dead?"

The Secretary, who happened to be foremost, drew himself together for a dignified outburst.

"No, sir," he said sternly, "there has been no massacre. I bring you news of no such disgusting spectacles."

"Disgusting spectacles?" repeated the President, with a bright, inquiring smile. "You mean Dr. Bull's spectacles?"

The Secretary choked for a moment, and the President went on with a sort of smooth appeal—

"Of course, we all have our opinions and even our eyes, but really to call them disgusting before the man himself——"

Dr. Bull tore off his spectacles and broke them on the table.

"My spectacles are blackguardly," he said, "but I'm not. Look at my face."

"I dare say it's the sort of face that grows on one," said the President, "in fact, it grows on you; and who am I to quarrel with the wild fruits upon the Tree of Life? I dare say it will grow on me some day."

"We have no time for tomfoolery," said the Secretary, breaking in savagely. "We have come to know what all this means. Who are you? What are you? Why did you get us all here? Do you know who and what we are? Are you a half-witted man playing the conspirator, or are you a clever man playing the fool? Answer me, I tell you."

"Candidates," murmured Sunday, "are only required to answer to eight out of the seventeen questions on the paper. As far as I can make out, you want me to tell you what I am, and what you are, and what this table is, and what this Council is, and what this world is for all I know. Well, I will go so far as to rend the veil of one mystery. If you want to know what you are, you are a set of highly well-intentioned young jackasses."

"And you," said Syme, leaning forward, "what are you?"

"I? What am I?" roared the President, and he rose slowly to an incredible height, like some enormous wave about to arch above them and break. "You want to know what I am, do you? Bull, you are a man of science. Grub in the roots of those trees and find out the truth about them. Syme, you are a poet. Stare at those morning clouds, and tell me or any one the truth about morning clouds. But I tell you this, that you will have found out the truth of the last tree and the topmost cloud before the truth about me. You will understand the sea, and I shall be still a riddle; you shall know what the stars are, and not know what I am. Since the beginning of the world all men have hunted me like a wolf—kings and sages, and poets and law-givers, all the churches, and all the philosophies. But I have never been caught yet, and the skies will fall in the time I turn to bay. I have given them a good run for their money, and I will now."

Before one of them could move, the monstrous man had swung himself like some huge ourang-outang over the balustrade of the balcony. Yet before he dropped he pulled himself up again as on a horizontal bar, and thrusting his great chin over the edge of the balcony, said solemnly—

"There's one thing I'll tell you though about who I am. I am the man in the dark room, who made you all policemen."

With that he fell from the balcony, bouncing on the stones below like a great ball of india-rubber, and went bounding off towards the corner of the Alhambra, where he hailed a hansom-cab and sprang inside it. The six detectives had been standing thunderstruck and livid in the light of his latest assertion; but when he disappeared into the cab, Syme's practical senses returned to him, and leaping over the balcony so recklessly as almost to break his legs, he called another cab.

He and Bull sprang into the cab together, the Professor and the Inspector into another, while the Secretary and the late Gogol scrambled into a third just in time to pursue the flying Syme, who was pursuing the flying President. Sunday led them a wild chase towards the northwest, his cabman, evidently under the influence of more than common inducements, urging the horse at breakneck speed. But Syme was in no mood for delicacies, and he stood up in his own cab shouting, "Stop thief!" until crowds ran along beside his cab, and policemen began to stop and ask questions. All this had its influence upon the President's cabman, who began to look dubious, and to slow down to a trot. He opened the trap to talk reasonably to his fare, and in so doing let the long whip droop over the front of the cab. Sunday leant forward, seized it, and jerked it violently out of the man's hand. Then standing up in front of the cab himself, he lashed the horse and roared aloud, so that they went down the streets like a flying storm. Through street after street and square after square went whirling this preposterous vehicle, in which the fare was urging the horse and driver trying desperately to stop it. The other three cabs came after it (if the phrase be permissible of a cab) like panting hounds. Shops and streets shot by like rattling arrows.

At the highest ecstasy of speed, Sunday turned round on the splashboard where he stood, and sticking his great grinning head out of the cab, with white hair whistling in the wind, he made a horrible face at his pursuers, like some colossal urchin. Then raising his right hand swiftly, he flung a ball of paper in Syme's face and vanished. Syme caught the thing while instinctively warding it off, and discovered that it consisted of two crumpled papers. One was addressed to himself, and the other to Dr. Bull, with a very long, and it is to be feared partly ironical, string of letters after his name. Dr. Bull's address was, at any rate, considerably longer than his communication, for the communication consisted entirely of the words:—

"What about Martin Tupper *now?*"

"What does the old maniac mean?" asked Bull, staring at the words. "What does yours say, Syme?"

Syme's message was, at any rate, longer, and ran as follows:—

"No one would regret anything in the nature of an interference by the Archdeacon more than I. I trust it will not come to that. But, for the last time, where are your goloshes? The thing is too bad, especially after what uncle said."

The President's cabman seemed to be regaining some control over his horse, and the pursuers gained a little as they swept round into the Edgware Road. And here there occurred what seemed to the allies a providential stoppage. Traffic of every kind was swerving to right or left or stopping, for down the long road was coming the unmistakable roar announcing the fire-engine, which in a few seconds went by like a brazen thunder-bolt. But quick as it went by, Sunday had bounded out of his cab, sprung at the fire-engine, caught it, slung himself on to it, and was seen as he disappeared in the noisy distance talking to the astonished fireman with explanatory gestures.

"After him!" howled Syme. "He can't go astray now. There's no mistaking a fire-engine."

The three cabmen, who had been stunned for a moment, whipped up their horses and slightly decreased the distance between themselves and their disappearing prey. The President acknowledged this proximity by coming to the back of the car, bowing repeatedly, kissing his hand, and finally flinging a neatly-folded note into the bosom of Inspector Ratcliffe. When that gentleman opened it, not without impatience, he found it contained the words:—

"Fly at once. The truth about your trouser-stretchers is known.—A FRIEND."

The fire-engine had struck still farther to the north, into a region that they did not recognise; and as it ran by a line of high railings shadowed with trees, the six friends were startled, but somewhat relieved, to see the President leap from the fire-engine, though whether through another whim or the increasing protest of his entertainers they could not see. Before the three cabs, however, could reach up to the spot, he had gone up the high railings like a huge grey cat, tossed himself over, and vanished in a darkness of leaves.

Syme with a furious gesture stopped his cab, jumped out, and sprang also to the escalade. When he had one leg over the fence and his friends were following, he turned a face on them which shone quite pale in the shadow.

"What place can this be?" he asked. "Can it be the old devil's house? I've heard he has a house in North London."

"All the better," said the Secretary grimly, planting a foot in a foothold, "we shall find him at home."

"No, but it isn't that," said Syme, knitting his brows. "I hear the most horrible noises, like devils laughing and sneezing and blowing their devilish noses!"

"His dogs barking, of course," said the Secretary.

"Why not say his black-beetles barking!" said Syme furiously, "snails barking! geraniums barking! Did you ever hear a dog bark like that?"

He held up his hand, and there came out of the thicket a long, growling roar that seemed to get under the skin and freeze the flesh—a low thrilling roar that made a throbbing in the air all about them.

"The dogs of Sunday would be no ordinary dogs," said Gogol, and shuddered.

Syme had jumped down on the other side, but he still stood listening impatiently.

"Well, listen to that," he said, "is that a dog—anybody's dog?"

There broke upon their ear a hoarse screaming as of things protesting and clamouring in sudden pain; and then, far off like an echo, what sounded like a long nasal trumpet.

"Well, his house ought to be hell!" said the Secretary; "and if it is hell, I'm going in!" and he sprang over the tall railings almost with one swing.

The others followed. They broke through a tangle of plants and shrubs, and came out on an open path. Nothing was in sight, but Dr. Bull suddenly struck his hands together.

"Why, you asses," he cried, "it's the Zoo!"

As they were looking round wildly for any trace of their wild quarry, a keeper in uniform came running along the path with a man in plain clothes.

"Has it come this way?" gasped the keeper.

"Has what?" asked Syme.

"The elephant!" cried the keeper. "An elephant has gone mad and run away!"

"He has run away with an old gentleman," said the other stranger breathlessly, "a poor old gentleman with white hair!"

"What sort of old gentleman?" asked Syme, with great curiosity.

"A very large and fat old gentleman in light grey clothes," said the keeper eagerly.

"Well," said Syme, "if he's that particular kind of old gentleman, if you're quite sure that he's a large and fat old gentleman in grey clothes, you may take my word for it that the elephant has not run away with him. He has run away with the elephant. The elephant is not made by God that could run away with him if he did not consent to the elopement. And, by thunder, there he is!"

There was no doubt about it this time. Clean across the space of grass, about two hundred yards away, with a crowd screaming and scampering vainly at his heels, went a huge grey elephant at an awful stride, with his trunk thrown out as rigid as a ship's bowsprit, and trumpeting like the trumpet of doom. On the back of the bellowing and plunging animal sat President Sunday with all the placidity of a sultan, but goading the animal to a furious speed with some sharp object in his hand.

"Stop him!" screamed the populace. "He'll be out of the gate!"

"Stop a landslide!" said the keeper. "He is out of the gate!"

And even as he spoke, a final crash and roar of terror announced that the great grey elephant had broken out of the gates of the Zoological Gardens, and was careering down Albany Street like a new and swift sort of omnibus.

"Great Lord!" cried Bull, "I never knew an elephant could go so fast. Well, it must be hansom-cabs again if we are even to keep him in sight."

As they raced along to the gate out of which the elephant had vanished, Syme felt a glaring panorama of the strange animals in the cages which they passed. Afterwards he thought it queer that he should have seen them so clearly. He remembered especially seeing pelicans, with their preposterous, pendant throats. He wondered why the pelican was the symbol of charity, except it was that it wanted a good deal of charity to admire a pelican. He remembered a hornbill, which was simply a huge yellow beak with a small bird tied on behind it. The whole gave him a sensation, the vividness of which he could not explain, that Nature was always making quite mysterious jokes. Sunday had told them that they would understand him when they had understood the stars. He wondered whether even the archangels understood the hornbill.

The six unhappy detectives flung themselves into cabs and followed the elephant, sharing the terror which he spread through the long stretch of the streets. This time Sunday did not turn round, but offered them the solid stretch of his unconscious back, which maddened them, if possible, more than his previous mockeries. Just before they came to Baker Street, however, he was seen to throw something far up into the air, as a boy does a ball meaning to catch it again. But at their rate of racing it fell far behind, just by the cab containing Gogol; and in faint hope of a clue or for some impulse unexplainable, he stopped his cab so as to pick it up. It was addressed to himself, and was quite a bulky parcel. On examination, however, its bulk was found to consist of thirty-three pieces of paper of no value wrapped one round the other. When the last covering was torn away it reduced itself to a small slip of paper, on which was written:—

"The word, I fancy, should be 'pink.' "

The man once known as Gogol said nothing, but the movements of his hands and feet were like those of a man urging a horse to renewed efforts.

Through street after street, through district after district, went the prodigy of the flying elephant, calling crowds to every window, and driving the traffic left and right. And still through all this insane publicity the three cabs toiled after it, until they came to be regarded as part of a procession, and perhaps the advertisement of a circus. They went at such a rate that distances were shortened beyond belief, and Syme saw the Albert Hall in Kensington when he thought that he was still in Paddington. The animal's pace was even more fast and free through the empty, aristocratic streets of South Kensington, and he finally headed towards that part of the sky-line where the enormous Wheel of Earl's Court stood up in the sky. The wheel grew larger and larger, till it filled heaven like the wheel of stars.

The beast outstripped the cabs. They lost him round several corners, and when they came to one of the gates of the Earl's Court Exhibition they found themselves finally blocked. In front of them was an enormous crowd; in the midst of it was an enormous elephant, heaving and shuddering as such shapeless creatures do. But the President had disappeared.

"Where has he gone to?" asked Syme, slipping to the ground.

"Gentleman rushed into the Exhibition, sir!" said an official in a dazed manner. Then he added in a injured voice: "Funny gentleman, sir. Asked me to hold his horse, and gave me this."

He held out with distaste a piece of folded paper, addressed: "To the Secretary of the Central Anarchist Council."

The Secretary, raging, rent it open, and found written inside it:—

"When the herring runs a mile,
Let the Secretary smile;
When the herring tries to *fly*,
Let the Secretary die.

Rustic Proverb."

"Why the eternal crikey," began the Secretary, "did you let the man in? Do people commonly come to your Exhibition riding on mad elephants? Do——"

"Look!" shouted Syme suddenly. "Look over there!"

"Look at what?" asked the Secretary savagely.

"Look at the captive balloon!" said Syme, and pointed in frenzy.

"Why the blazes should I look at a captive balloon?" demanded the Secretary. "What is there queer about a captive balloon?"

"Nothing," said Syme, "except that it isn't captive!"

They all turned their eyes to where the balloon swung and swelled above the Exhibition on a string, like a child's balloon. A second afterwards the string came in two just under the car, and the balloon, broken loose, floated away with the freedom of a soap bubble.

"Ten thousand devils!" shrieked the Secretary. "He's got into it!" and he shook his fists at the sky.

The balloon, borne by some chance wind, came right above them, and they could see the great white head of the President peering over the side and looking benevolently down on them.

"God bless my soul!" said the Professor with the elderly manner that he could never disconnect from his bleached beard and parchment face. "God bless my soul! I seemed to fancy that something fell on the top of my hat!"

He put up a trembling hand and took from that shelf a piece of twisted paper, which he opened absently, only to find it inscribed with a true lover's knot and the words:—

"Your beauty has not left me indifferent.—From LITTLE SNOWDROP."

There was a short silence, and then Syme said, biting his beard—

"I'm not beaten yet. The blasted thing must come down somewhere. Let's follow it!"

XIV
THE SIX PHILOSOPHERS

ACROSS GREEN fields, and breaking through blooming hedges, toiled six draggled detectives, about five miles out of London. The optimist of the party had at first proposed that they should follow the balloon across South England in hansom-cabs. But he was ultimately convinced of the persistent refusal of the balloon to follow the roads, and the still more persistent refusal of the cabmen to follow the balloon. Consequently the tireless though exasperated travellers broke through black thickets and ploughed through ploughed fields till each was turned into a figure too outrageous to be mistaken for a tramp. Those green hills of Surrey saw the final collapse and tragedy of the admirable light grey suit in which Syme had set out from Saffron Park. His silk hat was broken over his nose by a swinging bough, his coat-tails were torn to the shoulder by arresting thorns, the clay of England was splashed up to his collar; but he still carried his yellow beard forward with a silent and furious determination, and his eyes were still fixed on that floating ball of gas, which in the full flush of sunset seemed coloured like a sunset cloud.

"After all," he said, "it is very beautiful!"

"It is singularly and strangely beautiful!" said the Professor. "I wish the beastly gas-bag would burst!"

"No," said Dr. Bull, "I hope it won't. It might hurt the old boy."

"Hurt him!" said the vindictive Professor, "hurt him! Not as much as I'd hurt him if I could get up with him. Little Snowdrop!"

"I don't want him hurt, somehow," said Dr. Bull.

"What!" cried the Secretary bitterly. "Do you believe all that tale about his being our man in the dark room? Sunday would say he was anybody."

"I don't know whether I believe it or not," said Dr. Bull. "But it isn't that that I mean. I can't wish old Sunday's balloon to burst because—"

"Well," said Syme impatiently, "because?"

"Well, because he's so jolly like a balloon himself," said Dr. Bull desperately. "I don't understand a word of all that idea of his being the same man who gave us all our blue cards. It seems to make everything nonsense. But I don't care who knows it, I always had a sympathy for old Sunday himself, wicked as he was. Just as if he was a great bouncing baby. How can I explain what my queer sympathy was? It didn't prevent my fighting him like hell! Shall I make it clear if I say that I liked him because he was so fat?"

"You will not," said the Secretary.

"I've got it now," cried Bull, "it was because he was so fat and so light. Just like a balloon. We always think of fat people as heavy, but he could have danced against a sylph. I see now what I mean. Moderate strength is shown in violence, supreme strength is shown in levity. It was like the old speculations—what would happen if an elephant could leap up in the sky like a grasshopper?"

"Our elephant," said Syme, looking upwards, "has leapt into the sky like a grasshopper."

"And somehow," concluded Bull, "that's why I can't help liking old Sunday. No, it's not an admiration of force, or any silly thing like that. There is a kind of gaiety in the thing, as if he were bursting with some good news. Haven't you sometimes felt it on a spring day? You know Nature plays tricks, but somehow that day proves they are good-natured tricks. I never read the Bible myself, but that part they laugh at is literal truth, 'Why leap ye, ye high hills?' The hills do leap—at least, they try to. . . . Why do I like Sunday? . . . how can I tell you? . . . because he's such a Bounder."

There was a long silence, and then the Secretary said in a curious, strained voice—

"You do not know Sunday at all. Perhaps it is because you are better than I, and do not know hell. I was a fierce fellow, and a trifle morbid from the first. The man who sits in darkness, and who chose us all, chose me because I had all the crazy look of a conspirator—because my smile went crooked, and my eyes were gloomy, even when I smiled. But there must have been something in me that answered to the nerves in all these anarchic men. For when I first saw Sunday he expressed to me, not your airy vitality, but something both gross and sad in the Nature of Things. I found him smoking in a twilight room, a room with brown blind down, infinitely more depressing than the genial darkness in which our master lives. He sat there on a bench, a huge heap of a man, dark and out of shape. He listened to all my words without speaking or even stirring. I poured out my most passionate appeals, and asked my most eloquent questions. Then, after a long silence, the Thing began to shake, and I thought it was shaken by some secret malady. It shook like a loathsome and living jelly. It reminded me of everything I had ever read about the base bodies that are the origin of life—the deep sea lumps and protoplasm. It seemed like the final form of matter, the most shapeless and the most shameful. I could only tell myself, from its shudderings, that it was something at least that such a monster could be miserable. And then it broke upon me that the bestial mountain was shaking with a lonely laughter, and the laughter was at me. Do you ask me to forgive him that? It is no small thing to be laughed at by something at once lower and stronger than oneself."

"Surely you fellows are exaggerating wildly," cut in the clear voice of Inspector Ratcliffe. "President Sunday is a terrible fellow for one's intellect, but he is not such a Barnum's freak physically as you make out. He received me in an ordinary office, in a grey check coat, in broad daylight. He talked to me in an ordinary way. But I'll tell you what is a trifle creepy about Sunday. His room is neat, his clothes are neat, everything seems in order; but he's absent-minded. Sometimes his great bright eyes go quite blind. For hours he forgets that you are there. Now absent-mindedness is just a bit too awful in a bad man. We think of a wicked man as vigilant. We can't think of a wicked man who is honestly and sincerely dreamy, because we daren't think of a wicked man alone with himself. An absent-minded man means a good-natured man. It means a man who, if he happens to see you, will apologise. But how will you bear an absent-minded man who, if he happens to see you, will kill you? That is what tries the nerves, abstraction combined with cruelty. Men have felt it sometimes when they went through wild forests, and felt that the animals there were at once innocent and pitiless. They might ignore or slay. How would you like to pass ten mortal hours in a parlour with an absent-minded tiger?"

"And what do you think of Sunday, Gogol?" asked Syme.

"I don't think of Sunday on principle," said Gogol simply, "any more than I stare at the sun at noonday."

"Well, that is a point of view," said Syme thoughtfully. "What do you say, Professor?"

The Professor was walking with bent head and trailing stick, and he did not answer at all.

"Wake up, Professor!" said Syme genially. "Tell us what you think of Sunday."

The Professor spoke at last very slowly.

"I think something," he said, "that I cannot say clearly. Or, rather, I think something that I cannot even think clearly. But it is something like this. My early life, as you know, was a bit too large and loose. Well, when I saw Sunday's face I thought it was too large—everybody does, but I also thought it was too loose. The face was so big, that one couldn't focus it or make it a face at all. The eye was so far away from the nose, that it wasn't an eye. The mouth was so much by itself, that one had to think of it by itself. The whole thing is too hard to explain."

He paused for a little, still trailing his stick, and then went on—

"But put it this way. Walking up a road at night, I have seen a lamp and a lighted window and a cloud make together a most complete and unmistakable face. If any one in heaven has that face I shall know him again. Yet when I walked a little farther I found that there was no face, that the window was ten yards away, the lamp ten hundred yards, the cloud beyond the world. Well, Sunday's face escaped me; it ran away to right and left, as such chance pictures run away. And so his face has made me, somehow, doubt whether there are any faces. I don't know whether your face, Bull, is a face or a combination in perspective. Perhaps one black disc of your beastly glasses is quite close and another fifty miles away. Oh, the doubts of a materialist are not worth a dump. Sunday has taught me the last and the worst doubts, the doubts of a spiritualist. I am a Buddhist, I suppose; and Buddhism is not a creed, it is a doubt. My poor dear Bull, I do not believe that you really have a face. I have not faith enough to believe in matter."

Syme's eyes were still fixed upon the errant orb, which, reddened in the evening light, looked like some rosier and more innocent world.

"Have you noticed an odd thing," he said, "about all your descriptions? Each man of you finds Sunday quite different, yet each man of you can only find one thing to compare him to—the universe itself. Bull finds him like the earth in spring, Gogol like the sun at noonday. The Secretary is reminded of the shapeless protoplasm, and the Inspector of the carelessness of virgin forests. The Professor says he is like a changing landscape. This is queer, but it is queerer still that I also have had my odd notion about the President, and I also find that I think of Sunday as I think of the whole world."

"Get on a little faster, Syme," said Bull; "never mind the balloon."

"When I first saw Sunday," said Syme slowly, "I only saw his back; and when I saw his back, I knew he was the worst man in the world. His neck and shoulders were brutal, like those of some apish god. His head had a stoop that was hardly human, like the stoop of an ox. In fact, I had at once the revolting fancy that this was not a man at all, but a beast dressed up in men's clothes."

"Get on," said Dr. Bull.

"And then the queer thing happened. I had seen his back from the street, as he sat in the balcony. Then I entered the hotel, and coming round the other side of him, saw his face in the sunlight. His face frightened me, as it did every one; but not because it was brutal, not because it was evil. On the contrary, it frightened me because it was so beautiful, because it was so good."

"Syme," exclaimed the Secretary, "are you ill?"

"It was like the face of some ancient archangel, judging justly after heroic wars. There was laughter in the eyes, and in the mouth honour and sorrow. There was the same white hair, the same great, grey-clad shoulders that I had seen from behind. But when I saw him from behind I was certain he was an animal, and when I saw him in front I knew he was a god."

"Pan," said the Professor dreamily, "was a god and an animal."

"Then, and again and always," went on Syme, like a man talking to himself, "that has been for me the mystery of Sunday, and it is also the mystery of the world. When I see the horrible back, I am sure the noble face is but a mask. When I see the face but for an instant, I know the back is only a jest. Bad is so bad, that we cannot but think good an accident; good is so good, that we feel certain that evil could be explained. But the whole came to a kind of crest yesterday when I raced Sunday for the cab, and was just behind him all the way."

"Had you time for thinking then?" asked Ratcliffe.

"Time," replied Syme, "for one outrageous thought. I was suddenly possessed with the idea that the blind, blank back of his head really was his face—an awful, eyeless face staring at me! And I fancied that the figure running in front of me was really a figure running backwards, and dancing as he ran."

"Horrible!" said Dr. Bull, and shuddered.

"Horrible is not the word," said Syme. "It was exactly the worst instant of my life. And yet ten minutes afterwards, when he put his head out of the cab and made a grimace like a gargoyle, I knew that he was only like a father playing hide-and-seek with his children."

"It is a long game," said the Secretary, and frowned at his broken boots.

"Listen to me," cried Syme with extraordinary emphasis. "Shall I tell you the secret of the whole world? It is that we have only known the back of the world. We see everything from behind, and it looks brutal. That is not a tree, but the back of a tree. That is not a cloud, but the back of a cloud. Cannot you see that everything is stooping and hiding a face? If we could only get round in front——"

"Look!" cried out Bull clamorously, "the balloon is coming down!"

There was no need to cry out to Syme, who had never taken his eyes off it. He saw the great luminous globe suddenly stagger in the sky, right itself, and then sink slowly behind the trees like a setting sun.

The man called Gogol, who had hardly spoken through all their weary travels, suddenly threw up his hands like a lost spirit.

"He is dead!" he cried. "And now I know he was my friend—my friend in the dark!"

"Dead!" snorted the Secretary. "You will not find him dead easily. If he has been tipped out of the car, we shall find him rolling as a colt rolls in a field, kicking his legs for fun."

"Clashing his hoofs," said the Professor. "The colts do, and so did Pan."

"Pan again!" said Dr. Bull irritably. "You seem to think Pan is everything."

"So he is," said the Professor, "in Greek. He means everything."

"Don't forget," said the Secretary, looking down, "that he also means Panic."

Syme had stood without hearing any of the exclamations.

"It fell over there," he said shortly. "Let us follow it!"

Then he added with an indescribable gesture—

"Oh, if he has cheated us all by getting killed! It would be like one of his larks."

He strode off towards the distant trees with a new energy, his rags and ribbons fluttering in the wind. The others followed him in a more footsore and dubious manner. And almost at the same moment all six men realised that they were not alone in the little field.

Across the square of turf a tall man was advancing towards them, leaning on a strange long staff like a sceptre. He was clad in a fine but old-fashioned suit with knee-breeches; its colour was that shade between blue, violet and grey which can be seen in certain shadows of the woodland. His hair was whitish grey, and at the first glance, taken along with his knee-breeches, looked as if it was powdered. His advance was very quiet; but for the silver frost upon his head, he might have been one of the shadows of the wood.

"Gentlemen," he said, "my master has a carriage waiting for you in the road just by."

"Who is your master?" asked Syme, standing quite still.

"I was told you knew his name," said the man respectfully.

There was a silence, and then the Secretary said—

"Where is this carriage?"

"It has been waiting only a few moments," said the stranger. "My master has only just come home."

Syme looked left and right upon the patch of green field in which he found himself. The hedges were ordinary hedges, the trees seemed ordinary trees; yet he felt like a man entrapped in fairy-land.

He looked the mysterious ambassador up and down, but he could discover nothing except that the man's coat was the exact colour of the purple shadows, and that the man's face was the exact colour of the red and brown and golden sky.

"Show us the place," Syme said briefly, and without a word the man in the violet coat turned his back and walked towards a gap in the hedge, which let in suddenly the light of a white road.

As the six wanderers broke out upon this thoroughfare, they saw the white road blocked by what looked like a long row of carriages, such a row of carriages as might close the approach to some house in Park Lane. Along the side of these carriages stood a rank of splendid servants, all dressed in the grey-blue uniform, and all having a certain quality of stateliness and freedom which would not commonly belong to the servants of a gentleman, but rather to the officials and ambassadors of a great king. There were no less than six carriages waiting, one for each of the tattered and miserable band. All the attendants (as if in court-dress) wore swords, and as each man crawled into his carriage they drew them, and saluted with a sudden blaze of steel.

"What can it all mean?" asked Bull of Syme as they separated. "Is this another joke of Sunday's?"

"I don't know," said Syme as he sank wearily back in the cushions of his carriage; "but if it is, it's one of the jokes you talk about. It's a good-natured one."

The six adventurers had passed through many adventures, but not one had carried them so utterly off their feet as this last adventure of comfort. They had all become inured to things going roughly; but things suddenly going smoothly swamped them. They could not even feebly imagine what the carriages were; it was enough for them to know that they were carriages, and carriages with cushions. They could not conceive who the old man was who had led them; but it was quite enough that he had certainly led them to the carriages.

Syme drove through a drifting darkness of trees in utter abandonment. It was typical of him that while he had carried his bearded chin forward fiercely so long as anything could be done, when the whole business was taken out of his hands he fell back on the cushions in a frank collapse.

Very gradually and very vaguely he realised into what rich roads the carriage was carrying him. He saw that they passed the stone gates of what might have been a park, that they began gradually to climb a hill which, while wooded on both sides, was somewhat more orderly than a forest. Then there began to grow upon him, as upon a man slowly waking from a healthy sleep, a pleasure in everything. He felt that the hedges were what hedges should be, living walls; that a hedge is like a human army, disciplined, but all the more alive. He saw high elms behind the hedges, and vaguely thought how happy boys would be climbing there. Then his carriage took a turn of the path, and he saw suddenly and quietly, like a long, low, sunset cloud, a long, low house, mellow in the mild light of sunset. All the six friends compared notes afterwards and quarrelled; but they all agreed that in some unaccountable way the place reminded them of their boyhood. It was either this elm-top or that crooked path, it was either this scrap of orchard or that shape of a window; but each man of them declared that he could remember this place before he could remember his mother.

When the carriages eventually rolled up to a large, low, cavernous gateway, another man in the same uniform, but wearing a silver star on the grey breast of his coat, came out to meet them. This impressive person said to the bewildered Syme—

"Refreshments are provided for you in your room."

Syme, under the influence of the same mesmeric sleep of amazement, went up the large oaken stairs after the respectful attendant. He entered a splendid suite of apartments that seemed to be designed specially for him. He walked up to a long mirror with the ordinary instinct of his class, to pull his tie straight or to smooth his hair; and there he saw the frightful figure that he was—blood running down his face from where the bough had struck him, his hair standing out like yellow rags of rank grass, his clothes torn into long, wavering tatters. At once the whole enigma sprang up, simply as the question of how he had got there, and how he was to get out again. Exactly at the same moment a man in blue, who had been appointed as his valet, said very solemnly—

"I have put out your clothes, sir."

"Clothes!" said Syme sardonically. "I have no clothes except these," and he lifted two long strips of his frock-coat in fascinating festoons, and made a movement as if to twirl like a ballet girl.

"My master asks me to say," said the attendant, "that there is a fancy dress ball to-night, and that he desires you to put on the costume that I have laid out. Meanwhile, sir, there is a bottle of Burgundy and some cold pheasant, which he hopes you will not refuse, as it is some hours before supper."

"Cold pheasant is a good thing," said Syme reflectively, "and Burgundy is a spanking good thing. But really I do not want either of them so much as I want to know what the devil all this means, and what sort of costume you have got laid out for me. Where is it?"

The servant lifted off a kind of ottoman a long peacock-blue drapery, rather of the nature of a domino, on the front of which was emblazoned a large golden sun, and which was splashed here and there with flaming stars and crescents.

"You're to be dressed as Thursday, sir," said the valet somewhat affably.

"Dressed as Thursday!" said Syme in meditation. "It doesn't sound a warm costume."

"Oh, yes, sir," said the other eagerly, "the Thursday costume is quite warm, sir. It fastens up to the chin."

"Well, I don't understand anything," said Syme, sighing. "I have been used so long to uncomfortable adventures that comfortable adventures knock me out. Still, I may be allowed to ask why I should be particularly like Thursday in a green frock spotted all over with the sun and moon. Those orbs, I think, shine on other days. I once saw the moon on Tuesday, I remember."

"Beg pardon, sir," said the valet, "Bible also provided for you," and with a respectful and rigid finger he pointed out a passage in the first chapter of Genesis. Syme read it wondering. It was that in which the fourth day of the week is associated with the creation of the sun and moon. Here, however, they reckoned from a Christian Sunday.

"This is getting wilder and wilder," said Syme, as he sat down in a chair. "Who are these people who provide cold pheasant and Burgundy, and green clothes and Bibles? Do they provide everything?"

"Yes, sir, everything," said the attendant gravely. "Shall I help you on with your costume?"

"Oh, hitch the bally thing on!" said Syme impatiently.

But though he affected to despise the mummery, he felt a curious freedom and naturalness in his movements as the blue and gold garment fell about him; and when he found that he had to wear a sword, it stirred a boyish dream. As he passed out of the room he flung the folds across his shoulder with a gesture, his sword stood out at an angle, and he had all the swagger of a troubadour. For these disguises did not disguise, but reveal.

XV
THE ACCUSER

As Syme strode along the corridor he saw the Secretary standing at the top of a great flight of stairs. The man had never looked so noble. He was draped in a long robe of starless black, down the centre of which fell a band or broad stripe of pure white, like a single shaft of light. The whole looked like some very severe ecclesiastical vestment. There was no need for Syme to search his memory or the Bible in order to remember that the first day of creation marked the mere creation of light out of darkness. The vestment itself would alone have suggested the symbol; and Syme felt also how perfectly this pattern of pure white and black expressed the soul of the pale and austere Secretary, with his inhuman veracity and his cold frenzy, which made him so easily make war on the anarchists, and yet so easily pass for one of them. Syme was scarcely surprised to notice that, amid all the ease and hospitality of their new surroundings, this man's eyes were still stern. No smell of ale or orchards could make the Secretary cease to ask a reasonable question.

If Syme had been able to see himself, he would have realised that he, too, seemed to be for the first time himself and no one else. For if the Secretary stood for that philosopher who loves the original and formless light, Syme was a type of the poet who seeks always to make the light in special shapes, to split it up into sun and star. The philosopher may sometimes love the infinite; the poet always loves the finite. For him the great moment is not the creation of light, but the creation of the sun and moon.

As they descended the broad stairs together they overtook Ratcliffe, who was clad in spring green like a huntsman, and the pattern upon whose garment was a green tangle of trees. For he stood for that third day on which the earth and green things were made, and his square, sensible face, with its not unfriendly cynicism, seemed appropriate enough to it.

They were led out of another broad and low gateway into a very large old English garden, full of torches and bonfires, by the broken light of which a vast carnival of people were dancing in motley dress. Syme seemed to see every shape in Nature imitated in some crazy costume. There was a man dressed as a windmill with enormous sails, a man dressed as an elephant, a man dressed as a balloon; the two last, together, seemed to keep the thread of their farcical adventures. Syme even saw, with a queer thrill, one dancer dressed like an enormous hornbill, with a beak twice as big as himself—the queer bird which had fixed itself on his fancy like a living question while he was rushing down the long road at the Zoological Gardens. There were a thousand other such objects, however. There was a dancing lamp-post, a dancing apple tree, a dancing ship. One would have thought that the untamable tune of some mad musician had set all the common objects of field and street dancing an eternal jig. And long afterwards, when Syme was middle-aged and at rest, he could never see one of those particular objects—a lamp-post, or an apple tree, or a windmill—without thinking that it was a strayed reveller from that revel of masquerade.

On one side of this lawn, alive with dancers, was a sort of green bank, like the terrace in such old-fashioned gardens.

Along this, in a kind of crescent, stood seven great chairs, the thrones of the seven days. Gogol and Dr. Bull were already in their seats; the Professor was just mounting to his. Gogol, or Tuesday, had his simplicity well symbolised by a dress designed upon the division of the waters, a dress that separated upon his forehead and fell to his feet, grey and silver, like a sheet of rain. The Professor, whose day was that on which the birds and fishes—the ruder forms of life—were created, had a dress of dim purple, over which sprawled goggle-eyed fishes and outrageous tropical birds, the union in him of unfathomable fancy and of doubt. Dr. Bull, the last day of Creation, wore a coat covered with heraldic animals in red and gold, and on his crest a man rampant. He lay back in his chair with a broad smile, the picture of an optimist in his element.

One by one the wanderers ascended the bank and sat in their strange seats. As each of them sat down a roar of enthusiasm rose from the carnival, such as that with which crowds receive kings. Cups were clashed and torches shaken, and feathered hats flung in the air. The men for whom these thrones were reserved were men crowned with some extraordinary laurels. But the central chair was empty.

Syme was on the left hand of it and the Secretary on the right. The Secretary looked across the empty throne at Syme, and said, compressing his lips—

"We do not know yet that he is not dead in a field."

Almost as Syme heard the words, he saw on the sea of human faces in front of him a frightful and beautiful alteration, as if heaven had opened behind his head. But Sunday had only passed silently along the front like a shadow, and had sat in the central seat. He was draped plainly, in a pure and terrible white, and his hair was like a silver flame on his forehead.

For a long time—it seemed for hours—that huge masquerade of mankind swayed and stamped in front of them to marching and exultant music. Every couple dancing seemed a separate romance; it might be a fairy dancing with a pillar-box, or a peasant girl dancing with the moon; but in each case it was, somehow, as absurd as Alice in Wonderland, yet as grave and kind as a love story. At last, however, the thick crowd began to thin itself. Couples strolled away into the garden-walks, or began to drift towards that end of the building where stood smoking, in huge pots like fish-kettles, some hot and scented mixtures of old ale or wine. Above all these, upon a sort of black framework on the roof of the house, roared in its iron basket a gigantic bonfire, which lit up the land for miles. It flung the homely effect of firelight over the face of vast forests of grey or brown, and it seemed to fill with warmth even the emptiness of upper night. Yet this also, after a time, was allowed to grow fainter; the dim groups gathered more and more round the great cauldrons, or passed, laughing and clattering, into the inner passages of that ancient house. Soon there were only some ten loiterers in the garden; soon only four. Finally the last stray merry-maker ran into the house whooping to his companions. The fire faded, and the slow, strong stars came out. And the seven strange men were left alone, like seven stone statues on their chairs of stone. Not one of them had spoken a word.

They seemed in no haste to do so, but heard in silence the hum of insects and the distant song of one bird. Then Sunday spoke, but so dreamily that he might have been continuing a conversation rather than beginning one.

"We will eat and drink later," he said. "Let us remain together a little, we who have loved each other so sadly, and have fought so long. I seem to remember only centuries of heroic war, in which you were always heroes—epic on epic, iliad on iliad, and you always brothers in arms. Whether it was but recently (for time is nothing), or at the beginning of the world, I sent you out to war. I sat in the darkness, where there is not any created thing, and to you I was only a voice commanding valour and an unnatural virtue. You heard the voice in the dark, and you never heard it again. The sun in heaven denied it, the earth and sky denied it, all human wisdom denied it. And when I met you in the daylight I denied it myself."

Syme stirred sharply in his seat, but otherwise there was silence, and the incomprehensible went on.

"But you were men. You did not forget your secret honour, though the whole cosmos turned an engine of torture to tear it out of you. I knew how near you were to hell. I know how you, Thursday, crossed swords with King Satan, and how you, Wednesday, named me in the hour without hope."

There was complete silence in the starlit garden, and then the black-browed Secretary, implacable, turned in his chair towards Sunday, and said in a harsh voice—

"Who and what are you?"

"I am the Sabbath," said the other without moving. "I am the peace of God."

The Secretary started up, and stood crushing his costly robe in his hand.

"I know what you mean," he cried, "and it is exactly that that I cannot forgive you. I know you are contentment, optimism, what do they call the thing, an ultimate reconciliation. Well, I am not reconciled. If you were the man in the dark room, why were you also Sunday, an offence to the sunlight? If you were from the first our father and our friend, why were you also our greatest enemy? We wept, we fled in terror; the iron entered into our souls—and you are the peace of God! Oh, I can forgive God His anger, though it destroyed nations; but I cannot forgive Him His peace."

Sunday answered not a word, but very slowly he turned his face of stone upon Syme as if asking a question.

"No," said Syme, "I do not feel fierce like that. I am grateful to you, not only for wine and hospitality here, but for many a fine scamper and free fight. But I should like to know. My soul and heart are as happy and quiet here as this old garden, but my reason is still crying out. I should like to know."

Sunday looked at Ratcliffe, whose clear voice said—

"It seems so *silly* that you should have been on both sides and fought yourself."

Bull said—

"I understand nothing, but I am happy. In fact, I am going to sleep."

"I am not happy," said the Professor with his head in his hands, "because I do not understand. You let me stray a little too near to hell."

And then Gogol said, with the absolute simplicity of a child—

"I wish I knew why I was hurt so much."

Still Sunday said nothing, but only sat with his mighty chin upon his hand, and gazed at the distance. Then at last he said—

"I have heard your complaints in order. And here, I think, comes another to complain, and we will hear him also."

The falling fire in the great cresset threw a last long gleam, like a bar of burning gold, across the dim grass. Against this fiery band was outlined in utter black the advancing legs of a black-clad figure. He seemed to have a fine close suit with knee-breeches such as that which was worn by the servants of the house, only that it was not blue, but of this absolute sable. He had, like the servants, a kind of sword by his side. It was only when he had come quite close to the crescent of the seven and flung up his face to look at them, that Syme saw, with thunderstruck clearness, that the face was the broad, almost ape-like face of his old friend Gregory, with its rank red hair and its insulting smile.

"Gregory!" gasped Syme, half-rising from his seat. "Why, this is the real anarchist!"

"Yes," said Gregory, with a great and dangerous restraint, "I am the real anarchist."

" 'And there came a day,' " murmured Bull, who seemed really to have fallen asleep, " 'when the sons of God came before the Lord, and Satan also came with them.' "

"You are right," said Gregory, and gazed all round. "I am a destroyer. I would destroy the world if I could."

A sense of a pathos far under the earth stirred up in Syme, and he spoke brokenly and without sequence.

"Oh, most unhappy man," he cried, "try to be happy! You have red hair like your sister."

"My red hair, like red flames, shall burn up the world," said Gregory. "I thought I hated everything more than common men can hate anything; but I find that I do not hate everything so much as I hate you!"

"I never hated you," said Syme very sadly.

Then out of this unintelligible creature the last thunders broke. "You!" he cried. "You never hated because you never lived. I know what you are all of you, from first to last—you are the people in power! You are the police—the great fat, smiling men in blue and buttons! You are the Law, and you have never been broken. But is there a free soul alive that does not long to break you, only because you have never been broken? We in revolt talk all kind of nonsense doubtless about this crime or that crime of the Government. It is all folly! The only crime of the Government is that it governs. The unpardonable sin of the supreme power is that it is supreme. I do not curse you for being cruel. I do not curse you (though I might) for being kind. I curse you for being safe! You sit in your chairs of stone, and have never come down from them. You are the seven angels of heaven, and you have had no troubles. Oh, I could forgive you everything, you that rule all mankind, if I could feel for once that you had suffered for one hour a real agony such as I——"

Syme sprang to his feet, shaking from head to foot.

"I see everything," he cried, "everything that there is. Why does each thing on the earth war against each other thing? Why does each small thing in the world have to fight against the world itself? Why does a fly have to fight the whole universe? Why does a dandelion have to fight the whole universe? For the same reason that I had to be alone in the dreadful Council of the Days. So that each thing that obeys law may have the glory and isolation of the anarchist. So that each man fighting for order may be as brave and good a man as the dynamiter. So that the real lie of Satan may be flung back in the face of this blasphemer, so that by tears and torture we may earn the right to say to this man, 'You lie!' No agonies can be too great to buy the right to say to this accuser, 'We also have suffered.'

"It is not true that we have never been broken. We have been broken upon the wheel. It is not true that we have never descended from these thrones. We have descended into hell. We were complaining of unforgettable miseries even at the very moment when this man entered insolently to accuse us of happiness. I repel the slander; we have not been happy. I can answer for every one of the great guards of Law whom he has accused. At least——"

He had turned his eyes so as to see suddenly the great face of Sunday, which wore a strange smile.

"Have you," he cried in a dreadful voice, "have you ever suffered?"

As he gazed, the great face grew to an awful size, grew larger than the colossal mask of Memnon, which had made him scream as a child. It grew larger and larger, filling the whole sky; then everything went black. Only in the blackness before it entirely destroyed his brain he seemed to hear a distant voice saying a commonplace text that he had heard somewhere, "Can ye drink of the cup that I drink of?"

* * * * *

When men in books awake from a vision, they commonly find themselves in some place in which they might have fallen asleep; they yawn in a chair, or lift themselves with bruised limbs from a field. Syme's experience was something much more psychologically strange if there was indeed anything unreal, in the earthly sense, about the things he had gone through. For while he could always remember afterwards that he had swooned before the face of Sunday, he could not remember having ever come to at all. He could only remember that gradually and naturally he knew that he was and had been walking along a country lane with an easy and conversational companion. That companion had been a part of his recent drama; it was the red-haired poet Gregory. They were walking like old friends, and were in the middle of a conversation about some triviality. But Syme could only feel an unnatural buoyancy in his body and a crystal simplicity in his mind that seemed to be superior to everything that he said or did. He felt he was in possession of some impossible good news, which made every other thing a triviality, but an adorable triviality.

Dawn was breaking over everything in colours at once clear and timid; as if Nature made a first attempt at yellow and a first attempt at rose. A breeze blew so clean and sweet, that one could not think that it blew from the sky; it blew rather through some hole in the sky. Syme felt a simple surprise when he saw rising all round him on both sides of the road the red, irregular buildings of Saffron Park. He had no idea that he had walked so near London. He walked by instinct along one white road, on which early birds hopped and sang, and found himself outside a fenced garden. There he saw the sister of Gregory, the girl with the gold-red hair, cutting lilac before breakfast, with the great unconscious gravity of a girl.

THE END

Orthodoxy

TO MY MOTHER

Preface

THIS BOOK is meant to be a companion to "Heretics," and to put the positive side in addition to the negative. Many critics complained of the book called "Heretics" because it merely criticised current philosophies without offering any alternative philosophy. This book is an attempt to answer the challenge. It is unavoidably affirmative and therefore unavoidably autobiographical. The writer has been driven back upon somewhat the same difficulty as that which beset Newman in writing his Apologia; he has been forced to be egotistical only in order to be sincere. While everything else may be different the motive in both cases is the same. It is the purpose of the writer to attempt an explanation, not of whether the Christian Faith can be believed, but of how he personally has come to believe it. The book is therefore arranged upon the positive principle of a riddle and its answer. It deals first with all the writer's own solitary and sincere speculations and then with all the startling style in which they were all suddenly satisfied by the Christian Theology. The writer regards it as amounting to a convincing creed. But if it is not that it is at least a repeated and surprising coincidence.

GILBERT K. CHESTERTON.

Contents

I. INTRODUCTION IN DEFENCE OF EVERYTHING ELSE

THE ONLY possible excuse for this book is that it is an answer to a challenge. Even a bad shot is dignified when he accepts a duel. When some time ago I published a series of hasty but sincere papers, under the name of "Heretics," several critics for whose intellect I have a warm respect (I may mention specially Mr. G. S. Street) said that it was all very well for me to tell everybody to affirm his cosmic theory, but that I had carefully avoided supporting my precepts with example. "I will begin to worry about my philosophy," said Mr. Street, "when Mr. Chesterton has given us his." It was perhaps an incautious suggestion to make to a person only too ready to write books upon the feeblest provocation. But after all, though Mr. Street has inspired and created this book, he need not read it. If he does read it, he will find that in its pages I have attempted in a vague and personal way, in a set of mental pictures rather than in a series of deductions, to state the philosophy in which I have come to believe. I will not call it my philosophy; for I did not make it. God and humanity made it; and it made me.

I have often had a fancy for writing a romance about an English yachtsman who slightly miscalculated his course and discovered England under the impression that it was a new island in the South Seas. I always find, however, that I am either too busy or too lazy to write this fine work, so I may as well give it away for the purposes of philosophical illustration. There will probably be a general impression that the man who landed (armed to the teeth and talking by signs) to plant the British flag on that barbaric temple which turned out to be the Pavilion at Brighton, felt rather a fool. I am not here concerned to deny that he looked a fool. But if you imagine that he felt a fool, or at any rate that the sense of folly was his sole or his dominant emotion, then you have not studied with sufficient delicacy the rich romantic nature of the hero of this tale. His mistake was really a most enviable mistake; and he knew it, if he was the man I take him for. What could be more delightful than to have in the same few minutes all the fascinating terrors of going abroad combined with all the humane security of coming home again? What could be better than to have all the fun of discovering South Africa without the disgusting necessity of landing there? What could be more glorious than to brace one's self up to discover New South Wales and then realize, with a gush of happy tears, that it was really old South Wales. This at least seems to me the main problem for philosophers, and is in a manner the main problem of this book. How can we contrive to be at once astonished at the world and yet at home in it? How can this queer cosmic town, with its many-legged citizens, with its monstrous and ancient lamps, how can this world give us at once the fascination of a strange town and the comfort and honour of being our own town?

To show that a faith or a philosophy is true from every standpoint would be too big an undertaking even for a much bigger book than this; it is necessary to follow one path of argument; and this is the path that I here propose to follow. I wish to set forth my faith as particularly answering this double spiritual need, the need for that mixture of the familiar and the unfamiliar which Christendom has rightly named romance. For the very word "romance" has in it the mystery and ancient meaning of Rome. Any one setting out to dispute anything ought always to begin by saying what he does not dispute. Beyond stating what he proposes to prove he should always state what he does not propose to prove. The thing I do not propose to prove, the thing I propose to take as common ground between myself and any average reader, is this desirability of an active and imaginative life, picturesque and full of a poetical curiosity, a life such as western man at any rate always seems to have desired. If a man says that extinction is better than existence or blank existence better than variety and adventure, then he is not one of the ordinary people to whom I am talking. If a man prefers nothing I can give him nothing. But nearly all people I have ever met in this western society in which I live would agree to the general proposition that we need this life of practical romance; the combination of something that is strange with something that is secure. We need so to view the world as to combine an idea of wonder and an idea of welcome. We need to be happy in this wonderland without once being merely comfortable. It is *this* achievement of my creed that I shall chiefly pursue in these pages.

But I have a peculiar reason for mentioning the man in a yacht, who discovered England. For I am that man in a yacht. I discovered England. I do not see how this book can avoid being egotistical; and I do not quite see (to tell the truth) how it can avoid being dull. Dulness will, however, free me from the charge which I most lament; the charge of being flippant. Mere light sophistry is the thing that I happen to despise most of all things, and it is perhaps a wholesome fact that this is the thing of which I am generally accused. I know nothing so contemptible as a mere paradox; a mere ingenious defence of the indefensible. If it were true (as has been said) that Mr. Bernard Shaw lived upon paradox, then he ought to be a mere common millionaire; for a man of his mental activity could invent a sophistry every six minutes. It is as easy as lying; because it is lying. The truth is, of course, that Mr. Shaw is cruelly hampered by the fact that he cannot tell any lie unless he thinks it is the truth. I find myself under the same intolerable bondage. I never in my life said anything merely because I thought it funny; though of course, I have had ordinary human vainglory, and may have thought it funny because I had said it. It is one thing to describe an interview with a gorgon or a griffin, a creature who does not exist. It is another thing to discover that the rhinoceros does exist and then take pleasure in the fact that he looks as if he didn't. One searches for truth, but it may be that one pursues instinctively the more extraordinary truths. And I offer this book with the heartiest sentiments to all the jolly people who hate what I write, and regard it (very justly, for all I know) as a piece of poor clowning or a single tiresome joke.

For if this book is a joke it is a joke against me. I am the man who with the utmost daring discovered what had been discovered before. If there is an element of farce in what follows, the farce is at my own expense; for this book explains how I fancied I was the first to set foot in Brighton and then found I was the last. It recounts my elephantine adventures in pursuit of the obvious. No one can think my case more ludicrous than I think it myself; no reader can accuse me here of trying to make a fool of him: I am the fool of this story, and no rebel shall hurl me from my throne. I freely confess all the idiotic ambitions of the end of the nineteenth century. I did, like all other solemn little boys, try to be in advance of the age. Like them I tried to be some ten minutes in advance of the truth. And I found that I was eighteen hundred years behind it. I did strain my voice with a painfully juvenile exaggeration in uttering my truths. And I was punished in the fittest and funniest way, for I have kept my truths: but I have discovered, not that they were not truths, but simply that they were not mine. When I fancied that I stood alone I was really in the ridiculous position of being backed up by all Christendom. It may be, Heaven forgive me, that I did try to be original; but I only succeeded in inventing all by myself an inferior copy of the existing traditions of civilized religion. The man from the yacht thought he was the first to find England; I thought I was the first to find Europe. I did try to found a heresy of my own; and when I had put the last touches to it, I discovered that it was orthodoxy.

It may be that somebody will be entertained by the account of this happy fiasco. It might amuse a friend or an enemy to read how I gradually learnt from the truth of some stray legend or from the falsehood of some dominant philosophy, things that I might have learnt from my catechism—if I had ever learnt it. There may or may not be some entertainment in reading how I found at last in an anarchist club or a Babylonian temple what I might have found in the nearest parish church. If any one is entertained by learning how the flowers of the field or the phrases in an omnibus, the accidents of politics or the pains of youth came together in a certain order to produce a certain conviction of Christian orthodoxy, he may possibly read this book. But there is in everything a reasonable division of labour. I have written the book, and nothing on earth would induce me to read it.

I add one purely pedantic note which comes, as a note naturally should, at the beginning of the book. These essays are concerned only to discuss the actual fact that the central Christian theology (sufficiently summarized in the Apostles' Creed) is the best root of energy and sound ethics. They are not intended to discuss the very fascinating but quite different question of what is the present seat of authority for the proclamation of that creed. When the word "orthodoxy" is used here it means the Apostles' Creed, as understood by everybody calling himself Christian until a very short time ago and the general historic conduct of those who held such a creed. I have been forced by mere space to confine myself to what I have got from this creed; I do not touch the matter much disputed among modern Christians, of where we ourselves got it. This is not an ecclesiastical treatise but a sort of slovenly autobiography. But if any one wants my opinions about the actual nature of the authority, Mr. G. S. Street has only to throw me another challenge, and I will write him another book.

II. THE MANIAC

THOROUGHLY WORLDLY people never understand even the world; they rely altogether on a few cynical maxims which are not true. Once I remember walking with a prosperous publisher, who made a remark which I had often heard before; it is, indeed, almost a motto of the modern world. Yet I had heard it once too often, and I saw suddenly that there was nothing in it. The publisher said of somebody, "That man will get on; he believes in himself." And I remember that as I lifted my head to listen, my eye caught an omnibus on which was written "Hanwell." I said to him, "Shall I tell you where the men are who believe most in themselves? For I can tell you. I know of men who believe in themselves more colossally than Napoleon or Caesar. I know where flames the fixed star of certainty and success. I can guide you to the thrones of the Supermen. The men who really believe in themselves are all in lunatic asylums." He said mildly that there were a good many men after all who believed in themselves and who were not in lunatic asylums. "Yes, there are," I retorted, "and you of all men ought to know them. That drunken poet from whom you would not take a dreary tragedy, he believed in himself. That elderly minister with an epic from whom you were hiding in a back room, he believed in himself. If you consulted your business experience instead of your ugly individualistic philosophy, you would know that believing in himself is one of the commonest signs of a rotter. Actors who can't act believe in themselves; and debtors who won't pay. It would be much truer to say that a man will certainly fail, because he believes in himself. Complete self-confidence is not merely a sin; complete self-confidence is a weakness. Believing utterly in one's self is a hysterical and superstitious belief like believing in Joanna Southcote: the man who has it has 'Hanwell' written on his face as plain as it is written on that omnibus." And to all this my friend the publisher made this very deep and effective reply, "Well, if a man is not to believe in himself, in what is he to believe?" After a long pause I replied, "I will go home and write a book in answer to that question." This is the book that I have written in answer to it.

But I think this book may well start where our argument started—in the neighbourhood of the mad-house. Modern masters of science are much impressed with the need of beginning all inquiry with a fact. The ancient masters of religion were quite equally impressed with that necessity. They began with the fact of sin—a fact as practical as potatoes. Whether or not man could be washed in miraculous waters, there was no doubt at any rate that he wanted washing. But certain religious leaders in London, not mere materialists, have begun in our day not to deny the highly disputable water, but to deny the indisputable dirt. Certain new theologians dispute original sin, which is the only part of Christian theology which can really be proved. Some followers of the Reverend R. J. Campbell, in their almost too fastidious spirituality, admit divine sinlessness, which they cannot see even in their dreams. But they essentially deny human sin, which they can see in the street. The strongest saints and the strongest sceptics alike took positive evil as the starting-point of their argument. If it be true (as it certainly is) that a man can feel exquisite happiness in skinning a cat, then the religious philosopher can only draw one of two deductions. He must either deny the existence of God, as all atheists do; or he must deny the present union between God and man, as all Christians do. The new theologians seem to think it a highly rationalistic solution to deny the cat.

In this remarkable situation it is plainly not now possible (with any hope of a universal appeal) to start, as our fathers did, with the fact of sin. This very fact which was to them (and is to me) as plain as a pikestaff, is the very fact that has been specially diluted or denied. But though moderns deny the existence of sin, I do not think that they have yet denied the existence of a lunatic asylum. We all agree still that there is a collapse of the intellect as unmistakable as a falling house. Men deny hell, but not, as yet, Hanwell. For the purpose of our primary argument the one may very well stand where the other stood. I mean that as all thoughts and theories were once judged by whether they tended to make a man lose his soul, so for our present purpose all modern thoughts and theories may be judged by whether they tend to make a man lose his wits.

It is true that some speak lightly and loosely of insanity as in itself attractive. But a moment's thought will show that if disease is beautiful, it is generally some one else's disease. A blind man may be picturesque; but it requires two eyes to see the picture. And similarly even the wildest poetry of insanity can only be enjoyed by the sane. To the insane man his insanity is quite prosaic, because it is quite true. A man who thinks himself a chicken is to himself as ordinary as a chicken. A man who thinks he is a bit of glass is to himself as dull as a bit of glass. It is the homogeneity of his mind which makes him dull, and which makes him mad. It is only because we see the irony of his idea that we think him even amusing; it is only because he does not see the irony of his idea that he is put in Hanwell at all. In short, oddities only strike ordinary people. Oddities do not strike odd people. This is why ordinary people have a much more exciting time; while odd people are always complaining of the dulness of life. This is also why the new novels die so quickly, and why the old fairy tales endure for ever. The old fairy tale makes the hero a normal human boy; it is his adventures that are startling; they startle him because he is normal. But in the modern psychological novel the hero is abnormal; the centre is not central. Hence the fiercest adventures fail to affect him adequately, and the book is monotonous. You can make a story out of a hero among dragons; but not out of a dragon among dragons. The fairy tale discusses what a sane man will do in a mad world. The sober realistic novel of to-day discusses what an essential lunatic will do in a dull world.

Let us begin, then, with the mad-house; from this evil and fantastic inn let us set forth on our intellectual journey. Now, if we are to glance at the philosophy of sanity, the first thing to do in the matter is to blot out one big and common mistake. There is a notion adrift everywhere that imagination, especially mystical imagination, is dangerous to man's mental balance. Poets are commonly spoken of as psychologically unreliable; and generally there is a vague association between wreathing laurels in your hair and sticking straws in it. Facts and history utterly contradict this view. Most of the very great poets have been not only sane, but extremely business-like; and if Shakespeare ever really held horses, it was because he was much the safest man to hold them. Imagination does not breed insanity. Exactly what does breed insanity is reason. Poets do not go mad; but chess-players do. Mathematicians go mad, and cashiers; but creative artists very seldom. I am not, as will be seen, in any sense attacking logic: I only say that this danger does lie in logic, not in imagination.

Artistic paternity is as wholesome as physical paternity. Moreover, it is worthy of remark that when a poet really was morbid it was commonly because he had some weak spot of rationality on his brain. Poe, for instance, really was morbid; not because he was poetical, but because he was specially analytical. Even chess was too poetical for him; he disliked chess because it was full of knights and castles, like a poem. He avowedly preferred the black discs of draughts, because they were more like the mere black dots on a diagram. Perhaps the strongest case of all is this: that only one great English poet went mad, Cowper. And he was definitely driven mad by logic, by the ugly and alien logic of predestination. Poetry was not the disease, but the medicine; poetry partly kept him in health. He could sometimes forget the red and thirsty hell to which his hideous necessitarianism dragged him among the wide waters and the white flat lilies of the Ouse. He was damned by John Calvin; he was almost saved by John Gilpin. Everywhere we see that men do not go mad by dreaming. Critics are much madder than poets. Homer is complete and calm enough; it is his critics who tear him into extravagant tatters. Shakespeare is quite himself; it is only some of his critics who have discovered that he was somebody else. And though St. John the Evangelist saw many strange monsters in his vision, he saw no creature so wild as one of his own commentators. The general fact is simple. Poetry is sane because it floats easily in an infinite sea; reason seeks to cross the infinite sea, and so make it finite. The result is mental exhaustion, like the physical exhaustion of Mr. Holbein. To accept everything is an exercise, to understand everything a strain. The poet only desires exaltation and expansion, a world to stretch himself in. The poet only asks to get his head into the heavens. It is the logician who seeks to get the heavens into his head. And it is his head that splits.

It is a small matter, but not irrelevant, that this striking mistake is commonly supported by a striking misquotation. We have all heard people cite the celebrated line of Dryden as "Great genius is to madness near allied." But Dryden did not say that great genius was to madness near allied. Dryden was a great genius himself, and knew better. It would have been hard to find a man more romantic than he, or more sensible. What Dryden said was this, "Great wits are oft to madness near allied"; and that is true. It is the pure promptitude of the intellect that is in peril of a breakdown. Also people might remember of what sort of man Dryden was talking. He was not talking of any unworldly visionary like Vaughan or George Herbert.

He was talking of a cynical man of the world, a sceptic, a diplomatist, a great practical politician. Such men are indeed to madness near allied. Their incessant calculation of their own brains and other people's brains is a dangerous trade. It is always perilous to the mind to reckon up the mind. A flippant person has asked why we say, "As mad as a hatter." A more flippant person might answer that a hatter is mad because he has to measure the human head.

And if great reasoners are often maniacal, it is equally true that maniacs are commonly great reasoners. When I was engaged in a controversy with the *Clarion* on the matter of free will, that able writer Mr. R. B. Suthers said that free will was lunacy, because it meant causeless actions, and the actions of a lunatic would be causeless. I do not dwell here upon the disastrous lapse in determinist logic. Obviously if any actions, even a lunatic's, can be causeless, determinism is done for. If the chain of causation can be broken for a madman, it can be broken for a man. But my purpose is to point out something more practical. It was natural, perhaps, that a modern Marxian Socialist should not know anything about free will. But it was certainly remarkable that a modern Marxian Socialist should not know anything about lunatics. Mr. Suthers evidently did not know anything about lunatics. The last thing that can be said of a lunatic is that his actions are causeless. If any human acts may loosely be called causeless, they are the minor acts of a healthy man; whistling as he walks; slashing the grass with a stick; kicking his heels or rubbing his hands. It is the happy man who does the useless things; the sick man is not strong enough to be idle. It is exactly such careless and causeless actions that the madman could never understand; for the madman (like the determinist) generally sees too much cause in everything. The madman would read a conspiratorial significance into those empty activities. He would think that the lopping of the grass was an attack on private property. He would think that the kicking of the heels was a signal to an accomplice. If the madman could for an instant become careless, he would become sane. Every one who has had the misfortune to talk with people in the heart or on the edge of mental disorder, knows that their most sinister quality is a horrible clarity of detail; a connecting of one thing with another in a map more elaborate than a maze. If you argue with a madman, it is extremely probable that you will get the worst of it; for in many ways his mind moves all the quicker for not being delayed by the things that go with good judgment. He is not hampered by a sense of humour or by charity, or by the dumb certainties of experience. He is the more logical for losing certain sane affections. Indeed, the common phrase for insanity is in this respect a misleading one. The madman is not the man who has lost his reason. The madman is the man who has lost everything except his reason.

The madman's explanation of a thing is always complete, and often in a purely rational sense satisfactory. Or, to speak more strictly, the insane explanation, if not conclusive, is at least unanswerable; this may be observed specially in the two or three commonest kinds of madness. If a man says (for instance) that men have a conspiracy against him, you cannot dispute it except by saying that all the men deny that they are conspirators; which is exactly what conspirators would do. His explanation covers the facts as much as yours. Or if a man says that he is the rightful King of England, it is no complete answer to say that the existing authorities call him mad; for if he were King of England that might be the wisest thing for the existing authorities to do. Or if a man says that he is Jesus Christ, it is no answer to tell him that the world denies his divinity; for the world denied Christ's.

Nevertheless he is wrong. But if we attempt to trace his error in exact terms, we shall not find it quite so easy as we had supposed. Perhaps the nearest we can get to expressing it is to say this: that his mind moves in a perfect but narrow circle. A small circle is quite as infinite as a large circle; but, though it is quite as infinite, it is not so large. In the same way the insane explanation is quite as complete as the sane one, but it is not so large. A bullet is quite as round as the world, but it is not the world. There is such a thing as a narrow universality; there is such a thing as a small and cramped eternity; you may see it in many modern religions. Now, speaking quite externally and empirically, we may say that the strongest and most unmistakable *mark* of madness is this combination between a logical completeness and a spiritual contraction. The lunatic's theory explains a large number of things, but it does not explain them in a large way. I mean that if you or I were dealing with a mind that was growing morbid, we should be chiefly concerned not so much to give it arguments as to give it air, to convince it that there was something cleaner and cooler outside the suffocation of a single argument. Suppose, for instance, it were the first case that I took as typical; suppose it were the case of a man who accused everybody of conspiring against him. If we could express our deepest feelings of protest and appeal against this obsession, I suppose we should say something like this: "Oh, I admit that you have your case and have it by heart, and that many things do fit into other things as you say. I admit that your explanation explains a great deal; but what a great deal it leaves out! Are there no other stories in the world except yours; and are all men busy with your business? Suppose we grant the details; perhaps when the man in the street did not seem to see you it was only his cunning; perhaps when the policeman asked you your name it was only because he knew it already. But how much happier you would be if you only knew that these people cared nothing about you! How much larger your life would be if your self could become smaller in it; if you could really look at other men with common curiosity and pleasure; if you could see them walking as they are in their sunny selfishness and their virile indifference! You would begin to be interested in them, because they were not interested in you. You would break out of this tiny and tawdry theatre in which your own little plot is always being played, and you would find yourself under a freer sky, in a street full of splendid strangers." Or suppose it were the second case of madness, that of a man who claims the crown, your impulse would be to answer, "All right! Perhaps you know that you are the King of England; but why do you care? Make one magnificent effort and you will be a human being and look down on all the kings of the earth." Or it might be the third case, of the madman who called himself Christ. If we said what we felt, we should say, "So you are the Creator and Redeemer of the world: but what a small world it must be! What a little heaven you must inhabit, with angels no bigger than butterflies! How sad it must be to be God; and an inadequate God! Is there really no life fuller and no love more marvellous than yours; and is it really in your small and painful pity that all flesh must put its faith? How much happier you would be, how much more of you there would be, if the hammer of a higher God could smash your small cosmos, scattering the stars like spangles, and leave you in the open, free like other men to look up as well as down!"

And it must be remembered that the most purely practical science does take this view of mental evil; it does not seek to argue with it like a heresy but simply to snap it like a spell. Neither modern science nor ancient religion believes in complete free thought. Theology rebukes certain thoughts by calling them blasphemous. Science rebukes certain thoughts by calling them morbid. For example, some religious societies discouraged men more or less from thinking about sex. The new scientific society definitely discourages men from thinking about death; it is a fact, but it is considered a morbid fact. And in dealing with those whose morbidity has a touch of mania, modern science cares far less for pure logic than a dancing Dervish. In these cases it is not enough that the unhappy man should desire truth; he must desire health. Nothing can save him but a blind hunger for normality, like that of a beast. A man cannot think himself out of mental evil; for it is actually the organ of thought that has become diseased, ungovernable, and, as it were, independent. He can only be saved by will or faith. The moment his mere reason moves, it moves in the old circular rut; he will go round and round his logical circle, just as a man in a third-class carriage on the Inner Circle will go round and round the Inner Circle unless he performs the voluntary, vigorous, and mystical act of getting out at Gower Street. Decision is the whole business here; a door must be shut for ever. Every remedy is a desperate remedy. Every cure is a miraculous cure. Curing a madman is not arguing with a philosopher; it is casting out a devil. And however quietly doctors and psychologists may go to work in the matter, their attitude is profoundly intolerant—as intolerant as Bloody Mary. Their attitude is really this: that the man must stop thinking, if he is to go on living. Their counsel is one of intellectual amputation. If thy *head* offend thee, cut it off; for it is better, not merely to enter the Kingdom of Heaven as a child, but to enter it as an imbecile, rather than with your whole intellect to be cast into hell—or into Hanwell.

Such is the madman of experience; he is commonly a reasoner, frequently a successful reasoner. Doubtless he could be vanquished in mere reason, and the case against him put logically. But it can be put much more precisely in more general and even aesthetic terms. He is in the clean and well-lit prison of one idea: he is sharpened to one painful point. He is without healthy hesitation and healthy complexity. Now, as I explain in the introduction, I have determined in these early chapters to give not so much a diagram of a doctrine as some pictures of a point of view. And I have described at length my vision of the maniac for this reason: that just as I am affected by the maniac, so I am affected by most modern thinkers. That unmistakable mood or note that I hear from Hanwell, I hear also from half the chairs of science and seats of learning to-day; and most of the mad doctors are mad doctors in more senses than one. They all have exactly that combination we have noted: the combination of an expansive and exhaustive reason with a contracted common sense.

They are universal only in the sense that they take one thin explanation and carry it very far. But a pattern can stretch for ever and still be a small pattern. They see a chessboard white on black, and if the universe is paved with it, it is still white on black. Like the lunatic, they cannot alter their standpoint; they cannot make a mental effort and suddenly see it black on white.

Take first the more obvious case of materialism. As an explanation of the world, materialism has a sort of insane simplicity. It has just the quality of the madman's argument; we have at once the sense of it covering everything and the sense of it leaving everything out. Contemplate some able and sincere materialist, as, for instance, Mr. McCabe, and you will have exactly this unique sensation. He understands everything, and everything does not seem worth understanding. His cosmos may be complete in every rivet and cog-wheel, but still his cosmos is smaller than our world. Somehow his scheme, like the lucid scheme of the madman, seems unconscious of the alien energies and the large indifference of the earth; it is not thinking of the real things of the earth, of fighting peoples or proud mothers, or first love or fear upon the sea. The earth is so very large, and the cosmos is so very small. The cosmos is about the smallest hole that a man can hide his head in.

It must be understood that I am not now discussing the relation of these creeds to truth; but, for the present, solely their relation to health. Later in the argument I hope to attack the question of objective verity; here I speak only of a phenomenon of psychology. I do not for the present attempt to prove to Haeckel that materialism is untrue, any more than I attempted to prove to the man who thought he was Christ that he was labouring under an error. I merely remark here on the fact that both cases have the same kind of completeness and the same kind of incompleteness. You can explain a man's detention at Hanwell by an indifferent public by saying that it is the crucifixion of a god of whom the world is not worthy. The explanation does explain. Similarly you may explain the order in the universe by saying that all things, even the souls of men, are leaves inevitably unfolding on an utterly unconscious tree—the blind destiny of matter. The explanation does explain, though not, of course, so completely as the madman's. But the point here is that the normal human mind not only objects to both, but feels to both the same objection. Its approximate statement is that if the man in Hanwell is the real God, he is not much of a god. And, similarly, if the cosmos of the materialist is the real cosmos, it is not much of a cosmos. The thing has shrunk. The deity is less divine than many men; and (according to Haeckel) the whole of life is something much more grey, narrow, and trivial than many separate aspects of it. The parts seem greater than the whole.

For we must remember that the materialist philosophy (whether true or not) is certainly much more limiting than any religion. In one sense, of course, all intelligent ideas are narrow. They cannot be broader than themselves. A Christian is only restricted in the same sense that an atheist is restricted. He cannot think Christianity false and continue to be a Christian; and the atheist cannot think atheism false and continue to be an atheist. But as it happens, there is a very special sense in which materialism has more restrictions than spiritualism. Mr. McCabe thinks me a slave because I am not allowed to believe in determinism. I think Mr. McCabe a slave because he is not allowed to believe in fairies. But if we examine the two vetoes we shall see that his is really much more of a pure veto than mine. The Christian is quite free to believe that there is a considerable amount of settled order and inevitable development in the universe. But the materialist is not allowed to admit into his spotless machine the slightest speck of spiritualism or miracle. Poor Mr. McCabe is not allowed to retain even the tiniest imp, though it might be hiding in a pimpernel. The Christian admits that the universe is manifold and even miscellaneous, just as a sane man knows that he is complex. The sane man knows that he has a touch of the beast, a touch of the devil, a touch of the saint, a touch of the citizen. Nay, the really sane man knows that he has a touch of the madman. But the materialist's world is quite simple and solid, just as the madman is quite sure he is sane. The materialist is sure that history has been simply and solely a chain of causation, just as the interesting person before mentioned is quite sure that he is simply and solely a chicken. Materialists and madmen never have doubts.

Spiritual doctrines do not actually limit the mind as do materialistic denials. Even if I believe in immortality I need not think about it. But if I disbelieve in immortality I must not think about it. In the first case the road is open and I can go as far as I like; in the second the road is shut. But the case is even stronger, and the parallel with madness is yet more strange. For it was our case against the exhaustive and logical theory of the lunatic that, right or wrong, it gradually destroyed his humanity. Now it is the charge against the main deductions of the materialist that, right or wrong, they gradually destroy his humanity; I do not mean only kindness, I mean hope, courage, poetry, initiative, all that is human. For instance, when materialism leads men to complete fatalism (as it generally does), it is quite idle to pretend that it is in any sense a liberating force. It is absurd to say that you are especially advancing freedom when you only use free thought to destroy free will. The determinists come to bind, not to loose. They may well call their law the "chain" of causation. It is the worst chain that ever fettered a human being. You may use the language of liberty, if you like, about materialistic teaching, but it is obvious that this is just as inapplicable to it as a whole as the same language when applied to a man locked up in a mad-house. You may say, if you like, that the man is free to think himself a poached egg. But it is surely a more massive and important fact that if he is a poached egg he is not free to eat, drink, sleep, walk, or smoke a cigarette. Similarly you may say, if you like, that the bold determinist speculator is free to disbelieve in the reality of the will. But it is a much more massive and important fact that he is not free to raise, to curse, to thank, to justify, to urge, to punish, to resist temptations, to incite mobs, to make New Year resolutions, to pardon sinners, to rebuke tyrants, or even to say "thank you" for the mustard.

In passing from this subject I may note that there is a queer fallacy to the effect that materialistic fatalism is in some way favourable to mercy, to the abolition of cruel punishments or punishments of any kind. This is startlingly the reverse of the truth. It is quite tenable that the doctrine of necessity makes no difference at all; that it leaves the flogger flogging and the kind friend exhorting as before. But obviously if it stops either of them it stops the kind exhortation. That the sins are inevitable does not prevent punishment; if it prevents anything it prevents persuasion. Determinism is quite as likely to lead to cruelty as it is certain to lead to cowardice. Determinism is not inconsistent with the cruel treatment of criminals. What it is (perhaps) inconsistent with is the generous treatment of criminals; with any appeal to their better feelings or encouragement in their moral struggle. The determinist does not believe in appealing to the will, but he does believe in changing the environment. He must not say to the sinner, "Go and sin no more," because the sinner cannot help it. But he can put him in boiling oil; for boiling oil is an environment. Considered as a figure, therefore, the materialist has the fantastic outline of the figure of the madman. Both take up a position at once unanswerable and intolerable.

Of course it is not only of the materialist that all this is true. The same would apply to the other extreme of speculative logic. There is a sceptic far more terrible than he who believes that everything began in matter. It is possible to meet the sceptic who believes that everything began in himself. He doubts not the existence of angels or devils, but the existence of men and cows. For him his own friends are a mythology made up by himself. He created his own father and his own mother. This horrible fancy has in it something decidedly attractive to the somewhat mystical egoism of our day. That publisher who thought that men would get on if they believed in themselves, those seekers after the Superman who are always looking for him in the looking-glass, those writers who talk about impressing their personalities instead of creating life for the world, all these people have really only an inch between them and this awful emptiness. Then when this kindly world all round the man has been blackened out like a lie; when friends fade into ghosts, and the foundations of the world fail; then when the man, believing in nothing and in no man, is alone in his own nightmare, then the great individualistic motto shall be written over him in avenging irony. The stars will be only dots in the blackness of his own brain; his mother's face will be only a sketch from his own insane pencil on the walls of his cell. But over his cell shall be written, with dreadful truth, "He believes in himself."

All that concerns us here, however, is to note that this panegoistic extreme of thought exhibits the same paradox as the other extreme of materialism. It is equally complete in theory and equally crippling in practice. For the sake of simplicity, it is easier to state the notion by saying that a man can believe that he is always in a dream. Now, obviously there can be no positive proof given to him that he is not in a dream, for the simple reason that no proof can be offered that might not be offered in a dream. But if the man began to burn down London and say that his housekeeper would soon call him to breakfast, we should take him and put him with other logicians in a place which has often been alluded to in the course of this chapter. The man who cannot believe his senses, and the man who cannot believe anything else, are both insane, but their insanity is proved not by any error in their argument, but by the manifest mistake of their whole lives. They have both locked themselves up in two boxes, painted inside with the sun and stars; they are both unable to get out, the one into the health and happiness of heaven, the other even into the health and happiness of the earth.

Their position is quite reasonable; nay, in a sense it is infinitely reasonable, just as a threepenny bit is infinitely circular. But there is such a thing as a mean infinity, a base and slavish eternity. It is amusing to notice that many of the moderns, whether sceptics or mystics, have taken as their sign a certain eastern symbol, which is the very symbol of this ultimate nullity. When they wish to represent eternity, they represent it by a serpent with his tail in his mouth. There is a startling sarcasm in the image of that very unsatisfactory meal. The eternity of the material fatalists, the eternity of the eastern pessimists, the eternity of the supercilious theosophists and higher scientists of to-day is, indeed, very well presented by a serpent eating his tail, a degraded animal who destroys even himself.

This chapter is purely practical and is concerned with what actually is the chief mark and element of insanity; we may say in summary that it is reason used without root, reason in the void. The man who begins to think without the proper first principles goes mad; he begins to think at the wrong end. And for the rest of these pages we have to try and discover what is the right end. But we may ask in conclusion, if this be what drives men mad, what is it that keeps them sane? By the end of this book I hope to give a definite, some will think a far too definite, answer. But for the moment it is possible in the same solely practical manner to give a general answer touching what in actual human history keeps men sane. Mysticism keeps men sane. As long as you have mystery you have health; when you destroy mystery you create morbidity. The ordinary man has always been sane because the ordinary man has always been a mystic. He has permitted the twilight. He has always had one foot in earth and the other in fairyland. He has always left himself free to doubt his gods; but (unlike the agnostic of to-day) free also to believe in them. He has always cared more for truth than for consistency. If he saw two truths that seemed to contradict each other, he would take the two truths and the contradiction along with them. His spiritual sight is stereoscopic, like his physical sight: he sees two different pictures at once and yet sees all the better for that. Thus he has always believed that there was such a thing as fate, but such a thing as free will also. Thus he believed that children were indeed the kingdom of heaven, but nevertheless ought to be obedient to the kingdom of earth. He admired youth because it was young and age because it was not. It is exactly this balance of apparent contradictions that has been the whole buoyancy of the healthy man. The whole secret of mysticism is this: that man can understand everything by the help of what he does not understand. The morbid logician seeks to make everything lucid, and succeeds in making everything mysterious. The mystic allows one thing to be mysterious, and everything else becomes lucid. The determinist makes the theory of causation quite clear, and then finds that he cannot say "if you please" to the housemaid. The Christian permits free will to remain a sacred mystery; but because of this his relations with the housemaid become of a sparkling and crystal clearness. He puts the seed of dogma in a central darkness; but it branches forth in all directions with abounding natural health. As we have taken the circle as the symbol of reason and madness, we may very well take the cross as the symbol at once of mystery and of health. Buddhism is centripetal, but Christianity is centrifugal: it breaks out. For the circle is perfect and infinite in its nature; but it is fixed for ever in its size; it can never be larger or smaller. But the cross, though it has at its heart a collision and a contradiction, can extend its four arms for ever without altering its shape. Because it has a paradox in its centre it can grow without changing. The circle returns upon itself and is bound. The cross opens its arms to the four winds; it is a signpost for free travellers.

Symbols alone are of even a cloudy value in speaking of this deep matter; and another symbol from physical nature will express sufficiently well the real place of mysticism before mankind. The one created thing which we cannot look at is the one thing in the light of which we look at everything. Like the sun at noonday, mysticism explains everything else by the blaze of its own victorious invisibility. Detached intellectualism is (in the exact sense of a popular phrase) all moonshine; for it is light without heat, and it is secondary light, reflected from a dead world. But the Greeks were right when they made Apollo the god both of imagination and of sanity; for he was both the patron of poetry and the patron of healing. Of necessary dogmas and a special creed I shall speak later. But that transcendentalism by which all men live has primarily much the position of the sun in the sky. We are conscious of it as of a kind of splendid confusion; it is something both shining and shapeless, at once a blaze and a blur. But the circle of the moon is as clear and unmistakable, as recurrent and inevitable, as the circle of Euclid on a blackboard. For the moon is utterly reasonable; and the moon is the mother of lunatics and has given to them all her name.

III. THE SUICIDE OF THOUGHT

THE PHRASES of the street are not only forcible but subtle: for a figure of speech can often get into a crack too small for a definition. Phrases like "put out" or "off colour" might have been coined by Mr. Henry James in an agony of verbal precision. And there is no more subtle truth than that of the everyday phrase about a man having "his heart in the right place." It involves the idea of normal proportion; not only does a certain function exist, but it is rightly related to other functions. Indeed, the negation of this phrase would describe with peculiar accuracy the somewhat morbid mercy and perverse tenderness of the most representative moderns. If, for instance, I had to describe with fairness the character of Mr. Bernard Shaw, I could not express myself more exactly than by saying that he has a heroically large and generous heart; but not a heart in the right place. And this is so of the typical society of our time.

The modern world is not evil; in some ways the modern world is far too good. It is full of wild and wasted virtues. When a religious scheme is shattered (as Christianity was shattered at the Reformation), it is not merely the vices that are let loose. The vices are, indeed, let loose, and they wander and do damage. But the virtues are let loose also; and the virtues wander more wildly, and the virtues do more terrible damage. The modern world is full of the old Christian virtues gone mad. The virtues have gone mad because they have been isolated from each other and are wandering alone. Thus some scientists care for truth; and their truth is pitiless. Thus some humanitarians only care for pity; and their pity (I am sorry to say) is often untruthful. For example, Mr. Blatchford attacks Christianity because he is mad on one Christian virtue: the merely mystical and almost irrational virtue of charity. He has a strange idea that he will make it easier to forgive sins by saying that there are no sins to forgive.

Mr. Blatchford is not only an early Christian, he is the only early Christian who ought really to have been eaten by lions. For in his case the pagan accusation is really true: his mercy would mean mere anarchy. He really is the enemy of the human race—because he is so human. As the other extreme, we may take the acrid realist, who has deliberately killed in himself all human pleasure in happy tales or in the healing of the heart. Torquemada tortured people physically for the sake of moral truth. Zola tortured people morally for the sake of physical truth. But in Torquemada's time there was at least a system that could to some extent make righteousness and peace kiss each other. Now they do not even bow. But a much stronger case than these two of truth and pity can be found in the remarkable case of the dislocation of humility.

It is only with one aspect of humility that we are here concerned. Humility was largely meant as a restraint upon the arrogance and infinity of the appetite of man. He was always outstripping his mercies with his own newly invented needs. His very power of enjoyment destroyed half his joys. By asking for pleasure, he lost the chief pleasure; for the chief pleasure is surprise. Hence it became evident that if a man would make his world large, he must be always making himself small. Even the haughty visions, the tall cities, and the toppling pinnacles are the creations of humility. Giants that tread down forests like grass are the creations of humility. Towers that vanish upwards above the loneliest star are the creations of humility. For towers are not tall unless we look up at them; and giants are not giants unless they are larger than we. All this gigantesque imagination, which is, perhaps, the mightiest of the pleasures of man, is at bottom entirely humble. It is impossible without humility to enjoy anything—even pride.

But what we suffer from to-day is humility in the wrong place. Modesty has moved from the organ of ambition. Modesty has settled upon the organ of conviction; where it was never meant to be. A man was meant to be doubtful about himself, but undoubting about the truth; this has been exactly reversed. Nowadays the part of a man that a man does assert is exactly the part he ought not to assert—himself. The part he doubts is exactly the part he ought not to doubt—the Divine Reason. Huxley preached a humility content to learn from Nature. But the new sceptic is so humble that he doubts if he can even learn. Thus we should be wrong if we had said hastily that there is no humility typical of our time. The truth is that there is a real humility typical of our time; but it so happens that it is practically a more poisonous humility than the wildest prostrations of the ascetic. The old humility was a spur that prevented a man from stopping; not a nail in his boot that prevented him from going on. For the old humility made a man doubtful about his efforts, which might make him work harder. But the new humility makes a man doubtful about his aims, which will make him stop working altogether.

At any street corner we may meet a man who utters the frantic and blasphemous statement that he may be wrong. Every day one comes across somebody who says that of course his view may not be the right one. Of course his view must be the right one, or it is not his view. We are on the road to producing a race of men too mentally modest to believe in the multiplication table. We are in danger of seeing philosophers who doubt the law of gravity as being a mere fancy of their own. Scoffers of old time were too proud to be convinced; but these are too humble to be convinced. The meek do inherit the earth; but the modern sceptics are too meek even to claim their inheritance. It is exactly this intellectual helplessness which is our second problem.

The last chapter has been concerned only with a fact of observation: that what peril of morbidity there is for man comes rather from his reason than his imagination. It was not meant to attack the authority of reason; rather it is the ultimate purpose to defend it. For it needs defence. The whole modern world is at war with reason; and the tower already reels.

The sages, it is often said, can see no answer to the riddle of religion. But the trouble with our sages is not that they cannot see the answer; it is that they cannot even see the riddle. They are like children so stupid as to notice nothing paradoxical in the playful assertion that a door is not a door. The modern latitudinarians speak, for instance, about authority in religion not only as if there were no reason in it, but as if there had never been any reason for it. Apart from seeing its philosophical basis, they cannot even see its historical cause. Religious authority has often, doubtless, been oppressive or unreasonable; just as every legal system (and especially our present one) has been callous and full of a cruel apathy. It is rational to attack the police; nay, it is glorious. But the modern critics of religious authority are like men who should attack the police without ever having heard of burglars. For there is a great and possible peril to the human mind: a peril as practical as burglary. Against it religious authority was reared, rightly or wrongly, as a barrier. And against it something certainly must be reared as a barrier, if our race is to avoid ruin.

That peril is that the human intellect is free to destroy itself. Just as one generation could prevent the very existence of the next generation, by all entering a monastery or jumping into the sea, so one set of thinkers can in some degree prevent further thinking by teaching the next generation that there is no validity in any human thought. It is idle to talk always of the alternative of reason and faith. Reason is itself a matter of faith. It is an act of faith to assert that our thoughts have any relation to reality at all. If you are merely a sceptic, you must sooner or later ask yourself the question, "Why should *anything* go right; even observation and deduction? Why should not good logic be as misleading as bad logic? They are both movements in the brain of a bewildered ape." The young sceptic says, "I have a right to think for myself." But the old sceptic, the complete sceptic, says, "I have no right to think for myself. I have no right to think at all."

There is a thought that stops thought. That is the only thought that ought to be stopped. That is the ultimate evil against which all religious authority was aimed. It only appears at the end of decadent ages like our own: and already Mr. H. G. Wells has raised its ruinous banner; he has written a delicate piece of scepticism called "Doubts of the Instrument." In this he questions the brain itself, and endeavours to remove all reality from all his own assertions, past, present, and to come. But it was against this remote ruin that all the military systems in religion were originally ranked and ruled. The creeds and the crusades, the hierarchies and the horrible persecutions were not organized, as is ignorantly said, for the suppression of reason. They were organized for the difficult defence of reason. Man, by a blind instinct, knew that if once things were wildly questioned, reason could be questioned first. The authority of priests to absolve, the authority of popes to define the authority, even of inquisitors to terrify: these were all only dark defences erected round one central authority, more undemonstrable, more supernatural than all—the authority of a man to think. We know now that this is so; we have no excuse for not knowing it. For we can hear scepticism crashing through the old ring of authorities, and at the same moment we can see reason swaying upon her throne. In so far as religion is gone, reason is going. For they are both of the same primary and authoritative kind. They are both methods of proof which cannot themselves be proved.

And in the act of destroying the idea of Divine authority we have largely destroyed the idea of that human authority by which we do a long-division sum. With a long and sustained tug we have attempted to pull the mitre off pontifical man; and his head has come off with it.

Lest this should be called loose assertion, it is perhaps desirable, though dull, to run rapidly through the chief modern fashions of thought which have this effect of stopping thought itself. Materialism and the view of everything as a personal illusion have some such effect; for if the mind is mechanical, thought cannot be very exciting, and if the cosmos is unreal, there is nothing to think about. But in these cases the effect is indirect and doubtful. In some cases it is direct and clear; notably in the case of what is generally called evolution.

Evolution is a good example of that modern intelligence which, if it destroys anything, destroys itself. Evolution is either an innocent scientific description of how certain earthly things came about; or, if it is anything more than this, it is an attack upon thought itself. If evolution destroys anything, it does not destroy religion but rationalism. If evolution simply means that a positive thing called an ape turned very slowly into a positive thing called a man, then it is stingless for the most orthodox; for a personal God might just as well do things slowly as quickly, especially if, like the Christian God, he were outside time. But if it means anything more, it means that there is no such thing as an ape to change, and no such thing as a man for him to change into. It means that there is no such thing as a thing. At best, there is only one thing, and that is a flux of everything and anything. This is an attack not upon the faith, but upon the mind; you cannot think if there are no things to think about. You cannot think if you are not separate from the subject of thought. Descartes said, "I think; therefore I am." The philosophic evolutionist reverses and negatives the epigram. He says, "I am not; therefore I cannot think."

Then there is the opposite attack on thought: that urged by Mr. H. G. Wells when he insists that every separate thing is "unique," and there are no categories at all. This also is merely destructive. Thinking means connecting things, and stops if they cannot be connected. It need hardly be said that this scepticism forbidding thought necessarily forbids speech; a man cannot open his mouth without contradicting it. Thus when Mr. Wells says (as he did somewhere), "All chairs are quite different," he utters not merely a misstatement, but a contradiction in terms. If all chairs were quite different, you could not call them "all chairs."

Akin to these is the false theory of progress, which maintains that we alter the test instead of trying to pass the test. We often hear it said, for instance, "What is right in one age is wrong in another." This is quite reasonable, if it means that there is a fixed aim, and that certain methods attain at certain times and not at other times. If women, say, desire to be elegant, it may be that they are improved at one time by growing fatter and at another time by growing thinner. But you cannot say that they are improved by ceasing to wish to be elegant and beginning to wish to be oblong. If the standard changes, how can there be improvement, which implies a standard? Nietzsche started a nonsensical idea that men had once sought as good what we now call evil; if it were so, we could not talk of surpassing or even falling short of them. How can you overtake Jones if you walk in the other direction? You cannot discuss whether one people has succeeded more in being miserable than another succeeded in being happy. It would be like discussing whether Milton was more puritanical than a pig is fat.

It is true that a man (a silly man) might make change itself his object or ideal. But as an ideal, change itself becomes unchangeable. If the change-worshipper wishes to estimate his own progress, he must be sternly loyal to the ideal of change; he must not begin to flirt gaily with the ideal of monotony. Progress itself cannot progress. It is worth remark, in passing, that when Tennyson, in a wild and rather weak manner, welcomed the idea of infinite alteration in society, he instinctively took a metaphor which suggests an imprisoned tedium. He wrote—

> *Let the great world spin for ever down the ringing grooves of change.*

He thought of change itself as an unchangeable groove; and so it is. Change is about the narrowest and hardest groove that a man can get into.

The main point here, however, is that this idea of a fundamental alteration in the standard is one of the things that make thought about the past or future simply impossible. The theory of a complete change of standards in human history does not merely deprive us of the pleasure of honouring our fathers; it deprives us even of the more modern and aristocratic pleasure of despising them.

This bald summary of the thought-destroying forces of our time would not be complete without some reference to pragmatism; for though I have here used and should everywhere defend the pragmatist method as a preliminary guide to truth, there is an extreme application of it which involves the absence of all truth whatever. My meaning can be put shortly thus. I agree with the pragmatists that apparent objective truth is not the whole matter; that there is an authoritative need to believe the things that are necessary to the human mind. But I say that one of those necessities precisely is a belief in objective truth. The pragmatist tells a man to think what he must think and never mind the Absolute. But precisely one of the things that he must think is the Absolute. This philosophy, indeed, is a kind of verbal paradox. Pragmatism is a matter of human needs; and one of the first of human needs is to be something more than a pragmatist. Extreme pragmatism is just as inhuman as the determinism it so powerfully attacks. The determinist (who, to do him justice, does not pretend to be a human being) makes nonsense of the human sense of actual choice. The pragmatist, who professes to be specially human, makes nonsense of the human sense of actual fact.

To sum up our contention so far, we may say that the most characteristic current philosophies have not only a touch of mania, but a touch of suicidal mania. The mere questioner has knocked his head against the limits of human thought; and cracked it. This is what makes so futile the warnings of the orthodox and the boasts of the advanced about the dangerous boyhood of free thought. What we are looking at is not the boyhood of free thought; it is the old age and ultimate dissolution of free thought. It is vain for bishops and pious bigwigs to discuss what dreadful things will happen if wild scepticism runs its course. It has run its course. It is vain for eloquent atheists to talk of the great truths that will be revealed if once we see free thought begin. We have seen it end. It has no more questions to ask; it has questioned itself. You cannot call up any wilder vision than a city in which men ask themselves if they have any selves. You cannot fancy a more sceptical world than that in which men doubt if there is a world. It might certainly have reached its bankruptcy more quickly and cleanly if it had not been feebly hampered by the application of indefensible laws of blasphemy or by the absurd pretence that modern England is Christian. But it would have reached the bankruptcy anyhow. Militant atheists are still unjustly persecuted; but rather because they are an old minority than because they are a new one. Free thought has exhausted its own freedom. It is weary of its own success. If any eager freethinker now hails philosophic freedom as the dawn, he is only like the man in Mark Twain who came out wrapped in blankets to see the sun rise and was just in time to see it set. If any frightened curate still says that it will be awful if the darkness of free thought should spread, we can only answer him in the high and powerful words of Mr. Belloc, "Do not, I beseech you, be troubled about the increase of forces already in dissolution. You have mistaken the hour of the night: it is already morning." We have no more questions left to ask. We have looked for questions in the darkest corners and on the wildest peaks. We have found all the questions that can be found. It is time we gave up looking for questions and began looking for answers.

But one more word must be added. At the beginning of this preliminary negative sketch I said that our mental ruin has been wrought by wild reason, not by wild imagination. A man does not go mad because he makes a statue a mile high, but he may go mad by thinking it out in square inches. Now, one school of thinkers has seen this and jumped at it as a way of renewing the pagan health of the world. They see that reason destroys; but Will, they say, creates. The ultimate authority, they say, is in will, not in reason. The supreme point is not why a man demands a thing, but the fact that he does demand it. I have no space to trace or expound this philosophy of Will. It came, I suppose, through Nietzsche, who preached something that is called egoism. That, indeed, was simple-minded enough; for Nietzsche denied egoism simply by preaching it. To preach anything is to give it away. First, the egoist calls life a war without mercy, and then he takes the greatest possible trouble to drill his enemies in war. To preach egoism is to practise altruism. But however it began, the view is common enough in current literature. The main defence of these thinkers is that they are not thinkers; they are makers. They say that choice is itself the divine thing. Thus Mr. Bernard Shaw has attacked the old idea that men's acts are to be judged by the standard of the desire of happiness. He says that a man does not act for his happiness, but from his will. He does not say, "Jam will make me happy," but "I want jam." And in all this others follow him with yet greater enthusiasm. Mr. John Davidson, a remarkable poet, is so passionately excited about it that he is obliged to write prose. He publishes a short play with several long prefaces. This is natural enough in Mr. Shaw, for all his plays are prefaces:

Mr. Shaw is (I suspect) the only man on earth who has never written any poetry. But that Mr. Davidson (who can write excellent poetry) should write instead laborious metaphysics in defence of this doctrine of will, does show that the doctrine of will has taken hold of men. Even Mr. H. G. Wells has half spoken in its language; saying that one should test acts not like a thinker, but like an artist, saying, "I *feel* this curve is right," or "that line *shall* go thus." They are all excited; and well they may be. For by this doctrine of the divine authority of will, they think they can break out of the doomed fortress of rationalism. They think they can escape.

But they cannot escape. This pure praise of volition ends in the same break up and blank as the mere pursuit of logic. Exactly as complete free thought involves the doubting of thought itself, so the acceptation of mere "willing" really paralyzes the will. Mr. Bernard Shaw has not perceived the real difference between the old utilitarian test of pleasure (clumsy, of course, and easily misstated) and that which he propounds. The real difference between the test of happiness and the test of will is simply that the test of happiness is a test and the other isn't. You can discuss whether a man's act in jumping over a cliff was directed towards happiness; you cannot discuss whether it was derived from will. Of course it was. You can praise an action by saying that it is calculated to bring pleasure or pain to discover truth or to save the soul. But you cannot praise an action because it shows will; for to say that is merely to say that it is an action. By this praise of will you cannot really choose one course as better than another. And yet choosing one course as better than another is the very definition of the will you are praising.

The worship of will is the negation of will. To admire mere choice is to refuse to choose. If Mr. Bernard Shaw comes up to me and says, "Will something," that is tantamount to saying, "I do not mind what you will," and that is tantamount to saying, "I have no will in the matter." You cannot admire will in general, because the essence of will is that it is particular. A brilliant anarchist like Mr. John Davidson feels an irritation against ordinary morality, and therefore he invokes will—will to anything. He only wants humanity to want something. But humanity does want something. It wants ordinary morality. He rebels against the law and tells us to will something or anything. But we have willed something. We have willed the law against which he rebels.

All the will-worshippers, from Nietzsche to Mr. Davidson, are really quite empty of volition. They cannot will, they can hardly wish. And if any one wants a proof of this, it can be found quite easily. It can be found in this fact: that they always talk of will as something that expands and breaks out. But it is quite the opposite. Every act of will is an act of self-limitation. To desire action is to desire limitation. In that sense every act is an act of self-sacrifice. When you choose anything, you reject everything else. That objection, which men of this school used to make to the act of marriage, is really an objection to every act. Every act is an irrevocable selection and exclusion. Just as when you marry one woman you give up all the others, so when you take one course of action you give up all the other courses. If you become King of England, you give up the post of Beadle in Brompton. If you go to Rome, you sacrifice a rich suggestive life in Wimbledon. It is the existence of this negative or limiting side of will that makes most of the talk of the anarchic will-worshippers little better than nonsense. For instance, Mr. John Davidson tells us to have nothing to do with "Thou shalt not"; but it is surely obvious that "Thou shalt not" is only one of the necessary corollaries of "I will." "I will go to the Lord Mayor's Show, and thou shalt not stop me." Anarchism adjures us to be bold creative artists, and care for no laws or limits. But it is impossible to be an artist and not care for laws and limits. Art is limitation; the essence of every picture is the frame. If you draw a giraffe, you must draw him with a long neck. If, in your bold creative way, you hold yourself free to draw a giraffe with a short neck, you will really find that you are not free to draw a giraffe. The moment you step into the world of facts, you step into a world of limits. You can free things from alien or accidental laws, but not from the laws of their own nature. You may, if you like, free a tiger from his bars; but do not free him from his stripes. Do not free a camel of the burden of his hump: you may be freeing him from being a camel. Do not go about as a demagogue, encouraging triangles to break out of the prison of their three sides. If a triangle breaks out of its three sides, its life comes to a lamentable end. Somebody wrote a work called "The Loves of the Triangles"; I never read it, but I am sure that if triangles ever were loved, they were loved for being triangular. This is certainly the case with all artistic creation, which is in some ways the most decisive example of pure will. The artist loves his limitations: they constitute the *thing* he is doing. The painter is glad that the canvas is flat. The sculptor is glad that the clay is colourless.

In case the point is not clear, an historic example may illustrate it. The French Revolution was really an heroic and decisive thing, because the Jacobins willed something definite and limited. They desired the freedoms of democracy, but also all the vetoes of democracy. They wished to have votes and *not* to have titles. Republicanism had an ascetic side in Franklin or Robespierre as well as an expansive side in Danton or Wilkes. Therefore they have created something with a solid substance and shape, the square social equality and peasant wealth of France. But since then the revolutionary or speculative mind of Europe has been weakened by shrinking from any proposal because of the limits of that proposal. Liberalism has been degraded into liberality. Men have tried to turn "revolutionise" from a transitive to an intransitive verb. The Jacobin could tell you not only the system he would rebel against, but (what was more important) the system he would *not* rebel against, the system he would trust. But the new rebel is a sceptic, and will not entirely trust anything. He has no loyalty; therefore he can never be really a revolutionist. And the fact that he doubts everything really gets in his way when he wants to denounce anything. For all denunciation implies a moral doctrine of some kind; and the modern revolutionist doubts not only the institution he denounces, but the doctrine by which he denounces it. Thus he writes one book complaining that imperial oppression insults the purity of women, and then he writes another book (about the sex problem) in which he insults it himself. He curses the Sultan because Christian girls lose their virginity, and then curses Mrs. Grundy because they keep it. As a politician, he will cry out that war is a waste of life, and then, as a philosopher, that all life is a waste of time. A Russian pessimist will denounce a policeman for killing a peasant, and then prove by the highest philosophical principles that the peasant ought to have killed himself. A man denounces marriage as a lie, and then denounces aristocratic profligates for treating it as a lie. He calls a flag a bauble, and then blames the oppressors of Poland or Ireland because they take away that bauble. The man of this school goes first to a political meeting, where he complains that savages are treated as if they were beasts; then he takes his hat and umbrella and goes on to a scientific meeting, where he proves that they practically are beasts. In short, the modern revolutionist, being an infinite sceptic, is always engaged in undermining his own mines. In his book on politics he attacks men for trampling on morality; in his book on ethics he attacks morality for trampling on men.

Therefore the modern man in revolt has become practically useless for all purposes of revolt. By rebelling against everything he has lost his right to rebel against anything.

It may be added that the same blank and bankruptcy can be observed in all fierce and terrible types of literature, especially in satire. Satire may be mad and anarchic, but it presupposes an admitted superiority in certain things over others; it presupposes a standard. When little boys in the street laugh at the fatness of some distinguished journalist, they are unconsciously assuming a standard of Greek sculpture. They are appealing to the marble Apollo. And the curious disappearance of satire from our literature is an instance of the fierce things fading for want of any principle to be fierce about. Nietzsche had some natural talent for sarcasm: he could sneer, though he could not laugh; but there is always something bodiless and without weight in his satire, simply because it has not any mass of common morality behind it. He is himself more preposterous than anything he denounces. But, indeed, Nietzsche will stand very well as the type of the whole of this failure of abstract violence. The softening of the brain which ultimately overtook him was not a physical accident. If Nietzsche had not ended in imbecility, Nietzscheism would end in imbecility. Thinking in isolation and with pride ends in being an idiot. Every man who will not have softening of the heart must at last have softening of the brain.

This last attempt to evade intellectualism ends in intellectualism, and therefore in death. The sortie has failed. The wild worship of lawlessness and the materialist worship of law end in the same void. Nietzsche scales staggering mountains, but he turns up ultimately in Tibet. He sits down beside Tolstoy in the land of nothing and Nirvâna. They are both helpless—one because he must not grasp anything, and the other because he must not let go of anything. The Tolstoyan's will is frozen by a Buddhist instinct that all special actions are evil. But the Nietzscheite's will is quite equally frozen by his view that all special actions are good; for if all special actions are good, none of them are special. They stand at the cross-roads, and one hates all the roads and the other likes all the roads. The result is—well, some things are not hard to calculate. They stand at the cross-roads.

Here I end (thank God) the first and dullest business of this book—the rough review of recent thought. After this I begin to sketch a view of life which may not interest my reader, but which, at any rate, interests me. In front of me, as I close this page, is a pile of modern books that I have been turning over for the purpose—a pile of ingenuity, a pile of futility. By the accident of my present detachment, I can see the inevitable smash of the philosophies of Schopenhauer and Tolstoy, Nietzsche and Shaw, as clearly as an inevitable railway smash could be seen from a balloon. They are all on the road to the emptiness of the asylum. For madness may be defined as using mental activity so as to reach mental helplessness; and they have nearly reached it. He who thinks he is made of glass, thinks to the destruction of thought; for glass cannot think. So he who wills to reject nothing, wills the destruction of will; for will is not only the choice of something, but the rejection of almost everything. And as I turn and tumble over the clever, wonderful, tiresome, and useless modern books, the title of one of them rivets my eye. It is called "Jeanne d'Arc," by Anatole France. I have only glanced at it, but a glance was enough to remind me of Renan's "Vie de Jésus." It has the same strange method of the reverent sceptic. It discredits supernatural stories that have some foundation, simply by telling natural stories that have no foundation. Because we cannot believe in what a saint did, we are to pretend that we know exactly what he felt. But I do not mention either book in order to criticise it, but because the accidental combination of the names called up two startling images of sanity which blasted all the books before me. Joan of Arc was not stuck at the cross-roads, either by rejecting all the paths like Tolstoy, or by accepting them all like Nietzsche. She chose a path, and went down it like a thunderbolt. Yet Joan, when I came to think of her, had in her all that was true either in Tolstoy or Nietzsche, all that was even tolerable in either of them. I thought of all that is noble in Tolstoy, the pleasure in plain things, especially in plain pity, the actualities of the earth, the reverence for the poor, the dignity of the bowed back. Joan of Arc had all that and with this great addition, that she endured poverty as well as admiring it; whereas Tolstoy is only a typical aristocrat trying to find out its secret. And then I thought of all that was brave and proud and pathetic in poor Nietzsche, and his mutiny against the emptiness and timidity of our time. I thought of his cry for the ecstatic equilibrium of danger, his hunger for the rush of great horses, his cry to arms. Well, Joan of Arc had all that, and again with this difference, that she did not praise fighting, but fought. We *know* that she was not afraid of an army, while Nietzsche, for all we know, was afraid of a cow. Tolstoy only praised the peasant; she was the peasant. Nietzsche only praised the warrior; she was the warrior. She beat them both at their own antagonistic ideals; she was more gentle than the one, more violent than the other. Yet she was a perfectly practical person who did something, while they are wild speculators who do nothing. It was impossible that the thought should not cross my mind that she and her faith had perhaps some secret of moral unity and utility that has been lost. And with that thought came a larger one, and the colossal figure of her Master had also crossed the theatre of my thoughts. The same modern difficulty which darkened the subject-matter of Anatole France also darkened that of Ernest Renan. Renan also divided his hero's pity from his hero's pugnacity. Renan even represented the righteous anger at Jerusalem as a mere nervous breakdown after the idyllic expectations of Galilee. As if there were any inconsistency between having a love for humanity and having a hatred for inhumanity! Altruists, with thin, weak voices, denounce Christ as an egoist. Egoists (with even thinner and weaker voices) denounce Him as an altruist. In our present atmosphere such cavils are comprehensible enough. The love of a hero is more terrible than the hatred of a tyrant. The hatred of a hero is more generous than the love of a philanthropist. There is a huge and heroic sanity of which moderns can only collect the fragments. There is a giant of whom we see only the lopped arms and legs walking about. They have torn the soul of Christ into silly strips, labelled egoism and altruism, and they are equally puzzled by His insane magnificence and His insane meekness. They have parted His garments among them, and for His vesture they have cast lots; though the coat was without seam woven from the top throughout.

IV. THE ETHICS OF ELFLAND

When the business man rebukes the idealism of his office-boy, it is commonly in some such speech as this: "Ah, yes, when one is young, one has these ideals in the abstract and these castles in the air; but in middle age they all break up like clouds, and one comes down to a belief in practical politics, to using the machinery one has and getting on with the world as it is." Thus, at least, venerable and philanthropic old men now in their honoured graves used to talk to me when I was a boy. But since then I have grown up and have discovered that these philanthropic old men were telling lies. What has really happened is exactly the opposite of what they said would happen. They said that I should lose my ideals and begin to believe in the methods of practical politicians. Now, I have not lost my ideals in the least; my faith in fundamentals is exactly what it always was. What I have lost is my old childlike faith in practical politics. I am still as much concerned as ever about the Battle of Armageddon; but I am not so much concerned about the General Election. As a babe I leapt up on my mother's knee at the mere mention of it. No; the vision is always solid and reliable. The vision is always a fact. It is the reality that is often a fraud. As much as I ever did, more than I ever did, I believe in Liberalism. But there was a rosy time of innocence when I believed in Liberals.

I take this instance of one of the enduring faiths because, having now to trace the roots of my personal speculation, this may be counted, I think, as the only positive bias. I was brought up a Liberal, and have always believed in democracy, in the elementary liberal doctrine of a self-governing humanity. If any one finds the phrase vague or threadbare, I can only pause for a moment to explain that the principle of democracy, as I mean it, can be stated in two propositions. The first is this: that the things common to all men are more important than the things peculiar to any men. Ordinary things are more valuable than extraordinary things; nay, they are more extraordinary. Man is something more awful than men; something more strange. The sense of the miracle of humanity itself should be always more vivid to us than any marvels of power, intellect, art, or civilization. The mere man on two legs, as such, should be felt as something more heartbreaking than any music and more startling than any caricature. Death is more tragic even than death by starvation. Having a nose is more comic even than having a Norman nose.

This is the first principle of democracy: that the essential things in men are the things they hold in common, not the things they hold separately. And the second principle is merely this: that the political instinct or desire is one of these things which they hold in common. Falling in love is more poetical than dropping into poetry. The democratic contention is that government (helping to rule the tribe) is a thing like falling in love, and not a thing like dropping into poetry. It is not something analogous to playing the church organ, painting on vellum, discovering the North Pole (that insidious habit), looping the loop, being Astronomer Royal, and so on. For these things we do not wish a man to do at all unless he does them well. It is, on the contrary, a thing analogous to writing one's own love-letters or blowing one's own nose. These things we want a man to do for himself, even if he does them badly. I am not here arguing the truth of any of these conceptions; I know that some moderns are asking to have their wives chosen by scientists, and they may soon be asking, for all I know, to have their noses blown by nurses. I merely say that mankind does recognize these universal human functions, and that democracy classes government among them. In short, the democratic faith is this: that the most terribly important things must be left to ordinary men themselves—the mating of the sexes, the rearing of the young, the laws of the state. This is democracy; and in this I have always believed.

But there is one thing that I have never from my youth up been able to understand. I have never been able to understand where people got the idea that democracy was in some way opposed to tradition. It is obvious that tradition is only democracy extended through time. It is trusting to a consensus of common human voices rather than to some isolated or arbitrary record. The man who quotes some German historian against the tradition of the Catholic Church, for instance, is strictly appealing to aristocracy. He is appealing to the superiority of one expert against the awful authority of a mob. It is quite easy to see why a legend is treated, and ought to be treated, more respectfully than a book of history. The legend is generally made by the majority of people in the village, who are sane. The book is generally written by the one man in the village who is mad. Those who urge against tradition that men in the past were ignorant may go and urge it at the Carlton Club, along with the statement that voters in the slums are ignorant. It will not do for us. If we attach great importance to the opinion of ordinary men in great unanimity when we are dealing with daily matters, there is no reason why we should disregard it when we are dealing with history or fable. Tradition may be defined as an extension of the franchise. Tradition means giving votes to the most obscure of all classes, our ancestors. It is the democracy of the dead. Tradition refuses to submit to the small and arrogant oligarchy of those who merely happen to be walking about. All democrats object to men being disqualified by the accident of birth; tradition objects to their being disqualified by the accident of death. Democracy tells us not to neglect a good man's opinion, even if he is our groom; tradition asks us not to neglect a good man's opinion, even if he is our father. I, at any rate, cannot separate the two ideas of democracy and tradition; it seems evident to me that they are the same idea. We will have the dead at our councils. The ancient Greeks voted by stones; these shall vote by tombstones. It is all quite regular and official, for most tombstones, like most ballot papers, are marked with a cross.

I have first to say, therefore, that if I have had a bias, it was always a bias in favour of democracy, and therefore of tradition. Before we come to any theoretic or logical beginnings I am content to allow for that personal equation; I have always been more inclined to believe the ruck of hard-working people than to believe that special and troublesome literary class to which I belong. I prefer even the fancies and prejudices of the people who see life from the inside to the clearest demonstrations of the people who see life from the outside. I would always trust the old wives' fables against the old maids' facts. As long as wit is mother wit it can be as wild as it pleases.

Now, I have to put together a general position, and I pretend to no training in such things. I propose to do it, therefore, by writing down one after another the three or four fundamental ideas which I have found for myself, pretty much in the way that I found them Then I shall roughly synthesise them, summing up my persona philosophy or natural religion; then I shall describe my startling discovery that the whole thing had been discovered before. It had been discovered by Christianity. But of these profound persuasions which I have to recount in order, the earliest was concerned with this element of popular tradition. And without the foregoing explanation touching tradition and democracy I could hardly make my mental experience clear. As it is, I do not know whether I can make it clear, but I now propose to try.

My first and last philosophy, that which I believe in with unbroken certainty, I learnt in the nursery. I generally learnt it from a nurse; that is, from the solemn and star-appointed priestess at once of democracy and tradition. The things I believed most then, the things I believe most now, are the things called fairy tales. They seem to me to be the entirely reasonable things. They are not fantasies: compared with them other things are fantastic. Compared with them religion and rationalism are both abnormal, though religion is abnormally right and rationalism abnormally wrong. Fairyland is nothing but the sunny country of common sense. It is not earth that judges heaven, but heaven that judges earth; so for me at least it was not earth that criticised elfland, but elfland that criticised the earth. I knew the magic beanstalk before I had tasted beans; I was sure of the Man in the Moon before I was certain of the moon. This was at one with all popular tradition. Modern minor poets are naturalists, and talk about the bush or the brook; but the singers of the old epics and fables were supernaturalists, and talked about the gods of brook and bush. That is what the moderns mean when they say that the ancients did not "appreciate Nature," because they said that Nature was divine. Old nurses do not tell children about the grass, but about the fairies that dance on the grass; and the old Greeks ould not see the trees for the dryads.

But I deal here with what ethic and philosophy come from being l on fairy tales. If I were describing them in detail I could note ny noble and healthy principles that arise from them. There is the alrous lesson of "Jack the Giant Killer"; that giants should be d because they are gigantic. It is a manly mutiny against pride ch. For the rebel is older than all the kingdoms, and the n has more tradition than the Jacobite. There is the lesson of rella," which is the same as that of the Magnificat—*exaltavit* There is the great lesson of "Beauty and the Beast"; that a ıst be loved *before* it is loveable. There is the terrible allegory leeping Beauty," which tells how the human creature was blessed with all birthday gifts, yet cursed with death; and how death also may perhaps be softened to a sleep. But I am not concerned with any of the separate statutes of elfland, but with the whole spirit of its law, which I learnt before I could speak, and shall retain when I cannot write. I am concerned with a certain way of looking at life, which was created in me by the fairy tales, but has since been meekly ratified by the mere facts.

It might be stated this way. There are certain sequences or developments (cases of one thing following another), which are, in the true sense of the word, reasonable. They are, in the true sense of the word, necessary. Such are mathematical and merely logical sequences. We in fairyland (who are the most reasonable of all creatures) admit that reason and that necessity. For instance, if the Ugly Sisters are older than Cinderella, it is (in an iron and awful sense) *necessary* that Cinderella is younger than the Ugly Sisters. There is no getting out of it. Haeckel may talk as much fatalism about that fact as he pleases: it really must be. If Jack is the son of a miller, a miller is the father of Jack. Cold reason decrees it from her awful throne: and we in fairyland submit. If the three brothers all ride horses, there are six animals and eighteen legs involved: that is true rationalism, and fairyland is full of it. But as I put my head over the hedge of the elves and began to take notice of the natural world, I observed an extraordinary thing. I observed that learned men in spectacles were talking of the actual things that happened—dawn and death and so on—as if *they* were rational and inevitable. They talked as if the fact that trees bear fruit were just as *necessary* as the fact that two and one trees make three. But it is not. There is an enormous difference by the test of fairyland; which is the test of the imagination. You cannot *imagine* two and one not making three. But you can easily imagine trees not growing fruit; you can imagine them growing golden candlesticks or tigers hanging on by the tail. These men in spectacles spoke much of a man named Newton, who was hit by an apple, and who discovered a law. But they could not be got to see the distinction between a true law, a law of reason, and the mere fact of apples falling. If the apple hit Newton's nose, Newton's nose hit the apple. That is a true necessity: because we cannot conceive the one occurring without the other. But we can quite well conceive the apple not falling on his nose; we can fancy it flying ardently through the air to hit some other nose, of which it had a more definite dislike. We have always in our fairy tales kept this sharp distinction between the science of mental relations, in which there really are laws, and the science of physical facts, in which there are no laws, but only weird repetitions. We believe in bodily miracles, but not in mental impossibilities. We believe that a Bean-stalk climbed up to Heaven; but that does not at all confuse our convictions on the philosophical question of how many beans make five.

Here is the peculiar perfection of tone and truth in the nursery tales. The man of science says, "Cut the stalk, and the apple will fall"; but he says it calmly, as if the one idea really led up to the other. The witch in the fairy tale says, "Blow the horn, and the ogre's castle will fall"; but she does not say it as if it were something in which the effect obviously arose out of the cause. Doubtless she has given the advice to many champions, and has seen many castles fall, but she does not lose either her wonder or her reason. She does not muddle her head until it imagines a necessary mental connection between a horn and a falling tower. But the scientific men do muddle their heads, until they imagine a necessary mental connection between an apple leaving the tree and an apple reaching the ground. They do really talk as if they had found not only a set of marvellous facts, but a truth connecting those facts. They do talk as if the connection of two strange things physically connected them philosophically. They feel that because one incomprehensible thing constantly follows another incomprehensible thing the two together somehow make up a comprehensible thing. Two black riddles make a white answer.

In fairyland we avoid the word "law"; but in the land of science they are singularly fond of it. Thus they will call some interesting conjecture about how forgotten folks pronounced the alphabet, Grimm's Law. But Grimm's Law is far less intellectual than Grimm's Fairy Tales. The tales are, at any rate, certainly tales; while the law is not a law. A law implies that we know the nature of the generalisation and enactment; not merely that we have noticed some of the effects. If there is a law that pick-pockets shall go to prison, it implies that there is an imaginable mental connection between the idea of prison and the idea of picking pockets. And we know what the idea is. We can say why we take liberty from a man who takes liberties. But we cannot say why an egg can turn into a chicken any more than we can say why a bear could turn into a fairy prince. As *ideas,* the egg and the chicken are further off from each other than the bear and the prince; for no egg in itself suggests a chicken, whereas some princes do suggest bears. Granted, then, that certain transformations do happen, it is essential that we should regard them in the philosophic manner of fairy tales, not in the unphilosophic manner of science and the "Laws of Nature." When we are asked why eggs turn to birds or fruits fall in autumn, we must answer exactly as the fairy godmother would answer if Cinderella asked her why mice turned to horses or her clothes fell from her at twelve o'clock. We must answer that it is *magic*. It is not a "law," for we do not understand its general formula. It is not a necessity, for though we can count on it happening practically, we have no right to say that it must always happen. It is no argument for unalterable law (as Huxley fancied) that we count on the ordinary course of things. We do not count on it; we bet on it. We risk the remote possibility of a miracle as we do that of a poisoned pancake or a world-destroying comet. We leave it out of account, not because it is a miracle, and therefore an impossibility, but because it is a miracle, and therefore an exception. All the terms used in the science books, "law," "necessity," "order," "tendency," and so on, are really unintellectual, because they assume an inner synthesis, which we do not possess. The only words that ever satisfied me as describing Nature are the terms used in the fairy books, "charm," "spell," "enchantment." They express the arbitrariness of the fact and its mystery. A tree grows fruit because it is a *magic* tree. Water runs downhill because it is bewitched. The sun shines because it is bewitched.

I deny altogether that this is fantastic or even mystical. We may have some mysticism later on; but this fairy-tale language about things is simply rational and agnostic. It is the only way I can express in words my clear and definite perception that one thing is quite distinct from another; that there is no logical connection between flying and laying eggs. It is the man who talks about "a law" that he has never seen who is the mystic. Nay, the ordinary scientific man is strictly a sentimentalist. He is a sentimentalist in this essential sense, that he is soaked and swept away by mere associations. He has so often seen birds fly and lay eggs that he feels as if there must be some dreamy, tender connection between the two ideas, whereas there is none. A forlorn lover might be unable to dissociate the moon from lost love; so the materialist is unable to dissociate the moon from the tide. In both cases there is no connection, except that one has seen them together. A sentimentalist might shed tears at the smell of apple-blossom, because, by a dark association of his own, it reminded him of his boyhood. So the materialist professor (though he conceals his tears) is yet a sentimentalist, because, by a dark association of his own, apple-blossoms remind him of apples. But the cool rationalist from fairyland does not see why, in the abstract, the apple tree should not grow crimson tulips; it sometimes does in his country.

This elementary wonder, however, is not a mere fancy derived from the fairy tales; on the contrary, all the fire of the fairy tales is derived from this. Just as we all like love tales because there is an instinct of sex, we all like astonishing tales because they touch the nerve of the ancient instinct of astonishment. This is proved by the fact that when we are very young children we do not need fairy tales: we only need tales. Mere life is interesting enough. A child of seven is excited by being told that Tommy opened a door and saw a dragon. But a child of three is excited by being told that Tommy opened a door. Boys like romantic tales; but babies like realistic tales—because they find them romantic. In fact, a baby is about the only person, I should think, to whom a modern realistic novel could be read without boring him. This proves that even nursery tales only echo an almost pre-natal leap of interest and amazement. These tales say that apples were golden only to refresh the forgotten moment when we found that they were green. They make rivers run with wine only to make us remember, for one wild moment, that they run with water. I have said that this is wholly reasonable and even agnostic. And, indeed, on this point I am all for the higher agnosticism; its better name is Ignorance. We have all read in scientific books, and, indeed, in all romances, the story of the man who has forgotten his name. This man walks about the streets and can see and appreciate everything; only he cannot remember who he is. Well, every man is that man in the story. Every man has forgotten who he is. One may understand the cosmos, but never the ego; the self is more distant than any star. Thou shalt love the Lord thy God; but thou shalt not know thyself. We are all under the same mental calamity; we have all forgotten our names. We have all forgotten what we really are. All that we call common sense and rationality and practicality and positivism only means that for certain dead levels of our life we forget that we have forgotten. All that we call spirit and art and ecstasy only means that for one awful instant we remember that we forget.

But though (like the man without memory in the novel) we walk the streets with a sort of half-witted admiration, still it is admiration. It is admiration in English and not only admiration in Latin. The wonder has a positive element of praise. This is the next milestone to be definitely marked on our road through fairyland. I shall speak in the next chapter about optimists and pessimists in their intellectual aspect, so far as they have one. Here I am only trying to describe the enormous emotions which cannot be described. And the strongest emotion was that life was as precious as it was puzzling. It was an ecstasy because it was an adventure; it was an adventure because it was an opportunity. The goodness of the fairy tale was not affected by the fact that there might be more dragons than princesses; it was good to be in a fairy tale. The test of all happiness is gratitude; and I felt grateful, though I hardly knew to whom. Children are grateful when Santa Claus puts in their stockings gifts of toys or sweets. Could I not be grateful to Santa Claus when he put in my stockings the gift of two miraculous legs? We thank people for birthday presents of cigars and slippers. Can I thank no one for the birthday present of birth?

There were, then, these two first feelings, indefensible and indisputable. The world was a shock, but it was not merely shocking; existence was a surprise, but it was a pleasant surprise. In fact, all my first views were exactly uttered in a riddle that stuck in my brain from boyhood. The question was, "What did the first frog say?" And the answer was, "Lord, how you made me jump!" That says succinctly all that I am saying. God made the frog jump; but the frog prefers jumping. But when these things are settled there enters the second great principle of the fairy philosophy.

Any one can see it who will simply read "Grimm's Fairy Tales" or the fine collections of Mr. Andrew Lang. For the pleasure of pedantry I will call it the Doctrine of Conditional Joy. Touchstone talked of much virtue in an "if"; according to elfin ethics all virtue is in an "if." The note of the fairy utterance always is, "You may live in a palace of gold and sapphire, *if* you do not say the word 'cow'"; or "You may live happily with the King's daughter, *if* you do not show her an onion." The vision always hangs upon a veto. All the dizzy and colossal things conceded depend upon one small thing withheld. All the wild and whirling things that are let loose depend upon one thing that is forbidden. Mr. W. B. Yeats, in his exquisite and piercing elfin poetry, describes the elves as lawless; they plunge in innocent anarchy on the unbridled horses of the air—

Ride on the crest of the dishevelled tide,
And dance upon the mountains like a flame.

It is a dreadful thing to say that Mr. W. B. Yeats does not understand fairyland. But I do say it. He is an ironical Irishman, full of intellectual reactions. He is not stupid enough to understand fairyland. Fairies prefer people of the yokel type like myself; people who gape and grin and do as they are told. Mr. Yeats reads into elfland all the righteous insurrection of his own race. But the lawlessness of Ireland is a Christian lawlessness, founded on reason and justice. The Fenian is rebelling against something he understands only too well; but the true citizen of fairyland is obeying something that he does not understand at all. In the fairy tale an incomprehensible happiness rests upon an incomprehensible condition. A box is opened, and all evils fly out. A word is forgotten, and cities perish. A lamp is lit, and love flies away. A flower is plucked, and human lives are forfeited. An apple is eaten, and the hope of God is gone.

This is the tone of fairy tales, and it is certainly not lawlessness or even liberty, though men under a mean modern tyranny may think it liberty by comparison. People out of Portland Gaol might think Fleet Street free; but closer study will prove that both fairies and journalists are the slaves of duty. Fairy godmothers seem at least as strict as other godmothers. Cinderella received a coach out of Wonderland and a coachman out of nowhere, but she received a command—which might have come out of Brixton—that she should be back by twelve. Also, she had a glass slipper; and it cannot be a coincidence that glass is so common a substance in folk-lore. This princess lives in a glass castle, that princess on a glass hill; this one sees all things in a mirror; they may all live in glass houses if they will not throw stones. For this thin glitter of glass everywhere is the expression of the fact that the happiness is bright but brittle, like the substance most easily smashed by a housemaid or a cat. And this fairy-tale sentiment also sank into me and became my sentiment towards the whole world. I felt and feel that life itself is as bright as the diamond, but as brittle as the window-pane; and when the heavens were compared to the terrible crystal I can remember a shudder. I was afraid that God would drop the cosmos with a crash.

Remember, however, that to be breakable is not the same as to be perishable. Strike a glass, and it will not endure an instant; simply do not strike it, and it will endure a thousand years. Such, it seemed, was the joy of man, either in elfland or on earth; the happiness depended on *not doing something* which you could at any moment do and which, very often, it was not obvious why you should not do. Now, the point here is that to *me* this did not seem unjust. If the miller's third son said to the fairy, "Explain why I must not stand on my head in the fairy palace," the other might fairly reply, "Well, if it comes to that, explain the fairy palace." If Cinderella says, "How is it that I must leave the ball at twelve?" her godmother might answer, "How is it that you are going there till twelve?" If I leave a man in my will ten talking elephants and a hundred winged horses, he cannot complain if the conditions partake of the slight eccentricity of the gift. He must not look a winged horse in the mouth. And it seemed to me that existence was itself so very eccentric a legacy that I could not complain of not understanding the limitations of the vision when I did not understand the vision they limited. The frame was no stranger than the picture. The veto might well be as wild as the vision; it might be as startling as the sun, as elusive as the waters, as fantastic and terrible as the towering trees.

For this reason (we may call it the fairy godmother philosophy) I never could join the young men of my time in feeling what they called the general sentiment of *revolt*. I should have resisted, let us hope, any rules that were evil, and with these and their definition I shall deal in another chapter. But I did not feel disposed to resist any rule merely because it was mysterious. Estates are sometimes held by foolish forms, the breaking of a stick or the payment of a peppercorn: I was willing to hold the huge estate of earth and heaven by any such feudal fantasy. It could not well be wilder than the fact that I was allowed to hold it at all. At this stage I give only one ethical instance to show my meaning. I could never mix in the common murmur of that rising generation against monogamy, because no restriction on sex seemed so odd and unexpected as sex itself. To be allowed, like Endymion, to make love to the moon and then to complain that Jupiter kept his own moons in a harem seemed to me (bred on fairy tales like Endymion's) a vulgar anti-climax. Keeping to one woman is a small price for so much as seeing one woman. To complain that I could only be married once was like complaining that I had only been born once. It was incommensurate with the terrible excitement of which one was talking. It showed, not an exaggerated sensibility to sex, but a curious insensibility to it. A man is a fool who complains that he cannot enter Eden by five gates at once. Polygamy is a lack of the realization of sex; it is like a man plucking five pears in mere absence of mind. The aesthetes touched the last insane limits of language in their eulogy on lovely things. The thistledown made them weep; a burnished beetle brought them to their knees. Yet their emotion never impressed me for an instant, for this reason, that it never occurred to them to pay for their pleasure in any sort of symbolic sacrifice. Men (I felt) might fast forty days for the sake of hearing a blackbird sing. Men might go through fire to find a cowslip. Yet these lovers of beauty could not even keep sober for the blackbird. They would not go through common Christian marriage by way of recompense to the cowslip. Surely one might pay for extraordinary joy in ordinary morals. Oscar Wilde said that sunsets were not valued because we could not pay for sunsets. But Oscar Wilde was wrong; we can pay for sunsets. We can pay for them by not being Oscar Wilde.

Well, I left the fairy tales lying on the floor of the nursery, and I have not found any books so sensible since. I left the nurse guardian of tradition and democracy, and I have not found any modern type so sanely radical or so sanely conservative. But the matter for important comment was here: that when I first went out into the mental atmosphere of the modern world, I found that the modern world was positively opposed on two points to my nurse and to the nursery tales. It has taken me a long time to find out that the modern world is wrong and my nurse was right. The really curious thing was this: that modern thought contradicted this basic creed of my boyhood on its two most essential doctrines. I have explained that the fairy tales founded in me two convictions; first, that this world is a wild and startling place, which might have been quite different, but which is quite delightful; second, that before this wildness and delight one may well be modest and submit to the queerest limitations of so queer a kindness. But I found the whole modern world running like a high tide against both my tendernesses; and the shock of that collision created two sudden and spontaneous sentiments, which I have had ever since and which, crude as they were, have since hardened into convictions.

First, I found the whole modern world talking scientific fatalism; saying that everything is as it must always have been, being unfolded without fault from the beginning. The leaf on the tree is green because it could never have been anything else. Now, the fairy-tale philosopher is glad that the leaf is green precisely because it might have been scarlet. He feels as if it had turned green an instant before he looked at it. He is pleased that snow is white on the strictly reasonable ground that it might have been black. Every colour has in it a bold quality as of choice; the red of garden roses is not only decisive but dramatic, like suddenly spilt blood. He feels that something has been *done.* But the great determinists of the nineteenth century were strongly against this native feeling that something had happened an instant before. In fact, according to them, nothing ever really had happened since the beginning of the world. Nothing ever had happened since existence had happened; and even about the date of that they were not very sure.

The modern world as I found it was solid for modern Calvinism, for the necessity of things being as they are. But when I came to ask them I found they had really no proof of this unavoidable repetition in things except the fact that the things were repeated. Now, the mere repetition made the things to me rather more weird than more rational. It was as if, having seen a curiously shaped nose in the street and dismissed it as an accident, I had then seen six other noses of the same astonishing shape. I should have fancied for a moment that it must be some local secret society. So one elephant having a trunk was odd; but all elephants having trunks looked like a plot. I speak here only of an emotion, and of an emotion at once stubborn and subtle. But the repetition in Nature seemed sometimes to be an excited repetition, like that of an angry schoolmaster saying the same thing over and over again. The grass seemed signalling to me with all its fingers at once; the crowded stars seemed bent upon being understood. The sun would make me see him if he rose a thousand times. The recurrences of the universe rose to the maddening rhythm of an incantation, and I began to see an idea.

All the towering materialism which dominates the modern mind rests ultimately upon one assumption; a false assumption. It is supposed that if a thing goes on repeating itself it is probably dead; a piece of clockwork. People feel that if the universe was personal it would vary; if the sun were alive it would dance. This is a fallacy even in relation to known fact. For the variation in human affairs is generally brought into them, not by life, but by death; by the dying down or breaking off of their strength or desire. A man varies his movements because of some slight element of failure or fatigue. He gets into an omnibus because he is tired of walking; or he walks because he is tired of sitting still. But if his life and joy were so gigantic that he never tired of going to Islington, he might go to Islington as regularly as the Thames goes to Sheerness. The very speed and ecstacy of his life would have the stillness of death. The sun rises every morning. I do not rise every morning; but the variation is due not to my activity, but to my inaction. Now, to put the matter in a popular phrase, it might be true that the sun rises regularly because he never gets tired of rising. His routine might be due, not to a lifelessness, but to a rush of life. The thing I mean can be seen, for instance, in children, when they find some game or joke that they specially enjoy. A child kicks his legs rhythmically through excess, not absence, of life. Because children have abounding vitality, because they are in spirit fierce and free, therefore they want things repeated and unchanged. They always say, "Do it again"; and the grown-up person does it again until he is nearly dead. For grown-up people are not strong enough to exult in monotony. But perhaps God is strong enough to exult in monotony. It is possible that God says every morning, "Do it again" to the sun; and every evening, "Do it again" to the moon. It may not be automatic necessity that makes all daisies alike; it may be that God makes every daisy separately, but has never got tired of making them. It may be that He has the eternal appetite of infancy; for we have sinned and grown old, and our Father is younger than we. The repetition in Nature may not be a mere recurrence; it may be a theatrical *encore.* Heaven may *encore* the bird who laid an egg. If the human being conceives and brings forth a human child instead of bringing forth a fish, or a bat, or a griffin, the reason may not be that we are fixed in an animal fate without life or purpose. It may be that our little tragedy has touched the gods, that they admire it from their starry galleries, and that at the end of every human drama man is called again and again before the curtain. Repetition may go on for millions of years, by mere choice, and at any instant it may stop. Man may stand on the earth generation after generation, and yet each birth be his positively last appearance.

This was my first conviction; made by the shock of my childish emotions meeting the modern creed in mid-career. I had always vaguely felt facts to be miracles in the sense that they are wonderful: now I began to think them miracles in the stricter sense that they were *wilful*. I mean that they were, or might be, repeated exercises of some will. In short, I had always believed that the world involved magic: now I thought that perhaps it involved a magician. And this pointed a profound emotion always present and sub-conscious; that this world of ours has some purpose; and if there is a purpose, there is a person. I had always felt life first as a story: and if there is a story there is a story-teller.

But modern thought also hit my second human tradition. It went against the fairy feeling about strict limits and conditions. The one thing it loved to talk about was expansion and largeness. Herbert Spencer would have been greatly annoyed if any one had called him an imperialist, and therefore it is highly regrettable that nobody did.

But he was an imperialist of the lowest type. He popularized this contemptible notion that the size of the solar system ought to over-awe the spiritual dogma of man. Why should a man surrender his dignity to the solar system any more than to a whale? If mere size proves that man is not the image of God, then a whale may be the image of God; a somewhat formless image; what one might call an impressionist portrait. It is quite futile to argue that man is small compared to the cosmos; for man was always small compared to the nearest tree. But Herbert Spencer, in his headlong imperialism, would insist that we had in some way been conquered and annexed by the astronomical universe. He spoke about men and their ideals exactly as the most insolent Unionist talks about the Irish and their ideals. He turned mankind into a small nationality. And his evil influence can be seen even in the most spirited and honourable of later scientific authors; notably in the early romances of Mr. H. G. Wells. Many moralists have in an exaggerated way represented the earth as wicked. But Mr. Wells and his school made the heavens wicked. We should lift up our eyes to the stars from whence would come our ruin.

But the expansion of which I speak was much more evil than all this. I have remarked that the materialist, like the madman, is in prison; in the prison of one thought. These people seemed to think it singularly inspiring to keep on saying that the prison was very large. The size of this scientific universe gave one no novelty, no relief. The cosmos went on for ever, but not in its wildest constellation could there be anything really interesting; anything, for instance, such as forgiveness or free will. The grandeur or infinity of the secret of its cosmos added nothing to it. It was like telling a prisoner in Reading Gaol that he would be glad to hear that the gaol now covered half the county. The warder would have nothing to show the man except more and more long corridors of stone lit by ghasdy lights and empty of all that is human. So these expanders of the universe had nothing to show us except more and more infinite corridors of space lit by ghastly suns and empty of all that is divine.

In fairyland there had been a real law; a law that could be broken, for the definition of a law is something that can be broken. But the machinery of this cosmic prison was something that could not be broken; for we ourselves were only a part of its machinery. We were either unable to do things or we were destined to do them. The idea of the mystical condition quite disappeared; one can neither have the firmness of keeping laws nor the fun of breaking them. The largeness of this universe had nothing of that freshness and airy outbreak which we have praised in the universe of the poet. This modern universe is literally an empire; that is, it was vast, but it is not free. One went into larger and larger windowless rooms, rooms big with Babylonian perspective; but one never found the smallest window or a whisper of outer air.

Their infernal parallels seemed to expand with distance; but for me all good things come to a point, swords for instance. So finding the boast of the big cosmos so unsatisfactory to my emotions I began to argue about it a little; and I soon found that the whole attitude was even shallower than could have been expected. According to these people the cosmos was one thing since it had one unbroken rule. Only (they would say) while it is one thing it is also the only thing there is. Why, then, should one worry particularly to call it large? There is nothing to compare it with. It would be just as sensible to call it small. A man may say, "I like this vast cosmos, with its throng of stars and its crowd of varied creatures." But if it comes to that why should not a man say, "I like this cosy little cosmos, with its decent number of stars and as neat a provision of live stock as I wish to see"? One is as good as the other; they are both mere sentiments. It is mere sentiment to rejoice that the sun is larger than the earth; it is quite as sane a sentiment to rejoice that the sun is no larger than it is. A man chooses to have an emotion about the largeness of the world; why should he not choose to have an emotion about its smallness?

It happened that I had that emotion. When one is fond of anything one addresses it by diminutives, even if it is an elephant or a life-guardsman. The reason is, that anything, however huge, that can be conceived of as complete, can be conceived of as small. If military moustaches did not suggest a sword or tusks a tail, then the object would be vast because it would be immeasurable. But the moment you can imagine a guardsman you can imagine a small guardsman. The moment you really see an elephant you can call it "Tiny." If you can make a statue of a thing you can make a statuette of it. These people professed that the universe was one coherent thing; but they were not fond of the universe. But I was frightfully fond of the universe and wanted to address it by a diminutive. I often did so; and it never seemed to mind. Actually and in truth I did feel that these dim dogmas of vitality were better expressed by calling the world small than by calling it large. For about infinity there was a sort of carelessness which was the reverse of the fierce and pious care which I felt touching the pricelessness and the peril of life. They showed only a dreary waste; but I felt a sort of sacred thrift. For economy is far more romantic than extravagance. To them stars were an unending income of halfpence; but I felt about the golden sun and the silver moon as a schoolboy feels if he has one sovereign and one shilling.

These subconscious convictions are best hit off by the colour and tone of certain tales. Thus I have said that stories of magic alone can express my sense that life is not only a pleasure but a kind of eccentric privilege. I may express this other feeling of cosmic cosiness by allusion to another book always read in boyhood, "Robinson Crusoe," which I read about this time, and which owes its eternal vivacity to the fact that it celebrates the poetry of limits, nay, even the wild romance of prudence. Crusoe is a man on a small rock with a few comforts just snatched from the sea: the best thing in the book is simply the list of things saved from the wreck. The greatest of poems is an inventory. Every kitchen tool becomes ideal because Crusoe might have dropped it in the sea. It is a good exercise, in empty or ugly hours of the day, to look at anything, the coal-scuttle or the bookcase, and think how happy one could be to have brought it out of the sinking ship on to the solitary island. But it is a better exercise still to remember how all things have had this hair-breadth escape: everything has been saved from a wreck. Every man has had one horrible adventure: as a hidden untimely birth he had not been, as infants that never see the light. Men spoke much in my boyhood of restricted or ruined men of genius: and it was common to say that many a man was a Great Might-Have-Been. To me it is a more solid and startling fact that any man in the street is a Great Might-Not-Have-Been.

But I really felt (the fancy may seem foolish) as if all the order and number of things were the romantic remnant of Crusoe's ship. That there are two sexes and one sun, was like the fact that there were two guns and one axe. It was poignantly urgent that none should be lost; but somehow, it was rather fun that none could be added. The trees and the planets seemed like things saved from the wreck: and when I saw the Matterhorn I was glad that it had not been overlooked in the confusion. I felt economical about the stars as if they were sapphires (they are called so in Milton's Eden): I hoarded the hills. For the universe is a single jewel, and while it is a natural cant to talk of a jewel as peerless and priceless, of this jewel it is literally true. This cosmos is indeed without peer and without price: for there cannot be another one.

Thus ends, in unavoidable inadequacy, the attempt to utter the unutterable things. These are my ultimate attitudes towards life; the soils for the seeds of doctrine. These in some dark way I thought before I could write, and felt before I could think: that we may proceed more easily afterwards, I will roughly recapitulate them now. I felt in my bones; first, that this world does not explain itself. It may be a miracle with a supernatural explanation; it may be a conjuring trick, with a natural explanation. But the explanation of the conjuring trick, if it is to satisfy me, will have to be better than the natural explanations I have heard. The thing is magic, true or false. Second, I came to feel as if magic must have a meaning, and meaning must have some one to mean it. There was something personal in the world, as in a work of art; whatever it meant it meant violently. Third, I thought this purpose beautiful in its old design, in spite of its defects, such as dragons. Fourth, that the proper form of thanks to it is some form of humility and restraint: we should thank God for beer and Burgundy by not drinking too much of them. We owed, also, an obedience to whatever made us. And last, and strangest, there had come into my mind a vague and vast impression that in some way all good was a remnant to be stored and held sacred out of some primordial ruin. Man had saved his good as Crusoe saved his goods: he had saved them from a wreck. All this I felt and the age gave me no encouragement to feel it. And all this time I had not even thought of Christian theology.

V. THE FLAG OF THE WORLD

When I was a boy there were two curious men running about who were called the optimist and the pessimist. I constantly used the words myself, but I cheerfully confess that I never had any very special idea of what they meant. The only thing which might be considered evident was that they could not mean what they said; for the ordinary verbal explanation was that the optimist thought this world as good as it could be, while the pessimist thought it as bad as it could be. Both these statements being obviously raving non-sense, one had to cast about for other explanations. An optimist could not mean a man who thought everything right and nothing wrong. For that is meaningless; it is like calling everything right and nothing left. Upon the whole, I came to the conclusion that the optimist thought everything good except the pessimist, and that the pessimist thought everything bad, except himself. It would be unfair to omit altogether from the list the mysterious but suggestive def-inition said to have been given by a little girl, "An optimist is a man who looks after your eyes, and a pessimist is a man who looks after your feet." I am not sure that this is not the best definition of all. There is even a sort of allegorical truth in it. For there might, per-haps, be a profitable distinction drawn between that more dreary thinker who thinks merely of our contact with the earth from moment to moment, and that happier thinker who considers rather our primary power of vision and of choice of road.

But this is a deep mistake in this alternative of the optimist and the pessimist. The assumption of it is that a man criticises this world as if he were house-hunting, as if he were being shown over a new suite of apartments. If a man came to this world from some other world in full possession of his powers he might discuss whether the advantage of midsummer woods made up for the disadvantage of mad dogs, just as a man looking for lodgings might balance the presence of a telephone against the absence of a sea view. But no man is in that position. A man belongs to this world before he begins to ask if it is nice to belong to it. He has fought for the flag, and often won heroic victories for the flag long before he has ever enlisted. To put shortly what seems the essential matter, he has a loyalty long before he has any admiration.

In the last chapter it has been said that the primary feeling that this world is strange and yet attractive is best expressed in fairy tales. The reader may, if he likes, put down the next stage to that bellicose and even jingo literature which commonly comes next in the history of a boy. We all owe much sound morality to the penny dreadfuls. Whatever the reason, it seemed and still seems to me that our attitude towards life can be better expressed in terms of a kind of military loyalty than in terms of criticism and approval. My acceptance of the universe is not optimism, it is more like patriotism. It is a matter of primary loyalty. The world is not a lodging-house at Brighton, which we are to leave because it is miserable. It is the fortress of our family, with the flag flying on the turret, and the more miserable it is the less we should leave it. The point is not that this world is too sad to love or too glad not to love; the point is that when you do love a thing, its gladness is a reason for loving it, and its sadness a reason for loving it more. All optimistic thoughts about England and all pessimistic thoughts about her are alike reasons for the English patriot. Similarly, optimism and pessimism are alike arguments for the cosmic patriot.

Let us suppose we are confronted with a desperate thing—say Pimlico. If we think what is really best for Pimlico we shall find the thread of thought leads to the throne or the mystic and the arbitrary. It is not enough for a man to disapprove of Pimlico: in that case he will merely cut his throat or move to Chelsea. Nor, certainly, is it enough for a man to approve of Pimlico: for then it will remain Pimlico, which would be awful. The only way out of it seems to be for somebody to love Pimlico: to love it with a transcendental tie and without any earthly reason. If there arose a man who loved Pimlico, then Pimlico would rise into ivory towers and golden pinnacles; Pimlico would attire herself as a woman does when she is loved. For decoration is not given to hide horrible things: but to decorate things already adorable. A mother does not give her child a blue bow because he is so ugly without it. A lover does not give a girl a necklace to hide her neck. If men loved Pimlico as mothers love children, arbitrarily, because it is *theirs,* Pimlico in a year or two might be fairer than Florence. Some readers will say that this is a mere fantasy. I answer that this is the actual history of mankind. This, as a fact, is how cities did grow great. Go back to the darkest roots of civilization and you will find them knotted round some sacred stone or encircling some sacred well. People first paid honour to a spot and afterwards gained glory for it. Men did not love Rome because she was great. She was great because they had loved her.

The eighteenth-century theories of the social contract have been exposed to much clumsy criticism in our time; in so far as they meant that there is at the back of all historic government an idea of content and co-operation, they were demonstrably right. But they really were wrong, in so far as they suggested that men had ever aimed at order or ethics directly by a conscious exchange of interests. Morality did not begin by one man saying to another, "I will not hit you if you do not hit me"; there is no trace of such a transaction. There *is* a trace of both men having said, "We must not hit each other in the holy place." They gained their morality by guarding their religion. They did not cultivate courage. They fought for the shrine, and found they had become courageous. They did not cultivate cleanliness. They purified themselves for the altar, and found that they were clean. The history of the Jews is the only early document known to most Englishmen, and the facts can be judged sufficiently from that. The Ten Commandments which have been found substantially common to mankind were merely military commands; a code of regimental orders, issued to protect a certain ark across a certain desert. Anarchy was evil because it endangered the sanctity. And only when they made a holy day for God did they find they had made a holiday for men.

If it be granted that this primary devotion to a place or thing is a source of creative energy, we can pass on to a very peculiar fact. Let us reiterate for an instant that the only right optimism is a sort of universal patriotism. What is the matter with the pessimist? I think it can be stated by saying that he is the cosmic anti-patriot. And what is the matter with the anti-patriot? I think it can be stated, without undue bitterness, by saying that he is the candid friend. And what is the matter with the candid friend? There we strike the rock of real life and immutable human nature.

I venture to say that what is bad in the candid friend is simply that he is not candid. He is keeping something back—his own gloomy pleasure in saying unpleasant things. He has a secret desire to hurt, not merely to help. This is certainly, I think, what makes a certain sort of anti-patriot irritating to healthy citizens. I do not speak (of course) of the anti-patriotism which only irritates feverish stockbrokers and gushing actresses; that is only patriotism speaking plainly. A man who says that no patriot should attack the Boer War until it is over is not worth answering intelligently; he is saying that no good son should warn his mother off a cliff until she has fallen over it. But there is an anti-patriot who honestly angers honest men, and the explanation of him is, I think, what I have suggested: he is the uncandid candid friend; the man who says, "I am sorry to say we are ruined," and is not sorry at all. And he may be said, without rhetoric, to be a traitor; for he is using that ugly knowledge which was allowed him to strengthen the army, to discourage people from joining it. Because he is allowed to be pessimistic as a military adviser he is being pessimistic as a recruiting sergeant. Just in the same way the pessimist (who is the cosmic anti-patriot) uses the freedom that life allows to her counsellors to lure away the people from her flag. Granted that he states only facts, it is still essential to know what are his emotions, what is his motive. It may be that twelve hundred men in Tottenham are down with smallpox; but we want to know whether this is stated by some great philosopher who wants to curse the gods, or only by some common clergyman who wants to help the men.

The evil of the pessimist is, then, not that he chastises gods and men, but that he does not love what he chastises—he has not this primary and supernatural loyalty to things. What is the evil of the man commonly called an optimist? Obviously, it is felt that the optimist, wishing to defend the honour of this world, will defend the indefensible. He is the jingo of the universe; he will say, "My cosmos, right or wrong." He will be less inclined to the reform of things; more inclined to a sort of front-bench official answer to all attacks, soothing every one with assurances. He will not wash the world, but whitewash the world. All this (which is true of a type of optimist) leads us to the one really interesting point of psychology, which could not be explained without it.

We say there must be a primal loyalty to life: the only question is, shall it be a natural or a supernatural loyalty? If you like to put it so, shall it be a reasonable or an unreasonable loyalty? Now, the extraordinary thing is that the bad optimism (the whitewashing, the weak defence of everything) comes in with the reasonable optimism. Rational optimism leads to stagnation: it is irrational optimism that leads to reform. Let me explain by using once more the parallel of patriotism. The man who is most likely to ruin the place he loves is exactly the man who loves it with a reason. The man who will improve the place is the man who loves it without a reason. If a man loves some feature of Pimlico (which seems unlikely), he may find himself defending that feature against Pimlico itself. But if he simply loves Pimlico itself, he may lay it waste and turn it into the New Jerusalem. I do not deny that reform may be excessive; I only say that it is the mystic patriot who reforms. Mere jingo self-contentment is commonest among those who have some pedantic reason for their patriotism. The worst jingoes do not love England, but a theory of England. If we love England for being an empire, we may overrate the success with which we rule the Hindoos. But if we love it only for being a nation, we can face all events: for it would be a nation even if the Hindoos ruled us. Thus also only those will permit their patriotism to falsify history whose patriotism depends on history. A man who loves England for being English will not mind how she arose. But a man who loves England for being Anglo-Saxon may go against all facts for his fancy. He may end (like Carlyle and Freeman) by maintaining that the Norman Conquest was a Saxon Conquest. He may end in utter unreason—because he has a reason. A man who loves France for being military will palliate the army of 1870. But a man who loves France for being France will improve the army of 1870. This is exactly what the French have done, and France is a good instance of the working paradox. Nowhere else is patriotism more purely abstract and arbitrary; and nowhere else is reform more drastic and sweeping. The more transcendental is your patriotism, the more practical are your politics.

Perhaps the most everyday instance of this point is in the case of women; and their strange and strong loyalty. Some stupid people started the idea that because women obviously back up their own people through everything, therefore women are blind and do not see anything. They can hardly have known any women. The same women who are ready to defend their men through thick and thin are (in their personal intercourse with the man) almost morbidly lucid about the thinness of his excuses or the thickness of his head. A man's friend likes him but leaves him as he is: his wife loves him and is always trying to turn him into somebody else. Women who are utter mystics in their creed are utter cynics in their criticism. Thackeray expressed this well when he made Pendennis' mother, who worshipped her son as a god, yet assume that he would go wrong as a man. She underrated his virtue, though she overrated his value. The devotee is entirely free to criticise; the fanatic can safely be a sceptic. Love is not blind; that is the last thing that it is. Love is bound; and the more it is bound the less it is blind.

This at least had come to be my position about all that was called optimism, pessimism, and improvement. Before any cosmic act of reform we must have a cosmic oath of allegiance. A man must be interested in life, then he could be disinterested in his views of it. "My son give me thy heart"; the heart must be fixed on the right thing: the moment we have a fixed heart we have a free hand. I must pause to anticipate an obvious criticism. It will be said that a rational person accepts the world as mixed of good and evil with a decent satisfaction and a decent endurance. But this is exactly the attitude which I maintain to be defective. It is, I know, very common in this age; it was perfectly put in those quiet lines of Matthew Arnold which are more piercingly blasphemous than the shrieks of Schopenhauer—

Enough we live:—and if a life,
With large results so little rife,
Though bearable, seem hardly worth
This pomp of worlds, this pain of birth.

I know this feeling fills our epoch, and I think it freezes our epoch. For our Titanic purposes of faith and revolution, what we need is not the cold acceptance of the world as a compromise, but some way in which we can heartily hate and heartily love it. We do not want joy and anger to neutralize each other and produce a surly contentment; we want a fiercer delight and a fiercer discontent. We have to feel the universe at once as an ogre's castle, to be stormed, and yet as our own cottage, to which we can return at evening.

No one doubts that an ordinary man can get on with this world: but we demand not strength enough to get on with it, but strength enough to get it on. Can he hate it enough to change it, and yet love it enough to think it worth changing? Can he look up at its colossal good without once feeling acquiescence? Can he look up at its colossal evil without once feeling despair? Can he, in short, be at once not only a pessimist and an optimist, but a fanatical pessimist and a fanatical optimist? Is he enough of a pagan to die for the world, and enough of a Christian to die to it? In this combination,

I maintain, it is the rational optimist who fails, the irrational optimist who succeeds. He is ready to smash the whole universe for the sake of itself.

I put these things not in their mature logical sequence, but as they came: and this view was cleared and sharpened by an accident of the time. Under the lengthening shadow of Ibsen, an argument arose whether it was not a very nice thing to murder one's self. Grave moderns told us that we must not even say "poor fellow," of a man who had blown his brains out, since he was an enviable person, and had only blown them out because of their exceptional excellence. Mr. William Archer even suggested that in the golden age there would be penny-in-the-slot machines, by which a man could kill himself for a penny. In all this I found myself utterly hostile to many who called themselves liberal and humane. Not only is suicide a sin, it is the sin. It is the ultimate and absolute evil, the refusal to take an interest in existence; the refusal to take the oath of loyalty to life. The man who kills a man, kills a man. The man who kills himself, kills all men; as far as he is concerned he wipes out the world. His act is worse (symbolically considered) than any rape or dynamite outrage. For it destroys all buildings: it insults all women. The thief is satisfied with diamonds; but the suicide is not: that is his crime. He cannot be bribed, even by the blazing stones of the Celestial City. The thief compliments the things he steals, if not the owner of them. But the suicide insults everything on earth by not stealing it. He defiles every flower by refusing to live for its sake. There is not a tiny creature in the cosmos at whom his death is not a sneer. When a man hangs himself on a tree, the leaves might fall off in anger and the birds fly away in fury: for each has received a personal affront. Of course there may be pathetic emotional excuses for the act. There often are for rape, and there almost always are for dynamite. But if it comes to clear ideas and the intelligent meaning of things, then there is much more rational and philosophic truth in the burial at the cross-roads and the stake driven through the body, than in Mr. Archer's suicidal automatic machines. There is a meaning in burying the suicide apart. The man's crime is different from other crimes—for it makes even crimes impossible.

About the same time I read a solemn flippancy by some free-thinker: he said that a suicide was only the same as a martyr. The open fallacy of this helped to clear the question. Obviously a suicide is the opposite of a martyr. A martyr is a man who cares so much for something outside him, that he forgets his own personal life.

A suicide is a man who cares so little for anything outside him, that he wants to see the last of everything. One wants something to begin: the other wants everything to end. In other words, the martyr is noble, exactly because (however he renounces the world or execrates all humanity) he confesses this ultimate link with life; he sets his heart outside himself: he dies that something may live. The suicide is ignoble because he has not this link with being: he is a mere destroyer; spiritually, he destroys the universe. And then I remembered the stake and the cross-roads, and the queer fact that Christianity had shown this weird harshness to the suicide. For Christianity had shown a wild encouragement of the martyr. Historic Christianity was accused, not entirely without reason, of carrying martyrdom and asceticism to a point, desolate and pessimistic. The early Christian martyrs talked of death with a horrible happiness. They blasphemed the beautiful duties of the body: they smelt the grave afar off like a field of flowers. All this has seemed to many the very poetry of pessimism. Yet there is the stake at the cross-roads to show what Christianity thought of the pessimist.

This was the first of the long train of enigmas with which Christianity entered the discussion. And there went with it a peculiarity of which I shall have to speak more markedly, as a note of all Christian notions, but which distinctly began in this one. The Christian attitude to the martyr and the suicide was not what is so often affirmed in modern morals. It was not a matter of degree. It was not that a line must be drawn somewhere, and that the self-slayer in exaltation fell within the line, the self-slayer in sadness just beyond it. The Christian feeling evidently was not merely that the suicide was carrying martyrdom too far. The Christian feeling was furiously for one and furiously against the other: these two things that looked so much alike were at opposite ends of heaven and hell. One man flung away his life; he was so good that his dry bones could heal cities in pestilence. Another man flung away life; he was so bad that his bones would pollute his brethren's. I am not saying this fierceness was right; but why was it so fierce?

Here it was that I first found that my wandering feet were in some beaten track. Christianity had also felt this opposition of the martyr to the suicide: had it perhaps felt it for the same reason? Had Christianity felt what I felt, but could not (and cannot) express—this need for a first loyalty to things, and then for a ruinous reform of things? Then I remembered that it was actually the charge against Christianity that it combined these two things which I was wildly trying to combine. Christianity was accused, at one and the same time, of being too optimistic about the universe and of being too pessimistic about the world. The coincidence made me suddenly stand still.

An imbecile habit has arisen in modern controversy of saying that such and such a creed can be held in one age but cannot be held in another. Some dogma, we are told, was credible in the twelfth century, but is not credible in the twentieth. You might as well say that a certain philosophy can be believed on Mondays, but cannot be believed on Tuesdays. You might as well say of a view of the cosmos that it was suitable to half-past three, but not suitable to half-past four. What a man can believe depends upon his philosophy, not upon the clock or the century. If a man believes in unalterable natural law, he cannot believe in any miracle in any age. If a man believes in a will behind law, he can believe in any miracle in any age. Suppose, for the sake of argument, we are concerned with a case of thaumaturgic healing. A materialist of the twelfth century could not believe it any more than a materialist of the twentieth century. But a Christian Scientist of the twentieth century can believe it as much as a Christian of the twelfth century. It is simply a matter of a man's theory of things. Therefore in dealing with any historical answer, the point is not whether it was given in our time, but whether it was given in answer to our question. And the more I thought about when and how Christianity had come into the world, the more I felt that it had actually come to answer this question.

It is commonly the loose and latitudinarian Christians who pay quite indefensible compliments to Christianity. They talk as if there had never been any piety or pity until Christianity came, a point on which any mediaeval would have been eager to correct them. They represent that the remarkable thing about Christianity was that it was the first to preach simplicity or self-restraint, or inwardness and sincerity. They will think me very narrow (whatever that means) if I say that the remarkable thing about Christianity was that it was the first to preach Christianity. Its peculiarity was that it was peculiar, and simplicity and sincerity are not peculiar, but obvious ideals for all mankind. Christianity was the answer to a riddle, not the last truism uttered after a long talk. Only the other day I saw in an excellent weekly paper of Puritan tone this remark, that Christianity when stripped of its armour of dogma (as who should speak of a man stripped of his armour of bones), turned out to be nothing but the Quaker doctrine of the Inner Light. Now, if I were to say that

Christianity came into the world specially to destroy the doctrine of the Inner Light, that would be an exaggeration. But it would be very much nearer to the truth. The last Stoics, like Marcus Aurelius, were exactly the people who did believe in the Inner Light. Their dignity, their weariness, their sad external care for others, their incurable internal care for themselves, were all due to the Inner Light, and existed only by that dismal illumination. Notice that Marcus Aurelius insists, as such introspective moralists always do, upon small things done or undone; it is because he has not hate or love enough to make a moral revolution. He gets up early in the morning, just as our own aristocrats living the Simple Life get up early in the morning; because such altruism is much easier than stopping the games of the amphitheatre or giving the English people back their land. Marcus Aurelius is the most intolerable of human types. He is an unselfish egoist. An unselfish egoist is a man who has pride without the excuse of passion. Of all conceivable forms of enlightenment the worst is what these people call the Inner Light. Of all horrible religions the most horrible is the worship of the god within. Any one who knows any body knows how it would work; any one who knows any one from the Higher Thought Centre knows how it does work. That Jones shall worship the god within him turns out ultimately to mean that Jones shall worship Jones. Let Jones worship the sun or moon, anything rather than the Inner Light; let Jones worship cats or crocodiles, if he can find any in his street, but not the god within. Christianity came into the world firstly in order to assert with violence that a man had not only to look inwards, but to look outwards, to behold with astonishment and enthusiasm a divine company and a divine captain. The only fun of being a Christian was that a man was not left alone with the Inner Light, but definitely recognized an outer light, fair as the sun, clear as the moon, terrible as an army with banners.

All the same, it will be as well if Jones does not worship the sun and moon. If he does, there is a tendency for him to imitate them; to say, that because the sun burns insects alive, he may burn insects alive. He thinks that because the sun gives people sun-stroke, he may give his neighbour measles. He thinks that because the moon is said to drive men mad, he may drive his wife mad. This ugly side of mere external optimism had also shown itself in the ancient world. About the time when the Stoic idealism had begun to show the weaknesses of pessimism, the old nature worship of the ancients had begun to show the enormous weaknesses of optimism. Nature worship is natural enough while the society is young, or, in other words, Pantheism is all right as long as it is the worship of Pan. But Nature has another side which experience and sin are not slow in finding out, and it is no flippancy to say of the god Pan that he soon showed the cloven hoof. The only objection to Natural Religion is that somehow it always becomes unnatural. A man loves Nature in the morning for her innocence and amiability, and at nightfall, if he is loving her still, it is for her darkness and her cruelty. He washes at dawn in clear water as did the Wise Man of the Stoics, yet, somehow at the dark end of the day, he is bathing in hot bull's blood, as did Julian the Apostate. The mere pursuit of health always leads to something unhealthy. Physical nature must not be made the direct object of obedience; it must be enjoyed, not worshipped. Stars and mountains must not be taken seriously. If they are, we end where the pagan nature worship ended. Because the earth is kind, we can imitate all her cruelties. Because sexuality is sane, we can all go mad about sexuality. Mere optimism had reached its insane and appropriate termination. The theory that everything was good had become an orgy of everything that was bad.

On the other side our idealist pessimists were represented by the old remnant of the Stoics. Marcus Aurelius and his friends had really given up the idea of any god in the universe and looked only to the god within. They had no hope of any virtue in nature, and hardly any hope of any virtue in society. They had not enough interest in the outer world really to wreck or revolutionise it. They did not love the city enough to set fire to it. Thus the ancient world was exactly in our own desolate dilemma. The only people who really enjoyed this world were busy breaking it up; and the virtuous people did not care enough about them to knock them down. In this dilemma (the same as ours) Christianity suddenly stepped in and offered a singular answer, which the world eventually accepted as *the* answer. It was the answer then, and I think it is the answer now.

This answer was like the slash of a sword; it sundered; it did not in any sense sentimentally unite. Briefly, it divided God from the cosmos. That transcendence and distinctness of the deity which some Christians now want to remove from Christianity, was really the only reason why any one wanted to be a Christian. It was the whole point of the Christian answer to the unhappy pessimist and the still more unhappy optimist. As I am here only concerned with their particular problem, I shall indicate only briefly this great metaphysical suggestion. All descriptions of the creating or sustaining principle in things must be metaphorical, because they must be verbal. Thus the pantheist is forced to speak of God *in* all things as if he were in a box. Thus the evolutionist has, in his very name, the idea of being unrolled like a carpet. All terms, religious and irreligious, are open to this charge. The only question is whether all terms are useless, or whether one can, with such a phrase, cover a distinct *idea* about the origin of things. I think one can, and so evidently does the evolutionist, or he would not talk about evolution. And the root phrase for all Christian theism was this, that God was a creator, as an artist is a creator. A poet is so separate from his poem that he himself speaks of it as a little thing he has "thrown off." Even in giving it forth he has flung it away. This principle that all creation and procreation is a breaking off is at least as consistent through the cosmos as the evolutionary principle that all growth is a branching out. A woman loses a child even in having a child. All creation is separation. Birth is as solemn a parting as death.

It was the prime philosophic principle of Christianity that this divorce in the divine act of making (such as severs the poet from the poem or the mother from the new-born child) was the true description of the act whereby the absolute energy made the world. According to most philosophers, God in making the world enslaved it. According to Christianity, in making it, He set it free. God had written, not so much a poem, but rather a play; a play he had planned as perfect, but which had necessarily been left to human actors and stage-managers, who had since made a great mess of it. I will discuss the truth of this theorem later. Here I have only to point out with what a startling smoothness it passed the dilemma we have discussed in this chapter. In this way at least one could be both happy and indignant without degrading one's self to be either a pessimist or an optimist. On this system one could fight all the forces of existence without deserting the flag of existence. One could be at peace with the universe and yet be at war with the world. St. George could still fight the dragon, however big the monster bulked in the cosmos, though he were bigger than the mighty cities or bigger than the everlasting hills. If he were as big as the world he could yet be killed in the name of the world. St. George had not to consider any obvious odds or proportions in the scale of things, but only the original secret of their design. He can shake his sword at the dragon, even if it is everything; even if the empty heavens over his head are only the huge arch of its open jaws.

And then followed an experience impossible to describe. It was as if I had been blundering about since my birth with two huge and unmanageable machines, of different shapes and without apparent connection—the world and the Christian tradition. I had found this hole in the world: the fact that one must somehow find a way of loving the world without trusting it; somehow one must love the world without being worldly. I found this projecting feature of Christian theology, like a sort of hard spike, the dogmatic insistence that God was personal, and had made a world separate from Himself. The spike of dogma fitted exactly into the hole in the world—it had evidently been meant to go there—and then the strange thing began to happen. When once these two parts of the two machines had come together, one after another, all the other parts fitted and fell in with an eerie exactitude. I could hear bolt after bolt over all the machinery falling into its place with a kind of click of relief. Having got one part right, all the other parts were repeating that rectitude, as clock after clock strikes noon. Instinct after instinct was answered by doctrine after doctrine. Or, to vary the metaphor, I was like one who had advanced into a hostile country to take one high fortress. And when that fort had fallen the whole country surrendered and turned solid behind me. The whole land was lit up, as it were, back to the first fields of my childhood. All those blind fancies of boyhood which in the fourth chapter I have tried in vain to trace on the darkness, became suddenly transparent and sane. I was right when I felt that roses were red by some sort of choice: it was the divine choice. I was right when I felt that I would almost rather say that grass was the wrong colour than say it must by necessity have been that colour: it might verily have been any other. My sense that happiness hung on the crazy thread of a condition did mean something when all was said: it meant the whole doctrine of the Fall. Even those dim and shapeless monsters of notions which I have not been able to describe, much less defend, stepped quietly into their places like colossal caryatides of the creed. The fancy that the cosmos was not vast and void, but small and cosy, had a fulfilled significance now, for anything that is a work of art must be small in the sight of the artist; to God the stars might be only small and dear, like diamonds. And my haunting instinct that somehow good was not merely a tool to be used, but a relic to be guarded, like the goods from Crusoe's ship—even that had been the wild whisper of something originally wise, for, according to Christianity, we were indeed the survivors of a wreck, the crew of a golden ship that had gone down before the beginning of the world.

But the important matter was this, that it entirely reversed the reason for optimism. And the instant the reversal was made it felt like the abrupt ease when a bone is put back in the socket. I had often called myself an optimist, to avoid the too evident blasphemy of pessimism. But all the optimism of the age had been false and disheartening for this reason, that it had always been trying to prove that we fit in to the world. The Christian optimism is based on the fact that we do *not* fit in to the world. I had tried to be happy by telling myself that man is an animal, like any other which sought its meat from God. But now I really was happy, for I had learnt that man is a monstrosity. I had been right in feeling all things as odd, for I myself was at once worse and better than all things. The optimist's pleasure was prosaic, for it dwelt on the naturalness of everything; the Christian pleasure was poetic, for it dwelt on the unnaturalness of everything in the light of the supernatural. The modern philosopher had told me again and again that I was in the right place, and I had still felt depressed even in acquiescence. But I had heard that I was in the *wrong* place, and my soul sang for joy, like a bird in spring. The knowledge found out and illuminated forgotten chambers in the dark house of infancy. I knew now why grass had always seemed to me as queer as the green beard of a giant, and why I could feel homesick at home.

VI. THE PARADOXES OF CHRISTIANITY

THE REAL trouble with this world of ours is not that it is an unreasonable world, nor even that it is a reasonable one. The commonest kind of trouble is that it is nearly reasonable, but not quite. Life is not an illogicality; yet it is a trap for logicians. It looks just a little more mathematical and regular than it is; its exactitude is obvious, but its inexactitude is hidden; its wildness lies in wait. I give one coarse instance of what I mean. Suppose some mathematical creature from the moon were to reckon up the human body; he would at once see that the essential thing about it was that it was duplicate. A man is two men, he on the right exactly resembling him on the left. Having noted that there was an arm on the right and one on the left, a leg on the right and one on the left, he might go further and still find on each side the same number of fingers, the same number of toes, twin eyes, twin ears, twin nostrils, and even twin lobes of the brain. At last he would take it as a law; and then, where he found a heart on one side, would deduce that there was another heart on the other. And just then, where he most felt he was right, he would be wrong.

It is this silent swerving from accuracy by an inch that is the uncanny element in everything. It seems a sort of secret treason in the universe. An apple or an orange is round enough to get itself called round, and yet is not round after all. The earth itself is shaped like an orange in order to lure some simple astronomer into calling it a globe. A blade of grass is called after the blade of a sword, because it comes to a point; but it doesn't. Everywhere in things there is this element of the quiet and incalculable. It escapes the rationalists, but it never escapes till the last moment. From the grand curve of our earth it could easily be inferred that every inch of it was thus curved. It would seem rational that as a man has a brain on both sides, he should have a heart on both sides. Yet scientific men are still organizing expeditions to find the North Pole, because they are so fond of flat country. Scientific men are also still organizing expeditions to find a man's heart; and when they try to find it, they generally get on the wrong side of him.

Now, actual insight or inspiration is best tested by whether it guesses these hidden malformations or surprises. If our mathematician from the moon saw the two arms and the two ears, he might deduce the two shoulder-blades and the two halves of the brain. But if he guessed that the man's heart was in the right place, then I should call him something more than a mathematician. Now, this is exactly the claim which I have since come to propound for Christianity. Not merely that it deduces logical truths, but that when it suddenly becomes illogical, it has found, so to speak, an illogical truth. It not only goes right about things, but it goes wrong (if one may say so) exactly where the things go wrong. Its plan suits the secret irregularities, and expects the unexpected. It is simple about the simple truth; but it is stubborn about the subtle truth. It will admit that a man has two hands, it will not admit (though all the Modernists wail to it) the obvious deduction that he has two hearts. It is my only purpose in this chapter to point this out; to show that whenever we feel there is something odd in Christian theology, we shall generally find that there is something odd in the truth.

I have alluded to an unmeaning phrase to the effect that such and such a creed cannot be believed in our age. Of course, anything can be believed in any age. But, oddly enough, there really is a sense in which a creed, if it is believed at all, can be believed more fixedly in a complex society than in a simple one. If a man finds Christianity true in Birmingham, he has actually clearer reasons for faith than if he had found it true in Mercia. For the more complicated seems the coincidence, the less it can be a coincidence. If snowflakes fell in the shape, say, of the heart of Midlothian, it might be an accident. But if snowflakes fell in the exact shape of the maze at Hampton Court, I think one might call it a miracle. It is exactly as of such a miracle that I have since come to feel of the philosophy of Christianity. The complication of our modern world proves the truth of the creed more perfectly than any of the plain problems of the ages of faith. It was in Notting Hill and Battersea that I began to see that Christianity was true. This is why the faith has that elaboration of doctrines and details which so much distresses those who admire Christianity without believing in it. When once one believes in a creed, one is proud of its complexity, as scientists are proud of the complexity of science. It shows how rich it is in discoveries. If it is right at all, it is a compliment to say that it's elaborately right. A stick might fit a hole or a stone a hollow by accident. But a key and a lock are both complex. And if a key fits a lock, you know it is the right key.

But this involved accuracy of the thing makes it very difficult to do what I now have to do, to describe this accumulation of truth. It is very hard for a man to defend anything of which he is entirely convinced. It is comparatively easy when he is only partially convinced. He is partially convinced because he has found this or that proof of the thing, and he can expound it. But a man is not really convinced of a philosophic theory when he finds that something proves it. He is only really convinced when he finds that everything proves it. And the more converging reasons he finds pointing to this conviction, the more bewildered he is if asked suddenly to sum them up. Thus, if one asked an ordinary intelligent man, on the spur of the moment, "Why do you prefer civilization to savagery?" he would look wildly round at object after object, and would only be able to answer vaguely, "Why, there is that bookcase . . . and the coals in the coal-scuttle . . . and pianos . . . and policemen." The whole case for civilization is that the case for it is complex. It has done so many things. But that very multiplicity of proof which ought to make reply overwhelming makes reply impossible.

There is, therefore, about all complete conviction a kind of huge helplessness. The belief is so big that it takes a long time to get it into action. And this hesitation chiefly arises, oddly enough, from an indifference about where one should begin. All roads lead to Rome; which is one reason why many people never get there. In the case of this defence of the Christian conviction I confess that I would as soon begin the argument with one thing as another; I would begin it with a turnip or a taximeter cab. But if I am to be at all careful about making my meaning clear, it will, I think, be wiser to continue the current arguments of the last chapter, which was concerned to urge the first of these mystical coincidences, or rather ratifications. All I had hitherto heard of Christian theology had alienated me from it. I was a pagan at the age of twelve, and a complete agnostic by the age of sixteen; and I cannot understand any one passing the age of seventeen without having asked himself so simple a question.

I did, indeed, retain a cloudy reverence for a cosmic deity and a great historical interest in the Founder of Christianity. But I certainly regarded Him as a man; though perhaps I thought that, even in that point, He had an advantage over some of His modern critics. I read the scientific and sceptical literature of my time—all of it, at least, that I could find written in English and lying about; and I read nothing else; I mean I read nothing else on any other note of philosophy. The penny dreadfuls which I also read were indeed in a healthy and heroic tradition of Christianity; but I did not know this at the time. I never read a line of Christian apologetics. I read as little as I can of them now. It was Huxley and Herbert Spencer and Bradlaugh who brought me back to orthodox theology. They sowed in my mind my first wild doubts of doubt. Our grandmothers were quite right when they said that Tom Paine and the freethinkers unsettled the mind. They do. They unsettled mine horribly. The rationalist made me question whether reason was of any use whatever; and when I had finished Herbert Spencer I had got as far as doubting (for the first time) whether evolution had occurred at all. As I laid down the last of Colonel Ingersoll's atheistic lectures the dreadful thought broke across my mind, "Almost thou persuadest me to be a Christian." I was in a desperate way.

This odd effect of the great agnostics in arousing doubts deeper than their own might be illustrated in many ways. I take only one. As I read and re-read all the non-Christian or anti-Christian accounts of the faith, from Huxley to Bradlaugh, a slow and awful impression grew gradually but graphically upon my mind—the impression that Christianity must be a most extraordinary thing. For not only (as I understood) had Christianity the most flaming vices, but it had apparently a mystical talent for combining vices which seemed inconsistent with each other. It was attacked on all sides and for all contradictory reasons. No sooner had one rationalist demonstrated that it was too far to the east than another demonstrated with equal clearness that it was much too far to the west. No sooner had my indignation died down at its angular and aggressive squareness than I was called up again to notice and condemn its enervating and sensual roundness. In case any reader has not come across the thing I mean, I will give such instances as I remember at random of this self-contradiction in the sceptical attack. I give four or five of them; there are fifty more.

Thus, for instance, I was much moved by the eloquent attack on Christianity as a thing of inhuman gloom; for I thought (and still think) sincere pessimism the unpardonable sin. Insincere pessimism is a social accomplishment, rather agreeable than otherwise; and fortunately nearly all pessimism is insincere. But if Christianity was, as these people said, a thing purely pessimistic and opposed to life, then I was quite prepared to blow up St. Paul's Cathedral. But the extraordinary thing is this. They did prove to me in Chapter I. (to my complete satisfaction) that Christianity was too pessimistic; and then, in Chapter II., they began to prove to me that it was a great deal too optimistic. One accusation against Christianity was that it prevented men, by morbid tears and terrors, from seeking joy and liberty in the bosom of Nature. But another accusation was that it comforted men with a fictitious providence, and put them in a pink-and-white nursery. One great agnostic asked why Nature was not beautiful enough, and why it was hard to be free. Another great agnostic objected that Christian optimism, "the garment of make-believe woven by pious hands," hid from us the fact that Nature was ugly, and that it was impossible to be free. One rationalist had hardly done calling Christianity a nightmare before another began to call it a fool's paradise. This puzzled me; the charges seemed inconsistent. Christianity could not at once be the black mask on a white world, and also the white mask on a black world. The state of the Christian could not be at once so comfortable that he was a coward to cling to it, and so uncomfortable that he was a fool to stand it. If it falsified human vision it must falsify it one way or another; it could not wear both green and rose-coloured spectacles. I rolled on my tongue with a terrible joy, as did all young men of that time, the taunts which Swinburne hurled at the dreariness of the creed—

Thou hast conquered, O pale Galilaean, the world has
grown gray with Thy breath.

But when I read the same poet's accounts of paganism (as in "Atalanta"), I gathered that the world was, if possible, more gray before the Galilaean breathed on it than afterwards. The poet maintained, indeed, in the abstract, that life itself was pitch dark. And yet, somehow, Christianity had darkened it. The very man who denounced Christianity for pessimism was himself a pessimist. I thought there must be something wrong. And it did for one wild moment cross my mind that, perhaps, those might not be the very best judges of the relation of religion to happiness who, by their own account, had neither one nor the other.

It must be understood that I did not conclude hastily that the accusations were false or the accusers fools. I simply deduced that Christianity must be something even weirder and wickeder than they made out. A thing might have these two opposite vices; but it must be a rather queer thing if it did. A man might be too fat in one place and too thin in another; but he would be an odd shape. At this point my thoughts were only of the odd shape of the Christian religion; I did not allege any odd shape in the rationalistic mind.

Here is another case of the same kind. I felt that a strong case against Christianity lay in the charge that there is something timid, monkish, and unmanly about all that is called "Christian," especially in its attitude towards resistance and fighting. The great sceptics of the nineteenth century were largely virile. Bradlaugh in an expansive way, Huxley, in a reticent way, were decidedly men. In comparison, it did seem tenable that there was something weak and over patient about Christian counsels. The Gospel paradox about the other cheek, the fact that priests never fought, a hundred things made plausible the accusation that Christianity was an attempt to make a man too like a sheep. I read it and believed it, and if I had read nothing different, I should have gone on believing it. But I read something very different. I turned the next page in my agnostic manual, and my brain turned upside down. Now I found that I was to hate Christianity not for fighting too little, but for fighting too much. Christianity, it seemed, was the mother of wars. Christianity had deluged the world with blood. I had got thoroughly angry with the Christian, because he never was angry. And now I was told to be angry with him because his anger had been the most huge and horrible thing in human history; because his anger had soaked the earth and smoked to the sun. The very people who reproached Christianity with the meekness and non-resistance of the monasteries were the very people who reproached it also with the violence and valour of the Crusades. It was the fault of poor old Christianity (somehow or other) both that Edward the Confessor did not fight and that Richard Coeur de Leon did. The Quakers (we were told) were the only characteristic Christians; and yet the massacres of Cromwell and Alva were characteristic Christian crimes. What could it all mean? What was this Christianity which always forbade war and always produced wars? What could be the nature of the thing which one could abuse first because it would not fight, and second because it was always fighting? In what world of riddles was born this monstrous murder and this monstrous meekness? The shape of Christianity grew a queerer shape every instant.

I take a third case; the strangest of all, because it involves the one real objection to the faith. The one real objection to the Christian religion is simply that it is one religion. The world is a big place, full of very different kinds of people. Christianity (it may reasonably be said) is one thing confined to one kind of people; it began in Palestine, it has practically stopped with Europe. I was duly impressed with this argument in my youth, and I was much drawn towards the doctrine often preached in Ethical Societies—I mean the doctrine that there is one great unconscious church of all humanity founded on the omnipresence of the human conscience. Creeds, it was said, divided men; but at least morals united them. The soul might seek the strangest and most remote lands and ages and still find essential ethical common sense. It might find Confucius under Eastern trees, and he would be writing "Thou shalt not steal." It might decipher the darkest hieroglyphic on the most primeval desert, and the meaning when deciphered would be "Little boys should tell the truth." I believed this doctrine of the brotherhood of all men in the possession of a moral sense, and I believe it still—with other things. And I was thoroughly annoyed with Christianity for suggesting (as I supposed) that whole ages and empires of men had utterly escaped this light of justice and reason. But then I found an astonishing thing. I found that the very people who said that mankind was one church from Plato to Emerson were the very people who said that morality had changed altogether, and that what was right in one age was wrong in another. If I asked, say, for an altar, I was told that we needed none, for men our brothers gave us clear oracles and one creed in their universal customs and ideals. But if I mildly pointed out that one of men's universal customs was to have an altar, then my agnostic teachers turned clean round and told me that men had always been in darkness and the superstitions of savages. I found it was their daily taunt against Christianity that it was the light of one people and had left all others to die in the dark. But I also found that it was their special boast for themselves that science and progress were the discovery of one people, and that all other peoples had died in the dark. Their chief insult to Christianity was actually their chief compliment to themselves, and there seemed to be a strange unfairness about all their relative insistence on the two things. When considering some pagan or agnostic, we were to remember that all men had one religion; when considering some mystic or spiritualist, we were only to consider what absurd religions some men had. We could trust the ethics of Epictetus, because ethics had never changed. We must not trust the ethics of Bossuet, because ethics had changed. They changed in two hundred years, but not in two thousand.

This began to be alarming. It looked not so much as if Christianity was bad enough to include any vices, but rather as if any stick was good enough to beat Christianity with. What again could this astonishing thing be like which people were so anxious to contradict, that in doing so they did not mind contradicting themselves? I saw the same thing on every side. I can give no further space to this discussion of it in detail; but lest any one supposes that I have unfairly selected three accidental cases I will run briefly through a few others. Thus, certain sceptics wrote that the great crime of Christianity had been its attack on the family; it had dragged women to the loneliness and contemplation of the cloister, away from their homes and their children. But, then, other sceptics (slightly more advanced) said that the great crime of Christianity was forcing the family and marriage upon us; that it doomed women to the drudgery of their homes and children, and forbade them loneliness and contemplation. The charge was actually reversed. Or, again, certain phrases in the Epistles or the marriage service, were said by the anti-Christians to show contempt for woman's intellect. But I found that the anti-Christians themselves had a contempt for woman's intellect; for it was their great sneer at the Church on the Continent that "only women" went to it. Or again, Christianity was reproached with its naked and hungry habits; with its sackcloth and dried peas. But the next minute Christianity was being reproached with its pomp and its ritualism; its shrines of porphyry and its robes of gold. It was abused for being too plain and for being too coloured. Again Christianity had always been accused of restraining sexuality too much, when Bradlaugh the Malthusian discovered that it restrained it too little. It is often accused in the same breath of prim respectability and of religious extravagance. Between the covers of the same atheistic pamphlet I have found the faith rebuked for its disunion, "One thinks one thing, and one another," and rebuked also for its union, "It is difference of opinion that prevents the world from going to the dogs." In the same conversation a freethinker, a friend of mine, blamed Christianity for despising Jews, and then despised it himself for being Jewish.

I wished to be quite fair then, and I wish to be quite fair now; and I did not conclude that the attack on Christianity was all wrong. I only concluded that if Christianity was wrong, it was very wrong indeed. Such hostile horrors might be combined in one thing, but that thing must be very strange and solitary. There are men who are misers, and also spendthrifts; but they are rare. There are men sensual and also ascetic; but they are rare. But if this mass of mad contradictions really existed, quakerish and bloodthirsty, too gorgeous and too thread-bare, austere, yet pandering preposterously to the lust of the eye, the enemy of women and their foolish refuge, a solemn pessimist and a silly optimist, if this evil existed, then there was in this evil something quite supreme and unique. For I found in my rationalist teachers no explanation of such exceptional corruption. Christianity (theoretically speaking) was in their eyes only one of the ordinary myths and errors of mortals. *They* gave me no key to this twisted and unnatural badness. Such a paradox of evil rose to the stature of the supernatural. It was, indeed, almost as supernatural as the infallibility of the Pope. An historic institution, which never went right, is really quite as much of a miracle as an institution that cannot go wrong. The only explanation which immediately occurred to my mind was that Christianity did not come from heaven, but from hell. Really, if Jesus of Nazareth was not Christ, He must have been Antichrist.

And then in a quiet hour a strange thought struck me like a still thunderbolt. There had suddenly come into my mind another explanation. Suppose we heard an unknown man spoken of by many men. Suppose we were puzzled to hear that some men said he was too tall and some too short; some objected to his fatness, some lamented his leanness; some thought him too dark, and some too fair. One explanation (as has been already admitted) would be that he might be an odd shape. But there is another explanation. He might be the right shape. Outrageously tall men might feel him to be short. Very short men might feel him to be tall. Old bucks who are growing stout might consider him insufficiendy filled out; old beaux who were growing thin might feel that he expanded beyond the narrow lines of elegance. Perhaps Swedes (who have pale hair like tow) called him a dark man, while negroes considered him distinctly blonde. Perhaps (in short) this extraordinary thing is really the ordinary thing; at least the normal thing, the centre. Perhaps, after all, it is Christianity that is sane and all its critics that are mad—in various ways. I tested this idea by asking myself whether there was about any of the accusers anything morbid that might explain the accusation. I was startled to find that this key fitted a lock. For instance, it was certainly odd that the modern world charged Christianity at once with bodily austerity and with artistic pomp. But then it was also odd, very odd, that the modern world itself combined extreme bodily luxury with an extreme absence of artistic pomp. The modern man thought Becket's robes too rich and his meals too poor. But then the modern man was really exceptional in history; no man before ever ate such elaborate dinners in such ugly clothes. The modern man found the church too simple exactly where modern life is too complex; he found the church too gorgeous exactly where modern life is too dingy. The man who disliked the plain fasts and feasts was mad on *entrées.* The man who disliked vestments wore a pair of preposterous trousers. And surely if there was any insanity involved in the matter at all it was in the trousers, not in the simply falling robe. If there was any insanity at all, it was in the extravagant *entrées*, not in the bread and wine.

I went over all the cases, and I found the key fitted so far. The fact that Swinburne was irritated at the unhappiness of Christians and yet more irritated at their happiness was easily explained. It was no longer a complication of diseases in Christianity, but a complication of diseases in Swinburne. The restraints of Christians saddened him simply because he was more hedonist than a healthy man should be. The faith of Christians angered him because he was more pessimist than a healthy man should be. In the same way the Malthusians by instinct attacked Christianity; not because there is anything especially anti-Malthusian about Christianity, but because there is something a little anti-human about Malthusianism.

Nevertheless it could not, I felt, be quite true that Christianity was merely sensible and stood in the middle. There was really an element in it of emphasis and even frenzy which had justified the secularists in their superficial criticism. It might be wise, I began more and more to think that it was wise, but it was not merely worldly wise; it was not merely temperate and respectable. Its fierce crusaders and meek saints might balance each other; still, the crusaders were very fierce and the saints were very meek, meek beyond all decency. Now, it was just at this point of the speculation that I remembered my thoughts about the martyr and the suicide. In that matter there had been this combination between two almost insane positions which yet somehow amounted to sanity. This was just such another contradiction; and this I had already found to be true.

This was exactly one of the paradoxes in which sceptics found the creed wrong; and in this I had found it right. Madly as Christians might love the martyr or hate the suicide, they never felt these passions more madly than I had felt them long before I dreamed of Christianity. Then the most difficult and interesting part of the mental process opened, and I began to trace this idea darkly through all the enormous thoughts of our theology. The idea was that which I had outlined touching the optimist and the pessimist; that we want not an amalgam or compromise, but both things at the top of their energy; love and wrath both burning. Here I shall only trace it in relation to ethics. But I need not remind the reader that the idea of this combination is indeed central in orthodox theology. For orthodox theology has specially insisted that Christ was not a being apart from God and man, like an elf, nor yet a being half human and half not, like a centaur, but both things at once and both things thoroughly, very man and very God. Now let me trace this notion as I found it.

All sane men can see that sanity is some kind of equilibrium; that one may be mad and eat too much, or mad and eat too little. Some moderns have indeed appeared with vague versions of progress and evolution which seeks to destroy the μέσον or balance of Aristotle. They seem to suggest that we are meant to starve progressively, or to go on eating larger and larger breakfasts every morning for ever. But the great truism of the μέσον remains for all thinking men, and these people have not upset any balance except their own. But granted that we have all to keep a balance, the real interest comes in with the question of how that balance can be kept. That was the problem which Paganism tried to solve: that was the problem which I think Christianity solved and solved in a very strange way.

Paganism declared that virtue was in a balance; Christianity declared it was in a conflict: the collision of two passions apparently opposite. Of course they were not really inconsistent; but they were such that it was hard to hold simultaneously. Let us follow for a moment the clue of the martyr and the suicide; and take the case of courage. No quality has ever so much addled the brains and tangled the definitions of merely rational sages. Courage is almost a contradiction in terms. It means a strong desire to live taking the form of a readiness to die. "He that will lose his life, the same shall save it," is not a piece of mysticism for saints and heroes. It is a piece of everyday advice for sailors or mountaineers. It might be printed in an Alpine guide or a drill book. This paradox is the whole principle of courage; even of quite earthly or quite brutal courage. A man cut off by the sea may save his life if he will risk it on the precipice. He can only get away from death by continually stepping within an inch of it. A soldier surrounded by enemies, if he is to cut his way out, needs to combine a strong desire for living with a strange carelessness about dying. He must not merely cling to life, for then he will be a coward, and will not escape. He must not merely wait for death, for then he will be a suicide, and will not escape, He must seek his life in a spirit of furious indifference to it; he must desire life like water and yet drink death like wine. No philosopher, I fancy, has ever expressed this romantic riddle with adequate lucidity, and I certainly have not done so. But Christianity has done more: it has marked the limits of it in the awful graves of the suicide and the hero, showing the distance between him who dies for the sake of living and him who dies for the sake of dying. And it has held up ever since above the European lances the banner of the mystery of chivalry: the Christian courage, which is a disdain of death; not the Chinese courage, which is a disdain of life.

And now I began to find that this duplex passion was the Christian key to ethics everywhere. Everywhere the creed made a moderation out of the still crash of two impetuous emotions. Take, for instance, the matter of modesty, of the balance between mere pride and mere prostration. The average pagan, like the average agnostic, would merely say that he was content with himself, but not insolently self-satisfied, that there were many better and many worse, that his deserts were limited, but he would see that he got them. In short, he would walk with his head in the air; but not necessarily with his nose in the air. This is a manly and rational position, but it is open to the objection we noted against the compromise between optimism and pessimism—the "resignation" of Matthew Arnold. Being a mixture of two things, it is a dilution of two things; neither is present in its full strength or contributes its full colour. This proper pride does not lift the heart like the tongue of trumpets; you cannot go clad in crimson and gold for this. On the other hand, this mild rationalist modesty does not cleanse the soul with fire and make it clear like crystal; it does not (like a strict and searching humility) make a man as a little child, who can sit at the feet of the grass. It does not make him look up and see marvels; for Alice must grow small if she is to be Alice in Wonderland. Thus it loses both the poetry of being proud and the poetry of being humble. Christianity sought by this same strange expedient to save both of them.

It separated the two ideas and then exaggerated them both. In one way Man was to be haughtier than he had ever been before; in another way he was to be humbler than he had ever been before. In so far as I am Man I am the chief of creatures. In so far as I am *a* man I am the chief of sinners. All humility that had meant pessimism, that had meant man taking a vague or mean view of his whole destiny—all that was to go. We were to hear no more the wail of Ecclesiastes that humanity had no pre-eminence over the brute, or the awful cry of Homer that man was only the saddest of all the beasts of the field. Man was a statue of God walking about the garden. Man had pre-eminence over all the brutes; man was only sad because he was not a beast, but a broken god. The Greek had spoken of men creeping on the earth, as if clinging to it. Now Man was to tread on the earth as if to subdue it. Christianity thus held a thought of the dignity of man that could only be expressed in crowns rayed like the sun and fans of peacock plumage. Yet at the same time it could hold a thought about the abject smallness of man that could only be expressed in fasting and fantastic submission, in the gray ashes of St. Dominic and the white snows of St. Bernard. When one came to think of *one's self*, there was vista and void enough for any amount of bleak abnegation and bitter truth. There the realistic gentleman could let himself go—as long as he let himself go at himself. There was an open playground for the happy pessimist. Let him say anything against himself short of blaspheming the original aim of his being; let him call himself a fool and even a damned fool (though that is Calvinistic); but he must not say that fools are not worth saving. He must not say that a man, *quâ* man, can be valueless. Here, again in short, Christianity got over the difficulty of combining furious opposites, by keeping them both, and keeping them both furious. The Church was positive on both points. One can hardly think too little of one's self. One can hardly think too much of one's soul.

Take another case: the complicated question of charity, which some highly uncharitable idealists seem to think quite easy. Charity is a paradox, like modesty and courage. Stated baldly, charity certainly means one of two things—pardoning unpardonable acts, or loving unlovable people. But if we ask ourselves (as we did in the case of pride) what a sensible pagan would feel about such a subject, we shall probably be beginning at the bottom of it. A sensible pagan would say that there were some people one could forgive, and some one couldn't: a slave who stole wine could be laughed at; a slave who betrayed his benefactor could be killed, and cursed even after he was killed. In so far as the act was pardonable, the man was pardonable. That again is rational, and even refreshing; but it is a dilution. It leaves no place for a pure horror of injustice, such as that which is a great beauty in the innocent. And it leaves no place for a mere tenderness for men as men, such as is the whole fascination of the charitable. Christianity came in here as before. It came in startlingly with a sword, and clove one thing from another. It divided the crime from the criminal. The criminal we must forgive unto seventy times seven. The crime we must not forgive at all. It was not enough that slaves who stole wine inspired partly anger and partly kindness. We must be much more angry with theft than before, and yet much kinder to thieves than before. There was room for wrath and love to run wild. And the more I considered Christianity, the more I found that while it had established a rule and order, the chief aim of that order was to give room for good things to run wild.

Mental and emotional liberty are not so simple as they look. Really they require almost as careful a balance of laws and conditions as do social and political liberty. The ordinary aesthetic anarchist who sets out to feel everything freely gets knotted at last in a paradox that prevents him feeling at all. He breaks away from home limits to follow poetry. But in ceasing to feel home limits he has ceased to feel the "Odyssey." He is free from national prejudices and outside patriotism. But being outside patriotism he is outside "Henry V." Such a literary man is simply outside all literature: he is more of a prisoner than any bigot. For if there is a wall between you and the world, it makes little difference whether you describe yourself as locked in or as locked out. What we want is not the universality that is outside all normal sentiments; we want the universality that is inside all normal sentiments. It is all the difference between being free from them, as a man is free from a prison, and being free of them as a man is free of a city. I am free from Windsor Castle (that is, I am not forcibly detained there), but I am by no means free of that building. How can man be approximately free of fine emotions, able to swing them in a clear space without breakage or wrong? *This* was the achievement of this Christian paradox of the parallel passions. Granted the primary dogma of the war between divine and diabolic, the revolt and ruin of the world, their optimism and pessimism, as pure poetry, could be loosened like cataracts.

St. Francis, in praising all good, could be a more shouting optimist than Walt Whitman. St. Jerome, in denouncing all evil, could paint the world blacker than Schopenhauer. Both passions were free because both were kept in their place. The optimist could pour out all the praise he liked on the gay music of the march, the golden trumpets, and the purple banners going into battle. But he must not call the fight needless. The pessimist might draw as darkly as he chose the sickening marches or the sanguine wounds. But he must not call the fight hopeless. So it was with all the other moral problems, with pride, with protest, and with compassion. By defining its main doctrine, the Church not only kept seemingly inconsistent things side by side, but, what was more, allowed them to break out in a sort of artistic violence otherwise possible only to anarchists. Meekness grew more dramatic than madness. Historic Christianity rose into a high and strange *coup de théatre* of morality—things that are to virtue what the crimes of Nero are to vice. The spirits of indignation and of charity took terrible and attractive forms, ranging from that monkish fierceness that scourged like a dog the first and greatest of the Plantagenets, to the sublime pity of St. Catherine, who, in the official shambles, kissed the bloody head of the criminal. Poetry could be acted as well as composed. This heroic and monumental manner in ethics has entirely vanished with supernatural religion. They, being humble, could parade themselves: but we are too proud to be prominent. Our ethical teachers write reasonably for prison reform; but we are not likely to see Mr. Cadbury, or any eminent philanthropist, go into Reading Gaol and embrace the strangled corpse before it is cast into the quicklime. Our ethical teachers write mildly against the power of millionaires; but we are not likely to see Mr. Rockefeller, or any modern tyrant, publicly whipped in Westminster Abbey.

Thus, the double charges of the secularists, though throwing nothing but darkness and confusion on themselves, throw a real light on the faith. It *is* true that the historic Church has at once emphasised celibacy and emphasised the family; has at once (if one may put it so) been fiercely for having children and fiercely for not having children. It has kept them side by side like two strong colours, red and white, like the red and white upon the shield of St. George. It has always had a healthy hatred of pink. It hates that combination of two colours which is the feeble expedient of the philosophers. It hates that evolution of black into white which is tantamount to a dirty gray. In fact, the whole theory of the Church on virginity might be symbolized in the statement that white is a colour: not merely the absence of a colour. All that I am urging here can be expressed by saying that Christianity sought in most of these cases to keep two colours coexistent but pure. It is not a mixture like russet or purple; it is rather like a shot silk, for a shot silk is always at right angles, and is in the pattern of the cross.

So it is also, of course, with the contradictory charges of the anti-Christians about submission and slaughter. It *is* true that the Church told some men to fight and others not to fight; and it *is* true that those who fought were like thunderbolts and those who did not fight were like statues. All this simply means that the Church preferred to use its Supermen and to use its Tolstoyans. There must be *some* good in the life of battle, for so many good men have enjoyed being soldiers. There must be *some* good in the idea of non-resistance, for so many good men seem to enjoy being Quakers. All that the Church did (so far as that goes) was to prevent either of these good things from ousting the other. They existed side by side. The Tolstoyans, having all the scruples of monks, simply became monks. The Quakers became a club instead of becoming a sect. Monks said all that Tolstoy says; they poured out lucid lamentations about the cruelty of battles and the vanity of revenge. But the Tolstoyans are not quite right enough to run the whole world; and in the ages of faith they were not allowed to run it. The world did not lose the last charge of Sir James Douglas or the banner of Joan the Maid. And sometimes this pure gentleness and this pure fierceness met and justified their juncture; the paradox of all the prophets was fulfilled, and, in the soul of St. Louis, the lion lay down with the lamb. But remember that this text is too lightly interpreted. It is constantly assured, especially in our Tolstoyan tendencies, that when the lion lies down with the lamb the lion becomes lamb-like. But that is brutal annexation and imperialism on the part of the lamb. That is simply the lamb absorbing the lion instead of the lion eating the lamb. The real problem is—Can the lion lie down with the lamb and still retain his royal ferocity? *That* is the problem the Church attempted; *that* is the miracle she achieved.

This is what I have called guessing the hidden eccentricities of life. This is knowing that a man's heart is to the left and not in the middle. This is knowing not only that the earth is round, but knowing exactly where it is flat. Christian doctrine detected the oddities of life. It not only discovered the law, but it foresaw the exceptions. Those underrate Christianity who say that it discovered mercy; any one might discover mercy. In fact every one did. But to discover a plan for being merciful and also severe—*that* was to anticipate a strange need of human nature. For no one wants to be forgiven for a big sin as if it were a little one. Any one might say that we should be neither quite miserable nor quite happy. But to find out how far one *may* be quite miserable without making it impossible to be quite happy—that was a discovery in psychology. Any one might say, "Neither swagger nor grovel"; and it would have been a limit. But to say, "Here you can swagger and there you can grovel"—that was an emancipation.

This was the big fact about Christian ethics; the discovery of the new balance. Paganism had been like a pillar of marble, upright because proportioned with symmetry. Christianity was like a huge and ragged and romantic rock, which, though it sways on its pedestal at a touch, yet, because its exaggerated excrescences exactly balance each other, is enthroned there for a thousand years. In a Gothic cathedral the columns were all different, but they were all necessary. Every support seemed an accidental and fantastic support; every buttress was a flying buttress. So in Christendom apparent accidents balanced. Becket wore a hair shirt under his gold and crimson, and there is much to be said for the combination; for Becket got the benefit of the hair shirt while the people in the street got the benefit of the crimson and gold. It is at least better than the manner of the modern millionaire, who has the black and the drab outwardly for others, and the gold next his heart. But the balance was not always in one man's body as in Becket's; the balance was often distributed over the whole body of Christendom. Because a man prayed and fasted on the Northern snows, flowers could be flung at his festival in the Southern cities; and because fanatics drank water on the sands of Syria, men could still drink cider in the orchards of England. This is what makes Christendom at once so much more perplexing and so much more interesting than the Pagan empire; just as Amiens Cathedral is not better but more interesting than the Parthenon. If any one wants a modern proof of all this, let him consider the curious fact that, under Christianity, Europe (while remaining a unity) has broken up into individual nations. Patriotism is a perfect example of this deliberate balancing of one emphasis against another emphasis. The instinct of the Pagan empire would have said, "You shall all be Roman citizens, and grow alike; let the German grow less slow and reverent; the Frenchmen less experimental and swift." But the instinct of Christian Europe says, "Let the German remain slow and reverent, that the Frenchman may the more safely be swift and experimental. We will make an equipoise out of these excesses. The absurdity called Germany shall correct the insanity called France."

Last and most important, it is exactly this which explains what is so inexplicable to all the modern critics of the history of Christianity. I mean the monstrous wars about small points of theology, the earthquakes of emotion about a gesture or a word. It was only a matter of an inch; but an inch is everything when you are balancing. The Church could not afford to swerve a hair's breadth on some things if she was to continue her great and daring experiment of the irregular equilibrium. Once let one idea become less powerful and some other idea would become too powerful. It was no flock of sheep the Christian shepherd was leading, but a herd of bulls and tigers, of terrible ideals and devouring doctrines, each one of them strong enough to turn to a false religion and lay waste the world. Remember that the Church went in specifically for dangerous ideas; she was a lion tamer. The idea of birth through a Holy Spirit, of the death of a divine being, of the forgiveness of sins, or the fulfilment of prophecies, are ideas which, any one can see, need but a touch to turn them into something blasphemous or ferocious. The smallest link was let drop by the artificers of the Mediterranean, and the lion of ancestral pessimism burst his chain in the forgotten forests of the north. Of these theological equalisations I have to speak afterwards. Here it is enough to notice that if some small mistake were made in doctrine, huge blunders might be made in human happiness. A sentence phrased wrong about the nature of symbolism would have broken all the best statues in Europe. A slip in the definitions might stop all the dances; might wither all the Christmas trees or break all the Easter eggs. Doctrines had to be defined within strict limits, even in order that man might enjoy general human liberties. The Church had to be careful, if only that the world might be careless.

This is the thrilling romance of Orthodoxy. People have fallen into a foolish habit of speaking of orthodoxy as something heavy, humdrum, and safe. There never was anything so perilous or so exciting as orthodoxy. It was sanity: and to be sane is more dramatic than to be mad. It was the equilibrium of a man behind madly rushing horses, seeming to stoop this way and to sway that, yet in every attitude having the grace of statuary and the accuracy of arithmetic. The Church in its early days went fierce and fast with any warhorse; yet it is utterly unhistoric to say that she merely went mad along one idea, like a vulgar fanaticism. She swerved to left and right, so exactly as to avoid enormous obstacles. She left on one hand the huge bulk of Arianism, buttressed by all the worldly powers to make Christianity too worldly. The next instant she was swerving to avoid an orientalism, which would have made it too unworldly. The orthodox Church never took the tame course or accepted the conventions; the orthodox Church was never respectable. It would have been easier to have accepted the earthly power of the Arians. It would have been easy, in the Calvinistic seventeenth century, to fall into the bottomless pit of predestination. It is easy to be a madman: it is easy to be a heretic. It is always easy to let the age have its head; the difficult thing is to keep one's own. It is always easy to be a modernist; as it is easy to be a snob. To have fallen into any of those open traps of error and exaggeration which fashion after fashion and sect after sect set along the historic path of Christendom—that would indeed have been simple. It is always simple to fall; there are an infinity of angles at which one falls, only one at which one stands. To have fallen into any one of the fads from Gnosticism to Christian Science would indeed have been obvious and tame. But to have avoided them all has been one whirling adventure; and in my vision the heavenly chariot flies thundering through the ages, the dull heresies sprawling and prostrate, the wild truth reeling but erect.

VII. THE ETERNAL REVOLUTION

THE FOLLOWING propositions have been urged: First, that some faith in our life is required even to improve it; second, that some dissatisfaction with things as they are is necessary even in order to be satisfied; third, that to have this necessary content and necessary discontent it is not sufficient to have the obvious equilibrium of the Stoic. For mere resignation has neither the gigantic levity of pleasure nor the superb intolerance of pain. There is a vital objection to the advice merely to grin and bear it. The objection is that if you merely bear it, you do not grin. Greek heroes do not grin: but gargoyles do—because they are Christian. And when a Christian is pleased, he is (in the most exact sense) frightfully pleased; his pleasure is frightful. Christ prophesied the whole of Gothic architecture in that hour when nervous and respectable people (such people as now object to barrel organs) objected to the shouting of the gutter-snipes of Jerusalem. He said, "If these were silent, the very stones would cry out." Under the impulse of His spirit arose like a clamorous chorus the facades of the mediaeval cathedrals, thronged with shouting faces and open mouths. The prophecy has fulfilled itself: the very stones cry out.

If these things be conceded, though only for argument, we may take up where we left it the thread of the thought of the natural man, called by the Scotch (with regrettable familiarity), "The Old Man." We can ask the next question so obviously in front of us. Some satisfaction is needed even to make things better. But what do we mean by making things better? Most modern talk on this matter is a mere argument in a circle—that circle which we have already made the symbol of madness and of mere rationalism. Evolution is only good if it produces good; good is only good if it helps evolution. The elephant stands on the tortoise, and the tortoise on the elephant.

Obviously, it will not do to take our ideal from the principle in nature; for the simple reason that (except for some human or divine theory), there is no principle in nature. For instance, the cheap anti-democrat of to-day will tell you solemnly that there is no equality in nature. He is right, but he does not see the logical addendum. There is no equality in nature; also there is no inequality in nature. Inequality, as much as equality, implies a standard of value. To read aristocracy into the anarchy of animals is just as sentimental as to read democracy into it. Both aristocracy and democracy are human ideals: the one saying that all men are valuable, the other that some men are more valuable. But nature does not say that cats are more valuable than mice; nature makes no remark on the subject. She does not even say that the cat is enviable or the mouse pitiable. We think the cat superior because we have (or most of us have) a particular philosophy to the effect that life is better than death. But if the mouse were a German pessimist mouse, he might not think that the cat had beaten him at all. He might think he had beaten the cat by getting to the grave first. Or he might feel that he had actually inflicted frightful punishment on the cat by keeping him alive. Just as a microbe might feel proud of spreading a pestilence, so the pessimistic mouse might exult to think that he was renewing in the cat the torture of conscious existence. It all depends on the philosophy of the mouse. You cannot even say that there is victory or superiority in nature unless you have some doctrine about what things are superior. You cannot even say that the cat scores unless there is a system of scoring. You cannot even say that the cat gets the best of it unless there is some best to be got.

We cannot, then, get the ideal itself from nature, and as we follow here the first and natural speculation, we will leave out (for the present) the idea of getting it from God. We must have our own vision. But the attempts of most moderns to express it are highly vague.

Some fall back simply on the clock: they talk as if mere passage through time brought some superiority; so that even a man of the first mental calibre carelessly uses the phrase that human morality is never up to date. How can anything be up to date?—a date has no character. How can one say that Christmas celebrations are not suitable to the twenty-fifth of a month? What the writer meant, of course, was that the majority is behind his favourite minority—or in front of it. Other vague modern people take refuge in material metaphors; in fact, this is the chief mark of vague modern people. Not daring to define their doctrine of what is good, they use physical figures of speech without stint or shame, and, what is worst of all, seem to think these cheap analogies are exquisitely spiritual and superior to the old morality. Thus they think it intellectual to talk about things being "high." It is at least the reverse of intellectual; it is a mere phrase from a steeple or a weathercock. "Tommy was a good boy" is a pure philosophical statement, worthy of Plato or Aquinas. "Tommy lived the higher life" is a gross metaphor from a ten-foot rule.

This, incidentally, is almost the whole weakness of Nietzsche, whom some are representing as a bold and strong thinker. No one will deny that he was a poetical and suggestive thinker; but he was quite the reverse of strong. He was not at all bold. He never put his own meaning before himself in bald abstract words: as did Aristotle and Calvin, and even Karl Marx, the hard, fearless men of thought. Nietzsche always escaped a question by a physical metaphor, like a cheery minor poet. He said, "beyond good and evil," because he had not the courage to say, "more good than good and evil," or, "more evil than good and evil." Had he faced his thought without metaphors, he would have seen that it was nonsense. So, when he describes his hero, he does not dare to say, "the purer man," or "the happier man," or "the sadder man," for all these are ideas; and ideas are alarming. He says "the upper man," or "over man," a physical metaphor from acrobats or alpine climbers. Nietzsche is truly a very timid thinker. He does not really know in the least what sort of man he wants evolution to produce. And if he does not know, certainly the ordinary evolutionists, who talk about things being "higher," do not know either.

Then again, some people fall back on sheer submission and sitting still. Nature is going to do something some day; nobody knows what, and nobody knows when. We have no reason for acting, and no reason for not acting. If anything happens it is right: if anything is prevented it was wrong. Again, some people try to anticipate nature by doing something, by doing anything. Because we may possibly grow wings they cut off their legs. Yet nature may be trying to make them centipedes for all they know.

Lastly, there is a fourth class of people who take whatever it is that they happen to want, and say that that is the ultimate aim of evolution. And these are the only sensible people. This is the only really healthy way with the word evolution, to work for what you want, and to call *that* evolution. The only intelligible sense that progress or advance can have among men, is that we have a definite vision, and that we wish to make the whole world like that vision. If you like to put it so, the essence of the doctrine is that what we have around us is the mere method and preparation for something that we have to create. This is not a world, but rather the material for a world. God has given us not so much the colours of a picture as the colours of a palette. But he has also given us a subject, a model, a fixed vision. We must be clear about what we want to paint. This adds a further principle to our previous list of principles. We have said we must be fond of this world, even in order to change it. We now add that we must be fond of another world (real or imaginary) in order to have something to change it to.

We need not debate about the mere words evolution or progress: personally I prefer to call it reform. For reform implies form. It implies that we are trying to shape the world in a particular image; to make it something that we see already in our minds. Evolution is a metaphor from mere automatic unrolling. Progress is a metaphor from merely walking along a road—very likely the wrong road. But reform is a metaphor for reasonable and determined men: it means that we see a certain thing out of shape and we mean to put it into shape. And we know what shape.

Now here comes in the whole collapse and huge blunder of our age. We have mixed up two different things, two opposite things. Progress should mean that we are always changing the world to suit the vision. Progress does mean (just now) that we are always changing the vision. It should mean that we are slow but sure in bringing justice and mercy among men: it does mean that we are very swift in doubting the desirability of justice and mercy: a wild page from any Prussian sophist makes men doubt it. Progress should mean that we are always walking towards the New Jerusalem. It does mean that the New Jerusalem is always walking away from us. We are not altering the real to suit the ideal. We are altering the ideal: it is easier.

Silly examples are always simpler; let us suppose a man wanted a particular kind of world; say, a blue world. He would have no cause to complain of the slightness or swiftness of his task; he might toil for a long time at the transformation; he could work away (in every sense) until all was blue. He could have heroic adventures; the putting of the last touches to a blue tiger. He could have fairy dreams; the dawn of a blue moon. But if he worked hard, that high-minded reformer would certainly (from his own point of view) leave the world better and bluer than he found it. If he altered a blade of grass to his favourite colour every day, he would get on slowly. But if he altered his favourite colour every day, he would not get on at all. If, after reading a fresh philosopher, he started to paint everything red or yellow, his work would be thrown away: there would be nothing to show except a few blue tigers walking about, specimens of his early bad manner. This is exactly the position of the average modern thinker. It will be said that this is avowedly a preposterous example. But it is literally the fact of recent history. The great and grave changes in our political civilization all belonged to the early nineteenth century, not to the later. They belonged to the black and white epoch when men believed fixedly in Toryism, in Protestantism, in Calvinism, in Reform, and not unfrequently in Revolution. And whatever each man believed in he hammered at steadily, without scepticism: and there was a time when the Established Church might have fallen, and the House of Lords nearly fell. It was because Radicals were wise enough to be constant and consistent; it was because Radicals were wise enough to be Conservative. But in the existing atmosphere there is not enough time and tradition in Radicalism to pull anything down. There is a great deal of truth in Lord Hugh Cecil's suggestion (made in a fine speech) that the era of change is over, and that ours is an era of conservation and repose. But probably it would pain Lord Hugh Cecil if he realized (what is certainly the case) that ours is only an age of conservation because it is an age of complete unbelief. Let beliefs fade fast and frequently, if you wish institutions to remain the same. The more the life of the mind is unhinged, the more the machinery of matter will be left to itself. The net result of all our political suggestions, Collectivism, Tolstoyanism, Neo-Feudalism, Communism, Anarchy, Scientific Bureaucracy—the plain fruit of all of them is that the Monarchy and the House of Lords will remain. The net result of all the new religions will be that the Church of England will not (for heaven knows how long) be disestablished. It was Karl Marx, Nietzsche, Tolstoy, Cunninghame Grahame, Bernard Shaw and Auberon Herbert, who between them, with bowed gigantic backs, bore up the throne of the Archbishop of Canterbury.

We may say broadly that free thought is the best of all the safeguards against freedom. Managed in a modern style the emancipation of the slave's mind is the best way of preventing the emancipation of the slave. Teach him to worry about whether he wants to be free, and he will not free himself. Again, it may be said that this instance is remote or extreme. But, again, it is exactly true of the men in the streets around us. It is true that the negro slave, being a debased barbarian, will probably have either a human affection of loyalty, or a human affection for liberty. But the man we see every day—the worker in Mr. Gradgrind's factory, the little clerk in Mr. Gradgrind's office—he is too mentally worried to believe in freedom. He is kept quiet with revolutionary literature. He is calmed and kept in his place by a constant succession of wild philosophies. He is a Marxian one day, a Nietzscheite the next day, a Superman (probably) the next day; and a slave every day. The only thing that remains after all the philosophies is the factory. The only man who gains by all the philosophies is Gradgrind. It would be worth his while to keep his commercial helotry supplied with sceptical literature. And now I come to think of it, of course, Gradgrind is famous for giving libraries. He shows his sense. All modern books are on his side. As long as the vision of heaven is always changing, the vision of earth will be exactly the same. No ideal will remain long enough to be realized, or even partly realized. The modern young man will never change his environment; for he will always change his mind.

This, therefore, is our first requirement about the ideal towards which progress is directed; it must be fixed. Whistler used to make many rapid studies of a sitter; it did not matter if he tore up twenty portraits. But it would matter if he looked up twenty times, and each time saw a new person sitting placidly for his portrait. So it does not matter (comparatively speaking) how often humanity fails to imitate its ideal; for then all its old failures are fruitful. But it does frightfully matter how often humanity changes its ideal; for then all its old failures are fruitless. The question therefore becomes this: How can we keep the artist discontented with his pictures while preventing him from being vitally discontented with his art? How can we make a man always dissatisfied with his work, yet always satisfied with working? How can we make sure that the portrait painter will throw the portrait out of window instead of taking the natural and more human course of throwing the sitter out of window?

A strict rule is not only necessary for ruling; it is also necessary for rebelling. This fixed and familiar ideal is necessary to any sort of revolution. Man will sometimes act slowly upon new ideas; but he will only act swiftly upon old ideas. If I am merely to float or fade or evolve, it may be towards something anarchic; but if I am to riot, it must be for something respectable. This is the whole weakness of certain schools of progress and moral evolution. They suggest that there has been a slow movement towards morality, with an imperceptible ethical change in every year or at every instant. There is only one great disadvantage in this theory. It talks of a slow movement towards justice; but it does not permit a swift movement. A man is not allowed to leap up and declare a certain state of things to be intrinsically intolerable. To make the matter clear, it is better to take a specific example. Certain of the idealistic vegetarians, such as Mr. Salt, say that the time has now come for eating no meat; by implication they assume that at one time it was right to eat meat, and they suggest (in words that could be quoted) that some day it may be wrong to eat milk and eggs. I do not discuss here the question of what is justice to animals. I only say that whatever is justice ought, under given conditions, to be prompt justice. If an animal is wronged, we ought to be able to rush to his rescue. But how can we rush if we are, perhaps, in advance of our time? How can we rush to catch a train which may not arrive for a few centuries? How can I denounce a man for skinning cats, if he is only now what I may possibly become in drinking a glass of milk? A splendid and insane Russian sect ran about taking all the cattle out of all the carts. How can I pluck up courage to take the horse out of my hansom-cab, when I do not know whether my evolutionary watch is only a little fast or the cabman's a little slow? Suppose I say to a sweater, "Slavery suited one stage of evolution." And suppose he answers, "And sweating suits this stage of evolution." How can I answer if there is no eternal test? If sweaters can be behind the current morality, why should not philanthropists be in front of it? What on earth is the current morality, except in its literal sense—the morality that is always running away?

Thus we may say that a permanent ideal is as necessary to the innovator as to the conservative; it is necessary whether we wish the king's orders to be promptly executed or whether we only wish the king to be promptly executed. The guillotine has many sins, but to do it justice there is nothing evolutionary about it. The favourite evolutionary argument finds its best answer in the axe. The Evolutionist says, "Where do you draw the line?" the Revolutionist answers, "I draw it *here:* exactly between your head and body." There must at any given moment be an abstract right and wrong if any blow is to be struck; there must be something eternal if there is to be anything sudden. Therefore for all intelligible human purposes, for altering things or for keeping things as they are, for founding a system for ever, as in China, or for altering it every month as in the early French Revolution, it is equally necessary that the vision should be a fixed vision. This is our first requirement.

When I had written this down, I felt once again the presence of something else in the discussion: as a man hears a church bell above the sound of the street. Something seemed to be saying, "My ideal at least is fixed; for it was fixed before the foundations of the world. My vision of perfection assuredly cannot be altered; for it is called Eden. You may alter the place to which you are going; but you cannot alter the place from which you have come. To the orthodox there must always be a case for revolution; for in the hearts of men God has been put under the feet of Satan. In the upper world hell once rebelled against heaven. But in this world heaven is rebelling against hell. For the orthodox there can always be a revolution; for a revolution is a restoration. At any instant you may strike a blow for the perfection which no man has seen since Adam. No unchanging custom, no changing evolution can make the original good any thing but good. Man may have had concubines as long as cows have had horns: still they are not a part of him if they are sinful. Men may have been under oppression ever since fish were under water; still they ought not to be, if oppression is sinful. The chain may seem as natural to the slave, or the paint to the harlot, as does the plume to the bird or the burrow to the fox; still they are not, if they are sinful. I lift my prehistoric legend to defy all your history. Your vision is not merely a fixture: it is a fact." I paused to note the new coincidence of Christianity: but I passed on.

I passed on to the next necessity of any ideal of progress. Some people (as we have said) seem to believe in an automatic and impersonal progress in the nature of things. But it is clear that no political activity can be encouraged by saying that progress is natural and inevitable; that is not a reason for being active, but rather a reason for being lazy. If we are bound to improve, we need not trouble to improve. The pure doctrine of progress is the best of all reasons for not being a progressive. But it is to none of these obvious comments that I wish primarily to call attention.

The only arresting point is this: that if we suppose improvement to be natural, it must be fairly simple. The world might conceivably be working towards one consummation, but hardly towards any particular arrangement of many qualities. To take our original simile: Nature by herself may be growing more blue; that is, a process so simple that it might be impersonal. But Nature cannot be making a careful picture made of many picked colours, unless

Nature is personal. If the end of the world were mere darkness or mere light it might come as slowly and inevitably as dusk or dawn. But if the end of the world is to be a piece of elaborate and artistic chiaroscuro, then there must be design in it, either human or divine. The world, through mere time, might grow black like an old picture, or white like an old coat; but if it is turned into a particular piece of black and white art—then there is an artist.

If the distinction be not evident, I give an ordinary instance. We constantly hear a particularly cosmic creed from the modern humanitarians; I use the word humanitarian in the ordinary sense, as meaning one who upholds the claims of all creatures against those of humanity. They suggest that through the ages we have been growing more and more humane, that is to say, that one after another, groups or sections of beings, slaves, children, women, cows, or what not, have been gradually admitted to mercy or to justice. They say that we once thought it right to eat men (we didn't); but I am not here concerned with their history, which is highly unhistorical. As a fact, anthropophagy is certainly a decadent thing, not a primitive one. It is much more likely that modern men will eat human flesh out of affectation than that primitive man ever ate it out of ignorance. I am here only following the outlines of their argument, which consists in maintaining that man has been progressively more lenient, first to citizens, then to slaves, then to animals, and then (presumably) to plants. I think it wrong to sit on a man. Soon, I shall think it wrong to sit on a horse. Eventually (I suppose) I shall think it wrong to sit on a chair. That is the drive of the argument. And for this argument it can be said that it is possible to talk of it in terms of evolution or inevitable progress. A perpetual tendency to touch fewer and fewer things might—one feels, be a mere brute unconscious tendency, like that of a species to produce fewer and fewer children. This drift may be really evolutionary, because it is stupid.

Darwinism can be used to back up two mad moralities, but it cannot be used to back up a single sane one. The kinship and competition of all living creatures can be used as a reason for being insanely cruel or insanely sentimental; but not for a healthy love of animals. On the evolutionary basis you may be inhumane, or you may be absurdly humane; but you cannot be human. That you and a tiger are one may be a reason for being tender to a tiger. Or it may be a reason for being as cruel as the tiger. It is one way to train the tiger to imitate you, it is a shorter way to imitate the tiger. But in neither case does evolution tell you how to treat a tiger reasonably, that is, to admire his stripes while avoiding his claws.

If you want to treat a tiger reasonably, you must go back to the garden of Eden. For the obstinate reminder continued to recur: only the supernatural has taken a sane view of Nature. The essence of all pantheism, evolutionism, and modern cosmic religion is really in this proposition: that Nature is our mother. Unfortunately, if you regard Nature as a mother, you discover that she is a step-mother. The main point of Christianity was this: that Nature is not our mother: Nature is our sister. We can be proud of her beauty, since we have the same father; but she has no authority over us; we have to admire, but not to imitate. This gives to the typically Christian pleasure in this earth a strange touch of lightness that is almost frivolity. Nature was a solemn mother to the worshippers of Isis and Cybele. Nature was a solemn mother to Wordsworth or to Emerson. But Nature is not solemn to Francis of Assisi or to George Herbert. To St. Francis, Nature is a sister, and even a younger sister: a little, dancing sister, to be laughed at as well as loved.

This, however, is hardly our main point at present; I have admitted it only in order to show how constantly, and as it were accidentally, the key would fit the smallest doors. Our main point is here, that if there be a mere trend of impersonal improvement in Nature, it must presumably be a simple trend towards some simple triumph. One can imagine that some automatic tendency in biology might work for giving us longer and longer noses. But the question is, do we want to have longer and longer noses? I fancy not; I believe that we most of us want to say to our noses, "thus far, and no farther; and here shall thy proud point be stayed": we require a nose of such length as may ensure an interesting face. But we cannot imagine a mere biological trend towards producing interesting faces; because an interesting face is one particular arrangement of eyes, nose, and mouth, in a most complex relation to each other. Proportion cannot be a drift: it is either an accident or a design. So with the ideal of human morality and its relation to the humanitarians and the anti-humanitarians. It is conceivable that we are going more and more to keep our hands off things: not to drive horses; not to pick flowers. We may eventually be bound not to disturb a man's mind even by argument; not to disturb the sleep of birds even by coughing. The ultimate apotheosis would appear to be that of a man sitting quite still, nor daring to stir for fear of disturbing a fly, nor to eat for fear of incommoding a microbe. To so crude a consummation as that we might perhaps unconsciously drift. But do we want so crude a consummation? Similarly, we might unconsciously evolve along the opposite or Nietzschean line of development—superman crushing superman in one tower of tyrants until the universe is smashed up for fun. But do we want the universe smashed up for fun? Is it not quite clear that what we really hope for is one particular management and proposition of these two things; a certain amount of restraint and respect, a certain amount of energy and mastery? If our life is ever really as beautiful as a fairy-tale, we shall have to remember that all the beauty of a fairy-tale lies in this: that the prince has a wonder which just stops short of being fear. If he is afraid of the giant, there is an end of him; but also if he is not astonished at the giant, there is an end of the fairy-tale. The whole point depends upon his being at once humble enough to wonder, and haughty enough to defy. So our attitude to the giant of the world must not merely be increasing delicacy or increasing contempt: it must be one particular proportion of the two—which is exactly right. We must have in us enough reverence for all things outside us to make us tread fearfully on the grass. We must also have enough disdain for all things outside us, to make us, on due occasion, spit at the stars. Yet these two things (if we are to be good or happy) must be combined, not in any combination, but in one particular combination. The perfect happiness of men on the earth (if it ever comes) will not be a flat and solid thing, like the satisfaction of animals. It will be an exact and perilous balance; like that of a desperate romance. Man must have just enough faith in himself to have adventures, and just enough doubt of himself to enjoy them.

This, then, is our second requirement for the ideal of progress. First, it must be fixed; second, it must be composite. It must not (if it is to satisfy our souls) be the mere victory of some one thing swallowing up everything else, love or pride or peace or adventure; it must be a definite picture composed of these elements in their best proportion and relation. I am not concerned at this moment to deny that some such good culmination may be, by the constitution of things, reserved for the human race. I only point out that if this composite happiness is fixed for us it must be fixed by some mind; for only a mind can place the exact proportions of a composite happiness. If the beatification of the world is a mere work of nature, then it must be as simple as the freezing of the world, or the burning up of the world. But if the beatification of the world is not a work of nature but a work of art, then it involves an artist. And here again my contemplation was cloven by the ancient voice which said, "I could have told you all this a long time ago. If there is any certain progress it can only be my kind of progress, the progress towards a complete city of virtues and dominations where righteousness and peace contrive to kiss each other. An impersonal force might be leading you to a wilderness of perfect flatness or a peak of perfect height. But only a personal God can possibly be leading you (if, indeed, you are being led) to a city with just streets and architectural proportions, a city in which each of you can contribute exactly the right amount of your own colour to the many coloured coat of Joseph."

Twice again, therefore, Christianity had come in with the exact answer that I required. I had said, "The ideal must be fixed," and the Church had answered, "Mine is literally fixed, for it existed before anything else." I said secondly, "It must be artistically combined, like a picture"; and the Church answered, "Mine is quite literally a picture, for I know who painted it." Then I went on to the third thing, which, as it seemed to me, was needed for a Utopia or goal of progress. And of all the three it is infinitely the hardest to express. Perhaps it might be put thus: that we need watchfulness even in Utopia, lest we fall from Utopia as we fell from Eden.

We have remarked that one reason offered for being a progressive is that things naturally tend to grow better. But the only real reason for being a progressive is that things naturally tend to grow worse. The corruption in things is not only the best argument for being progressive; it is also the only argument against being conservative. The conservative theory would really be quite sweeping and unanswerable if it were not for this one fact. But all conservatism is based upon the idea that if you leave things alone you leave them as they are. But you do not. If you leave a thing alone you leave it to a torrent of change. If you leave a white post alone it will soon be a black post. If you particularly want it to be white you must be always painting it again; that is, you must be always having a revolution. Briefly, if you want the old white post you must have a new white post. But this which is true even of inanimate things is in a quite special and terrible sense true of all human things. An almost unnatural vigilance is really required of the citizen because of the horrible rapidity with which human institutions grow old. It is the custom in passing romance and journalism to talk of men suffering under old tyrannies. But, as a fact, men have almost always suffered under new tyrannies; under tyrannies that had been public liberties hardly twenty years before. Thus England went mad with joy over the patriotic monarchy of Elizabeth; and then (almost immediately afterwards) went mad with rage in the trap of the tyranny of Charles the First. So, again, in France the monarchy became intolerable, not just after it had been tolerated, but just after it had been adored. The son of Louis the well-beloved was Louis the guillotined. So in the same way in England in the nineteenth century the Radical manufacturer was entirely trusted as a mere tribune of the people, until suddenly we heard the cry of the Socialist that he was a tyrant eating the people like bread. So again, we have almost up to the last instant trusted the newspapers as organs of public opinion. Just recently some of us have seen (not slowly, but with a start) that they are obviously nothing of the kind. They are, by the nature of the case, the hobbies of a few rich men. We have not any need to rebel against antiquity; we have to rebel against novelty. It is the new rulers, the capitalist or the editor, who really hold up the modern world. There is no fear that a modern king will attempt to override the constitution; it is more likely that he will ignore the constitution and work behind its back; he will take no advantage of his kingly power; it is more likely that he will take advantage of his kingly powerlessness, of the fact that he is free from criticism and publicity. For the king is the most private person of our time. It will not be necessary for any one to fight again against the proposal of a censorship of the press. We do not need a censorship of the press. We have a censorship by the press.

This startling swiftness with which popular systems turn oppressive is the third fact for which we shall ask our perfect theory of progress to allow. It must always be on the look out for every privilege being abused, for every working right becoming a wrong. In this matter I am entirely on the side of the revolutionists. They are really right to be always suspecting human institutions; they are right not to put their trust in princes nor in any child of man. The chieftain chosen to be the friend of the people becomes the enemy of the people; the newspaper started to tell the truth now exists to prevent the truth being told. Here, I say, I felt that I was really at last on the side of the revolutionary. And then I caught my breath again: for I remembered that I was once again on the side of the orthodox.

Christianity spoke again and said: "I have always maintained that men were naturally backsliders; that human virtue tended of its own nature to rust or to rot; I have always said that human beings as such go wrong, especially happy human beings, especially proud and prosperous human beings. This eternal revolution, this suspicion sustained through centuries, you (being a vague modern) call the doctrine of progress. If you were a philosopher you would call it, as I do, the doctrine of original sin. You may call it the cosmic advance as much as you like; I call it what it is—the Fall."

I have spoken of orthodoxy coming in like a sword; here I confess it came in like a battle-axe. For really (when I came to think of it) Christianity is the only thing left that has any real right to question the power of the well-nurtured or the well-bred. I have listened often enough to Socialists, or even to democrats, saying that the physical conditions of the poor must of necessity make them mentally and morally degraded. I have listened to scientific men (and there are still scientific men not opposed to democracy) saying that if we give the poor healthier conditions vice and wrong will disappear. I have listened to them with a horrible attention, with a hideous fascination. For it was like watching a man energetically sawing from the tree the branch he is sitting on. If these happy democrats could prove their case, they would strike democracy dead. If the poor are thus utterly demoralized, it may or may not be practical to raise them. But it is certainly quite practical to disfranchise them. If the man with a bad bedroom cannot give a good vote, then the first and swiftest deduction is that he shall give no vote. The governing class may not unreasonably say: "It may take us some time to reform his bedroom. But if he is the brute you say, it will take him very little time to ruin our country. Therefore we will take your hint and not give him the chance." It fills me with horrible amusement to observe the way in which the earnest Socialist industriously lays the foundation of all aristocracy, expatiating blandly upon the evident unfitness of the poor to rule. It is like listening to somebody at an evening party apologising for entering without evening dress, and explaining that he had recently been intoxicated, had a personal habit of taking off his clothes in the street, and had, moreover, only just changed from prison uniform. At any moment, one feels, the host might say that really, if it was as bad as that, he need not come in at all. So it is when the ordinary Socialist, with a beaming face, proves that the poor, after their smashing experiences, cannot be really trustworthy. At any moment the rich may say, "Very well, then, we won't trust them," and bang the door in his face. On the basis of Mr. Blatchford's view of heredity and environment, the case for the aristocracy is quite overwhelming. If clean homes and clean air make clean souls, why not give the power (for the present at any rate) to those who undoubtedly have the clean air? If better conditions will make the poor more fit to govern themselves, why should not better conditions already make the rich more fit to govern them? On the ordinary environment argument the matter is fairly manifest. The comfortable class must be merely our vanguard in Utopia.

Is there any answer to the proposition that those who have had the best opportunities will probably be our best guides? Is there any answer to the argument that those who have breathed clean air had better decide for those who have breathed foul? As far as I know, there is only one answer, and that answer is Christianity. Only the Christian Church can offer any rational objection to a complete confidence in the rich. For she has maintained from the beginning that the danger was not in man's environment, but in man. Further, she has maintained that if we come to talk of a dangerous environment, the most dangerous environment of all is the commodious environment. I know that the most modern manufacture has been really occupied in trying to produce an abnormally large needle. I know that the most recent biologists have been chiefly anxious to discover a very small camel. But if we diminish the camel to his smallest, or open the eye of the needle to its largest—if, in short, we assume the words of Christ to have meant the very least that they could mean, His words must at the very least mean this—that rich men are not very likely to be morally trustworthy. Christianity even when watered down is hot enough to boil all modern society to rags. The mere minimum of the Church would be a deadly ultimatum to the world. For the whole modern world is absolutely based on the assumption, not that the rich are necessary (which is tenable), but that the rich are trustworthy, which (for a Christian) is not tenable. You will hear everlastingly, in all discussions about newspapers, companies, aristocracies, or party politics, this argument that the rich man cannot be bribed. The fact is, of course, that the rich man is bribed; he has been bribed already. That is why he is a rich man. The whole case for Christianity is that a man who is dependent upon the luxuries of this life is a corrupt man, spiritually corrupt, politically corrupt, financially corrupt. There is one thing that Christ and all the Christian saints have said with a sort of savage monotony. They have said simply that to be rich is to be in peculiar danger of moral wreck. It is not demonstrably un-Christian to kill the rich as violators of definable justice. It is not demonstrably un-Christian to crown the rich as convenient rulers of society. It is not certainly un-Christian to rebel against the rich or to submit to the rich. But it is quite certainly un-Christian to trust the rich, to regard the rich as more morally safe than the poor. A Christian may consistently say, "I respect that man's rank, although he takes bribes." But a Christian cannot say, as all modern men are saying at lunch and breakfast, "a man of that rank would not take bribes." For it is a part of Christian dogma that any man in any rank may take bribes. It is a part of Christian dogma; it also happens by a curious coincidence that it is a part of obvious human history. When people say that a man "in that position" would be incorruptible, there is no need to bring Christianity into the discussion. Was Lord Bacon a bootblack? Was the Duke of Marlborough a crossing sweeper? In the best Utopia, I must be prepared for the moral fall of any man in any position at any moment; especially for my fall from my position at this moment.

Much vague and sentimental journalism has been poured out to the effect that Christianity is akin to democracy, and most of it is scarcely strong or clear enough to refute the fact that the two things have often quarrelled. The real ground upon which Christianity and democracy are one is very much deeper. The one specially and peculiarly un-Christian idea is the idea of Carlyle—the idea that the man should rule who feels that he can rule. Whatever else is Christian, this is heathen. If our faith comments on government at all, its comment must be this—that the man should rule who does *not* think that he can rule. Carlyle's hero may say, "I will be king"; but the Christian saint must say "Nolo episcopari." If the great paradox of Christianity means anything, it means this—that we must take the crown in our hands, and go hunting in dry places and dark corners of the earth until we find the one man who feels himself unfit to wear it. Carlyle was quite wrong; we have not got to crown the exceptional man who knows he can rule. Rather we must crown the much more exceptional man who knows he can't.

Now, this is one of the two or three vital defences of working democracy. The mere machinery of voting is not democracy, though at present it is not easy to effect any simpler democratic method. But even the machinery of voting is profoundly Christian in this practical sense—that it is an attempt to get at the opinion of those who would be too modest to offer it. It is a mystical adventure; it is specially trusting those who do not trust themselves. That enigma is strictly peculiar to Christendom. There is nothing really humble about the abnegation of the Buddhist; the mild Hindoo is mild, but he is not meek. But there is something psychologically Christian about the idea of seeking for the opinion of the obscure rather than taking the obvious course of accepting the opinion of the prominent. To say that voting is particularly Christian may seem somewhat curious. To say that canvassing is Christian may seem quite crazy. But canvassing is very Christian in its primary idea. It is encouraging the humble; it is saying to the modest man, "Friend, go up higher." Or if there is some slight defect in canvassing, that is in its perfect and rounded piety, it is only because it may possibly neglect to encourage the modesty of the canvasser.

Aristocracy is not an institution: aristocracy is a sin; generally a very venial one. It is merely the drift or slide of men into a sort of natural pomposity and praise of the powerful, which is the most easy and obvious affair in the world.

It is one of the hundred answers to the fugitive perversion of modern "force" that the promptest and boldest agencies are also the most fragile or full of sensibility. The swiftest things are the softest things. A bird is active, because a bird is soft. A stone is helpless, because a stone is hard. The stone must by its own nature go downwards, because hardness is weakness. The bird can of its nature go upwards, because fragility is force. In perfect force there is a kind of frivolity, an airiness that can maintain itself in the air. Modern investigators of miraculous history have solemnly admitted that a characteristic of the great saints is their power of "levitation." They might go further; a characteristic of the great saints is their power of levity. Angels can fly because they can take themselves lightly. This has been always the instinct of Christendom, and especially the instinct of Christian art. Remember how Fra Angelico represented all his angels, not only as birds, but almost as butterflies. Remember how the most earnest mediaeval art was full of light and fluttering draperies, of quick and capering feet. It was the one thing that the modern Pre-raphaelites could not imitate in the real Pre-raphaelites. Burne-Jones could never recover the deep levity of the Middle Ages. In the old Christian pictures the sky over every figure is like a blue or gold parachute. Every figure seems ready to fly up and float about in the heavens. The tattered cloak of the beggar will bear him up like the rayed plumes of the angels. But the kings in their heavy gold and the proud in their robes of purple will all of their nature sink downwards, for pride cannot rise to levity or levitation. Pride is the downward drag of all things into an easy solemnity.

One "settles down" into a sort of selfish seriousness; but one has to rise to a gay self-forgetfulness. A man "falls" into a brown study; he reaches up at a blue sky. Seriousness is not a virtue. It would be a heresy, but a much more sensible heresy, to say that seriousness is a vice. It is really a natural trend or lapse into taking one's self gravely, because it is the easiest thing to do. It is much easier to write a good *Times* leading article than a good joke in *Punch*. For solemnity flows out of men naturally; but laughter is a leap. It is easy to be heavy: hard to be light. Satan fell by the force of gravity.

Now, it is the peculiar honour of Europe since it has been Christian that while it has had aristocracy it has always at the back of its heart treated aristocracy as a weakness—generally as a weakness that must be allowed for. If any one wishes to appreciate this point, let him go outside Christianity into some other philosophical atmosphere. Let him, for instance, compare the classes of Europe with the castes of India. There aristocracy is far more awful, because it is far more intellectual. It is seriously felt that the scale of classes is a scale of spiritual values; that the baker is better than the butcher in an invisible and sacred sense. But no Christianity, not even the most ignorant or perverse, ever suggested that a baronet was better than a butcher in that sacred sense. No Christianity, however ignorant or extravagant, ever suggested that a duke would not be damned. In pagan society there may have been (I do not know) some such serious division between the free man and the slave. But in Christian society we have always thought the gentleman a sort of joke, though I admit that in some great crusades and councils he earned the right to be called a practical joke. But we in Europe never really and at the root of our souls took aristocracy seriously. It is only an occasional non-European alien (such as Dr. Oscar Levy, the only intelligent Nietzscheite) who can even manage for a moment to take aristocracy seriously. It may be a mere patriotic bias, though I do not think so, but it seems to me that the English aristocracy is not only the type, but is the crown and flower of all actual aristocracies; it has all the oligarchical virtues as well as all the defects. It is casual, it is kind, it is courageous in obvious matters; but it has one great merit that overlaps even these. The great and very obvious merit of the English aristocracy is that nobody could possibly take it seriously.

In short, I had spelled out slowly, as usual, the need for an equal law in Utopia; and, as usual, I found that Christianity had been there before me. The whole history of my Utopia has the same amusing sadness. I was always rushing out of my architectural study with plans for a new turret only to find it sitting up there in the sunlight, shining, and a thousand years old. For me, in the ancient and partly in the modern sense, God answered the prayer, "Prevent us, O Lord, in all our doings." Without vanity, I really think there was a moment when I could have invented the marriage vow (as an institution) out of my own head; but I discovered, with a sigh, that it had been invented already. But, since it would be too long a business to show how, fact by fact and inch by inch, my own conception of Utopia was only answered in the New Jerusalem, I will take this one case of the matter of marriage as indicating the converging drift, I may say the converging crash of all the rest.

When the ordinary opponents of Socialism talk about impossibilities and alterations in human nature they always miss an important distinction. In modern ideal conceptions of society there are some desires that are possibly not attainable: but there are some desires that are not desirable. That all men should live in equally beautiful houses is a dream that may or may not be attained. But that all men should live in the same beautiful house is not a dream at all; it is a nightmare. That a man should love all old women is an ideal that may not be attainable. But that a man should regard all old women exactly as he regards his mother is not only an unattainable ideal, but an ideal which ought not to be attained. I do not know if the reader agrees with me in these examples; but I will add the example which has always affected me most. I could never conceive or tolerate any Utopia which did not leave to me the liberty for which I chiefly care, the liberty to bind myself. Complete anarchy would not merely make it impossible to have any discipline or fidelity; it would also make it impossible to have any fun. To take an obvious instance, it would not be worth while to bet if a bet were not binding. The dissolution of all contracts would not only ruin morality but spoil sport. Now betting and such sports are only the stunted and twisted shapes of the original instinct of man for adventure and romance, of which much has been said in these pages. And the perils, rewards, punishments, and fulfilments of an adventure must be real, or the adventure is only a shifting and heartless nightmare. If I bet I must be made to pay, or there is no poetry in betting. If I challenge I must be made to fight, or there is no poetry in challenging. If I vow to be faithful I must be cursed when I am unfaithful, or there is no fun in vowing. You could not even make a fairy tale from the experiences of a man who, when he was swallowed by a whale, might find himself at the top of the Eiffel Tower, or when he was turned into a frog might begin to behave like a flamingo. For the purpose even of the wildest romance results must be real; results must be irrevocable. Christian marriage is the great example of a real and irrevocable result; and that is why it is the chief subject and centre of all our romantic writing. And this is my last instance of the things that I should ask, and ask imperatively, of any social paradise; I should ask to be kept to my bargain, to have my oaths and engagements taken seriously; I should ask Utopia to avenge my honour on myself.

All my modern Utopian friends look at each other rather doubtfully, for their ultimate hope is the dissolution of all special ties. But again I seem to hear, like a kind of echo, an answer from beyond the world. "You will have real obligations, and therefore real adventures when you get to my Utopia. But the hardest obligation and the steepest adventure is to get there."

VIII. THE ROMANCE OF ORTHODOXY

It is customary to complain of the bustle and strenuousness of our epoch. But in truth the chief mark of our epoch is a profound laziness and fatigue; and the fact is that the real laziness is the cause of the apparent bustle. Take one quite external case; the streets are noisy with taxicabs and motorcars; but this is not due to human activity but to human repose. There would be less bustle if there were more activity, if people were simply walking about. Our world would be more silent if it were more strenuous. And this which is true of the apparent physical bustle is true also of the apparent bustle of the intellect. Most of the machinery of modern language is labour-saving machinery; and it saves mental labour very much more than it ought. Scientific phrases are used like scientific wheels and piston-rods to make swifter and smoother yet the path of the comfortable. Long words go rattling by us like long railway trains. We know they are carrying thousands who are too tired or too indolent to walk and think for themselves. It is a good exercise to try for once in a way to express any opinion one holds in words of one syllable. If you say "The social utility of the indeterminate sentence is recognized by all criminologists as a part of our sociological evolution towards a more humane and scientific view of punishment," you can go on talking like that for hours with hardly a movement of the gray matter inside your skull. But if you begin "I wish Jones to go to gaol and Brown to say when Jones shall come out," you will discover, with a thrill of horror, that you are obliged to think. The long words are not the hard words, it is the short words that are hard. There is much more metaphysical subtlety in the word "damn" than in the word "degeneration."

But these long comfortable words that save modern people the toil of reasoning have one particular aspect in which they are especially ruinous and confusing. This difficulty occurs when the same long word is used in different connections to mean quite different things. Thus, to take a well-known instance, the word "idealist" has one meaning as a piece of philosophy and quite another as a piece of moral rhetoric. In the same way the scientific materialists have had just reason to complain of people mixing up "materialist" as a term of cosmology with "materialist" as a moral taunt. So, to take a cheaper instance, the man who hates "progressives" in London always calls himself a "progressive" in South Africa.

A confusion quite as unmeaning as this has arisen in connection with the word "liberal" as applied to religion and as applied to politics and society. It is often suggested that all Liberals ought to be freethinkers, because they ought to love everything that is free. You might just as well say that all idealists ought to be High Churchmen, because they ought to love everything that is high. You might as well say that Low Churchmen ought to like Low Mass, or that Broad Churchmen ought to like broad jokes. The thing is a mere accident of words. In actual modern Europe a freethinker does not mean a man who thinks for himself. It means a man who, having thought for himself, has come to one particular class of conclusions, the material origin of phenomena, the impossibility of miracles, the improbability of personal immortality and so on. And none of these ideas are particularly liberal. Nay, indeed almost all these ideas are definitely illiberal, as it is the purpose of this chapter to show.

In the few following pages I propose to point out as rapidly as possible that on every single one of the matters most strongly insisted on by liberalisers of theology their effect upon social practice would be definitely illiberal. Almost every contemporary proposal to bring freedom into the church is simply a proposal to bring tyranny into the world. For freeing the church now does not even mean freeing it in all directions. It means freeing that peculiar set of dogmas loosely called scientific, dogmas of monism, of pantheism, or of Arianism, or of necessity. And every one of these (and we will take them one by one) can be shown to be the natural ally of oppression. In fact, it is a remarkable circumstance (indeed not so very remarkable when one comes to think of it) that most things are the allies of oppression. There is only one thing that can never go past a certain point in its alliance with oppression—and that is orthodoxy. I may, it is true, twist orthodoxy so as partly to justify a tyrant. But I can easily make up a German philosophy to justify him entirely.

Now let us take in order the innovations that are the notes of the new theology or the modernist church. We concluded the last chapter with the discovery of one of them. The very doctrine which is called the most old-fashioned was found to be the only safeguard of the new democracies of the earth. The doctrine seemingly most unpopular was found to be the only strength of the people. In short, we found that the only logical negation of oligarchy was in the affirmation of original sin. So it is, I maintain, in all the other cases.

I take the most obvious instance first, the case of miracles. For some extraordinary reason, there is a fixed notion that it is more liberal to disbelieve in miracles than to believe in them. Why, I cannot imagine, nor can anybody tell me. For some inconceivable cause a "broad" or "liberal" clergyman always means a man who wishes at least to diminish the number of miracles; it never means a man who wishes to increase that number. It always means a man who is free to disbelieve that Christ came out of His grave; it never means a man who is free to believe that his own aunt came out of her grave. It is common to find trouble in a parish because the parish priest cannot admit that St. Peter walked on water; yet how rarely do we find trouble in a parish because the clergyman says that his father walked on the Serpentine? And this is not because (as the swift secularist debater would immediately retort) miracles cannot be believed in our experience. It is not because "miracles do not happen," as in the dogma which Matthew Arnold recited with simple faith. More supernatural things are *alleged* to have happened in our time than would have been possible eighty years ago. Men of science believe in such marvels much more than they did: the most perplexing, and even horrible, prodigies of mind and spirit are always being unveiled in modern psychology. Things that the old science at least would frankly have rejected as miracles are hourly being asserted by the new science. The only thing which is still old-fashioned enough to reject miracles is the New Theology. But in truth this notion that it is "free" to deny miracles has nothing to do with the evidence for or against them. It is a lifeless verbal prejudice of which the original life and beginning was not in the freedom of thought, but simply in the dogma of materialism. The man of the nineteenth century did not disbelieve in the Resurrection because his liberal Christianity allowed him to doubt it. He disbelieved in it because his very strict materialism did not allow him to believe it. Tennyson, a very typical nineteenth-century man, uttered one of the instinctive truisms of his contemporaries when he said that there was faith in their honest doubt. There was indeed. Those words have a profound and even a horrible truth. In their doubt of miracles there was a faith in a fixed and godless fate; a deep and sincere faith in the incurable routine of the cosmos. The doubts of the agnostic were only the dogmas of the monist.

Of the fact and evidence of the supernatural I will speak afterwards. Here we are only concerned with this clear point; that in so far as the liberal idea of freedom can be said to be on either side in the discussion about miracles, it is obviously on the side of miracles. Reform or (in the only tolerable sense) progress means simply the gradual control of matter by mind. A miracle simply means the swift control of matter by mind. If you wish to feed the people, you may think that feeding them miraculously in the wilderness is impossible—but you cannot think it illiberal. If you really want poor children to go to the seaside, you cannot think it illiberal that they should go there on flying dragons; you can only think it unlikely. A holiday, like Liberalism, only means the liberty of man. A miracle only means the liberty of God. You may conscientiously deny either of them, but you cannot call your denial a triumph of the liberal idea. The Catholic Church believed that man and God both had a sort of spiritual freedom. Calvinism took away the freedom from man, but left it to God. Scientific materialism binds the Creator Himself; it chains up God as the Apocalypse chained the devil. It leaves nothing free in the universe. And those who assist this process are called the "liberal theologians."

This, as I say, is the lightest and most evident case. The assumption that there is something in the doubt of miracles akin to liberality or reform is literally the opposite of the truth. If a man cannot believe in miracles there is an end of the matter; he is not particularly liberal, but he is perfectly honourable and logical, which are much better things. But if he can believe in miracles, he is certainly the more liberal for doing so; because they mean first, the freedom of the soul, and secondly, its control over the tyranny of circumstance. Sometimes this truth is ignored in a singularly naïve way, even by the ablest men. For instance, Mr. Bernard Shaw speaks with hearty old-fashioned contempt for the idea of miracles, as if they were a sort of breach of faith on the part of nature: he seems strangely unconscious that miracles are only the final flowers of his own favourite tree, the doctrine of the omnipotence of will. Just in the same way he calls the desire for immortality a paltry selfishness, forgetting that he has just called the desire for life a healthy and heroic selfishness. How can it be noble to wish to make one's life infinite and yet mean to wish to make it immortal? No, if it is desirable that man should triumph over the cruelty of nature or custom, then miracles are certainly desirable; we will discuss afterwards whether they are possible.

But I must pass on to the larger cases of this curious error; the notion that the "liberalising" of religion in some way helps the liberation of the world. The second example of it can be found in the question of pantheism—or rather of a certain modern attitude which is often called immanentism, and which often is Buddhism. But this is so much more difficult a matter that I must approach it with rather more preparation.

The things said most confidently by advanced persons to crowded audiences are generally those quite opposite to the fact; it is actually our truisms that are untrue. Here is a case. There is a phrase of facile liberality uttered again and again at ethical societies and parliaments of religion: "the religions of the earth differ in rites and forms, but they are the same in what they teach." It is false; it is the opposite of the fact. The religions of the earth do *not* greatly differ in rites and forms; they do greatly differ in what they teach. It is as if a man were to say, "Do not be misled by the fact that the *Church Times* and the *Freethinker* look utterly different, that one is painted on vellum and the other carved on marble, that one is triangular and the other hectagonal; read them and you will see that they say the same thing." The truth is, of course, that they are alike in everything except in the fact that they don't say the same thing. An atheist stockbroker in Surbiton looks exactly like a Swedenborgian stockbroker in Wimbledon. You may walk round and round them and subject them to the most personal and offensive study without seeing anything Swedenborgian in the hat or anything particularly godless in the umbrella. It is exactly in their souls that they are divided. So the truth is that the difficulty of all the creeds of the earth is not as alleged in this cheap maxim: that they agree in meaning, but differ in machinery. It is exactly the opposite. They agree in machinery; almost every great religion on earth works with the same external methods, with priests, scriptures, altars, sworn brotherhoods, special feasts. They agree in the mode of teaching; what they differ about is the thing to be taught. Pagan optimists and Eastern pessimists would both have temples, just as Liberals and Tories would both have newspapers. Creeds that exist to destroy each other both have scriptures, just as armies that exist to destroy each other both have guns.

The great example of this alleged identity of all human religions is the alleged spiritual identity of Buddhism and Christianity. Those who adopt this theory generally avoid the ethics of most other creeds, except, indeed, Confucianism, which they like because it is not a creed. But they are cautious in their praises of Mahometanism, generally confining themselves to imposing its morality only upon the refreshment of the lower classes. They seldom suggest the Mahometan view of marriage (for which there is a great deal to be said), and towards Thugs and fetish worshippers their attitude may even be called cold. But in the case of the great religion of Gautama they feel sincerely a similarity.

Students of popular science, like Mr. Blatchford, are always insisting that Christianity and Buddhism are very much alike, especially Buddhism. This is generally believed, and I believed it myself until I read a book giving the reasons for it. The reasons were of two kinds: resemblances that meant nothing because they were common to all humanity, and resemblances which were not resemblances at all. The author solemnly explained that the two creeds were alike in things in which all creeds are alike, or else he described them as alike in some point in which they are quite obviously different. Thus, as a case of the first class, he said that both Christ and Buddha were called by the divine voice coming out of the sky, as if you would expect the divine voice to come out of the coal-cellar. Or, again, it was gravely urged that these two Eastern teachers, by a singular coincidence, both had to do with the washing of feet. You might as well say that it was a remarkable coincidence that they both had feet to wash. And the other class of similarities were those which simply were not similar. Thus this reconciler of the two religions draws earnest attention to the fact that at certain religious feasts the robe of the Lama is rent in pieces out of respect, and the remnants highly valued. But this is the reverse of a resemblance, for the garments of Christ were not rent in pieces out of respect, but out of derision; and the remnants were not highly valued except for what they would fetch in the rag shops. It is rather like alluding to the obvious connection between the two ceremonies of the sword: when it taps a man's shoulder, and when it cuts off his head. It is not at all similar for the man. These scraps of puerile pedantry would indeed matter little if it were not also true that the alleged philosophical resemblances are also of these two kinds, either proving too much or not proving anything. That Buddhism approves of mercy or of self-restraint is not to say that it is specially like Christianity; it is only to say that it is not utterly unlike all human existence. Buddhists disapprove in theory of cruelty or excess because all sane human beings disapprove in theory of cruelty or excess. But to say that Buddhism and Christianity give the same philosophy of these things is simply false. All humanity does agree that we are in a net of sin. Most of humanity agrees that there is some way out. But as to what is the way out, I do not think that there are two institutions in the universe which contradict each other so flatly as Buddhism and Christianity.

Even when I thought, with most other well-informed, though unscholarly, people, that Buddhism and Christianity were alike, there was one thing about them that always perplexed me; I mean the startling difference in their type of religious art. I do not mean in its technical style of representation, but in the things that it was manifestly meant to represent. No two ideals could be more opposite than a Christian saint in a Gothic cathedral and a Buddhist saint in a Chinese temple. The opposition exists at every point; but perhaps the shortest statement of it is that the Buddhist saint always has his eyes shut, while the Christian saint always has them very wide open. The Buddhist saint has a sleek and harmonious body, but his eyes are heavy and sealed with sleep. The mediaeval saint's body is wasted to its crazy bones, but his eyes are frightfully alive. There cannot be any real community of spirit between forces that produced symbols so different as that. Granted that both images are extravagances, are perversions of the pure creed, it must be a real divergence which could produce such opposite extravagances. The Buddhist is looking with a peculiar intentness inwards. The Christian is staring with a frantic intentness outwards. If we follow that clue steadily we shall find some interesting things.

A short time ago Mrs. Besant, in an interesting essay, announced that there was only one religion in the world, that all faiths were only versions or perversions of it, and that she was quite prepared to say what it was. According to Mrs. Besant this universal Church is simply the universal self. It is the doctrine that we are really all one person; that there are no real walls of individuality between man and man. If I may put it so, she does not tell us to love our neighbours; she tells us to be our neighbours. That is Mrs. Besant's thoughtful and suggestive description of the religion in which all men must find themselves in agreement. And I never heard of any suggestion in my life with which I more violently disagree. I want to love my neighbour not because he is I, but precisely because he is not I. I want to adore the world, not as one likes a looking-glass, because it is one's self, but as one loves a woman, because she is entirely different. If souls are separate love is possible. If souls are united love is obviously impossible. A man may be said loosely to love himself, but he can hardly fall in love with himself, or, if he does, it must be a monotonous courtship. If the world is full of real selves, they can be really unselfish selves. But upon Mrs. Besant's principle the whole cosmos is only one enormously selfish person.

It is just here that Buddhism is on the side of modern pantheism and immanence. And it is just here that Christianity is on the side of humanity and liberty and love. Love desires personality; therefore love desires division. It is the instinct of Christianity to be glad that God has broken the universe into little pieces, because they are living pieces. It is her instinct to say "little children love one another" rather than to tell one large person to love himself. This is the intellectual abyss between Buddhism and Christianity; that for the Buddhist or Theosophist personality is the fall of man, for the Christian it is the purpose of God, the whole point of his cosmic idea. The world-soul of the Theosophists asks man to love it only in order that man may throw himself into it. But the divine centre of Christianity actually threw man out of it in order that he might love it. The oriental deity is like a giant who should have lost his leg or hand and be always seeking to find it; but the Christian power is like some giant who in a strange generosity should cut off his right hand, so that it might of its own accord shake hands with him. We come back to the same tireless note touching the nature of Christianity; all modern philosophies are chains which connect and fetter; Christianity is a sword which separates and sets free. No other philosophy makes God actually rejoice in the separation of the universe into living souls. But according to orthodox Christianity this separation between God and man is sacred, because this is eternal. That a man may love God it is necessary that there should be not only a God to be loved, but a man to love him. All those vague theosophical minds for whom the universe is an immense melting-pot are exactly the minds which shrink instinctively from that earthquake saying of our Gospels, which declare that the Son of God came not with peace but with a sundering sword. The saying rings entirely true even considered as what it obviously is; the statement that any man who preaches real love is bound to beget hate. It is as true of democratic fraternity as a divine love; sham love ends in compromise and common philosophy; but real love has always ended in bloodshed. Yet there is another and yet more awful truth behind the obvious meaning of this utterance of our Lord. According to Himself the Son was a sword separating brother and brother that they should for an aeon hate each other. But the Father also was a sword, which in the black beginning separated brother and brother, so that they should love each other at last.

This is the meaning of that almost insane happiness in the eyes of the mediaeval saint in the picture. This is the meaning of the sealed eyes of the superb Buddhist image. The Christian saint is happy because he has verily been cut off from the world; he is separate from things and is staring at them in astonishment. But why should the Buddhist saint be astonished at things?—since there is really only one thing, and that being impersonal can hardly be astonished at itself. There have been many pantheist poems suggesting wonder, but no really successful ones. The pantheist cannot wonder, for he cannot praise God or praise anything as really distinct from himself. Our immediate business here, however, is with the effect of this Christian admiration (which strikes outwards, towards a deity distinct from the worshipper) upon the general need for ethical activity and social reform. And surely its effect is sufficiently obvious. There is no real possibility of getting out of pantheism any special impulse to moral action. For pantheism implies in its nature that one thing is as good as another; whereas action implies in its nature that one thing is greatly preferable to another. Swinburne, in the high summer of his scepticism, tried in vain to wrestle with this difficulty. In "Songs before Sunrise," written under the inspiration of Garibaldi and the revolt of Italy he proclaimed the newer religion and the purer God which should wither up all the priests of the world:

What doest thou now
Looking Godward to cry
I am I, thou art thou,
I am low, thou art high,
I am thou that thou seekest to find him, find
thou but thyself, thou art I.

Of which the immediate and evident deduction is that tyrants are as much the sons of God as Garibaldis; and that King Bomba of Naples having, with the utmost success, "found himself" is identical with the ultimate good in all things. The truth is that the western energy that dethrones tyrants has been directly due to the western theology that says "I am I, thou art thou." The same spiritual separation which looked up and saw a good king in the universe looked up and saw a bad king in Naples. The worshippers of Bomba's god dethroned Bomba. The worshippers of Swinburne's god have covered Asia for centuries and have never dethroned a tyrant. The Indian saint may reasonably shut his eyes because he is looking at that which is I and Thou and We and They and It. It is a rational occupation: but it is not true in theory and not true in fact that it helps the Indian to keep an eye on Lord Curzon. That external vigilance which has always been the mark of Christianity (the command that we should *watch* and pray) has expressed itself both in typical western orthodoxy and in typical western politics: but both depend on the idea of a divinity transcendent, different from ourselves, a deity that disappears. Certainly the most sagacious creeds may suggest that we should pursue God into deeper and deeper rings of the labyrinth of our own ego. But only we of Christendom have said that we should hunt God like an eagle upon the mountains: and we have killed all monsters in the chase.

Here again, therefore, we find that in so far as we value democracy and the self-renewing energies of the west, we are much more likely to find them in the old theology than the new. If we want reform, we must adhere to orthodoxy: especially in this matter (so much disputed in the counsels of Mr. R.J. Campbell), the matter of insisting on the immanent or the transcendent deity. By insisting specially on the immanence of God we get introspection, self-isolation, quietism, social indifference—Tibet. By insisting specially on the transcendence of God we get wonder, curiosity, moral and political adventure, righteous indignation—Christendom. Insisting that God is inside man, man is always inside himself. By insisting that God transcends man, man has transcended himself.

If we take any other doctrine that has been called old-fashioned we shall find the case the same. It is the same, for instance, in the deep matter of the Trinity. Unitarians (a sect never to be mentioned without a special respect for their distinguished intellectual dignity and high intellectual honour) are often reformers by the accident that throws so many small sects into such an attitude. But there is nothing in the least liberal or akin to reform in the substitution of pure monotheism for the Trinity. The complex God of the Athanasian Creed may be an enigma for the intellect; but He is far less likely to gather the mystery and cruelty of a Sultan than the lonely god of Omar or Mahomet. The god who is a mere awful unity is not only a king but an Eastern king. The *heart* of humanity, especially of European humanity, is certainly much more satisfied by the strange hints and symbols that gather round the Trinitarian idea, the image of a council at which mercy pleads as well as justice, the conception of a sort of liberty and variety existing even in the inmost chamber of the world. For Western religion has always felt keenly the idea "it is not well for man to be alone." The social instinct asserted itself everywhere as when the Eastern idea of hermits was practically expelled by the Western idea of monks. So even asceticism became brotherly; and the Trappists were sociable even when they were silent. If this love of a living complexity be our test, it is certainly healthier to have the Trinitarian religion than the Unitarian. For to us Trinitarians (if I may say it with reverence)—to us God Himself is a society. It is indeed a fathomless mystery of theology, and even if I were theologian enough to deal with it directly, it would not be relevant to do so here. Suffice it to say here that this triple enigma is as comforting as wine and open as an English fireside; that this thing that bewilders the intellect utterly quiets the heart: but out of the desert, from the dry places and the dreadful suns, come the cruel children of the lonely God; the real Unitarians who with scimitar in hand have laid waste the world. For it is not well for God to be alone.

Again, the same is true of that difficult matter of the danger of the soul, which has unsettled so many just minds. To hope for all souls is imperative; and it is quite tenable that their salvation is inevitable. It is tenable, but it is not specially favourable to activity or progress. Our fighting and creative society ought rather to insist on the danger of everybody, on the fact that every man is hanging by a thread or clinging to a precipice. To say that all will be well anyhow is a comprehensible remark: but it cannot be called the blast of a trumpet. Europe ought rather to emphasize possible perdition; and Europe always has emphasized it. Here its highest religion is at one with all its cheapest romances. To the Buddhist or the eastern fatalist existence is a science or a plan, which must end up in a certain way. But to a Christian existence is a *story*, which may end up in any way. In a thrilling novel (that purely Christian product) the hero is not eaten by cannibals; but it is essential to the existence of the thrill that he *might* be eaten by cannibals. The hero must (so to speak) be an eatable hero. So Christian morals have always said to the man, not that he would lose his soul, but that he must take care that he didn't. In Christian morals, in short, it is wicked to call a man "damned": but it is strictly religious and philosophic to call him damnable.

All Christianity concentrates on the man at the cross-roads. The vast and shallow philosophies, the huge syntheses of humbug, all talk about ages and evolution and ultimate developments. The true philosophy is concerned with the instant. Will a man take this road or that?—that is the only thing to think about, if you enjoy thinking. The aeons are easy enough to think about, any one can think about them. The instant is really awful: and it is because our religion has intensely felt the instant, that it has in literature dealt much with battle and in theology dealt much with hell. It is full of *danger,* like a boy's book: it is at an immortal crisis. There is a great deal of real similarity between popular fiction and the religion of the western people. If you say that popular fiction is vulgar and tawdry, you only say what the dreary and well-informed say also about the images in the Catholic churches. Life (according to the faith) is very like a serial story in a magazine: life ends with the promise (or menace) "to be continued in our next." Also, with a noble vulgarity, life imitates the serial and leaves off at the exciting moment. For death is distinctly an exciting moment.

But the point is that a story is exciting because it has in it so strong an element of will, of what theology calls free will. You cannot finish a sum how you like. But you can finish a story how you like. When somebody discovered the Differential Calculus there was only one Differential Calculus he could discover. But when Shakespeare killed Romeo he might have married him to Juliet's old nurse if he had felt inclined. And Christendom has excelled in the narrative romance exactly because it has insisted on the theological free will. It is a large matter and too much to one side of the road to be discussed adequately here; but this is the real objection to that torrent of modern talk about treating crime as disease, about making a prison merely a hygienic environment like a hospital, of healing sin by slow scientific methods. The fallacy of the whole thing is that evil is a matter of active choice whereas disease is not. If you say that you are going to cure a profligate as you cure an asthmatic, my cheap and obvious answer is, "Produce the people who want to be asthmatics as many people want to be profligates." A man may lie still and be cured of a malady. But he must not lie still if he wants to be cured of a sin; on the contrary, he must get up and jump about violently. The whole point indeed is perfectly expressed in the very word which we use for a man in hospital; "patient" is in the passive mood; "sinner" is in the active. If a man is to be saved from influenza, he may be a patient. But if he is to be saved from forging, he must be not a patient but an *impatient*. He must be personally impatient with forgery. All moral reform must start in the active not the passive will.

Here again we reach the same substantial conclusion. In so far as we desire the definite reconstructions and the dangerous revolutions which have distinguished European civilization, we shall not discourage the thought of possible ruin; we shall rather encourage it. If we want, like the Eastern saints, merely to contemplate how right things are, of course we shall only say that they must go right. But if we particularly want to *make* them go right, we must insist that they may go wrong.

Lastly, this truth is yet again true in the case of the common modern attempts to diminish or to explain away the divinity of Christ. The thing may be true or not; that I shall deal with before I end. But if the divinity is true it is certainly terribly revolutionary. That a good man may have his back to the wall is no more than we knew already; but that God could have his back to the wall is a boast for all insurgents for ever. Christianity is the only religion on earth that has felt that omnipotence made God incomplete. Christianity alone has felt that God, to be wholly God, must have been a rebel as well as a king. Alone of all creeds, Christianity has added courage to the virtues of the Creator. For the only courage worth calling courage must necessarily mean that the soul passes a breaking point—and does not break. In this indeed I approach a matter more dark and awful than it is easy to discuss; and I apologise in advance if any of my phrases fall wrong or seem irreverent touching a matter which the greatest saints and thinkers have justly feared to approach. But in that terrific tale of the Passion there is a distinct emotional suggestion that the author of all things (in some unthinkable way) went not only through agony, but through doubt. It is written, "Thou shalt not tempt the Lord thy God." No; but the Lord thy God may tempt Himself; and it seems as if this was what happened in Gethsemane. In a garden Satan tempted man: and in a garden God tempted God. He passed in some superhuman manner through our human horror of pessimism. When the world shook and the sun was wiped out of heaven, it was not at the crucifixion, but at the cry from the cross: the cry which confessed that God was forsaken of God. And now let the revolutionists choose a creed from all the creeds and a god from all the gods of the world, carefully weighing all the gods of inevitable recurrence and of unalterable power. They will not find another god who has himself been in revolt. Nay (the matter grows too difficult for human speech), but let the atheists themselves choose a god. They will find only one divinity who ever uttered their isolation; only one religion in which God seemed for an instant to be an atheist.

These can be called the essentials of the old orthodoxy, of which the chief merit is that it is the natural fountain of revolution and reform; and of which the chief defect is that it is obviously only an abstract assertion. Its main advantage is that it is the most adventurous and manly of all theologies. Its chief disadvantage is simply that it is a theology. It can always be urged against it that it is in its nature arbitrary and in the air. But it is not so high in the air but that great archers spend their whole lives in shooting arrows at it—yes, and their last arrows; there are men who will ruin themselves and ruin their civilization if they may ruin also this old fantastic tale. This is the last and most astounding fact about this faith; that its enemies will use any weapon against it, the swords that cut their own fingers, and the firebrands that burn their own homes. Men who begin to fight the Church for the sake of freedom and humanity end by flinging away freedom and humanity if only they may fight the Church. This is no exaggeration; I could fill a book with the instances of it. Mr. Blatchford set out, as an ordinary Bible-smasher, to prove that Adam was guiltless of sin against God; in manoeuvring so as to maintain this he admitted, as a mere side issue, that all the tyrants, from Nero to King Leopold, were guiltless of any sin against humanity. I know a man who has such a passion for proving that he will have no personal existence after death that he falls back on the position that he has no personal existence now. He invokes Buddhism and says that all souls fade into each other; in order to prove that he cannot go to heaven he proves that he cannot go to Hartlepool. I have known people who protested against religious education with arguments against any education, saying that the child's mind must grow freely or that the old must not teach the young. I have known people who showed that there could be no divine judgment by showing that there can be no human judgment, even for practical purposes. They burned their own corn to set fire to the church; they smashed their own tools to smash it; any stick was good enough to beat it with, though it were the last stick of their own dismembered furniture. We do not admire, we hardly excuse, the fanatic who wrecks this world for love of the other. But what are we to say of the fanatic who wrecks this world out of hatred of the other? He sacrifices the very existence of humanity to the non-existence of God. He offers his victims not to the altar, but merely to assert the idleness of the altar and the emptiness of the throne. He is ready to ruin even that primary ethic by which all things live, for his strange and eternal vengeance upon some one who never lived at all.

And yet the thing hangs in the heavens unhurt. Its opponents only succeed in destroying all that they themselves justly hold dear. They do not destroy orthodoxy; they only destroy political and common courage sense. They do not prove that Adam was not responsible to God; how could they prove it? They only prove (from their premises) that the Czar is not responsible to Russia. They do not prove that Adam should not have been punished by God; they only prove that the nearest sweater should not be punished by men. With their oriental doubts about personality they do not make certain that we shall have no personal life hereafter; they only make certain that we shall not have a very jolly or complete one here. With their paralysing hints of all conclusions coming out wrong they do not tear the book of the Recording Angel; they only make it a little harder to keep the books of Marshall & Snelgrove. Not only is the faith the mother of all worldly energies, but its foes are the fathers of all worldly confusion. The secularists have not wrecked divine things; but the secularists have wrecked secular things, if that is any comfort to them. The Titans did not scale heaven; but they laid waste the world.

IX. AUTHORITY AND THE ADVENTURER

THE LAST chapter has been concerned with the contention that orthodoxy is not only (as is often urged) the only safe guardian of morality or order, but is also the only logical guardian of liberty, innovation and advance. If we wish to pull down the prosperous oppressor we cannot do it with the new doctrine of human perfectibility; we can do it with the old doctrine of Original Sin. If we want to uproot inherent cruelties or lift up lost populations we cannot do it with the scientific theory that matter precedes mind; we can do it with the supernatural theory that mind precedes matter. If we wish specially to awaken people to social vigilance and tireless pursuit of practise, we cannot help it much by insisting on the Immanent God and the Inner Light: for these are at best reasons for contentment; we can help it much by insisting on the transcendent God and the flying and escaping gleam; for that means divine discontent. If we wish particularly to assert the idea of a generous balance against that of a dreadful autocracy we shall instinctively be Trinitarian rather than Unitarian. If we desire European civilization to be a raid and a rescue, we shall insist rather that souls are in real peril than that their peril is ultimately unreal. And if we wish to exalt the outcast and the crucified, we shall rather wish to think that a veritable God was crucified, rather than a mere sage or hero. Above all, if we wish to protect the poor we shall be in favour of fixed rules and clear dogmas. The *rules* of a club are occasionally in favour of the poor member. The drift of a club is always in favour of the rich one.

And now we come to the crucial question which truly concludes the whole matter. A reasonable agnostic, if he has happened to agree with me so far, may justly turn round and say, "You have found a practical philosophy in the doctrine of the Fall; very well. You have found a side of democracy now dangerously neglected wisely asserted in Original Sin; all right. You have found a truth in the doctrine of hell; I congratulate you. You are convinced that worshippers of a personal God look outwards and are progressive; I congratulate them. But even supposing that those doctrines do include those truths, why cannot you take the truths and leave the doctrines? Granted that all modern society is trusting the rich too much because it does not allow for human weakness; granted that orthodox ages have had a great advantage because (believing in the Fall) they did allow for human weakness, why cannot you simply allow for human weakness without believing in the Fall? If you have discovered that the idea of damnation represents a healthy idea of danger, why can you not simply take the idea of danger and leave the idea of damnation? If you see clearly the kernel of common sense in the nut of Christian orthodoxy, why cannot you simply take the kernel and leave the nut? Why cannot you (to use that cant phrase of the newspapers which I, as a highly scholarly agnostic, am a little ashamed of using) why cannot you simply take what is good in Christianity, what you can define as valuable, what you can comprehend, and leave all the rest, all the absolute dogmas that are in their nature incomprehensible?" This is the real question; this is the last question; and it is a pleasure to try to answer it.

The first answer is simply to say that I am a rationalist. I like to have some intellectual justification for my intuitions. If I am treating man as a fallen being it is an intellectual convenience to me to believe that he fell; and I find, for some odd psychological reason, that I can deal better with a man's exercise of free will if I believe that he has got it. But I am in this matter yet more definitely a rationalist. I do not propose to turn this book into one of ordinary Christian apologetics; I should be glad to meet at any other time the enemies of Christianity in that more obvious arena. Here I am only giving an account of my own growth in spiritual certainty. But I may pause to remark that the more I saw of the merely abstract arguments against the Christian cosmology the less I thought of them. I mean that having found the moral atmosphere of the Incarnation to be common sense, I then looked at the established intellectual arguments against the Incarnation and found them to be common nonsense. In case the argument should be thought to suffer from the absence of the ordinary apologetic I will here very briefly summarise my own arguments and conclusions on the purely objective or scientific truth of the matter.

If I am asked, as a purely intellectual question, why I believe in Christianity, I can only answer, "For the same reason that an intelligent agnostic disbelieves in Christianity." I believe in it quite rationally upon the evidence. But the evidence in my case, as in that of the intelligent agnostic, is not really in this or that alleged demonstration; it is in an enormous accumulation of small but unanimous facts. The secularist is not to be blamed because his objections to Christianity are miscellaneous and even scrappy; it is precisely such scrappy evidence that does convince the mind. I mean that a man may well be less convinced of a philosophy from four books, than from one book, one battle, one landscape, and one old friend. The very fact that the things are of different kinds increases the importance of the fact that they all point to one conclusion. Now, the non-Christianity of the average educated man to-day is almost always, to do him justice, made up of these loose but living experiences. I can only say that my evidences for Christianity are of the same vivid but varied kind as his evidences against it. For when I look at these various anti-Christian truths, I simply discover that none of them are true. I discover that the true tide and force of all the facts flows the other way. Let us take cases. Many a sensible modern man must have abandoned Christianity under the pressure of three such converging convictions as these: first, that men, with their shape, structure, and sexuality, are, after all, very much like beasts, a mere variety of the animal kingdom; second, that primeval religion arose in ignorance and fear; third, that priests have blighted societies with bitterness and gloom. Those three anti-Christian arguments are very different; but they are all quite logical and legitimate; and they all converge. The only objection to them (I discover) is that they are all untrue. If you leave off looking at books about beasts and men, if you begin to look at beasts and men then (if you have any humour or imagination, any sense of the frantic or the farcical) you will observe that the startling thing is not how like man is to the brutes, but how unlike he is. It is the monstrous scale of his divergence that requires an explanation. That man and brute are like is, in a sense, a truism; but that being so like they should then be so insanely unlike, that is the shock and the enigma. That an ape has hands is far less interesting to the philosopher than the fact that having hands he does next to nothing with them; does not play knuckle-bones or the violin; does not carve marble or carve mutton. People talk of barbaric architecture and debased art. But elephants do not build colossal temples of ivory even in a rococo style; camels do not paint even bad pictures, though equipped with the material of many camel's-hair brushes. Certain modern dreamers say that ants and bees have a society superior to ours. They have, indeed, a civilization; but that very truth only reminds us that it is an inferior civilization. Who ever found an ant-hill decorated with the statues of celebrated ants? Who has seen a bee-hive carved with the images of gorgeous queens of old? No; the chasm between man and other creatures may have a natural explanation, but it is a chasm. We talk of wild animals; but man is the only wild animal. It is man that has broken out. All other animals are tame animals; following the rugged respectability of the tribe or type. All other animals are domestic animals; man alone is ever undomestic, either as a profligate or a monk. So that this first superficial reason for materialism is, if anything, a reason for its opposite; it is exactly where biology leaves off that all religion begins.

It would be the same if I examined the second of the three chance rationalist arguments; the argument that all that we call divine began in some darkness and terror. When I did attempt to examine the foundations of this modern idea I simply found that there were none. Science knows nothing whatever about pre-historic man; for the excellent reason that he is pre-historic. A few professors choose to conjecture that such things as human sacrifice were once innocent and general and that they gradually dwindled; but there is no direct evidence of it, and the small amount of indirect evidence is very much the other way. In the earliest legends we have, such as the tales of Isaac and of Iphigenia, human sacrifice is not introduced as something old, but rather as something new; as a strange and frightful exception darkly demanded by the gods. History says nothing; and legends all say that the earth was kinder in its earliest time. There is no tradition of progress; but the whole human race has a tradition of the Fall. Amusingly enough, indeed, the very dissemination of this idea is used against its authenticity. Learned men literally say that this pre-historic calamity cannot be true because every race of mankind remembers it. I cannot keep pace with these paradoxes.

And if we took the third chance instance, it would be the same; the view that priests darken and embitter the world. I look at the world and simply discover that they don't. Those countries in

Europe which are still influenced by priests, are exactly the countries where there is still singing and dancing and coloured dresses and art in the open-air. Catholic doctrine and discipline may be walls; but they are the walls of a playground. Christianity is the only frame which has preserved the pleasure of Paganism. We might fancy some children playing on the flat grassy top of some tall island in the sea. So long as there was a wall round the cliff's edge they could fling themselves into every frantic game and make the place the noisiest of nurseries. But the walls were knocked down, leaving the naked peril of the precipice. They did not fall over; but when their friends returned to them they were all huddled in terror in the centre of the island; and their song had ceased.

Thus these three facts of experience, such facts as go to make an agnostic, are, in this view, turned totally round. I am left saying, "Give me an explanation, first, of the towering eccentricity of man among the brutes; second, of the vast human tradition of some ancient happiness; third, of the partial perpetuation of such pagan joy in the countries of the Catholic Church." One explanation, at any rate, covers all three: the theory that twice was the natural order interrupted by some explosion or revelation such as people now call "psychic." Once Heaven came upon the earth with a power or seal called the image of God, whereby man took command of Nature; and once again (when in empire after empire men had been found wanting) Heaven came to save mankind in the awful shape of a man. This would explain why the mass of men always look backwards; and why the only corner where they in any sense look forwards is the little continent where Christ has His Church. I know it will be said that Japan has become progressive. But how can this be an answer when even in saying "Japan has become progressive," we really only mean, "Japan has become European"? But I wish here not so much to insist on my own explanation as to insist on my original remark. I agree with the ordinary unbelieving man in the street in being guided by three or four odd facts all pointing to something; only when I came to look at the facts I always found they pointed to something else.

I have given an imaginary triad of such ordinary anti-Christian arguments; if that be too narrow a basis I will give on the spur of the moment another. These are the kind of thoughts which in combination create the impression that Christianity is something weak and diseased. First, for instance, that Jesus was a gentle creature, sheepish and unworldly, a mere ineffectual appeal to the world;

second, that Christianity arose and flourished in the dark ages of ignorance, and that to these the Church would drag us back; third, that the people still strongly religious or (if you will) superstitious—such people as the Irish—are weak, unpractical, and behind the times. I only mention these ideas to affirm the same thing: that when I looked into them independently I found, not that the conclusions were unphilosophical, but simply that the facts were not facts. Instead of looking at books and pictures about the New Testament I looked at the New Testament. There I found an account, not in the least of a person with his hair parted in the middle or his hands clasped in appeal, but of an extraordinary being with lips of thunder and acts of lurid decision, flinging down tables, casting out devils, passing with the wild secrecy of the wind from mountain isolation to a sort of dreadful demagogy; a being who often acted like an angry god—and always like a god. Christ had even a literary style of his own, not to be found, I think, elsewhere; it consists of an almost furious use of the *a fortiori*. His "how much more" is piled one upon another like castle upon castle in the clouds. The diction used *about* Christ has been, and perhaps wisely, sweet and submissive. But the diction used by Christ is quite curiously gigantesque; it is full of camels leaping through needles and mountains hurled into the sea. Morally it is equally terrific; he called himself a sword of slaughter, and told men to buy swords if they sold their coats for them. That he used other even wilder words on the side of non-resistance greatly increases the mystery; but it also, if anything, rather increases the violence. We cannot even explain it by calling such a being insane; for insanity is usually along one consistent channel. The maniac is generally a monomaniac. Here we must remember the difficult definition of Christianity already given; Christianity is a superhuman paradox whereby two opposite passions may blaze beside each other. The one explanation of the Gospel language that does explain it, is that it is the survey of one who from some supernatural height beholds some more startling synthesis.

I take in order the next instance offered: the idea that Christianity belongs to the Dark Ages. Here I did not satisfy myself with reading modern generalisations; I read a little history. And in history I found that Christianity, so far from belonging to the Dark Ages, was the one path across the Dark Ages that was not dark. It was a shining bridge connecting two shining civilizations. If any one says that the faith arose in ignorance and savagery the answer is simple: it didn't.

It arose in the Mediterranean civilization in the full summer of the Roman Empire. The world was swarming with sceptics, and pantheism was as plain as the sun, when Constantine nailed the cross to the mast. It is perfectly true that afterwards the ship sank; but it is far more extraordinary that the ship came up again: repainted and glittering, with the cross still at the top. This is the amazing thing the religion did: it turned a sunken ship into a submarine. The ark lived under the load of waters; after being buried under the débris of dynasties and clans, we arose and remembered Rome. If our faith had been a mere fad of the fading empire, fad would have followed fad in the twilight, and if the civilization ever re-emerged (and many such have never re-emerged) it would have been under some new barbaric flag. But the Christian Church was the last life of the old society and was also the first life of the new. She took the people who were forgetting how to make an arch and she taught them to invent the Gothic arch. In a word, the most absurd thing that could be said of the Church is the thing we have all heard said of it. How can we say that the Church wishes to bring us back into the Dark Ages? The Church was the only thing that ever brought us out of them.

I added in this second trinity of objections an idle instance taken from those who feel such people as the Irish to be weakened or made stagnant by superstition. I only added it because this is a peculiar case of a statement of fact that turns out to be a statement of falsehood. It is constantly said of the Irish that they are impractical. But if we refrain for a moment from looking at what is said about them and look at what is *done* about them, we shall see that the Irish are not only practical, but quite painfully successful. The poverty of their country, the minority of their members are simply the conditions under which they were asked to work; but no other group in the British Empire has done so much with such conditions. The Nationalists were the only minority that ever succeeded in twisting the whole British Parliament sharply out of its path. The Irish peasants are the only poor men in these islands who have forced their masters to disgorge. These people, whom we call priest-ridden, are the only Britons who will not be squire-ridden. And when I came to look at the actual Irish character, the case was the same. Irishmen are best at the specially *hard* professions—the trades of iron, the lawyer, and the soldier. In all these cases, therefore, I came back to the same conclusion: the sceptic was quite right to go by the facts, only he had not looked at the facts. The sceptic is too credulous; he believes in newspapers or even in encyclopaedias. Again the three questions left me with three very antagonistic questions. The average sceptic wanted to know how I explained the namby-pamby note in the Gospel, the connection of the creed with mediaeval darkness and the political impracticability of the Celtic Christians. But I wanted to ask, and to ask with an earnestness amounting to urgency, "What is this incomparable energy which appears first in one walking the earth like a living judgment and this energy which can die with a dying civilization and yet force it to a resurrection from the dead; this energy which last of all can inflame a bankrupt peasantry with so fixed a faith in justice that they get what they ask, while others go empty away; so that the most helpless island of the Empire can actually help itself?"

There is an answer: it is an answer to say that the energy is truly from outside the world; that it is psychic, or at least one of the results of a real psychical disturbance. The highest gratitude and respect are due to the great human civilizations such as the old Egyptian or the existing Chinese. Nevertheless it is no injustice for them to say that only modern Europe has exhibited incessantly a power of self-renewal recurring often at the shortest intervals and descending to the smallest facts of building or costume. All other societies die finally and with dignity. We die daily. We are always being born again with almost indecent obstetrics. It is hardly an exaggeration to say that there is in historic Christendom a sort of unnatural life: it could be explained as a supernatural life. It could be explained as an awful galvanic life working in what would have been a corpse. For our civilization *ought* to have died, by all parallels, by all sociological probability, in the Ragnorak of the end of Rome. That is the weird inspiration of our estate: you and I have no business to be here at all. We are all *revenants;* all living Christians are dead pagans walking about. Just as Europe was about to be gathered in silence to Assyria and Babylon, something entered into its body. And Europe has had a strange life—it is not too much to say that it has had the *jumps*—ever since.

I have dealt at length with such typical triads of doubt in order to convey the main contention—that my own case for Christianity is rational; but it is not simple. It is an accumulation of varied facts, like the attitude of the ordinary agnostic. But the ordinary agnostic has got his facts all wrong. He is a non-believer for a multitude of reasons; but they are untrue reasons. He doubts because the Middle Ages were barbaric, but they weren't; because Darwinism is demonstrated, but it isn't; because miracles do not happen, but they do; because monks were lazy, but they were very industrious; because nuns are unhappy, but they are particularly cheerful; because Christian art was sad and pale, but it was picked out in peculiarly bright colours and gay with gold; because modern science is moving away from the supernatural, but it isn't, it is moving towards the supernatural with the rapidity of a railway train.

But among these million facts all flowing one way there is, of course, one question sufficiently solid and separate to be treated briefly, but by itself; I mean the objective occurrence of the supernatural. In another chapter I have indicated the fallacy of the ordinary supposition that the world must be impersonal because it is orderly. A person is just as likely to desire an orderly thing as a disorderly thing. But my own positive conviction that personal creation is more conceivable than material fate, is, I admit, in a sense, undiscussable. I will not call it a faith or an intuition, for those words are mixed up with mere emotion, it is strictly an intellectual conviction; but it is a *primary* intellectual conviction like the certainty of self of the good of living. Any one who likes, therefore, may call my belief in God merely mystical; the phrase is not worth fighting about. But my belief that miracles have happened in human history is not a mystical belief at all; I believe in them upon human evidences as I do in the discovery of America. Upon this point there is a simple logical fact that only requires to be stated and cleared up. Somehow or other an extraordinary idea has arisen that the disbelievers in miracles consider them coldly and fairly, while believers in miracles accept them only in connection with some dogma. The fact is quite the other way. The believers in miracles accept them (rightly or wrongly) because they have evidence for them. The disbelievers in miracles deny them (rightly or wrongly) because they have a doctrine against them. The open, obvious, democratic thing is to believe an old apple-woman when she bears testimony to a miracle, just as you believe an old apple-woman when she bears testimony to a murder. The plain, popular course is to trust the peasant's word about the ghost exactly as far as you trust the peasant's word about the landlord. Being a peasant he will probably have a great deal of healthy agnosticism about both. Still you could fill the British Museum with evidence uttered by the peasant, and given in favour of the ghost. If it comes to human testimony there is a choking cataract of human testimony in favour of the supernatural. If you reject it, you can only mean one of two things.

You reject the peasant's story about the ghost either because the man is a peasant or because the story is a ghost story. That is, you either deny the main principle of democracy, or you affirm the main principle of materialism—the abstract impossibility of miracle. You have a perfect right to do so; but in that case you are the dogmatist. It is we Christians who accept all actual evidence—it is you rationalists who refuse actual evidence being constrained to do so by your creed. But I am not constrained by any creed in the matter, and looking impartially into certain miracles of mediaeval and modern times, I have come to the conclusion that they occurred. All argument against these plain facts is always argument in a circle. If I say, "Mediaeval documents attest certain miracles as much as they attest certain battles," they answer, "But mediaevals were superstitious"; if I want to know in what they were superstitious, the only ultimate answer is that they believed in the miracles. If I say "a peasant saw a ghost," I am told, "But peasants are so credulous." If I ask, "Why credulous?" the only answer is—that they see ghosts. Iceland is impossible because only stupid sailors have seen it; and the sailors are only stupid because they say they have seen Iceland. It is only fair to add that there is another argument that the unbeliever may rationally use against miracles, though he himself generally forgets to use it.

He may say that there has been in many miraculous stories a notion of spiritual preparation and acceptance: in short, that the miracle could only come to him who believed in it. It may be so, and if it is so how are we to test it? If we are inquiring whether certain results follow faith, it is useless to repeat wearily that (if they happen) they do follow faith. If faith is one of the conditions, those without faith have a most healthy right to laugh. But they have no right to judge. Being a believer may be, if you like, as bad as being drunk; still if we were extracting psychological facts from drunkards, it would be absurd to be always taunting them with having been drunk. Suppose we were investigating whether angry men really saw a red mist before their eyes. Suppose sixty excellent householders swore that when angry they had seen this crimson cloud: surely it would be absurd to answer "Oh, but you admit you were angry at the time." They might reasonably rejoin (in a stentorian chorus), "How the blazes could we discover, without being angry, whether angry people see red?" So the saints and ascetics might rationally reply, "Suppose that the question is whether believers can see visions—even then, if you are interested in visions it is no point to object to believers." You are still arguing in a circle—in that old mad circle with which this book began.

The question of whether miracles ever occur is a question of common sense and of ordinary historical imagination: not of any final physical experiment. One may here surely dismiss that quite brainless piece of pedantry which talks about the need for "scientific conditions" in connection with alleged spiritual phenomena. If we are asking whether a dead soul can communicate with a living it is ludicrous to insist that it shall be under conditions in which no two living souls in their senses would seriously communicate with each other. The fact that ghosts prefer darkness no more disproves the existence of ghosts than the fact that lovers prefer darkness disproves the existence of love. If you choose to say, "I will believe that Miss Brown called her *fiancé* a periwinkle or, any other endearing term, if she will repeat the word before seventeen psychologists," then I shall reply, "Very well, if those are your conditions, you will never get the truth, for she certainly will not say it." It is just as unscientific as it is unphilosophical to be surprised that in an unsympathetic atmosphere certain extraordinary sympathies do not arise. It is as if I said that I could not tell if there was a fog because the air was not clear enough; or as if I insisted on perfect sunlight in order to see a solar eclipse.

As a common-sense conclusion, such as those to which we come about sex or about midnight (well knowing that many details must in their own nature be concealed) I conclude that miracles do happen. I am forced to it by a conspiracy of facts: the fact that the men who encounter elves or angels are not the mystics and the morbid dreamers, but fishermen, farmers, and all men at once coarse and cautious; the fact that we all know men who testify to spiritualistic incidents but are not spiritualists, the fact that science itself admits such things more and more every day. Science will even admit the Ascension if you call it Levitation, and will very likely admit the Resurrection when it has thought of another word for it. I suggest the Regalvanisation. But the strongest of all is the dilemma above mentioned, that these supernatural things are never denied except on the basis either of anti-democracy or of materialist dogmatism—I may say materialist mysticism. The sceptic always takes one of the two positions; either an ordinary man need not be believed, or an extraordinary event must not be believed. For I hope we may dismiss the argument against wonders attempted in the mere recapitulation of frauds, of swindling mediums or trick miracles. That is not an argument at all, good or bad. A false ghost disproves the reality of ghosts exactly as much as a forged banknote disproves the existence of the Bank of England—if anything, it proves its existence.

Given this conviction that the spiritual phenomena do occur (my evidence for which is complex but rational), we then collide with one of the worst mental evils of the age. The greatest disaster of the nineteenth century was this: that men began to use the word "spiritual" as the same as the word "good." They thought that to grow in refinement and uncorporeality was to grow in virtue. When scientific evolution was announced, some feared that it would encourage mere animality. It did worse: it encouraged mere spirituality. It taught men to think that so long as they were passing from the ape they were going to the angel. But you can pass from the ape and go to the devil. A man of genius, very typical of that time of bewilderment, expressed it perfectly. Benjamin Disraeli was right when he said he was on the side of the angels. He was indeed; he was on the side of the fallen angels. He was not on the side of any mere appetite or animal brutality; but he was on the side of all the imperialism of the princes of the abyss; he was on the side of arrogance and mystery, and contempt of all obvious good. Between this sunken pride and the towering humilities of heaven there are, one must suppose, spirits of shapes and sizes. Man, in encountering them, must make much the same mistakes that he makes in encountering any other varied types in any other distant continent. It must be hard at first to know who is supreme and who is subordinate. If a shade arose from the under world, and stared at Piccadilly, that shade would not quite understand the idea of an ordinary closed carriage. He would suppose that the coachman on the box was a triumphant conqueror, dragging behind him a kicking and imprisoned captive. So, if we see spiritual facts for the first time, we may mistake who is uppermost. It is not enough to find the gods; they are obvious; we must find God, the real chief of the gods. We must have a long historic experience in supernatural phenomena—in order to discover which are really natural. In this light I find the history of Christianity, and even of its Hebrew origins, quite practical and clear. It does not trouble me to be told that the Hebrew god was one among many. I know he was, without any research to tell me so. Jehovah and Baal looked equally important, just as the sun and the moon looked the same size. It is only slowly that we learn that the sun is immeasurably our master, and the small moon only our satellite. Believing that there is a world of spirits, I shall walk in it as I do in the world of men, looking for the thing that I like and think good. Just as I should seek in a desert for clean water, or toil at the North Pole to make a comfortable fire, so I shall search the land of void and vision until I find something fresh like water, and comforting like fire; until I find some place in eternity, where I am literally at home. And there is only one such place to be found.

I have now said enough to show (to any one to whom such an explanation is essential) that I have in the ordinary arena of apologetics, a ground of belief. In pure records of experiment (if these be taken democratically without contempt or favour) there is evidence first, that miracles happen, and second that the nobler miracles belong to our tradition. But I will not pretend that this curt discussion is my real reason for accepting Christianity instead of taking the moral good of Christianity as I should take it out of Confucianism.

I have another far more solid and central ground for submitting to it as a faith, instead of merely picking up hints from it as a scheme. And that is this: that the Christian Church in its practical relation to my soul is a living teacher, not a dead one. It not only certainly taught me yesterday, but will almost certainly teach me to-morrow. Once I saw suddenly the meaning of the shape of the cross; some day I may see suddenly the meaning of the shape of the mitre. One fine morning I saw why windows were pointed; some fine morning I may see why priests were shaven. Plato has told you a truth; but Plato is dead. Shakespeare has startled you with an image; but Shakespeare will not startle you with any more. But imagine what it would be to live with such men still living, to know that Plato might break out with an original lecture to-morrow, or that at any moment Shakespeare might shatter everything with a single song. The man who lives in contact with what he believes to be a living Church is a man always expecting to meet Plato and Shakespeare to-morrow at breakfast. He is always expecting to see some truth that he has never seen before. There is one only other parallel to this position; and that is the parallel of the life in which we all began. When your father told you, walking about the garden, that bees stung or that roses smelt sweet, you did not talk of taking the best out of his philosophy. When the bees stung you, you did not call it an entertaining coincidence. When the rose smelt sweet you did not say "My father is a rude, barbaric symbol, enshrining (perhaps unconsciously) the deep delicate truths that flowers smell." No: you believed your father, because you had found him to be a living fountain of facts, a thing that really knew more than you; a thing that would tell you truth to-morrow, as well as to-day. And if this was true of your father, it was even truer of your mother; at least it was true of mine, to whom this book is dedicated. Now, when society is in a rather futile fuss about the subjection of women, will no one say how much every man owes to the tyranny and privilege of women, to the fact that they alone rule education until education becomes futile: for a boy is only sent to be taught at school when it is too late to teach him anything. The real thing has been done already, and thank God it is nearly always done by women. Every man is womanised, merely by being born. They talk of the masculine woman; but every man is a feminised man. And if ever men walk to Westminster to protest against this female privilege, I shall not join their procession.

For I remember with certainty this fixed psychological fact; that the very time when I was most under a woman's authority, I was most full of flame and adventure. Exactly because when my mother said that ants bit they did bite, and because snow did come in winter (as she said); therefore the whole world was to me a fairyland of wonderful fulfilments, and it was like living in some Hebraic age, when prophecy after prophecy came true. I went out as a child into the garden, and it was a terrible place to me, precisely because I had a clue to it: if I had held no clue it would not have been terrible, but tame. A mere unmeaning wilderness is not even impressive. But the garden of childhood was fascinating, exactly because everything had a fixed meaning which could be found out in its turn. Inch by inch I might discover what was the object of the ugly shape called a rake; or form some shadowy conjecture as to why my parents kept a cat.

So, since I have accepted Christendom as a mother and not merely as a chance example, I have found Europe and the world once more like the little garden where I stared at the symbolic shapes of cat and rake; I look at everything with the old elvish ignorance and expectancy. This or that rite or doctrine may look as ugly and extraordinary as a rake; but I have found by experience that such things end somehow in grass and flowers. A clergyman may be apparently as useless as a cat, but he is also as fascinating, for there must be some strange reason for his existence. I give one instance out of a hundred; I have not myself any instinctive kinship with that enthusiasm for physical virginity, which has certainly been a note of historic Christianity. But when I look not at myself but at the world, I perceive that this enthusiasm is not only a note of Christianity, but a note of Paganism, a note of high human nature in many spheres. The Greeks felt virginity when they carved Artemis, the Romans when they robed the vestals, the worst and wildest of the great Elizabethan playwrights clung to the literal purity of a woman as to the central pillar of the world. Above all, the modern world (even while mocking sexual innocence) has flung itself into a generous idolatry of sexual innocence—the great modern worship of children. For any man who loves children will agree that their peculiar beauty is hurt by a hint of physical sex. With all this human experience, allied with the Christian authority, I simply conclude that I am wrong, and the church right; or rather that I am defective, while the church is universal. It takes all sorts to make a church; she does not ask me to be celibate. But the fact that I have no appreciation of the celibates, I accept like the fact that I have no ear for music. The best human experience is against me, as it is on the subject of Bach. Celibacy is one flower in my father's garden, of which I have not been told the sweet or terrible name. But I may be told it any day.

This, therefore, is, in conclusion, my reason for accepting the religion and not merely the scattered and secular truths out of the religion. I do it because the thing has not merely told this truth or that truth, but has revealed itself as a truth-telling thing. All other philosophies say the things that plainly seem to be true; only this philosophy has again and again said the thing that does not seem to be true, but is true. Alone of all creeds it is convincing where it is not attractive; it turns out to be right, like my father in the garden. Theosophists for instance will preach an obviously attractive idea like re-incarnation; but if we wait for its logical results, they are spiritual superciliousness and the cruelty of caste. For if a man is a beggar by his own pre-natal sins, people will tend to despise the beggar. But Christianity preaches an obviously unattractive idea, such as original sin; but when we wait for its results, they are pathos and brotherhood, and a thunder of laughter and pity; for only with original sin we can at once pity the beggar and distrust the king. Men of science offer us health, an obvious benefit; it is only afterwards that we discover that by health, they mean bodily slavery and spiritual tedium. Orthodoxy makes us jump by the sudden brink of hell; it is only afterwards that we realise that jumping was an athletic exercise highly beneficial to our health. It is only afterwards that we realise that this danger is the root of all drama and romance. The strongest argument for the divine grace is simply its ungraciousness. The unpopular parts of Christianity turn out when examined to be the very props of the people. The outer ring of Christianity is a rigid guard of ethical abnegations and professional priests; but inside that inhuman guard you will find the old human life dancing like children, and drinking wine like men; for Christianity is the only frame for pagan freedom. But in the modern philosophy the case is opposite; it is its outer ring that is obviously artistic and emancipated; its despair is within.

And its despair is this, that it does not really believe that there is any meaning in the universe; therefore it cannot hope to find any romance; its romances will have no plots. A man cannot expect any adventures in the land of anarchy. But a man can expect any number of adventures if he goes travelling in the land of authority. One can find no meanings in a jungle of scepticism; but the man will find more and more meanings who walks through a forest of doctrine and design. Here everything has a story tied to its tail, like the tools or pictures in my father's house; for it is my father's house. I end where I began—at the right end. I have entered at last the gate of all good philosophy. I have come into my second childhood.

But this larger and more adventurous Christian universe has one final mark difficult to express; yet as a conclusion of the whole matter I will attempt to express it. All the real argument about religion turns on the question of whether a man who was born upside down can tell when he comes right way up. The primary paradox of Christianity is that the ordinary condition of man is not his sane or sensible condition; that the normal itself is an abnormality. That is the inmost philosophy of the Fall. In Sir Oliver Lodge's interesting new Catechism, the first two questions were: "What are you?" and "What, then, is the meaning of the Fall of Man?" I remember amusing myself by writing my own answers to the questions; but I soon found that they were very broken and agnostic answers. To the question, "What are you?" I could only answer, "God knows." And to the question, "What is meant by the Fall?" I could answer with complete sincerity, "That whatever I am, I am not myself." This is the prime paradox of our religion; something that we have never in any full sense known, is not only better than ourselves, but even more natural to us than ourselves. And there is really no test of this except the merely experimental one with which these pages began, the test of the padded cell and the open door. It is only since I have known orthodoxy that I have known mental emancipation. But, in conclusion, it has one special application to the ultimate idea of joy.

It is said that Paganism is a religion of joy and Christianity of sorrow; it would be just as easy to prove that Paganism is pure sorrow and Christianity pure joy. Such conflicts mean nothing and lead nowhere. Everything human must have in it both joy and sorrow; the only matter of interest is the manner in which the two things are balanced or divided. And the really interesting thing is this, that the pagan was (in the main) happier and happier as he approached the earth, but sadder and sadder as he approached the heavens. The gaiety of the best Paganism, as in the playfulness of Catullus or Theocritus, is, indeed, an eternal gaiety never to be forgotten by a grateful humanity. But it is all a gaiety about the facts of life, not about its origin. To the pagan the small things are as sweet as the small brooks breaking out of the mountain; but the broad things are as bitter as the sea. When the pagan looks at the very core of the cosmos he is struck cold. Behind the gods, who are merely despotic, sit the fates, who are deadly. Nay, the fates are worse than deadly; they are dead. And when rationalists say that the ancient world was more enlightened than the Christian, from their point of view they are right. For when they say "enlightened" they mean darkened with incurable despair. It is profoundly true that the ancient world was more modern than the Christian. The common bond is in the fact that ancients and moderns have both been miserable about existence, about everything, while mediaevals were happy about that at least. I freely grant that the pagans, like the moderns, were only miserable about everything—they were quite jolly about everything else. I concede that the Christians of the Middle Ages were only at peace about everything—they were at war about everything else. But if the question turn on the primary pivot of the cosmos, then there was more cosmic contentment in the narrow and bloody streets of Florence than in the theatre of Athens or the open garden of Epicurus. Giotto lived in a gloomier town than Euripides, but he lived in a gayer universe.

The mass of men have been forced to be gay about the little things, but sad about the big ones. Nevertheless (I offer my last dogma defiantly) it is not native to man to be so. Man is more himself, man is more manlike, when joy is the fundamental thing in him, and grief the superficial. Melancholy should be an innocent interlude, a tender and fugitive frame of mind; praise should be the permanent pulsation of the soul. Pessimism is at best an emotional half-holiday; joy is the uproarious labour by which all things live. Yet, according to the apparent estate of man as seen by the pagan or the agnostic, this primary need of human nature can never be fulfilled. Joy ought to be expansive; but for the agnostic it must be contracted, it must cling to one corner of the world. Grief ought to be a concentration; but for the agnostic its desolation is spread through an unthinkable eternity. This is what I call being born upside down. The sceptic may truly be said to be topsy-turvy; for his feet are dancing upwards in idle ecstasies, while his brain is in the abyss. To the modern man the heavens are actually below the earth. The explanation is simple; he is standing on his head; which is a very weak pedestal to stand on. But when he has found his feet again he knows it. Christianity satisfies suddenly and perfectly man's ancestral instinct for being the right way up; satisfies it supremely in this; that by its creed joy becomes something gigantic and sadness something special and small. The vault above us is not deaf because the universe is an idiot; the silence is not the heartless silence of an endless and aimless world. Rather the silence around us is a small and pitiful stillness like the prompt stillness in a sick-room. We are perhaps permitted tragedy as a sort of merciful comedy: because the frantic energy of divine things would knock us down like a drunken farce. We can take our own tears more lightly than we could take the tremendous levities of the angels. So we sit perhaps in a starry chamber of silence, while the laughter of the heavens is too loud for us to hear.

Joy, which was the small publicity of the pagan, is the gigantic secret of the Christian. And as I close this chaotic volume I open again the strange small book from which all Christianity came; and I am again haunted by a kind of confirmation. The tremendous figure which fills the Gospels towers in this respect, as in every other, above all the thinkers who ever thought themselves tall. His pathos was natural, almost casual. The Stoics, ancient and modern, were proud of concealing their tears. He never concealed His tears; He showed them plainly on His open face at any daily sight, such as the far sight of His native city. Yet He concealed something. Solemn supermen and imperial diplomatists are proud of restraining their anger. He never restrained His anger. He flung furniture down the front steps of the Temple, and asked men how they expected to escape the damnation of Hell. Yet He restrained something. I say it with reverence; there was in that shattering personality a thread that must be called shyness. There was something that He hid from all men when He went up a mountain to pray. There was something that He covered constantly by abrupt silence or impetuous isolation. There was some one thing that was too great for God to show us when He walked upon our earth; and I have sometimes fancied that it was His mirth.

The Club of Queer Trades

With All 32 Original Illustrations
by the Author

Contents

Illustrations

I. THE TREMENDOUS ADVENTURES OF MAJOR BROWN

RABELAIS, OR his wild illustrator Gustave Doré, must have had something to do with the designing of the things called flats in England and America. There is something entirely Gargantuan in the idea of economising space by piling houses on top of each other, front doors and all. And in the chaos and complexity of those perpendicular streets anything may dwell or happen, and it is in one of them, I believe, that the inquirer may find the offices of the Club of Queer Trades. It may be thought at the first glance that the name would attract and startle the passer-by, but nothing attracts or startles in these dim immense hives. The passer-by is only looking for his own melancholy destination, the Montenegro Shipping Agency or the London office of the *Rutland Sentinel,* and passes through the twilight passages as one passes through the twilight corridors of a dream. If the Thugs set up a Strangers' Assassination Company in one of the great buildings in Norfolk Street, and sent in a mild man in spectacles to answer inquiries, no inquiries would be made. And the Club of Queer Trades reigns in a great edifice hidden like a fossil in a mighty cliff of fossils.

The nature of this society, such as we afterwards discovered it to be, is soon and simply told. It is an eccentric and Bohemian Club, of which the absolute condition of membership lies in this, that the candidate must have invented the method by which he earns his living. It must be an entirely new trade. The exact definition of this requirement is given in the two principal rules. First, it must not be a mere application or variation of an existing trade. Thus, for instance, the Club would not admit an insurance agent simply because instead of insuring men's furniture against being burnt in a fire, he insured, let us say, their trousers against being torn by a mad dog.

The principle (as Sir Bradcock Burnaby-Bradcock, in the extraordinarily eloquent and soaring speech to the Club on the occasion of the question being raised in the Stormby Smith affair, said wittily and keenly) is the same. Secondly, the trade must be a genuine commercial source of income, the support of its inventor. Thus the Club would not receive a man simply because he chose to pass his days collecting broken sardine tins, unless he could drive a roaring trade in them. Professor Chick made that quite clear. And when one remembers what Professor Chick's own new trade was, one doesn't know whether to laugh or cry.

The discovery of this strange society was a curiously refreshing thing; to realise that there were ten new trades in the world was like looking at the first ship or the first plough. It made a man feel what he should feel, that he was still in the childhood of the world. That I should have come at last upon so singular a body was, I may say without vanity, not altogether singular, for I have a mania for belonging to as many societies as possible: I may be said to collect clubs, and I have accumulated a vast and fantastic variety of specimens ever since, in my audacious youth, I collected the Athenæum. At some future day, perhaps, I may tell tales of some of the other bodies to which I have belonged. I will recount the doings of the Dead Man's Shoes Society (that superficially immoral, but darkly justifiable communion); I will explain the curious origin of the Cat and Christian, the name of which has been so shamefully misinterpreted; and the world shall know at least why the Institute of Typewriters coalesced with the Red Tulip League. Of the Ten Teacups, of course I dare not say a word. The first of my revelations, at any rate, shall be concerned with the Club of Queer Trades, which, as I have said, was one of this class, one which I was almost bound to come across sooner or later, because of my singular hobby. The wild youth of the metropolis call me facetiously "The King of Clubs." They also call me "The Cherub," in allusion to the roseate and youthful appearance I have presented in my declining years. I only hope the spirits in the better world have as good dinners as I have. But the finding of the Club of Queer Trades has one very curious thing about it. The most curious thing about it is that it was not discovered by me: it was discovered by my friend Basil Grant, a star-gazer, a mystic, and a man who scarcely stirred out of his attic.

Very few people knew anything of Basil; not because he was in the least unsociable, for if a man out of the street had walked into his rooms he would have kept him talking till morning. Few people knew him, because, like all poets, he could do without them; he welcomed a human face as he might welcome a sudden blend of colour in a sunset; but he no more felt the need of going out to parties than he felt the need of altering the sunset clouds. He lived in a queer and comfortable garret in the roofs of Lambeth. He was surrounded by a chaos of things that were in odd contrast to the slums around him: old fantastic books, swords, armour—the whole dust-hole of romanticism. But his face, amid all these quixotic relics, appeared curiously keen and modern—a powerful, legal face. And no one but I knew who he was.

Long ago as it is, every one remembers the terrible and grotesque scene that occurred in——, when one of the most acute and forcible of the English judges suddenly went mad on the bench. I had my own view of that occurrence; but about the facts themselves there is no question at all. For some months, indeed for some years, people had detected something curious in the judge's conduct. He seemed to have lost interest in the law, in which he had been beyond expression brilliant and terrible as a K.C., and to be occupied in giving personal and moral advice to the people concerned. He talked more like a priest or a doctor, and a very outspoken one at that. The first thrill was probably given when he said to a man who had attempted a crime of passion: "I sentence you to three years' imprisonment, under the firm, and solemn, and God-given conviction, that what you require is three months at the seaside." He accused criminals from the bench, not so much of their obvious legal crimes, but of things that had never been heard of in a court of justice, monstrous egoism, lack of humour, and morbidity deliberately encouraged. Things came to a head in that celebrated diamond case in which the Prime Minister himself, that brilliant patrician, had to come forward, gracefully and reluctantly, to give evidence against his valet. After the detailed life of the household had been thoroughly exhibited, the judge requested the Premier again to step forward, which he did with quiet dignity. The judge then said, in a sudden, grating voice: "Get a new soul. That thing's not fit for a dog. Get a new soul." All this, of course, in the eyes of the sagacious, was premonitory of that melancholy and farcical day when his wits actually deserted him in open court. It was a libel case between two very eminent and powerful financiers, against both of whom charges of considerable defalcation were brought. The case was long and complex; the advocates were long and eloquent; but at last, after weeks of work and rhetoric, the time came for the great judge to give a summing-up; and one of his celebrated masterpieces of lucidity and pulverising logic was eagerly looked for. He had spoken very little during the prolonged affair, and he looked sad and lowering at the end of it. He was silent for a few moments, and then burst into a stentorian song. His remarks (as reported) were as follows:—

"O Rowty-owty tiddly-owty
Tiddly-owty tiddly-owty
Highty-ighty tiddly-ighty
Tiddly-ighty ow."

He then retired from public life and took the garret in Lambeth.

I was sitting there one evening, about six o'clock, over a glass of that gorgeous Burgundy which he kept behind a pile of black-letter folios; he was striding about the room, fingering, after a habit of his, one of the great swords in his collection; the red glare of the strong fire struck his square features and his fierce grey hair; his blue eyes were even unusually full of dreams, and he had opened his mouth to speak dreamily, when the door was flung open, and a pale, fiery man, with red hair and a huge furred overcoat, swung himself panting into the room.

"Sorry to bother you, Basil," he gasped. "I took a liberty—made an appointment here with a man—a client—in five minutes—I beg your pardon, sir," and he gave me a bow of apology.

Basil smiled at me. "You didn't know," he said, "that I had a practical brother. This is Rupert Grant, Esquire, who can and does all there is to be done. Just as I was a failure at one thing, he is a success at everything. I remember him as a journalist, a house-agent, a naturalist, an inventor, a publisher, a schoolmaster, a—what are you now, Rupert?"

"I am and have been for some time," said Rupert, with some dignity, "a private detective, and there's my client."

A loud rap at the door had cut him short, and, on permission being given, the door was thrown sharply open and a stout, dapper man walked swiftly into the room, set his silk hat with a clap on the table, and said, "Good-evening, gentle*men*," with a stress on the last syllable that somehow marked him out as a martinet, military, literary and social. He had a large head streaked with black and grey, and an abrupt black moustache, which gave him a look of fierceness which was contradicted by his sad sea-blue eyes.

Basil immediately said to me, "Let us come into the next room, Gully," and was moving towards the door, but the stranger said:—

"Not at all. Friends remain. Assistance possibly."

The moment I heard him speak I remembered who he was, a certain Major Brown I had met years before in Basil's society. I had forgotten altogether the black dandified figure and the large solemn head, but I remembered the peculiar speech, which consisted of only saying about a quarter of each sentence, and that sharply, like the crack of a gun. I do not know, it may have come from giving orders to troops.

Major Brown was a V.C., and an able and distinguished soldier, but he was anything but a warlike person. Like many among the iron men who recovered British India, he was a man with the natural belief and tastes of an old maid. In his dress he was dapper and yet demure; in his habits he was precise to the point of the exact adjustment of a tea-cup. One enthusiasm he had, which was of the nature of a religion—the cultivation of pansies. And when he talked about his collection, his blue eyes glittered like a child's at a new toy, the eyes that had remained untroubled when the troops were roaring victory round Roberts at Candahar.

"Well, Major," said Rupert Grant, with a lordly heartiness, flinging himself into a chair, "what is the matter with you?"

"Yellow pansies. Coal cellar. P. G. Northover," said the Major, with righteous indignation.

We glanced at each other with inquisitiveness. Basil, who had his eyes shut in his abstracted way, said simply:—

"I beg your pardon."

"Fact is. Street, you know, man, pansies. On wall. Death to me. Something. Preposterous."

We shook our heads gently. Bit by bit, and mainly by the seemingly sleepy assistance of Basil Grant, we pieced together the Major's fragmentary, but excited narration. It would be infamous to submit the reader to what we endured; therefore I will tell the story of Major Brown in my own words. But the reader must imagine the scene. The eyes of Basil closed as in a trance, after his habit, and the eyes of Rupert and myself getting rounder and rounder as we listened to one of the most astounding stories in the world, from the lips of the little man in black, sitting bolt upright in his chair and talking like a telegram.

Major Brown was, I have said, a successful soldier, but by no means an enthusiastic one. So far from regretting his retirement on half-pay, it was with delight that he took a small neat villa, very like a doll's house, and devoted the rest of his life to pansies and weak tea. The thought that battles were over when he had once hung up his sword in the little front hall (along with two patent stew-pots and a bad water-colour), and betaken himself instead to wielding the rake in his little sunlit garden, was to him like having come into a harbour in heaven. He was Dutch-like and precise in his taste in gardening, and had, perhaps, some tendency to drill his flowers like soldiers. He was one of those men who are capable of putting four umbrellas in the stand rather than three, so that two may lean one way and two another; he saw life like a pattern in a freehand drawing-book. And assuredly he would not have believed, or even understood, any one who had told him that within a few yards of his brick paradise he was destined to be caught in a whirlpool of incredible adventures, such as he had never seen or dreamed of in the horrible jungle, or the heart of battle.

One certain bright and windy afternoon, the Major, attired in his usual faultless manner, had set out for his usual constitutional. In crossing from one great residential thoroughfare to another, he happened to pass along one of those aimless-looking lanes which lie along the back-garden walls of a row of mansions, and which in their empty and discoloured appearance give one an odd sensation as of being behind the scenes of a theatre. But mean and sulky as the scene might be in the eyes of most of us, it was not altogether so in the Major's, for along the coarse gravel footway was coming a thing which was to him what the passing of a religious procession is to a devout person. A large, heavy man, with fish-blue eyes and a ring of irradiating red beard, was pushing before him a barrow, which was ablaze with incomparable flowers. There were splendid specimens of almost every order, but the Major's own favourite pansies predominated. The Major stopped and fell into conversation, and then into bargaining. He treated the man after the manner of collectors and other mad men, that is to say, he carefully and with a sort of anguish selected the best roots from the less excellent, praised some, disparaged others, made a subtle scale ranging from a thrilling worth and rarity to a degraded insignificance, and then bought them all. The man was just pushing off his barrow when he stopped and came close to the Major.

"I'll tell you what, sir," he said. "If you're interested in them things, you just get on to that wall."

"On the wall!" cried the scandalised Major, whose conventional soul quailed within him at the thought of such fantastic trespass.

"Finest show of yellow pansies in England in that there garden, sir," hissed the tempter. "I'll help you up, sir."

How it happened no one will ever know, but that positive enthusiasm of the Major's life triumphed over all its negative traditions, and with an easy leap and swing that showed that he was in no need of physical assistance, he stood on the wall at the end of the strange garden. The second after, the flapping of the frock-coat at his knees made him feel inexpressibly a fool. But the next instant all such trifling sentiments were swallowed up by the most appalling shock of surprise the old soldier had ever felt in all his bold and wandering existence. His eyes fell upon the garden, and there across a large bed in the centre of the lawn was a vast pattern of pansies; they were splendid flowers, but for once it was not their horticultural aspects that Major Brown beheld, for the pansies were arranged in gigantic capital letters so as to form the sentence—

"DEATH TO MAJOR BROWN"

A kindly looking old man, with white whiskers, was watering them.

Brown looked sharply back at the road behind him; the man with the barrow had suddenly vanished. Then he looked again at the lawn with its incredible inscription. Another man might have thought he had gone mad, but Brown did not. When romantic ladies gushed over his V.C. and his military exploits, he sometimes felt himself to be a painfully prosaic person, but by the same token he knew he was incurably sane. Another man, again, might have thought himself a victim of a passing practical joke, but Brown could not easily believe this. He knew from his own quaint learning that the garden arrangement was an elaborate and expensive one; he thought it extravagantly improbable that any one would pour out money like water for a joke against him. Having no explanation whatever to offer, he admitted the fact to himself, like a clear-headed man, and waited as he would have done in the presence of a man with six legs.

At this moment the stout old man with white whiskers looked up, and the watering-can fell from his hand, shooting a swirl of water down the gravel path.

"Who on earth are you?" he gasped, trembling violently.

"I am Major Brown," said that individual, who was always cool in the hour of action.

The old man gaped helplessly like some monstrous fish. At last he stammered wildly, "Come down—come down here!"

"At your service," said the Major, and alighted at a bound on the grass beside him without disarranging his silk hat.

The old man turned his broad back and set off at a sort of waddling run towards the house, followed with swift steps by the Major. His guide led him through the back passages of a gloomy, but gorgeously appointed house, until they reached the door of the front room. Then the old man turned with a face of apoplectic terror dimly showing in the twilight.

"For heaven's sake," he said, "don't mention jackals."

Then he threw open the door, releasing a burst of red lamplight, and ran downstairs with a clatter.

The Major stepped into a rich, glowing room, full of red copper, and peacock and purple hangings, hat in hand. He had the finest manners in the world, and though mystified, was not in the least embarrassed to see that the only occupant was a lady, sitting by the window, looking out.

"Madam," he said, bowing simply, "I am Major Brown."

"Sit down," said the lady; but she did not turn her head.

She was a graceful, green-clad figure, with fiery red hair and a flavour of Bedford Park. "You have come, I suppose," she said mournfully, "to tax me about the hateful title-deeds."

"I have come, madam," he said, "to know what is the matter. To know why my name is written across your garden. Not amicably either."

He spoke grimly, for the thing had hit him. It is impossible to describe the effect produced on the mind by that quiet and sunny garden scene, the frame for a stunning and brutal personality. The evening air was still, and the grass was golden in the place where the little flowers he studied cried to heaven for his blood.

"You know I must not turn around," said the lady; "every afternoon till the stroke of six I must keep my face turned to the street."

Some queer and unusual inspiration made the prosaic soldier resolute to accept these outrageous riddles without surprise.

"It is almost six," he said; and even as he spoke the barbaric copper clock upon the wall clanged the first stroke of the hour. At the sixth the lady sprung up and turned on the Major one of the queerest and yet most attractive faces he had ever seen in his life; open, and yet tantalising, the face of an elf.

"That makes the third year I have waited," she cried. "This is an anniversary. The waiting almost makes one wish the frightful thing would happen once and for all."

And even as she spoke, a sudden rending cry broke the stillness. From low down on the pavement of the dim street (it was already twilight) a voice cried out with a raucous and merciless distinctness:—

"Major Brown, Major Brown, where does the jackal dwell?"

Brown was decisive and silent in action. He strode to the front door and looked out. There was no sign of life in the blue gloaming of the street, where one or two lamps were beginning to light their lemon sparks. On returning, he found the lady in green trembling.

"It is the end," she cried, with shaking lips; "it may be death for both of us. Whenever—"

But even as she spoke her speech was cloven by another hoarse proclamation from the dark street, again horribly articulate.

"Major Brown, Major Brown, how did the jackal die?"

Brown dashed out of the door and down the steps, but again he was frustrated; there was no figure in sight, and the street was far too long and empty for the shouter to have run away. Even the rational Major was a little shaken as he returned at a certain time to the drawing-room. Scarcely had he done so than the terrific voice came:—

"Major Brown, Major Brown, where did——"

Brown was in the street almost at a bound, and he was in time—in time to see something which at first glance froze the blood. The cries appeared to come from a decapitated head resting on the pavement.

The next moment the pale Major understood. It was the head of a man thrust through the coal-hole in the street. The next moment, again, it had vanished, and Major Brown turned to the lady. "Where's your coal cellar?" he said, and stepped out into the passage.

She looked at him with wild grey eyes. "You will not go down," she cried, "alone, into the dark hole, with that beast?"

"Is this the way?" replied Brown, and descended the kitchen stairs three at a time. He flung open the door of a black cavity and stepped in, feeling in his pocket for matches. As his right hand was thus occupied, a pair of great slimy hands came out of the darkness, hands clearly belonging to a man of gigantic stature, and seized him by the back of the head. They forced him down, down in the suffocating darkness, a brutal image of destiny. But the Major's head,

"The cries appeared to come from a decapitated head resting on the pavement"

though upside down, was perfectly clear and intellectual. He gave quietly under the pressure until he had slid down almost to his hands and knees. Then finding the knees of the invisible monster within a foot of him, he simply put out one of his long, bony, and skilful hands, and gripping the leg by a muscle pulled it off the ground, and laid the huge living man, with a crash, along the floor. He strove to rise, but Brown was on top like a cat. They rolled over and over. Big as the man was, he had evidently now no desire but to escape; he made sprawls hither and thither to get past the Major to the door, but that tenacious person had him hard by the coat collar and hung with the other hand to a beam. At length there came a strain in holding back this human bull, a strain under which Brown expected his hand to rend and part from the arm. But something else rent and parted; and the dim fat figure of the giant vanished out of the cellar, leaving the torn coat in the Major's hand; the only fruit of his adventure and the only clue to the mystery. For when he went up and out at the front door, the lady, the rich hangings, and the whole equipment of the house had disappeared. It had only bare boards and whitewashed walls.

"The lady was in the conspiracy, of course," said Rupert, nodding. Major Brown turned brick red. "I beg your pardon," he said, "I think not."

Rupert raised his eyebrows and looked at him for a moment, but said nothing. When next he spoke he asked:—

"Was there anything in the pockets of the coat?"

"There was sevenpence halfpenny in coppers and a threepenny-bit," said the Major, carefully; "there was a cigarette-holder, a piece of string, and this letter," and he laid it on the table. It ran as follows:—

"DEAR MR. PLOVER,

"I am annoyed to hear that some delay has occurred in the arrangements *re* Major Brown. Please see that he is attacked as per arrangement to-morrow. The coal-cellar, of course.

"Yours faithfully,
"P. G. NORTHOVER."

Rupert Grant was leaning forward listening with hawk-like eyes. He cut in:—

"Is it dated from anywhere?"

"A pair of great slimy hands came out of the darkness and seized him by the back of the head"

"No—oh, yes!" replied Brown, glancing upon the paper; "14 Tanner's Court, North——"

Rupert sprang up and struck his hands together.

"Then why are we hanging here? Let's get along. Basil, lend me your revolver."

Basil was staring into the embers like a man in a trance; and it was some time before he answered:—

"I don't think you'll need it."

"Perhaps not," said Rupert, getting into his fur coat. "One never knows. But going down a dark court to see criminals—"

"Do you think they are criminals?" asked his brother.

Rupert laughed stoutly. "Giving orders to a subordinate to strangle a harmless stranger in a coal-cellar may strike you as a very blameless experiment, but——"

"Do you think they wanted to strangle the Major?" asked Basil, in the same distant and monotonous voice.

"My dear fellow, you've been asleep. Look at the letter."

"I am looking at the letter," said the mad judge calmly; though, as a matter of fact, he was looking at the fire. "I don't think it's the sort of letter one criminal would write to another."

"My dear boy, you are glorious," cried Rupert, turning round, with laughter in his bright blue eyes. "Your methods amaze me. Why, there *is* the letter. It *is* written, and it does give orders for a crime. You might as well say that the Nelson Column was not at all the sort of thing that was likely to be set up in Trafalgar Square."

Basil Grant shook all over with a sort of silent laughter, but did not otherwise move.

"That's rather good," he said; "but, of course, logic like that's not what is really wanted. It's a question of spiritual atmosphere. It's not a criminal letter."

"It is. It's a matter of fact," cried the other in an agony of reasonableness.

"Facts," murmured Basil, like one mentioning some strange, far-off animals, "how facts obscure the truth. I may be silly—in fact, I'm off my head—but I never could believe in that man—what's his name, in those capital stories?—Sherlock Holmes. Every detail points to something, certainly; but generally to the wrong thing. Facts point in all directions, it seems to me, like the thousands of twigs on a tree. It's only the life of the tree that has unity and goes up—only the green blood that springs, like a fountain, at the stars."

"But what the deuce else can the letter be but criminal?"

"We have eternity to stretch our legs in," replied the mystic. "It can be an infinity of things. I haven't seen any of them—I've only seen the letter. I look at that, and say it's not criminal."

"Then what's the origin of it?"

"I haven't the vaguest idea."

"Then why don't you accept the ordinary explanation?"

Basil continued for a little to glare at the coals, and seemed collecting his thoughts in a humble and even painful way. Then he said:—

"Suppose you went out into the moonlight. Suppose you passed through silent, silvery streets and squares until you came into an open and deserted space, set with a few monuments, and you beheld one dressed as a ballet girl dancing in the argent glimmer. And suppose you looked, and saw it was a man disguised. And suppose you looked again, and saw it was Lord Kitchener. What would you think?"

He paused a moment, and went on:—

"You could not adopt the ordinary explanation. The ordinary explanation of putting on singular clothes is that you look nice in them; you would not think that Lord Kitchener dressed up like a ballet girl out of ordinary personal vanity. You would think it much more likely that he inherited a dancing madness from a great grandmother; or had been hypnotised at a séance; or threatened by a secret society with death if he refused the ordeal. With Baden-Powell, say, it might be a bet—but not with Kitchener. I should know all that, because in my public days I knew him quite well. So I know that letter quite well, and criminals quite well. It's not a criminal's letter. It's all atmospheres." And he closed his eyes and passed his hand over his forehead.

Rupert and the Major were regarding him with a mixture of respect and pity. The former said:—

"Well, I'm going, anyhow, and shall continue to think—until your spiritual mystery turns up—that a man who sends a note recommending a crime, that is, actually a crime that is actually carried out, at least tentatively, is, in all probability, a little casual in his moral tastes. Can I have that revolver?"

"Certainly," said Basil, getting up. "But I am coming with you." And he flung an old cape or cloak round him, and took a sword-stick from the corner.

"You!" said Rupert, with some surprise, "you scarcely ever leave your hole to look at anything on the face of the earth."

Basil fitted on a formidable old white hat.

"I scarcely ever," he said, with an unconscious and colossal arrogance, "hear of anything on the face of the earth that I do not understand at once, without going to see it."

And he led the way out into the purple night.

We four swung along the flaring Lambeth streets, across Westminster Bridge, and along the Embankment in the direction of that part of Fleet Street which contained Tanner's Court. The erect, black figure of Major Brown, seen from behind, was a quaint contrast to the hound-like stoop and flapping mantle of young Rupert Grant, who adopted, with childlike delight, all the dramatic poses of the detective of fiction. The finest among his many fine qualities was his boyish appetite for the colour and poetry of London. Basil, who walked behind, with his face turned blindly to the stars, had the look of a somnambulist.

Rupert paused at the corner of Tanner's Court, with a quiver of delight at danger, and gripped Basil's revolver in his greatcoat pocket.

"Shall we go in now?" he asked.

"Not get police?" asked Major Brown, glancing sharply up and down the street.

"I am not sure," answered Rupert, knitting his brows. "Of course, it's quite clear, the thing's all crooked. But there are three of us, and——"

"I shouldn't get the police," said Basil in a queer voice. Rupert glanced at him and stared hard.

"Basil," he cried, "you're trembling. What's the matter—are you afraid?"

"Cold, perhaps," said the Major, eyeing him. There was no doubt that he was shaking.

At last, after a few moments' scrutiny, Rupert broke into a curse.

"You're laughing," he cried. "I know that confounded, silent, shaky laugh of yours. What the deuce is the amusement, Basil? Here we are, all three of us, within a yard of a den of ruffians——"

"But I shouldn't call the police," said Basil. "We four heroes are quite equal to a host," and he continued to quake with his mysterious mirth.

Rupert turned with impatience and strode swiftly down the court, the rest of us following. When he reached the door of No. 14 he turned abruptly, the revolver glittering in his hand.

"Stand close," he said in the voice of a commander. "The scoundrel may be attempting an escape at this moment. We must fling open the door and rush in."

"'You!' said Rupert . . . 'you scarcely ever leave your hole to look at anything'"

The four of us cowered instantly under the archway, rigid, except for the old judge and his convulsion of merriment.

"Now," hissed Rupert Grant, turning his pale face and burning eyes suddenly over his shoulder, "when I say 'Four,' follow me with a rush. If I say 'Hold him,' pin the fellows down, whoever they are. If I say 'Stop,' stop. I shall say that if there are more than three. If they attack us I shall empty my revolver on them. Basil, have your sword-stick ready. Now—one, two, three, four!"

With the sound of the word the door burst open, and we fell into the room like an invasion, only to stop dead.

The room, which was an ordinary and neatly-appointed office, appeared, at the first glance, to be empty. But on a second and more careful glance, we saw seated behind a very large desk with pigeon-holes and drawers of bewildering multiplicity, a small man with a black waxed moustache, and the air of a very average clerk, writing hard. He looked up as we came to a standstill.

"Did you knock?" he asked pleasantly. "I am sorry if I did not hear. What can I do for you?"

There was a doubtful pause, and then, by general consent, the Major himself, the victim of the outrage, stepped forward.

The letter was in his hand, and he looked unusually grim.

"Is your name P. G. Northover?" he asked.

"That is my name," replied the other, smiling.

"I think," said Major Brown, with an increase in the dark glow of his face, "that this letter was written by you." And with a loud clap he struck open the letter on the desk with his clenched fist. The man called Northover looked at it with unaffected interest, and merely nodded.

"Well, sir," said the Major, breathing hard, "what about that?"

"What about it, precisely," said the man with the moustache.

"I am Major Brown," said that gentleman sternly.

Northover bowed. "Pleased to meet you, sir. What have you to say to me?"

"Say!" cried the Major, loosing a sudden tempest; "why, I want this confounded thing settled. I want——"

"Certainly, sir," said Northover, jumping up with a slight elevation of the eyebrows. "Will you take a chair for a moment." And he pressed an electric bell just above him, which thrilled and tinkled in a room beyond. The Major put his hand on the back of the chair offered him, but stood chafing and beating the floor with his polished boot.

The next moment an inner glass door was opened, and a fair, weedy, young man, in a frock-coat, entered from within.

“ ‘Stand close,’ he said . . . ‘we must fling open the door and rush in’ ”

"Mr. Hopson," said Northover, "this is Major Brown. Will you please finish that thing for him I gave you this morning and bring it in?"

"Yes, sir," said Mr. Hopson, and vanished like lightning.

"You will excuse me, gentlemen," said the egregious Northover, with his radiant smile, "if I continue to work until Mr. Hopson is ready. I have some books that must be cleared up before I get away on my holiday to-morrow. And we all like a whiff of the country, don't we? Ha! ha!"

The criminal took up his pen with a child-like laugh, and a silence ensued; a placid and busy silence on the part of Mr. P. G. Northover; a raging silence on the part of everybody else.

At length the scratching of Northover's pen in the stillness was mingled with a knock at the door, almost simultaneous with the turning of the handle, and Mr. Hopson came in again with the same silent rapidity, placed a paper before his principal, and disappeared again.

The man at the desk pulled and twisted his spiky moustache for a few moments as he ran his eye up and down the paper presented to him. He took up his pen, with a slight, instantaneous frown, and altered something, muttering—"Careless." Then he read it again with the same impenetrable reflectiveness, and finally handed it to the frantic Brown, whose hand was beating the devil's tattoo on the back of the chair.

"I think you will find that all right, Major," he said briefly.

The Major looked at it; whether he found it all right or not will appear later, but he found it like this:

Major Brown to P. G. Northover.

	£	s.	d.
January 1, to account rendered	5	6	0
May 9, to potting and embedding of 200 pansies	2	0	0
To cost of trolley with flowers	0	15	0
To hiring of man with trolley	0	5	0
To hire of house and garden for one day	1	0	0
To furnishing of room in peacock curtains, copper ornaments, &c	3	0	0

To salary of Miss Jameson	1	0	0
To salary of Mr. Plover	1	0	0
Total	£14	6	0

A remittance will oblige.

"What," said Brown, after a dead pause, and with eyes that seemed slowly rising out of his head. "What in heaven's name is this?"

"What is it?" repeated Northover, cocking his eyebrow with amusement. "It's your account, of course."

"My account!" The Major's ideas appeared to be in a vague stampede. "My account. And what have I got to do with it?"

"Well," said Northover, laughing outright, "naturally I prefer you to pay it."

The Major's hand was still resting on the back of the chair as the words came. He scarcely stirred otherwise, but he lifted the chair bodily into the air with one hand and hurled it at Northover's head.

The legs crashed against the desk, so that Northover only got a blow on the elbow as he sprang up with clenched fists, only to be seized by the united rush of the rest of us. The chair had fallen clattering on the empty floor.

"Let me go, you scamps," he shouted. "Let me——"

"Stand still," cried Rupert, authoritatively. "Major Brown's action is excusable. The abominable crime you have attempted——"

"A customer has a perfect right," said Northover hotly, "to question an alleged overcharge, but confound it all, not to throw furniture."

"What, in God's name, do you mean by your customers and overcharges?" shrieked Major Brown, whose keen feminine nature, steady in pain or danger, became almost hysterical in the presence of a long and exasperating mystery. "Who are you? I've never seen you or your insolent tomfool bills. I know one of your cursed brutes tried to choke me——"

"Mad," said Northover, gazing blankly round; "all of them mad. I didn't know they travelled in quartettes."

"Enough of this prevarication," said Rupert; "your crimes are discovered. A policeman is stationed at the corner of the court. Though only a private detective myself, I will take the responsibility of telling you that anything you say——"

"Mad," repeated Northover, with a weary air.

And at this moment, for the first time, there struck in among them the strange, sleepy voice of Basil Grant.

"Major Brown," he said, "may I ask you a question?"

The Major turned his head with an increased bewilderment.

"You?" he cried; "certainly, Mr. Grant."

"Can you tell me," said the mystic, with sunken head and lowering brow, as he traced a pattern in the dust with his sword-stick, "can you tell me what was the name of the man who lived in your house before you?"

The unhappy Major was only faintly more disturbed by this last and futile irrelevancy, and he answered vaguely:

"Yes, I think so; a man named Gurney something—a name with a hyphen—Gurney-Brown; that was it."

"And when did the house change hands?" said Basil, looking up sharply. His strange eyes were burning brilliantly.

"I came in last month," said the Major.

And at the mere word the criminal Northover suddenly fell into his great office chair and shouted with a volleying laughter.

"Oh! it's too perfect—it's too exquisite," he gasped, beating the arms with his fists. He was laughing deafeningly; Basil Grant was laughing voicelessly; and the rest of us only felt that our heads were like weathercocks in a whirlwind.

"Confound it, Basil," cried Rupert, stamping. "If you don't want me to go mad and blow your metaphysical brains out, tell me what all this means?"

Northover rose.

"Permit me, sir, to explain," he said. "And, first of all, permit me to apologise to you, Major Brown, for a most abominable and unpardonable blunder, which has caused you menace and inconvenience, in which, if you will allow me to say so, you have behaved with astonishing courage and dignity. Of course you need not trouble about the bill. We will stand the loss." And, tearing the paper across, he flung the halves into the waste-paper basket and bowed.

Poor Brown's face was still a picture of distraction. "But I don't even begin to understand," he cried. "What bill? what blunder? what loss?"

Mr. P. G. Northover advanced in the centre of the room, thoughtfully, and with a great deal of unconscious dignity. On closer consideration, there were apparent about him other things beside a screwed moustache, especially a lean, sallow face, hawk-like, and not without a careworn intelligence. Then he looked up abruptly.

"Do you know where you are, Major?" he said.

"God knows I don't," said the warrior, with fervour.

"You are standing," replied Northover, "in the office of the Adventure and Romance Agency, Limited."

"And what's that?" blankly inquired Brown.

The man of business leaned over the back of the chair, and fixed his dark eyes on the other's face.

"Major," said he, "did you ever, as you walked along the empty street upon some idle afternoon, feel the utter hunger for something to happen—something, in the splendid words of Walt Whitman: 'Something pernicious and dread; something far removed from a puny and pious life; something unproved; something in a trance; something loosed from its anchorage, and driving free.' Did you ever feel that?"

"Certainly not," said the Major shortly.

"Then I must explain with more elaboration," said Mr. Northover, with a sigh. "The Adventure and Romance Agency has been started to meet a great modern desire. On every side, in conversation and in literature, we hear of the desire for a larger theatre of events—for something to waylay us and lead us splendidly astray. Now the man who feels this desire for a varied life pays a yearly or a quarterly sum to the Adventure and Romance Agency; in return, the Adventure and Romance Agency undertakes to surround him with startling and weird events. As a man is leaving his front door, an excited sweep approaches him and assures him of a plot against his life; he gets into a cab, and is driven to an opium den; he receives a mysterious telegram or a dramatic visit, and is immediately in a vortex of incidents. A very picturesque and moving story is first written by one of the staff of distinguished novelists who are at present hard at work in the adjoining room. Yours, Major Brown (designed by our Mr. Grigsby), I consider peculiarly forcible and pointed; it is almost a pity you did not see the end of it. I need scarcely explain further the monstrous mistake. Your predecessor in your present house, Mr. Gurney-Brown, was a subscriber to our agency, and our foolish clerks, ignoring alike the dignity of the hyphen and the glory of military rank, positively imagined that Major Brown and Mr. Gurney-Brown were the same person. Thus you were suddenly hurled into the middle of another man's story."

"How on earth does the thing work?" asked Rupert Grant, with bright and fascinated eyes.

"We believe that we are doing a noble work," said Northover warmly. "It has continually struck us that there is no element in modern life that is more lamentable than the fact that the modern man has to seek all artistic existence in a sedentary state. If he wishes to float into fairyland, he reads a book; if he wishes to dash into the thick of battle, he reads a book; if he wishes to soar into heaven, he reads a book; if he wishes to slide down the banisters, he reads a book. We give him these visions, but we give him exercise at the same time, the necessity of leaping from wall to wall, of fighting strange gentlemen, of running down long streets from pursuers—all healthy and pleasant exercises. We give him a glimpse of that great morning world of Robin Hood or the Knights Errant, when one great game was played under the splendid sky. We give him back his childhood, that godlike time when we can act stories, be our own heroes, and at the same instant dance and dream."

Basil gazed at him curiously. The most singular psychological discovery had been reserved to the end, for as the little business man ceased speaking he had the blazing eyes of a fanatic.

Major Brown received the explanation with complete simplicity and good humour.

"Of course; awfully dense, sir," he said. "No doubt at all, the scheme excellent. But I don't think—" He paused a moment, and looked dreamily out of the window. "I don't think you will find me in it. Somehow, when one's seen—seen the thing itself, you know—blood and men screaming, one feels about having a little house and a little hobby; in the Bible, you know, 'There remaineth a rest.' "

Northover bowed. Then after a pause, he said:

"Gentlemen, may I offer you my card. If any of the rest of you desire, at any time, to communicate with me, despite Major Brown's view of the matter——"

"I should be obliged for your card, sir," said the Major, in his abrupt but courteous voice. "Pay for chair."

The agent of Romance and Adventure handed his card, laughing.

It ran, "P. G. Northover, B.A., C.Q.T., Adventure and Romance Agency, 14 Tanner's Court, Fleet Street."

"What on earth is 'C.Q.T.?' " asked Rupert Grant, looking over the Major's shoulder.

"Don't you know?" returned Northover. "Haven't you ever heard of the Club of Queer Trades?"

"There seems to be a confounded lot of funny things we haven't heard of," said the little Major, reflectively. "What's this one?"

"The Club of Queer Trades is a society consisting exclusively of people who have invented some new and curious way of making money. I was one of the earliest members."

"You deserve to be," said Basil, taking up his great white hat, with a smile, and speaking for the last time that evening.

When they had passed out the Adventure and Romance agent wore a queer smile, as he trod down the fire and locked his desk up. "A fine chap, that Major; when one hasn't a touch of the poet one stands some chance of being a poem. But to think of such a clockwork little creature of all people getting into the nets of one of Grigsby's tales," and he laughed out aloud in the silence.

Just as the laugh echoed away, there came a sharp knock at the door. An owlish head, with dark moustaches, was thrust in, with deprecating and somewhat absurd inquiry.

"What! back again, Major?" cried Northover in surprise. "What can I do for you?"

The Major shuffled feverishly into the room.

"It's horribly absurd," he said. "Something must have got started in me that I never knew before. But upon my soul I feel the most desperate desire to know the end of it all."

"The end of it all?"

"Yes," said the Major, " 'Jackals,' and the title-deeds, and 'death to Major Brown.' "

The agent's face grew grave, but his eyes were amused.

"I am terribly sorry, Major," said he, "but what you ask is impossible. I don't know any one I would sooner oblige than you; but the rules of the agency are strict. The Adventures are confidential; you are an outsider; I am not allowed to let you know an inch more than I can help. I do hope you understand——"

"There is no one," said Brown, "who understands discipline better than I do. Thank you very much. Good-night."

And the little man withdrew for the last time.

He married Miss Jameson, the lady with the red hair and the green garments. She was an actress, employed (with many others) by the Romance Agency; and her marriage with the prim old veteran caused some stir in her languid and intellectualised set. She always replied very quietly that she had met scores of men who acted splendidly in the charades provided for them by Northover, but that she had only met one man who went down into a coal-cellar when he really thought it contained a murderer.

The Major and she are living as happily as birds, in an absurd villa, and the former has taken to smoking. Otherwise he is unchanged—except, perhaps, there are moments when, alert and full of feminine unselfishness as the Major is by nature, he falls into a trance of abstraction. Then his wife recognises with a concealed smile, by the blind look in his blue eyes, that he is wondering what were the title-deeds, and why he was not allowed to mention jackals. But, like so many old soldiers, Brown is religious, and believes that he will realise the rest of those purple adventures in a better world.

II. THE PAINFUL FALL OF A GREAT REPUTATION

Basil Grant and I were talking one day in what is perhaps the most perfect place for talking on earth—the top of a tolerably deserted tramcar. To talk on the top of a hill is superb, but to talk on the top of a flying hill is a fairy tale.

The vast blank space of North London was flying by; the very pace gave us a sense of its immensity and its meanness. It was, as it were, a base infinitude, a squalid eternity, and we felt the real horror of the poor parts of London, the horror that is so totally missed and misrepresented by the sensational novelists who depict it as being a matter of narrow streets, filthy houses, criminals and maniacs, and dens of vice. In a narrow street, in a den of vice, you do not expect civilisation, you do not expect order. But the horror of this was the fact that there was civilisation, that there was order, but that civilisation only showed its morbidity, and order only its monotony. No one would say in going through a criminal slum, "I see no statues. I notice no cathedrals." But here there were public buildings; only they were mostly lunatic asylums. Here there were statues; only they were mostly statues of railway engineers and philanthropists—two dingy classes of men united by their common contempt for the people. Here there were churches; only they were the churches of dim and erratic sects, Agapemonites or Irvingites. Here, above all, there were broad roads and vast crossings and tramway lines and hospitals and all the real marks of civilisation. But though one never knew, in one sense, what one would see next, there was one thing we knew we should not see—anything really great, central, of the first class, anything that humanity had adored. And with revulsion indescribable our emotions returned, I think, to those really close and crooked entries, to those really mean streets, to those genuine slums which lie round the Thames and the City, in which nevertheless a real possibility remains that at any chance corner the great cross of the great cathedral of Wren may strike down the street like a thunderbolt.

"But you must always remember also," said Grant to me, in his heavy abstracted way, when I had urged this view, "that the very vileness of the life of these ordered plebeian places, bears witness to the victory of the human soul. I agree with you. I agree that they have to live in something worse than barbarism. They have to live in a fourth-rate civilisation. But yet I am practically certain that the majority of people here are good people. And being good is an adventure far more violent and daring than sailing round the world. Besides——"

"Go on," I said.

No answer came.

"Go on," I said, looking up.

The big blue eyes of Basil Grant were standing out of his head and he was paying no attention to me. He was staring over the side of the tram.

"What is the matter?" I asked, peering over also.

"It is very odd," said Grant at last, grimly, "that I should have been caught out like this at the very moment of my optimism. I said all these people were good, and there is the wickedest man in London."

"Where?" I asked, leaning over further, "where?"

"Oh, I was right enough," he went on, in that strange continuous and sleepy tone which always angered his hearers at acute moments, "I was right enough when I said all these people were good. They are heroes; they are saints. Now and then they may perhaps steal a spoon or two; they may beat a wife or two with the poker. But they are saints all the same; they are angels; they are robed in white; they are clad with wings and haloes—at any rate compared to that man."

"Which man?" I cried again, and then my eye caught the figure at which Basil's bull's eyes were glaring.

He was a slim, smooth person, passing very quickly among the quickly passing crowd, but though there was nothing about him sufficient to attract a startled notice, there was quite enough to demand a curious consideration when once that notice was attracted. He wore a black top-hat, but there was enough in it of those strange curves whereby the decadent artist of the eighties tried to turn the top-hat into something as rhythmic as an Etruscan vase. His hair, which was largely grey, was curled with the instinct of one who appreciated the gradual beauty of grey and silver. The rest of his face was oval and I thought, rather Oriental; he had two black tufts of moustache.

"What has he done?" I asked.

"I am not sure of the details," said Grant, "but his besetting sin is a desire to intrigue to the disadvantage of others. Probably he has adopted some imposture or other to effect his plan."

"What plan?" I asked. "If you know all about him why don't you tell me why he is the wickedest man in England? What is his name?"

Basil Grant stared at me for some moments.

"I think you've made a mistake in my meaning," he said. "I don't know his name. I never saw him before in my life."

"Never saw him before!" I cried, with a kind of anger; "then what in heaven's name do you mean by saying that he is the wickedest man in England?"

"I meant what I said," said Basil Grant calmly. "The moment I saw that man, I saw all these people stricken with a sudden and splendid innocence. I saw that while all ordinary poor men in these streets were being themselves, he was not being himself. I saw that all the men in these slums, cadgers, pickpockets, hooligans, are all, in the deepest sense, trying to be good. And I saw that that man was trying to be evil."

"But if you never saw him before——" I began.

"In God's name, look at his face," cried out Basil in a voice that startled the driver. "Look at the eyebrows. They mean that infernal pride which made Satan so proud that he sneered even at heaven when he was one of the first angels in it. Look at his moustaches, they are so grown as to insult humanity. In the name of the sacred heavens, look at his hair. In the name of God and the stars, look at his hat."

I stirred uncomfortably.

"But after all," I said, "this is very fanciful—perfectly absurd. Look at the mere facts. You have never seen the man before, you——"

"Oh, the mere facts," he cried out in a kind of despair. "The mere facts! Do you really admit—are you still so sunk in superstitions, so clinging to dim and prehistoric altars, that you believe in facts? Do you not trust an immediate impression?"

"Well, an immediate impression may be," I said, "a little less practical than facts."

"Bosh," he said. "On what else is the whole world run but immediate impressions? What is more practical? My friend, the philosophy of this world may be founded on facts, its business is run

" 'Why don't you tell me why he is the wickedest man in England?' "

on spiritual impressions and atmospheres. Why do you refuse or accept a clerk? Do you measure his skull? Do you read up his physiological state in a handbook? Do you go upon facts at all? Not a scrap. You accept the clerk who may save your business—you refuse the clerk that may rob your till, entirely upon those immediate mystical impressions under the pressure of which I pronounce, with a perfect sense of certainty and sincerity, that that man walking in that street beside us is a humbug and a villain of some kind."

"You always put things well," I said, "but, of course, such things cannot immediately be put to the test."

Basil sprang up straight and swayed with the swaying car.

"Let us get off and follow him," he said. "I bet you five pounds it will turn out as I say."

And with a scuttle, a jump, and a run, we were off the car.

The man with the curved silver hair and the curved Eastern face walked along for some time, his long splendid frock coat flying behind him. Then he swung sharply out of the great glaring road and disappeared down an ill-lit alley. We swung silently after him.

"This is an odd turning for a man of that kind to take," I said.

"A man of what kind?" asked my friend.

"Well," I said, "a man with that kind of expression and those boots. I thought it rather odd, to tell the truth, that he should be in this part of the world at all."

"Ah, yes," said Basil, and said no more.

We tramped on, looking steadily in front of us. The elegant figure, like the figure of a black swan, was silhouetted suddenly against the glare of intermittent gaslight and then swallowed again in night. The intervals between the lights were long, and a fog was thickening on the whole city. Our pace, therefore, had become swift and mechanical between the lamp-posts; but Basil came to a standstill suddenly like a reined horse; I stopped also. We had almost run into the man. A great part of the solid darkness in front of us was the darkness of his body.

At first I thought he had turned to face us. But though we were hardly a yard off he did not realise that we were there. He tapped four times on a very low and dirty door in the dark, crabbed street. A gleam of gas cut the darkness as it opened slowly. We listened intently, but the interview was short and simple and inexplicable as an interview could be. Our exquisite friend handed in what looked like a paper or a card and said:

"At once. Take a cab."

A heavy, deep voice from inside said:

"Right you are."

And with a click we were in blackness again, and striding on after the striding stranger through a labyrinth of London lanes, the lights just helping us. It was only five o'clock, but winter and the fog had made it like midnight.

"This is really an extraordinary walk for the patent-leather boots," I repeated.

"I don't know," said Basil humbly. "It leads to Berkeley Square."

As I tramped on I strained my eyes through the dusky atmosphere and tried to make out the direction described. For some ten minutes I wondered and doubted; at the end of that I saw that my friend was right. We were coming to the great dreary spaces of fashionable London—more dreary, one must admit, even than the dreary plebeian spaces.

"This is very extraordinary!" said Basil Grant, as we turned into Berkeley Square.

"What is extraordinary?" I asked. "I thought you said it was quite natural."

"I do not wonder," answered Basil, "at his walking through nasty streets; I do not wonder at his going to Berkeley Square. But I do wonder at his going to the house of a very good man."

"What very good man?" I asked with exasperation.

"The operation of time is a singular one," he said with his imperturbable irrelevancy. "It is not a true statement of the case to say that I have forgotten my career when I was a judge and a public man. I remember it all vividly, but it is like remembering some novel. But fifteen years ago I knew this square as well as Lord Rosebery does, and a confounded long sight better than that man who is going up the steps of old Beaumont's house."

"Who is old Beaumont?" I asked, irritably.

"A perfectly good fellow. Lord Beaumont of Foxwood—don't you know his name? He is a man of transparent sincerity, a nobleman who does more work than a navvy, a socialist, an anarchist, I don't know what; anyhow, he's a philosopher and philanthropist. I admit he has the slight disadvantage of being, beyond all question, off his head. He has that real disadvantage which has arisen out of the modern worship of progress and novelty; and he thinks anything odd and new must be an advance. If you went to him and proposed to eat your grandmother, he would agree with you, so long as you put it on hygienic and public grounds, as a cheap alternative to cremation. So long as you progress fast enough it seems a matter of indifference to him whether you are progressing to the stars or the devil. So his house is filled with an endless succession of literary and political fashions; men who wear long hair because it is romantic; men who wear short hair because it is medical; men who walk on their feet only to exercise their hands; and men who walk on their hands for fear of tiring their feet. But though the inhabitants of his *salons* are generally fools, like himself, they are almost always, like himself, good men. I am really surprised to see a criminal enter there."

"My good fellow," I said firmly, striking my foot on the pavement, "the truth of this affair is very simple. To use your own eloquent language, you have the 'slight disadvantage' of being off *your* head. You see a total stranger in a public street; you choose to start certain theories about his eyebrows. You then treat him as a burglar because he enters an honest man's door. The thing is too monstrous. Admit that it is, Basil, and come home with me. Though these people are still having tea, yet with the distance we have to go, we shall be late for dinner."

Basil's eyes were shining in the twilight like lamps.

"I thought," he said, "that I had outlived vanity."

"What do you want now?" I cried.

"I want," he cried out, "what a girl wants when she wears her new frock; I want what a boy wants when he goes in for a slanging match with a monitor—I want to show somebody what a fine fellow I am. I am as right about that man as I am about your having a hat on your head. You say it cannot be tested. I say it can. I will take you to see my old friend Beaumont. He is a delightful man to know."

"Do you really mean——?" I began.

"I will apologise," he said calmly, "for our not being dressed for a call," and walking across the vast misty square, he walked up the dark stone steps and rang at the bell.

A severe servant in black and white opened the door to us: on receiving my friend's name his manner passed in a flash from astonishment to respect. We were ushered into the house very quickly, but not so quickly but that our host, a white-haired man with a fiery face, came out quickly to meet us.

"My dear fellow," he cried, shaking Basil's hand again and again, "I have not seen you for years. Have you been—er—" he said, rather wildly, "have you been in the country?"

"Our exquisite friend handed in what looked like a paper"

"Not for all that time," answered Basil, smiling. "I have long given up my official position, my dear Philip, and have been living in a deliberate retirement. I hope I do not come at an inopportune moment."

"An inopportune moment," cried the ardent gentleman. "You come at the most opportune moment I could imagine. Do you know who is here?"

"I do not," answered Grant, with gravity. Even as he spoke a roar of laughter came from the inner room.

"Basil," said Lord Beaumont, solemnly, "I have Wimpole here."

"And who is Wimpole?"

"Basil," cried the other, "you must have been in the country. You must have been in the antipodes. You must have been in the moon. Who is Wimpole? Who was Shakespeare?"

"As to who Shakespeare was," answered my friend placidly, "my views go no further than thinking that he was not Bacon. More probably he was Mary Queen of Scots. But as to who Wimpole is——" and his speech also was cloven with a roar of laughter from within.

"Wimpole!" cried Lord Beaumont, in a sort of ecstasy. "Haven't you heard of the great modern wit? My dear fellow, he has turned conversation, I do not say into an art—for that, perhaps, it always was—but into a great art, like the statuary of Michael Angelo—an art of masterpieces. His repartees, my good friend, startle one like a man shot dead. They are final; they are——"

Again there came the hilarious roar from the room, and almost with the very noise of it, a big, panting, apoplectic old gentleman came out of the inner house into the hall where we were standing.

"Now, my dear chap," began Lord Beaumont, hastily.

"I tell you, Beaumont, I won't stand it," exploded the large old gentleman. "I won't be made game of by a twopenny literary adventurer like that. I won't be made a guy. I won't——"

"Come, come," said Beaumont, feverishly. "Let me introduce you. This is Mr. Justice Grant—that is, Mr. Grant. Basil, I am sure you have heard of Sir Walter Cholmondeliegh."

"Who has not?" asked Grant, and bowed to the worthy old baronet, eyeing him with some curiosity. He was hot and heavy in his momentary anger, but even that could not conceal the noble though opulent outline of his face and body, the florid white hair, the Roman nose, the body stalwart though corpulent, the chin aristocratic though double. He was a magnificent courtly gentleman; so much of a gentleman that he could show an unquestionable

" 'Now, my dear chap,' began Lord Beaumont, hastily"

weakness of anger without altogether losing dignity; so much of a gentleman that even his *faux pas* were well-bred.

"I am distressed beyond expression, Beaumont," he said gruffly, "to fail in respect to these gentlemen, and even more especially to fail in it in your house. But it is not you or they that are in any way concerned, but that flashy half-caste jackanapes——"

At this moment a young man with a twist of red moustache and a sombre air came out of the inner room. He also did not seem to be greatly enjoying the intellectual banquet within.

"I think you remember my friend and secretary, Mr. Drummond," said Lord Beaumont, turning to Grant, "even if you only remember him as a schoolboy."

"Perfectly," said the other. Mr. Drummond shook hands pleasantly and respectfully, but the cloud was still on his brow. Turning to Sir Walter Cholmondeliegh, he said:

"I was sent by Lady Beaumont to express her hope that you were not going yet, Sir Walter. She says she has scarcely seen anything of you."

The old gentleman, still red in the face, had a temporary internal struggle; then his good manners triumphed, and with a gesture of obeisance and a vague utterance of, "If Lady Beaumont . . . a lady, of course," he followed the young man back into the *salon*. He had scarcely been deposited there half a minute before another peal of laughter told that he had (in all probability) been scored off again.

"Of course I can excuse dear old Cholmondeliegh," said Beaumont, as he helped us off with our coats. "He has not the modern mind."

"What is the modern mind?" asked Grant.

"Oh, it's enlightened you know and progressive—and faces the facts of life seriously." At this moment another roar of laughter came from within.

"I only ask," said Basil, "because of the last two friends of yours who had the modern mind, one thought it wrong to eat fishes and the other thought it right to eat men. I beg your pardon—this way, if I remember right."

"Do you know," said Lord Beaumont, with a sort of feverish entertainment, as he trotted after us towards the interior, "I can never quite make out which side you are on. Sometimes you seem so liberal and sometimes so reactionary. *Are* you a modern, Basil?"

"No," said Basil, loudly and cheerfully, as he entered the crowded drawing-room.

This caused a slight diversion, and some eyes were turned away from our slim friend with the Oriental face for the first time that afternoon. Two people, however, still looked at him. One was the daughter of the house, Muriel Beaumont, who gazed at him with great violet eyes and with the intense and awful thirst of the female upper class for verbal amusement and stimulus. The other was Sir Walter Cholmondeliegh, who looked at him with a still and sullen but unmistakable desire to throw him out of the window.

He sat there, coiled rather than seated on the easy chair; everything from the curves of his smooth limbs to the coils of his silvered hair suggesting the circles of a serpent more than the straight limbs of a man—the unmistakable, splendid serpentine gentleman we had seen walking in North London, his eyes shining with repeated victory.

"What I can't understand, Mr. Wimpole," said Muriel Beaumont eagerly, "is how you contrive to treat all this so easily. You say things quite philosophical and yet so wildly funny. If I thought of such things, I'm sure I should laugh outright when the thought first came."

"I agree with Miss Beaumont," said Sir Walter, suddenly exploding with indignation. "If I had thought of anything so futile, I should find it difficult to keep my countenance."

"Difficult to keep your countenance," cried Mr. Wimpole, with an air of alarm; "oh, do keep your countenance! Keep it in the British Museum."

Every one laughed uproariously, as they always do at an already admitted readiness, and Sir Walter, turning suddenly purple, shouted out:

"Do you know who you are talking to, with your confounded tomfooleries?"

"I never talk tomfooleries," said the other, "without first knowing my audience."

Grant walked across the room and tapped the red-moustached secretary on the shoulder. That gentleman was leaning against the wall regarding the whole scene with a great deal of gloom; but, I fancied, with very particular gloom when his eyes fell on the young lady of the house rapturously listening to Wimpole.

"May I have a word with you outside, Drummond?" asked Grant. "It is about business. Lady Beaumont will excuse us."

I followed my friend, at his own request, greatly wondering, to this strange external interview. We paused abruptly, into a kind of side room out of the hall.

"Drummond," said Basil, sharply, "there are a great many good people, and a great many sane people here this afternoon. Unfortunately, by a kind of coincidence, all the good people are mad, and all the sane people are wicked. You are the only person I know of here who is honest and has also some common sense. What do you make of Wimpole?"

Mr. Secretary Drummond had a pale face and red hair; but at this his face became suddenly as red as his moustache.

"I am not a fair judge of him," he said.

"Why not?" asked Grant.

"Because I hate him like hell," said the other, after a long pause and violently.

Neither Grant nor I needed to ask the reason; his glances towards Miss Beaumont and the stranger were sufficiently illuminating. Grant said quietly:

"But before—before you came to hate him, what did you really think of him?"

"I am in a terrible difficulty," said the young man, and his voice told us, like a clear bell, that he was an honest man. "If I spoke about him as I feel about him now, I could not trust myself. And I should like to be able to say that when I first saw him I thought he was charming. But, again, the fact is I didn't. I hate him, that is my private affair. But I also disapprove of him—really I do believe I disapprove of him quite apart from my private feelings. When first he came, I admit he was much quieter, but I did not like, so to speak, the moral swell of him. Then that jolly old Sir Walter Cholmondeliegh got introduced to us, and this fellow, with his cheap-jack wit, began to score off the old man in the way he does now. Then I felt that he must be a bad lot; it must be bad to fight the old and the kindly. And he fights the poor old chap savagely, unceasingly, as if he hated old age and kindliness. Take, if you want it, the evidence of a prejudiced witness. I admit that I hate the man because a certain person admires him. But I believe that apart from that I should hate the man because old Sir Walter hates him."

This speech affected me with a genuine sense of esteem and pity of the young man; that is, of pity for him because of his obviously hopeless worship of Miss Beaumont, and of esteem for him because of the direct realistic account of the history of Wimpole which he had given. Still, I was sorry that he seemed so steadily set against the man, and could not help referring it to an instinct of his personal relations, however nobly disguised from himself.

In the middle of these meditations, Grant whispered in my ear what was perhaps the most startling of all interruptions.

"In the name of God, let's get away."

I have never known exactly in how odd a way this odd old man affected me. I only know that for some reason or other he so affected me that I was, within a few minutes, in the street outside.

"This," he said, "is a beastly but amusing affair."

"What is?" I asked, baldly enough.

"This affair. Listen to me, my old friend. Lord and Lady Beaumont have just invited you and me to a grand dinner-party this very night, at which Mr. Wimpole will be in all his glory. Well, there is nothing very extraordinary about that. The extraordinary thing is that we are not going."

"Well, really," I said, "it is already six o'clock and I doubt if we could get home and dress. I see nothing extraordinary in the fact that we are not going."

"Don't you?" said Grant. "I'll bet you'll see something extraordinary in what we're doing instead."

I looked at him blankly.

"Doing instead?" I asked. "What are we doing instead?"

"Why," said he, "we are waiting for one or two hours outside this house on a winter evening. You must forgive me; it is all my vanity. It is only to show you that I am right. Can you, with the assistance of this cigar, wait until both Sir Walter Cholmondeliegh and the mystic Wimpole have left this house?"

"Certainly," I said. "But I do not know which is likely to leave first. Have you any notion?"

"No," he said. "Sir Walter may leave first in a glow of rage. Or again, Mr. Wimpole may leave first, feeling that his last epigram is a thing to be flung behind him like a firework. And Sir Walter may remain some time to analyse Mr. Wimpole's character. But they will both have to leave within reasonable time, for they will both have to get dressed and come back to dinner here to-night."

As he spoke the shrill double whistle from the porch of the great house drew a dark cab to the dark portal. And then a thing happened that we really had not expected. Mr. Wimpole and Sir Walter Cholmondeliegh came out at the same moment.

They paused for a second or two opposite each other in a natural doubt; then a certain geniality, fundamental perhaps in both of them, made Sir Walter smile and say: "The night is foggy. Pray take my cab."

Before I could count twenty the cab had gone rattling up the street with both of them. And before I could count twenty-three Grant had hissed in my ear:

"Run after the cab; run as if you were running from a mad dog—run."

We pelted on steadily, keeping the cab in sight, through dark mazy streets. God only, I thought, knows why we are running at all, but we are running hard. Fortunately we did not run far. The cab pulled up at the fork of two streets and Sir Walter paid the cabman, who drove away rejoicing, having just come in contact with the more generous among the rich. Then the two men talked together as men do talk together after giving and receiving great insults, the talk which leads either to forgiveness or a duel—at least so it seemed as we watched it from ten yards off. Then the two men shook hands heartily, and one went down one fork of the road and one down another.

Basil, with one of his rare gestures, flung his arms forward.

"Run after that scoundrel," he cried; "let us catch him now."

We dashed across the open space and reached the juncture of two paths.

"Stop!" I shouted wildly to Grant. "That's the wrong turning."

He ran on.

"Idiot!" I howled. "Sir Walter's gone down there. Wimpole has slipped us. He's half a mile down the other road. You're wrong. . . . Are you deaf? You're wrong!"

"I don't think I am," he panted, and ran on.

"But I saw him!" I cried. "Look in front of you. Is that Wimpole? It's the old man. . . . What are you doing? What are we to do?"

"Keep running," said Grant.

Running soon brought us up to the broad back of the pompous old baronet, whose white whiskers shone silver in the fitful lamplight. My brain was utterly bewildered. I grasped nothing.

"Charlie," said Basil, hoarsely, "can you believe in my common sense for four minutes?"

"Of course," I said, panting.

"Then help me to catch that man in front and hold him down. Do it at once when I say 'Now.' Now!"

"We sprang on Sir Walter Cholmondeliegh"

We sprang on Sir Walter Cholmondeliegh, and rolled that portly old gentleman on his back. He fought with a commendable valour, but we got him tight. I had not the remotest notion why. He had a splendid and full-blooded vigour; when he could not box he kicked, and we bound him; when he could not kick he shouted, and we gagged him. Then, by Basil's arrangement, we dragged him into a small court by the street side and waited. As I say, I had no notion why.

"I am sorry to incommode you," said Basil calmly out of the darkness; "but I have made an appointment here."

"An appointment!" I said blankly.

"Yes," he said, glancing calmly at the apoplectic old aristocrat gagged on the ground, whose eyes were starting impotently from his head. "I have made an appointment here with a thoroughly nice young fellow. An old friend. Jasper Drummond his name is—you may have met him this afternoon at the Beaumonts'. He can scarcely come though till the Beaumonts' dinner is over."

For I do not know how many hours we stood there calmly in the darkness. By the time those hours were over I had thoroughly made up my mind that the same thing had happened which had happened long ago on the bench of a British Court of Justice. Basil Grant had gone mad. I could imagine no other explanation of the facts, with the portly, purple-faced old country gentleman flung there strangled on the floor like a bundle of wood.

After about four hours a lean figure in evening dress rushed into the court. A glimpse of gaslight showed the red moustache and white face of Jasper Drummond.

"Mr. Grant," he said blankly, "the thing is incredible. You were right; but what did you mean? All through this dinner-party, where dukes and duchesses and editors of Quarterlies had come especially to hear him, that extraordinary Wimpole kept perfectly silent. He didn't say a funny thing. He didn't say anything at all. What does it mean?"

Grant pointed to the portly old gentleman on the ground.

"That is what it means," he said.

Drummond, on observing a fat gentleman lying so calmly about the place, jumped back, as from a mouse.

"What?" he said weakly, " . . . what?"

Basil bent suddenly down and tore a paper out of Sir Walter's breast-pocket, a paper which the baronet, even in his hampered state, seemed to make some effort to retain.

"Tore a paper out of Sir Walter's breast-pocket"

It was a large loose piece of white wrapping paper, which Mr. Jasper Drummond read with a vacant eye and undisguised astonishment. As far as he could make out, it consisted of a series of questions and answers, or at least of remarks and replies, arranged in the manner of a catechism. The greater part of the document had been torn and obliterated in the struggle, but the termination remained. It ran as follows:

"C. Says——Keep countenance.

"*W.* Keep——British Museum.

"C. Know whom talk——absurdities.

"*W.* Never talk absurdities without——"

"What is it?" cried Drummond, flinging the paper down in a sort of final fury.

"What is it?" replied Grant, his voice rising into a kind of splendid chant. "What is it? It is a great new profession. A great new trade. A trifle immoral, I admit, but still great, like piracy."

"A new profession!" said the young man with the red moustache vaguely; "a new trade!"

"A new trade," repeated Grant, with a strange exultation, "a new profession! What a pity it is immoral."

"But what the deuce is it?" cried Drummond and I in a breath of blasphemy.

"It is," said Grant calmly, "the great new trade of the Organiser of Repartee. This fat old gentleman lying on the ground strikes you, as I have no doubt, as very stupid and very rich. Let me clear his character. He is, like ourselves, very clever and very poor. He is also not really at all fat; all that is stuffing. He is not particularly old, and his name is not Cholmondeliegh. He is a swindler, and a swindler of a perfectly delightful and novel kind. He hires himself out at dinner parties to lead up to other people's repartees. According to a preconcerted scheme (which you may find on that piece of paper), he says the stupid things he has arranged for himself, and his client says the clever things arranged for him. In short, he allows himself to be scored off for a guinea a night."

"And this fellow Wimpole—" began Drummond with indignation.

"This fellow Wimpole," said Basil Grant, smiling, "will not be an intellectual rival in the future. He had some fine things, elegance and silvered hair, and so on. But the intellect is with our friend on the floor."

"That fellow," cried Drummond furiously, "that fellow ought to be in gaol."

"Not at all," said Basil, indulgently; "he ought to be in the Club of Queer Trades."

III. THE AWFUL REASON OF THE VICAR'S VISIT

THE REVOLT of Matter against Man (which I believe to exist) has now been reduced to a singular condition. It is the small things rather than the large things which make war against us and, I may add, beat us. The bones of the last mammoth have long ago decayed, a mighty wreck; the tempests no longer devour our navies, nor the mountains with hearts of fire heap hell over our cities. But we are engaged in a bitter and eternal war with small things; chiefly with microbes and with collar studs. The stud with which I was engaged (on fierce and equal terms) as I made the above reflections, was one which I was trying to introduce into my shirt collar when a loud knock came at the door.

My first thought was as to whether Basil Grant had called to fetch me. He and I were to turn up at the same dinner-party (for which I was in the act of dressing), and it might be that he had taken it into his head to come my way, though we had arranged to go separately. It was a small and confidential affair at the table of a good but unconventional political lady, an old friend of his. She had asked us both to meet a third guest, a Captain Fraser, who had made something of a name and was an authority on chimpanzees. As Basil was an old friend of the hostess and I had never seen her, I felt that it was quite possible that he (with his usual social sagacity) might have decided to take me along in order to break the ice. The theory, like all my theories, was complete; but as a fact it was not Basil.

I was handed a visiting card inscribed: "Rev. Ellis Shorter," and underneath was written in pencil, but in a hand in which even hurry could not conceal a depressing and gentlemanly excellence, "Asking the favour of a few moments' conversation on a most urgent matter."

I had already subdued the stud, thereby proclaiming that the image of God has supremacy over all matters (a valuable truth), and throwing on my dress-coat and waistcoat, hurried into the drawing-room. He rose at my entrance, flapping like a seal; I can use no other description. He flapped a plaid shawl over his right arm; he flapped a pair of pathetic black gloves; he flapped his clothes; I may say, without exaggeration, that he flapped his eyelids, as he rose. He was a bald-browed, white-haired, white-whiskered old clergyman, of a flappy and floppy type. He said:

"I am so sorry. I am so very sorry. I am so extremely sorry. I come—I can only say—I can only say in my defence, that I come—upon an important matter. Pray forgive me."

I told him I forgave perfectly and waited.

"What I have to say," he said, brokenly, "is so dreadful—it is so dreadful—I have lived a quiet life."

I was burning to get away, for it was already doubtful if I should be in time for dinner. But there was something about the old man's honest air of bitterness that seemed to open to me the possibilities of life larger and more tragic than my own.

I said gently: "Pray go on."

Nevertheless the old gentleman, being a gentleman as well as old, noticed my secret impatience and seemed still more unmanned.

"I'm so sorry," he said weakly; "I wouldn't have come—but for—your friend Major Brown recommended me to come here."

"Major Brown!" I said, with some interest.

"Yes," said the Reverend Mr. Shorter, feverishly flapping his plaid shawl about. "He told me you helped him in a great difficulty—and my difficulty! Oh, my dear sir, it's a matter of life and death."

I rose abruptly, in an acute perplexity. "Will it take long, Mr. Shorter?" I asked. "I have to go out to dinner almost at once."

He rose also, trembling from head to foot, and yet somehow, with all his moral palsy, he rose to the dignity of his age and his office.

"I have no right, Mr. Swinburne—I have no right at all," he said. "If you have to go out to dinner, you have of course—a perfect right—of course a perfect right. But when you come back—a man will be dead."

And he sat down, quaking like a jelly.

The triviality of the dinner had been in those two minutes dwarfed and drowned in my mind. I did not want to go and see a political widow, and a captain who collected apes; I wanted to hear what had brought this dear, doddering old vicar into relation with immediate perils.

"Will you have a cigar?" I said.

"No thank you," he said, with indescribable embarrassment, as if not smoking cigars was a social disgrace.

"A glass of wine?" I said.

"No, thank you, no, thank you; not just now," he repeated with that hysterical eagerness with which people who do not drink at all often try to convey that on any other night of the week they would sit up all night drinking rum-punch. "Not just now, thank you."

"Nothing else I can get for you?" I said, feeling genuinely sorry for the well-mannered old donkey. "A cup of tea?"

I saw a struggle in his eye and I conquered. When the cup of tea came he drank it like a dipsomaniac gulping brandy. Then he fell back and said:

"I have had such a time, Mr. Swinburne. I am not used to these excitements. As Vicar of Chuntsey, in Essex"—he threw this in with an indescribable airiness of vanity—"I have never known such things happen."

"What things happen?" I asked.

He straightened himself with sudden dignity.

"As Vicar of Chuntsey, in Essex," he said, "I have never been forcibly dressed up as an old woman and made to take part in a crime in the character of an old woman. Never once. My experience may be small. It may be insufficient. But it has never occurred to me before."

"I have never heard of it," I said, "as among the duties of a clergyman. But I am not well up in church matters. Excuse me if perhaps I failed to follow you correctly. Dressed up—as what?"

"As an old woman," said the vicar solemnly, "as an old woman."

I thought in my heart that it required no great transformation to make an old woman of him, but the thing was evidently more tragic than comic, and I said respectfully:

"May I ask how it occurred?"

"I will begin at the beginning," said Mr. Shorter, "and I will tell my story with the utmost possible precision. At seventeen minutes past eleven this morning I left the vicarage to keep certain appointments and pay certain visits in the village. My first visit was to Mr. Jervis, the treasurer of our League of Christian Amusements, with whom I concluded some business touching the claim made by Parkes the gardener in the matter of the rolling of our tennis lawn. I then visited

Mrs. Arnett, a very earnest church-woman, but permanently bedridden. She is the author of several small works of devotion, and of a book of verse, entitled (unless my memory misleads me) 'Eglantine.' "

He uttered all this not only with deliberation, but with something that can only be called, by a contradictory phrase, eager deliberation. He had, I think, a vague memory in his head of the detectives in the detective stories, who always sternly require that nothing should be kept back.

"I then proceeded," he went on, with the same maddening conscientiousness of manner, "to Mr. Carr (not Mr. James Carr, of course; Mr. Robert Carr) who is temporarily assisting our organist, and having consulted with him (on the subject of a choir boy who is accused, I cannot as yet say whether justly or not, of cutting holes in the organ pipes), I finally dropped in upon a Dorcas meeting at the house of Miss Brett. The Dorcas meetings are usually held at the vicarage, but my wife being unwell, Miss Brett, a new-comer in our village, but very active in church work, had very kindly consented to hold them. The Dorcas society is entirely under my wife's management as a rule, and except for Miss Brett, who, as I say, is very active, I scarcely know any members of it. I had, however, promised to drop in on them, and I did so.

"When I arrived there were only four other maiden ladies with Miss Brett, but they were sewing very busily. It is very difficult, of course, for any person, however strongly impressed with the necessity in these matters of full and exact exposition of the facts, to remember and repeat the actual details of a conversation, particularly a conversation which (though inspired with a most worthy and admirable zeal for good work) was one which did not greatly impress the hearer's mind at the time and was, in fact—er—mostly about socks. I can, however, remember distinctly that one of the spinster ladies (she was a thin person with a woollen shawl, who appeared to feel the cold, and I am almost sure she was introduced to me as Miss James) remarked that the weather was very changeable. Miss Brett then offered me a cup of tea, which I accepted, I cannot recall in what words. Miss Brett is a short and stout lady with white hair. The only other figure in the group that caught my attention was a Miss Mowbray, a small and neat lady of aristocratic manners, silver hair, and a high voice and colour. She was the most emphatic member of the party; and her views on the subject of pinafores, though expressed with a natural deference to myself, were in themselves strong and advanced. Besides her (although all five ladies were dressed simply in black) it could not be denied that the others looked in some way what you men of the world would call dowdy.

"After about ten minutes' conversation I rose to go, and as I did so I heard something which—I cannot describe it—something which seemed to—but I really cannot describe it."

"What did you hear?" I asked, with some impatience.

"I heard," said the vicar solemnly, "I heard Miss Mowbray (the lady with the silver hair) say to Miss James (the lady with the woollen shawl), the following extraordinary words. I committed them to memory on the spot, and as soon as circumstances set me free to do so, I noted them down on a piece of paper. I believe I have it here." He fumbled in his breast-pocket, bringing out mild things, note-books, circulars and programmes of village concerts. "I heard Miss Mowbray say to Miss James, the following words: 'Now's your time, Bill.' "

He gazed at me for a few moments after making this announcement, gravely and unflinchingly, as if conscious that here he was unshaken about his facts. Then he resumed, turning his bald head more towards the fire.

"This appeared to me remarkable. I could not by any means understand it. It seemed to me first of all peculiar that one maiden lady should address another maiden lady as 'Bill.' My experience, as I have said, may be incomplete; maiden ladies may have among themselves and in exclusively spinster circles wilder customs than I am aware of. But it seemed to me odd, and I could almost have sworn (if you will not misunderstand the phrase) I should have been strongly impelled to maintain at the time that the words, 'Now's your time, Bill,' were by no means pronounced with that upper-class intonation which, as I have already said, had up to now characterised Miss Mowbray's conversation. In fact, the words, 'Now's your time, Bill,' would have been, I fancy, unsuitable if pronounced with that upper-class intonation.

"I was surprised, I repeat, then, at the remark. But I was still more surprised, when looking round me in bewilderment, my hat and umbrella in hand, I saw the lean lady with the woollen shawl leaning upright against the door out of which I was just about to make my exit. She was still knitting, and I supposed that this erect posture against the door was only an eccentricity of spinsterhood and an oblivion of my intended departure.

"I said genially, 'I am so sorry to disturb you, Miss James, but I must really be going. I have—er——' I stopped here, for the

"A big revolver in her hand"

words she had uttered in reply, though singularly brief and in tone extremely businesslike, were such as to render that arrest of my remarks, I think, natural and excusable. I have these words also noted down. I have not the least idea of their meaning; so I have only been able to render them phonetically. But she said," and Mr. Shorter peered short-sightedly at his papers, "she said: 'Chuck it, fat 'ead,' and she added something that sounded like, 'It's a kop,' or (possibly) 'a kopt.' And then the last cord, either of my sanity or the sanity of the universe, snapped suddenly. My esteemed friend and helper, Miss Brett, standing by the mantelpiece, said: 'Put 'is old 'ead in a bag, Sam, and tie 'im up before you start jawin'. You'll be kopt yourselves some o' these days with this way of doin' things, har lar theater.'

"My head went round and round. Was it really true, as I had suddenly fancied a moment before, that unmarried ladies had some dreadful riotous society of their own from which all others were excluded? I remembered dimly in my classical days (I was a scholar in a small way once, but now, alas! rusty), I remembered the mysteries of the Bona Dea and their strange female freemasonry. I remembered the witches' Sabbaths. I was just in my absurd lightheadedness, trying to remember a line of verse about Diana's nymphs, when Miss Mowbray threw her arm round me from behind. The moment it held me I knew it was not a woman's arm.

"Miss Brett—or what I had called Miss Brett—was standing in front of me with a big revolver in her hand and a broad grin on her face. Miss James was still leaning against the door, but had fallen into an attitude so totally new, and so totally unfeminine, that it gave one a shock. She was kicking her heels, with her hands in her pockets and her cap on one side. She was a man. I mean he was a wo——no, that is, I saw that instead of being a woman she—he, I mean—that is, it was a man."

Mr. Shorter became indescribably flurried and flapping in endeavouring to arrange these genders and his plaid shawl at the same time. He resumed with a higher fever of nervousness:

"As for Miss Mowbray, she—he, held me in a ring of iron. He had her arm—that is she had his arm—round her neck—my neck I mean—and I could not cry out. Miss Brett—that is, Mr. Brett, at least Mr. something who was not Miss Brett—had the revolver pointed at me. The other two ladies—or—er—gentlemen, were rummaging in some bag in the background. It was all clear at last: they were criminals dressed up as women, to kidnap me!

To kidnap the Vicar of Chuntsey, in Essex. But why? Was it to be Nonconformists?

"The brute leaning against the door called out carelessly, ''Urry up, 'Arry. Show the old bloke what the game is and let's get off.'

" 'Curse 'is eyes,' said Miss Brett—I mean the man with the revolver—'why should we show 'im the game?'

" 'If you take my advice you bloomin' well will,' said the man at the door, whom they called Bill. 'A man wot knows wot 'e's doin' is worth ten wot don't, even if 'e's a potty old parson.'

" 'Bill's right enough,' said the coarse voice of the man who held me (it had been Miss Mowbray's). 'Bring out the picture, 'Arry.'

"The man with the revolver walked across the room to where the other two women—I mean men—were turning over baggage, and asked them for something which they gave him. He came back with it across the room and held it out in front of me. And compared to the surprise of that display, all the previous surprises of this awful day shrank suddenly.

"It was a portrait of myself. That such a picture should be in the hands of these scoundrels might in any case have caused a mild surprise; but no more. It was no mild surprise that I felt. The likeness was an extremely good one, worked up with all the accessories of the conventional photographic studio. I was leaning my head on my hand and was relieved against a painted landscape of woodland. It was obvious that it was no snapshot; it was clear that I had sat for this photograph. And the truth was that I had never sat for such a photograph. It was a photograph that I had never had taken.

"I stared at it again and again. It seemed to me to be touched up a good deal; it was glazed as well as framed, and the glass blurred some of the details. But there unmistakably was my face, my eyes, my nose and mouth, my head and hand, posed for a professional photographer. And I had never posed so for any photographer.

" 'Be'old the bloomin' miracle,' said the man with the revolver, with ill-timed facetiousness. 'Parson, prepare to meet your God.' And with this he slid the glass out of the frame. As the glass moved, I saw that part of the picture was painted on it in Chinese white, notably a pair of white whiskers and a clerical collar. And underneath was a portrait of an old lady in a quiet black dress, leaning her head on her hand against the woodland landscape. The old lady was as like me as one pin is like another. It had required only the whiskers and the collar to make it me in every hair.

" 'Entertainin', ain't it?' said the man described as 'Arry, as he shot the glass back again. 'Remarkable resemblance, parson. Gratifyin' to the lady. Gratifyin' to you. And hi may hadd, particlery gratifyin' to us, as bein' the probable source of a very tolerable haul. You know Colonel Hawker, the man who's come to live in these parts, don't you?'

"I nodded.

" 'Well,' said the man 'Arry, pointing to the picture, 'that's 'is mother. 'Oo ran to catch 'im when 'e fell? She did,' and he flung his fingers in a general gesture towards the photograph of the old lady who was exactly like me.

" 'Tell the old gent wot 'e's got to do and be done with it,' broke out Bill from the door. 'Look 'ere, Reverend Shorter, we ain't goin' to do you no 'arm. We'll give you a sov. for your trouble if you like. And as for the old woman's clothes—why, you'll look lovely in 'em.'

" 'You ain't much of a 'and at a description, Bill,' said the man behind me. 'Mr. Shorter, it's like this. We've got to see this man Hawker to-night. Maybe he'll kiss us all and 'ave up the champagne when 'e sees us. Maybe on the other 'and—'e won't. Maybe 'e'll be dead when we goes away. Maybe not. But we've got to see 'im. Now as you know, 'e shuts 'isself up and never opens the door to a soul; only you don't know why and we does. The only one as can ever get at 'im is 'is mother. Well, it's a confounded funny coincidence,' he said, accenting the penultimate, 'it's a very unusual piece of good luck, but you're 'is mother.'

" 'When first I saw 'er picture,' said the man Bill, shaking his head in a ruminant manner, 'when I first saw it I said—old Shorter. Those were my exact words—old Shorter.'

" 'What do you mean, you wild creatures?' I gasped. 'What am I to do?'

" 'That's easy said, your 'oliness,' said the man with the revolver good-humouredly; 'you've got to put on those clothes,' and he pointed to a poke-bonnet and a heap of female clothes in the corner of the room.

"I will not dwell, Mr. Swinburne, upon the details of what followed. I had no choice. I could not fight five men, to say nothing of a loaded pistol. In five minutes, sir, the Vicar of Chuntsey was dressed as an old woman—as somebody else's mother, if you please, and was dragged out of the house to take part in a crime.

"It was already late in the afternoon, and the nights of winter were closing in fast. On a dark road, in a blowing wind, we set out towards the lonely house of Colonel Hawker, perhaps the queerest cortege that ever straggled up that or any other road. To every human eye, in every external, we were six very respectable old ladies of small means, in black dresses and refined but antiquated bonnets; and we were really five criminals and a clergyman.

"I will cut a long story short. My brain was whirling like a windmill as I walked, trying to think of some manner of escape. To cry out, so long as we were far from houses, would be suicidal, for it would be easy for the ruffians to knife me or to gag me and fling me in a ditch. On the other hand, to attempt to stop strangers and explain the situation was impossible, because of the frantic folly of the situation itself. Long before I had persuaded the chance postman or carrier of so absurd a story, my companions would certainly have got off themselves, and in all probability would have carried me off, as a friend of theirs who had the misfortune to be mad or drunk. The last thought, however, was an inspiration; though a very terrible one. Had it come to this, that the Vicar of Chuntsey must pretend to be mad or drunk? It had come to this.

"I walked along with the rest up the deserted road, imitating and keeping pace, as far as I could, with their rapid and yet lady-like step, until at length I saw a lamp-post and a policeman standing under it. I had made up my mind. Until we reached them, we were all equally demure and silent and swift. When we reached them I suddenly flung myself against the railings and roared out: 'Hooray! Hooray! Hooray! Rule Britannia! Get your 'air cut. Houp-la! Boo!' It was a condition of no little novelty for a man of my position.

"The constable instantly flashed his lantern on me, or the draggled, drunken old woman that was my travesty. 'Now then, mum,' he began gruffly.

" 'Come along quiet, or I'll eat your heart,' cried Sam in my ear hoarsely. 'Stop, or I'll flay you.' It was frightful to hear the words and see the neatly-shawled old spinster who whispered them.

"I yelled, and yelled—I was in for it now. I screamed comic refrains that vulgar young men had sung, to my regret, at our village concerts; I rolled to and fro like a ninepin about to fall.

" 'If you can't get your friend on quiet, ladies,' said the policeman, 'I shall have to take 'er up. Drunk and disorderly she is right enough.'

"I redoubled my efforts. I had not been brought up to this sort of thing; but I believe I eclipsed myself. Words that I did not know I had ever heard of seemed to come pouring out of my open mouth.

" 'When we get you past,' whispered Bill, 'you'll howl louder; you'll howl louder when we're burning your feet off.'

"I screamed in my terror those awful songs of joy. In all the nightmares that men have ever dreamed, there has never been anything so blighting and horrible as the faces of those five men, looking out of their poke-bonnets; the figures of district visitors with the faces of devils. I cannot think there is anything so heart-breaking in hell.

"For a sickening instant I thought that the bustle of my companions and the perfect respectability of all our dresses would overcome the policeman and induce him to let us pass. He wavered, so far as one can describe anything so solid as a policeman as wavering. I lurched suddenly forward and ran my head into his chest, calling out (if I remember correctly), 'Oh, crikey, blimy, Bill.' It was at that moment that I remembered most clearly that I was the Vicar of Chuntsey, in Essex.

"My desperate coup saved me. The policeman had me hard by the back of the neck.

" 'You come along with me," he began, but Bill cut in with his perfect imitation of a lady's finnicking voice.'

" 'Oh, pray, constable, don't make a disturbance with our poor friend. We will get her quietly home. She does drink too much, but she is quite a lady—only eccentric.'

" 'She butted me in the stomach,' said the policeman, briefly.

" 'Eccentricities of genius,' said Sam earnestly.

" 'Pray let me take her home,' reiterated Bill, in the resumed character of Miss James, 'she wants looking after.'

" 'She does,' said the policeman, 'but I'll look after her.'

" 'That's no good,' cried Bill, feverishly. 'She wants her friends. She wants a particular medicine we've got.'

" 'Yes,' assented Miss Mowbray, with excitement, 'no other medicine any good, constable. Complaint quite unique.'

" 'I'm all righ'. Cutchy, cutchy, coo!' remarked, to his eternal shame, the Vicar of Chuntsey.

" 'Look here, ladies,' said the constable sternly, 'I don't like the eccentricity of your friend, and I don't like 'er songs, or 'er 'ead in my stomach. And now I come to think of it, I don't like the looks of you. I've seen many as quiet-dressed as you as was wrong 'uns. Who are you?'

" 'We've not our cards with us,' said Miss Mowbray, with indescribable dignity. 'Nor do we see why we should be insulted by any

Jack-in-office who chooses to be rude to ladies, when he is paid to protect them. If you choose to take advantage of the weakness of our unfortunate friend, no doubt you are legally entitled to take her. But if you fancy you have any legal right to bully us, you will find yourself in the wrong box.'

"The truth and dignity of this staggered the policeman for a moment. Under cover of their advantage my five persecutors turned for an instant on me faces like faces of the damned and then swished off into the darkness. When the constable first turned his lantern and his suspicions on to them, I had seen the telegraphic look flash from face to face saying that only retreat was possible now.

"By this time I was sinking slowly to the pavement, in a state of acute reflection. So long as the ruffians were with me, I dared not quit the rôle of drunkard. For if I had begun to talk reasonably and explain the real case, the officer would merely have thought that I was slightly recovered and would have put me in charge of my friends. Now, however, if I liked I might safely undeceive him.

"But I confess I did not like. The chances of life are many, and it may doubtless sometimes lie in the narrow path of duty for a clergyman of the Church of England to pretend to be a drunken old woman; but such necessities are, I imagine, sufficiently rare to appear to many improbable. Suppose the story got about that I had pretended to be drunk. Suppose people did not all think it was pretence!

"I lurched up, the policeman half-lifting me. I went along weakly and quietly for about a hundred yards. The officer evidently thought that I was too sleepy and feeble to effect an escape, and so held me lightly and easily enough. Past one turning, two turnings, three turnings, four turnings, he trailed me with him, a limp and slow and reluctant figure. At the fourth turning, I suddenly broke from his hand and tore down the street like a maddened stag. He was unprepared, he was heavy, and it was dark. I ran and ran and ran, and in five minutes' running, found I was gaining. In half an hour I was out in the fields under the holy and blessed stars, where I tore off my accursed shawl and bonnet and buried them in clean earth."

The old gentleman had finished his story and leant back in his chair. Both the matter and the manner of his narration had, as time went on, impressed me favourably. He was an old duffer and pedant, but behind these things he was a country-bred man and gentleman, and had showed courage and a sporting instinct in the hour of desperation. He had told his story with many quaint formalities of diction, but also with a very convincing realism.

"And now——" I began.

"And now," said Shorter, leaning forward again with something like servile energy, "and now, Mr. Swinburne, what about that unhappy man Hawker? I cannot tell what those men meant, or how far what they said was real. But surely there is danger. I cannot go to the police, for reasons that you perceive. Among other things, they wouldn't believe me. What is to be done?"

I took out my watch. It was already half-past twelve.

"My friend Basil Grant," I said, "is the best man we can go to. He and I were to have gone to the same dinner to-night; but he will just have come back by now. Have you any objection to taking a cab?"

"Not at all," he replied, rising politely, and gathering up his absurd plaid shawl.

A rattle in a hansom brought us underneath the sombre pile of workmen's flats in Lambeth which Grant inhabited; a climb up a wearisome wooden staircase brought us to his garret. When I entered that wooden and scrappy interior, the white gleam of Basil's shirt-front and the lustre of his fur coat flung on the wooden settle, struck me as a contrast. He was drinking a glass of wine before retiring. I was right; he had come back from the dinner-party.

He listened to the repetition of the story of the Rev. Ellis Shorter with the genuine simplicity and respect which he never failed to exhibit in dealing with any human being. When it was over he said simply:

"Do you know a man named Captain Fraser?"

I was so startled at this totally irrelevant reference to the worthy collector of chimpanzees with whom I ought to have dined that evening, that I glanced sharply at Grant. The result was that I did not look at Mr. Shorter. I only heard him answer, in his most nervous tone, "No."

Basil, however, seemed to find something very curious about his answer or his demeanour generally, for he kept his big blue eyes fixed on the old clergyman, and though the eyes were quite quiet they stood out more and more from his head.

"You are quite sure, Mr. Shorter," he repeated, "that you don't know Captain Fraser?"

"Quite," answered the vicar, and I was certainly puzzled to find him returning so much to the timidity, not to say the demoralisation of his tone when he first entered my presence.

Basil sprang smartly to his feet.

“ *‘I tore off my accursed shawl and bonnet’* ”

"Then our course is clear," he said. "You have not even begun your investigation, my dear Mr. Shorter; the first thing for us to do is to go together to see Captain Fraser."

"When?" asked the clergyman, stammering.

"Now," said Basil, putting one arm in his fur coat.

The old clergyman rose to his feet, quaking all over.

"I really do not think that it is necessary," he said.

Basil took his arm out of the fur coat, threw it over the chair again, and put his hands in his pockets.

"Oh," he said, with emphasis. "Oh—you don't think it necessary; then," and he added the words with great clearness and deliberation, "then, Mr. Ellis Shorter, I can only say that I would like to see you without your whiskers."

And at these words I also rose to my feet, for the great tragedy of my life had come. Splendid and exciting as life was in continual contact with an intellect like Basil's, I had always the feeling that that splendour and excitement were on the borderland of sanity. He lived perpetually near the vision of the reason of things which makes men lose their reason. And I felt of his insanity as men feel of the death of friends with heart disease. It might come anywhere, in a field, in a hansom cab, looking at a sunset, smoking a cigarette. It had come now. At the very moment of delivering a judgment for the salvation of a fellow creature, Basil Grant had gone mad.

"Your whiskers," he cried, advancing with blazing eyes. "Give me your whiskers. And your bald head."

The old vicar naturally retreated a step or two. I stepped between.

"Sit down, Basil," I implored, "you're a little excited. Finish your wine."

"Whiskers," he answered sternly, "whiskers."

And with that he made a dash at the old gentleman, who made a dash for the door, but was intercepted. And then, before I knew where I was, the quiet room was turned into something between a pantomime and a pandemonium by those two. Chairs were flung over with a crash, tables were vaulted with a noise like thunder, screens were smashed, crockery scattered in smithereens, and still Basil Grant bounded and bellowed after the Rev. Ellis Shorter.

And now I began to perceive something else, which added the last half-witted touch to my mystification. The Rev. Ellis Shorter, of Chuntsey, in Essex, was by no means behaving as I had previously noticed him to behave, or, as considering his age and station I should have expected him to behave. His power of dodging, leaping, and

" *'Whiskers,' he answered sternly, 'whiskers'* "

fighting would have been amazing in a lad of seventeen, and in this doddering old vicar looked like a sort of farcical fairy-tale. Moreover, he did not seem to be so much astonished as I had thought. There was even a look of something like enjoyment in his eyes; so there was in the eye of Basil. In fact, the unintelligible truth must be told. They were both laughing.

At length Shorter was cornered.

"Come, come, Mr. Grant," he panted, "you can't do anything to me. It's quite legal. And it doesn't do any one the least harm. It's only a social fiction. A result of our complex society, Mr. Grant."

"I don't blame you, my man," said Basil coolly. "But I want your whiskers. And your bald head. Do they belong to Captain Fraser?"

"No, no," said Mr. Shorter, laughing, "we provide them ourselves. They don't belong to Captain Fraser."

"What the deuce does all this mean?" I almost screamed. "Are you all in an infernal nightmare? Why should Mr. Shorter's bald head belong to Captain Fraser? How could it? What the deuce has Captain Fraser to do with the affair? What is the matter with him? You dined with him, Basil."

"No," said Grant, "I didn't."

"Didn't you go to Mrs. Thornton's dinner party?" I asked, staring. "Why not?"

"Well," said Basil, with a slow and singular smile, "the fact is I was detained by a visitor. I have him as a point of fact, in my bedroom."

"In your bedroom?" I repeated; but my imagination had reached that point when he might have said in his coal scuttle or his waistcoat pocket.

Grant stepped to the door of an inner room, flung it open, and walked in. Then he came out again with the last of the bodily wonders of that wild night. He introduced into the sitting-room, in an apologetic manner, and by the nape of the neck, a limp clergyman with a bald head, white whiskers and a plaid shawl.

"Sit down, gentlemen," cried Grant, striking his hands heartily. "Sit down all of you and have a glass of wine. As you say, there is no harm in it, and if Captain Fraser had simply dropped me a hint I could have saved him from dropping a good sum of money. Not that you would have liked that, eh?"

The two duplicate clergymen, who were sipping their Burgundy with two duplicate grins, laughed heartily at this, and one of them carelessly pulled off his whiskers and laid them on the table.

"Basil," I said, "if you are my friend, save me. What is all this?"

He laughed again.

"Only another addition, Cherub, to your collection of Queer Trades. These two gentlemen (whose health I have now the pleasure of drinking) are Professional Detainers."

"And what on earth's that?" I asked.

"It's really very simple, Mr. Swinburne," began he who had once been the Rev. Ellis Shorter, of Chuntsey, in Essex; and it gave me a shock indescribable to hear out of that pompous and familiar form come no longer its own pompous and familiar voice, but the brisk sharp tones of a young city man. "It is really nothing very important. We are paid by our clients to detain in conversation, on some harmless pretext, people whom they want out of the way for a few hours. And Captain Fraser——" and with that he hesitated and smiled.

Basil smiled also. He intervened.

"The fact is that Captain Fraser, who is one of my best friends, wanted us both out of the way very much. He is sailing to-night for East Africa, and the lady with whom we were all to have dined is—er—what is I believe described as 'the romance of his life.' He wanted that two hours with her, and employed these two reverend gentlemen to detain us at our houses so as to let him have the field to himself."

"And of course," said the late Mr. Shorter, apologetically to me, "as I had to keep a gentleman at home from keeping an appointment with a lady, I had to come with something rather hot and strong—rather urgent. It wouldn't have done to have been tame."

"Oh," I said, "I acquit you of tameness."

"Thank you, sir," said the man, respectfully, "always very grateful for any recommendation, sir."

The other man idly pushed back his artificial bald head, revealing close red hair, and spoke dreamily, perhaps under the influence of Basil's admirable Burgundy.

"It's wonderful how common it's getting, gentlemen. Our office is busy from morning till night. I've no doubt you've often knocked up against us before. You just take notice. When an old bachelor goes on boring you with hunting stories, when you're burning to be introduced to somebody, he's from our bureau. When a lady calls on parish work and stops hours, just when you wanted to go to the Robinsons', she's from our bureau. The Robinson hand, sir, may be darkly seen."

"There is one thing I don't understand," I said. "Why you are both vicars."

A shade crossed the brow of the temporary incumbent of Chuntsey, in Essex.

"That may have been a mistake, sir," he said. "But it was not our fault. It was all the munificence of Captain Fraser. He requested that the highest price and talent on our tariff should be employed to detain you gentlemen. Now the highest payment in our office goes to those who impersonate vicars, as being the most respectable and more of a strain. We are paid five guineas a visit. We have had the good fortune to satisfy the firm with our work; and we are now permanently vicars. Before that we had two years as colonels, the next in our scale. Colonels are four guineas."

"We are now permanently vicars"

IV. THE SINGULAR SPECULATION OF THE HOUSE-AGENT

LIEUTENANT DRUMMOND Keith was a man about whom conversation always burst like a thunderstorm the moment he left the room. This arose from many separate touches about him. He was a light, loose person, who wore light, loose clothes, generally white, as if he were in the tropics; he was lean and graceful, like a panther, and he had restless black eyes.

He was very impecunious. He had one of the habits of the poor in a degree so exaggerated as immeasurably to eclipse the most miserable of the unemployed: I mean the habit of continual change of lodgings. There are inland tracts of London where, in the very heart of artificial civilisation, humanity has almost become nomadic once more. But in that restless interior there was no ragged tramp so restless as the elegant officer in the loose white clothes. He had shot a great many things in his time, to judge from his conversation, from partridges to elephants, but his slangier acquaintances were of opinion that "the moon" had been not unfrequently amid the victims of his victorious rifle. The phrase is a fine one, and suggests a mystic, elvish, nocturnal hunting.

He carried from house to house and from parish to parish a kit which consisted practically of five articles. Two odd-looking, large-bladed spears, tied together, the weapons, I suppose, of some savage tribe, a green umbrella, a huge and tattered copy of the "Pickwick Papers," a big game rifle, and a large sealed jar of some unholy Oriental wine. These always went into every new lodging, even for one night; and they went in quite undisguised, tied up in wisps of string or straw, to the delight of the poetic gutter boys in the little grey streets.

"They went in quite undisguised, tied up in wisps of string or straw, to the delight of the poetic gutter boys"

I had forgotten to mention that he always carried also his old regimental sword. But this raised another odd question about him. Slim and active as he was, he was no longer very young. His hair, indeed, was quite grey, though his rather wild almost Italian moustache retained its blackness, and his face was careworn under its almost Italian gaiety. To find a middle-aged man who has left the army at the primitive rank of lieutenant is unusual and not necessarily encouraging. With the more cautious and solid this fact, like his endless flitting, did the mysterious gentleman no good.

Lastly, he was a man who told the kind of adventures which win a man admiration, but not respect. They came out of queer places, where a good man would scarcely find himself, out of opium dens and gambling hells; they had the heat of the thieves' kitchens or smelled of a strange smoke from cannibal incantations. These are the kind of stories which discredit a person almost equally whether they are believed or no. If Keith's tales were false he was a liar; if they were true he had had, at any rate, every opportunity of being a scamp.

He had just left the room in which I sat with Basil Grant and his brother Rupert, the voluble amateur detective. And as I say was invariably the case, we were all talking about him. Rupert Grant was a clever young fellow, but he had that tendency which youth and cleverness, when sharply combined, so often produce, a somewhat extravagant scepticism. He saw doubt and guilt everywhere, and it was meat and drink to him. I had often got irritated with this boyish incredulity of his, but on this particular occasion I am bound to say that I thought him so obviously right that I was astounded at Basil's opposing him, however banteringly.

I could swallow a good deal, being naturally of a simple turn, but I could not swallow Lieutenant Keith's autobiography.

"You don't seriously mean, Basil," I said, "that you think that that fellow really did go as a stowaway with Nansen and pretend to be the Mad Mullah and——"

"He has one fault," said Basil, thoughtfully, "or virtue, as you may happen to regard it. He tells the truth in too exact and bald a style; he is too veracious."

"Oh! if you are going to be paradoxical," said Rupert contemptuously, "be a bit funnier than that. Say, for instance, that he has lived all his life in one ancestral manor."

"No, he's extremely fond of change of scene," replied Basil dispassionately, "and of living in odd places. That doesn't prevent his chief trait being verbal exactitude. What you people don't understand is that telling a thing crudely and coarsely as it happened makes it sound frightfully strange. The sort of things Keith recounts are not the sort of things that a man would make up to cover himself with honour; they are too absurd. But they are the sort of things that a man would do if he were sufficiently filled with the soul of skylarking."

"So far from paradox," said his brother, with something rather like a sneer, "you seem to be going in for journalese proverbs. Do you believe that truth is stranger than fiction?"

"Truth must of necessity be stranger than fiction," said Basil placidly. "For fiction is the creation of the human mind, and therefore is congenial to it."

"Well, your lieutenant's truth is stranger, if it is truth, than anything I ever heard of," said Rupert, relapsing into flippancy. "Do you, on your soul, believe in all that about the shark and the camera?"

"I believe Keith's words," answered the other. "He is an honest man."

"I should like to question a regiment of his landladies," said Rupert cynically.

"I must say, I think you can hardly regard him as unimpeachable merely in himself," I said mildly; "his mode of life——"

Before I could complete the sentence the door was flung open and Drummond Keith appeared again on the threshold, his white Panama on his head.

"I say, Grant," he said, knocking off his cigarette ash against the door, "I've got no money in the world till next April. Could you lend me a hundred pounds? There's a good chap."

Rupert and I looked at each other in an ironical silence. Basil, who was sitting by his desk, swung the chair round idly on its screw and picked up a quill-pen.

"Shall I cross it?" he asked, opening a cheque-book.

"Really," began Rupert, with a rather nervous loudness, "since Lieutenant Keith has seen fit to make this suggestion to Basil before his family, I——"

"Here you are, Ugly," said Basil, fluttering a cheque in the direction of the quite nonchalant officer. "Are you in a hurry?"

"Yes," replied Keith, in a rather abrupt way. "As a matter of fact I want it now. I want to see my—er—business man."

Rupert was eyeing him sarcastically, and I could see that it was on the tip of his tongue to say, inquiringly, "Receiver of stolen goods, perhaps." What he did say was:

"A business man? That's rather a general description, Lieutenant Keith."

Keith looked at him sharply, and then said, with something rather like ill-temper:

"He's a thingum-my-bob, a house-agent, say. I'm going to see him."

"Oh, you're going to see a house-agent, are you?" said Rupert Grant grimly. "Do you know, Mr. Keith, I think I should very much like to go with you?"

Basil shook with his soundless laughter. Lieutenant Keith started a little; his brow blackened sharply.

"I beg your pardon," he said. "What did you say?"

Rupert's face had been growing from stage to stage of ferocious irony, and he answered:

"I was saying that I wondered whether you would mind our strolling along with you to this house-agent's."

The visitor swung his stick with a sudden whirling violence.

"Oh, in God's name, come to my house-agent's! Come to my bedroom. Look under my bed. Examine my dust-bin. Come along!" And with a furious energy which took away our breath he banged his way out of the room.

Rupert Grant, his restless blue eyes dancing with his detective excitement, soon shouldered alongside him, talking to him with that transparent camaraderie which he imagined to be appropriate from the disguised policeman to the disguised criminal. His interpretation was certainly corroborated by one particular detail, the unmistakable unrest, annoyance, and nervousness of the man with whom he walked. Basil and I tramped behind, and it was not necessary for us to tell each other that we had both noticed this.

Lieutenant Drummond Keith led us through very extraordinary and unpromising neighbourhoods in the search for his remarkable house-agent. Neither of the brothers Grant failed to notice this fact. As the streets grew closer and more crooked and the roofs lower and the gutters grosser with mud, a darker curiosity deepened on the brows of Basil, and the figure of Rupert seen from behind seemed to fill the street with a gigantic swagger of success. At length, at the end of the fourth or fifth lean grey street in that sterile district we came suddenly to a halt, the mysterious lieutenant looking once more about him with a sort of sulky desperation. Above a row of shutters and a door, all indescribably dingy in appearance and in size scarce sufficient even for a penny toyshop, ran the inscription: "P. Montmorency, House-Agent."

"Our eyes were fixed where his were fixed, upon something on the counter. It was a ferret"

"This is the office of which I spoke," said Keith, in a cutting voice. "Will you wait here a moment, or does your astonishing tenderness about my welfare lead you to wish to overhear everything I have to say to my business adviser?"

Rupert's face was white and shaking with excitement; nothing on earth would have induced him now to have abandoned his prey.

"If you will excuse me," he said, clenching his hands behind his back, "I think I should feel myself justified in——"

"Oh! Come along in," exploded the lieutenant. He made the same gesture of savage surrender. And he slammed into the office, the rest of us at his heels.

P. Montmorency, house-agent, was a solitary old gentleman sitting behind a bare brown counter. He had an egglike head, froglike jaws, and a grey hairy fringe of aureole round the lower part of his face; the whole combined with a reddish, aquiline nose. He wore a shabby black frock coat, a sort of semiclerical tie worn at a very unclerical angle, and looked, generally speaking, about as unlike a house-agent as anything could look, short of something like a sandwich-man or a Scotch Highlander.

We stood inside the room for fully forty seconds, and the odd old gentleman did not look at us. Neither, to tell the truth, odd as he was, did we look at him. Our eyes were fixed, where his were fixed, upon something that was crawling about on the counter in front of him. It was a ferret.

The silence was broken by Rupert Grant. He spoke in that sweet and steely voice which he reserved for great occasions and practised for hours together in his bedroom. He said:

"Mr. Montmorency, I think?"

The old gentleman started, lifted his eyes with a bland bewilderment, picked up the ferret by the neck, stuffed it alive into his trousers pocket, smiled apologetically, and said:

"Sir."

"You are a house-agent, are you not?" asked Rupert.

To the delight of that criminal investigator, Mr. Montmorency's eyes wandered unquietly towards Lieutenant Keith, the only man present that he knew.

"A house-agent," cried Rupert again, bringing out the word as if it were "burglar."

"Yes . . . oh, yes," said the man, with a quavering and almost coquettish smile. "I am a house-agent . . . oh, yes."

"Well, I think," said Rupert, with a sardonic sleekness, "that Lieutenant Keith wants to speak to you. We have come in by his request."

Lieutenant Keith was lowering gloomily, and now he spoke.

"I have come, Mr. Montmorency, about that house of mine."

"Yes, sir," said Montmorency, spreading his fingers on the flat counter. "It's all ready, sir. I've attended to all your suggestions—er—about the br——"

"Right," cried Keith, cutting the word short with the startling neatness of a gunshot. "We needn't bother about all that. If you've done what I told you, all right."

And he turned sharply towards the door.

Mr. Montmorency, house-agent, presented a picture of pathos. After stammering a moment he said: "Excuse me . . . Mr. Keith . . . there was another matter . . . about which I wasn't quite sure. I tried to get all the heating apparatus possible under the circumstances . . . but in winter . . . at that elevation . . ."

"Can't expect much, eh?" said the lieutenant, cutting in with the same sudden skill. "No, of course not. That's all right, Montmorency. There can't be any more difficulties," and he put his hand on the handle of the door.

"I think," said Rupert Grant, with a satanic suavity, "that Mr. Montmorency has something further to say to you, lieutenant."

"Only," said the house-agent, in desperation, "what about the birds?"

"I beg your pardon," said Rupert, in a general blank.

"What about the birds?" said the house-agent, doggedly.

Basil, who had remained throughout the proceedings in a state of Napoleonic calm, which might be more accurately described as a state of Napoleonic stupidity, suddenly lifted his leonine head.

"Before you go, Lieutenant Keith," he said. "Come now. Really, what about the birds?"

"I'll take care of them," said Lieutenant Keith, still with his long back turned to us; "they sha'n't suffer."

"Thank you, sir, thank you," cried the incomprehensible house-agent, with an air of ecstacy. "You'll excuse my concern, sir. You know I'm wild on wild animals. I'm as wild as any of them on that. Thank you, sir, but there's another thing . . ."

The lieutenant, with his back turned to us, exploded with an indescribable laugh and swung round to face us. It was a laugh, the purport of which was direct and essential, and yet which one cannot exactly express. As near as it said anything, verbally speaking, it said: "Well, if you must spoil it, you must. But you don't know what you're spoiling."

"There is another thing," continued Mr. Montmorency weakly. "Of course if you don't want to be visited you'll paint the house green, but——"

"Green!" shouted Keith. "Green! Let it be green or nothing. I won't have a house of another colour. Green!" and before we could realise anything the door had banged between us and the street.

Rupert Grant seemed to take a little time to collect himself; but he spoke before the echoes of the door died away.

"Your client, Lieutenant Keith, appears somewhat excited," he said. "What is the matter with him? Is he unwell?"

"Oh, I should think not," said Mr. Montmorency, in some confusion. "The negotiations have been somewhat difficult—the house is rather——"

"Green," said Rupert calmly. "That appears to be a very important point. It must be rather green. May I ask you, Mr. Montmorency, before I rejoin my companion outside, whether, in your business, it is usual to ask for houses by their colour? Do clients write to a house-agent asking for a pink house or a blue house? Or, to take another instance, for a green house?"

"Only," said Montmorency, trembling, "only to be inconspicuous."

Rupert had his ruthless smile. "Can you tell me any place on earth in which a green house would be inconspicuous?"

The house-agent was fidgeting nervously in his pocket. Slowly drawing out a couple of lizards and leaving them to run on the counter, he said:

"No; I can't."

"You can't suggest an explanation?"

"No," said Mr. Montmorency, rising slowly and yet in such a way as to suggest a sudden situation. "I can't. And may I, as a busy man, be excused if I ask you, gentlemen, if you have any demand to make of me in connection with my business. What kind of house would you desire me to get for you, sir?"

He opened his blank blue eyes on Rupert, who seemed for the second staggered. Then he recovered himself with perfect common sense and answered:

"The lieutenant . . . swung round to face us"

"I am sorry, Mr. Montmorency. The fascination of your remarks has unduly delayed us from joining our friend outside. Pray excuse my apparent impertinence."

"Not at all, sir," said the house-agent, taking a South American spider idly from his waistcoat pocket and letting it climb up the slope of his desk. "Not at all, sir. I hope you will favour me again."

Rupert Grant dashed out of the office in a gust of anger, anxious to face Lieutenant Keith. He was gone. The dull, starlit street was deserted.

"What do you say now?" cried Rupert to his brother. His brother said nothing now.

We all three strode down the street in silence, Rupert feverish, myself dazed, Basil, to all appearance, merely dull. We walked through grey street after grey street, turning corners, traversing squares, scarcely meeting any one, except occasional drunken knots of two or three.

In one small street, however, the knots of two or three began abruptly to thicken into knots of five or six and then into great groups and then into a crowd. The crowd was stirring very slightly. But any one with a knowledge of the eternal populace knows that if the outside rim of a crowd stirs ever so slightly it means that there is madness in the heart and core of the mob. It soon became evident that something really important had happened in the centre of this excitement. We wormed our way to the front, with the cunning which is known only to cockneys, and once there we soon learned the nature of the difficulty. There had been a brawl concerned with some six men, and one of them lay almost dead on the stones of the street. Of the other four, all interesting matters were, as far as we were concerned, swallowed up in one stupendous fact. One of the four survivors of the brutal and perhaps fatal scuffle was the immaculate Lieutenant Keith, his clothes torn to ribbons, his eyes blazing, blood on his knuckles. One other thing, however, pointed at him in a worse manner. A short sword, or very long knife, had been drawn out of his elegant walking-stick, and lay in front of him upon the stones. It did not, however, appear to be bloody.

The police had already pushed into the centre with their ponderous omnipotence, and even as they did so, Rupert Grant sprang forward with his incontrollable and intolerable secret.

"That is the man, constable," he shouted, pointing at the battered lieutenant. "He is a suspicious character. He did the murder."

"There's been no murder done, sir," said the policeman, with his automatic civility. "The poor man's only hurt. I shall only be able to take the names and addresses of the men in the scuffle and have a good eye kept on them."

"Have a good eye kept on that one," said Rupert, pale to the lips, and pointing to the ragged Keith.

"All right, sir," said the policeman, unemotionally, and went the round of the people present, collecting the addresses. When he had completed his task the dusk had fallen and most of the people not immediately connected with the examination had gone away. He still found, however, one eager-faced stranger lingering on the outskirts of the affair. It was Rupert Grant.

"Constable," he said, "I have a very particular reason for asking you a question. Would you mind telling me whether that military fellow who dropped his sword-stick in the row gave you an address or not?"

"Yes, sir," said the policeman, after a reflective pause; "yes, he gave me his address."

"My name is Rupert Grant," said that individual, with some pomp. "I have assisted the police on more than one occasion. I wonder whether you would tell me, as a special favour, what address?"

The constable looked at him.

"Yes," he said slowly, "if you like. His address is: 'The Elms, Buxton Common, near Purley, Surrey.' "

"Thank you," said Rupert, and ran home through the gathering night as fast as his legs could carry him, repeating the address to himself.

Rupert Grant generally came down late in a rather lordly way to breakfast; he contrived, I don't know how, to achieve always the attitude of the indulged younger brother. Next morning, however, when Basil and I came down we found him ready and restless.

"Well," he said, sharply to his brother almost before we sat down to the meal. "What do you think of your Drummond Keith now?"

"What do I think of him?" inquired Basil slowly. "I don't think anything of him."

"I'm glad to hear it," said Rupert, buttering his toast with an energy that was somewhat exultant. "I thought you'd come round to my view, but I own I was startled at your not seeing it from the beginning. The man is a translucent liar and knave."

"I think," said Basil, in the same heavy monotone as before, "that I did not make myself clear. When I said that I thought nothing of him I meant grammatically what I said. I meant that I did not think about him; that he did not occupy my mind. You, however, seem to me to think a lot of him, since you think him a knave. I should say he was glaringly good myself."

"I sometimes think you talk paradox for its own sake," said Rupert, breaking an egg with unnecessary sharpness. "What the deuce is the sense of it? Here's a man whose original position was, by our common agreement, dubious. He's a wanderer, a teller of tall tales, a man who doesn't conceal his acquaintance with all the blackest and bloodiest scenes on earth. We take the trouble to follow him to one of his appointments, and if ever two human beings were plotting together and lying to every one else, he and that impossible house-agent were doing it. We followed him home, and the very same night he is in the thick of a fatal, or nearly fatal, brawl, in which he is the only man armed. Really, if this is being glaringly good, I must confess that the glare does not dazzle me."

Basil was quite unmoved. "I admit his moral goodness is of a certain kind, a quaint, perhaps a casual kind. He is very fond of change and experiment. But all the points you so ingeniously make against him are mere coincidence or special pleading. It's true he didn't want to talk about his house business in front of us. No man would. It's true that he carries a sword-stick. Any man might. It's true he drew it in the shock of a street fight. Any man would. But there's nothing really dubious in all this. There's nothing to confirm——"

As he spoke a knock came at the door.

"If you please, sir," said the landlady, with an alarmed air, "there's a policeman wants to see you."

"Show him in," said Basil, amid the blank silence.

The heavy, handsome constable who appeared at the door spoke almost as soon as he appeared there.

"I think one of you gentlemen," he said, curtly but respectfully, "was present at the affair in Copper Street last night, and drew my attention very strongly to a particular man."

Rupert half rose from his chair, with eyes like diamonds, but the constable went on calmly, referring to a paper.

"A young man with grey hair. Had light grey clothes, very good, but torn in the struggle. Gave his name as Drummond Keith."

"This is amusing," said Basil, laughing. "I was in the very act of clearing that poor officer's character of rather fanciful aspersions. What about him?"

"Well, sir," said the constable, "I took all the men's addresses and had them watched. It wasn't serious enough to do more than that. All the other addresses are all right. But this man Keith gave a false address. The place doesn't exist."

The breakfast table was nearly flung over as Rupert sprang up, slapping both his thighs.

"Well, by all that's good," he cried. "This is a sign from heaven."

"It's certainly very extraordinary," said Basil quietly, with knitted brows. "It's odd the fellow should have given a false address, considering he was perfectly innocent in the——"

"Oh, you jolly old early Christian duffer," cried Rupert, in a sort of rapture, "I don't wonder you couldn't be a judge. You think every one as good as yourself. Isn't the thing plain enough now? A doubtful acquaintance; rowdy stories, a most suspicious conversation, mean streets, a concealed knife, a man nearly killed, and, finally, a false address. That's what we call glaring goodness."

"It's certainly very extraordinary," repeated Basil. And he strolled moodily about the room. Then he said: "You are quite sure, constable, that there's no mistake? You got the address right, and the police have really gone to it and found it was a fraud?"

"It was very simple, sir," said the policeman, chuckling. "The place he named was a well-known common quite near London, and our people were down there this morning before any of you were awake. And there's no such house. In fact, there are hardly any houses at all. Though it is so near London, it's a blank moor with hardly five trees on it, to say nothing of Christians. Oh, no, sir, the address was a fraud right enough. He was a clever rascal, and chose one of those scraps of lost England that people know nothing about. Nobody could say off-hand that there was not a particular house dropped somewhere about the heath. But as a fact, there isn't."

Basil's face during this sensible speech had been growing darker and darker with a sort of desperate sagacity. He was cornered almost for the first time since I had known him; and to tell the truth I rather wondered at the almost childish obstinacy which kept him so close to his original prejudice in favour of the wildly questionable lieutenant. At length he said:

"You really searched the common? And the address was really not known in the district—by the way, what was the address?"

The constable selected one of his slips of paper and consulted it, but before he could speak Rupert Grant, who was leaning in the window in a perfect posture of the quiet and triumphant detective, struck in with the sharp and suave voice he loved so much to use.

"Why, I can tell you that, Basil," he said graciously, as he idly plucked leaves from a plant in the window. "I took the precaution to get this man's address from the constable last night."

"And what was it?" asked his brother gruffly.

"The constable will correct me if I am wrong," said Rupert, looking sweetly at the ceiling. "It was 'The Elms, Buxton Common, near Purley, Surrey.' "

"Right, sir," said the policeman, laughing and folding up his papers.

There was a silence, and the blue eyes of Basil looked blindly for a few seconds into the void. Then his head fell back in his chair so suddenly that I started up, thinking him ill. But before I could move further his lips had flown apart (I can use no other phrase) and a peal of gigantic laughter struck and shook the ceiling—laughter that shook the laughter, laughter redoubled, laughter incurable, laughter that could not stop.

Two whole minutes afterwards it was still unended; Basil was ill with laughter; but still he laughed. The rest of us were by this time ill almost with terror.

"Excuse me," said the insane creature, getting at last to his feet. "I am awfully sorry. It is horribly rude. And stupid, too. And also unpractical, because we have not much time to lose if we're to get down to that place. The train service is confoundedly bad, as I happen to know. It's quite out of proportion to the comparatively small distance."

"Get down to that place?" I repeated blankly. "Get down to what place?"

"I have forgotten its name," said Basil vaguely, putting his hands in his pockets as he rose. "Something Common near Purley. Has any one got a time-table?"

"You don't seriously mean," cried Rupert, who had been staring in a sort of confusion of emotions. "You don't mean that you want to go to Buxton Common, do you? You can't mean that!"

"Why shouldn't I go to Buxton Common?" asked Basil, smiling.

"Why should you?" said his brother, catching hold again restlessly of the plant in the window and staring at the speaker.

"To find our friend, the lieutenant, of course," said Basil Grant. "I thought you wanted to find him?"

Rupert broke a branch brutally from the plant and flung it impatiently on the floor. "And in order to find him," he said, "you suggest the admirable expedient of going to the only place on the habitable earth where we know he can't be."

The constable and I could not avoid breaking into a kind of assenting laugh, and Rupert, who had family eloquence, was encouraged to go on with a reiterated gesture:

"He may be in Buckingham Palace; he may be sitting astride the cross of St. Paul's; he may be in jail (which I think most likely); he may be in the Great Wheel; he may be in my pantry; he may be in your store cupboard; but out of all the innumerable points of space, there is only one where he has just been systematically looked for and where we know that he is not to be found—and that, if I understand you rightly, is where you want us to go."

"Exactly," said Basil calmly, getting into his great coat; "I thought you might care to accompany me. If not, of course, make yourselves jolly here till I come back."

It is our nature always to follow vanishing things and value them if they really show a resolution to depart. We all followed Basil, and I cannot say why, except that he was a vanishing thing, that he vanished decisively with his great coat and his stick. Rupert ran after him with a considerable flurry of rationality.

"My dear chap," he cried, "do you really mean that you see any good in going down to this ridiculous scrub, where there is nothing but beaten tracks and a few twisted trees, simply because it was the first place that came into a rowdy lieutenant's head when he wanted to give a lying reference in a scrape?"

"Yes," said Basil, taking out his watch, "and, what's worse, we've lost the train."

He paused a moment and then added: "As a matter of fact, I think we may just as well go down later in the day. I have some writing to do, and I think you told me, Rupert, that you thought of going to the Dulwich Gallery. I was rather too impetuous. Very likely he wouldn't be in. But if we get down by the 5.15, which gets to Purley about 6,1 expect we shall just catch him."

"Catch him!" cried his brother, in a kind of final anger. "I wish we could. Where the deuce shall we catch him now?"

"I keep forgetting the name of the common," said Basil, as he buttoned up his coat. "The Elms—what is it? Buxton Common, near Purley. That's where we shall find him."

"But there is no such place," groaned Rupert; but he followed his brother downstairs.

We all followed him. We snatched our hats from the hat-stand and our sticks from the umbrella-stand; and why we followed him we did not and do not know. But we always followed him, whatever was the meaning of the fact, whatever was the nature of his mastery. And the strange thing was that we followed him the more completely the more nonsensical appeared the thing which he said. At bottom, I believe, if he had risen from our breakfast table and said, "I am going to find the Holy Pig with Ten Tails," we should have followed him to the end of the world.

I don't know whether this mystical feeling of mine about Basil on this occasion has got any of the dark and cloudy colour, so to speak, of the strange journey that we made the same evening. It was already very dense twilight when we struck southward from Purley. Suburbs and things on the London border may be, in most cases, commonplace and comfortable. But if ever by any chance they really are empty solitudes they are to the human spirit more desolate and dehumanised than any Yorkshire moors or Highland hills, because the suddenness with which the traveller drops into that silence has something about it as of evil elf-land. It seems to be one of the ragged suburbs of the cosmos half-forgotten by God—such a place was Buxton Common, near Purley.

There was certainly a sort of grey futility in the landscape itself. But it was enormously increased by the sense of grey futility in our expedition. The tracts of drab turf looked useless, the occasional wind-stricken trees looked useless, but we, the human beings, more useless than the hopeless turf or the idle trees. We were maniacs akin to the foolish landscape, for we were come to chase the wild goose which has led men and left men in bogs from the beginning. We were three dazed men under the captaincy of a madman going to look for a man whom we knew was not there in a house that had no existence. A livid sunset seemed to look at us with a sort of sickly smile before it died.

Basil went on in front with his coat collar turned up, looking in the gloom rather like a grotesque Napoleon. We crossed swell after swell of the windy common in increasing darkness and entire silence. Suddenly Basil stopped and turned to us, his hands in his pockets. Through the dusk I could just detect that he wore a broad grin as of comfortable success.

"Well," he cried, taking his heavily gloved hands out of his pockets and slapping them together, "here we are at last."

"Suddenly Basil stopped and turned to us, his hands in his pockets"

The wind swirled sadly over the homeless heath; two desolate elms rocked above us in the sky like shapeless clouds of grey. There was not a sign of man or beast to the sullen circle of the horizon, and in the midst of that wilderness Basil Grant stood rubbing his hands with the air of an innkeeper standing at an open door.

"How jolly it is," he cried, "to get back to civilisation. That notion that civilisation isn't poetical is a civilised delusion. Wait till you've really lost yourself in nature, among the devilish woodlands and the cruel flowers. Then you'll know that there's no star like the red star of man that he lights on his hearth-stone; no river like the red river of man, the good red wine, which you, Mr. Rupert Grant, if I have any knowledge of you, will be drinking in two or three minutes in enormous quantities."

Rupert and I exchanged glaces of fear. Basil went on heartily, as the wind died in the dreary trees.

"You'll find our host a much more simple kind of fellow in his own house. I did when I visited him when he lived in the cabin at Yarmouth, and again in the loft at the city warehouse. He's really a very good fellow. But his greatest virtue remains what I said originally."

"What do you mean?" I asked, finding his speech straying towards a sort of sanity. "What is his greatest virtue?"

"His greatest virtue," replied Basil, "is that he always tells the literal truth."

"Well, really," cried Rupert, stamping about between cold and anger, and slapping himself like a cabman, "he doesn't seem to have been very literal or truthful in this case, nor you either. Why the deuce, may I ask, have you brought us out to this infernal place?"

"He was too truthful, I confess," said Basil, leaning against the tree; "too hardly veracious, too severely accurate. He should have indulged in a little more suggestiveness and legitimate romance. But come, it's time we went in. We shall be late for dinner."

Rupert whispered to me with a white face:

"Is it a hallucination, do you think? Does he really fancy he sees a house?"

"I suppose so," I said. Then I added aloud, in what was meant to be a cheery and sensible voice, but which sounded in my ears almost as strange as the wind:

"Come, come, Basil, my dear fellow. Where do you want us to go?"

"Why, up here," cried Basil, and with a bound and a swing he was above our heads, swarming up the grey column of the colossal tree.

"Come up, all of you," he shouted out of the darkness, with the voice of a schoolboy. "Come up. You'll be late for dinner."

The two great elms stood so close together that there was hardly a yard anywhere, and in some places not more than a foot, between them. Thus occasional branches and even bosses and boles formed a series of footholds that almost amounted to a rude natural ladder. They must, I supposed, have been some sport of growth, Siamese twins of vegetation.

Why we did it I cannot think; perhaps, as I have said, the mystery of the waste and dark had brought out and made primary something wholly mystical in Basil's supremacy. But we only felt that there was a giant's staircase going somewhere, perhaps to the stars; and the victorious voice above called to us out of heaven. We hoisted ourselves up after him.

Half-way up some cold tongue of the night air struck and sobered me suddenly. The hypnotism of the madman above fell from me, and I saw the whole map of our silly actions as clearly as if it were printed. I saw three modern men in black coats who had begun with a perfectly sensible suspicion of a doubtful adventurer and who had ended, God knows how, half-way up a naked tree on a naked moorland, far from that adventurer and all his works, that adventurer who was at that moment, in all probability, laughing at us in some dirty Soho restaurant. He had plenty to laugh at us about, and no doubt he was laughing his loudest; but when I thought what his laughter would be if he knew where we were at that moment, I nearly let go of the tree and fell.

"Swinburne," said Rupert, suddenly, from above, "what are we doing? Let's get down again," and by the mere sound of his voice I knew that he too felt the shock of wakening to reality.

"We can't leave poor Basil," I said. "Can't you call to him or get hold of him by the leg?"

"He's too far ahead," answered Rupert; "he's nearly at the top of the beastly thing. Looking for Lieutenant Keith in the rooks' nests, I suppose."

We were ourselves by this time far on our frantic vertical journey. The mighty trunks were beginning to sway and shake slightly in the wind. Then I looked down and saw something which made me feel that we were far from the world in a sense and to a degree that I cannot easily describe. I saw that the almost straight lines of the tall elm trees diminished a little in perspective as they fell. I was used to seeing parallel lines taper towards the sky. But to see them taper towards the earth made me feel lost in space, like a falling star.

"Can nothing be done to stop Basil?" I called out.

"No," answered my fellow climber. "He's too far up. He must get to the top, and when he finds nothing but wind and leaves he may go sane again. Hark at him above there; you can just hear him talking to himself."

"Perhaps he's talking to us," I said.

"No," said Rupert, "he'd shout if he was. I've never known him to talk to himself before; I'm afraid he really is bad to-night; it's a known sign of the brain going."

"Yes," I said sadly, and listened. Basil's voice certainly was sounding above us, and not by any means in the rich and riotous tones in which he had hailed us before. He was speaking quietly, and laughing every now and then, up there among the leaves and stars.

After a silence mingled with this murmur, Rupert Grant suddenly said, "My God!" with a violent voice.

"What's the matter—are you hurt?" I cried alarmed.

"No. Listen to Basil," said the other in a very strange voice. "He's not talking to himself."

"Then he is talking to us," I cried.

"No," said Rupert simply, "he's talking to somebody else."

Great branches of the elm loaded with leaves swung about us in a sudden burst of wind, but when it died down I could still hear the conversational voice above. I could hear two voices.

Suddenly from aloft came Basil's boisterous hailing voice as before: "Come up, you fellows. Here's Lieutenant Keith."

And a second afterwards came the half-American voice we had heard in our chambers more than once. It called out:

"Happy to see you, gentlemen; pray come in."

Out of a hole in an enormous dark egg-shaped thing pendant in the branches like a wasp's nest, was protruding the pale face and fierce moustache of the lieutenant, his teeth shining with that slightly Southern air that belonged to him.

Somehow or other, stunned and speechless, we lifted ourselves heavily into the opening. We fell into the full glow of a lamp-lit, cushioned, tiny room, with a circular wall lined with books, a circular table, and a circular seat around it. At this table sat three people. One was Basil, who, in the instant after alighting there, had fallen into an attitude of marmoreal ease as if he had been there from boyhood; he was smoking a cigar with a slow pleasure. The second was Lieutenant Drummond Keith, who looked happy also, but feverish and doubtful compared with his granite guest. The third

"'Happy to see you, gentlemen; pray come in'"

was the little bald-headed house-agent with the wild whiskers, who called himself Montmorency. The spears, the green umbrella, and the cavalry sword hung in parallels on the wall. The sealed jar of strange wine was on the mantelpiece, the enormous rifle in the corner. In the middle of the table was a magnum of champagne. Glasses were already set for us.

The wind of the night roared far below us, like an ocean at the foot of a light-house. The room stirred slightly, as a cabin might in a mild sea.

Our glasses were filled, and we still sat there dazed and dumb. Then Basil spoke.

"You seem still a little doubtful, Rupert. Surely there is no further question about the cold veracity of our injured host."

"I don't quite grasp it all," said Rupert, blinking still in the sudden glare. "Lieutenant Keith said his address was——"

"It's really quite right, sir," said Keith, with an open smile. "The bobby asked me where I lived. And I said, quite truthfully, that I lived in the elms on Buxton Common, near Purley. So I do. This gentleman, Mr. Montmorency, whom I think you have met before, is an agent for houses of this kind. He has a special line in arboreal villas. It's being kept rather quiet at present, because the people who want these houses don't want them to get too common. But it's just the sort of thing that a fellow like myself, racketing about in all sorts of queer corners of London, naturally knocks up against."

"Are you really an agent for arboreal villas?" asked Rupert eagerly, recovering his ease with the romance of the reality.

Mr. Montmorency, in his embarrassment, fingered one of his pockets and nervously pulled out a snake, which crawled about the table.

"W-well, yes, sir," he said. "The fact was—er—my people wanted me very much to go into the house-agency business. But I never cared myself for anything but natural history and botany and things like that. My poor parents have been dead some years now, but—naturally I like to respect their wishes. And I thought somehow that an arboreal villa agency was a sort of—of compromise between being a botanist and being a house-agent."

Rupert could not help laughing. "Do you have much custom?" he asked.

"N-not much," replied Mr. Montmorency, and then he glanced at Keith, who was (I am convinced) his only client. "But what there is—very select."

" *'N-not much,' replied Mr. Montmorency, 'but what there is—very select'* "

"My dear friends," said Basil, puffing his cigar, "always remember two facts. The first is that though, when you are guessing about any one who is sane, the sanest thing is the most likely; when you are guessing about any one who is, like our host, insane, the maddest thing is the most likely. The second is to remember that very plain literal fact always seems fantastic. If Keith had taken a little brick box of a house in Clapham with nothing but railings in front of it and had written 'The Elms' over it, you wouldn't have thought there was anything fantastic about that. Simply because it was a great blaring, swaggering lie you would have believed it."

"Drink your wine, gentlemen," said Keith, laughing, "for this confounded wind will upset it."

We drank, and as we did so, although the hanging house, by a cunning mechanism, swung only slightly, we knew that the great head of the elm-tree swayed in the sky like a stricken thistle.

V. THE NOTICEABLE CONDUCT OF PROFESSOR CHADD

Basil Grant had comparatively few friends besides myself; yet he was the reverse of an unsociable man. He would talk to any one anywhere, and talk not only well but with perfectly genuine concern and enthusiasm for that person's affairs. He went through the world, as it were, as if he were always on the top of an omnibus or waiting for a train. Most of these chance acquaintances, of course, vanished into darkness out of his life. A few here and there got hooked on to him, so to speak, and became his lifelong intimates, but there was an accidental look about all of them as if they were windfalls, samples taken at random, goods fallen from a goods train or presents fished out of a bran-pie. One would be, let us say, a veterinary surgeon with the appearance of a jockey; another, a mild prebendary with a white beard and vague views; another a young captain in the Lancers, seemingly exactly like other captains in the Lancers; another, a small dentist from Fulham, in all reasonable certainty precisely like every other dentist from Fulham. Major Brown, small, dry, and dapper, was one of these; Basil had made his acquaintance over a discussion in a hotel cloak-room about the right hat, a discussion which reduced the little major almost to a kind of masculine hysterics, the compound of the selfishness of an old bachelor and the scrupulosity of an old maid. They had gone home in a cab together and then dined with each other twice a week until they died. I myself was another. I had met Grant while he was still a judge, on the balcony of the National Liberal Club, and exchanged a few words about the weather. Then we had talked for about half an hour about politics and God; for men always talk about the most important things to total strangers. It is because in the total stranger we perceive man himself; the image of God is not disguised by resemblances to an uncle or doubts of the wisdom of a moustache.

One of the most interesting of Basil's motley group of acquaintances was Professor Chadd. He was known to the ethnological world (which is a very interesting world, but a long way off this one) as the second greatest, if not the greatest, authority on the relations of savages to language. He was known to the neighbourhood of Hart Street, Bloomsbury, as a bearded man with a bald head, spectacles, and a patient face, the face of an unaccountable Nonconformist who had forgotten how to be angry. He went to and fro between the British Museum and a selection of blameless tea-shops, with an armful of books and a poor but honest umbrella. He was never seen without the books and the umbrella, and was supposed (by the lighter wits of the Persian MS. room) to go to bed with them in his little brick villa in the neighbourhood of Shepherd's Bush. There he lived with three sisters, ladies of solid goodness, but sinister demeanour. His life was happy, as are almost all the lives of methodical students, but one would not have called it exhilarating. His only hours of exhilaration occurred when his friend Basil Grant came into the house, late at night, a tornado of conversation.

Basil, though close on sixty, had moods of boisterous babyishness, and these seemed for some reason or other to descend upon him, particularly in the house of his studious and almost dingy friend. I can remember vividly (for I was acquainted with both parties and often dined with them) the gaiety of Grant on that particular evening when the strange calamity fell upon the professor. Professor Chadd was, like most of his particular class and type (the class that is at once academic and middle-class), a Radical of a solemn and old-fashioned type. Grant was a Radical himself, but he was that more discriminating and not uncommon type of Radical who passes most of his time in abusing the Radical party. Chadd had just contributed to a magazine an article called "Zulu Interests and the New Makango Frontier," in which a precise scientific report of his study of the customs of the people of T'Chaka was reinforced by a severe protest against certain interference with these customs both by the British and the Germans. He was sitting with the magazine in front of him, the lamplight shining on his spectacles, a wrinkle in his forehead, not of anger, but of perplexity, as Basil Grant strode up and down the room, shaking it with his voice, with his high spirits and his heavy tread.

"It's not your opinions that I object to, my esteemed Chadd," he was saying, "it's you. You are quite right to champion the Zulus, but for all that you do not sympathise with them. No doubt you know the Zulu way of cooking tomatoes and the Zulu prayer before blowing one's nose; but for all that you don't understand them as well as I do, who don't know an assegai from an alligator. You are more learned, Chadd, but I am more Zulu. Why is it that the jolly old barbarians of this earth are always championed by people who are their antithesis? Why is it? You are sagacious, you are benevolent, you are well informed, but, Chadd, you are not savage. Live no longer under that rosy illusion. Look in the glass. Ask your sisters. Consult the librarian of the British Museum. Look at this umbrella." And he held up that sad but still respectable article. "Look at it. For ten mortal years to my certain knowledge you have carried that object under your arm, and I have no sort of doubt that you carried it at the age of eight months, and it never occurred to you to give one wild yell and hurl it like a javelin—thus——"

And he sent the umbrella whizzing past the professor's bald head, so that it knocked over a pile of books with a crash and left a vase rocking.

Professor Chadd appeared totally unmoved, with his face still lifted to the lamp and the wrinkle cut in his forehead.

"Your mental processes," he said, "always go a little too fast. And they are stated without method. There is no kind of inconsistency"—and no words can convey the time he took to get to the end of the word—"between valuing the right of the aborigines to adhere to their stage in the evolutionary process, so long as they find it congenial and requisite to do so. There is, I say, no inconsistency between this concession which I have just described to you and the view that the evolutionary stage in question is, nevertheless, so far as we can form any estimate of values in the variety of cosmic processes, definable in some degree as an inferior evolutionary stage."

Nothing but his lips had moved as he spoke, and his glasses still shone like two pallid moons.

Grant was shaking with laughter as he watched him.

"True," he said, "there is no inconsistency, my son of the red spear. But there is a great deal of incompatibility of temper. I am very far from being certain that the Zulu is on an inferior evolutionary stage, whatever the blazes that may mean. I do not think there is anything stupid or ignorant about howling at the moon or being afraid of devils in the dark. It seems to me perfectly philosophical. Why should a man be thought a sort of idiot because he feels the mystery and peril of existence itself? Suppose, my dear Chadd, suppose it is we who are the idiots because we are not afraid of devils in the dark?"

Professor Chadd slit open a page of the magazine with a bone paper-knife and the intent reverence of the bibliophile.

"Beyond all question," he said, "it is a tenable hypothesis. I allude to the hypothesis which I understand you to entertain, that our civilisation is not or may not be an advance upon, and indeed (if I apprehend you) is, or may be a retrogression from states identical with or analogous to the state of the Zulus. Moreover, I shall be inclined to concede that such a proposition is of the nature, in some degree at least, of a primary proposition, and cannot adequately be argued, in the same sense, I mean, that the primary proposition of pessimism, or the primary proposition of the nonexistence of matter, cannot adequately be argued. But I do not conceive you to be under the impression that you have demonstrated anything more concerning this proposition than that it is tenable, which, after all, amounts to little more than the statement that it is not a contradiction in terms."

Basil threw a book at his head and took out a cigar.

"You don't understand," he said, "but, on the other hand, as a compensation, you don't mind smoking. Why you don't object to that disgustingly barbaric rite I can't think. I can only say that I began it when I began to be a Zulu, about the age of ten. What I maintained was that although you knew more about Zulus in the sense that you are a scientist, I know more about them in the sense that I am a savage. For instance, your theory of the origin of language, something about its having come from the formulated secret language of some individual creature, though you knocked me silly with facts and scholarship in its favour, still does not convince me, because I have a feeling that that is not the way that things happen. If you ask me why I think so I can only answer that I am a Zulu; and if you ask me (as you most certainly will) what is my definition of a Zulu, I can answer that also. He is one who has climbed a Sussex apple-tree at seven and been afraid of a ghost in an English lane."

"Your process of thought—" began the immovable Chadd, but his speech was interrupted. His sister, with that masculinity which always in such families concentrates in sisters, flung open the door with a rigid arm and said:

"James, Mr. Bingham of the British Museum wants to see you again."

The philosopher rose with a dazed look, which always indicates in such men the fact that they regard philosophy as a familiar thing, but practical life as a weird and unnerving vision, and walked dubiously out of the room.

"I hope you do not mind my being aware of it, Miss Chadd," said Basil Grant, "but I hear that the British Museum has recognised one of the men who have deserved well of their commonwealth. It is true, is it not, that Professor Chadd is likely to be made keeper of Asiatic manuscripts?"

The grim face of the spinster betrayed a great deal of pleasure and a great deal of pathos also. "I believe it's true," she said. "If it is, it will not only be great glory which women, I assure you, feel a great deal, but great relief, which they feel more; relief from worry from a lot of things. James's health has never been good, and while we are as poor as we are he had to do journalism and coaching, in addition to his own dreadful grinding notions and discoveries, which he loves more than man, woman, or child. I have often been afraid that unless something of this kind occurred we should really have to be careful of his brain. But I believe it is practically settled."

"I am delighted," began Basil, but with a worried face, "but these red-tape negotiations are so terribly chancy that I really can't advise you to build on hope, only to be hurled down into bitterness. I've known men, and good men like your brother, come nearer than this and be disappointed. Of course, if it is true——"

"If it is true," said the woman fiercely, "it means that people who have never lived may make an attempt at living."

Even as she spoke the professor came into the room still with the mazed look in his eyes.

"Is it true?" asked Basil, with burning eyes.

"Not a bit true," answered Chadd after a moment's bewilderment. "Your argument was in three points fallacious."

"What do you mean?" demanded Grant.

"Well," said the professor slowly, "in saying that you could possess a knowledge of the essence of Zulu life distinct from——"

"Oh! confound Zulu life," cried Grant, with a burst of laughter. "I mean, have you got the post?"

"You mean the post of keeper of the Asiatic manuscripts," he said, opening his eye with childlike wonder. "Oh, yes, I got that. But the real objection to your argument, which has only, I admit, occurred

“‘What do you make of that?’”

to me since I have been out of the room, is that it does not merely presuppose a Zulu truth apart from the facts, but infers that the discovery of it is absolutely impeded by the facts."

"I am crushed," said Basil, and sat down to laugh, while the professor's sister retired to her room, possibly to laugh, possibly not.

It was extremely late when we left the Chadds, and it is an extremely long and tiresome journey from Shepherd's Bush to Lambeth. This may be our excuse for the fact that we (for I was stopping the night with Grant) got down to breakfast next day at a time inexpressibly criminal, a time, in point of fact, close upon noon. Even to that belated meal we came in a very lounging and leisurely fashion. Grant, in particular, seemed so dreamy at table that he scarcely saw the pile of letters by his plate, and I doubt if he would have opened any of them if there had not lain on the top that one thing which has succeeded amid modern carelessness in being really urgent and coercive—a telegram. This he opened with the same heavy distraction with which he broke his egg and drank his tea. When he read it he did not stir a hair or say a word, but something, I know not what, made me feel that the motionless figure had been pulled together suddenly as strings are tightened on a slack guitar. Though he said nothing and did not move, I knew that he had been for an instant cleared and sharpened with a shock of cold water. It was scarcely any surprise to me when a man had drifted sullenly to his seat and fallen into it, kicked it away like a cur from under him and came round to me in two strides.

"What do you make of that?" he said, and flattened out the wire in front of me.

It ran: "Please come at once. James's mental state dangerous. Chadd."

"What does the woman mean?" I said after a pause, irritably. "Those women have been saying that the poor old professor was mad ever since he was born."

"You are mistaken," said Grant composedly. "It is true that all sensible women think all studious men mad. It is true, for the matter of that, all women of any kind think all men of any kind mad. But they don't put it in telegrams, any more than they wire to you that grass is green or God all-merciful. These things are truisms, and often private ones at that. If Miss Chadd has written down under the eye of a strange woman in a post-office that her brother is off his head you may be perfectly certain that she did it because it was a matter of life and death, and she can think of no other way of forcing us to come promptly."

"It will force us of course," I said, smiling.

"Oh, yes," he replied; "there is a cab-rank near."

Basil scarcely said a word as we drove across Westminster Bridge, through Trafalgar Square, along Piccadilly, and up the Uxbridge Road. Only as he was opening the gate he spoke.

"I think you may take my word for it, my friend," he said; "this is one of the most queer and complicated and astounding incidents that ever happened in London or, for that matter, in any high civilisation."

"I confess with the greatest sympathy and reverence that I don't quite see it," I said. "Is it so very extraordinary or complicated that a dreamy somnambulant old invalid who has always walked on the borders of the inconceivable should go mad under the shock of great joy? Is it so very extraordinary that a man with a head like a turnip and a soul like a spider's web should not find his strength equal to a confounding change of fortunes? Is it, in short, so very extraordinary that James Chadd should lose his wits from excitement?"

"It would not be extraordinary in the least," answered Basil, with placidity. "It would not be extraordinary in the least," he repeated, "if the professor had gone mad. That was not the extraordinary circumstance to which I referred."

"What," I asked, stamping my foot, "was the extraordinary thing?"

"The extraordinary thing," said Basil, ringing the bell, "is that he has not gone mad from excitement."

The tall and angular figure of the eldest Miss Chadd blocked the doorway as the door opened. Two other Miss Chadds seemed in the same way to be blocking the narrow passage and the little parlour. There was a general sense of their keeping something from view. They seemed like three black-clad ladies in some strange play of Maeterlinck, veiling the catastrophe from the audience in the manner of the Greek chorus.

"Sit down, won't you?" said one of them, in a voice that was somewhat rigid with pain. "I think you had better be told first what has happened."

Then, with her bleak face looking unmeaningly out of the window, she continued, in an even and mechanical voice:

"I had better state everything that occurred just as it occurred. This morning I was clearing away the breakfast things, my sisters were both somewhat unwell, and had not come down. My brother had just gone out of the room, I believe, to fetch a book. He came back again, however, without it, and stood for some time staring at the empty grate. I said, 'Were you looking for anything I could get?' He did not answer, but this constantly happens, as he is often very abstracted. I repeated my question, and still he did not answer. Sometimes he is so wrapped up in his studies that nothing but a touch on the shoulder would make him aware of one's presence, so I came round the table towards him. I really do not know how to describe the sensation which I then had. It seems simply silly, but at the moment it seemed something enormous, upsetting one's brain. The fact is, James was standing on one leg."

Grant smiled slowly and rubbed his hands with a kind of care.

"Standing on one leg?" I repeated.

"Yes," replied the dead voice of the woman, without an inflection to suggest that she felt the fantasticality of her statement. "He was standing on the left leg and had the right drawn up at a sharp angle, the toe pointing downwards. I asked him if his leg hurt him. His only answer was to shoot the leg straight at right angles to the other, as if pointing to the other with his toe to the wall. He was still looking quite gravely at the fireplace.

" 'James, what is the matter?' I cried, for I was thoroughly frightened. James gave three kicks in the air with the right leg, flung up the other, gave three kicks in the air with it also and spun round like a teetotum the other way. 'Are you mad?' I cried. 'Why don't you answer me?' He had come to a standstill, facing me, and was looking at me as he always does, with his lifted eyebrows and great spectacled eyes. When I had spoken he remained a second or two motionless, and then his only reply was to lift his left foot slowly from the floor and describe circles with it in the air. I rushed to the door and shouted for Christina. I will not dwell on the dreadful hours that followed. All three of us talked to him, implored him to speak to us with appeals that might have brought back the dead, but he has done nothing but hop and dance and kick with a solemn silent face. It looks as if his legs belonged to some one else or were possessed by devils. He has never spoken to us from that time to this."

"Where is he now?" I said, getting up in some agitation. "We ought not to leave him alone."

"Doctor Colman is with him," said Miss Chadd calmly. "They are in the garden. Doctor Colman thought the air would do him good. And he can scarcely go into the street."

"James was standing on one leg"

Basil and I walked rapidly to the window which looked out on the garden. It was a small and somewhat snug suburban garden; the flower beds a little too neat and like the pattern of a coloured carpet; but on this shining and opulent summer day even they had the exuberance of something natural, I had almost said tropical. In the middle of a bright and verdant but painfully circular lawn stood two figures. One of them was a small, sharp-looking man with black whiskers and a very polished hat (I presume Dr. Colman), who was talking very quietly and clearly, yet with a nervous twitch, as it were, in his face. The other was our old friend, listening with his old forbearing expression and owlish eyes, the strong sunlight gleaming on his glasses as the lamplight had gleamed the night before, when the boisterous Basil had rallied him on his studious decorum. But for one thing the figure of this morning might have been the identical figure of last night. That one thing was that while the face listened reposefully the legs were industriously dancing like the legs of a marionette. The neat flowers and the sunny glitter of the garden lent an indescribable sharpness and incredibility to the prodigy—the prodigy of the head of a hermit and the legs of a harlequin. For miracles should always happen in broad daylight. The night makes them credible and therefore commonplace.

The second sister had by this time entered the room and came somewhat drearily to the window.

"You know, Adelaide," she said, "that Mr. Bingham from the Museum is coming again at three."

"I know," said Adelaide Chadd bitterly. "I suppose we shall have to tell him about this. I thought that no good fortune would ever come easily to us."

Grant suddenly turned round. "What do you mean?" he said. "What will you have to tell Mr. Bingham?"

"You know what I shall have to tell him," said the professor's sister, almost fiercely. "I don't know that we need give it its wretched name. Do you think that the keeper of Asiatic manuscripts will be allowed to go on like that?" And she pointed for an instant at the figure in the garden, the shining, listening face and the unresting feet.

Basil Grant took out his watch with an abrupt movement. "When did you say the British Museum man was coming?" he said.

"Three o'clock," said Miss Chadd briefly.

"Then I have an hour before me," said Grant, and without another word threw up the window and jumped out into the garden. He did not walk straight up to the doctor and lunatic, but strolling round the garden path drew near them cautiously and yet apparently carelessly. He stood a couple of feet off them, seemingly counting halfpence out of his trousers pocket, but, as I could see, looking up steadily under the broad brim of his hat.

Suddenly he stepped up to Professor Chadd's elbow, and said, in a loud familiar voice, "Well, my boy, do you still think the Zulus our inferiors?"

The doctor knitted his brows and looked anxious, seeming to be about to speak. The professor turned his bald and placid head towards Grant in a friendly manner, but made no answer, idly flinging his left leg about.

"Have you converted Dr. Colman to your views?" Basil continued, still in the same loud and lucid tone.

Chadd only shuffled his feet and kicked a little with the other leg, his expression still benevolent and inquiring. The doctor cut in rather sharply. "Shall we go inside, professor?" he said. "Now you have shown me the garden. A beautiful garden. A most beautiful garden. Let us go in," and he tried to draw the kicking ethnologist by the elbow, at the same time whispering to Grant: "I must ask you not to trouble him with questions. Most risky. He must be soothed."

Basil answered in the same tone, with great coolness:

"Of course your directions must be followed out, doctor. I will endeavour to do so, but I hope it will not be inconsistent with them if you will leave me alone with my poor friend in this garden for an hour. I want to watch him. I assure you, Dr. Colman, that I shall say very little to him, and that little shall be as soothing as—as syrup."

The doctor wiped his eyeglass thoughtfully.

"It is rather dangerous for him," he said, "to be long in this strong sun without his hat. With his bald head, too."

"That is soon settled," said Basil composedly, and took off his own big hat and clapped it on the egglike skull of the professor. The latter did not turn round but danced away with his eyes on the horizon.

The doctor put on his glasses again, looked severely at the two for some seconds, with his head on one side, like a bird's, and then saying, shortly, "All right," strutted away into the house, where the three Misses Chadd were all looking out from the parlour window on to the garden. They looked out on it with hungry eyes for a full hour without moving, and they saw a sight which was more extraordinary than madness itself.

Basil Grant addressed a few questions to the madman, without succeeding in making him do anything but continue to caper, and when he had done this slowly took a red note-book out of one pocket and a large pencil out of another.

He began hurriedly to scribble notes. When the lunatic skipped away from him he would walk a few yards in pursuit, stop, and make notes again. Thus they followed each other round and round the foolish circle of turf, the one writing in pencil with the face of a man working out a problem, the other leaping and playing like a child.

After about three-quarters of an hour of this imbecile scene, Grant put the pencil in his pocket, but kept the note-book open in his hand, and walking round the mad professor, planted himself directly in front of him.

Then occurred something that even those already used to that wild morning had not anticipated or dreamed. The professor, on finding Basil in front of him, stared with a blank benignity for a few seconds, and then drew up his left leg and hung it bent in the attitude that his sister had described as being the first of all his antics. And the moment he had done it Basil Grant lifted his own leg and held it out rigid before him, confronting Chadd with the flat sole of his boot. The professor dropped his bent leg, and swinging his weight on to it kicked out the other behind, like a man swimming. Basil crossed his feet like a Saltire cross, and then flung them apart again, giving a leap into the air. Then before any of the spectators could say a word or even entertain a thought about the matter, both of them were dancing a sort of jig or hornpipe opposite each other; and the sun shone down on two madmen instead of one.

They were so stricken with the deafness and blindness of monomania that they did not see the eldest Miss Chadd come out feverishly into the garden with gestures of entreaty, a gentleman following her. Professor Chadd was in the wildest posture of a *pas-de-quatre*. Basil Grant seemed about to turn a cartwheel, when they were frozen in their follies by the steely voice of Adelaide Chadd saying, "Mr. Bingham, of the British Museum."

Mr. Bingham was a slim, well-clad gentleman with a pointed and slightly effeminate grey beard, unimpeachable gloves, and formal but agreeable manners. He was the type of the over-civilised, as Professor Chadd was of the uncivilised pedant. His formality and agreeableness did him some credit under the circumstances. He had a vast experience of books and a considerable experience of the

"They followed each other round and round . . . one writing in pencil with the face of a man working out a problem, the other leaping and playing like a child"

more dilettante fashionable salons. But neither branch of knowledge had accustomed him to the spectacle of two grey-haired middle-class gentlemen in modern costume throwing themselves about like acrobats as a substitute for an after-dinner nap.

The professor continued his antics with perfect placidity, but Grant stopped abruptly. The doctor had reappeared on the scene, and his shiny black eyes, under his shiny black hat, moved restlessly from one of them to the other.

"Dr. Colman," said Basil, turning to him, "will you entertain Professor Chadd again for a little while? I am sure that he needs you. Mr. Bingham, might I have the pleasure of few moments' private conversation? My name is Grant."

Mr. Bingham, of the British Museum, bowed in a manner that was respectful but a trifle bewildered.

"Miss Chadd will excuse me," continued Basil easily, "if I know my way about the house." And he led the dazed librarian rapidly through the back door into the parlour.

"Mr. Bingham," said Basil, setting a chair for him, "I imagine that Miss Chadd has told you of this distressing occurrence."

"She has, Mr. Grant," said Bingham, looking at the table with a sort of compassionate nervousness. "I am more pained than I can say by this dreadful calamity. It seems quite heart-rending that the thing should have happened just as we have decided to give your eminent friend a position which falls far short of his merits. As it is, of course—really, I don't know what to say. Professor Chadd may, of course, retain—I sincerely trust he will—his extraordinary valuable intellect. But I am afraid—I am really afraid—that it would not do to have the curator of the Asiatic manuscripts—er—dancing about."

"I have a suggestion to make," said Basil, and sat down abruptly in his chair, drawing it up to the table.

"I am delighted, of course," said the gentleman from the British Museum, coughing and drawing up his chair also.

The clock on the mantelpiece ticked for just the moments required for Basil to clear his throat and collect his words, and then he said:

"My proposal is this. I do not know that in the strict use of words you could altogether call it a compromise, still it has something of that character. My proposal is that the Government (acting, as I presume, through your Museum) should pay Professor Chadd £800 a year until he stops dancing."

"Eight hundred a year!" said Mr. Bingham, and for the first time lifted his mild blue eyes to those of his interlocutor—and he raised them with a mild blue stare. "I think I have not quite understood you. Did I understand you to say that Professor Chadd ought to be employed, in his present state, in the Asiatic manuscript department at eight hundred a year?"

Grant shook his head resolutely.

"No," he said firmly. "No. Chadd is a friend of mine, and I would say anything for him I could. But I do not say, I cannot say, that he ought to take on the Asiatic manuscripts. I do not go so far as that. I merely say that until he stops dancing you ought to pay him £800. Surely you have some general fund for the endowment of research."

Mr. Bingham looked bewildered.

"I really don't know," he said, blinking his eyes, "what you are talking about. Do you ask us to give this obvious lunatic nearly a thousand a year for life?"

"Not at all," cried Basil, keenly and triumphantly. "I never said for life. Not at all."

"What for then?" asked the meek Bingham, suppressing an instinct meekly to tear his hair. "How long is this endowment to run? Not till his death? Till the Judgment day?"

"No," said Basil, beaming, "but just what I said. Till he has stopped dancing." And he lay back with satisfaction and his hands in his pockets.

Bingham had by this time fastened his eyes keenly on Basil Grant and kept them there.

"Come, Mr. Grant," he said. "Do I seriously understand you to suggest that the Government pay Professor Chadd an extraordinarily high salary simply on the ground that he has (pardon the phrase) gone mad? That he should be paid more than four good clerks solely on the ground that he is flinging his boots about in the back yard?"

"Precisely," said Grant, composedly.

"That this absurd payment is not only to run on with the absurd dancing, but actually to stop with the absurd dancing?"

"One must stop somewhere," said Grant. "Of course."

Bingham rose and took up his perfect stick and gloves.

"There is really nothing more to be said, Mr. Grant," he said coldly. "What you are trying to explain to me may be a joke—a slightly unfeeling joke. It may be your sincere view, in which case I ask your pardon for the former suggestion. But, in any case, it appears quite irrelevant to my duties. The mental morbidity, the mental downfall, of Professor Chadd, is a thing so painful to me that I cannot easily endure to speak of it. But it is clear there is a limit to everything. And if the Archangel Gabriel went mad it would sever his connection, I am sorry to say, with the British Museum Library."

He was stepping towards the door, but Grant's hand, flung out in dramatic warning, arrested him.

"Stop!" said Basil sternly. "Stop while there is yet time. Do you want to take part in a great work, Mr. Bingham? Do you want to help in the glory of Europe—in the glory of science? Do you want to carry your head in the air when it is bald or white because of the part that you bore in a great discovery? Do you want——"

Bingham cut in sharply:

"And if I do want this, Mr. Grant——"

"Then," said Basil lightly, "your task is easy. Get Chadd £800 a year till he stops dancing."

With a fierce flap of his swinging gloves Bingham turned impatiently to the door, but in passing out of it found it blocked. Dr. Colman was coming in.

"Forgive me, gentlemen," he said, in a nervous, confidential voice, "the fact is, Mr. Grant, I—er—have made a most disturbing discovery about Mr. Chadd."

Bingham looked at him with grave eyes.

"I was afraid so," he said. "Drink, I imagine."

"Drink!" echoed Colman, as if that were a much milder affair. "Oh, no, it's not drink."

Mr. Bingham became somewhat agitated, and his voice grew hurried and vague. "Homicidal mania——" he began.

"No, no," said the medical man impatiently.

"Thinks he's made of glass," said Bingham feverishly, "or says he's God—or——"

"No," said Dr. Colman sharply; "the fact is, Mr. Grant, my discovery is of a different character. The awful thing about him is——"

"Oh, go on, sir," cried Bingham, in agony.

"The awful thing about him is," repeated Colman, with deliberation, "that he isn't mad."

"Not mad!"

"There are quite well-known physical tests of lunacy," said the doctor shortly; "he hasn't got any of them."

" 'The awful thing about him is that he isn't mad' "

"But why does he dance?" cried the despairing Bingham. "Why doesn't he answer us? Why hasn't he spoken to his family?"

"The devil knows," said Dr. Colman coolly. "I'm paid to judge of lunatics, but not of fools. The man's not mad."

"What on earth can it mean? Can't we make him listen?" said Mr. Bingham. "Can none get into any kind of communication with him?"

Grant's voice struck in sudden and clear, like a steel bell:

"I shall be very happy," he said, "to give him any message you like to send."

Both men stared at him.

"Give him a message?" they cried simultaneously. "How will you give him a message?"

Basil smiled in his slow way.

"If you really want to know how I shall give him your message," he began, but Bingham cried:

"Of course, of course," with a sort of frenzy.

"Well," said Basil, "like this." And he suddenly sprang a foot into the air, coming down with crashing boots, and then stood on one leg.

His face was stern, though this effect was slightly spoiled by the fact that one of his feet was making wild circles in the air.

"You drive me to it," he said. "You drive me to betray my friend. And I will, for his own sake, betray him."

The sensitive face of Bingham took on an extra expression of distress as of one anticipating some disgraceful disclosure. "Anything painful, of course——" he began.

Basil let his loose foot fall on the carpet with a crash that struck them all rigid in their feeble attitudes.

"Idiots!" he cried. "Have you seen the man? Have you looked at James Chadd going dismally to and fro from his dingy house to your miserable library, with his futile books and his confounded umbrella, and never seen that he has the eyes of a fanatic? Have you never noticed, stuck casually behind his spectacles and above his seedy old collar, the face of a man who might have burned heretics, or died for the philosopher's stone? It is all my fault, in a way: I lit the dynamite of his deadly faith. I argued against him on the score of his famous theory about language—the theory that language was complete in certain individuals and was picked up by others simply by watching them. I also chaffed him about not understanding things in rough and ready practice. What has this glorious bigot done? He has answered me. He has worked out a system of language of his own (it would take too long to explain); he has made up, I say, a language of his own. And he has sworn that till people understand it, till he can speak to us in this language, he will not speak in any other. And he shall not. I have understood, by taking careful notice; and, by heaven, so shall the others. This shall not be blown upon. He shall finish his experiment. He shall have £800 a year from somewhere till he has stopped dancing. To stop him now is an infamous war on a great idea. It is religious persecution."

Mr. Bingham held out his hand cordially.

"I thank you, Mr. Grant," he said. "I hope I shall be able to answer for the source of the £800, and I fancy that I shall. Will you come in my cab?"

"No, thank you very much, Mr. Bingham," said Grant heartily, "I think I will go and have a chat with the professor in the garden."

The conversation between Chadd and Grant appeared to be personal and friendly. They were still dancing when I left.

VI. THE ECCENTRIC SECLUSION OF THE OLD LADY

THE CONVERSATION of Rupert Grant had two great elements of interest—first, the long fantasias of detective deduction in which he was engaged, and, second, his genuine romantic interest in the life of London. His brother Basil said of him: "His reasoning is particularly cold and clear, and invariably leads him wrong. But his poetry comes in abruptly and leads him right." Whether this was true of Rupert as a whole, or no, it was certainly curiously supported by one story about him which I think worth telling.

We were walking along a lonely terrace in Brompton together. The street was full of that bright blue twilight which comes about half-past eight in summer, and which seems for the moment to be not so much a coming of darkness as the turning on of a new azure illuminator, as if the earth were lit suddenly by a sapphire sun. In the cool blue the lemon tint of the lamps had already begun to flame, and as Rupert and I passed them, Rupert talking excitedly, one after another the pale sparks sprang out of the dusk. Rupert was talking excitedly because he was trying to prove to me the nine hundred and ninety-ninth of his amateur detective theories. He would go about London, with this mad logic in his brain, seeing a conspiracy in a cab accident, and a special providence in a falling fusee. His suspicions at the moment were fixed upon an unhappy milkman who walked in front of us. So arresting were the incidents which afterwards overtook us that I am really afraid that I have forgotten what were the main outlines of the milkman's crime. I think it had something to do with the fact that he had only one small can of milk to carry, and that of that he had left the lid loose and walked so quickly that he spilled milk on the pavement. This showed that he was not thinking of his small burden, and this again

" 'I'll bet you half a crown that wherever he comes to a real stop I'll find out something curious' "

showed that he anticipated some other than lacteal business at the end of his walk, and this (taken in conjunction with something about muddy boots) showed something else that I have entirely forgotten. I am afraid that I derided this detailed revelation unmercifully; and I am afraid that Rupert Grant, who, though the best of fellows, had a good deal of the sensitiveness of the artistic temperament, slightly resented my derision. He endeavoured to take a whiff of his cigar with the placidity which he associated with his profession, but the cigar, I think, was nearly bitten through.

"My dear fellow," he said acidly, "I'll bet you half a crown that wherever that milkman comes to a real stop I'll find out something curious."

"My resources are equal to that risk," I said, laughing. "Done."

We walked on for about a quarter of an hour in silence in the trail of the mysterious milkman. He walked quicker and quicker, and we had some ado to keep up with him; and every now and then he left a splash of milk, silver in the lamplight. Suddenly, almost before we could note it, he disappeared down the area steps of a house. I believe Rupert really believed that the milkman was a fairy; for a second he seemed to accept him as having vanished. Then calling something to me which somehow took no hold on my mind, he darted after the mystic milkman, and disappeared himself into the area.

I waited for at least five minutes, leaning against a lamp-post in the lonely street. Then the milkman came swinging up the steps without his can and hurried off clattering down the road. Two or three minutes more elapsed and then Rupert came bounding up also, his face pale but yet laughing; a not uncommon contradiction in him, denoting excitement.

"My friend," he said, rubbing his hands, "so much for all your scepticism. So much for your philistine ignorance of the possibilities of a romantic city. Two and sixpence, my boy, is the form in which your prosaic good nature will have to express itself."

"What?" I said incredulously, "do you mean to say that you really did find anything the matter with the poor milkman?"

His face fell.

"Oh, the milkman," he said, with a miserable affectation at having misunderstood me. "No, I—I—didn't exactly bring anything home to the milkman himself, I——"

"What did the milkman say and do?" I said, with inexorable sternness.

" 'Just listen to that,' he said"

"Well, to tell the truth," said Rupert, shifting restlessly from one foot to another, "the milkman himself, as far as merely physical appearances went, just said, 'Milk, Miss,' and handed in the can. That is not to say, of course, that he did not make some secret sign or some——"

I broke into a violent laugh. "You idiot," I said, "why don't you own yourself wrong and have done with it? Why should he have made a secret sign any more than anyone else? You own he said nothing and did nothing worth mentioning. You own that, don't you?"

His face grew grave.

"Well, since you ask me, I must admit that I do. It is possible that the milkman did not betray himself. It is even possible that I was wrong about him."

"Then come along with you," I said, with a certain amicable anger, "and remember that you owe me half a crown."

"As to that, I differ from you," said Rupert coolly. "The milkman's remarks may have been quite innocent. Even the milkman may have been. But I do not owe you half a crown. For the terms of the bet were, I think, as follows, as I propounded them, that wherever that milkman came to a real stop I should find out something curious."

"Well?" I said.

"Well," he answered, "I jolly well have. You just come with me," and before I could speak he had turned tail once more and whisked through the blue dark into the moat or basement of the house. I followed almost before I made my decision.

When we got down into the area I felt indescribably foolish—literally, as the saying is, in a hole. There was nothing but a closed door, shuttered windows, the steps down which we had come, the ridiculous well in which I found myself, and the ridiculous man who had brought me there, and who stood there with dancing eyes. I was just about to turn back when Rupert caught me by the elbow.

"Just listen to that," he said, and keeping my coat gripped in his right hand, he rapped with the knuckles of his left on the shutters of the basement window. His air was so definite that I paused and even inclined my head for a moment towards it. From inside was coming the murmur of an unmistakable human voice.

"Have you been talking to somebody inside?" I asked suddenly, turning to Rupert.

"No, I haven't," he replied, with a grim smile, "but I should very much like to. Do you know what somebody is saying in there?"

"No, of course not," I replied.

"Then I recommend you to listen," said Rupert sharply.

In the dead silence of the aristocratic street at evening, I stood a moment and listened. From behind the wooden partition, in which there was a long lean crack, was coming a continuous and moaning sound which took the form of the words: "When shall I get out? When shall I get out? Will they ever let me out?" or words to that effect.

"Do you know anything about this?" I said, turning upon Rupert very abruptly.

"Perhaps you think I am the criminal," he said sardonically, "instead of being in some small sense the detective. I came into this area two or three minutes ago, having told you that I knew there was something funny going on, and this woman behind the shutters (for it evidently is a woman) was moaning like mad. No, my dear friend, beyond that I do not know anything about her. She is not, startling as it may seem, my disinherited daughter, or a member of my secret seraglio. But when I hear a human being wailing that she can't get out, and talking to herself like a mad woman and beating on the shutters with her fists, as she was doing two or three minutes ago, I think it worth mentioning, that is all."

"My dear fellow," I said, "I apologise; this is no time for arguing. What is to be done?"

Rupert Grant had a long clasp-knife naked and brilliant in his hand.

"First of all," he said, "house-breaking." And he forced the blade into the crevice of the wood and broke away a huge splinter, leaving a gap and glimpse of the dark window-pane inside. The room within was entirely unlighted, so that for the first few seconds the window seemed a dead and opaque surface, as dark as a strip of slate. Then came a realisation which, though in a sense gradual, made us step back and catch our breath. Two large dim human eyes were so close to us that the window itself seemed suddenly to be a mask. A pale human face was pressed against the glass within, and with increased distinctness, with the increase of the opening came the words:

"When shall I get out?"

"What can all this be?" I said.

Rupert made no answer, but lifting his walking-stick and pointing the ferrule like a fencing sword at the glass, punched a hole in it, smaller and more accurate than I should have supposed possible. The moment he had done so the voice spouted out of the hole, so to speak, piercing and querulous and clear, making the same demand for liberty.

"Can't you get out, madam?" I said, drawing near the hole in some perturbation.

"Get out. Of course I can't," moaned the unknown female bitterly. "They won't let me. I told them I would be let out. I told them I'd call the police. But it's no good. Nobody knows, nobody comes. They could keep me as long as they liked only——"

I was in the very act of breaking the window finally with my stick, when Rupert held my arm hard, held it with a curious, still, and secret rigidity as if he desired to stop me, but did not desire to be observed to do so. I paused a moment, and in the act swung slightly round, so that I was facing the supporting wall of the front door steps. The act froze me into a sudden stillness like that of Rupert, for a figure almost as motionless as the pillars of the portico, but unmistakably human, had put his head out from between the doorposts and was gazing down into the area. One of the lighted lamps of the street was just behind his head, throwing it into abrupt darkness. Consequently, nothing whatever could be seen of his face beyond one fact, that he was unquestionably staring at us. I must say I thought Rupert's calmness magnificent. He rang the area bell quite idly, and went on talking to me with the easy end of a conversation which had never had any beginning. The black glaring figure in the portico did not stir. I almost thought it was really a statue. In another moment the grey area was golden with gaslight as the basement door was opened suddenly and a small and decorous housemaid stood in it.

"Pray excuse me," said Rupert, in a voice which he contrived to make somehow or other at once affable and underbred, "but we thought perhaps that you might do something for the Waifs and Strays. We don't expect——"

"Not here," said the small servant, with the incomparable severity of the menial of the non-philanthropic, and slammed the door in our faces.

"Very sad, very sad—the indifference of these people," said the philanthropist, with gravity as we went together up the steps. As we did so the motionless figure in the portico suddenly disappeared.

"Discussing religion with the booking-office clerk"

"Well, what do you make of that?" asked Rupert, slapping his gloves together when we got into the street.

I do not mind admitting that I was seriously upset. Under such conditions I had but one thought.

"Don't you think," I said a trifle timidly, "that we had better tell your brother?"

"Oh, if you like," said Rupert, in a lordly way. "He is quite near, as I promised to meet him at Gloucester Road Station. Shall we take a cab? Perhaps, as you say, it might amuse him."

Gloucester Road Station had, as if by accident, a somewhat deserted look. After a little looking about we discovered Basil Grant with his great head and his great white hat blocking the ticket-office window. I thought at first that he was taking a ticket for somewhere and being an astonishingly long time about it. As a matter of fact, he was discussing religion with the booking-office clerk, and had almost got his head through the hole in his excitement. When we dragged him away it was some time before he would talk of anything but the growth of an Oriental fatalism in modern thought, which had been well typified by some of the official's ingenious but perverse fallacies. At last we managed to get him to understand that we had made an astounding discovery. When he did listen, he listened attentively, walking between us up and down the lamp-lit street, while we told him in a rather feverish duet of the great house in South Kensington, of the equivocal milkman, of the lady imprisoned in the basement, and the man staring from the porch. At length he said:

"If you're thinking of going back to look the thing up, you must be careful what you do. It's no good you two going there. To go twice on the same pretext would look dubious. To go on a different pretext would look worse. You may be quite certain that the inquisitive gentleman who looked at you looked thoroughly, and will wear, so to speak, your portraits next his heart. If you want to find out if there is anything in this without a police raid I fancy you had better wait outside. I'll go in and see them."

His slow and reflective walk brought us at length within sight of the house. It stood up ponderous and purple against the last pallor of twilight. It looked like an ogre's castle. And so apparently it was.

"Do you think it's safe, Basil," said his brother, pausing, a little pale, under the lamp, "to go into that place alone? Of course we shall be near enough to hear if you yell, but these devils might do something—something sudden—or odd. I can't feel it's safe."

"I know of nothing that is safe," said Basil composedly, "except, possibly—death," and he went up the steps and rang at the bell. When the massive respectable door opened for an instant, cutting a square of gaslight in the gathering dark, and then closed with a bang, burying our friend inside, we could not repress a shudder. It had been like the heavy gaping and closing of the dim lips of some evil leviathan. A freshening night breeze began to blow up the street, and we turned up the collars of our coats. At the end of twenty minutes, in which we had scarcely moved or spoken, we were as cold as icebergs, but more, I think, from apprehension than the atmosphere. Suddenly Rupert made an abrupt movement towards the house.

"I can't stand this," he began, but almost as he spoke sprang back into the shadow, for the panel of gold was again cut out of the black house front, and the burly figure of Basil was silhouetted against it coming out. He was roaring with laughter and talking so loudly that you could have heard every syllable across the street. Another voice, or, possibly, two voices, were laughing and talking back at him from within.

"No, no, no," Basil was calling out, with a sort of hilarious hostility. "That's quite wrong. That's the most ghastly heresy of all. It's the soul, my dear chap, the soul that's the arbiter of cosmic forces. When you see a cosmic force you don't like, trick it, my boy. But I must really be off."

"Come and pitch into us again," came the laughing voice from out of the house. "We still have some bones unbroken."

"Thanks, very much, I will—good-night," shouted Grant, who had by this time reached the street.

"Good-night," came the friendly call in reply, before the door closed.

"Basil," said Rupert Grant, in a hoarse whisper, "what are we to do?"

The elder brother looked thoughtfully from one of us to the other.

"What is to be done, Basil?" I repeated in uncontrollable excitement.

"I'm not sure," said Basil doubtfully. "What do you say to getting some dinner somewhere and going to the Court Theatre to-night? I tried to get those fellows to come, but they couldn't."

We stared blankly.

"Go to the Court Theatre?" repeated Rupert. "What would be the good of that?"

"Good? What do you mean?" answered Basil, staring also. "Have you turned Puritan or Passive Resister, or something? For fun, of course."

"But, great God in heaven! What are we going to do, I mean!" cried Rupert. "What about the poor woman locked up in that house? Shall I go for the police?"

Basil's face cleared with immediate comprehension, and he laughed.

"Oh, that," he said. "I'd forgotten that. That's all right. Some mistake, possibly. Or some quite trifling private affair. But I'm sorry those fellows couldn't come with us. Shall we take one of these green omnibuses? There is a restaurant in Sloane Square."

"I sometimes think you play the fool to frighten us," I said irritably. "How can we leave that woman locked up? How can it be a mere private affair? How can crime and kidnapping and murder, for all I know, be private affairs? If you found a corpse in a man's drawing-room, would you think it bad taste to talk about it just as if it was a confounded dado or an infernal etching?"

Basil laughed heartily.

"That's very forcible," he said. "As a matter of fact, though, I know it's all right in this case. And there comes the green omnibus."

"How do you know it's all right in this case?" persisted his brother angrily.

"My dear chap, the thing's obvious," answered Basil, holding a return ticket between his teeth while he fumbled in his waistcoat pocket. "Those two fellows never committed a crime in their lives. They're not the kind. Have either of you chaps got a halfpenny? I want to get a paper before the omnibus comes."

"Oh, curse the paper!" cried Rupert, in a fury. "Do you mean to tell me, Basil Grant, that you are going to leave a fellow creature in pitch darkness in a private dungeon, because you've had ten minutes' talk with the keepers of it and thought them rather good men?"

"Good men do commit crimes sometimes," said Basil, taking the ticket out of his mouth. "But this kind of good man doesn't commit that kind of crime. Well, shall we get on this omnibus?"

The great green vehicle was indeed plunging and lumbering along the dim wide street towards us. Basil had stepped from the curb, and for an instant it was touch and go whether we should all have leaped on to it and been borne away to the restaurant and the theatre.

"Basil," I said, taking him firmly by the shoulder. "I simply won't leave this street and this house."

"Nor will I," said Rupert, glaring at it and biting his fingers. "There's some black work going on there. If I left it I should never sleep again."

Basil Grant looked at us both seriously.

"Of course if you feel like that," he said, "we'll investigate further. You'll find it's all right, though. They're only two young Oxford fellows. Extremely nice, too, though rather infected with this pseudo-Darwinian business. Ethics of evolution and all that."

"I think," said Rupert darkly, ringing the bell, "that we shall enlighten you further about their ethics."

"And may I ask," said Basil gloomily, "what it is that you propose to do?"

"I propose, first of all," said Rupert, "to get into this house; secondly, to have a look at these nice young Oxford men; thirdly, to knock them down, bind them, gag them, and search the house."

Basil stared indignantly for a few minutes. Then he was shaken for an instant with one of his sudden laughs.

"Poor little boys," he said. "But it almost serves them right for holding such silly views, after all," and he quaked again with amusement; "there's something confoundedly Darwinian about it."

"I suppose you mean to help us?" said Rupert.

"Oh, yes, I'll be in it," answered Basil, "If it's only to prevent your doing the poor chaps any harm."

He was standing in the rear of our little procession, looking indifferent and sometimes even sulky, but somehow the instant the door opened he stepped first into the hall, glowing with urbanity.

"So sorry to haunt you like this," he said. "I met two friends outside who very much want to know you. May I bring them in?"

"Delighted, of course," said a young voice, the unmistakable voice of the Isis, and I realised that the door had been opened, not by the decorous little servant girl, but by one of our hosts in person. He was a short, but shapely young gentleman, with curly dark hair and a square, snub-nosed face. He wore slippers and a sort of blazer of some incredible college purple.

"This way," he said; "mind the steps by the staircase. This house is more crooked and old-fashioned than you would think from its snobbish exterior. There are quite a lot of odd corners in the place really."

"That," said Rupert, with a savage smile, "I can quite believe."

We were by this time in the study or back parlour, used by the young inhabitants as a sitting-room, an apartment littered with magazines and books ranging from Dante to detective stories. The other youth, who stood with his back to the fire smoking a corncob, was big and burly, with dead brown hair brushed forward and a Norfolk jacket. He was that particular type of man whose every feature and action is heavy and clumsy, and yet who is, you would say, rather exceptionally a gentleman.

"Any more arguments?" he said, when introduction had been effected. "I must say, Mr. Grant, you were rather severe upon eminent men of science such as we. I've half a mind to chuck my D.Sc. and turn minor poet."

"Bosh," answered Grant. "I never said a word against eminent men of science. What I complain of is a vague popular philosophy which supposes itself to be scientific when it is really nothing but a sort of new religion and an uncommonly nasty one. When people talked about the fall of man they knew they were talking about a mystery, a thing they didn't understand. Now that they talk about the survival of the fittest they think they do understand it, whereas they have not merely no notion, they have an elaborately false notion of what the words mean. The Darwinian movement has made no difference to mankind, except that, instead of talking unphilosophically about philosophy, they now talk unscientifically about science."

"That is all very well," said the big young man, whose name appeared to be Burrows. "Of course, in a sense, science, like mathematics or the violin, can only be perfectly understood by specialists. Still, the rudiments may be of public use. Greenwood here," indicating the little man, in the blazer, "doesn't know one note of music from another. Still, he knows something. He knows enough to take off his hat when they play 'God save the King.' He doesn't take it off by mistake when they play 'Oh, dem Golden Slippers.' Just in the same way science——"

Here Mr. Burrows stopped abruptly. He was interrupted by an argument uncommon in philosophical controversy and perhaps not wholly legitimate. Rupert Grant had bounded on him from behind, flung an arm round his throat, and bent the giant backwards.

"Knock the other fellow down, Swinburne," he called out, and before I knew where I was I was locked in a grapple with the man in the purple blazer. He was a wiry fighter, who bent and sprang like whalebone, but I was heavier and had taken him

"Smoking a corn-cob"

utterly by surprise. I twitched one of his feet from under him; he swung for a moment on the single foot, and then we fell with a crash amid the litter of newspapers, myself on top.

My attention for a moment released by victory, I could hear Basil's voice finishing some long sentence of which I had not heard the beginning.

" . . . wholly, I must confess, unintelligible to me, my dear sir, and I need not say unpleasant. Still one must side with one's old friends against the most fascinating new ones. Permit me, therefore, in tying you up in this antimacassar, to make it as commodious as handcuffs can reasonably be while . . ."

I had staggered to my feet. The gigantic Burrows was toiling in the garrotte of Rupert, while Basil was striving to master his mighty hands. Rupert and Basil were both particularly strong, but so was Mr. Burrows; how strong, we knew a second afterwards. His head was held back by Rupert's arm, but a convulsive heave went over his whole frame. An instant after his head plunged forward like a bull's, and Rupert Grant was slung head over heels, a Catherine wheel of legs, on the floor in front of him. Simultaneously the bull's head butted Basil in the chest, bringing him also to the ground with a crash, and the monster, with a Berserker roar, leaped at me and knocked me into the corner of the room, smashing the waste-paper basket. The bewildered Greenwood sprang furiously to his feet. Basil did the same. But they had the best of it now.

Greenwood dashed to the bell and pulled it violently, sending peals through the great house. Before I could get panting to my feet, and before Rupert, who had been literally stunned for a few moments, could even lift his head from the floor, two footmen were in the room. Defeated even when we were in a majority, we were now outnumbered. Greenwood and one of the footmen flung themselves upon me, crushing me back into the corner upon the wreck of the paper basket. The other two flew at Basil, and pinned him against the wall. Rupert lifted himself on his elbow, but he was still dazed.

In the strained silence of our helplessness I heard the voice of Basil come with a loud incongruous cheerfulness.

"Now this," he said, "is what I call enjoying oneself."

I caught a glimpse of his face, flushed and forced against the bookcase, from between the swaying limbs of my captors and his. To my astonishment his eyes were really brilliant with pleasure, like those of a child heated by a favourite game.

I made several apoplectic efforts to rise, but the servant was on top of me so heavily that Greenwood could afford to leave me to him. He turned quickly to come to reinforce the two who were mastering Basil. The latter's head was already sinking lower and lower, like a leaning ship, as his enemies pressed him down. He flung up one hand just as I thought him falling and hung on to a huge tome in the bookcase, a volume, I afterwards discovered, of St. Chrysostom's theology. Just as Greenwood bounded across the room towards the group, Basil plucked the ponderous tome bodily out of the shelf, swung it, and sent it spinning through the air, so that it struck Greenwood flat in the face and knocked him over like a rolling ninepin. At the same instant Basil's stiffness broke, and he sank, his enemies closing over him.

Rupert's head was clear, but his body shaken; he was hanging as best he could on to the half-prostrate Greenwood. They were rolling over each other on the floor, both somewhat enfeebled by their falls, but Rupert certainly the more so. I was still successfully held down. The floor was a sea of torn and trampled papers and magazines, like an immense waste-paper basket. Burrows and his companion were almost up to the knees in them, as in a drift of dead leaves. And Greenwood had his leg struck right through a sheet of the *Pall Mall Gazette*, which clung to it ludicrously, like some fantastic trouser frill.

Basil, shut from me in a human prison, a prison of powerful bodies, might be dead for all I knew. I fancied, however, that the broad back of Mr. Burrows, which was turned towards me, had a certain bend of effort in it as if my friend still needed some holding down. Suddenly that broad back swayed hither and thither. It was swaying on one leg; Basil, somehow, had hold of the other. Burrows' huge fist and those of the footmen were battering Basil's sunken head like an anvil, but nothing could get the giant's ankle out of his sudden and savage grip. While his own head was forced slowly down in darkness and great pain, the right leg of his captor was being forced in the air. Burrows swung to and fro with a purple face. Then suddenly the floor and the walls and the ceiling shook together, as the colossus fell, all his length seeming to fill the floor. Basil sprang up with dancing eyes, and with three blows like battering-rams knocked the footman into a cocked hat. Then he sprang on top of Burrows, with one antimacassar in his hand and another in his teeth, and bound him hand and foot almost before he knew clearly that his head had struck the floor. Then Basil sprang at Greenwood, whom Rupert was struggling to hold down, and between them they secured him easily. The man who had hold of me let go and turned to his rescue, but I leaped up like a spring released, and, to my infinite satisfaction, knocked the fellow down. The other footman, bleeding at the mouth and quite demoralised, was stumbling out of the room. My late captor, without a word, slunk after him, seeing that the battle was won. Rupert was sitting astride the pinioned Mr. Greenwood, Basil astride the pinioned Mr. Burrows.

To my surprise the latter gentleman, lying bound on his back, spoke in a perfectly calm voice to the man who sat on top of him.

"And now, gentlemen," he said, "since you have got your own way, perhaps you wouldn't mind telling us what the deuce all this is?"

"This," said Basil, with a radiant face, looking down at his captive, "this is what we call the survival of the fittest."

Rupert, who had been steadily collecting himself throughout the later phases of the fight, was intellectually altogether himself again at the end of it. Springing up from the prostrate Greenwood, and knotting a handkerchief round his left hand, which was bleeding from a blow, he sang out quite coolly:

"Basil, will you mount guard over the captive of your bow and spear and antimacassar? Swinburne and I will clear out the prison downstairs."

"All right," said Basil, rising also and seating himself in a leisured way in an armchair. "Don't hurry for us," he said, glancing round at the litter of the room, "we have all the illustrated papers."

Rupert lurched thoughtfully out of the room, and I followed him even more slowly; in fact, I lingered long enough to hear, as I passed through the room, the passages and the kitchen stairs, Basil's voice continuing conversationally:

"And now, Mr. Burrows," he said, settling himself sociably in the chair, "there's no reason why we shouldn't go on with that amusing argument. I'm sorry that you have to express yourself lying on your back on the floor, and, as I told you before, I've no more notion why you are there than the man in the moon. A conversationalist like yourself, however, can scarcely be seriously handicapped by any bodily posture. You were saying, if I remember right, when this incidental fracas occurred, that the rudiments of science might with advantage be made public."

"Precisely," said the large man on the floor in an easy tone. "I hold that nothing more than a rough sketch of the universe as seen by science can be . . ."

"This is what we call the survival of the fittest"

And here the voices died away as we descended into the basement. I noticed that Mr. Greenwood did not join in the amicable controversy. Strange as it may appear, I think he looked back upon our proceedings with a slight degree of resentment. Mr. Burrows, however, was all philosophy and chattiness. We left them, as I say, together, and sank deeper and deeper into the underworld of that mysterious house, which perhaps appeared to us somewhat more Tartarian than it really was, owing to our knowledge of its semi-criminal mystery and of the human secret locked below.

The basement floor had several doors, as is usual in such a house; doors that would naturally lead to the kitchen, the scullery, the pantry, the servants' hall, and so on. Rupert flung open all the doors with indescribable rapidity. Four out of the five opened on entirely empty apartments. The fifth was locked. Rupert broke the door in like a bandbox, and we fell into the sudden blackness of the sealed, unlighted room.

Rupert stood on the threshold, and called out like a man calling into an abyss:

"Whoever you are, come out. You are free. The people who held you captive are captives themselves. We heard you crying and we came to deliver you. We have bound your enemies upstairs hand and foot. You are free."

For some seconds after he had spoken into the darkness there was a dead silence in it. Then there came a kind of muttering and moaning. We might easily have taken it for the wind or rats if we had not happened to have heard it before. It was unmistakably the voice of the imprisoned woman, drearily demanding liberty, just as we had heard her demand it.

"Has anybody got a match?" said Rupert grimly. "I fancy we have come pretty near the end of this business."

I struck a match and held it up. It revealed a large, bare yellow-papered apartment with a dark-clad figure at the other end of it near the window. An instant after it burned my fingers and dropped, leaving darkness. It had, however, revealed something more practical—an iron gas bracket just above my head. I struck another match and lit the gas. And we found ourselves suddenly and seriously in the presence of the captive.

At a sort of workbox in the window of this subterranean breakfast-room sat an elderly lady with a singularly high colour and almost startling silver hair. She had, as if designedly to relieve these effects, a pair of Mephistophelean black eyebrows and a very neat black dress. The glare of the gas lit up her piquant hair and face perfectly against the brown background of the shutters. The background was blue and not brown in one place; at the place where Rupert's knife had torn a great opening in the wood about an hour before.

"Madam," said he, advancing with a gesture of the hat, "permit me to have the pleasure of announcing to you that you are free. Your complaints happened to strike our ears as we passed down the street, and we have therefore ventured to come to your rescue."

The old lady with the red face and the black eyebrows looked at us for a moment with something of the apoplectic stare of a parrot. Then she said, with a sudden gust or breathing of relief:

"Rescue? Where is Mr. Greenwood? Where is Mr. Burrows? Did you say you had rescued me?"

"Yes, madam," said Rupert, with a beaming condescension. "We have very satisfactorily dealt with Mr. Greenwood and Mr. Burrows. We have settled affairs with them very satisfactorily."

The old lady rose from her chair and came very quickly towards us.

"What did you say to them? How did you persuade them?" she cried.

"We persuaded them, my dear madam," said Rupert, laughing, "by knocking them down and tying them up. But what is the matter?"

To the surprise of every one the old lady walked slowly back to her seat by the window.

"Do I understand," she said, with the air of a person about to begin knitting, "that you have knocked down Mr. Burrows and tied him up?"

"We have," said Rupert proudly; "we have resisted their oppression and conquered it."

"Oh, thanks," answered the old lady, and sat down by the window.

A considerable pause followed.

"The road is quite clear for you, madam," said Rupert pleasantly.

The old lady rose, cocking her black eyebrows and her silver crest at us for an instant.

"But what about Greenwood and Burrows?" she said. "What did I understand you to say had become of them?"

"They are lying on the floor upstairs," said Rupert, chuckling. "Tied hand and foot."

"Well, that settles it," said the old lady, coming with a kind of bang into her seat again, "I must stop where I am."

Rupert looked bewildered.

"Stop where you are?" he said. "Why should you stop any longer where you are? What power can force you now to stop in this miserable cell?"

"The question rather is," said the old lady, with composure, "what power can force me to go anywhere else?"

We both stared wildly at her and she stared tranquilly at us both.

At last I said, "Do you really mean to say that we are to leave you here?"

"I suppose you don't intend to tie me up," she said, "and carry me off? I certainly shall not go otherwise."

"But, my dear madam," cried out Rupert, in a radiant exasperation, "we heard you with our own ears crying because you could not get out."

"Eavesdroppers often hear rather misleading things," replied the captive grimly. "I suppose I did break down a bit and lose my temper and talk to myself. But I have some sense of honour for all that."

"Some sense of honour?" repeated Rupert, and the last light of intelligence died out of his face, leaving it the face of an idiot with rolling eyes.

He moved vaguely towards the door and I followed. But I turned yet once more in the toils of my conscience and curiosity. "Can we do nothing for you, madam?" I said forlornly.

"Why," said the lady, "if you are particularly anxious to do me a little favour you might untie the gentlemen upstairs."

Rupert plunged heavily up the kitchen staircase, shaking it with his vague violence. With mouth open to speak he stumbled to the door of the sitting-room and scene of battle.

"Theoretically speaking, that is no doubt true," Mr. Burrows was saying, lying on his back and arguing easily with Basil; "but we must consider the matter as it appears to our senses. The origin of morality . . ."

"Basil," cried Rupert, gasping, "she won't come out."

"Who won't come out?" asked Basil, a little cross at being interrupted in an argument.

"The lady downstairs," replied Rupert. "The lady who was locked up. She won't come out. And she says that all she wants is for us to let these fellows loose."

"And a jolly sensible suggestion," cried Basil, and with a bound he was on top of the prostrate Burrows once more and was unknotting his bonds with hands and teeth.

"A brilliant idea. Swinburne, just undo Mr. Greenwood."

In a dazed and automatic way I released the little gentleman in the purple jacket, who did not seem to regard any of the proceedings as particularly sensible or brilliant. The gigantic Burrows, on the other hand, was heaving with herculean laughter.

"Well," said Basil, in his cheeriest way, "I think we must be getting away. We've so much enjoyed our evening. Far too much regard for you to stand on ceremony. If I may so express myself, we've made ourselves at home. Good-night. Thanks so much. Come along, Rupert."

"Basil," said Rupert desperately, "for God's sake come and see what you can make of the woman downstairs. I can't get the discomfort out of my mind. I admit that things look as if we had made a mistake. But these gentlemen won't mind perhaps . . ."

"No, no," cried Burrows, with a sort of Rabelaisian uproariousness. "No, no, look in the pantry, gentlemen. Examine the coalhole. Make a tour of the chimneys. There are corpses all over the house, I assure you."

This adventure of ours was destined to differ in one respect from others which I have narrated. I had been through many wild days with Basil Grant, days for the first half of which the sun and the moon seemed to have gone mad. But it had almost invariably happened that towards the end of the day and its adventure things had cleared themselves like the sky after rain, and a luminous and quiet meaning had gradually dawned upon me. But this day's work was destined to end in confusion worse confounded. Before we left that house, ten minutes afterwards, one half-witted touch was added which rolled all our minds in cloud. If Rupert's head had suddenly fallen off on the floor, if wings had begun to sprout out of Greenwood's shoulders, we could scarcely have been more suddenly stricken. And yet of this we had no explanation. We had to go to bed that night with the prodigy and get up next morning with it and let it stand in our memories for weeks and months. As will be seen, it was not until months afterwards that by another accident and in another way it was explained. For the present I only state what happened.

When all five of us went down the kitchen stairs again, Rupert leading, the two hosts bringing up the rear, we found the door of the prison again closed. Throwing it open we found the place again as black as pitch. The old lady, if she was still there, had turned out the gas; she seemed to have a weird preference for sitting in the dark.

Without another word Rupert lit the gas again. The little old lady turned her bird-like head as we all stumbled forward in the strong gaslight. Then, with a quickness that almost made me jump, she sprang up and swept a sort of old-fashioned curtsey or reverence. I looked quickly at Greenwood and Burrows, to whom it was natural to suppose this subservience had been offered. I felt irritated at what was implied in this subservience, and desired to see the faces of the tyrants as they received it. To my surprise they did not seem to have seen it at all; Burrows was paring his nails with a small penknife. Greenwood was at the back of the group and had hardly entered the room. And then an amazing fact became apparent. It was Basil Grant who stood foremost of the group, the golden gaslight lighting up his strong face and figure. His face wore an expression indescribably conscious, with the suspicion of a very grave smile. His head was slightly bent with a restrained bow. It was he who had acknowledged the lady's obeisance. And it was he, beyond any shadow of reasonable doubt, to whom it had really been directed.

"So I hear," he said, in a kindly yet somehow formal voice, "I hear, madam, that my friends have been trying to rescue you. But without success."

"No one, naturally, knows my faults better than you," answered the lady with a high colour. "But you have not found me guilty of treachery."

"I willingly attest it, madam," replied Basil, in the same level tones, "and the fact is that I am so much gratified with your exhibition of loyalty that I permit myself the pleasure of exercising some very large discretionary powers. You would not leave this room at the request of these gentlemen. But you know that you can safely leave it at mine."

The captive made another reverence. "I have never complained of your injustice," she said. "I need scarcely say what I think of your generosity."

And before our staring eyes could blink she had passed out of the room, Basil holding the door open for her.

He turned to Greenwood with a relapse into joviality. "This will be a relief to you," he said.

"Yes, it will," replied that immovable young gentleman with a face like a sphinx.

" 'Basil,' said Rupert, 'I always thought you were my brother. But are you a man? I mean—are you only a man?' "

We found ourselves outside in the dark blue night, shaken and dazed as if we had fallen into it from some high tower.

"Basil," said Rupert at last, in a weak voice. "I always thought you were my brother. But are you a man? I mean—are you only a man?"

"At present," replied Basil, "my mere humanity is proved by one of the most unmistakable symbols—hunger. We are too late for the theatre in Sloane Square. But we are not too late for the restaurant. Here comes the green omnibus!" and he had leaped on it before we could speak.

As I said, it was months after that Rupert Grant suddenly entered my room, swinging a satchel in his hand and with a general air of having jumped over the garden wall, and implored me to go with him upon the latest and wildest of his expeditions. He proposed to himself no less a thing than the discovery of the actual origin, whereabouts, and headquarters of the source of all our joys and sorrows—the Club of Queer Trades. I should expand this story for ever if I explained how ultimately we ran this strange entity to its lair. The process meant a hundred interesting things. The tracking of a member, the bribing of a cabman, the fighting of roughs, the lifting of a paving stone, the finding of a cellar, the finding of a cellar below the cellar, the finding of the subterranean passage, the finding of the Club of Queer Trades.

I have had many strange experiences in my life, but never a stranger one than that I felt when I came out of those rambling, sightless, and seemingly hopeless passages into the sudden splendour of a sumptuous and hospitable dining-room, surrounded upon almost every side by faces that I knew. There was Mr. Montmorency, the Arboreal House-Agent, seated between the two brisk young men who were occasionally vicars, and always Professional Detainers. There was P. G. Northover, founder of the Adventure and Romance Agency. There was Professor Chadd, who invented the Dancing Language.

As we entered all the members seemed to sink suddenly into their chairs, and with the very action the vacancy of the presidential seat gaped at us like a missing tooth.

"The president's not here," said Mr. P. G. Northover, turning suddenly to Professor Chadd.

"N-no," said that philosopher, with more than his ordinary vagueness. "I can't imagine where he is."

"Good heavens," said Mr. Montmorency, jumping up, "I really feel a little nervous. I'll go and see." And he ran out of the room.

An instant after he ran back again, twittering with a timid ecstasy.

"Mr. Montmorency, the Arboreal House-Agent"

" 'The President's not here' "

"He's there, gentlemen—he's there all right—he's coming in now," he cried, and sat down. Rupert and I could hardly help feeling the beginnings of a sort of wonder as to who this person might be who was the first member of this insane brotherhood. Who, we thought indistinctly, could be maddest in this world of madmen; what fantastic was it whose shadow filled all these fantastics with so loyal an expectation?

Suddenly we were answered. The door flew open and the room was filled and shaken with a shout, in the midst of which Basil Grant, smiling and in evening dress, took his seat at the head of the table.

How we ate that dinner I have no idea. In the common way I am a person particularly prone to enjoy the long luxuriance of the club dinner. But on this occasion it seemed a hopeless and endless string of courses. *Hors-d'oeuvres* sardines seemed as big as herrings, soup seemed a sort of ocean, larks were ducks, ducks were ostriches until that dinner was over. The cheese course was maddening. I had often heard of the moon being made of green cheese. That night I thought the green cheese was made of the moon. And all the time Basil Grant went on laughing and eating and drinking, and never threw one glance at us to tell us why he was there, the king of these capering idiots.

At last came the moment which I knew must in some way enlighten us, the time of the club speeches and the club toasts. Basil Grant rose to his feet amid a surge of song and cheers.

"Gentlemen," he said, "it is a custom in this society that the president for the year opens the proceedings not by any general toast or sentiment, but by calling upon each member to give a brief account of his trade. We then drink to that calling and to all who follow it. It is my business, as the senior member, to open by stating my claim to membership of this club. Years ago, gentlemen, I was a judge; I did my best in that capacity to do justice and to administer the law. But it gradually dawned on me that in my work, as it was, I was not touching even the fringe of justice. I was seated in the seat of the mighty, I was robed in scarlet and ermine; nevertheless, I held a small and lowly and futile post. I had to go by a mean rule as much as a postman, and my red and gold was worth no more than his. Daily there passed before me taut and passionate problems, the stringency of which I had to pretend to relieve by silly imprisonments or silly damages, while I knew all the time, by the light of my living common sense, that they would have been far better relieved by a kiss or a thrashing, or a few words of explanation, or a duel, or a tour in the West Highlands.

Then, as this grew on me, there grew on me continuously the sense of a mountainous frivolity. Every word said in the court, a whisper or an oath, seemed more connected with life than the words I had to say. Then came the time when I publicly blasphemed the whole bosh, was classed as a madman and melted from public life."

Something in the atmosphere told me that it was not only Rupert and I who were listening with intensity to this statement.

"Well, I discovered that I could be of real use. I offered myself privately as a purely moral judge to settle purely moral differences. Before very long these unofficial courts of honour (kept strictly secret) had spread over the whole of society. People were tried before me not for the practical trifles for which nobody cares, such as committing a murder, or keeping a dog without a licence. My criminals were tried for the faults which really make social life impossible. They were tried before me for selfishness, or for an impossible vanity, or for scandal-mongering, or for stinginess to guests or dependents. Of course these courts had no sort of real coercive powers. The fulfilment of their punishments rested entirely on the honour of the ladies and gentlemen involved, including the honour of the cuprits. But you would be amazed to know how completely our orders were always obeyed. Only lately I had a most pleasing example. A maiden lady in South Kensington whom I had condemned to solitary confinement for being the means of breaking off an engagement through backbiting, absolutely refused to leave her prison, although some well-meaning persons had been inopportune enough to rescue her."

Rupert Grant was staring at his brother, his mouth fallen agape. So, for the matter of that, I expect, was I. This, then, was the explanation of the old lady's strange discontent and her still stranger content with her lot. She was one of the culprits of his Voluntary Criminal Court. She was one of the clients of his Queer Trade.

We were still dazed when we drank, amid a crash of glasses, the health of Basil's new judiciary. We had only a confused sense of everything having been put right, the sense men will have when they come into the presence of God. We dimly heard Basil say:

"Mr. P. G. Northover will now explain the Adventure and Romance Agency."

And we heard equally dimly Northover beginning the statement he had made long ago to Major Brown. Thus our epic ended where it had begun, like a true cycle.

THE END

Essays

ON ESSAYS

Come to Think of It

THERE ARE dark and morbid moods in which I am tempted to feel that Evil re-entered the world in the form of Essays. The Essay is like the Serpent, smooth and graceful and easy of movement, also wavering or wandering. Besides, I suppose that the very word Essay had the original meaning of "trying it on." The serpent was in every sense of the word tentative. The tempter is always feeling his way, and finding out how much other people will stand. That misleading air of irresponsibility about the Essay is very disarming through appearing to be disarmed. But the serpent can strike without claws, as it can run without legs. It is the emblem of all those arts which are elusive, evasive, impressionistic, and shading away from tint to tint. I suppose that the Essay, so far as England at least is concerned, was almost invented by Francis Bacon. I can well believe it. I always thought he was the villain of English history.

It may be well to explain that I do not really regard all Essayists as wicked men. I have myself been an essayist, or tried to be an essayist; or pretended to be an essayist. Nor do I in the least dislike essays. I take perhaps my greatest literary pleasure in reading them; after such really serious necessities of the intellect as detective stories and tracts written by madmen. There is no better reading in the world than some contemporary essays, like those of Mr. E.V. Lucas or Mr. Robert Lynd. And though, unlike Mr. Lucas and Mr. Lynd, I am quite incapable of writing a really good essay, the motive of my dark suggestion is not a diabolic jealousy or envy. It is merely a natural taste for exaggeration, when dealing with a point too subtle to permit of exactitude. If I may myself imitate the timid and tentative tone of the true essayist, I will confine myself to saying that there is something in what I say. There is really an element in modern letters which is at once indefinite and dangerous.

What I mean is this. The distinction between certain old forms and certain relatively recent forms of literature is that the old were limited by a logical purpose. The Drama and the Sonnet were of the old kind; the Essay and the Novel are of the new. If a sonnet breaks out of the sonnet form, it ceases to be a sonnet. It may become a wild and inspiring specimen of free verse; but you do not have to call it a sonnet because you have nothing else to call it. But in the case of the new sort of novel, you do very often have to call it a novel because you have nothing else to call it. It is sometimes called a novel when it is hardly even a narrative. There is nothing to test or define it, except that it is not spaced like an epic poem, and often has even less of a story. The same applies to the apparently attractive leisure and liberty of the essay. By its very nature it does not exactly explain what it is trying to do, and thus escapes a decisive judgment about whether it has really done it. But in the case of the essay there is a practical peril; precisely because it deals so often with theoretical matters. It is always dealing with theoretical matters without the responsibility of being theoretical, or of propounding a theory.

For instance, there is any amount of sense and nonsense talked both for and against what is called mediævalism. There is also any amount of sense and nonsense talked for and against what is called modernism. I have occasionally tried to talk a little of the sense, with the result that I have been generally credited with all the nonsense. But if a man wanted one real and rational test, which really does distinguish the mediæval from the modern mood, it might be stated thus. The mediæval man thought in terms of the Thesis, where the modern man thinks in terms of the Essay. It would be unfair, perhaps, to say that the modern man only essays to think—or, in other words, makes a desperate attempt to think. But it would be true to say that the modern man often only essays, or attempts, to come to a conclusion. Whereas the mediæval man hardly thought it worth while to think at all, unless he could come to a conclusion. That is why he took a definite thing called a Thesis, and proposed to prove it. That is why Martin Luther, a very mediæval man in most ways, nailed up on the door the theses he proposed to prove. Many people suppose that he was doing something revolutionary, and even modernist, in doing this. In fact, he was doing exactly what all the other mediæval students and doctors had done ever since the twilight of the Dark Ages. If the really modern Modernist attempted to do it, he would probably find that he had never arranged his thoughts in the forms of theses at all. Well, it is quite an error to suppose, so far as I am concerned, that it is any question of restoring the rigid apparatus of the mediæval system. But I do think that the Essay has wandered too far away from the Thesis.

There is a sort of irrational and indefensible quality in many of the most brilliant phrases of the most beautiful essays. There is no essayist I enjoy more than Stevenson; there is probably no man now alive who admires Stevenson more than I. But if we take some favourite and frequently quoted sentence, such as, "To travel hopefully is better than to arrive," we shall see that it gives a loophole for every sort of sophistry and unreason. If it could be stated as a thesis, it could not be defended as a thought. A man would not travel hopefully at all, if he thought that the goal would be disappointing as compared with the travels. It is tenable that travel is the more enjoyable; but in that case it cannot be called hopeful. For the traveller is here presumed to hope for the end of travel, not merely for its continuance.

Now, of course, I do not mean that pleasant paradoxes of this sort have not a place in literature; and because of them the essay has a place in literature. There is room for the merely idle and wandering essayist, as for the merely idle and wandering traveller. The trouble is that the essayists have become the only ethical philosophers. The wandering thinkers have become the wandering preachers, and our only substitute for preaching friars. And whether our system is to be materialist or moralist, or sceptical or transcendental, we need more of a system than that. After a certain amount of wandering the mind wants either to get there or to go home. It is one thing to travel hopefully, and say half in jest that it is better than to arrive. It is another thing to travel hopelessly, because you know you will never arrive.

I was struck by the same tendency in re-reading some of the best essays ever written, which were especially enjoyed by Stevenson—the essays of Hazlitt. "You can live like a gentleman on Hazlitt's ideas," as Mr. Augustine Birrell truly remarked; but even in these we see the beginning of this inconsistent and irresponsible temper. For instance, Hazlitt was a Radical and constantly railed at Tories for not trusting men or mobs. I think it was he who lectured Walter Scott for so small a matter as making the mediæval mob in *Ivanhoe* jeer ungenerously at the retreat of the Templars. Anyhow, from any number of passages, one would infer that Hazlitt offered himself as a friend of the people. But he offered himself most furiously as an enemy of the Public. When he began to write about the Public, he described exactly the same many-headed monster of ignorance and cowardice and cruelty which the worst Tories called the Mob.

Now, if Hazlitt has been obliged to set forth his thoughts on Democracy in the theses of a mediæval schoolman, he would have had to think much more clearly and make up his mind much more decisively. I will leave the last word with the essayist; and admit that I am not sure whether he would have written such good essays.

A PIECE OF CHALK

Tremendous Trifles

I REMEMBER one splendid morning, all blue and silver, in the summer holidays when I reluctantly tore myself away from the task of doing nothing in particular, and put on a hat of some sort and picked up a walking-stick, and put six very bright-coloured chalks in my pocket. I then went into the kitchen (which, along with the rest of the house, belonged to a very square and sensible old woman in a Sussex village), and asked the owner and occupant of the kitchen if she had any brown paper. She had a great deal; in fact, she had too much; and she mistook the purpose and the rationale of the existence of brown paper. She seemed to have an idea that if a person wanted brown paper he must be wanting to tie up parcels; which was the last thing I wanted to do; indeed, it is a thing which I have found to be beyond my mental capacity. Hence she dwelt very much on the varying qualities of toughness and endurance in the material. I explained to her that I only wanted to draw pictures on it, and that I did not want them to endure in the least; and that from my point of view, therefore, it was a question, not of tough consistency, but of responsive surface, a thing comparatively irrelevant in a parcel. When she understood that I wanted to draw she offered to overwhelm me with note-paper, apparently supposing that I did my notes and correspondence on old brown paper wrappers from motives of economy.

I then tried to explain the rather delicate logical shade, that I not only liked brown paper, but liked the quality of brownness in paper, just as I liked the quality of brownness in October woods, or in beer, or in the peat-streams of the North. Brown paper represents the primal twilight of the first toil of creation, and with a bright-coloured chalk or two you can pick out points of fire in it, sparks of gold, and blood-red, and sea-green, like the first fierce stars that sprang out of divine darkness. All this I said (in an off-hand way) to the old woman; and I put the brown paper in my pocket along with the chalks, and possibly other things. I suppose everyone must have reflected how primeval and how poetical are the things that one carries in one's pocket; the pocket-knife, for instance, the type of all human tools, the infant of the sword. Once I planned to write a book of poems entirely about the things in my pockets. But I found it would be too long; and the age of the great epics is past.

With my stick and my knife, my chalks and my brown paper, I went out on to the great downs. I crawled across those colossal contours that express the best quality of England, because they are at the same time soft and strong. The smoothness of them has the same meaning as the smoothness of great cart-horses, or the smoothness of the beech-tree; it declares in the teeth of our timid and cruel theories that the mighty are merciful. As my eye swept the landscape, the landscape was as kindly as any of its cottages, but for power it was like an earthquake. The villages in the immense valley were safe, one could see, for centuries; yet the lifting of the whole land was like the lifting of one enormous wave to wash them all away.

I crossed one swell of living turf after another, looking for a place to sit down and draw. Do not, for heaven's sake, imagine I was going to sketch from Nature. I was going to draw devils and seraphim, and blind old gods that men worshipped before the dawn of right, and saints in robes of angry crimson, and seas of strange green, and all the sacred or monstrous symbols that look so well in bright colours on brown paper. They are much better worth drawing than Nature; also they are much easier to draw. When a cow came slouching by in the field next to me, a mere artist might have drawn it; but I always get wrong in the hind legs of quadrupeds. So I drew the soul of the cow; which I saw there plainly walking before me in the sunlight; and the soul was all purple and silver, and had seven horns and the mystery that belongs to all the beasts. But though I could not with a crayon get the best out of the landscape, it does not follow that the landscape was not getting the best out of me. And this, I think, is the mistake that people make about the old poets who lived before Wordsworth, and were supposed not to care very much about Nature because they did not describe it much.

They preferred writing about great men to writing about great hills; but they sat on the great hills to write it. They gave out much less about Nature, but they drank in, perhaps, much more. They painted the white robes of their holy virgins with the blinding snow, at which they had stared all day. They blazoned the shields of their paladins with the purple and gold of many heraldic sunsets. The greenness of a thousand green leaves clustered into the live green figure of Robin Hood. The blueness of a score of forgotten skies became the blue robes of the Virgin. The inspiration went in like sunbeams and came out like Apollo.

But as I sat scrawling these silly figures on the brown paper, it began to dawn on me, to my great disgust, that I had left one chalk, and that a most exquisite and essential chalk, behind. I searched all my pockets, but I could not find any white chalk. Now, those who are acquainted with all the philosophy (nay, religion) which is typified in the art of drawing on brown paper, know that white is positive and essential. I cannot avoid remarking here upon a moral significance. One of the wise and awful truths which this brown-paper art reveals, is this, that white is a colour. It is not a mere absence of colour; it is a shining and affirmative thing, as fierce as red, as definite as black. When, so to speak, your pencil grows red-hot, it draws roses; when it grows white-hot, it draws stars. And one of the two or three defiant verities of the best religious morality, of real Christianity, for example, is exactly this same thing; the chief assertion of religious morality is that white is a colour. Virtue is not the absence of vices or the avoidance of moral dangers; virtue is a vivid and separate thing, like pain or a particular smell. Mercy does not mean not being cruel or sparing people revenge or punishment; it means a plain and positive thing like the sun, which one has either seen or not seen.

Chastity does not mean abstention from sexual wrong; it means something flaming, like Joan of Arc. In a word, God paints in many colours, but He never paints so gorgeously, I had almost said so gaudily, as when He paints in white. In a sense our age has realised this fact, and expressed it in our sullen costume. For if it were really true that white was a blank and colourless thing, negative and non-committal, then white would be used instead of black and grey for the funeral dress of this pessimistic period. We should see city gentlemen in frock coats of spotless silver linen, with top hats as white as wonderful arum lilies. Which is not the case.

Meanwhile, I could not find my chalk.

I sat on the hill in a sort of despair. There was no town nearer than Chichester at which it was even remotely probable that there would be such a thing as an artist's colourman. And yet, without white, my absurd little pictures would be as pointless as the world would be if there were no good people in it. I stared stupidly round, racking my brain for expedients. Then I suddenly stood up and roared with laughter, again and again, so that the cows stared at me and called a committee. Imagine a man in the Sahara regretting that he had no sand for his hour-glass. Imagine a gentleman in mid-ocean wishing that he had brought some salt water with him for his chemical experiments. I was sitting on an immense warehouse of white chalk. The landscape was made entirely out of white chalk. White chalk was piled more miles until it met the sky I stooped and broke a piece off the rock I sat on: it did not mark so well as the shop chalks do; but it gave the effect. And I stood there in a trance of pleasure, realising that this Southern England is not only a grand peninsula, and a tradition and a civilisation; it is something even more admirable. It is a piece of chalk.

THE ROMANTIC IN THE RAIN

A Miscellany of Men

The middle classes of modern England are quite fanatically fond of washing; and are often enthusiastic for teetotalism. I cannot therefore comprehend why it is that they exhibit a mysterious dislike of rain. Rain, that inspiring and delightful thing, surely combines the qualities of these two ideals with quite a curious perfection. Our philanthropists are eager to establish public baths everywhere. Rain surely is a public bath; it might almost be called mixed bathing. The appearance of persons coming fresh from this great natural lustration is not perhaps polished or dignified; but for the matter of that, few people are dignified when coming out of a bath. But the scheme of rain in itself is one of an enormous purification. It realises the dream of some insane hygienist: it scrubs the sky. Its giant brooms and mops seem to reach the starry rafters and starless corners of the cosmos; it is a cosmic spring-cleaning.

If the Englishman is really fond of cold baths, he ought not to grumble at the English climate for being a cold bath. In these days we are constantly told that we should leave our little special possessions and join in the enjoyment of common social institutions and a common social machinery I offer the rain as a thoroughly Socialistic institution. It disregards that degraded delicacy which has hitherto led each gentleman to take his shower-bath in private. It is a better shower-bath, because it is public and communal; and, best of all, because somebody else pulls the string.

As for the fascination of rain for the water drinker, it is a fact the neglect of which I simply cannot comprehend. The enthusiastic water drinker must regard a rainstorm as a sort of universal banquet and debauch of his own favourite beverage. Think of the imaginative intoxication of the wine drinker if the crimson clouds sent down claret or the golden clouds hock. Paint upon primitive darkness some such scenes of apocalypse, towering and gorgeous skyscapes in which champagne falls like fire from heaven or the dark skies grow purple and tawny with the terrible colours of port. All this must the wild abstainer feel, as he rolls in the long soaking grass, kicks his ecstatic heels to heaven, and listens to the roaring rain. It is he, the water drinker, who ought to be the true bacchanal of the forests; for all the forests are drinking water. Moreover, the forests are apparently enjoying it: the trees rave and reel to and fro like drunken giants; they clash boughs as revellers clash cups; they roar undying thirst and howl the health of the world.

All around me as I write is a noise of Nature drinking; and Nature makes a noise when she is drinking, being by no means refined. If I count it Christian mercy to give a cup of cold water to a sufferer, shall I complain of these multitudinous cups of cold water handed round to all living things; a cup of water for every shrub; a cup of water for every weed? I would be ashamed to grumble at it. As Sir Philip Sidney said, their need is greater than mine—especially for water.

There is a wild garment that still carries nobly the name of a wild Highland clan: a clan come from those hills where rain is not so much an incident as an atmosphere. Surely every man of imagination must feel a tempestuous flame of Celtic romance spring up within him whenever he puts on a mackintosh. I could never reconcile myself to carrying an umbrella; it is a pompous Eastern business, carried over the heads of despots in the dry, hot lands. Shut up, an umbrella is an unmanageable walking-stick; open, it is an inadequate tent. For my part, I have no taste for pretending to be a walking pavilion; I think nothing of my hat, and precious little of my head. If I am to be protected against wet, it must be by some closer and more careless protection, something that I can forget altogether. It might be a Highland plaid. It might be that yet more Highland thing, a mackintosh.

And there is really something in the mackintosh of the military qualities of the Highlander. The proper cheap mackintosh has a blue and white sheen as of steel or iron; it gleams like armour. I like to think of it as the uniform of that ancient clan in some of its old and misty raids. I like to think of all the Macintoshes, in their mackintoshes, descending on some doomed Lowland village, their wet waterproofs flashing in the sun or moon. For indeed this is one of the real beauties of rainy weather, that while the amount of original and direct light is commonly lessened, the number of things that reflect light is unquestionably increased. There is less sunshine; but there are more shiny things; such beautifully shiny things as pools and puddles and mackintoshes. It is like moving in a world of mirrors.

And indeed this is the last and not the least gracious of the casual works of magic wrought by rain: that while it decreases light, yet it doubles it. If it dims the sky, it brightens the earth. It gives the roads (to the sympathetic eye) something of the beauty of Venice. Shallow lakes of water reiterate every detail of earth and sky; we dwell in a double universe. Sometimes walking upon bare and lustrous pavements, wet under numerous lamps, a man seems a black blot on all that golden looking-glass, and could fancy he was flying in a yellow sky. But wherever trees and towns hang head downwards in a pigmy puddle, the sense of Celestial topsy-turvydom is the same. This bright, wet, dazzling confusion of shape and shadow, of reality and reflection, will appeal strongly to any one with the transcendental instinct about this dreamy and dual life of ours. It will always give a man the strange sense of looking down at the skies.

A MUCH REPEATED REPETITION

Daily News

He must have been a man with a very dim and strange mind who said, "History repeats itself." Of course, there is a grain of veracity in it, but surely the correct way of stating the matter would be, "The Universe repeats itself, with the possible exception of history." Of all earthly studies history is the only one that does not repeat itself. This is the very definition of the divinity of man. Astronomy repeats itself; botany repeats itself; trigonometry repeats itself; mechanics repeats itself; compound long division repeats itself. Every sum if worked out in the same way at any time will bring out the same answer. But it is the peculiarity and fascination of the sums of history that with the most perfect calculation the sum comes out with a slight mysterious difference every time. There is a certain amount of the divine in every government or society. In most governments and societies it is a very small amount indeed; but there is just enough of it to do the noble and needful work; there is just enough, that is to say, to make that government or society go where it doesn't want to go, and produce something entirely different from what it had intended.

A great many moderns say that history is a science; if so it occupies a solitary and splendid elevation among the sciences; it is the only science the conclusions of which are always wrong. History has filled itself with many and bewildering crimes. It has consumed continents; it has destroyed nations and empires and civilisations; it has given birth to men who seemed to be like demons let loose, like monsters from an immoral planet. But there is one unendurable thing that it has never done; there is one unpardonable sin that it has never committed. It has never repeated itself. It has never asked to agonise once more with precisely the same agony; it has never asked us to look again upon the same living and hateful face. Carlyle said admirably of the Court chaplains who spoke of Louis XV as having "fallen asleep in the Lord" that after all the main matter was that he did fall asleep. "Curtained in thick night, under what keeping we ask not, he at least will never, through unending ages, insult the face of the sun any more."

The life of man is a terrible thing at many times and in many places: he has much to put up with in any case. But he has not to put up with the horror of history repeating itself. That is the freedom and glory of the god which he has bought by so much suffering. That is what he has won by giving up the Nirvans of the Cabbages; by surrendering the perfect heaven of matter. When a man has struck a tyrant dead he does not have to say, "A precise replica of this tyrant will be standing in this spot a year hence. I have only cut down a poppy." When a man takes the trouble to go mad and break down and lay waste a temple, he does not have to say, "An exact reproduction of this temple will grow out of the ground in twelve months. I have only plucked a blade of grass." To man is spared the hideous and frantic and violent farce of repetition. Politicians do not come again like the flowers of spring. Eminent public persons do not rise again like the sun.

Imagine what it would be if things were so! A perfect Chamberlain, with eyeglass and orchid, would grow out of the ground at regular seasons; there might be clusters, nay, there might be fields full of them. There would be a regular month for them. They would be sowed and reaped and all that sort of thing. But fortunately for us, things do not in history happen in that way. In history a thing recurs, but it never recurs quite exactly. It comes back, but it is never quite the same. Mr. Chamberlain, for instance, will undoubtedly repeat himself. He will come back in human history; or the type of man he is will come back; but he will not be quite the same in every detail. The differences might be many. Personally, I believe he will have red whiskers and will understand the nature of war. But no one can prophesy.

I need scarcely insist further upon the fearful prospect if history really repeated itself. There is something about the actual demeanour of mankind, as I perceive it, which leads me to believe that they do not think the Flood will repeat itself. There is something about the demeanour of the ruling classes which leads me to believe that they do not think that the French Revolution will repeat itself. There is an indefinable air about the splendid, hardy, victorious

Anglo-Saxon generals of our age which leads me to believe that they do not think that Napoleon will repeat himself. Everybody really assumes in human affairs and in human relations that everything that comes will be something that has never exactly come before; it may be good, it may be bad, it may be excellent, it may be atrocious, but it will at least be new. Novelty is the one element which we demand of all human things. It is the one element that we always have. Even the awful blow which awaits us all at last has one great human peculiarity; it is mysterious. It awakens regret, terror, and curiosity.

All this is the origin of the one distinctly human thing—the story. There can be as good science about a turnip as about a man. There can be, properly considered, as good philosophy about a turnip as about a man. There can be, I should strongly, though reverently, suspect, as good theology about a turnip as about a man. There can be, without any question at all, as good higher mathematics about a turnip as about a man. But I do not think, though I speak in a manner somewhat tentative, that there could be as good a novel written about a turnip as about a man. I am not sure; there may be a quiet, silvery school of fiction, to which a turnip would lend itself. But I think, on the whole, that even in the most quiet and silvery school there would be needed a certain swell and ebb of events. No; in this matter of the story comes in the real supremacy of man. Of a mechanical thing we have a full knowledge. Of a living thing we have a divine ignorance; and a divine ignorance may be called the definition of romance. The Christian gospel is not a system; a system is fit for turnips. The Christian gospel is literally a story; that is, a thing in which one does not know what is to happen next. This thing, called Fiction, then, is the main fact of our human supremacy. If you want to know what is our human kinship with Nature, with the brutes, and with the stars, you can find cartloads of big philosophical volumes to show it you. You will find our kinship with Nature in books on geology and books on metaphysics. But if you want to find our isolation and divinity, you must pick up a penny novelette.

CHEESE

Alarms and Discursions

My forthcoming work in five volumes, "The Neglect of Cheese in European Literature," is a work of such unprecedented and laborious detail that it is doubtful if I shall live to finish it. Some overflowings from such a fountain of information may therefore be permitted to sprinkle these pages. I cannot yet wholly explain the neglect to which I refer. Poets have been mysteriously silent on the subject of cheese. Virgil, if I remember right, refers to it several times, but with too much Roman restraint. He does not let himself go on cheese. The only other poet I can think of just now who seems to have had some sensibility on the point was the nameless author of the nursery rhyme which says: "If all the trees were bread and cheese"—which is, indeed, a rich and gigantic vision of the higher gluttony. If all the trees were bread and cheese there would be considerable deforestation—in any part of England where I was living. Wild and wide woodlands would reel and fade before me as rapidly as they ran after Orpheus. Except Virgil and this anonymous rhymer, I can recall no verse about cheese. Yet it has every quality which we require in exalted poetry. It is a short, strong word; it rhymes to "breeze" and "seas" (an essential point); that it is emphatic in sound is admitted even by the civilisation of the modern cities. For their citizens, with no apparent intention except emphasis, will often say, "Cheese it!" or even "Quite the cheese." The substance itself is imaginative. It is ancient—sometimes in the individual case, always in the type and custom. It is simple, being directly derived from milk, which is one of the ancestral drinks, not lightly to be corrupted with soda-water. You know, I hope (though I myself have only just thought of it), that the four rivers of Eden were milk, water, wine, and ale. Aerated waters only appeared after the Fall.

But cheese has another quality, which is also the very soul of song. Once in endeavouring to lecture in several places at once, I made an eccentric journey across England, a journey of so irregular and even illogical shape that it necessitated my having lunch on four successive days in four roadside inns in four different counties. In each inn they had nothing but bread and cheese; nor can I imagine why a man should want more than bread and cheese, if he can get enough of it. In each inn the cheese was good; and in each inn it was different. There was a noble Wensleydale cheese in Yorkshire, a Cheshire cheese in Cheshire, and so on. Now, it is just here that true poetic civilisation differs from that paltry and mechanical civilisation which holds us all in bondage. Bad customs are universal and rigid, like modern militarism. Good customs are universal and varied, like native chivalry and self-defence. Both the good and bad civilisation cover us as with a canopy, and protect us from all that is outside. But a good civilisation spreads over us freely like a tree, varying and yielding because it is alive. A bad civilisation stands up and sticks out above us like an umbrella—artificial, mathematical in shape; not merely universal, but uniform. So it is with the contrast between the substances that vary and the substances that are the same wherever they penetrate. By a wise doom of heaven men were commanded to eat cheese, but not the same cheese. Being really universal it varies from valley to valley. But if, let us say, we compare cheese with soap (that vastly inferior substance), we shall see that soap tends more and more to be merely Smith's Soap or Brown's Soap, sent automatically all over the world. If the Red Indians have soap it is Smith's Soap. If the Grand Lama has soap it is Brown's soap. There is nothing subtly and strangely Buddhist, nothing tenderly Tibetan, about his soap. I fancy the Grand Lama does not eat cheese (he is not worthy), but if he does it is probably a local cheese, having some real relation to his life and outlook. Safety matches, tinned foods, patent medicines are sent all over the world; but they are not produced all over the world. Therefore there is in them a mere dead identity, never that soft play of slight variation which exists in things produced everywhere out of the soil, in the milk of the kine, or the fruits of the orchard. You can get a whisky and soda at every outpost of the Empire: that is why so many Empire-builders go mad. But you are not tasting or touching any environment, as in the cider of Devonshire or the grapes of the Rhine. You are not approaching Nature in one of her myriad tints of mood, as in the holy act of eating cheese.

When I had done my pilgrimage in the four wayside public-houses I reached one of the great northern cities, and there I proceeded, with great rapidity and complete inconsistency, to a large and elaborate restaurant, where I knew I could get many other things besides bread and cheese. I could get that also, however; or at least I expected to get it; but I was sharply reminded that I had entered Babylon, and left England behind. The waiter brought me cheese, indeed, but cheese cut up into contemptibly small pieces; and it is the awful fact that, instead of Christian bread, he brought me biscuits. Biscuits—to one who had eaten the cheese of four great countrysides! Biscuits—to one who had proved anew for himself the sanctity of the ancient wedding between cheese and bread! I addressed the waiter in warm and moving terms. I asked him who he was that he should put asunder those whom Humanity had joined. I asked him if he did not feel, as an artist, that a solid but yielding substance like cheese went naturally with a solid, yielding substance like bread; to eat it off biscuits is like eating it off slates. I asked him if, when he said his prayers, he was so supercilious as to pray for his daily biscuits. He gave me generally to understand that he was only obeying a custom of Modern Society. I have therefore resolved to raise my voice, not against the waiter, but against Modern Society, for this huge and unparalleled modern wrong.

ON GARGOYLES

Alarms and Discursions

Alone at some distance from the wasting walls of a disused abbey I found half sunken in the grass the grey and goggle-eyed visage of one of those graven monsters that made the ornamental water-spouts in the cathedrals of the Middle Ages. It lay there, scoured by ancient rains or striped by recent fungus, but still looking like the head of some huge dragon slain by a primeval hero. And as I looked at it, I thought of the meaning of the grotesque, and passed into some symbolic reverie of the three great stages of art.

I

Once upon a time there lived upon an island a merry and innocent people, mostly shepherds and tillers of the earth. They were republicans, like all primitive and simple souls; they talked over their affairs under a tree, and the nearest approach they had to a personal ruler was a sort of priest or white witch who said their prayers for them. They worshipped the sun, not idolatrously, but as the golden crown of the god whom all such infants see almost as plainly as the sun.

Now this priest was told by his people to build a great tower, pointing to the sky in salutation of the Sun-god; and he pondered long and heavily before he picked his materials. For he was resolved to use nothing that was not almost as clear and exquisite as sunshine itself; he would use nothing that was not washed as white as the rain can wash the heavens, nothing that did not sparkle as spotlessly as that crown of God. He would have nothing grotesque or obscure; he would not have even anything emphatic or even anything mysterious. He would have all the arches as light as laughter and as candid as logic. He built the temple in three concentric courts, which were cooler and more exquisite in substance each than the other. For the outer wall was a hedge of white lilies, ranked so thick that a green stalk was hardly to be seen; and the wall within that was of crystal, which smashed the sun into a million stars. And the wall within that, which was the tower itself, was a tower of pure water, forced up in an everlasting fountain; and upon the very tip and crest of that foaming spire was one big and blazing diamond, which the water tossed up eternally and caught again as a child catches a ball.

"Now," said the priest, "I have made a tower which is a little worthy of the sun."

II

But about this time the island was caught in a swarm of pirates; and the shepherds had to turn themselves into rude warriors and seamen; and at first they were utterly broken down in blood and shame; and the pirates might have taken the jewel flung up for ever from their sacred fount. And then, after years of horror and humiliation, they gained a little and began to conquer because they did not mind defeat. And the pride of the pirates went sick within them after a few unexpected foils; and at last the invasion rolled back into the empty seas and the island was delivered. And for some reason after this men began to talk quite differently about the temple and the sun. Some, indeed, said, "You must not touch the temple; it is classical; it is perfect, since it admits no imperfections." But the others answered, "In that it differs from the sun, that shines on the evil and the good and on mud and monsters everywhere. The temple is of the noon; it is made of white marble clouds and sapphire sky. But the sun is not always of the noon. The sun dies daily; every night he is crucified in blood and fire."

Now the priest had taught and fought through all the war, and his hair had grown white, but his eyes had grown young. And he said, "I was wrong and they are right. The sun, the symbol of our father, gives life to those earthly things that are full of ugliness and energy. All the exaggerations are right, if they exaggerate the right thing. Let us point to heaven with tusks and horns and fins and trunks and tails so long as they all point to heaven. The ugly animals praise God as much as the beautiful. The frog's eyes stand out of his head because he is staring at heaven. The giraffe's neck is long because he is stretching towards heaven. The donkey has ears to hear—let him hear."

And under the new inspiration they planned a gorgeous cathedral in the Gothic manner, with all the animals of the earth crawling over it, and all the possible ugly things making up one common beauty, because they all appealed to the god. The columns of the temple were carved like the necks of giraffes; the dome was like an ugly tortoise; and the highest pinnacle was a monkey standing on his head with his tail pointing at the sun. And yet the whole was beautiful, because it was lifted up in one living and religious gesture as a man lifts his hands in prayer.

III

But this great plan was never properly completed. The people had brought up on great wagons the heavy tortoise roof and the huge necks of stone, and all the thousand and one oddities that made up that unity, the owls and the efts and the crocodiles and the kangaroos, which hideous by themselves might have been magnificent if reared in one definite proportion and dedicated to the sun. For this was Gothic, this was romantic, this was Christian art; this was the whole advance of Shakespeare upon Sophocles. And that symbol which was to crown it all, the ape upside down, was really Christian; for man is the ape upside down.

But the rich, who had grown riotous in the long peace, obstructed the thing, and in some squabble a stone struck the priest on the head and he lost his memory. He saw piled in front of him frogs and elephants, monkeys and giraffes, toadstools and sharks, all the ugly things of the universe which he had collected to do honour to God. But he forgot why he had collected them. He could not remember the design or the object. He piled them all wildly into one heap fifty feet high; and when he had done it all the rich and influential went into a passion of applause and cried, "This is real art! This is Realism! This is things as they really are!"

That, I fancy, is the only true origin of Realism. Realism is simply Romanticism that has lost its reason. This is so not merely in the sense of insanity but of suicide. It has lost its reason; that is its reason for existing. The old Greeks summoned godlike things to worship their god. The mediæval Christians summoned all things to worship theirs, dwarfs and pelicans, monkeys and madmen. The modern realists summon all these million creatures to worship their god; and then have no god for them to worship. Paganism was in art a pure beauty; that was the dawn. Christianity was a beauty created by controlling a million monsters of ugliness; and that in my belief was the zenith and the noon. Modern art and science practically mean having the million monsters and being unable to control them; and I will venture to call that the disruption and the decay. The finest lengths of the Elgin marbles consist of splendid horses going to the temple of a virgin. Christianity, with its gargoyles and grotesques, really amounted to saying this: that a donkey could go before all the horses of the world when it was really going to the temple. Romance means a holy donkey going to the temple. Realism means a lost donkey going nowhere.

The fragments of futile journalism or fleeting impression which are here collected are very like the wrecks and riven blocks that were piled in a heap round my imaginary priest of the sun. They are very like that grey and gaping head of stone that I found overgrown with the grass. Yet I will venture to make even of these trivial fragments the high boast that I am a mediævalist and not a modern. That is, I really have a notion of why I have collected all the nonsensical things there are. I have not the patience nor perhaps the constructive intelligence to state the connecting link between all these chaotic papers. But it could be stated. This row of shapeless and ungainly monsters which I now set before the reader does not consist of separate idols cut out capriciously in lonely valleys or various islands. These monsters are meant for the gargoyles of a definite cathedral. I have to carve the gargoyles, because I can carve nothing else; I leave to others the angels and the arches and the spires. But I am very sure of the style of the architecture and of the consecration of the church.

ON VULGARITY

Come to Think of It

MOST OF us must have wondered if we could find a real definition of Vulgarity. For it is generally difficult to destroy, or even to defy, a thing that we cannot define. I suspect, to begin with, that we should discover, in the case of this word, a difficulty that exists with regard to a great many modern words. They were invented after the age of doctrine and definition. They are at best artistic and atmospheric. They have come to stand for strong impressions which are real enough, but to stand for them merely as symbols, sometimes poetical, sometimes arbitrary and accidental. And I rather fancy that, in the case of Vulgarity and other verbal symbols, we should find that the inquiry ended in an odd way. When we had really managed to put into other words the thing we meant by this particular word, we should probably find that it was a very incorrect word for it.

Thus Vulgarity, as a vice which we can all feel rather vividly (I should imagine) in the affairs and fashions around us, is not really connected with the ancient *vulgus;* not even with the *profanum vulgus* [the common crowd]. The mob has its own vices, but it is not necessarily vulgar. The mass of mankind has its own weaknesses, but we do not necessarily feel those weaknesses as vulgarizing. The particular thing we mean, or at any rate the thing I mean, when I use this word, is something much more subtle and certainly much more poisonous. But I really do not know any other word for it. I could easily give examples of it from the press, but this would be a rather cheap and unfair way of filling the pages in this book. So, with a full sense of the rashness of the experiment, I will make an attempt to state the real nature of the thing I call Vulgarity; and I wish I knew a worse name for it.

What I mean by Vulgarity is this. When six men stand up and we suddenly see that one of them is a dwarf, we are startled to find him so stunted. We only realise that he is stunted because he is standing up; because he is stretching himself to his full height. When the mind of man stretches itself, in order to show off, and is still stunted, that is the revelation that I mean. It is by the showing off that we see how little there is to show. When somebody tries to impress us, either with his wit or assurance, or knowledge of the world, or power, or grace, or even poetry and ideality, and in the very act of doing so shows he has low ideas of all these things—that is Vulgarity. In other words, a thing is only vulgar when its best is base.

That is why many things commonly called vulgar do not seem to me vulgar at all. The red-nosed comedian, the man who sits on his hat, the joke about the drunken man, these are not the sort of thing of which I am thinking; indeed, they are the very reverse. For the man who sits on his hat is not standing up. The drunkard is not stretching himself; he is (as he will explain) enjoying relaxation. The red-nosed comedian is not pretending to be at his best. These things may have dangers or weaknesses of their own, but they do not indicate that a man is base even at his best. The man who sits on his hat on the stage may be perfectly dignified when he sits on his chair at home, or takes off his hat in church. The red-nosed comedian, when he has hung up his red nose along with his little hat, may be in private life a blend of Bayard and Socrates. We can appeal from Philip drunk to Philip sober. But we can appeal no further, if we find that even Philip sober is a boor and a brute. If he is base at his best, and baser in his attempt to impress us with his best, then we have a certain sensation for which I know no other name. It appears when the man does pretend to be Bayard, and can only manage to be Barnum. It appears when the man does go to church and take off his hat, and seems to care more about the hat than the church. It appears, in short, when there is something about him that seems to debase and flatten everything he touches; and most of all when he touches worthy and exalted things. Thus there is the man who wishes first to prove that he is a gentleman, and only proves two things; first, that he is vulgar enough to prefer being a gentleman to being a man; and second, that he has a hideously stunted and half-witted notion even of being a gentleman. There is the man who wishes to show that he has lived in the best society; and shows even in showing it that he does not know the best society from the worst.

There are any number of lesser and often more excusable examples, but this is the touch that makes the difference. There is the man who is always being tactful without tact. There is the man who jokes loudly and laughs heartily, and so proves that he has no sense of humour. There is the man who talks a great deal about understanding women, and with every word helps us with a ghastly clarity to understand him. There is the man who tells stories of the wonderful affability and friendliness of very rich men he has known, and thereby reveals his secret religion—that rich men are gods and that he is a fortunate favourite of the gods. All these men have the mark that I call for convenience vulgar; the mark that they give us their own moral and spiritual measure by stretching themselves to their full stature. If they had been a little lax and casual and humble, we might never have found them out. If they had not been so clever, we might never have known that they were fools. If they had not been so gentlemanly, we should not have seen that they were cads.

If I have in any faint degree described this indescribable thing, I would ask the reader to run his eye down a large number of current columns, and see whether there is not something hurting our heritage of culture, something all the more vulgar because it is subtle. It is seldom or never indecent, at any rate in England. It would perhaps be less dangerous if it were less decent. It keeps on one side of one line, but its very posture in balancing on that line is offensive. As I have said, in my sense, the notion of going on the spree is not vulgar, but the perpetual implication that everybody is going nowhere except to the best restaurants is vulgar. For Vulgarity is a thing of visions and even ideals; and men are judged by their dreams.

THE ROMANCE OF CHILDHOOD

All is Grist

I AM just old enough to remember the world before telephones. And I remember that my father and my uncle fitted up with their own metal and chemicals the first telephone I ever saw: a miniature telephone reaching from the top bedroom under the roof to the remote end of the garden. I was really impressed imaginatively by this; and I do not think I have ever been so much impressed since by any extension of it. The point is rather important in the whole theory of imagination. It did startle me that a voice should sound in the room when it was really as distant as the next street. It would hardly have startled me more if it had been as distant as the next town. It does not startle me any more if it is as distant as the next continent. The miracle is over. Thus I admired even the large scientific things most on a small scale. So I always found that I was much more attracted by the microscope than the telescope. I was not overwhelmed in childhood by being told of remote stars which the sun never reached, any more than in manhood by being told of the empire on which the sun never set. I had no use for an empire that had no sunsets. But I was inspired and thrilled by looking through a little hole at a crystal like a pin's head, and seeing it change pattern and colour like a pygmy sunset.

I have already picked two quarrels with better men than myself, who were enthusiasts for childish romance, upon the reality of the romance of childhood. First, I disagree with them when they treat the infantile imagination as a sort of dream; whereas I remember it rather as a man dreaming might remember the world where he was awake. And second, I deny that children have suffered under a tyranny of moral tales. For I remember the time when it would have seemed the most hideous tyranny to take my moral tales away from me. And, in order to make this clear, I must contradict yet another common assumption in the romantic description of the dawn of life. The point is not very easy to explain; indeed, I have spent the greater part of my life in an unsuccessful attempt to explain it. Upon the cartloads of ill-constructed books in which I have completely failed to do so I have no desire to dwell. But perhaps, as a general definition, this might be useful; or, if not as a definition, at least a suggestion. From the first vaguely, and of late more and more clearly, I have felt that the world is conceiving liberty as something that merely works outwards. And I have always conceived it as something that works inwards.

The ordinary poetic description of the first dreams of life is a description of mere longing for larger and larger horizons. The imagination is supposed to work towards the infinite; though in that sense the infinite is the opposite of the imagination. For the imagination deals with an image, and an image is in its nature a thing that has an outline, and therefore a limit. Now I will maintain, paradoxical as it may seem, that the child does not desire merely to fall out of the window, or even to fly through the air or to be drowned in the sea. When he wishes to go to other places, they are still places, even if nobody has ever been there. But, in truth, the case is much stronger than that. It is plain on the face of the facts that the child is positively in love with limits. He uses his imagination to invent imaginary limits. The nurse and the governess have never told him that it is his moral duty to step on alternate paving-stones. He deliberately deprives this world of half its paving-stones, in order to exult in a challenge that he has offered to himself. I played that kind of game with myself all over the mats and boards and carpets of the house; and, at the risk of being detained during His Majesty's pleasure, I will admit that I often play it still. In that sense I have constantly tried to cut down the actual space at my disposal; to divide and subdivide, into these happy prisons, the house in which I was quite free to run wild. I believe that there is in this psychological freak a truth without which the whole modern world is missing its main opportunity. If we look at the favourite nursery romances, or at least if we have the patience to look at them twice, we shall find that they all really support this view, even when they have largely been accepted as supporting the opposite view. The charm of Robinson Crusoe is not in the fact that he could find his way to a remote island, but in the fact that he could not find any way of getting away from it. It is that fact which gives an intensive interest and excitement to all the things that he had with him on the island; the axe and the parrot and the guns and the little hoard of grain. The tale of *Treasure Island* is not the record of a vague desire to go on a sea voyage for one's health. It ends where it began; and it began with Stevenson drawing a map of the island, with all its bays and capes cut out as clearly as fretwork. The eternal interest of the Noah's Ark, considered as a toy, consists in its complete suggestion of compactness and isolation; of creatures so comically remote and fantastic being all locked up in one box; as if Noah had been told to pack up the sun and moon with his luggage. In other words, it is exactly the same game that I have played myself, by piling all the things I wanted on a sofa, and imagining that the carpet around me was the surrounding sea.

This game of self-limitation is one of the secret pleasures of life. As it says in the little manuals about such sports, the game is played in several forms. One very good way of playing it is to look at the nearest bookcase and wonder whether you would find sufficient entertainment in that chance collection, even if you had no other books. But always it is dominated by this principle of division and restriction, which begins with the game played by the child with the paving-stones. But I dwell upon it here because it must be understood as something real and rooted, so far as I am concerned, in order that the other views I have offered about these things may make any sort of sense. If anybody chooses to say that I have founded all my social philosophy on the antics of a baby, I am quite satisfied to bow and smile.

I have no great hopes that my own private Utopia, the Utopia of subdivision and self-limitation, is likely to be rapidly established in the real world. I do not immediately expect that the landlord with five hundred acres will instantly cut it down to fifty acres, and stand in startled admiration of the fresh and pleasing shape, the entirely new and attractive map or outline of his domains. I hardly suppose that he will be romantically enraptured, all at once, at the discovery of the enchanted island that I have cut out for him, out of the dull and dreary sea of his solid landed estate. I doubt whether the simple kindly act of stealing half his books will drive him to reading the other half; I am not sure that the traditional childish present, of a little garden marked out in the middle of his large garden, will instantly change him to a little child. But I do know that great historic changes always begin at exactly the opposite end to the end the world is pursuing, and that the human search, so long turned outwards, will turn inwards very soon.